KATHERINE
MANSFIELD
THE STORY-TELLER

Biography
A Glorious Fame: The Life of Margaret Cavendish, Duchess of Newcastle, 1623–1673
Learning not to be First: The Life of Christina Rossetti
A Passionate Sisterhood: The Sisters, Wives and Daughters of the Lake Poets
Catherine Cookson: The Biography
Margaret Forster: An Introduction
Seeking Catherine Cookson's 'Da': The Real Story of Finding Her Father

Non-fiction (as Kate Gordon)
Rites and Ceremonies: A Practical Guide to Alternative Baptism and Baby-naming
Rites and Ceremonies: A Practical Guide to Alternative Weddings
Rites and Ceremonies: A Practical Guide to Alternative Funerals

Poetry
Unwritten Lives

KATHERINE MANSFIELD
THE STORY-TELLER

KATHLEEN JONES

EDINBURGH UNIVERSITY PRESS

How blind we little creatures are! It's only the fairy tales we really live by. If we set out upon a journey, the more wonderful the treasure, the greater the temptations and perils to be overcome. And if someone rebels and says, Life isn't good enough on those terms, one can only say: 'It is!'

KATHERINE MANSFIELD TO JOHN MIDDLETON MURRY, 1920

© 2010 Ferber Jones Ltd

First published by Penguin Group (NZ), 2010

Edinburgh University Press Ltd
22 George Square, Edinburgh

www.euppublishing.com

Typeset in Joanna
by Pindar NZ, Auckland, New Zealand, and
printed and bound in Great Britain by
CPI Antony Rowe, Chippenham and Eastbourne

A CIP record for this book is available from the British Library

ISBN 978 0 7486 4354 7 (hardback)

Contents

Acknowledgements

This book has taken me almost ten years to write and during that time I have had a considerable amount of help from a large number of people. Particular thanks must go to Carol O'Brien at Constable Publishers, who started this project off, and to Margaret Scott, who encouraged me from the beginning, read the chapters as I wrote them and made sure that I didn't give up. My thanks, also, to Peter Day, who talked to me about Ida Baker, read the book and gave me permission to quote from Ida's letters and unpublished papers. I am particularly grateful for the considerable scholarship of Vincent O'Sullivan, who answered my questions, gave me good advice and took time to read the manuscript. Thanks are due to Oroya Day and everyone at the Katherine Mansfield Birthplace Trust, who have given me hospitality and answered innumerable queries; the staff of the Alexander Turnbull Library for their friendly assistance; the staff of the British Library who found obscure texts for me and gave me permission to quote from the papers of Samuel Koteliansky, Ida Baker, Katherine Mansfield's letters to Ida Baker, Elizabeth Countess Russell, letters between Frederick Goodyear and Katherine Mansfield, and between Sydney Schiff and Wyndham Lewis. I am also grateful to Reinhard F. E. Wolf, for supplying information about the Pension Müller and Bad Wörishofen and for permission to use one of the illustrations, and to Jill Armsby, who looked up the genealogy of the le Maistre family for me.

I would also like to thank the University of Edinburgh library, Jennifer Kinnear at the Fergusson Archive in Perth who have given permission to use the J. D. Fergusson image, the Charles Deering McCormick Library of Special Collections, Northwestern University Library, particularly Russell Maylone, who patiently answered my queries regarding the papers of Dorothy Brett, and Professor Lee Roloff, who gave me permission to quote from them; Mrs G. C. Drey for permission to use the photograph of Anne Estelle (Rice) Drey and quote from her letters; Mrs A. F. G. Alpers for permission to quote from unpublished letters and other material relating to the late Antony Alpers; and the Harry Ransom Humanities Research Centre, who hold manuscripts relating to Ruth Mantz and John Middleton Murry. I would also like to remember the late Dr Jim Leitch, who took the trouble to talk to me at length about tuberculosis and Katherine Mansfield's medical conditions, and Dr Clare McKenna, who tried to make sure that I didn't go off on the wrong track.

Several Mansfield scholars have given me their time and shared knowledge, including Dr Angela Smith, Dr Gerri Kimber and Dr Janet Wilson, and I would also like to acknowledge the assistance and support of the Katherine Mansfield Society. Members of the Beauchamp family have brought the personalities alive for me, particularly Janine Renshaw Beauchamp, who was brought up by Katherine's sister Jeanne. She has given permission to use some of the photographs that illustrate this book. I would also like to thank Roger Beauchamp, whom I met in New Zealand. A particular debt is owed to the family of John Middleton Murry. This book could not have been written without their co-operation and I am profoundly grateful.

I would also like to thank: the Society of Authors for permission to use material from the estates of John Middleton Murry and Katherine Mansfield; the University of Nottingham; Pollinger Ltd and the estates of D. H. Lawrence and Frieda Lawrence Ravagli for permission to use photographs and to quote from material, published and unpublished; the estates of Virginia and Leonard Woolf for permission to quote from letters and diaries; the Center for Biographical Research at the University of Hawai'i at Manoa for permission to quote from an article by Jeffrey Meyers; the family of Garnet Carrington Trowell; and Dr Carol Nathanson and the Hollis Taggart Gallery in New York for tracking down a photograph of Anne Estelle (Rice) Drey. I thank Kettle's Yard in Cambridge for permission to quote from the work of J. S. Ede and the papers of Sophie Brzeska and Henri Gaudier.

I would like to thank Northern Arts, the British Council and the Royal Literary Fund for supporting this book financially. Thanks to all the friends and family who gave me bed and board while I did research in New Zealand, France, Italy, Switzerland, Germany, England and Scotland; to Neil Ferber, who lived through it with me and who spent hours in libraries doing research and more hours at home constructing websites; to my agent Isobel Dixon at Blake Friedmann; and particularly to my publisher Geoff Walker, all the staff at Penguin New Zealand and my editor Anna Rogers, who saved me from many an error! Any that remain are my own. Every effort has been made to locate the current owners of copyright material; I would be grateful to hear from anyone I was unable to trace.

Introduction

What, think you, causes me truest joy
Down by the sea — the wild mad storm of waves
The fierce rushing swirl of waters together
The cruel salt spray that blows, that beats upon my face . . .
The song of the wind as I stretch out my arms and embrace it
This indeed gives me joy.

KATHLEEN BEAUCHAMP, 2 MARCH 1906

The first thing you notice in Wellington is the wind. A full southerly buster was blowing as I drove in around the bays of the harbour, hurling the waves onto the rocks. At the hotel on Tinakori Road, shutters slapped and banged in a crazy percussion, just as Katherine described in one of her earliest stories, 'The Wind Blows'. I recognised the way it blew the stinging dust 'in waves, in clouds, in big round whirls', heard the 'loud roaring sound' from the tree ferns and the pohutukawa trees in the botanic garden, the clanking of the overhead cables for the trolley buses. Clinging to the car door to steady myself, the street map levitating from my grasp, I experienced the exactness of Katherine's images – 'a newspaper wagged in the air like a lost kite' before spiking itself onto a pine tree; sentences blew away 'like little narrow ribbons'.

Tinakori Road, where Katherine was born and where her father occupied progressively larger houses as his status rose, runs along a steep hillside with spectacular views of the city. Above it, a tree-clad slope climbs

13

upwards towards the ridge and below it, houses stagger downhill towards the brief fringe of level ground that edges the circular bay, enclosed by hills. The street follows a major fault line in an area that remains seismically active, and tremors were part of Katherine's childhood experience.

Katherine loved the view from Tinakori Road, writing in her youthful notebook how 'all in a fever myself I rushed out of the stifling house . . . on to the gorse golden hills. A white road round the hills – there I walked. And below me, like a beautiful Pre-Raphaelite picture, lay the sea and the violet mountains. The sky all a riot of rose and yellow – amethyst and purple. At the foot of the hill – the city – but all curtained by a blue mist that hung over it in pale wreaths of Beauty.'[1] Though engulfed by the expanding capital, the old houses renumbered to accommodate the new, Tinakori Road has changed little in a hundred and twenty years. It is still lined by brightly painted wooden houses, and you can have a drink in the local working men's pub, where Katherine's inscrutable face looks down from the wall. The prime minister now occupies the residence where Katherine was given a farewell garden party before leaving for England in 1908 and which she used as material for one of her best-known stories.

The fabric of her narratives is laid out in front of me as I look from the motel window. The curve of the bay where Katherine spent her summers, the quays where she and her brother watched the steamers depart and dreamed of one day leaving themselves; the botanic garden where she wandered with her sisters, conscious always of the untamed wilderness just on the other side of the garden fence. 'Here is laughter and movement and bright sunlight – but behind me – is it near, or miles and miles away? – the bush lies hidden in the shadow.'[2] Katherine's childhood was spent on the insecure margin between a recent immigrant civilisation and the encroaching wilderness, inhabited by an older, non-European culture that was being dispossessed.

As a visitor to Wellington you can walk along the road Katherine took each day to school, visit the cemetery where her family were buried, see 'the gully' where their servants lived in relative poverty, and visit the house where she was born, now meticulously restored. A square, white, plain, two-storey weatherboard house behind a picket fence, it has four bedrooms, two reception rooms, a kitchen, scullery and 'other offices'.

In the space of a decade Harold Beauchamp would be able to move his family to a sprawling mansion further up the street – opposite, and similar in size, to the prime minister's house. The increasing opulence of Harold

Beauchamp's houses signified his changing position in the city as he rose from a mere finance clerk to become chairman and director of the Bank of New Zealand and a member of the Wellington Harbour Board, and of a dozen other public companies. Eventually he was given a knighthood. In the New World, where the infrastructure was still unformed and flexible, ambition was worthy, ability was rewarded and anything was possible. It was an optimistic country where women would become the first in the world to win the right to vote in 1893, and where they worked alongside men to develop frontier land and commercial enterprises. This was the atmosphere that formed Katherine, and shaped her own dreams and ambitions.

Katherine's grandfather, Arthur Beauchamp, was a self-made extrovert who came to New Zealand from England by way of the Australian goldfields, settled at Picton at the upper end of the South Island and became active in local politics, being elected briefly to the New Zealand parliament. His son Harold, Katherine's father, started out working for Arthur at the family store. Lively and enterprising, Harold realised that the future lay in the capital rather than the provinces and a family story tells how he and a friend made plans to move there, raffling their horse and boat – the only things they possessed – in order to finance the trip. Raffling was a novel notion to raise more money and they sold a lot of tickets. But the two young men also bought a couple of tickets themselves and were suspected of foul play when they won both the boat and the horse. They got the money and kept the goods, but had to leave town quickly. In Wellington, Harold found a job as a finance clerk in the import-export business of W. M. Bannatyne & Co., and prospered. Marriage to Annie Dyer, the beautiful daughter of another Australian immigrant, in 1884 established him socially and, when his employer died, he was made a partner.

In New Zealand terms, the Beauchamps were not part of the colonial aristocracy, but of the vigorous, commercial class that underpinned and would eventually overtake it. Harold traced his origins back to a London silversmith at the time of Samuel Pepys, and several Beauchamp relatives in England were upper middle class professionals – doctors, lawyers and businessmen. Katherine's cousin Mary Beauchamp, known as Elizabeth, made a very advantageous marriage in 1891 to the German Count Henning August von Arnim, which gives some indication of the social classes on whose fringes the family moved. Respectable, solid, but not above taking a gamble occasionally, they were the backbone of the Victorian commercial empire – the class so authentically portrayed by John Galsworthy in his *Forsyte Saga*.

The girl who would eventually become known internationally as Katherine Mansfield was born on 14 October 1888. She was christened Kathleen Mansfield Beauchamp in the wooden cathedral church of St Paul's in the centre of Wellington, though her siblings called her Kass. She was the third daughter and her entrance into the world was something of a (never publicly acknowledged) disappointment to parents who wanted a son to be heir to the growing Beauchamp estate. Katherine's two elder sisters, Vera and Charlotte (known as Chaddie), were already attractive, intelligent, unexceptionable young girls who would grow up to do everything expected of them by their parents and social peers. A younger sister, Jeanne, and a brother, Leslie, were equally conventional. Katherine, with all the privilege of the middle child, always believed herself to be different and this conviction was reinforced by her parents' response to a girl who refused to conform or to be pleasing in order to please. Her resistance showed itself in the stubborn, direct gaze scowling at the observer from family photographs, the penetrating point-blank questions that disconcerted both her family and their social circle.

There were physical differences too. Katherine wore glasses and was plumper than her sisters. She did not smile as often. She could be awkward and was regarded as the most demanding of the five children. She felt herself to be loved less than her siblings and as a result became more difficult to love. The feelings of rejection grew. When her parents went off to Europe, leaving Katherine with her grandmother, her mother's first returning words to the eager little girl waiting on the quayside were 'Well, Kathleen, I see you're still as fat as ever!' Katherine's answer was to cultivate her difference and develop a keen inner life that divided her ever more sharply from her family.

She was always imaginative. A school friend remembered playing with Katherine in the garden at Tinakori Road and hearing 'a noise which to ordinary people would have sounded like a lawn mower'. To Katherine it was 'Bronzo the dragon gnashing his teeth'. The spiral of smoke from a bonfire became the dragon spitting fire. Katherine armed herself and her friend with spears and shields cut from aloe and flax plants and stealthily crept through the mysterious, forbidden, green door that led to the neighbour's garden. The dragon was quickly revealed as 'an irate gardener' who chased the two girls with a rake. They ran out of the gate and in a panic turned the wrong way, rushing up the drive instead of into the street. They were trapped. 'It was tea time, but to go up past the dragon and his rake was unthinkable.' But Katherine had the answer and approached a 'kindly looking man' walking past. They were, she told him, two princesses who had been chased by a gardener, who was 'really a dragon in disguise'. The man, who knew Katherine's family, entered into the spirit of the occasion and escorted the girls home 'as though we really were fairy princesses'.[3]

Katherine received yet another scolding and would always be labelled an actress and a liar. But the adventures that took place in her head were as real as anything that happened outside it. She published her first story at the age of nine. 'Enna Blake' – printed in the Wellington Girls' High School magazine – is an imaginary trip to Torquay, relocated to rural New Zealand, where girls go on walks to collect ferns and mosses. It opens in Enna's voice with a directness that already presages Mansfield's mature style: '"Oh mother, it is still raining, and you say I can't go out." It was a girl who spoke; she looked about ten. She was standing in a well-furnished room, and was looking out of a large bay window.' The editor comments: 'This story, written by one of the girls who have lately entered the school, shows promise of great merit'.[4]

The house at 25 (once 11) Tinakori Road is a shrine to Katherine's memory, its fussy Victorian colonial interior carefully matched to the period. The rooms seem crowded now with even two or three visitors. How they contained the expansive personality of Harold Beauchamp, his languid wife Annie, her two unmarried sisters, her mother, Margaret Dyer, three children and a live-in servant, is difficult to imagine. It perhaps gives an insight into the adult Katherine's love of Japanese minimalism, her hatred of clutter, and her obsession with order.

The Katherine Mansfield Birthplace Society, founded by Oroya Day, has several treasures that belonged to Katherine. In pride of place are her typewriter, locked away in a glass case, and an exquisite black, embroidered jacket – narrow-waisted and buttoned Chinese fashion. These items found their way back to New Zealand after Katherine's death, gifted by Ida Baker, her lifelong companion, through the scholar Margaret Scott, who has dedicated her life to the transcription of Katherine's letters and notebooks. While Oroya painstakingly restored the house, Margaret decoded the work and, through her friendship with Ida, returned a number of surviving artefacts to New Zealand – some to the Birthplace Society and some to the Alexander Turnbull Library, where the memory of New Zealand's most famous writer is preserved.

Although the Katherine Mansfield Birthplace Society thrives on visitors,

Harold's own memorial to his daughter, erected in 1933, is run down and neglected. When I went to see it, graffiti had been scrawled on the pergola, and the filthy water of the concrete pool contained the body of a dead bird. There were no flowers and the paint was peeling. Katherine's portrait, a triumphant statement of personality by the American Colourist Anne Estelle Rice, is hidden away in the vaults of the Museum of New Zealand Te Papa Tongarewa, along with much of the art collection Harold Beauchamp gave as an endowment to the capital city he helped to build.

Katherine's literary fortunes have fluctuated since she died in 1923. For many years her work was undervalued in her birth country, as her first biographer Ruth Mantz discovered, and there were those who considered her to be more European than authentically a New Zealander. In the Oral History Centre of the Alexander Turnbull Library, listening to the cultured Kensington accents of her sisters on tape, one can well imagine how this might happen – after all, Katherine spent a large part of her life in Europe. But there are other voices there too, reassuringly New Zealand voices. Edie Bendall, the object of Katherine's eighteen-year-old passion, talks of the stifling atmosphere of Katherine's family, the social calendars of fashionable young women, the corseting of young minds along with their bodies, and how she and Katherine walked every evening to talk of literature and art and the world beyond their limited horizons. 'I am ashamed of young New Zealand,' Katherine wrote in a letter. 'All the firm, fat framework of their brains must be demolished before they can begin to learn. They want a purifying influence – a mad wave of Pre-Raphaelitism, of Super-aestheticism, should intoxicate the country.'[5] Katherine and Edie's views were in direct conflict with the prevailing mores, expressed by one of Annie Beauchamp's contemporaries. 'After all that is said of the advantages of art & high civilisation & the way some girls consider home ties, duties & affection mere dust in the balance when weighed against European culture & advantages, I had far rather my children & grandchildren grew up loving dunces than have them value intellectual gains as the supreme objects to be striven for in life.'[6]

The teenage Katherine was on the side of intellectual gain and European culture, but against the Victorian straitjacket its social conventions imposed. It was a dichotomy she struggled with. 'On one hand lay the mode bohème – alluring, knowledge-bringing, full of work and sensation, full of impulse, pulsating with the cry of Youth Youth Youth . . . On the other hand lay the Suitable Appropriate Existence. The days full of perpetual

Society functions, the hours full of clothes discussions – the waste of life. The stifling atmosphere would kill me . . .'[7] Part of her would always be rooted in an older, non-European heritage. In Wellington Katherine had a passionate adolescent love affair with a Maori girl, Maata Mahupuku. Even after the affair was over, they remained friends. Maata's nephew talks on tape of her funeral, and asserts that draft chapters of an early autobiographical novel called 'Maata', which Katherine sent to her from England, as well as their personal letters, were put into the coffin when Maata was buried.

In the novel, fragments of which exist elsewhere in manuscript, Katherine herself takes on the Maori persona of the heroine. Her fictional and actual relationships with Maata illustrate her fascination with the double heritage of her birth country – the balance between Maori and Pakeha. As early as 1906, in a piece called 'Summer Idylle', Katherine assumes a Maori identity, but with a Pakeha name – Marina. She imagines the 'slow, tranquil surrender of the Night Spirits' and dreams of eating 'eggs and bread and honey and peaches' with her female Pakeha counterpart, who bears the Maori name Hinemoa. The whole of Katherine's sexual and racial ambivalence is there – the crossover of names, Marina and Hinemoa's erotic exchange in a room redolent of tea tree blossom, and Hinemoa saying 'it is because you are so utterly the foreign element . . .'[8]

Leaving Wellington on the ferry as Katherine did, I crossed Cook Strait to the South Island, the vessel edging its way through narrow fjords of impossibly turquoise water to the small port of Picton, where Arthur Beauchamp, Katherine's entrepreneurial grandfather, ran a store and tried to farm. She remembered visiting him, 'lying to one side of an immense bed . . . like a very old wide-awake bird'.[9] Further south, the city of Christchurch was the last place in New Zealand Katherine saw before she left for England. She arrived by ferry from Wellington and transferred to the liner anchored in the deep-water terminal at Lyttelton, over the hill from Christchurch, which now takes container ships and oil tankers. I went there to visit Margaret Scott, whose home nearby Diamond Harbour is a focus for scholars and writers from all over the world who want to share a bottle of wine and talk Mansfield.

Margaret describes the almost impossible task of learning to read Katherine's handwriting as like translating a foreign language, and the specimens on show in the Alexander Turnbull Library support this description.

Margaret once spent an entire week deciphering one word, the blown-up photocopy propped in front of her at breakfast, lunch and dinner in the hope that some blinding flash of insight would eventually occur. And it did. Katherine's habit of choosing the unusual, the least expected, word – as in the phrase 'the swooning sun' – added to the difficulty of the task.

Margaret is one of the few people still alive to have known Katherine's surviving family and friends. She visited Katherine's sister, Vera, in the United States, stayed with John Middleton Murry's fourth wife in Norfolk and became a trusted friend of Ida Baker – the famous 'L.M.' of Katherine's diaries and letters. Margaret tells wry stories of Ida's haphazard house-keeping. On one occasion Ida, her eyesight very poor, cooked some rather elderly mushrooms she had kept for too long in a paper bag. 'Lesley, dear, they're crawling with maggots!' Margaret said, as they sizzled and seethed in the pan. Ida was mortified, throwing them out into the garden with profuse apologies to the maggots she had almost cremated. 'Of course,' she said, 'they had eaten so much mushroom they would have been more mushroom than maggot. So it wouldn't have been too bad if we had eaten them.' Margaret glimpsed the infuriatingly irrational logic that had so enraged Katherine, as well as the naivety and honesty that kept Ida loyal.[10]

On subsequent visits to New Zealand, I spent weeks in the archives of the Alexander Turnbull Library, reading Katherine's letters and original notebooks, which reveal much more than their printed transcriptions. They are human documents that show their author's method of working and her fluctuating moods. Katherine liked to write in 'cahiers' – French school exercise books – but she also used Strakers' diaries and pocket-sized notebooks with board covers. She wrote on the right-hand side of the page, leaving the left-hand side free for annotations. The notebooks are well used: there are pages torn out, corners folded down and sometimes pressed flowers between the pages. In the margins, she scribbled comments and doodles, shopping lists and occasionally, in a fit of boredom, snatches of music hall songs and jokes. You can tell by her handwriting when she is angry or exhausted.

John Middleton Murry's diaries and letters are there too. For the first time it is possible to put them side by side with Katherine's to provide a complete narrative of their years together. John's diaries, which he kept until his death in 1957, and his fragments of autobiography, are a harrow-ing record of emotional inadequacy and how his obsession with Katherine destroyed two of his three subsequent marriages and adversely affected the lives of his four children. He is often accused of being 'the man who made Mansfield miserable' and, before I went to New Zealand, my background reading had reinforced that view. I began my research prepared to be critical. But, after reading his diaries, I found myself much more compassionate and better able to understand why he had behaved as he did, and why Katherine went on loving him 'in spite of all'. Mansfield scholar and author Vincent O'Sullivan, who co-edited *The Letters of Katherine Mansfield* with Margaret Scott, was a sane and objective adviser in my quest to understand their complex relationship and to unravel the 'Mansfield myth' that John Murry's editing of her work created.

To go to New Zealand in search of Katherine Mansfield is to be aware of the heart of her duality. This remains one of the least urbanised places on earth. Small oases of human habitation exist in a vast wild landscape still largely unshaped by humans, full of dramatic contrasts and contradictions. Snow-covered alps, volcanoes, glaciers, craters and geysers, glacial torrents in wide flood plains, impenetrable rain forests and tropical beaches give place to each other just as they did in Katherine's time. She experienced this landscape with a passionate physicality. It became a metaphor for the disordered adolescent landscape within her that resisted 'European cultivation' as forcefully as the Maori had resisted appropriation of their traditions and their land by the white immigrants – the Pakeha. The hinterland of Maori culture, ancient and powerful, exerted a strong influence on Katherine. Harold Beauchamp learned their language in order to do business with Maori. His cousin married a Maori and had five children. Katherine's Maori relatives and friends showed her a different view from the European perspective, a new way of living and experiencing the world around her, and a way of resisting colonisation. Katherine knew she had 'the taint of the Pioneer' in her blood. She was aware of the role of Pakeha as usurpers, insensitive to any kind of right that was not expressed in a legal document. Katherine could see, when she looked out into the bush, 'vague forms lurking in the shadow, staring at me malevolently, wildly, the thief of their birthright'. She imagined a shadowy host of dispossessed, 'passing, passing'. And the sound of water, the wind swaying in the trees suddenly became 'the sound of weeping'. Yet the bush was a source of strength and creativity as she fed on its erotic power. 'There is bush, silent and splendid . . . and everywhere that strange indefinable scent. As I breathe it, it seems to absorb, to become part of me – and I am old with the age of centuries, strong with the strength of savagery.'[11]

Born across two cultures, educated in yet another, Katherine would always struggle for one definitive identity. And her work, edited for a European audience, reflected the divisions, though it remained always recognisably antipodean. As one of Katherine's compatriots remarked,

> It touches neither fiord nor geyser certainly but it has the feel of the land. – If she mentioned neither street nor tree that New Zealand knows, if her work were set before us unknown and unplaced I think we would lift our noses like dogs to the wind and smell our country. I think we would know the Picton boat and morning At the Bay . . . I cannot pass a certain house in Tinakori Road without a stir of pain for the girl who they say lived there as Cassie Beauchamp. It is a far cry from Tinakori to Fontainebleau where from the nettle, danger, she plucked the flower, safety.[12]

PART I

Leaving All Fair

All my manuscripts I leave entirely to you to do what you like with. Go through them one day, dear love, and destroy all you do not use. Please destroy all letters you do not wish to keep & all papers. You know my love of tidiness. Have a clean sweep, Bogey, and leave all fair — will you?

KATHERINE MANSFIELD TO JOHN MURRY, 7 AUGUST 1923

PART I

Leaving An Heir

1

Fontainebleau

When Miss Katherine Mansfield, the brilliant novelist, passed away the other day in almost the spring of her promise, it was in a curious little oasis in the historic Forest of Fontainebleau, some forty miles from Paris, where a movement, started by an Eastern philosopher-mystic called Gurdjieff, has been attracting much attention . . .

THE GRAPHIC, 10 MARCH 1923

9 January 1923, La Prieuré, Fontainebleau

Katherine has been up since 7.30 a.m. The curtains have been drawn back and the tall shutters pushed open to let in the winter sun. The first-floor room she has been given at the Institute for the Harmonious Development of Man is square, high and decorated after the French style – the walls a chilly blue, the ceiling painted with gold stars. A draughty window gives a view down across the bare January garden to the gatehouse of the chateau. The room has a worn and rather shabby grandeur. The antique furniture is a relic of more prosperous times – a wooden bed, the two chairs pulled up close to the fireplace, the washstand in the corner, the vast clothes press occupying most of one wall. There are French engravings on the walls and a rug on the floor to give a touch of colour but the whole impression is comfortless. The room has been imprinted by the character of its history – once a luxurious French chateau owned by a king's mistress, subsequently occupied as a Carmelite foundation, converted back into a private

25

residence in the nineteenth century and then abandoned to dereliction before the war in 1914. Although now reoccupied by George Ivanovich Gurdjieff's Eastern tribe, it still has something of the monastic spirit. There is a damp stain in the corner of the ceiling and that smell peculiar to old buildings – a mingling of last night's ashes, wood polish, damp plaster and the indefinable odour left by generations of human occupation. Underlying everything is the persistent smell of Russian cooking – fermented milk and cabbage soup – that seeps up from the kitchens below.

Katherine is sitting at a table underneath the window with a fur coat clutched around her shoulders. She's holding a pen, but the ink has long been dry on the words written in the notebook before her. She puts down her pen to blow on her fingers and read the lines she had hoped to complete when she came here: '. . . an exquisite day . . . one of those days, so clear, so still, so silent, you almost feel the earth itself has stopped in astonishment at its own beauty . . .'[1]

It is a beginning. Katherine has spent the last twelve weeks systematically tearing up a series of beginnings, but today, as she picks up her pen again, she feels new possibilities, though they are qualified by a series of conditional clauses. If only it were not so cold; if only spring were not so far away; if only she did not cough so much . . . The fire in the grate is almost out, but the log basket is empty. In her journal, just above that last entry, is a list of Russian words and phrases she's been learning. They read like a poem.

> I am cold
> Bring paper to light a fire
> paper
> cinders
> wood
> matches
> flame, smoke . . .

In the leather writing case at Katherine's elbow are two unfinished letters. The one she has been trying to write to her sisters tails away in an exhausted scrawl halfway down the second page. It's dated 31 December – over a week ago – but she simply lacks the energy to finish it at present. And what more can she say? How could Jeanne and Chaddie, with their Kensington and country house mentalities, ever understand what she's doing here? Ridiculous even to try. 'As you know I came here for a "cure" but it's not a "cure" in any ordinary sense of the word, the cure consists in leading as full and as different a life as possible, in entering into as many new interests as possible. In taking up all kinds of new things of any sort and description. Purely medical treatment there is none, as we understand it, or not enough to mention. We are about 50–60, mainly Russians, established here in a colony, and leading a very particular kind of communal life . . .'[2]

In a few hours her husband John will be here. His photograph – a recent Christmas present – sits on her table – the dark rumpled hair, the slim, almost feminine face, in three-quarter profile, the troubled expression that is irresistible to women. Katherine has been musing about John throughout her stay here, through the sleepless hours of those interminable nights when her lungs burn, her heart pounds and thrashes in her chest and all the terrors and regrets of her life parade themselves around the room. In October, when she arrived here, she had written, in a fit of depression, to tell him that it was all over between them. 'I now know that I must grow a shell away from you. I want, I "ask" for my independence.'[3] Her desire to cut herself adrift had been inspired by the need for absolute truth. Their relationship has so often been a lie – a romantic fiction played out in their letters. How easy it was to colour things differently in retrospect. 'Looking back, my boat is almost swamped sometimes by seas of sentiment. "Ah what have I missed. How sweet it was, how clear, how warm, how simple, how precious!" And I think of the garden at Isola Bella and the furry bees . . . But then I remember what we really felt – the blanks, the silences, the anguish of continual misunderstandings.'[4]

So why has she given in to this sudden sentimental desire for John's presence? Katherine can't really answer that question. It's the paradox of their relationship – to be together proved impossible, yet to be apart was to long for him again, despite the fact that he had hurt her so much, first by falling in love with her friend Dorothy Brett, and then with Princess Elizabeth Bibesco – such a stupid girl! He had also picked up a prostitute and then, instead of going with her to a hotel room, had taken her to a restaurant in the Tottenham Court Road, bought her a dinner and talked to her. That was so typical of John. His inability to act maddened Katherine, but it was also somehow endearing. He was like a perpetual child abroad in the world. His need to tell her about his misdeeds was also thoroughly juvenile. Did he know how much it hurt when he stood before her – metaphorically – in his letters, explaining and absolving himself, crestfallen, lip trembling, like a naughty child who hopes to be forgiven because he's had the courage to confess before being found out?

But then, inevitably, her own sins rise up to reproach her: Francis Carco (pointless to argue that she had not been married to John at the time), Garnet's baby (a hurt too deep to quantify), her teenage passion for Maata, Floryan's blackmail, that first ridiculous marriage, her cruelty to Ida, and other unspeakable sins: 'There's always just one secret – just one – that never can be told'.[5] People advised her to write it all down to experience, but there was pain, terror, suffering, 'waste – destruction, too'. She has spent years of her life trying to make sense of it.

Then in London last summer there had been a crisis. Everything she had ever written seemed full of showiness and those 'writerly tricks' she so despised in others.[6] Her whole existence had suddenly seemed stale and false – she had concealed too much for too long, tried to be too many things to too many people until she hardly knew who she was. She had written sarcastically in her notebook: 'Let me take the case of K.M. She has led, ever since she can remember, a very typically false life.'[7] It was not sufficient just to be able to write – 'Literature is not enough!' – one had to know how to live too. Katherine had tried to explain to John around Christmas that she was longing for 'a far more truthful existence . . . I want to be real.'[8] That is why she had had to come here: to heal the psyche, to make herself whole, in the hope that a perfect balance of flesh, intellect and spirit – what Gurdjieff called Hand, Head and Heart – might enable her ravaged body to be healed. This is what he had promised her. He had studied widely in Persia, Afghanistan, India and Tibet, and told his followers that 'too much attention has been paid in the West to the development of the mind, and too little to the emotions'. His aim was to discover 'faculties and forces' that are innate but dormant in the human organism.[9] Katherine, who has tried every conventional cure in Europe as well as the latest and most risky medical theories, with no perceivable benefit, is putting her faith in Gurdjieff as a last resort. She's aware, in the rational part of her mind, that a thousand people a week are dying from tuberculosis, but she doesn't want to accept that she might be one of them. Here, at the institute, people treat her as a person, not a hopeless invalid. The illness that has crept through her body and dulled her mind, obliterating her personality, absorbing too much of her energy and precious writing time, can be shrugged off and left in the corner of the room. Here she is neither Katherine Mansfield the writer, nor Mrs Murry the patient. There is only the inner life. Nothing is expected of her.

A note from Ida is on the table at her elbow, its tone hurt and chiding. It says only 'I am enclosing the coat and the underwear you asked me to buy', but Katherine knows that Ida is fretting and thinking, 'Why have you invited John who is so thoughtless and unkind to you? Why not me, your own L.M.,[10] the person who has loved you so devotedly, so steadfastly all our lives, since I first met you when you were fourteen and fresh from New Zealand?'

Katherine can feel Ida's powerful emotional eye directed towards her from the farm where she is living and working at Lisieux – a job chosen so that she can be close by, hoping that Katherine will send for her, wanting to be the one person Katherine cannot do without. (*Very anxious about K. Woke in the night hearing her call me – so distinctly that I answered aloud – such a cold wind.*) Katherine can see Ida's self-conscious, awkward body, her stolid face, the slight moustache above her lip, her big hands, her dark brown eyes, full of need. Ida's love is absolute and unendurable. (*Received letter from K with great relief – Also annoyed ps evidently an answer to my letter. I shouldn't have sent that letter – it was a weakness. If only I could always keep the personality of independence – going on living – I could write to her – wrote today . . .*)

Ida's letters are full of questions about clothes – she worries about Katherine's comfort. (*Has she all those beautiful things she misses?*)[11] She has sent a camisole, some stockings and a pair of shoes. Would Katherine like another skirt? A blouse? Her purchases are often unsuitable. Katherine knows as she unpacks a hideous jacket from the excessive brown paper and string that Ida deems necessary for posting, that she has spent hours agonising in the shop between the coral and the green – only to choose the very one that Katherine is bound to hate. Inevitably she will realise her mistake only after she has arrived home, and feel obliged to tuck apologetic notes into the parcel to excuse the fault. Worst of all is the undertone of love and grief in every letter. Katherine is reminded with every communication that, for Ida, she is already dead. Why must Ida be so tragic? It is the one thing that Ida and John have in common: both have nailed down her coffin and, in their own ways, are already tending her grave. John even talks in his letters of 'meeting her on the other side'.

Although Ida's unconditional devotion has almost driven her mad at times, here, at Fontainebleau, Katherine is conscious more than ever of their interdependence. The second letter in her well-worn writing case, which accompanies her everywhere, is for Ida: 'Dear Ida . . . you have been in my mind all day . . .' She remembers that it was a gift from Ida at Isola Bella at Menton – the 'one perfect thing' that cancelled out all the imperfect things – and looking at it takes Katherine vividly back to the villa they had shared, 'the olive trees before and the cotton tree along the twisted fence and the red roses and big starry-eyed daisies'.[12] With difficulty Katherine wrenches her mind away from the sentimental reflections she has forbidden herself.

> We are in the throes of theatre building which ought to be ready by January 13th. Gurdjieff has bought 63 carpets for it and the same number of fur rugs. The carpets which were displayed one by one in the salon last night are like living things – worlds of beauty. And what a joy to begin to learn which is a garden, which a café, which a prayer mat, which 'l'histoire de ses troupeaux' and so on. My thoughts are full of carpets and Persia and Samarkand.

When Ida had brought her to Fontainebleau for the first time, Katherine had commented that Gurdjieff, with his astrakhan hat and handlebar moustache, looked like a Turkish carpet dealer and they had both laughed. It is ironic to discover now that he is – at least in one of his incarnations. He has almost as many selves as she has herself.

Katherine lifts her pen again. 'I am looking for signs of Spring already. Under the espalier pear trees there were wonderful Xmas roses which I saw for the first time this year. They reminded me of Switzerland; and somebody found four primroses the other day . . .' This is the domestic language that Ida understands, the practicalities of the physical world. Katherine jokes about Ida being 'my wife', but it is very close to the truth. Ida has always looked after her physical needs; she understands the little, trivial necessities of female life. Only to Ida can Katherine confess that the depilatory cream she had used to remove hair from her upper lip has stained her skin navy blue, or that she is planning to have her hair rinsed in henna; only to Ida can she describe the horrors of shopping for a hat with John in Paris. It is difficult for Katherine to imagine how important those things once were to her. Appearances mean nothing here. 'My blue dress is in large holes. Those cashmere cardigans look as if rats have gnawed them.

As to my fur coat – it's like a wet London cat. The last time I was in the stable I caught one of the goats nibbling it . . . Write and tell me how you are will you? Dear Ida?'[13]

The letter is folded into her blotter. John will post it for her when he comes. Ida – who otherwise knows her so well – has never understood about John, about the ties that bind them to each other. (*I am jealous – no. It's not jealousy – only it hurts to feel that K wants a life with Jack – not with me – with someone – not me – I can't make a life with her – I can't understand. It seems to me that in friendship your life is quite alone . . .*)[14] Katherine tells herself that she has forgiven him, that it is time for reconciliation. In anticipation of his visit she has reinstated her fringe; when she came here she preferred simply to draw her hair back from her face. The fringe is somehow symbolic. Today, she is once more Mrs John Middleton Murry.

At least in this place she has learned to deal with fear. Did anyone know what it was to live constantly with the fear of death? It was in France with Ida that she had first coughed bright red blood into her hand. The terror of that moment – to die perhaps with everything in her mind and nothing written or finished. To know what one was capable of but might not be given the chance to show. She had vowed then that she would write like a demon, not waste a single second of whatever life she had left.

But what has she accomplished in the four years since then? A few stories, far too few to count for anything, a multitude of book reviews, written out of financial necessity, endless useless letters. But not the novel that sits inside her like a gigantic growth, rooted in her mind, not yet committed to paper. She has no energy to write it yet. In the mornings she has scarcely the strength to put on the warm underclothes that Ida has sent and go downstairs. She has written nothing worth keeping for months, but the ideas have begun to flow again and she had told her friend A. R. Orage a few nights ago about this revival of the old belief: 'I want to write a book. This is after a long period of passivity; I am going to write a wonderful book. I must soon get well enough to start to work on it[15]. . . I have begun many times, but I am not yet ready, it seems. However the idea is clear enough . . . Two people fall in love and marry. One, or perhaps both of them has had previous affairs, the remains of which still linger like ghosts in the home. Both wish to forget, but the ghosts still walk . . .'[16]

John Murry arrives from Paris after lunch. He had written a few days earlier to tell Katherine that he had to finish an editorial for the *Times Literary
Supplement* and would take the night boat from Newhaven, arriving in Paris
early on Tuesday morning. He went first to a hotel to collect some clothes
and a pair of shoes that had been bought for Katherine and brought over
on the ferry by an acquaintance. Dorothy Brett had suggested that customs
might be suspicious of him if he travelled with women's clothes in his
luggage, so he had asked a Mrs Nelson to take them for him. It did not
occur to John that he might simply have told the customs officials that
they were a present for his wife. Katherine, knowing John's incompetence
in the business of travel, has sent him precise instructions on how to get
to La Prieuré from Paris. 'You get out of the train at Avon and take a cab
here which costs 8 francs with tip. Ring the bell at the porter's lodge
and I'll open the gate . . . I hope Tchehov's wife will be here. I have gone
back to my big lovely room too, so we should have plenty of space to
ourselves.'[17]

For John the meeting, their first in four months, is fraught with anxiety. He vacillates between total denial and profound despair. He wants to
believe that she can recover, but in his dark moments is convinced that she
will not. The Katherine who comes towards him is 'more like a wraith than
a woman'. She reminds observers 'of a candle light, pale, tiny, bright but
frail, to be extinguished by a draught'.[18] Her face, by contrast, is radiant,
her cheeks flushed with tuberculosis, and her feverish eyes appear enormous above the gaunt cheekbones. John, in his self-delusion, believes her
to be better. Katherine introduces him to her friend Olga Ivanovna, known
as Olgivanna, her doctor James Young, a young Lithuanian girl called Adele
Kufian, who has fallen under Katherine's spell, and then the great man
Gurdjieff himself, who speaks so little English, French or German that the
possibilities of conversation are almost nil. Then Katherine takes John up
to her room for a private talk.

She tries to explain why she had felt the need to cut John off. Her
love for him had had to die: 'It was killing us both . . . I felt that I could
not bear it – tearing my heart away from yours. But I managed to do it.'
John blames the teachings of her mentor Gurdjieff and assumes that this
is 'part of the spiritual discipline of the place . . . thus to sacrifice one's
earthly affections'. Although he is happy when she tells him – 'I have won
through, at last . . . My love for you has all come back to me, renewed and
purified, – and greater than ever. That was why I wanted you to come'[19]

– he is aware of underlying feelings of confusion and dread. Katherine's heightened emotional state worries him; her unquestioning espousal of esoteric philosophies is at odds with his own devotion to logic and reason, and she is surrounded by men he fears may be charlatans. Over the last few months he has read books recommended by Katherine in an attempt to understand what she is doing, but the ideas they contain remain mysterious in the light of his agnosticism. He can't follow her leap of faith. John is out of his depth among people who have embraced an alien philosophy, though he finds an instant rapport with James Young. The doctor had been first a surgeon, then studied under Jung to become a psychotherapist. At Fontainebleau he is exploring the healing possibilities of Gurdjieff's theories and sharing a room with A. R. Orage, a man John detests and regards as a negative influence on Katherine's life and health. He blames Orage for introducing Katherine to Gurdjieff. Without him, John believes, she would never have entered the institute and might have spent the winter in a more comfortable environment.

Gurdjieff is in the middle of a massive project, the details of which have filled Katherine's letters. He has recently bought an old aircraft hangar used by the French during the war and transported it to the garden of the priory. There it is being transformed into a huge performance space called the Study House, big enough to accommodate three hundred people. The metal walls are being decorated with murals and a floor has been constructed of clay bricks made in the Russian fashion. There is a perfumed fountain in front of a dais used by performers, a gigantic throne under a canopy for Gurdjieff himself, and raised terraces around the walls covered with Russian furs and oriental carpets for spectators to sit on. To please Katherine, John takes a paintbrush and helps Olga to decorate some glass panels. She tries to explain the principles they live by, telling John that in the institute they try to create an atmosphere of overwhelming love; that this love is a healing, creative force.

When the bell rings for dinner, it has begun to rain, but Katherine refuses an umbrella to walk across to the main house. 'I love the rain tonight,' she tells Olga. 'I want the feeling of it on my face.' After supper they all go into the salon for an evening performance of music and dance. Katherine has a special seat beside the fireplace where big logs are spitting and crackling. Tambourines jingle in the background and they can hear musicians tuning their instruments. Katherine seems agitated and aloof. 'I want music,' she says to Olga. 'Why don't they begin? . . . I simply must see the "group" tonight. Will they do the "group"?' She wants John to see the centre piece of La Prieuré's philosophy transmuted into dance – a 'prayer' in movement and music, a synthesis of body and mind that comes from the Sufi tradition. The music begins; the dancers prepare themselves. Katherine's thin face is glowing with expectation.[20] For her, though not for John, the music is a spiritual experience.

When the performance ends at 10.30 p.m., many of the participants, including Olga, go back to the Study House to continue working. There is very little time now before the Russian new year on 13 January and it has to be made ready for the celebration. Katherine, exhausted by the effort of the day, goes back to her room, escorted by John and Adele. Climbing the stairs steadily, without support, hoping to show John just how well she is, strains Katherine's body and her lungs to the limit.

She begins to cough and, as she enters the bedroom, bright, arterial blood spurts through the fingers she puts over her mouth. 'I think . . . I am going to die,' she gasps. John, terrified, runs downstairs to call for a doctor. Adele tries to staunch the flow of blood with a towel. When John returns, James and another doctor push him aside and he leaves the room with one last, anguished glance at his wife. Though she can no longer speak, the expression in Katherine's eyes is beseeching.

All efforts to stop the haemorrhage are useless and, at eleven o'clock, Katherine is pronounced dead. John is comforted by Olga and Adele, who have waited on the landing outside the door with him. They are all in shock, barely able to function. A telegram is sent to Ida at Lisieux, asking her to come immediately.

The following day, Ida arrives on the afternoon train and moves into Katherine's room at La Prieuré. Ida had felt when they parted in October that she would never see Katherine again, and just before Christmas she had woken in the early hours of the morning in her room at Lisieux 'from a dream of the knowledge of death', the tears coursing down her cheeks. Katherine had wanted to deny the fact of dying; had wanted everyone around her to ignore her illness and behave as if nothing was the matter. But that's not always possible when one loves someone so much. Ida doesn't like to think of Katherine dying in such a cold, inhospitable place, surrounded by strangers. She finds some comfort when Olga tells her that this was not the case – that on the last evening Katherine had been 'so full of the spirit of love that she was transformed'.

Katherine's body has been laid out in the priory chapel. Ida is horrified by the cheap white wooden coffin that John has chosen – 'cold and bare'. She goes up to the room and brings down the 'brilliantly embroidered black silk Spanish shawl' given to Katherine by Ottoline Morrell and covers the casket with it.[21] Remembering her friend's love of flowers, she brings in whatever winter blooms she can find in the garden – Christmas roses and snowdrops – and arranges them on the coffin.

Ida tries to contain her grief and concentrate on the practical aspects of the task in front of her. While John negotiates with funeral directors Pompes Funèbres and sends telegrams to friends and family informing them of Katherine's death and the date and time of the funeral, Ida has the personal, distressing job of sorting through Katherine's clothes and belongings, packing what must be taken back to England, identifying the keepsakes that Katherine has bequeathed to her friends. Ida had been with Katherine at the hotel in Switzerland last summer when the will had been drawn up and witnessed by the maid and the proprietor, so – even though it will be several days before it is given to John – she is familiar with its contents. The making of the will had seemed an ominous event to Ida, but Katherine had passed it off light-heartedly. After she reached La Prieuré she had written to Ida that though she felt better, 'as a precaution I shall send my will to the Bank in case of accidents'.[22] Katherine's gold watch and chain, placed on the mantelpiece after her death, have been left to Ida as a 'symbol or pledge . . . to assure me that she was still going forward and on'.[23] The fur coat has been left to John's mother, though it has suffered dreadfully at Fontainebleau and is now unfit for anything. Katherine had practically lived in it to keep out the cold, even scraped carrots in it when on kitchen duty. The embroidered Spanish shawl now draped over Katherine's coffin has to be given to Anne Estelle (Rice) Drey. The rest of her clothes are for Ida. She knows by heart the list of other small bequests to friends and family. Everything else has been left to Jack.

Ida, whose own parents died while she was young, has more experience of funerals than John. He remains stunned, incapable of rational thought. Katherine had once instructed him humorously to choose a young and pretty wife to follow her and 'give your little girl the pearl ring'.[24] John immediately gives it to Adele and a disgusted Ida interprets it as an engagement. Adele is sensible enough to return the ring after a tactful interval.

On Thursday several of John's associates arrive from London for the funeral. Among them is the novelist Henry Tomlinson, whom Katherine had been encouraging just before she died. Millar Dunning, who scarcely knew Katherine but has become close to John in the months since she left, has come to support his friend. John's assistant editor J. W. N. Sullivan has also come, despite the fact that Katherine had thought him 'a queer fish'. She once complained that he 'set her teeth on edge'. John's brother Richard – who had to some extent taken the place of Katherine's own brother in her life – is there, but not her greatest friend, the Russian writer Samuel Koteliansky, who is deeply distressed that the authorities have refused him a travel permit. Being a Russian immigrant, he is not free to come and go as he pleases. It is a strange mixture of people who knew Katherine only slightly and are there because John has invited them, and those for whom her death is a personal tragedy.

In the evening they all have dinner at the Chalet de la Fôret in Fontainebleau, where some of them are staying. Before the meal Ida, upset, walks up and down the garden outside with Orage, comforted by the fact that he is one of Katherine's closest and oldest friends. Both of them have known Katherine longer than anyone else in the room and have memories no one else can share. Orage tells friends that Katherine is the only woman he has ever truly loved.[25]

Given that the guests have only Katherine in common, dinner is a rather strained social occasion. The conversation ranges widely and attitudes towards Katherine, and why she came here, are sometimes critical. There are strong differences of opinion between John and his associates and Katherine's friends from the institute – Orage in particular. Ida stands up and tells them she does not think they should be 'speaking in this manner' talking about Katherine when she is not there 'to defend or explain herself'.[26] Her disconcerting outburst breaks up the party.

Katherine's sisters, Jeanne and Chaddie, and her friend Dorothy Brett, arrive on Friday morning, in clear winter sunshine. After lunch, Katherine's coffin, still draped in Ottoline's shawl and decorated with flowers Ida has ordered from Paris, is loaded onto a hearse drawn by four black-plumed horses to be taken to the small Protestant church. Brett has brought a basket of lily of the valley tied with pink ribbon. There are very few wreaths. Because the funeral is not in London many of the people prominent in Katherine's life are missing: the Bloomsbury contingent – Virginia and Leonard Woolf, Ottoline Morrell, Bertrand Russell, Katherine's literary cousin Elizabeth von

Arnim (now the estranged wife of the Earl Russell), T. S. Eliot, Mark Gertler and E. M. Forster – as well as close personal friends such as Koteliansky and the painter, Anne Estelle Rice. Katherine's eldest sister Vera is in Canada and the Lawrences are in Mexico.

Even so, the little church is quite crowded, the congregation swelled by people from the institute. The service is in French. The eulogy, written by John, is given by a minister who did not know Katherine at all. After the service the coffin has to be taken to the cemetery. It seems to the mourners 'a very long way'. The funeral cars are forced to travel at a 'crawling pace' behind the horses. Ida can't bear it and gets out to walk beside the hearse, 'miles and miles very slowly'.[27] Winter days are short in the Northern hemisphere and by the time the cortège arrives it is 'bitterly cold and almost dark'. There is confusion as the coffin is lowered into the grave. The minister, 'his white hair shining in the dim light',[28] waits for John to throw in the traditional handful of earth, but he is immobilised by grief and can't be prompted. Ida, realising that something is called for, tosses in the small bunch of marigolds – one of Katherine's favourite flowers – that she has been holding.

That evening a funeral meal is served in the new Study House with 'an immense number of dishes . . . carried round to everyone', and there are 'dancers, with music and many lights'. Tomorrow is the Russian new year. Wine is served and John, who has never had much of a head for alcohol, is observed 'talking far too much and laughing hysterically'. Orage asks Ida to take John up to his room.

In her own room, lying on the bed where Katherine has so recently died, Ida feels *'completely numb, as though I had been shattered, like some brittle thing, into tiny fragments all scattered and no more LM left at all'*.[29]

2

The Husband's Story

Once upon a time a sensitive soul was born in New Zealand, took the name Katherine Mansfield and came to Europe, where she wrote evocative fragments, loved delicately, and died young – technically of pulmonary tuberculosis but really because life was too gross for her . . . Fortunately, this banal person never existed.

BRIGID BROPHY, *MICHIGAN REVIEW*, 1966

Katherine has been the centre of John's life since he was a twenty-two-year-old undergraduate at Oxford. Back in England, in a fit of depression, he climbs onto his motor cycle and, leaving Dorothy Brett's house in London, travels out to the cottage in Sussex lent to him by his friend Millar Dunning. There, sitting alone by the fire, he has an acute mystical experience. 'The room was filled with a presence and I knew I was not alone – that I never could be alone any more . . . I could never be afraid in the old ways or cowardly with the old cowardice . . . The "presence" was definitely connected with the person of Katherine Mansfield . . . It had a moral quality, or a moral effect: I was immediately and deeply convinced that "all was well with her".'[1] He is convinced that Katherine's love has survived her death and will now be with him always. She will live on through her work, recreated by his own love for her; he is determined not to let her die. The altar is now 'draped for the Katherine Mansfield cult'.[2]

Within a couple of weeks of the funeral John is already writing businesslike letters to Katherine's agent J. B. Pinker. 'After consulting Katherine Mansfield's cousin and friend, Countess Russell ... I have decided that the best method to follow with regard to her unpublished work is this: I intend to bring out a volume containing all the stories & fragments of stories written by my wife since the publication of "The Garden Party". These will make only a small volume, to be sold, I should imagine, at 5/-. This volume must be published as soon as possible, while her name and reputation is still fresh in the public mind.'[3] He has already discussed this with Michael Sadleir at Constable and they have planned an ambitious schedule. The 'Dove's Nest', a collection of the stories written in her last two years, is to be published immediately. In the summer John will bring out a complete volume of Katherine's poems, then in the autumn of 1923 and the spring of 1924 two volumes of early, unpublished, stories written between 'The German Pension' and 'Bliss'. John aims to have the manuscripts for all three volumes ready by the end of April. Then he intends to start work on a volume of extracts from her notebooks he calls 'Journal & Sketches'. 'This will contain some of her finest & most individual work. But is one of the hardest volumes to collect & arrange.'[4] He intends to publish this in the summer of 1924, to be followed by a two-volume edition of her letters in the autumn of 1924 and the spring of 1925. In addition he has already decided that, during the next twelve months, every edition of the *Adelphi* – the periodical he edits – will contain something of Katherine's, giving her the widest possible literary publicity. When others protest at this overexposure, he tells them that 'Katherine's work is sacred – a bad word, but the best I have – to me'.[5] But John is never able to keep to this ambitious schedule and editing her letters and manuscripts will take him almost the whole of his life: the final volume will appear in 1954.

John has complete control of her unpublished work, thanks to the Copyright Act, only a decade old and with its influence on an author's estate relatively untried. The new legislation gives John control of Katherine's published work for fifty years, but her unpublished work – by far the largest part of the gift – becomes his absolute property in perpetuity. In leaving the whole of her literary estate to her husband without any legal provisos, Katherine was probably unaware of the implications. She had written a simple will and a letter to her husband concerning her manuscripts, without ever consulting a solicitor. They leave her intentions unclear and give ammunition to those who consider John's actions unethical.

According to the will drawn up on 14 August 1922 at a hotel in Switzerland, 'all manuscripts notebooks papers letters I leave to John M. Murry likewise I should like him to publish as little as possible and to tear up and burn as much as possible he will understand that I desire to leave as few traces of my camping ground as possible.'[6] But the letter she had written to John on 7 August is subtly different. 'All my manuscripts I leave entirely to you to do what you like with. Go through them one day, dear love, and destroy all you do not use. Please destroy all letters you do not wish to keep & all papers. You know my love of tidiness. Have a clean sweep, Bogey, and leave all fair – will you?'[7]

Katherine destroyed some material at Fontainebleau before she died, but most of her manuscripts, letters and journals were in trunks and boxes scattered throughout Europe – some left in Switzerland, some at her flat in London, some in storage. It is also clear that she believed, as many terminally ill patients do, that she would be given more time to finish her work. When she had contemplated death the previous summer and written both the will and the letter she seems to have envisaged John publishing only complete stories that he knew had met her exacting standards. She trusted him to use his editorial instincts to prune out sub-standard material – the sketches and extracts she was still hoping to work on when she died. It also seems clear, from the tone of both documents, that she did not foresee him publishing utterly private material – her journals and her letters; she talks of him destroying any that he does not wish to 'keep'. This accords with her sentiments about posthumous publication in a letter to Ottoline in 1921, criticising the editors of a new edition of Chekhov's notebooks: 'It's not fair to glean a man's buttons and pins and hawk them after his death'.[8]

But her wishes – both expressed and implied – are in direct conflict with John's own instincts, his feelings towards Katherine after her death and his need to earn a living. Consumed by grief and guilt at his treatment of Katherine while she was alive, he will spend the rest of his life nurturing her literary reputation and editing her work, constructing a literary legend from the fragments available to him and living on the proceeds. To many he is a ghoul 'boiling Katherine's bones to make soup',[9] but to others he is preserving and publishing some of her best work, keeping her name alive for future generations. It is probable that, without his obsession, she would have been forgotten. As with Sylvia Plath and her husband Ted Hughes, the tragedy of Katherine Mansfield's life and early death, and the part played by John Murry, have created a seductive myth that is hard to penetrate.

Garnet Trowell, Katherine's first lover and the father of her child, reads the news of her death in the London papers. He is still working as what his family terms 'a bow jockey' – a peripatetic violinist with touring orchestras. A shy, self-effacing man, he had never married while Katherine was alive, but now in 1923 he weds a Canadian girl and they plan to return to her home in Windsor, Ontario and settle there. Like his father, Garnet intends to teach music. Katherine's love letters, and the gifts that she had given him during their affair, are in his luggage when he leaves.

At Hogarth House, where Virginia and Leonard Woolf had first published Katherine's story 'Prelude', Virginia learns the news of her death from the cook. 'Nelly said in her sensational way at breakfast on Friday "Mrs Murry's dead! It says so in the paper!" At that one feels what? A shock of relief? A rival the less? Then confusion at feeling so little then, gradually, blankness & disappointment; then a depression which I could not rouse myself from all that day. When I began to write, it seemed to me there was no point in writing. Katherine wont read it. Katherine's my rival no longer.'[10] A dream of the dead Katherine in a white wreath haunts Virginia for several months.

Like John, Ida, who is going through what she later describes as a severe nervous breakdown, claims to have been visited by Katherine. Living at Brett's house in London, she is helping John to sort Katherine's manuscripts and transcribing some of her work. One evening, 'I always think due to my great need in my hopeless despair – she was suddenly, unexpectedly with me. I saw her face full of light like a halo, as, with a lovely smile she assured me all was well with her and so, of course, with me.'[11]

In Bloomsbury there are other psychic experiences. The Honourable Dorothy Brett, Bloomsbury groupie and Slade graduate, has finally, after years of courtship and persuasion, given her advanced virginity to John Murry and is expecting him to marry her. She claims to have encountered Katherine on the stairs of her house in Pond Street and Brett's charwoman says she has seen Katherine sitting in the room where she had stayed just before leaving for Fontainebleau. Encouraged by these psychic revelations, Brett declares that she can feel Katherine's presence constantly with her. She begins a journal addressed directly to her main rival for John's attention. 'Tig, My Beautiful little friend . . . I have felt you so close to me these last few days – only you do not come so often now or so clearly = dearest,

I've been worried – what am I to do with your little lad – I hear you still saying – "Look after the little lad for me, Brett, oh do look after him" – and then I remember all my looking after led to . . .' What it had led to is confided in another entry: 'Dearest Tig, For the first time in my life I slept with a man and that man was yours . . .'[12]

Ever since Katherine went to Fontainebleau, John has been searching for comfort in all the women around him. Apart from Brett, he has developed what he calls 'a warm physical passion' for Millar Dunning's wife, Bill, living next door to his cottage in Sussex.[13] Bill, a self-advertised medium, now claims to be possessed by Katherine's spirit. When she talks, it is Katherine who speaks through her. Brett believes it and comments that 'her voice makes me shiver'.[14] Some of his friends believe that, through his affairs, John is seeking to make contact with his dead wife. He proposes to Vere Bartrick-Baker, Katherine's school friend, and – possibly – former lover. Frieda Lawrence, whose wedding ring Katherine wore to her grave, also appears again during the summer of 1923 and, despite having a husband still alive in Mexico, tries to seduce John. Though he admits that he is in love with her, John refuses on the grounds of his loyalty to Lawrence. Most people believe they are lovers. Brett is grief-stricken, writing to Katherine in her diary, 'I want to tell you, dear, of Frieda = of the appalling indecency of her to me and JMM. Oh, why are people so indelicate . . . I feel as though a bucket of dirty water has been thrown over me . . .'[15] But not all John's affairs are connected with Katherine. Unknown to the others, he also has a liaison with a woman he describes as 'an Australian whore' and brings her down to the cottage to stay for the weekend.[16]

He is suffering from immense sexual frustration. During the last years Katherine had been too ill to be physically attractive. Hurt, she had noticed how he turned his mouth away from her when she went to kiss him on their wedding day in 1918; how her cough, the deep, gurgling cough of the consumptive, followed often by blood-stained expectoration, disgusted him. And her body, even if he had still wanted her, was too frail – the bones too near the skin, the heart too weak – for healthy, animal activity. John had tried to explain: 'My longing to hold you in my arms was terrible; but more terrible was the thought which held me back. "No, I mustn't; I shall hurt her." At that moment the knowledge of your illness blinded me like a flash of lightning – tore right through my heart.'[17] It was something Katherine, also sexually deprived, needing so desperately to be loved and comforted, could not understand.

John is inexperienced where women are concerned, and has always suffered from what he calls 'the fearful shyness of sex'.[18] He allows women to seduce him, but is rarely bold enough to make the first move. He later regrets not having had a complete physical affair with Princess Elizabeth Bibesco; since everyone had believed them to be lovers it would have made no difference. He feels, too, that Katherine should have been kinder about his love affair with Brett and others after she had gone to Fontainebleau – affairs that, according to John, rarely went further than kissing, cuddling and exchanging love letters. 'Those years of sexual deprivation I underwent in my young manhood were indeed pretty grim, and I marvel a little that Katherine was not a little more understanding towards me in that respect. Not that it matters. But I know something about "married chastity".'[19] But however much he knows about sexual abstinence, John knows nothing about how women think and feel. It had not occurred to him, when he confessed his misdemeanours to Katherine, that she would 'mind' him making love with someone else as she lay dying, or that Brett – a lonely, profoundly deaf woman of thirty-nine – might now mistake his need for comfort for a genuine relationship.

On the same day, 1 February, that he is writing to Katherine's agent about her work, John is also writing to Brett, telling her that she must not think of marriage just yet. His excuse is that he is too full of grief to make a new commitment so soon. But Brett, who has been sharing a bed with him, is not to be deterred. Having discouraged John's advances all autumn out of loyalty to Katherine, she now thinks she has a right to Katherine's husband, and believes her role as close friend and the next Mrs Murry, entitles her to participate in the arrangements for Katherine's estate. While John is at Ditchling, Brett is horrified by the sight of Ida, wearing Katherine's gold watch, sorting the precious belongings and manuscripts that Brett is forbidden to touch. There is a quarrel and afterwards Brett writes to John, venting her jealousy and her snobbery about a woman she regards as her social inferior. (Brett is, after all, the daughter of a viscount.) She accuses Ida of complete insensitivity and of 'torturing' Katherine when she was alive. John writes another letter, this time much stronger. 'I tell you frankly I don't like it. You make a great many insinuations about Ida which I don't like.' Some of them he finds 'intolerable'. 'Why this pretence of superiority to her? "This solid school-girl type." Really! Do you imagine that Katherine would have relied on her for twenty years, had she been that?' As for torturing her, 'Do you imagine you never tortured Tig? Or I, for that matter?'[20]

Less than a month after writing to Brett, John is in bed with Katherine's old friend Vere Bartrick-Baker, staying at her house in Chobham and contemplating a more lasting attachment. He writes a letter afterwards, telling Vere that he had asked her to consider living with him only 'because I suddenly had the feeling that you might care to live with me the absurd kind of life which is the only one possible for me'. A couple of weeks later marriage is more explicitly discussed. 'I don't want you to marry me because I may appear charming; nor because we're both a bit tired and weary . . . But because we're both out to make something positive out of it. We're not too old to be profoundly happy; we are too old to make a stupid mistake.'[21] A fortnight later he is backtracking at top speed, as he had with Brett. John seems also to have talked to D. H. Lawrence, now settled at Taos in Mexico, about the possibility of marriage to one or other of these women, because Lawrence writes in April: 'I don't see you with another wife. But it will be as it will be.'[22]

A month after Katherine's death John publishes, in the February 1923 issue of *Adelphi*, an autobiographical account of his psychic experience in the cottage in Sussex. 'I became aware of myself as a little island against whose slender shores a cold, dark, boundless ocean lapped devouring. Somehow, in that moment, I knew I had reached a pinnacle of personal being . . . The love I had lost was still mine, but now more durable, being knit into the very substance of the universe I had feared.' His public parade of feeling is ridiculed by both friends and critics, who know very well where he has been spending his nights. Virginia Woolf writes a little sketch of a Bloomsbury dinner party conversation in her diary, and Aldous Huxley lampoons him as Burlap in his novel *Point Counter Point*. 'When Susan died Burlap exploited the grief he felt, or at any rate loudly said he felt, in a more than usually painful series of those always painfully personal articles which were the secret of his success as a journalist . . . Pages of a rather hysterical lyricism about the dead child-woman . . .'[23]

Lawrence, himself suffering from advanced tuberculosis, writes a letter of condolence to John, which heals a long breach between the two men. Katherine's death leads to a temporary truce. Lawrence says that he had been on the point of sending her a book. 'I wanted Katherine to read it. She'll know, though. The dead don't die.' The death of a contemporary disturbs him: '. . . it makes me afraid. As if worse were coming.' He feels 'as if old moorings [are] breaking . . . It has been a savage enough pilgrimage these last four years.'[24] But to others Lawrence complains that John is putting Katherine's 'waste paper basket' before the public. Lawrence thinks that he is trying to make her out to be a genius and a saint and, worst of all, he is making 'capital out of her death'.[25]

Lawrence is referring to *The Dove's Nest*, published in London in June, followed by publication in the United States two months later. It contains one of her New Zealand stories, 'The Doll's House', and a few masterpieces written in Switzerland – particularly 'The Fly' and 'A Married Man's Story'. But it is bulked out by commercial stories, a long way from her best work, which Katherine had been writing under a magazine contract that paid for her medical treatment, and fragments among her papers which John has himself edited into shape. Katherine had been writing and rewriting the title story, 'The Dove's Nest', during her time at Sierre in Switzerland. At one time it had grown to the size of a 'short novel' and she had been intrigued to see if that was what it would become. But in the end the bloated manuscript did not come up to her standards and was among the things she burned when she came to Fontainebleau. Its slimmed down offspring is published by John, though it is difficult to know what Katherine would have done with it had she lived. Lawrence is right in his judgement that this uneven collection falls short of Katherine's critical demands.

When Frieda sails from New York on 18 August 1923 Lawrence asks John to take care of her. 'I wish you'd look after her a bit: would it be a nuisance?' Lawrence is reluctant to come to a country he now regards as hostile. 'I don't want to go: don't know why.' He repeatedly makes the excuse that he is working on another novel, but the reality probably lies in another comment he makes in a letter to a friend. 'I feel England has insulted me, and I stomach that feeling badly.'[26]

In September Lawrence tells John that he does not know where Frieda is. 'From Frieda not a word – suppose Germany has swallowed her.' But Lawrence has also been travelling so he is not altogether surprised at the lack of contact.[27] In fact Frieda has gone to Europe with John – she is going to Germany, he is going to Switzerland and they travel to Freiburg together via Paris. John tells Brett he is going to collect Katherine's manuscripts from Sierre and others that he is intending to find out about psychotherapy for T. S. Eliot's troubled wife, Vivien. During the journey he and Frieda, always attracted to each other, become very close. 'On the journey we declared our love to each other. She was sweet and lovely, altogether adorable, and she wanted us to stay together in Freiburg for a few days anyhow, and I wanted it terribly. The idea of our sleeping together, waking in each other's arms, seemed like heaven on earth.'[28] Frieda has told friends that Lawrence is impotent, and that they are estranged. She has already had other affairs. John's rejection of her advances makes Frieda very sad and in her letters she taunts him about his timidity.[29] John also experiences regret; he believes himself in love with Frieda and his erotic feelings towards her make him realise that he must do something about his personal relationships. He comes to a decision. In October he writes to Brett from Switzerland to tell her that he wants to end their affair and will no longer live with her when he returns. She pours out her anguish to Katherine.

> I have been through a bad time = ever since JMM wrote telling me of his decision to leave my little house and move into his flat, I have felt chilled = he is right in his way = it is difficult for us to live so intimately together unless we go further and marry = and so the crack is widening = I understand him perfectly but it does not lessen the regret = I would have liked a deeper relationship but I do not now think that it will ever be for me = For the first time since early youth he feels free = there are young women = and to man they are eternally exciting, mysterious and perhaps desirable = Oh, Tig, of what use to torment oneself =[30]

Although John shares a bed with her again briefly when he comes back to England, he moves out of her house in Pond Street a couple of weeks later and the affair is over – at least as far as John is concerned – though Brett is still claiming that he is occasionally her lover until February. 'I never refuse him,' she tells Koteliansky.[31]

Ida's services are also dispensed with. She has taken Katherine's command to 'look after Jack' very seriously, but John, understandably, finds her company either in London or at Ditchling inconvenient. He consults Katherine's cousin, Elizabeth, and Ida is offered the position of companion housekeeper to Elizabeth at her London house. Ida travels out to Switzerland with Elizabeth during the winter and eventually moves into a small cottage in the New Forest, bought by Elizabeth as a retreat, where Ida lives with a female friend she had known in London. At this point John loses touch with Ida and as a result a great deal of valuable knowledge that only Ida has is lost and Katherine's estate becomes the victim of John's inadequate organisational skills. When Katherine died, John had commissioned a simple stone to cover her grave, inscribed with her name, her dates and the proprietorial statement 'Wife of John Middleton Murry', but in the emotional chaos of his life he has forgotten to pay for Katherine's burial so her body is soon moved into a communal grave, designed to be reused by those who cannot afford an individual plot. Even in death, Katherine is not allowed to remain in one place.

Katherine's Poems, edited by John, are published in November. Many of them are juvenilia, including children's poems she had written in New Zealand to be illustrated by a friend. Others are 'emotional safety valve' poems from her notebooks that she had never intended to be published and had never been revised. Katherine was not a good poet and the verses included in the anthology are slight – more interesting for what they say about Katherine than as individual poems. John, whose own poetry is excruciating, is emotionally ill equipped to judge Katherine's output. Even his editorial comments are inaccurate. Ida, who had been present when some of the poems were written, annotates her own copy with pencilled corrections as she reads through them and shares her comments with Elizabeth.

A poem called 'Jangling Memory' had been written for Garnet Trowell, much earlier than the date John has given it. Ida puts it into a group with 'The Arabian Shawl', the poignant 'Sleeping Together' and 'The Quarrel' – all belonging to the 1908–9 period when Katherine had been staying with the Trowell family in London. A poem called 'The Secret' had originally been written in 1911 as a dedication on the flyleaf of a book Katherine had given to Ida. But 'The Gulf', which John also dates as 1911, had not been written until after Katherine's brother Leslie died four years later. The 1917 poem 'Night scented Stock' had been written for Garsington, recalling a skinny dipping episode at one of Ottoline's house parties.

> 'Is the moon a virgin or is she a harlot?'
> Asked somebody. Nobody would tell.
> The faces and the hands moved in a pattern
> As the music rose and fell.

The accuracy of Ida's memory can now be checked with reference to Katherine's notebooks, which John, in his haste to put her work before the public, had not had time to read.

Frieda is still in John's life. She writes to her husband that she likes England and does not want to go back to Mexico. Her children are in England, her family in Germany and she misses them when she is on the other side of the Atlantic. Lawrence, sensing his wife's estrangement, realises that he will have to go to Europe in order to persuade her to return home. Frieda sends him a telegram with one word, 'Come'. (It is scrambled to 'Cone' by the telegraph operator, but Lawrence understands it.) He arrives at the beginning of December.

Immediately there is trouble between Lawrence and John. The former had been invited to write an article for the *Adelphi*, and given carte blanche, but John does not like the result. 'He went green at my first article, and wouldn't print it. "No, Lorenzo, you'll only make enemies." – As if that weren't what I want.' Lawrence describes John as one of the 'suburbanians', and thinks his editorial conservatism will be the death of the magazine by making it too safe. John is by nature timid and 'approval seeking'; Lawrence enjoys controversy. 'I hate this slime of "all the world's my friend".'[32]

Lawrence tries to persuade John and Brett to go out to Taos with him when he returns. It is to be his dream of Rananim – the ideal artistic community they had talked about when John and Katherine lived next door to the Lawrences in Cornwall. Brett, whose reputation as a painter is rapidly growing, is very keen. She likes the idea of America and can see a new direction for her work. John considers it, but will not commit himself. He would have to abandon his career as an editor to live solely on writing, and there is the question of Katherine's literary estate and the nurturing of her reputation. How could he manage that from Mexico? And there are more complicated sexual politics to be considered. There is his brief fling with Frieda in the autumn; Brett is still hoping to marry him and has recently miscarried (or aborted) his child; and he has just met a young woman he finds disturbingly attractive.

There is another negative too. John is always conscious of Lawrence's intense emotional feelings towards him. The homo-erotic passage in *Women in Love* between Gerald Crich and Rupert Birkin is believed to have been based on an episode Katherine once described taking place between Lawrence and John. Katherine had been fully conscious of Lawrence's interest in her husband and often complained that when they were together she was totally ignored. John is only just beginning to realise what Katherine, with her own ambiguous sexuality, had known instinctively. When he leans over to Lawrence at the Café Royal – they are both rather drunk – kisses him and says, 'I love you, Lorenzo, but I cannot promise never to betray you!', John believes he has guessed 'Lawrence's secret', which he knows by a 'preternatural illumination'.[33]

A year later, when their relationship is foundering again, Lawrence writes to John:

> You remember that charming dinner at the Café Royal that night? You remember saying: I love you, Lorenzo, but I won't promise not to betray you? Well, you CAN'T betray me, and that's all there is to that. Ergo, just leave off loving me. Let's wipe off all that Judas-Jesus slime. Remember, you have betrayed everything and everybody up to now. It may have been your destiny . . . All I want to say is, don't think you can either love me or betray me. Learn that I am not lovable: hence not betrayable.[34]

In January 1924, John publishes in the *Adelphi* a poem in archaic mode that is false not only in tone, but in fact and sentiment. The poem had been written eight years earlier and he has recycled it for the first anniversary of Katherine's death.

> *A child of other worlds, a perfect thing*
> *Vouchsafed to justify this world's imagining? . . .*
> *A princess manifest, a child withouten stain.*

Throughout the autumn his eulogies in editorial prefaces and articles in the *Adelphi* have become increasingly hagiographic. He is beginning to mythologise Katherine – to the horror of her friends. They believe that by overstating his claims for her writing he risks having her work ridiculed. 'Great?' asks Lawrence. 'Why say great?'[35] Katherine's friend Koteliansky, and her cousin Sydney Waterlow, openly question John's wisdom in filling the *Adelphi* with her work and the disagreement escalates into a row over editorial control of the magazine. Sydney thinks that John is treating Kot, its business manager, very badly. John, who still blames Kot for encouraging Katherine to go to Gurdjieff, replies with four words in giant letters on four pieces of paper: 'GO BOIL YOUR HEAD'.[36]

Virginia Woolf, contemplating the revelations of Brett's charwoman and John's sickly sentimentality, asks her diary what Katherine could possibly have done to deserve 'this cheap posthumous life'.[37] Woolf remembers a different Katherine, 'who dressed like a tart and behaved like a bitch';[38] a caustic, self-mocking woman who could recount wicked anecdotes about acquaintances that had Leonard Woolf weeping with laughter; a woman who despised maudlin sentiment and was not afraid to admit she had sometimes lived outside the tramlines of respectable convention and who claimed to have 'gone every sort of hog since she was seventeen'.[39]

In a letter from Germany early in 1924 Lawrence queries John's motivations and future direction. 'I don't know if you really want to go to Taos . . . You seemed to me really very unsure . . . Can't you focus yourself outside yourself? Not for ever focused on yourself, ad nauseam?'[40] When John finally tells him that he can't come to Mexico, though without admitting the main reason for his withdrawal, Lawrence feels let down. In March the Lawrences leave, taking only Brett, who writes to Katherine in her diary: 'I'm off to Mexico – I am leaving JMM – It's been fearfully hard to do – but I feel it is right – I've loved him, cherished him . . . but I am going because it is best for him to be alone for a little while – I've done all I can – and lately I've been held back, because I felt the need in him of being free – I have given no outward sign of affection – it's been difficult to restrain myself – but it is right – he must have freedom when he needs it – So I go – Lawrence, Frieda and I –'[41]

Elsewhere there is the acrid smell of burning paper as people who had known only one side of Katherine begin to get a distinct sense of what she might have been to others. Beatrice Hastings, one of Katherine's first friends in London, is particularly caustic, publishing a vicious attack that claims Katherine had 'twittered her way out of a world she had fouled wherever she went'.[42] Those who have no need to take account of the autograph value of Katherine's letters, begin to reread and destroy documents that might cast a poor light on their own conduct. Others, who had loved her, want to protect her reputation. One of these is Vere Bartrick-Baker, who had not only been the object of Katherine's teenage passion, but also the recipient of confidences about her affair with Floryan Sobieniowski. John writes to her that Katherine 'once confessed to me that she was afraid of you, and that she felt that one day you would "strike back at her". (I don't vouch for the actual phrase: but the sense of it is accurate enough.) I came (I don't know why) to the conclusion that there were some "incriminating" letters. Possibly, because I knew that at one period Katherine was rather addicted to such letters. But I never had the faintest doubt of the reality of her fear of you.'[43] Katherine need not have been afraid: Vere burns all her letters from Katherine, though she does keep a story, 'Leves Amores', of an ambiguous erotic episode. Edie Bendall, now Mrs G. G. S. Robison, tells enquirers that Katherine's love letters to her had been 'stolen' while she was on honeymoon. Ida has already made a bonfire of all the letters she had received from Katherine over those difficult early years in London, and the Floryan letters, ransomed after a blackmail attempt, have also been destroyed. Katherine's letters to Maata Mahupuku are buried with their recipient. Those closest to Katherine do what they can to ensure that John's description of her as 'withouten stain' is credible.

Meanwhile Katherine's work is accruing large American royalties – over £1000 for work sold during 1922, and Constable send John a cheque for another £1000 in advance for the new publications. It is more money than Katherine had ever earned in her life. With his own income from the *Adelphi* and other literary work, John is comfortably off and able to buy a car.

On 25 October 1923, just after John has returned from his European holiday with Frieda, a young woman walks into the *Adelphi* office to talk about a short story she has just submitted for the magazine. She is slim and dark, but, unlike Katherine, she is childlike, extremely naive and much younger than her twenty-two years. Her name is Violet le Maistre. That night she writes on the flyleaf of Chekhov's *The Darling and Other Stories*, which John has recommended her to read: 'Bought on a day of most wonderful elation. Mr Middleton Murry has been talking with me about my work. He says I show the most amazing promise and that he was astounded. He is going to print some of my stuff.'[44] Within six months of that meeting, they are married.

3

Ida's Story

I write of KM – what does anyone know of the truth of one they love?

IDA BAKER, *THE MEMORIES OF LM*

In 1969, in a small cottage in the New Forest, Ida Constance Baker sits down at her kitchen table, and, persuaded by friends, begins to write down her memories of Katherine Mansfield.

> It is almost impossible to suggest Katherine with the use of words – like catching a breath of light on a butterfly's wing or describing the shading of a rose . . . She was neither tall nor short . . . she had a sensitive, finely curved mouth – and deep, dark steady eyes that looked – but above all she was herself – clear cut & with clear clean edges. There was a bell like quality in her rich, low, voice, though her singing voice was a high, pure soprano.[1]

Ida is eighty-one and very frail. Her white hair, no longer thick, is pinned up on top of her head, her fine skin webbed by tiny lines, and her dark eyes almost opaque behind the huge glasses she needs in order to see. She still invites close friends to call her Lesley Moore, the name that Katherine had given her when they were at school together – Lesley for Katherine's brother and Moore for Ida's mother's maiden name. Her whole life has been defined by her relationship with Katherine. In her memoir, Ida remembers the sacrifices she had made for her friend. How she had left her father in Rhodesia because she felt that Katherine needed her more – the guilt of his lonely suicide still distresses her. Ida also remembers the unevenness of her relationship with Katherine – all the stupid things that she had done to avoid annoying her. How she had slept on Katherine's doorstep one night because she had missed the train home and didn't want to wake her up. How she had pretended not to be hungry, so that Katherine would not feel obliged to spend money to feed her. But it had been Ida who had taken all the informal photographs of family and friends, developing them in hotel bathrooms and lodging house kitchens; Ida who had sat up late at night listening to Katherine's intimate conversations. She is the recorder, the faithful witness to Katherine's most secret life.

Ida's decision to write at least some of what she knows, is motivated by a need to put the record straight before she dies. Biographers, particularly Antony Alpers and Ruth Mantz, have angered her by their interpretation of Katherine's life and their relationship. Ida believes that John Murry has, in his own self-serving way, also told the story to suit himself. Her story has not been told and she is the only witness to the early part of Katherine's life – the episodes that Katherine tried hardest to conceal. Biographers and scholars have been asking her to talk for years, but she has always refused. Most wrote polite letters, but some were rather more determined.

One biographer, denied an interview because Ida was too ill, had found out where she lived and gained entrance to her cottage without an invitation. Ida was in a chair beside the fire, wrapped in blankets. She told him that she was too tired to talk and wanted to rest, but he refused to leave. 'I had to restrain myself from saying, "You'll soon have plenty of time to rest. This is the time to *talk*."' He confessed afterwards that he had had 'to suppress a desire to pile a few more blankets on Ida and carefully go through her papers'.[2] According to Ida's friends, the biographer did not leave until Ida made a telephone call to neighbours. Small wonder that Ida's editors observe 'a whiff of gunpowder' in the sub-text of her memoir.[3]

Ida first met Katherine in 1903 when they were both students at Queen's College, a London establishment for the further education of young women. Katherine, sent with her two older sisters to be educated in England, was already a precocious adolescent. Ida was a shy, naive, young girl from the colonies, still grieving for her mother who had recently died. Trying to define herself on paper so many years later, she describes herself as 'much slower to reach maturity . . . I remember even much later feeling very like those small yellow water lilies with their long stalks firmly fixed at the bottom of the river – but with their heads always floating below the hurrying surface . . . at the bottom, in the still waters, I was doing my own growing.'[4]

Viewed by others, it was an odd friendship. Katherine was attractive, socially confident, articulate and rich; Ida, the daughter of an Indian army doctor with limited funds, was tall, pale-skinned, with a beautiful mass of auburn hair, gauche and physically awkward. But they both felt themselves to be 'different' from others – marked out in some way. Ida's description of herself as a child, 'a fat little girl in glasses' could also be Katherine's. As a young woman Ida, too, struggled with her weight, as several of her letters comment: 'I have grown no thinner!!! . . . so far I can see no signs of "skeletonism", I grieve to say'.[5] Both Ida and Katherine felt misunderstood or rejected and had had a difficult experience of family. They also shared a love of music: Katherine was studying the cello, determined to be a professional musician, and Ida played the violin with the intention of making it her career. She and Katherine practised together and, with another New Zealander, Ruth Herrick, had fun dressing as bohemian young musicians with black floppy ties and soft felt hats. They once scandalised contemporaries by dressing in clothes 'borrowed' from Ida's father's wardrobe. Ida, who would have liked the courage to be daring, lived by proxy through her more confident friends.

Katherine had already published stories, poems and sketches in school magazines in New Zealand and continued to do so at Queen's. Ida also wrote poetry, though she showed it to no one except Katherine. Once, Ida wrote a short story for the college magazine and took it to show Katherine, only to discover that she too had written a story on the same subject. As always, Ida retreated in the face of superior gifts: 'my dream-child was hastily smothered'. This was a pity, because Ida had some talent for words. She was homesick for Rhodesia, where her father finally settled, and when she writes of it, her prose sings. 'I loved the country with its vibrant silences – the high quiet rocks, & poppies scattered without apparent plan & almost empty of human beings. The eucalyptus trees glittering in the moonlight – the bent grasses, swaying in the cool early morning breeze, with their heavy, clinging dew drops – all burnt up half an hour after the sun took charge.' What she lacked, Katherine told her, was a 'critical faculty' and she had 'no strong opinions'.[6] Ida admits in her memoir that she had no sense of humour either and was often slow to pick up on Katherine's clever ironies. She was the 'good conduct' monitor in class; Katherine was one of a wild, experimental group, often in trouble. There were constant clashes with her mother's sister, Aunt Belle, who had been left behind in England to chaperone the three Beauchamp girls. Not only did Katherine want more freedom than Belle was prepared to allow her, she fought continually with her sisters – particularly Vera – and eventually had to be moved to another room. According to Ida, Belle Dyer was 'young & hard & more interested in her own affairs than with any wish to understand an evolving artist'.[7] She had her own agenda: to find the husband who had eluded her in New Zealand. Belle was soon being courted by a wealthy shipowner and had no intention of allowing her turbulent niece to get in the way of her own future career.

Katherine once asked Ida what she would do if Katherine did 'something awful – like killing someone with a hatpin'. Ida's first reaction was practical, more concerned with the disposal of the body than the morality of the act. Katherine was surprised, and it was then that Ida outlined what she thought friendship meant – absolute loyalty and being there for each other, whatever happened. Katherine is often accused of 'using' Ida and many assumed, like Brett, that the relationship was one-sided and based on servitude and slavish admiration, but there were deeper qualities of attraction and an unseen balance. Ida was emphatic about that. 'There was no domination in it,' she wrote.[8] What she gave, she gave willingly and this dedication made her feel valuable. Ida saw in Katherine all the things she would have liked to have been herself – socially confident, articulate and gifted. This was someone worth dedicating one's life to. And there was something else, an emotional pull she was too innocent to recognise.

For Katherine, Ida was the perfect counterpoint to her own mercurial disposition. Katherine suffered from what was called, in the eighteenth century, 'an excess of sensibility' – she was given to episodes of extreme nervous excitement or fear, when her heart raced and pounded, she became emotionally overwrought, utterly terrified, and often fainted. Her friends referred to these episodes as 'Katherine's stunts'; some even believed that she did it deliberately to draw attention to herself. Ida's phlegmatic character was a calming influence, and she could soothe Katherine's panic attacks and bring her back to earth. When Katherine said impulsively during a walk in Regents Park, 'Shall we be friends?', she did so because she recognised in Ida a quality of absolute dependability. Ida's affections, once fixed, would never deviate, and she could give Katherine the unconditional love she had never had within her family. From that moment on their lives were intricately connected. For Ida, Katherine became 'the roadway of my life'.[9] For Katherine, Ida became a pillar of rock in a turbulent ocean – an island she could always return to, like a wandering bird.[10]

At a very simple level the relationship worked because Ida needed someone to love and Katherine needed to be loved, for under her self-confident exterior, there was a much more insecure young girl, who felt it necessary to hide her real self under a succession of masks. 'There are many many people that I like very much, but they generally view my public rooms, and they call me false, and mad, and changeable. I would not show them what I was really like for worlds.'[11] Katherine was unpopular at school, mainly because she was thought to keep herself 'reserved'. This was the girl who had felt obliged to hide her inner life from her family since she was very young; the girl whose mother had abandoned her at a year old and then again at three to spend several months in England; the girl who had watched her dead baby sister being laid out in her grandmother's bedroom; the girl who suffered night terrors even as an adult. Ida was one of only three people, Katherine declared, with whom she could be completely 'real'. There were always other important relationships in her life, but her bond with Ida 'ran beneath or through these, untouched'.[12] Her sisters joked that Ida had become her 'walking shadow'.

Ida remembered their first meeting with the vividness of hindsight. Probably because she had already been friends with Katherine's cousin Sylvia Payne, for several years as a 'junior' at Queen's, the matron, Miss Wood, asked Ida to show the three Beauchamp sisters to their attic bedroom. Vera was barely noticed, Chaddie simply a well-dressed young woman with fair hair, but Katherine made an instant impression as she looked at Ida 'steadily with calm, deeply dark eyes'. A few nights later, going up to the stairs to their room, Ida saw Katherine standing at the top, 'in a full, soft silk dress, her head tilted a little, her eyes glowing, her lips a little open as she sang to herself . . .'[13] There was a kind of falling in love – 'It was not long before I knew that I had found what I was to have and to be for the next twenty years'.[14] Ida's devotion was never subservient; it was a willed act requiring considerable strength. Those who knew her throughout her life remarked that underneath a surface of calm and sweetness she was a powerful woman with the tenacity of a bulldog.

At fourteen Katherine was passionate, reckless, rebellious, avid for experience and, though widely read, innocent in worldly terms. She had led a very sheltered life within the protection of the privileged Beauchamp family, and her sexual education had been rudimentary. The Beauchamp girls, like most young Victorian women, were given little information about the life of the body. Interviewed in old age, Katherine's sisters admitted that they had been told almost nothing by their mother. Coming from a generation before the publication of Marie Stopes' revelatory work, they were so ignorant they feared they could become pregnant from a kiss. Katherine was sexually precocious in an age which refused to admit that adult women, and certainly not teenage girls, might have a physical appetite. There was a dangerous mixture of ignorance and desire.

Katherine's journal records her feelings in the draft of an autobiographical novel called 'Juliet' written at Queen's.

> 'Got a mood?' [Her friend asks.]
> 'Yes, said Juliet. It's the very Devil.'
> 'It's sure to be something physical . . .You feel sexual.'
> 'Horribly – and in need of a physical shock or violence. Perhaps a good smacking would be beneficial.'15

Like other young women in the same situation, Katherine's sensual passions were expended in a fantasy relationship with a red-haired young musician from New Zealand, Tom Trowell (always known as Arnold), the son of her Wellington cello teacher, to whom she wrote feverish, embarrassing letters, most of them unsent, and in a crush on her handsome German teacher, Walter Rippmann (*I am ashamed at the way in which I long for German. I simply can't help it.*).16 She also had strong feelings of physical attraction towards a number of young women. Katherine embarked on relationships with Ruth Herrick ('a wild New Zealander'), her cousin Sylvia Payne, who had ambitions to be a painter, and a girl called Evelyn Bartrick-Baker (usually known as Vere). Katherine was never physically attracted to Ida – something that Ida found painful without being able to analyse why. Only at the end of her life could she begin to approach certain aspects of their relationship and discuss, with a young male friend, 'my lesbian friendship' with Katherine. It is not a word she is comfortable with, though she acknowledges that this is how people have interpreted their relationship.

Ida would often go to Katherine's room to listen to her playing the cello, and formed a quartet with the three sisters – Chaddie singing, and Vera playing the piano. Both Katherine and Vera had real musical gifts – though Vera acknowledged Katherine's superiority – and composed songs and music for them all to play. Katherine wrote the words. Katherine had learnt all she could musically in New Zealand but, in London, she began to develop her other gifts. On most evenings, Ida and Katherine went up to Katherine's room which had 'a view high up out over the lead roofs and the mews behind the house where the horse carriages were kept and the coachmen lived'. They could clearly hear 'the sound of the horses' hooves on the paved ground mingling with the splashing of water and the voices and laughter of the cockney grooms'. Ida watched Katherine 'lean out of the window, breathing, listening, absorbed and dreaming'. She listened to Katherine talk of literature. 'To find Truth, Katherine said, she would go down into herself, deep down, like sinking to the bottom of a dark well. Waiting at the bottom Truth would come to her.'[17]

For an impressionable New Zealand girl, London was a magical place. 'It is totally beyond description! It is most marvellous!!!!' Katherine wrote excitedly to a friend in Wellington. She had experienced a snowstorm on ''Appy 'Ampstead 'Eath', ridden on the top of a horse-drawn bus, her hat tied on with a piece of strong elastic, and talked to the driver in his open cab, wrapped against the winter cold in rugs and gloves. There were hundreds of motor cars – a rare sight in New Zealand. She fell in love with Westminster Abbey and the tomb of Sophia, the infant daughter of James I – 'the tomb is of white marble. It is a baby's bassinette with a hood and deep curtains, and a little child asleep inside. I bent over and kissed the baby.' She did all the usual tourist things, overwhelmed by the richness of the culture now available to her. In St Paul's Cathedral the organ music filled her eyes with tears; in the British Museum she was moved by the sculpture; in the Tate Gallery it was paintings by Watts. 'The pictures . . . They take away all my adjectives!!!!!!' But one of her favourite places was Hyde Park with its parade of carriages, and people on horse-back and on foot, particularly the nannies walking their charges. The babies 'in their perambulators . . . remind me of little bits of wedding cake tied up with white ribbons'.[18] She was, Ida said, already 'practising the art of word painting, looking and seeing to make her true and perfect picture.'[19]

Though a year too young to be officially eligible, the clever Ida won the Professor's Scholarship at Queen's. If her mother had still been alive to encourage her, she might have gone on to develop her gifts. Katherine was careless of academic achievement, spending her time in class dreaming and rarely getting high marks for her work, though, according to her German teacher, she had a good mind and a gift for languages. She later regretted that she had spent so much time dreaming and scribbling and so little acquiring an education.

> My wasted, wasted, early girlhood . . . My college life, which is such a vivid and detailed memory, in one way, might never have contained a book or a lecture . . . What coherent account could I give of the history of English Literature? Or what of English History? None . . . I lived in the girls, the professors, the big, lovely building, the leaping fires in winter, all the pattern that was – weaving. Nobody saw it, I felt, as I did. My mind was just like a squirrel. I gathered and gathered and hid away, for that long 'winter' when I should discover all this treasure . . . Why didn't I listen . . . What an opportunity missed! What has it not cost me![20]

In her early novel, one of the characters – the sexually ambivalent, artistic Rudolf – urges Juliet to embrace experience in the interests of art. 'Live this life, Juliet. Did Chopin fear to satisfy the cravings of his nature, his natural desires? No, that is how he is so great. Why do you push away just that which you need – because of convention? Why do you dwarf your nature, spoil your life? . . . You are blind, and far worse, you are deaf to all that is worth living for.'[21] This was an appropriation of one of Oscar Wilde's aphorisms, which Katherine had copied into her notebook: 'To realise one's nature perfectly – that is what each of us is here for'. In 1906, however, the gaining of experience was considered desirable in a man, but not in a woman. Katherine, who copied out another Wilde quote – 'the only way to get rid of temptation is to yield to it', longed for male freedoms and chafed at the restrictions placed on her sex. She wrote to a friend: 'I am so keen upon all women having a definite future – are not you? The idea of sitting and waiting for a husband is absolutely revolting.'[22] Yet part of her yearned to fall in love and marry, have children, and a home. Her biology was already at war with her mind – the part of her personality that wanted to experience 'the full octave' of sex, travel, the world of art and letters. How could she be a writer without it? But she knew that, as a woman, ahead of her lay the 'Suitable, Appropriate Existence . . . The waste of life.'[23] At seventeen, in the attic room at Queen's College, Katherine was already aware of the paradoxes within herself: 'I say I am independent – I am utterly dependent. I say I am masculine – no-one could be more feminine. I say I am complete – I am hopelessly incomplete.'[24] Nothing reinforced her feeling of powerlessness more than the situation that arose in the early months of 1906.

Katherine longed to stay on in London to join Ida in studying music at the Royal Academy, but in the spring Harold Beauchamp returned to England to collect his daughters. Katherine begged to be allowed to stay, but it was not even considered. Katherine and Ida had secret meetings in the French classroom every evening. There, Katherine, 'unhappy and rather desolate', would practise her cello, finding some relief for her feelings in music. The two girls talked of a reunion, planning a future in which both could make independent careers as musicians. Katherine was going to use the pseudonym 'Katherine Mansfield', and Ida was persuaded to adopt the more androgynous name 'Lesley Moore'. It was the beginning of K.M. and L.M.

To Ida those evenings were 'precious beyond all things . . . like pearls slipped onto a string, to be counted and treasured'.[25] But the girls' plans were to receive a further blow when Katherine's father told her that he was 'greatly opposed' to her wish to be a professional cellist or to 'take up the 'cello to any great extent'. She felt hopeless in the face of such intransigence – 'my hope for a musical career is absolutely gone'. But, after the first spasm of anger and despair – 'I could not tell you what I have felt like – and do now when I think of it' – she began to realise that there was another way out. Like her cousin Elizabeth, who had played Liszt to the composer's daughter Cosima Wagner before embarking on a successful literary career, Katherine was gifted in both music and literature. It is possible that her decision was coloured by the role model Elizabeth provided. By this time Elizabeth had published five best-selling novels and was something of a celebrity. Her German stories, particularly The Adventures of Elizabeth in Rügen, may have had a considerable influence on Katherine's early work. Elizabeth's success was certainly helpful in Katherine's arguments with the family. She told friends that 'In the future I shall give all my time to writing'.[26]

Back in New Zealand a few months later, reluctantly dragged home from London and desperate to return, Katherine spent her time reading, practising her art and thinking about a way forward. After reading Come and Find Me, by American playwright, novelist, actor and suffragist Elizabeth

Robins, she writes: 'I feel that I do now realise, dimly, what women in the future will be capable of. They truly as yet have never had their chance. Talk of our enlightened days and our emancipated country – pure nonsense! We are firmly held with the self-fashioned chains of slavery. Yes, now I see that they are self-fashioned, and must be self-removed.'[27]

Katherine would pay an appalling price for removing the chains and exercising freedoms most women today take for granted and Ida, who had sworn to help Katherine dispose of a body if it had been necessary, would help her friend, just as she had promised, without moral judgement or recrimination.

PART II

Wanted: A New World

I am neither a short story, nor a sketch, nor an impression,
nor a tale. I am written in prose. I am a great deal shorter
than a novel; I may be only one page long, but, on the other
hand, there is no reason why I should not be thirty.
I have a special quality — a something, a something which
is immediately, perfectly recognisable. It belongs to me; it
is of my essence. In fact I am often given away in the first
sentence. I seem almost to stand or fall by it. It is to me
what the first phrase of the song is to the singer.
Those who know me feel, 'Yes, that is it.' And they are from
that moment prepared for what is to follow.

KATHERINE MANSFIELD, *ATHENAEUM*, 25 JUNE 1920

4

'The Wizard London'

Why tell lies and play a part? Yes, it is clear that I have the wish, if not the hope, of remaining on this earth by whatever means in my power. If I do not die young, I hope to survive as a great artist; but if I do, I will have my Journal published, which cannot fail to be interesting . . . There — suppose me famous. We begin: —

MARIE BASHKIRTSEFF, THE JOURNAL OF A YOUNG ARTIST 1806–1884

Wellington, New Zealand. A dark-haired girl sits at the window gazing out at the ships moored in the harbour below her parents' house, dreaming of London. Outside the door of her room she can hear the everyday sounds of family life – the squeak and rattle of the laundry basket, the chatter of siblings, the cook arguing about the daily butcher's order. Desperate to escape, she writes in her journal: 'Here, then, is a little summary of what I need – power, wealth, and freedom. It is the hopelessly insipid doctrine that love is the only thing in the world, taught, hammered into women from generation to generation which hampers us so cruelly. We must get rid of that bogey, and then they come – the opportunity of happiness and freedom.'[1]

It is 1907. Katherine is eighteen years old and has been at home in 75 Tinakori Road, the latest Beauchamp residence, for several months. She has mapped out her first juvenile novel 'Juliet', written a collection of children's poetry, filled several notebooks with sketches and poems and continued, despite parental indifference, to study the cello. She has also made herself thoroughly obnoxious with her rebellious moods, and her obvious contempt for a home life that constricts what she regards as her need to exercise artistic freedom. As for many teenagers, her parents have become the focus for her discontent. A friend describes the Beauchamps as 'bridge and golf' people,[2] and their upwardly mobile lifestyle, built around the pursuit of money and influence, is anathema to Katherine, who finds her family boring and accuses her father of being 'constantly suspicious, constantly overbearingly tyrannous', with her mother 'completely under his influence, suggestible & easily upset . . . I shall never be able to live at home – I can plainly see that. There would be constant friction. For more than a quarter of an hour they are quite unbearable.' London has alerted Katherine to her intellectual capacities. A mind that should have been extending itself at university is idling uselessly in Wellington without stimulation. Katherine remarks arrogantly, but perhaps accurately, that her parents are her 'mental inferiors'. She has a sense of waste and despair, and suffers what she describes as 'Heimweh'.[3]

All three sisters are suffering from having spent three years in a more sophisticated, metropolitan city. A miserable Chaddie writes to Sylvia Payne that 'we have absolutely no friends. All the girls we used to know have grown up and got married and don't seem the least bit interested in us . . .'[4] To make matters worse, the grandmother who had brought them up, taking the place of their delicate and abstracted mother, dies three weeks after their return.

Katherine writes endless, nostalgic letters to her Queen's College friends: 'I feel absolutely ill with grief and sadness . . . Life here's impossible . . . and my heart keeps flying off – Oxford Circus – Westminster Bridge at the Whistler hour . . . My old room . . . It haunts me all so much – and I feel it must come back soon.'[5] But whenever she mentions the idea of going back to London, her parents are horrified. 'My father spoke of my returning as damned rot, said look here he wouldn't have me fooling around in dark corners with fellows.' Nervous of Katherine's precocity, they regard her as headstrong and obdurate and hope that she will soon 'settle down'. But her father, though 'intensely curious and a little baffled',[6] understands more of her plight than she gives him credit for, and arranges readers' passes for Katherine and her sister Vera at the General Assembly Library, which is used by members of the New Zealand parliament. Soon Katherine is renewing her passion for Maeterlinck and reading Ibsen, Shaw, Meredith, Dickens,

Tolstoy and books by such women as Elizabeth Robins and Russian diarist, painter and sculptor Marie Bashkirtseff, which underline Katherine's developing need for emancipation. She realises that she is far from being alone in rejecting the traditional path laid out for women of her class and is determined to pursue her ambitions. 'Art,' Katherine writes in her notebook, 'is absolutely self-development.'[7]

But, while one part of her nature loathes the 'suitable appropriate existence', the other revels in dresses, balls, boyfriends and social diversions. The Beauchamp sisters are at the heart of fashionable Wellington and the columns of the local paper record their social calendar and their wardrobe. Katherine appears at a 'girls' tea' resplendent in mauve taffeta; at the Wellington College Sports she is glimpsed in 'green shantung with green hat'; for her mother's 'At Home', she wears 'a dress of ecru lace with narrow pipings of flame-coloured silk'.[8] There are visits to concerts and the theatre. She flirts, what she calls being 'tediously foolish', with two young men, one of whom keeps a dance programme with her name on it for many years. 'Engaged' to one of them for three weeks, she is in love with the idea of romance. Her emotions swing wildly between ecstasy and despair. After playing a Bach cello piece at a private concert, 'I went out into the streets. It was so beautiful – the full moon was like a strain of music heard through a closed door – mist over everything, the hills mere shadows . . . I became terribly unhappy, almost wept in the street . . .'[9]

Her parents are unaware that the main object of Katherine's passion at the moment is an older woman called Edith K. Bendall. 'I feel more powerfully all those so termed sexual impulses with her than I have with any men,' Katherine writes in her notebook. What she feels for Edie makes her realise that the strong physical attraction she had felt towards a member of the English cricket team – 'Adonis' – on the boat from England had been 'nothing but a pose' and her unrequited, fantasy love for Arnold Trowell is also completely overshadowed by Edith's reality. 'I love him – but I wonder, with all my soul – And here is the kernel of the whole matter – the Oscar-like thread.'[10]

Edie, nine years older than Katherine, has studied at an art school in Sydney and is trying to make a living as an illustrator. She's one of the few people Katherine knows who has experienced life outside New Zealand. They had known each other before Katherine went away to London: a notebook entry mentions going to church with Edie when Katherine is thirteen. Now she's a young woman and they meet again on a more equal footing. Katherine writes to Edie almost every day – 'beautiful', enthralling letters she has never received from anyone in her life, not even the man she is going to marry. Edie has a studio near Fitzherbert Terrace and at five o'clock every evening, when she finishes her work, they go for long walks and discuss art and life. They plan a book together and Edie does some drawings to illustrate the children's poetry and stories that Katherine is writing. The poems are as good as anything written for children at that period and the illustrations are charming, but they can't persuade a publisher to take them. At the beginning of June the two women have a weekend at the holiday cottage or bach that Harold Beauchamp has recently bought on the beach at Days Bay, on the other side of Wellington Harbour. It has 'a small poverty stricken sitting room . . . A cabin-like bedroom fitted with bunks, and an outhouse with a bath, and wood cellar, coal cellar, complete.' Behind it the sea laps right up to the cottage and at the front the bush grows down, wild, to the road.

Sharing a cottage, a bedroom, with Edie, stretches Katherine's restraint to the limit. All her life she has suffered from night terrors. 'Every night terrible dreams – all about when I was little & about people I'd quite forgotten.' Edie comforts Katherine and allows her to creep into her bed, but the physical proximity is more than Katherine can bear. 'I am half mad with love . . . clinging to her hands, her face against mine, I am child, woman, and more than half man.' She knows she would like to take this relationship physically as far as it would go, but knows that Edie is afraid '& Custom hedges her in . . .' Such intensity can't last.[11]

By the end of the weekend at Days Bay, some boundary has been crossed and Katherine feels rejected. On Sunday night 2 June, she is sitting in the living room 'almost dead with cold', unable to sleep, contemplating the end of the relationship. 'I cannot lie in my bed and not feel the magic of her body . . . She enthrals, enslaves me, and her personal self, her body absolute, is my worship. I feel that to lie with my head on her breast is to feel what Life can hold. All my troubles, my wretched fears are swept away.' But Edie is unresponsive, uncomfortable before the strong emotions of this eighteen-year-old, whose parents trust her to look after her. Katherine feels tortured. 'I am so shocked with grief that I feel I cannot continue my hard course of loving and being unloved.' Creeping back into the bedroom, Katherine leans out of the window, looking at the dark yard and the bush beyond, her imagination racing 'until the very fence became terrible'. The fenceposts become 'hideous forms' that grimace and gesticulate, taking human shapes. The top of one breaks off and rolls under the house; it is perhaps only a cat that has been sleeping on the fence, but to Katherine it becomes a vision of crucifixion and death. She sits on the edge of the bed 'trembling, half crying, hysterical with grief'. Edie wakes and folds Katherine into her arms again 'her voice whispering "Better now darling?"'. She strokes her hair, warms her cold body with her own and soothes her back into sleep. Katherine is in bliss. 'I drew close to her warm sweet body, happier than I had ever been than I could ever have imagined being, . . . clinging to her & wishing that this darkness might last for ever.'[12] Edie says later in an interview that Katherine must have misinterpreted her 'motherly gestures'. Although 'very taken' by the girl – 'a darling – I adored her' – Edie is already involved with the man she marries a year later.[13] It has been an affair of the heart rather than the body, but it has made Katherine realise things about herself; 'a thousand things which had been obscure' become plain – 'O Oscar!'[14]

By 29 June Katherine confesses that Edie bores her. Sensing that she has exposed herself too much, she perhaps now feels the need to withdraw completely. The affair is over, commuted to friendship. Edie has disappointed Katherine by not being able to throw over convention and respond to her passionate impulses. Her disillusionment brings out the dismissive cruelty of which Katherine is always capable. 'And now E.K.B is a thing of the Past, absolutely, irrevocably. Thank Heaven! It was, I consider retrospectively, a frantically maudlin relationship, & one better ended – also she will not achieve a great deal of greatness. She has not the necessary impetus of character.'[15] The truth is that someone has entered Katherine's life to replace Edie. In the same journal entry she begins to talk of her desire for Maata Mahupuku.

Maata is an altogether different young woman. Half Maori, she is of a similar age to Katherine and had known her before Katherine went to London. There are hints of some kind of adolescent romp while they were at school together. Maata herself has travelled to Europe and had once visited Katherine in London en route for Paris. Wealthy, exotic, less conventional than Edie, something of an adventuress, she has already been the inspiration for the erotic Marina and Hinemoa sketches written at Queen's College. Someone else who knew her commented afterwards that she was like the heroine of Kathleen Winsor's *Forever Amber*, having 'a distinct disinclination to sleep by herself'.[16] After their reunion in Wellington she quickly becomes the focus for Katherine's passionate nature. Speculating on her own 'susceptibility to sexual impulse', Katherine sometimes wonders whether she is 'normal'. 'Do other people of my own age feel as I do I wonder so absolutely powerful[ly] licentious, so almost physically ill?' The subject is never discussed: there are no women's magazines to offer advice about sexual desire and the church regards such thoughts as 'unclean'. Katherine is unusual in being able to write about it, even for her own eyes. 'This is unclean I know but true. What an extraordinary thing – I feel savagely crude . . .' Her claims to have 'had' Maata ('I want her as I have had her') have to be taken lightly, given the extent of her fantasy life and the way she uses her notebooks to explore it.[17] The only known facts are that Katherine admits being sexually attracted to Maata, and that, when Maata dies, Katherine's letters and the early drafts of the novel are interred with her.

Throughout her time in Wellington Katherine continues to be disturbed by strong feelings of attraction for other women. She wonders sometimes if she is going mad. Women's lives are still governed by the Victorian moral code, with its emphasis on ignorance and the complete denial of the realities of love and desire. Certain types of sexual indulgence and perversion are even seen as evidence of insanity. Masturbation, according to popular belief, can lead to madness and 'moral and physical decay'. Katherine shares her fears with a friend, Kitty Mackenzie, a doctor's daughter, who 'is afflicted with the same terror'.[18] With absolutely no information to guide them, both girls can only hopelessly accept their fate. But it helps to know that someone else feels the same impulses.

Some time in April 1907, just before Katherine's relationship with Edie, her father had been appointed chairman of the Bank of New Zealand. The Wellington papers acknowledged his success with mocking verses and ironic compliments: 'He is the beau ideal of a dapper, suave, acute commercial man who has always known what to do at the right time and has done it'.[19] To keep in step with his status, the family had moved from Tinakori Road to a more suitable residence lower down the hill at 4 Fitzherbert Terrace. It has a ballroom that can be used for concerts, a croquet lawn and a very large garden, perfect for summer parties. Katherine at last has a room of her own and can indulge her need for solitude. The house also has a smoking room and during this time Katherine takes up the habit. She spends a lot of time in the ballroom, which has the perfect sound for her cello, practising endlessly – 'All the morning I played – very difficult music – & was happy'.[20] A friend lends her a gramophone and some records, which she has to carry home on the tram, but she finds the effort worth it when she spends the afternoon listening to Beethoven. 'Life – it is playing past me in a torrent of divine melody.'

Katherine is spending much more time with the Trowells, who have gradually become her surrogate family. She calls them 'my people' and Thomas Trowell senior becomes 'my father'. Her music lessons are a great solace and she spends a lot of time at their house in Buller Street, talking about music, making friends with their fourteen-year-old daughter Dolly and being mothered by Kate Trowell. She's been having cello lessons with Thomas since she was twelve and had played chamber music with his red-haired twin sons, Garnet and Arnold, until the two boys were sent to Europe to study at the Frankfurt conservatoire at roughly the same time that the Beauchamp girls went to London. Katherine has been infatuated with the elder Trowell twin, Arnold, since she was thirteen, 'Because he poured into my virgin soul the Life essence of Music – Never an hour passes free from his influence.'[21] They have corresponded for four years and developed a close friendship. Arnold's Six morceaux pour violoncelle, written for his London debut and sent to Katherine for a Christmas present, are dedicated to his 'dear friend Kathleen Beauchamp'. Katherine and her sisters had visited the brothers in Brussels in 1906 and there, Katherine had met one of their friends, 'Rudolf', whose androgynous personality fascinated her. Confused by her own desires, this was her first close contact with someone who was attracted to their own sex – a real-life Oscar Wilde. When he shot himself shortly afterwards, his suicide made a deep impression on her and he was written into her novel 'Juliet'.

Like many adolescents, Katherine has chosen someone safe and unobtainable for her first heterosexual love affair. Thomas Trowell senior, who seems to have been aware of Katherine's interest in his son, warns her against a marriage with a musician. After her cello lesson they sit in the smoking room at 4 Fitzherbert Terrace listening to a Weber fugue and discussing 'Marriage and Music – the mistake that a woman makes ever to think that she is first in a musician's estimation – it must inevitably be first His Art . . . Mr Trowell said she must share his glories and always keep him on the heights.'[22] Katherine is sure that she can do this for Arnold, though she thinks that such self-sacrifice is 'curiously Christian' and it reminds her of Ida.

But the very next day, 28 August, her 'fantasy' love affair with Arnold, who is now making a name for himself in Europe as a composer, ends when letters arrive from friends in London telling her that he is involved with her school friend, Gwen Rouse. Katherine writes turgid, tragic love letters to him in her notebook in the character of 'Kätherine Schönfeld'. 'But whatever happens – tho' you marry another, tho we never meet again – I belong to you, we belong to each other. And whenever you want me, with both my hands I say – unashamed, fiercely proud, exultant, triumphant, satisfied at last – "take me".' These letters, which read like a cheap novel, are part of the fantasy, a dramatisation of her feelings – there is no evidence that they were ever sent. The reality of their correspondence is more prosaic. Another letter is drafted in German, a language she shares with Arnold: 'Last week Dr Crosby brought me – your "Reverie du Soir" – So I have to write something – I find this work so wonderfully beautiful – so dreamy – and so full of longing too. I hope I shall hear you play the Reverie du Soir in a concert this year! My good friend Ida Baker has given me several pages from the newspapers – what a succes merveille. Often in my thoughts I have congratulated you.'[23] Arnold's letters to Katherine are similarly friendly and polite, and there are few of them. If he had ever been the recipient of her private confessions, he could not have written as he does.

Katherine pours out her heart to Ida, who commiserates over the loss of the 'ideal lover'. Although Katherine's notebooks give the impression that she is having affairs with both men and women, they have a sexual character only in the world of her rich imagination. The little girl who once heard a lawnmower in a neighbouring garden and persuaded her friend it was a dragon, is now having grown-up adventures. Her family accuse her of 'embroidering' everything; the girls at Queen's College had thought she was something of a liar and an actress. But every now and then, as Ida observes, in solitude Katherine forces herself to face the truth. In June Katherine writes in her notebook: 'In my life – so much Love in Imagination, in reality 18 barren years'.[24] By the end of October, after her nineteenth birthday, Katherine is thanking heaven that 'at present, though I am damnable, I am in love with nobody – except myself'.[25] Still fascinated by his sexuality and daring attitude to life, she fills her notebook with quotations from Oscar Wilde. He is a comforting example of the androgyny she can feel within herself and becomes a paradigm of artistic and personal freedom.

But for Katherine there is only the tedium of evenings spent at home; her father yawning, dozing in his chair, telling everyone what he had for lunch and then what everyone else had for lunch ('they discuss only the food'); her mother deciding it is time for bed at ten o'clock, refusing lemon and soda because it gives her wind. Katherine is so bored she can scarcely breathe. In her room, by the light of a lamp, she lets her imagination loose.[26] 'I feel passionate & mad. Why not write something good. Here's a thought. Of course it may be nothing. My hands clasped idly in my lap. Sitting in my room I watch the window curtains blow to & fro.'[27] She has already written a vignette of childhood memory that will, ten years later, be developed into one of her most famous stories. 'Vera Margaret, Charlotte Mary & K.M. were cleaning out the doll's house. There were three dippers of water on the floor, three little pieces of real Monkey brand [soap] and in their hands they held three little rags . . .'[28] Katherine is developing her craft by introspection, reading and practice. A piece in her notebook in April 1907 shows how she approached a story. She calls it 'The Growing of Wings'.

> Try & make some sort of sketch of the whole – it will be far simpler, so to speak, block it in. For instance place your characters carefully and completely. Yvonne is born in New Zealand. At the death of her Father she is sent to London to Miss Pitts who keeps a boarding house for young girls who wish to study at the various Colleges. Here is the opportunity for sketching in, say Opal Vedron, Constance Foster, and Mrs Manners.[29]

The members of her family refuse to take her seriously and will not respect her need for privacy and solitude. If they come into a room and she is 'merely' reading a book, they interrupt her or give her more useful tasks to do. If she goes to her bedroom to write, her siblings come in to talk to her, particularly Jeanne, fascinated by her older sister and curious about what she is doing. 'She leans against the door rattling the handle and says – are you writing a colossal thing or an ordinary thing or anything exciting?'[30] In one vignette, Katherine describes herself facing punishment for hurling a book at one sister and an inkwell at the other.

In September, without any warning, the Trowells announce that they are leaving New Zealand to make a home for their sons Arnold and Garnet, already in England. Katherine is devastated. 'I used to think – as long as they are here I can bear it – & now?' Their departure makes her more determined than ever to get back to London. 'I shall somehow or other go too. You just see!'[31]

Her hopes are raised by the publication of her first stories. Harold Beauchamp had consulted a young journalist he knew called Tom Mills and asked him to read some of Katherine's work. Although rather surprised at the sensual element in the writing, Mills was impressed and recommended that Katherine should send her work to Edwin J. Brady at the Melbourne literary magazine, the *Native Companion*. Brady had written back querying their originality and commenting that they reminded him of Oscar Wilde.

On 23 September Katherine writes to him in the sophisticated persona she is currently assuming. 'With regard to the "Vignettes" I am sorry that [they] resemble their illustrious relatives to so marked an extent – and assure you – they feel very much my own ... It cannot be said that anything you have of mine is "cribbed" – Frankly – I hate plagiarism ... You ask for some details as to myself. I am poor – obscure – just eighteen years of age – with a rapacious appetite for everything and principles as light as my purse –.'[32] She stresses her wish for anonymity and asks that the work appear under the name K. Mansfield or K. M. Mills. Brady, who finds it hard to believe that the stories have been written by a girl of eighteen, writes to Katherine's father for confirmation. Harold replies that she is 'a very original character, and writing – whether it be good or bad – comes to her quite naturally'.[33]

A man of commerce, Katherine's father is beginning to see her work in a new light. He buys her a typewriter and, until she can learn to use it successfully, his secretary is persuaded to type up the manuscripts. Katherine is obviously worried by some of the content: 'I'm afraid you won't like "Leves Amores" – I can't think how I wrote it – it's partly a sort of dream'.[34] It is now widely interpreted as an erotic episode between two women, but can also be seen as being written in the persona of a male narrator. She was exploring the 'male' side of her personality and it may have been just such an experiment. One of her pieces, 'In the Botanical Gardens', published in the *Native Companion*, carries the pseudonym 'Julian Mark' and Katherine is also signing herself 'Karl Mansfield'. Brady decides to print three of the vignettes in successive issues and puts Katherine's first cheque in the post. She is ecstatic. The first piece, 'Silhouettes', appears in the November issue and Katherine describes running down to Lambton Quay with her brother Leslie to purchase a copy of the periodical, then reading it on the street corner. Publication gives her enormous encouragement. 'I ought to make a good author. I certainly have the ambition and the ideas but have I the power to carry it all through?' The answer to her question is London. 'Yes – if I get back but not unless I do.'[35] She is convinced that she will be unable to become a creative artist unless she goes back. 'O London – to write the word makes me feel that I could burst into tears. Isn't it terrible to love anything so much. I do not care at all for men – but London – it is Life.'[36]

Katherine is experiencing continued opposition to her plans and dreads the clashes with her father. 'I am frightened and trying to be brave. This is the greatest and most terrible torture that I have ever thought of enduring, but I can have courage, face him bravely with my head high, and fight – for Life, absolutely.'[37] Her notebook is full of entries where she tries to reassure and encourage herself. 'Do not at the last moment lose courage – argue wisely & quietly. Be more man than woman. Keep your brain perfectly clear. Keep your balance!!!!! Convince your Father that it is "la seule chose".'[38]

In the end, worn down by constant arguments, her parents give their permission reluctantly, with provisos. The biggest stumbling block is finding somewhere for Katherine to live where she will be supervised. Aunt Belle is now married in England, has a young baby and emphatically does not want to be saddled with her nieces again – particularly Katherine. Her second cousin, the son of grandfather Arthur's brother, Henry Heron Beauchamp, known as 'Guardy', is written to. He had been the Beauchamp girls' official guardian during their time at Queen's College and they had stayed at his house during the school holidays. But this time he refuses, reluctant to repeat the experience and take on a relative he does not much care for, though he is very tactful and manages not to state that Katherine, unlike her sisters, is too much trouble and just not charming enough. It is decided, provisionally, that if someone can be found to keep an eye on her, Katherine will travel back to England in April, chaperoned by the wife of the ship's captain. In the meantime, when one of Katherine's friends, Millie Parker, suggests that she join a family camping trip into the bush, the Beauchamps are very keen for Katherine to go and see something of her native country. Perhaps they are hoping she will change her mind.

On 18 November, Katherine writes to her sister Chaddie: 'Your humble servant is seated on the very top of I know not how much luggage – so excuse the writing. This is a most extraordinary experience.'[39] She is travelling with the Parker family and four of their friends, in two horse-drawn wagons, through the wild and remote Urewera region of the central North Island. The densely forested and hilly land with its occasional settlements and primitive beauty affects Katherine profoundly. 'The child spirit, hidden away under a thousand and one grey City wrappings, bursts its bonds & exults within me.'[40]

She has her first really close contact with Maori – 'Blue skirt, great piece of greenstone, black hair, beautiful bone earrings' – and she is fascinated by their difference. The party visit several Maori 'Pahs':

> at the summit a little Maori whare was painted black against the wide sky. Before it two cabbage trees stretched out phantom fingers, and a dog, watching me coming up the hill, barked madly . . . I neared the whare and a little Maori girl and three boys sprang from nowhere & waved & beckoned. At the door a beautiful old Maori woman sat cuddling a cat. She wore a white handkerchief round her black hair and a vivid green & black [check] rug wrapped round her body. Under the rug I caught a glimpse of a very full blue print dress, with native fashion, the skirt over the bodice.

In Katherine's romantic imagination, 'Visions of long dead Maoris, of forgotten battles and vanished feuds stirred in me . . .'[41]

The detailed journal she keeps will become the fabric of future stories, particularly 'The Woman at the Store', inspired directly by a lonely homestead she visits during the trip: 'lunch at Rangataiki. The store is so ugly – they do not seem glad or surprised to see us, give us fresh bread, all surly & familiar and they seem troubled . . . we say goodbye . . . and at nightfall rounding the bend reach our copse. It is a threatening evening, the farm child, the woman, her great boots – she has been digging.'[42] In the story Katherine captures perfectly the poverty and isolation, conveys the vague sense of threat that exists in most of her stories – a darkness lurking out of view that menaces the sunlight in the foreground. 'The blazing sun uplifts itself like a gigantic torch to light the bush – it is all so gigantic and tragic & even in the bright sunlight it is . . . passionately secret.'

Katherine is bitten to death by mosquitoes, despite being anointed with 'Oil of Camphor, Solomon solution and rose water', and is smoking cigarettes to keep them away. She bathes naked in hot thermal pools with the other women of the party, falls in love with Lake Taupo, but loathes Rotorua, which is full of honeymoon couples 'and the inevitable old man who becomes disgusted with everything'. In her notebook, writing sometimes in the first person, sometimes in the third, she records her daily impressions of the landscape, the people and the feelings that they inspire.

'Then suddenly a clearing of burnt manuka and they . . . cry aloud – There is the river. Savage, grey, fierce, rushing, tumbling, thrashing, sucking the life from the still placid flow of water behind – like waves of the sea, like fierce wolves. The noise is like thunder & right before them the lonely mountain outlined against a vivid orange sky . . . The very rock on which they climb is hot with the colour.' The musician in her is listening to the sounds – a bird cries like an oboe, water is dripping with intricate percussion – and, as her prose reveals, she has a painter's eye for colour and perspective. But though the wildness and savagery of the landscape strike a chord in her own passionate nature, Katherine is always aware of her longing to be somewhere else. On a grey morning when the river valley is shrouded in mist 'as she brushes her hair a wave of cold air strikes her, clamps cold fingers about her heart – it is the wizard London'.[43]

Back in Wellington, Harold Beauchamp, disappointed by Guardy's response, is having second thoughts about sending Katherine to London. 'Castles have been tumbling about my ears since Father came home,' writes Katherine in a letter, but she remains determined. 'Willy nilly – I GO.'[44] In January there is another setback when the Native Companion folds in Melbourne. Katherine has to begin looking for new outlets for her work and it is quickly apparent that the kind of literary publication she needs can't be found in either New Zealand or Australia. She has no intention of writing froth for leisured colonial ladies. Her attitude to her future career has become more businesslike. She enrols for classes at the Technical College to learn typing and bookkeeping – the practical skills she will need as a writer. She is working on 'Juliet' and has begun another novel, inspired by her recent Urewera trip, provisionally called 'The Youth of Rewa'.

Twenty-three-year-old Vera is already in Sydney, staying with relatives. The Beauchamps are unhappy with her choice of husband – James Macintosh Bell is not quite what they had wanted for their eldest daughter – so she has been sent to Australia to see if a change of place will bring about a change of heart. There is some talk of all three girls sharing a flat in London, though this comes to nothing. Vera, impatient with Katherine's self-dramatisation, tells her mother that Katherine needs 'a real sorrow' to bring her to her senses. Katherine, informed of this 'firm belief', indignantly refutes the idea. 'I can't really let that pass – Vera without saying it shows how little you know of my life. I was almost amused – deeply hurt – and not a little surprised . . . That rather cheap and distinctly simple philosophy of the ennobling power of sorrow does not surely belong to you – It is true in a very few cases but there is more strength required for permanent happiness in man than for sorrow . . . I am convinced times without number that in the future that silly statement "she ought to have real sorrow" will be as unintelligible as a book of "Elizabethan simples for the stomach ache".'[45]

Katherine is still hoping to be allowed to go to London in April, but in March this idea is suddenly abandoned. Ida remembers a letter from Katherine telling her that while her mother was in her daughter's bedroom, the wind had scattered some papers. Annie Beauchamp had picked them up and been utterly appalled by what she read. Tom Mills later told another story. He was now working for the local paper in Feilding, about 160 kilometres north of Wellington. He claimed to have been contacted by Katherine's father, because of his connections with the Wellington police, to sort out a blackmail attempt on Katherine. This he was able to do and some 'young man' had to leave Wellington quickly by boat. Such a story is hard to believe. Harold Beauchamp was quite capable of sorting out any importuning individuals himself without involving a journalist. It is also suspect because Tom was in love with Katherine – 'he has written me too many letters – told me too much of himself – and likes me far too much'. His visits to Wellington were 'a trying ordeal'. Given the explicit nature of Katherine's writing, Ida's explanation seems more likely. In her notebook Katherine sketches a father who rages at his daughter: 'You are behaving badly. You must learn to realize that the silken cords of parental authority are very tight ropes indeed. I want no erratic spasmodic daughter. I demand a sane healthy-minded girl – <close the shutters upon your lopsided ambitions> . . . it was so exactly like him – an undeniable trade atmosphere.'[46] The April departure is cancelled.

Katherine and Chaddie, feeling 'seedy' and low spirited, are sent to Days Bay with a maid to recuperate. Katherine has begun to worry about her heart. She has palpitations whenever she is anxious or upset and they terrify her. 'It is really most extraordinary that I should feel so confident of dying of heart failure . . .'[47] Her fears are grounded in family history. Grandfather Arthur had died of heart failure, and her mother's heart has been weak ever since a bout of rheumatic fever before the children were born. At Days Bay Katherine gradually recovers her health. The days are leisurely. It is autumn: when it is fine they walk or bathe; on stormy days Chaddie sews and the maid reads the sensational novels of Marie Corelli, which Katherine can't resist ridiculing in letters to Vera. Her own reading is much more serious. She has begun to tackle the major European novelists and lists them in her notebook with analytical comments. Balzac particularly appeals to her with his philosophy that 'La passion est toute l'humanité'. She analyses his 'thesis of the Human Comedy':

First – effects
Second – causes
Third – principles

and pictures Balzac sitting in his room, in a white dressing gown, writing feverishly. Nathaniel Hawthorne 'is with Tolstoi the only novelist of the soul'. Robert Louis Stevenson is 'A literary vagrant'. Zola 'defines Art as nature seen through a temperament'. Of Flaubert she writes in French, 'we don't follow the same route any more – don't navigate the same voyage. For myself, I don't seek the port, but the open sea.' She reads and rereads Maupassant's preface to the novel *Pierre et Jean*, which is a treatise on the art of the novel and the 'discipline of the writer's life'.[48]

Katherine is particularly fascinated by the journal of Marie Bashkirtseff, a friend of Maupassant's, who died tragically – of tuberculosis – at the age of twenty-six, after leading the kind of emancipated, artistic life that Katherine herself is yearning for. As she searches desperately for role models, this book becomes a seminal, visionary text that opens a window onto a world she knows she wants to inhabit. The confessional 'voice' of Bashkirtseff's journal is very similar to the one Katherine adopts for hers. She uses Bashkirtseff's journal as a template, aware of the ambiguities and the self consciousness of the form: '. . . the life of a woman must always be curious, told thus day by day, without any attempt at posing; as if no one in the world would ever read it, yet written with the intention of being read . . . And I tell all, yes all . . . Else what were the use of it? In fact, it will be sufficiently apparent that I tell everything . . .'[49] Bashkirtseff's work is edited to suit the morals of the time, but the erotic undertones persist, as do the outspoken criticisms of her society.

Katherine identifies completely with the young Russian rebel who defied convention to study art at the Académie Julian (his name was Rodolphe Julian – these names occur in Katherine's work at this time) in Paris towards the end of the nineteenth century. Bashkirtseff was a gifted musician and painter, dedicated to art and complaining about the shackles of convention that held women back. 'What I long for is the freedom of going about alone . . . Of stopping and looking at the artistic shops, of entering churches and museums, of walking about the old streets at night; that's what I long for; and that's the freedom without which one cannot become a real artist . . . Curse it all, it is this that makes me gnash my teeth to think I am a woman!'[50] The tragic image of Bashkirtseff fading out of life on a sofa, draped in soft white lace, her painting unfinished on the easel, is one that Katherine will remember later. The heroine of her unfinished novel 'Juliet' is given just such a tragic death after the failure of love. Katherine is still young and healthy enough to consider it romantic.

After an interval, Harold Beauchamp changes his mind again. He will 'stand in her light' no longer. Katherine's sisters say later that they are sure their mother persuaded him to let her go. Annie Beauchamp trusts her children absolutely and they worry about letting her down. Harold has agreed the amount of £100 a year for Katherine's allowance, and Henry Beauchamp, a professor at the Royal Academy of Music, has recommended a hostel for young female musicians called, by a coincidence, Beauchamp Lodge. 'If a place can be found for her there . . .' Soon Katherine is waiting for a cable from London in 'suspense and rapturous assurance'.[51] It arrives at the beginning of June after an unbearable interval. Katherine comes home from her classes at the Technical College – the rest of the family are out shopping – and the maid tells her the news. Katherine immediately rushes round to a friend's house to share her excitement, weeping tears of joy.

Life quickly becomes a succession of lists and visits to the dressmaker. 'I've nothing fashionable at all.'[52] At the end of June the prime minister's wife throws a garden party for Katherine's departure, and there is a 'violet tea', recorded by the local paper and revealing the full horror of the life Katherine is desperate to escape from. 'A great number of the guest of honour's girl friends came to wish her good luck. There was a pig-drawing competition during the afternoon . . . and afterwards the book was presented to Miss Beauchamp as a souvenir.' In another room there is a fortune teller – 'the tea table looked very pretty with bright-coloured lights in the centre and little bowls of violets and primroses scattered about'. 'Miss K. Beauchamp,' the columnist gushes, 'wore a dark brown coat and skirt, and black fox furs.'[53]

5

Freedom and Experience

Dim mist of a fog-bound day,
From the lilac trees that droop in St Mary's Square
The dead leaves fall, a silent fluttering crowd —
Dead thoughts that shivering fall on the barren earth.
Over and under it all the muttering murmur of London.

KATHERINE MANSFIELD, LONDON, 22.IX.08

'I come now to a very difficult time in Katherine's life,' Ida writes in her memoir, 'difficult both for her to live and for others to understand.'[1] And even more difficult since Ida has burnt all the letters she received from Katherine during this period. There are only the notebooks that escaped Katherine's own wilful destruction, some of her letters to Garnet Trowell, which he would keep for the rest of his life, her first husband's careful, puzzled account of their marriage and the reluctant memories of the participants, perhaps no longer to be relied on. The events of the next year will determine the course of Katherine's life and understanding them is essential to understanding her character and the decisions she later made. Some of what happens can be deduced from letters, journals and circumstantial evidence; much of it – too much – remains mysterious.

Katherine arrives in London on 24 August 1908 and Ida is there to meet her, waiting on the station platform in joyful anticipation. Ida is surprised that none of the Beauchamp family is there to welcome Katherine. Aunt

Belle has her own husband and family to occupy her; Katherine's great-uncle Henry and his wife – parents of the famous Elizabeth von Arnim – who are nominally 'keeping an eye' on Katherine, are old and frail. Their sons – one the professor of music at the Royal Academy, the other a doctor – have declined close involvement. The much older Elizabeth, whose contact with Katherine has been slight, is living in Germany. 'These relatives', to Ida, are part of 'a wealthy, old fashioned and formal generation', and thoroughly unsympathetic. She can't understand their lack of feeling for Katherine. 'I have always felt bitter towards them.'[2] If they had been there to help Katherine on her 'dangerous first steps in freedom and experience', Ida insists, the disastrous events of the next twelve months would not have happened.[3]

For two days Katherine stays with Ida and her sister at Colonel Baker's flat in Montagu Mansions before moving to Beauchamp Lodge in Paddington, where she takes a 'superior' room on the first floor at the back of the hostel. It has a french window leading out onto a balcony that overlooks the busy canal, but it is north facing and rather gloomy and Ida worries that Katherine, prone to 'despair and frustration',[4] will find it depressing. But at first everything is exciting. 'Westbourne Grove looked as she had always imagined Venice to look at night, mysterious, dark, even the hansoms were like gondolas dodging up and down, and the lights trailing luridly – tongues of flame licking the wet street – magic fish swimming in the Grand Canal.'[5] Katherine now has the 'room of one's own' that Virginia Woolf identified as being essential to the developing woman writer and she has an annual allowance of £100. But Katherine has never had to budget her own money. Everything has been paid for by her father and she has been used to the best of everything. Now, after paying for her room and board, she has only about 10s. a week to buy clothes, music lessons, theatre tickets, meals out and all other expenses. It is rather like living on a student grant and Katherine has no concept of economy, splashing out money on flowers and Egyptian cigarettes and presents for her friends. For Ida, Harold Beauchamp's greatest mistake was to give his daughter such a small allowance. But Katherine is delighted to be back in England again on any terms, and the allowance seems quite adequate at the time. The arrangement is that she must draw it monthly from a Mr Alexander Kay at the Bank of New Zealand, whom Harold Beauchamp has asked to keep an informal eye on Katherine and report immediately any anxieties that he may have.

As soon as she is settled in Beauchamp Lodge, Katherine goes to 52 Carlton Hill in St John's Wood to visit the Trowell family. She is shocked to discover that, in the two years since she last saw him, Arnold Trowell has changed and no longer resembles the romantic image in her memory. 'Caesar', as she had nicknamed him, is now, in Ida's words, 'a smallish, thin, quite ordinary boy'. It is his brother Garnet who claims her attention – 'gentle, sweet-tempered, quiet Garnet',[6] who had previously gone unnoticed. He is an unlikely object of romance – with a mop of unruly hair, a long, aquiline nose and a fine-boned, sensitive face – but Katherine immediately falls in love with him. For the shy nineteen-year-old, used to taking a back seat to his gifted twin, Katherine's interest strikes like a thunderbolt. Within a few days they are walking beside the canals, through Maida Vale, in all weathers, or sitting on Primrose Hill, huddled beneath Garnet's fur-lined overcoat, smoking Katherine's Abdullahs, declaring their feelings for each other and talking about marriage. Katherine is deeply in love and her emotions spill out into her letters, her notebooks, and numerous poems – some of which she sends to Garnet with her letters. A black and silver Egyptian shawl holds particular significance.

> 'It is cold outside, you will need a coat –
> What! This old Arabian shawl!
> Bind it about your head and throat,
> These steps . . . It is dark . . . my hand . . . you might fall.'
>
> What has happened? What strange, sweet charm
> Lingers about this Arabian shawl . . .
> Do not tremble so! There can be no harm
> In just remembering – that is all.
>
> 'I love you so – I will be your wife,'
> Here, in the dark of the Terrace wall,
> Say it again. Let that other life
> Fold us like the Arabian shawl.[7]

Katherine's earliest surviving letter to Garnet is dated the 10 September – less than two weeks after her arrival in London – and she seems to be staying overnight at Carlton Hill. 'I've wanted you ever since I saw you yesterday – I have been wretched – I don't know why exactly – but I feel we have so much to say and so little time to say it in before you go away.

Dearest – I love you so intensely that I feel I could tell you so now until we both are old – and then you wouldn't understand – You are my life, now; I feel as though your kisses had absorbed my very soul into yours . . . I love you. I shall see you tomorrow. Get up and wake me early and let's go for a walk before breakfast – you & I.'[8] Under the professional name of Carrington Garnet, Garnet has taken a job as a violinist in the orchestra of the Moody-Manners Opera Company and will be touring the country with them for weeks at a time. While he is away, Katherine becomes a frequent visitor to the Trowell family.

Ida is sometimes invited to Carlton Hill with Katherine and she, too, homesick for proper family life, is mesmerised by the atmosphere at the Trowells' loving, peaceful house, 'with a small garden at the back and flowering bushes and trees in front; a pleasant place. I remember sitting on the doorstep with the Trowells' young daughter, looking into the garden, the spring scented air drifting in, the large room with Arnold thundering on the piano playing consecutive 6ths – then very unusual and modern – or drifting into delicate Debussy melodies; old Mr Trowell talking to Katherine, which he always loved doing, and Garnet tall and pale passing in and out while "Mother" was bustling and talking, getting tea for us all in the kitchen.'[9] When Katherine and Ida remember Carlton Hill, it is always spring, though their visits take place through the autumn and winter. For Katherine, reared in New Zealand, October and November mean spring and Ida simply echoes her recollections.

By 16 September Garnet has gone again, this time to Birmingham, and Katherine writes passionate love letters that follow him round the country. She discusses music with him – she has just been to the Proms to hear Beethoven, 'Like a giant child walking over the earth' – but most of the content concerns her feelings and the reiteration of her passion for him. 'Garnet – take me – hold me – kiss me. Let me lose myself in you – for I am yours. When I think of you I feel that a flame leaps up in my body.'[10] There is no more talk of Oscar Wilde and no sense of decorous restraint. Katherine's unharnessed emotions are wild, voluptuous and extravagant. This is the love affair for which all the others have been a rehearsal. 'Oh, with you I could catch hold of the moon like a little silver sixpence – & play ball in the garden with Dolly – with any one of the planets.'[11] On the following day he sends her photographs. 'Now you are framed on my writing table – you are on a little low shelf by my bed – and even against my candlestick; so your face shall be the last thing I see when I blow out the light and go to sleep.'

She tells Garnet, now in Halifax, about the suffrage meeting she has just attended, intending to write a report on it and perhaps to join, but she had been repelled by the women she had met, intense, serious, and careless of physical appearance. 'Two women who looked like very badly upholstered chairs pounced upon me and begged me to become a voluntary worker. There were over two hundred present – all strange-looking, in deadly earnest – all looking, especially the older ones, particularly "run to seed".' Katherine can find no affinity there, although she shares the same sentiments. 'Decided I could not be a suffragette – the world was too full of laughter.' Garnet is going to be away until Christmas and she can hardly wait for his return. He writes to her every day. 'All that you say to me seems almost curiously familiar, for beloved . . . Know that I shall love you eternally . . .' She's already calling him 'Husband'.[12]

Katherine confides to her notebook that, for her, life and fiction 'are one thing indivisible'. Her love affair is translated into fiction, eventually becoming the basis of a story called 'Something Childish but Very Natural', where two young people, Henry and Edna, walk through London at night fantasising about being married and living together.

London became their playground. On Saturday afternoons they explored. They found their own shops where they bought cigarettes and sweets for Edna – and their own tea-shop with their own table – their own streets – and one night . . . they found their own village . . . The houses were small and covered with creepers and ivy. Some of them had worn wooden steps leading up to the doors. You had to go down a little flight of steps to enter some of the others; and just across the road – to be seen from every window – was the river, with a walk beside it and some high poplar trees.

'This is the place for us to live in,' said Henry. 'There's a house to let, too. I wonder if it would wait if we asked it. I'm sure it would.'

'Yes, I would like to live there,' said Edna. They crossed the road and she leaned against the trunk of a tree and looked up at the empty house with a dreamy smile.

In imagination they explore all the rooms of the house, sit at the kitchen table, make tea. There is a big blue chair for Edna and they have a maid called Euphemia. This is a game lovers play all over the world, but in the story, it is Henry who is the impatient lover; Edna who takes Garnet's part as the cautious realist.

The night was dark and warm. They did not want to go home. 'What I feel so certain of is,' said Henry, 'that we ought to be living there now. We oughtn't to wait for things. What's age? You're as old as you'll ever be and so am I. You know,' he said, 'I have a feeling often and often that it's dangerous to wait for things – that if you wait for things they only go further and further away.'

'But, Henry, – money! You see we haven't any money.'[13]

Money has begun to be a problem; after Katherine's rent is paid at Beauchamp Lodge there is simply not enough and there does not seem to be any prospect of earning a living from writing just yet. London is far more expensive than she had expected. Casting around for some other way of making money, she decides that she will have to sell her beloved cello. She and Ida take it back to the shop where it had been bought and are offered only £3, a fraction of the purchase price. Ida is horrified, but Katherine feels obliged to take it.

She has also begun to think of using her talents as a writer and as an accomplished mimic to make money – 'to write – and recite what I write', but not in a traditional way. She tells Garnet that 'nothing offends me so much as the conventional reciter – stiff – affected – awkward'. Katherine imagines a darkened stage set with a high-backed oak chair, flowers, books, a shaded reading lamp and herself in a 'simple, beautifully coloured dress' delivering the words like music. 'Tone should be my secret – each word a variety of tone . . . I know I possess the power of holding people.' She likes the idea of writing for performance – 'I feel there's a big opening for something sensational and new in this direction . . .'[14] Katherine practises reading her poems in front of a mirror, to the amusement of her friends.

She is writing a lot of poetry, filling her notebooks with verses and sending them to Garnet. One of these poems, called 'October' is dedicated to her sister Vera. It is a picture of London – not a romantic view, but the city in autumn, with winter waiting off stage, the kind of dreary, fog-bound day that Katherine hated.

Through the grey haze the carts loom heavy, gigantic
Down the dull street. Children at play in the gutter
Quarrel and cry; their voices are flat and toneless.
With a sound like the shuffling tread of some giant monster
I hear the trains escape from the station near, and tear their way into the country.
Everything looks fantastic, repellent. I see from my window
An old man pass, dull, formless, like the stump of a dead tree moving.

> *The virginia creeper, like blood, streams down the face of the houses.*
> *Even the railings, blackened and sharply defined, look evil and strangely malignant.*[15]

October, her birthday month, is also for Katherine 'my unfortunate month. I dislike exceedingly to have to pass through it – each day fills me with terror',[16] though she never explains why. Letters from her family in New Zealand depress her. When Vera remarks that they are so much happier and more united as a family since Katherine has gone, she feels hurt and alienated. 'I think the shadow of the old life creeps over me, and I feel so out of touch with them.' When the wind blows, she remembers 'that frightful sensation of grief that used to come over me in Wellington'.[17] She has a nightmare where she and Garnet are at a Tchaikovsky concert – 'And in a violin passage, swift & terrible – I saw to my horror, a great flock of black, wide winged birds – fly screaming over the orchestra . . .'[18] Fear and a presentiment of disaster are constantly with her; her emotions swing from ecstasy to despair in a single moment. She has a young person's fascination with death. Her heart and mind are in the turbulent romantic condition described by the young Percy Bysshe Shelley in 'Adonais'.

> . . .*When lofty thought*
> *Lifts a young heart above its mortal lair*
> *And love and life contend in it for what*
> *Shall be its earthly doom, the dead live there*
> *And move like winds of light on dark and stormy air.*

In her notebook, with the capitals she used liberally, Katherine contrasts the alternative visions of 'Youth' and 'Age', comparing them inevitably to 'Winter' and 'Summer'. Age is full of fear – she sees her naked soul 'tossed defenceless, in the fury of a thousand tempests' or 'torn, limb from limb, by Winter, by her last lover, by Death'. Youth is a 'laughing child, face lit with sunlight'. The autumn leaves fall on her, not as 'a kiss from the withered mouth of Death', but 'in a shining shower'. '"See," she cries exultantly to Age, "see the kisses of Summer".'[19] Katherine, in love with love, is walking between fear and joy, buoyed up by the optimism of youth.

She scribbles down phrases and impressions, and ideas for stories. Few are successfully realised. There are more sketches for the 'Youth of Rewa'. Other stories are written, read aloud to friends, but collect only rejection slips. She is having trouble finding an outlet for her work – only one piece of fiction finds a home, ironically in New Zealand. 'The Education of Audrey', a Wildean story written before she came to England, is published in the Wellington *Evening Post* in January 1909. But in London Oscar Wilde is losing his place as one of Katherine's main influences. 'Does Oscar still keep so firm a stronghold in my soul?' she writes in her notebook, 'No! Because now I am growing capable of seeing a wider vision.' Although her work is at times quite sophisticated, Katherine herself is still very young, as an entry in her journal demonstrates: 'now it would be colossally interesting if I could only write a really good novel. Something unusual that would surely catch on – a trifle outre in the main – something that would make me really famous. Let's see!!! K sat on the rug.'[20]

It is not as easy to work in London as Katherine had hoped. Apart from stiff competition for publication, there are too many distractions. Beauchamp Lodge is a noisy hostel for young female musicians. 'Above me a woman is practising the drum – not an inspiring instrument. It sounds like the growling of some colossal dog, and I know I shall have dreadful nightmares . . . Oh, dear, next door someone has started scales on the trombone – curiously like a Strauss Tone Poem of Domestic Snoring.'[21] The girls are very sociable and come to Katherine's room and interrupt her almost as often as her sisters had done in Wellington. But much of it is happy and careless. There is a picture of student life; 'I have just finished a little supper – cooked over my fire – and eaten with horn spoons, out of little French bowls de mariage – of boiled onions – of all things on earth! And we have laughed so much at nothing and been so gay that I feel it is senseless to go to bed.'[22]

There is schoolgirl jealousy between Katherine's friends. Ida, who visits almost every day, is very resentful that one or two girls are almost always in Katherine's room. Their attentions are 'too constant', Ida complains, 'suffocating her and preventing her from working.'[23] These two girls are Margaret Wishart and Amy Birch. Margaret feels particularly close to Katherine, finding her 'loving, sincere, and utterly unselfish, and so full of consideration in a thousand little ways'.[24] Both Margaret and Amy consider Ida 'a great bore' who worships Katherine 'in an abnormal fashion . . . Frantically jealous of her having any other associates.' The Beauchamp Lodge girls joke about Ida being 'an incubus'.[25] But Katherine, though she often feels smothered by the intensity of Ida's love, can't do without it.

On 14 October, Garnet sends Katherine a ring for her twentieth birthday, a symbol of their secret engagement. Katherine has already given him a large black opal set in a plain silver band given to her by an aunt in New Zealand as a leaving gift. From 15 to 19 October Katherine is at Melrose, the Surrey country home of Aunt Belle and her shipowner husband, set in an idyllic pastoral landscape. In letters she tells Garnet that Melrose is her perfect house – when they are married they must have one just like it. It 'has furniture and indeed whole fireplaces that I feel I would like to steal for us in the Future – such a beautiful gate table, and brass carved Flemish buckets for coal, and old oak chests.'[26] Like Henry in the story, Katherine is dreaming, without any thought for the practicalities.

When she returns from Surrey, Katherine goes to Carlton Hill to show off her birthday present and Garnet's ring is much admired, particularly by his younger sister Dolly, who takes it as incontrovertible proof that they are engaged. The Trowell parents are more reserved, unsure of the significance of the gift, suspecting what they can't prove and uneasy at the idea of Katherine being engaged to their son without her family's approval. Kate Trowell doesn't believe that Katherine can make her son happy. The social divide between the son of a humble music teacher and the daughter of the chairman of the Bank of New Zealand is just too wide. The couple are also much too young. Garnet is nineteen and still has to make his way in the world of music. They have no money to live on.

By the end of October, Katherine is beginning to wonder if she is pregnant. On 19 October she confides to her journal: 'Feel frightful & can't think why . . . Feel awful, shocking, terrible. What is to be done, I wonder.'[27] She tells the girls at Beauchamp Lodge a fantastic story of going ashore with a young man at Montevideo on the voyage from New Zealand, being drugged and subjected to some kind of assault. It is a typical Katherine story – a fiction woven from a small base of fact. Something has occurred to make Katherine, who had left New Zealand profoundly ignorant on sexual matters, fear pregnancy. There was certainly a shipboard romance during the seven-week voyage, with a young man called Sidney Hislop, still in touch with Katherine and generally described as 'a friend'. It is possible that Katherine is afraid she might have allowed herself to go too far. Avid for experience and on her own for the first time, she may well have done so. It is also possible she has already allowed Garnet to be her 'husband' in fact as well as imagination. The truth can only be guessed.

Katherine, according to her friends, is a natural liar. But it is not as straightforward as that. Like many young creative artists, Katherine is making a fiction out of her life, embroidering the ordinary to create the fantastic. She inhabits her fictions like rooms in a boarding house – being one person and then another, playing landlady to a number of different characters. According to a friend, 'her great delight was a game she played of being someone else. She would act the part completely, until she even got herself mixed up as to who and what she was. She would tell me that the acting became so real to her that she didn't always know which was her real self.'[28] It is Katherine's talent to become her characters and to see the world from within their minds. As early as Queen's College she had written to Sylvia Payne, 'I am enjoying this Hotel life. There is a kind of feeling of irresponsibility about it that is fascinating. Would you not like to try all sorts of lives – one is so very small – but that is the satisfaction of writing – one can impersonate so many people . . .'[29]

Away from home and family, with a new circle of friends, Katherine is free to be anyone she pleases. To the Trowells she is the animating heart of the family: 'I can bring happiness to that house . . . when Mr and Mrs Trowell do not look on the bright side of things – I talk Beethoven to the one – and play with the other – and kiss Doll – so it goes better'.[30] To her new friends at Beauchamp Lodge, Margaret and Amy, she is a bohemian sophisticate having the secrets of Swiss hairdressers and original sin. Another Katherine is also beginning to emerge, someone who inhabits the world of art and literature, not just as a member of the audience, but as a participant. Dr Caleb Saleeby, a musical friend of the Trowells whose wife is the daughter of the Victorian poet Alice Meynell, invites her to dinner. Saleeby, a former gynaecologist who has abandoned medicine for journalism, is science editor of the heavyweight *Pall Mall Gazette* and writes sometimes for a small, socialist periodical called the *New Age*, edited by A. R. Orage. Saleeby is a Fabian, an advocate of eugenics and a friend of George Bernard Shaw. Katherine meets a diverse group of people around his dining table and knows that these introductions are precious if she wants to break into literary circles. She is also quick to realise the advantages of her parents' social position in New Zealand. They had entertained the Venezuelan pianist Madame Teresa Carreno when she played in Wellington and in London Katherine visits her backstage at the theatre. Not only is Katherine remembered, but she is invited to visit Madame Carreno at home, where she spends the afternoon 'talking in the half dark

− in a fascinating room full of flowers and photographs − fine pictures of her famous friends, and Russian cigarets − and books and music and cushioned couches − you know the type of room − We talked, I think in the main − of Music in Relation to Life − of the splendid artist calling.'[31]

This is the world Katherine wants to be part of, a world where traditional conventions have less value than art. But Katherine is playing a dangerous game. To believe in the principles of sexual freedom when there is no freely available contraception can have only one consequence. Still worrying about her late period, unsure where to go for advice on her anxieties, Katherine consults an old school friend, Ruth Herrick − that other 'wild New Zealander' − who recommends a sympathetic female physician. On 29 October, after going with her friend Margaret to Paris for a wedding, Katherine visits Mrs Charley Boyd and at last puts her mind at rest.[32] If Katherine had been pregnant she would not have been the first Beauchamp girl to be in this predicament. A few years ago, her cousin Charlotte, Elizabeth's older sister, had conceived a child at the age of fifteen and been whisked off to Switzerland to have the baby conveniently spirited away. This is the way things are done in upper middle class circles: a few months away from home for reasons of health, or perhaps visiting a distant relative, a discreet adoption − a family secret never to be spoken of. Despite Katherine's relief at Mrs Boyd's reassurance, the false alarm disturbs her and she makes several good resolutions for the future. 'Now I must more definitely arrange my life. I'm being bad.'[33] Until now, Katherine's life has been lived within the disciplines and boundaries set by others. Freedom is more difficult than she had anticipated.

The Trowells, too, are having money problems. The move to London from New Zealand has been more expensive than they had expected and Thomas Trowell has not been able to find enough pupils to pay their way. The maid is given notice and other economies are proposed. One of the problems is that Britain in 1908 is experiencing a financial recession. Almost a million are unemployed. Katherine sees them from her hansom cab as she goes home from the theatre and describes the scene in a letter to Garnet − 'Dim men and women . . . clustering in broken groups round the doors of the public houses. From some of the bars came the sound of horrible laughter.' There are policemen on horseback waiting ominously at Marble Arch and crowds of people huddled together on the edge of the park 'and all the streets stretching out on every side like the black web of some monstrous spider. In the Edgware Road we passed a great procession of the unemployed. They carried a scarlet banner. You cannot think how horrible and sinister they looked – tramping along – hundreds of them – monotonously, insistently – like a grey procession of dead hours.'[34] Katherine is protected from the effects of the recession because her money comes from New Zealand, but the Trowells are dependent on the middle classes being able to pay for their children's music lessons and when economies are being made those luxuries are often the first to go.

Katherine, finding it hard to work at Beauchamp Lodge, suggests a remedy. Why doesn't she rent a room at Carlton Hill instead? She is longing for family life, a closer relationship with Garnet and a way to save money. For Katherine it seems the ideal solution for both parties. The family agree, but Kate Trowell, 'little mother', is uneasy. It hurts her pride to be beholden to a Beauchamp, and she is worried about Katherine's relationship with her son, which is too intense and has developed too rapidly. She does not understand, either, the switch of interest from Arnold to Garnet. She has known Katherine since she first came for cello lessons at the age of twelve and, though fond of her, does not necessarily want this mercurial, demanding and (she considers) rather spoilt, young woman as a daughter-in-law. Ida identifies Mrs Trowell's opposition as the greatest obstacle to a marriage between Katherine and Garnet.

Margaret Wishart suggests that Katherine, who has always had a fine soprano voice, should take up singing as well as recitation to earn extra money. She mentions a singing and elocution teacher called George Bowden. By coincidence Katherine has already met him at a musical evening. A former choral scholar at King's College, Cambridge, he is a friend of the Saleebys and part of the Trowells' circle. George, in his thirties, is a young man about town who takes himself very seriously. He is sincere, rather pompous and utterly conventional. Katherine bursts into his life with the destructive power of a comet. She is determined to charm him in order to realise her ambitions; he is flattered and fascinated. Katherine, in love with Garnet, is indifferent to him.

When Garnet returns from his tour with the Moody-Manners Opera Company on 22 November to stay at Carlton Hill for eight days of leave, the couple have not seen each other for over two months. 'What a journal we shall write in that week,'[35] Katherine exclaims in a letter, joyfully anticipating his arrival. In her notebook she takes on the persona of Maata and the Trowells become the (deliberately named) Close family. There are a father and a mother, a maid called Jenny, two brothers, Philip and Hal, and a younger sister of fourteen called Maisie, though Katherine sometimes calls her Dolly, then crosses it out, her mistake underlining the autobiographical nature of the story. The two main characters – Philip and Maata – are both nineteen. The whole narrative is full of the lively banter of an intimate, happy family. In one extended passage Maata arrives later than intended at the house. 'In the bright hot kitchen Mrs Close, an apron tied over her black dress, shook the rolling pin at Maata. "No," she said, "you shan't kiss me. Don't come near me, you bad girl. You've broken your promise – you said you'd come early."' The mother is making an apple pie and pricking Maata's name in the pastry with a fork. Maata loves the kitchen. 'She looked at the big black stove, shedding so bright a light from behind the open bars, at all the homely cooking things on the table, at the blue dinner set on the dresser, at Jenny peeling potatoes with a penny book of fortune-telling propped against the water bowl, at everything – so real & simple and human.'[36]

Maata runs upstairs, hearing the 'voice of the violin from the room above', and slips into the room where Philip is practising. There are symbols of future grief – Philip's shadow on the ceiling 'like a cross' and 'the violin case lying open on the white bed was like a little coffin'. Philip and Maata talk. He tells her how lonely he is and how difficult he finds it to have faith in his future. This strikes a chord with Maata and they admit their love for each other. Hal comes up to call them both to dinner and finds them sitting closely together, with flushed faces, and can't resist teasing his brother. 'Lucky fellow,' he says and shouts after them 'all the way to the dining room "I knew it, I knew it"'. After another homely scene in the drawing-room, roasting chestnuts and listening to Hal at the piano, Philip and Maata go out for a walk, though Maata knows his mother is uneasy about their relationship. As they stroll across Primrose Hill they talk about being together, fantasise about the houses they are going to live in, and the kind of life they will lead. Maata tells Philip that she thinks 'Patience a dreadful thing. Well – I just haven't any, where you are concerned. And I don't want to have any. Everything must happen now, here.'[37] This is the voice of the young, impetuous Kathleen Beauchamp, confident that she can get what she wants. They go back to the house and wait until the parents have gone to bed. 'Then the sound of the two doors closing. Philip put out the gas & gathered the beloved Maata into his arms.'

In reality the two courting couples compete for territory. Since the Trowell parents and Dolly are occupying the drawing-room, and Arnold and Gwen have staked out the dining room, Katherine and Garnet have to meet in Garnet's room, with its conveniently tempting bed. During his visit the Trowells have to go away for a couple of days and the young people are left alone together, just as, in the novel, the parents go out, leaving Philip and Maata in the house with Maisie. It is probably at this point that, already secretly engaged, Katherine and Garnet become lovers and are spied upon by Dolly. In the novel, Philip and Maata are in bed, entwined in each other's arms: 'Maisie discovers them, but says nothing – she thinks they have been secretly married. She is full of the secret . . .'[38]

On 4 December 1908 Katherine writes a poem that seems to refer to Garnet's visit. It describes a young couple sitting by the fire, talking and reading in complete harmony with each other.

> We two, it seemed, were shut apart
> Were fire bound from the Winter world
> And all the secrets of the past
> Lay, like a scroll unfurled.
>
> As through the Winter afternoon
> We dreaming, read of many lands
> And woke . . . to find the Book of Life
> Spread open in our hands.[39]

But after Garnet leaves on 30 November to rejoin the opera company, things deteriorate at Carlton Hill. The Trowells are glad of Katherine's rent money, but there is friction between the women. Katherine's presence in the household as a paying guest has subtly altered the relationships within it. Gwen and Katherine have already fallen out over something that Gwen has said. Katherine blames Gwen for causing trouble with the Trowells and writes to Garnet that 'She spoke of you and me in a way that made me exceedingly angry'.[40] They patch up the quarrel, but it is the end of any close friendship. Then Ida reports arguments between Katherine and Kate Trowell over money for the laundry – with no maid now at Carlton Hill, the washing is being sent out and must be paid for. Katherine regards herself as a member of the family and thinks it should be included in her rent. Kate feels that Katherine is taking advantage of her good nature and treating her like a servant. Katherine, too young to be aware of the older woman's sensibilities, is used to being waited on by maids and has never had to do anything for herself. In the fictional version, the Close family 'are sick of Maata's fine ways. And she is sick of their commonness. She goes away for the weekend & comes back to find Ma wants the money for the washing. No, she won't give it. How silent they are all growing.'[41] Katherine's relationship with Garnet is also under pressure: after the first week of December he ceases to keep her letters.

By Christmas the atmosphere is fragile. The family are all together and Katherine buys Garnet a travelling chess set, though she does not record his gift to her. Notebooks and letters have been concealed or destroyed, but it seems that at some point during the holiday there is an incident that blows Katherine and Garnet's carefully fabricated world apart. Their intimate relationship is discovered by the Trowells. Garnet's sister Dolly witnesses a terrible row: her mother in tears, her father and Garnet shouting, and Katherine hysterical. Thomas Trowell, a man of conventional morality and strict principles, is filled with disgust and loathing for his former pupil. He tells her she is emotionally unbalanced – why else would a well-brought-up girl behave like a street walker? – and a corrupting influence on his son. He will not allow Katherine to ruin Garnet's life, and orders her from the house forbidding her to return. 'Gentle, sweet-tempered, quiet Garnet', in total awe of his father, allows it to happen. Dolly, who cares deeply about Katherine and regards her as a sister, is not permitted to see her again and is never given any explanation of the event by her parents.

6

The Lost Child

I ran to the forest for shelter,
Breathless, half sobbing;
I put my arms round a tree,
Pillowed my head against the rough bark,
'Protect me,' I said, 'I am a lost child.'
But the tree showered silver drops on my face and hair.
A wind sprang up from the ends of the earth;
It lashed the forest together.
A huge green wave thundered and burst over my head.
I prayed, implored, 'Please take care of me!'
But the wind pulled at my cloak and the rain beat upon me.

KATHERINE MANSFIELD, 'THE STORM', BAD WÖRISHOFEN, 1909

Back at Beauchamp Lodge, in a cheaper room on the ground floor facing the road, Katherine, almost destroyed by the betrayal of the two people she had regarded as 'my father' and 'little mother', lies awake at night listening to the street sounds of London, and tries to come to terms with the reality of her position. 'Aunt Martha' – her period – is late and Katherine, more knowledgeable since her visit to Mrs Boyd, knows that this time there is real cause for concern. She is 'sick at heart until I am physically sick'. But there is also optimism. Garnet's parents are totally opposed to their relationship, but Garnet loves her and a way will be found to be together. She is disappointed by his inability to stand up to his father, but she still believes in him absolutely. The Trowells know that there is the possibility of a child and Katherine is sure that they will come round in the end. How could they be so barbaric as to deny their own grandchild? She convinces herself that everything will work out for the best and continues to write to Garnet, who is back on tour. Katherine tells no one at Beauchamp Lodge about her predicament. Ida knows only that Katherine's love affair is in serious trouble and that money is short.

Trained by George Bowden and given recommendations by him, Katherine is accepting bookings from hostesses wanting someone to entertain guests at their soirées. She sings simple songs with piano accompaniment and writes little comic sketches – in cockney or Irish dialect – which she performs. There is no sordid business transaction involved – she will go as a guest, sing for her supper and be given a guinea or two as a tip before she leaves. Katherine has new evening dresses made for these performances (which cost more than the fee) and Ida goes round to help her dress and do her hair. But Ida notices that Katherine is unreliable: sometimes she decides at the last moment that she does not want to go and Ida will be sent with a note to make Katherine's excuses. The dutiful Ida can't approve this capricious approach, but she says nothing.

Ida is also uncomfortable with George's increasingly amorous attitude towards Katherine. He has begun to send her flowers and presents and love letters 'full of humble devotion & understanding, really beautifully expressed'.[1] Katherine cruelly reads out extracts to the girls at Beauchamp Lodge, 'gurgling with laughter . . . interspersed with caustic comments'.[2] The girls protest that she is being unfair, but Katherine is too unhappy to care. George becomes Mr Peacock, the singing teacher in 'Reginald Peacock's Day', a vain caricature whose catchphrase is 'Dear lady, I should be only too charmed!' Katherine plays with George. He is balm for her rejection by the Trowells, but the only person she cares about is Garnet. As the weeks go by with no sign of 'Aunt Martha', and the Trowells remain intransigent, her optimism fades. Kate Trowell and Dolly cut her dead on the steps of the theatre when she bumps into them one evening, and she becomes increasingly agitated and despairing. It is only six months since she left New Zealand; she has failed to establish herself as a writer and the predicament she now faces is the one most feared by her parents. The thought of what her family might say makes Katherine wretched. The word 'failure' has never entered her vocabulary before.

The letters between Katherine and Garnet have not survived, but in the third week of January she visits him in Liverpool.[3] During the slow train journey from London via Hereford she occupies herself by reading Dante Gabriel Rossetti and writing little character sketches of the people in the carriage: an old man with a blue and white striped neckerchief who looks like a bargee; a couple with a raw, 'unfinished look'; a full-blooded man reading a book on 'Meat Inspection'. It is the details she notes: 'enormous tan boots & purple hands, a cut finger bound with a soiled cloth'. The tone is upbeat and optimistic.

The visit to Garnet does not, however, live up to Katherine's hopes. Far from standing firm with her and defying his family as she had expected, Garnet is wavering. He is still legally a minor and can't get married for another two years without his parents' permission. Their opposition is not something he can easily ignore. Katherine returns to London in despair. She continues to write to Garnet, long impassioned epistles 'begging him to come and see her or to answer her letters'. Ida posts these for her, hardly able to bear her friend's suffering. Every morning Katherine wakes to the devastating knowledge that he has not written and he will not come.[4]

The future looks increasingly bleak. By the middle of February, having missed two periods, Katherine knows for certain that she is carrying Garnet's child. Lying awake in the noisy room at Beauchamp Lodge, fear gnaws at her. Being an unmarried mother is the most shameful thing that can happen to a girl, regarded by society as morally contaminating. Katherine has seen the Victorian woodcuts of 'fallen women' living on the street with their babies and has no desire to become a social outcast. She feels completely alone – there is no possibility of asking her stuffy relatives for help. That would create the kind of family scandal she has been brought up to avoid. No, she has got herself into this mess, and she must now get herself out of it.

A solution unexpectedly presents itself. In the fictional version, Maata returns to London after her disastrous visit to Philip and has a meeting with her singing teacher, Mr Evershed. 'They sit on the sofa in Evershed's room. He proposes. She accepts. They are married [the] next afternoon.'[5] In real life, something very similar takes place.

Despite ridiculing his mannerisms and his devotion, Katherine has become dependent on George Bowden's friendship. They have a lot in common, including relatives in New Zealand, and spend hours talking about books and music. He is understanding, in favour of the emancipation of women and supportive of her ambitions. They also share an acute sense of the absurd. George remembers an occasion at a friend's musical evening, just after they had first met, when they were listening to a soprano singing, in an affected voice, 'Down in the forest something steer'd (stirred) / It was only the note of a beard (bird)'. He had inadvertently glanced at Katherine and realised that she, too, was struggling not to laugh out loud. For George, this was the defining moment, and he fell in love with her. He has a small service flat in Paddington, just round the corner from Beauchamp Lodge, which he shares with a male friend. There is a manservant who was once butler to the Marchioness of Aylesbury, 1.8 metres tall and so much like a music hall caricature that they christen him their 'Admirable Crichton'. Katherine becomes a regular visitor to lunch – 'three bachelors together'.[6]

One of George's attractions is that he has an established career and is financially secure. But for Katherine, cast off by the Trowells and fearing the same rejection from her own family, the most attractive thing about him is the sincerity of his love. He treats her like a precious object and is 'extremely persistent'. 'I think he knew she did not love him,' Ida writes, 'but he seemed to understand her and her needs, and offered security, peace – a place where she would be sheltered – able to work without anxiety. She was rather like a frightened young thing looking everywhere for a way of escape.' Ida adds, perceptively, that 'When KM was young she could never manage her life – always after a while things got too complicated for her & she had to escape.'[7]

The day after his proposal, Katherine sends George a note, asking him 'not to expect too much' of her. Their marriage is to be unconventional, and they will meet 'at the roadside camp-fire of life', rather than round the dining table.[8] George is quite happy about this, glad, he says, that their relationship can further her emancipation, rather than cripple it. Their engagement is announced at one of Dr Saleeby's dinners and George is taken to meet Katherine's Beauchamp cousins. There is a surreal tea party with Henry Beauchamp and Elizabeth von Arnim when George is formally vetted by the family. Whatever the Beauchamps feel about the match they are too polite to say anything to Katherine, but Henry writes immediately to her family in Wellington. Mr Kay at the Bank of New Zealand is also concerned. He tells Ida later that he had suspected 'from her face' that she might be pregnant. Katherine's parents are alarmed enough to take action. The timing is very inconvenient, since Vera is getting married in a few months' time, but Annie Beauchamp sends a cable telling of 'immense anxiety at home' and informing Katherine that she is getting on a boat to England straight away. In a panic, fearing that her mother is going to prevent the marriage, Katherine persuades George that they must be married very quickly, without any fuss and a date is set for 2 March at the Paddington register office. Katherine lies about her age, telling George that she is twenty-two, so that parental consent will not be required.

Only George, Katherine and Ida are at the ceremony, Katherine dressed in her best costume, head to toe in black 'with a dreadful shiny black straw hat on her head'. The register office is 'a horrible little place – a small room with . . . a long counter such as one would find in a cleaner's and dyer's . . . bare and very dirty, with an uncleaned window'.[9] As George has neglected to bring a best man, the registrar has to go out and find a second witness to the marriage. The ceremony is quickly over and Ida goes miserably home, leaving Katherine and George at the hotel where they are going to stay overnight. Ida has lent Katherine the dressing case she has just received for her twenty-first birthday and she tucks a little note into one of the pockets with the words 'Bear up' written on it.

George takes Katherine out to dinner and then to a show, and from his point of view the evening passes pleasantly enough. Outwardly Katherine seems calm and happy, if a little nervous. They go up to their room and George discreetly allows her to prepare for bed while he goes out to smoke a cigarette. Faced by the sight of the bed that she will shortly be expected to share with him, Katherine realises the enormity of what she has done. She is revolted by the idea of sleeping with a man she does not love. When George comes back to take his wife in a loving embrace he is unprepared for her 'sudden and complete frigidity'.[10] Katherine will not allow him to touch her. George is shocked, but, being a considerate man, convinces himself that such behaviour is perhaps due to wedding night nerves. Katherine needs time and tact. Next morning after breakfast they leave the hotel together and Katherine tells George that she is going back to Beauchamp Lodge to collect her belongings and will meet him at the flat. But she never appears. There is no communication from her and for almost a week he does not know where she is.

That morning, on her return to Beauchamp Lodge, she tells the girls breakfasting there that she is now a married woman. The theatrical announcement is greeted with complete consternation. Her friends Margaret and Amy are shocked and mystified. The hostel is rife with gossip. There are rumours that it is some kind of stunt, perhaps for a story she is going to write. In the afternoon Katherine, 'in a great state of despair and anxiety',[11] tells Ida that she has left George and is never going back. It has all been a terrible mistake. Her sardonic sense of humour comes into play: she says that she couldn't stand the pink satin bedspread or the pink tassels on the lampshades in the hotel room and had been unable to go through with it. But Katherine's new status has put her in a difficult situation: because Beauchamp Lodge is for single women only she must leave immediately.

Ida helps Katherine to move into an unfurnished room above the Swiss hairdresser they both use, and finds a bed and some essential furniture. There is a gas ring to cook on, but water and bathroom facilities are downstairs. The room is bare and cheerless but it is all they can afford since Katherine has spent the last of her month's allowance, 27s., on the hat for her wedding. Ida has only recently turned twenty-one and inherited a legacy from her mother. She generously gives Katherine money to help her out. They come to an agreement – 'after all,' Ida argues, 'you wouldn't hesitate to ask a friend for a cup of tea, so why make such a fuss over money?' Tea, abbreviated to T, becomes their code phrase for money. It is in this 'wretched bedroom', gaunt with lack of sleep, that George finally finds her a few days later, 'dry-eyed and firm in her determination to go her own way alone'.[12]

Ida is the only person Katherine can confide in; can trust absolutely. Katherine confesses that she's expecting Garnet's child.[13] Ida, though shocked and concerned, stands by her friend. Within a few days of the marriage Katherine decides that she must go and see Garnet again. Surely, face to face, without any interference from others, they can work something out? It is a desperate last effort.

The Moody-Manners Opera Company is playing in Glasgow for a two-week season, beginning on 8 March. Katherine makes the long train journey north and this episode becomes the basis for amusing anecdotes Katherine will later use to enliven Bloomsbury dinner parties – describing herself 'wandering round the moors of Scotland like a Gypsy', or 'cooking kippers over a gas-flame' in the bedroom of her lodging house.[14] She even tells friends that the opera company gave her a part in the chorus. The facts are harder to establish.

Scotland is bone-achingly cold, with a bitter wind and snow on the ground. Garnet is tired and irritable, worn out with work and anxiety. The lodgings he takes her to are cold and dirty. They pretend to the landlady that she is his wife. As she waits for him to come to bed, Katherine writes in her journal, just after the notes of her January journey to Liverpool, 'Night. J'attends pour la premiere fois dans ma vie le crise de ma vie [I wait, for the first time in my life, for the crisis of my life]. As I wait a flock of sheep pass down the street in the moonlight, I hear the cracking [of]

the whip & behind the dark heavy cart – like a death cart . . . I pray the dear
Lord I have not waited too long for my soul hungers as my body all day
has hungered & cried for him.' Garnet still does not know that Katherine
has married someone else and she understands exactly how delicate her
predicament is. 'Each moment . . . is a moment of supreme danger, but this
man I love with all my heart. The other I do not even care about.'[15] This
entry is connected to a poem she writes shortly afterwards – the beautiful 'Sleeping Together' which begins 'Sleeping together . . . How tired you
were . . .'

> *Was it a thousand years ago?*
> *I woke in your arms – you were sound asleep –*
> *And heard the pattering sound of sheep*
> *Softly I slipped to the floor and crept*
> *To the curtained window, then, while you slept,*
> *I watched the sheep pass by in the snow.*
>
> *O flock of thoughts with their shepherd Fear*
> *Shivering, desolate, out in the cold,*
> *That entered into my heart to fold!*
> *A thousand years . . .Was it yesterday*
> *When we, two children of far away,*
> *Clinging close to the darkness, lay*
> *Sleeping together? . . . How tired you were . . .*[16]

Garnet, one of forty-five orchestral musicians, is playing six evenings a
week, plus two matinées and rehearsals. Sunday, the company's only day
off, is usually spent travelling from one location to another. The repertoire
is large and demanding. During their fortnight in Glasgow the company
perform Lohengrin, Carmen, Tannhäuser, Die Meistersinger von Nürnberg, Faust, Madame
Butterfly, Aida, Cavalleria Rusticana, Pagliacci, Maritana, The Bohemian Girl and The
Lily of Killarney. It is an exhausting schedule. Any romantic ideas Katherine
might have had about the life of a travelling musician are eliminated by
her visit. A succession of scruffy lodging houses, the lack of money and
the absence of space and privacy to write make Katherine miserable. Ida
remembers that Katherine's fastidious tastes were offended by 'the squalor
of theatrical life'. And by the time she returns, the physical realities of living with Garnet have also tarnished her love for him. Katherine tells Ida

afterwards that she really couldn't bear 'to see the way that Garnet ate his egg'. Not only does Katherine encounter physical disillusionment, but her impression of Garnet's character is shaken by the visit. Since the end of August 1908, she has spent only three weeks in his company; the rest of their affair has been conducted by letter. Garnet turns out to be weaker and much more conventional than she had thought.

In the fictional version, Maata goes to see Philip at the theatre where he is playing. There are many similarities in the description of the train journey – often the same words and phrases. Maata goes back to Philip's lodgings in a 'dirty ugly house' and for one night they are 'wonderfully happy'. But the mood breaks. In the morning Maata discovers an upsetting letter from Mrs Close, which she reads and which precipitates a quarrel. Philip is 'suspicious & cold, his heart eaten with fatigue'; they spend a week in gloom.

The letter that arrives from Kate Trowell while Katherine is with Garnet is much more devastating: Katherine's marriage has been announced in *The Times* on 17 March and is common knowledge within a few days. Betrayed and hurt by Garnet's reaction, Katherine, like Maata, lashes out. 'On the morning of going away she wakes early & sees the sheep. She is cruel. "You're your Mother's boy . . . What's the good of pretending. I am not made to be poor."' There is no way of knowing whether Katherine goes on to Liverpool with the Moody-Manners performers when they leave Glasgow on 21 March. After the revelation of her marriage, nothing can ever be the same again. In Katherine's novel, Philip has a breakdown after he sees the announcement in the newspapers. The book ends with Philip's suicide and Maata's realisation that she must go on without him. 'Life is not gay. Life is never gay.'[17]

After her trip to Glasgow Katherine has to face the fact that she has finally, irrevocably, put herself beyond Garnet's reach. It does not seem to have occurred to Katherine that her mother might have been able to get her unconsummated marriage annulled on the grounds that she was a minor and therefore unable to consent, and subsequently put pressure on the Trowell family to allow her to marry Garnet. Katherine, distraught, can think of nothing but Garnet and the love she has lost. Ida records that: 'It became more than she could bear – & the Fear from which she suffered always afterwards – terrible night fears when she was alone – tormented her. As she could not sleep she went to a chemist & bought some Veronal – It made her sleep. So she got more & could not give it up.'[18]

One morning when Ida comes for breakfast she can't get an answer to her knock. Katherine has 'drugged herself so heavily to get through the long, empty, frightening night'.[19]

At Easter, one of the coldest on record, Katherine has a kind of crisis. Writing in her notebook on Maundy Thursday, 8 April 1909, she identifies herself closely with the agony of the crucified Christ. Can she believe in the risen Christ? Is He still alive and close to her like her much loved grandmother – 'surely all whom we love who have died are close to us . . . Oh, lend me your aid – I thirst too, I hang upon the cross. Let me be crucified so that I may cry "it is finished".'[20] She follows it with tortured verses:

> I could find no rest
> Tossed & turned, and cried aloud, I suffer
> In my tortured breast
> Turned the knife, & probed the flesh more deeply.
>
> Up against it – Life seemed like a wall
> Brick and fouled & grimed.[21]

She is now, on paper at least, a married woman and her child will be officially legitimate. But in all this no thought is given to George Bowden's position. Edie Bendall later accuses Katherine of deliberately using him as she feels that she was once used. It is, she says, a Beauchamp characteristic.[22] But it is not as straightforward or as calculated as that. Katherine is acting blindly, on instinct. Her sisters often accuse her of making decisions emotionally rather than after rational, logical analysis. Katherine puts it down to fear – the ruling force of her young life, she admits in a letter. 'All my mistakes have been because I was afraid.'[23]

Living in the dirty room, addicted to Veronal – a drug not calculated to benefit her unborn child – Katherine unexpectedly begins to write again. The experience she is going through adds greater depth to her characterisation and her stories lose their previous smart Wildean superficiality. Ida finds a young typist who can decipher Katherine's handwriting and she begins to work seriously. 'The Tiredness of Rosabel' is about a young girl working as a milliner, living in a single room in poverty, dreaming of a young man who comes into the shop to buy a hat for his girlfriend, and compliments her on her looks. 'How handsome he had been! She had thought of no one else all day; his face fascinated her; she could see clearly his fine, straight eyebrows, and his hair grew back from his forehead with just the slightest suspicion of crisp curl, his laughing, disdainful mouth. She saw again his slim hands counting the money into hers . . .'

Rosabel fantasises that, instead of returning wearily on the bus to a cold, sparsely furnished attic room, she goes home in the brougham with the young man, attended by a maid. 'The fire had been lighted in her boudoir, the curtains drawn, there were a great pile of letters waiting her . . . She glanced through them listlessly as she went upstairs to dress. A fire in her bedroom too, and her beautiful, shining dress spread on the bed . . .' Rosabel has to make do with a scone, a cup of tea and a boiled egg in a shabby café, but her fantasy counterpart enjoys the luxury that Kathleen Beauchamp has left behind. 'Oh, that lunch! The table covered with flowers, a band hidden behind a grove of palms playing music that fired her blood like wine – the soup, and oysters, and pigeons, and creamed potatoes, and champagne, of course, and afterwards coffee and cigarettes . . .'

Rosabel shivers her way to bed under a grimy quilt, and dreams that she is in the young man's arms. 'And the night passed. Presently the cold fingers of dawn closed over her uncovered hand; grey light flooded the dull room. Rosabel shivered, drew a little gasping breath, sat up. And because her heritage was that tragic optimism, which is all too often the only inheritance of youth, still half asleep, she smiled, with a little nervous tremor round her mouth.'[24]

Aware that her advancing pregnancy can't be concealed for much longer, and that her mother will be arriving in a few weeks, Katherine tries to make some kind of plan for the future. Sometime in April she travels to Brussels on the spur of the moment, perhaps thinking of moving to a different location – one with happier associations. 'I took a drug this afternoon & slept until after five – then Ida woke me – Still half asleep & terribly tired I packed. 'She takes the boat train to Harwich, which brings back memories of a 1906 journey to Brussels with her sisters and Aunt Belle to visit Arnold and Garnet while they were studying there. In her journal she addresses her entries to the man she still loves. 'Garnie, I feel that I am going home. To escape England is my great desire . . . Everybody sleeps but I – the train shatters through the darkness . . . I travel under the name of Mrs K. Bendall.' Edie's name has been borrowed, not only for Katherine's use, but for the character of Rhoda Bendall (a portrait of Ida) in her novel 'Maata'. On the boat Katherine downs brandy and soda and manages to sleep through the night, though she is still haunted by an 'intolerable headache'. She complains that her body feels 'self conscious'. 'Je pense of all the frightful things possible – "all this filthiness". . . with no home – no place in which I can hang up my hat – & say here I belong – for there is no such place in the wide world for me'. But she is still observing and reading and thinking. 'The intensity of an action is its truth,' she writes in her notebook. 'Not everyone can become the artist of his own life, or have the courage to go his own way.' She quotes Mallarmé: 'the principles of Art are eternal – the principles of Morality ebb and flow with the climate.'[25]

In Brussels she visits Cook's travel agency, and there is a mention in her notebook of going to New York. In the novel, Philip and Maata discuss going to New York together as a solution to their problems, though, as in reality, it does not happen. The trip to Belgium produces two vivid sketches, 'The Journey to Bruges' and 'A Truthful Adventure'. The first is simply an account of the journey; the second describes how the heroine arrives in Bruges intending to stay for at least a month, until a chance meeting with an old school friend from New Zealand precipitates her departure. Whatever Katherine's purpose in going to Belgium, by 29 April she is heading back to London. 'In this room. Almost before this is written I shall read it from another room and such is Life . . . Shall I ever be a happy woman again?' In the train she wonders 'when I shall sit & read aloud to my little son'.[26]

Katherine knows she can't possibly let her mother see the grimy room she lives in. Ida manages to find a small two-bedroom flat in Maida Vale – not a fashionable area – with flimsy bamboo furniture and cheap cotton curtains. The two girls naively imagine that it might be a suitable place for Katherine's mother to stay when she arrives. On 27 May the entire Beauchamp family gather on the station platform to greet the boat-train. Katherine is there, standing at the end of the platform, wearing the unsuitable hat she bought for her wedding and 'quite unacknowledged by any of the family'. In a hideous reprise of that childhood episode on the Wellington quayside, Katherine is noticed by her mother only as a kind of afterthought. Her first recorded words to Katherine are a criticism – not this time of the plumpness of her figure – but of the ugly black hat. Ida and Katherine feel deflated and inconsequential. 'I had never known, and I think Katherine had forgotten, the unquestioned assurance, security and authority of the rich, represented by her mother.'[27] Annie Beauchamp sweeps Katherine off to a quiet, private hotel in Manchester

Street where she has already booked a suite of rooms. The hat is given to the chambermaid.

What happens after the door closes on Ida's retreating figure is forever secret. The Beauchamps do not talk of it and Katherine burns her notebooks. Annie interviews George Bowden on 'the subject of Katherine's health' and he tells her the story of their unconsummated marriage. She consults the Beauchamp family, talks to Mr Kay, then to Ida's father. After her conversation with Colonel Baker it is decided that the wisest course is to separate the girls. Some have taken this to refer to their parents' belief in the existence of an 'unnatural friendship', but it is Katherine's heterosexual activities that are the immediate concern. In the eyes of a conventional parent, her pregnancy, and the undisciplined behaviour that has led to it, present a much greater moral danger to Ida. Even though Katherine's pregnancy is not generally known, her precipitate marriage leads many people to suspect something and rumours of her scandalous behaviour have even reached New Zealand: Vera's fiancé is warned against marrying into the family because of Katherine. Colonel Baker tells Ida he is sending her and her sister on a holiday to the Canary Islands. Katherine, Ida is told, is being taken abroad by her mother to a Bavarian convent, where Katherine can, in Annie's words, 'recover from all her adventures'. But, as Ida adds, it is actually 'for her family's sake,' so that Katherine can remain 'hidden and out of the way until all the scandal and shame [has] been forgotten'.[28] Ida is unsure whether Katherine's mother knows about the pregnancy, but her uncertainty is based – in hindsight – on the premise that Annie could never have treated her daughter as she did, had she known that Katherine was expecting a child.[29] Katherine's sisters, back in Wellington, are told nothing.

A few days after her mother's arrival Katherine is again on a train, bound for Europe, vanishing from the lives of her Beauchamp Lodge friends without any explanation – 'Suddenly, snap', they are cut off, to their 'utter hurt and bewilderment'. Katherine leaves behind her the impression of a girl who is not only morally reckless, but 'untruthful and insincere'.[30]

The long train journey across Europe passes through villages of 'white & green houses with red geraniums at the windows and lilac bushes in the garden'. Forests of pine and birch 'rush to surround the train like an army, and then fall back leaving fields again, and more fields threaded with streams and spanned with wooden bridges'.[31] Katherine is glad to be leaving England, though she continues to grieve for her separation from Garnet. She still wears his ring and her journal entries are addressed to him. 'Dearest, there is so much to tell you of, and yet all my impressions seem to be put into a lolly bag and jumbled up together . . . You know. Take one? . . . At the German frontier where all the baggage was examined – after it was done I went out of the station and ran down a little path and looked over a fence. Lilac filled the air – it seemed almost smudged with lilac, washed in it . . .'[32] The gardens and woods of Germany are full of lilac in bloom and for the rest of Katherine's life lilac has a special significance. Its colour, 'like half mourning', and its perfume, remind her of a profound emotional experience.

Bad Wörishofen lies on the flat German plateau south-west of Munich. There are a few wooded slopes beyond the town that might pass for hills in Holland and, in the distance on a clear day, the Alps are just visible on the horizon. It is a small spa town – so small you can walk from one end to the other in fifteen minutes. The narrow main street is dominated by a baroque cathedral and, attached to it, the massive Klosterhaus, which houses both priests and nuns and a Kinderasyl – children's asylum or orphanage. The spa had been founded in the late nineteenth century by Father Sebastian Kneipp, a Catholic priest, whose theories of water therapy, gentle exercise and a balanced vegetarian diet still form the basis of the treatments provided. The hotels and pensions in the surrounding streets are packed with those who have come to take the 'cure'.

Katherine's mother checks into the expensive Hotel Kreuzer and Katherine writes her name in the register as 'Käthe Beauchamp Bowden', defiantly giving her occupation as 'woman writer'. The hotel is only a few hundred metres away from the Klosterhaus, with its clearly visible 'little white tower', where Annie intends Katherine to have her baby. Religious foundations like this are very useful for the disposal of inconvenient children. Spa resorts are equally valuable for concealment. Bad Wörishofen provides both. A girl can be spirited away, for 'reasons of health', and come back several months later, apparently cured. Her inconvenient 'affliction' will be placed in the Kinderasyl behind the Klosterhaus,[33] cared for by the nuns, put up for adoption and vanish from view. Records are rarely kept and are not open to the scrutiny of anyone outside the Catholic church. The unfashionable spa may have been recommended by Katherine's second cousin Sydney Beauchamp, who had a West End general practice in London, specialising in obstetrics and whose sister Charlotte had given birth to an illegitimate son in just such a place several years earlier, or by Elizabeth von Arnim, who is currently in England visiting her Beauchamp relatives.

Katherine's mother stays only two or three days in Bad Wörishofen, long enough to make the necessary arrangements, then departs, leaving her daughter to face the birth alone. In different circumstances Annie may well have stayed with Katherine, but her daughter, typically, has chosen the worst possible time to get herself into trouble. Vera is to be married in Wellington's cathedral church on 23 September and Annie must get back in time to finalise the details of the wedding. Katherine's bad behaviour cannot be allowed to ruin her eldest sister's great occasion. By 10 June Annie is again on board a ship bound for New Zealand, having been in Europe less than two weeks. She arrives in New Zealand at the beginning of August and immediately arranges a meeting with her solicitor to dictate a codicil striking Katherine out of her will. In Bad Wörishofen, Katherine, having just experienced the 'icy steel' of her mother's character, believes that Annie has ceased to love her, though she sends her mother affectionate postcards of Bad Wörishofen – the convent and the Kinderasyl, and the Kurhaus (the spa) – addressed to 'Janey dear' – Annie's family nickname.

But she has no intention of giving up Garnet's baby. Within days of her mother's departure Katherine moves away from the convent into the Villa Pension Müller, a cheap boarding house on the outskirts of town, next to the railway line. The accommodation is very basic, with few comforts. The window is obscured by a chestnut tree, and there is a horse-hair sofa so hard Katherine prefers to curl up on the floor. The room is 'dark and cool'. 'Some day when I am asked – "Mother where was I born" and I answer – "In Bavaria, dear", I shall feel again I think this coldness – physical mental – heart coldness – hand coldness – soul coldness.'[34] Feeling totally abandoned, without family or friends, Katherine writes poems of longing and loneliness, among them 'The Sea Child', which owes something to Matthew Arnold.

> Into the world you sent her, mother,
>> Fashioned her body of coral and foam,
> Combed a wave in her hair's warm smother,
>> And drove her away from home.

In the dark of the night she crept to the town
And under a doorway she laid her down,
The little blue child in the foam-fringed gown.

And never a sister and never a brother
To hear her call, to answer her cry
Her face shone out from the hair's warm smother
Like a moonkin up in the sky.
She sold her corals; she sold her foam;
Her rainbow heart like a singing shell
Broke in her body; she crept back home.

Peace, go back to the world, my daughter,
Daughter, go back to the darkling land;
There is nothing here but sad sea water,
And a handful of shifting sand.[35]

In her room at the pension, Katherine's thoughts go back to New Zealand. She writes poems and stories about her brother Leslie, the only member of the family to whom she feels close, even though he is six years younger. Katherine remembers her grandmother lifting the corner of the shawl to show her the baby for the first time and how 'his mouth moved as if he were kissing'.[36] But there is also disillusion with family relationships. Katherine writes a story about a girl on a train telling a fellow passenger of her much-loved brother and her hopes for him. The other girl then relates the bitter story of her own brother whom she had idolised, believing that he had 'high ideals' and 'reverence for women'. But sometime later he had come to the house where she had been tricked into being a prostitute and, in the dark, tried to make love to her, muttering obscenities in her ear.

Katherine has begun to think quite a lot about prostitutes – she has her own experience of being treated as a 'scarlet woman'. The Trowells' disgust and revulsion and her own mother's rejection have made her feel 'soiled'. She has always questioned traditional views of morality – now she does so more actively. She knows she has stepped across a line and from now on the world will be divided between those who judge her actions and those who do not. Always a very private person, Katherine tells herself that her reserve must now be even stronger until she knows who she can trust. 'Don't lower your mask,' she will write much later, 'until you have another mask prepared beneath – As terrible as you like – but a mask.'[37]

During the day Katherine goes to the spa to take the treatment. She is trying to get her health back and wean herself off Veronal. 'There are no trees in the "Luft Bad". It boasts a collection of plain, wooden cells, a bath shelter, two swings and two odd clubs – one, presumably the lost property of Hercules or the German army, and the other to be used with safety in the cradle.[38] And there in all weathers we take the air – walking, or sitting in little companies talking over each other's ailments and measurements and ills that flesh is heir to . . . Over the wall on the right hand side, is the men's section. We hear them chopping down trees and sawing through planks, dashing heavy weights to the ground, and singing part songs. Yes, they take it far more seriously.'[39] Katherine follows the vegetarian diet served at the pension and goes for barefoot walks in the surrounding woods. She continues to write letters to Garnet in her notebook, though she knows she can't even send them to him. She has no way of knowing where the Moody-Manners Opera Company is playing and Ida is not in London to forward mail.

Once more Katherine is living a 'hotel life', surrounded by material for unwritten stories. Alone and fearful, she sews baby clothes and fills her notebooks with sketches of the people who live in the pension and frequent the spa, borrowing their names and their characters for the sharp satirical stories that will eventually become her first published collection, *In a German Pension*. There is Fräulein Stiegelauer, the owner of the Villa Pension Müller, who lives on fruit and sauerkraut; Frau Brechenmacher, the postman's wife, who reluctantly submits to her clumsy, insensitive husband in bed, shielding her face 'like a child who expects to be hurt'; the mysterious Baron who always eats alone; and the gross, silk-suited Herr Rat, whose voice opens the first of her German pension stories, 'Germans at Meat'.

'Bread soup was placed upon the table. "Ah," said the Herr Rat, leaning upon the table as he peered into the tureen, "that is what I need. My 'magen' has not been in order for several days. Bread soup, and just the right consistency . . ."' Apart from his preoccupation with food, Herr Rat tells exotic traveller's tales. His suit is made from silk smuggled through Russia wound around his body ('How I perspired! Every inch of it had to be washed afterwards.') and he tells his fellow guests of a Turkish expedition with 'a drunken guide who was bitten by a mad dog and fell over a precipice into a field of attar of roses'.[40] In its first version, the story is narrated in the third person by the English-speaking 'Kathleen', but this is later altered to an anonymous first-person narrator who sets herself primly apart, observing and recording, as reluctant to reveal her real identity as she is to expose her bare legs in the Luft Bad.

Katherine's fastidiousness is revolted by the obsession of those around her with bodily functions and she satirises them mercilessly. 'Ah, that is so strange about you English. You do not seem to enjoy discussing the functions of the body,' says Frau Fischer. 'As well speak of a railway train and refuse to mention the engine. How can we hope to understand anybody, knowing nothing of their stomachs? In my husband's most severe illness – the poultices –.'

It is Frau Fischer, the garrulous owner of a candle factory, who asks inconvenient questions about the narrator's marital status: 'Then, dear child, where is your husband?' The 'I' of the story replies that he is a sea captain 'on a long and perilous sea voyage'. When Frau Fischer tells her that all will be different when she has a child in her arms, that motherhood is the perfect antidote to loneliness, the narrator repudiates this: 'I consider child-bearing the most ignominious of all professions'. But Frau Fischer will not be silenced and the questions and observations continue. 'This husband that I had created for [her] benefit, became in her hands so substantial a figure that I could no longer see myself sitting on a rock with seaweed in my hair, awaiting that phantom ship for which all women love to suppose they hunger. Rather I saw myself pushing a perambulator up the gangway, and counting up the missing buttons on my husband's uniform jacket.' Frau Fischer squeezes the narrator's reluctant hand. '"So young and yet to suffer so cruelly," she murmurs. "There is nothing that sours a woman so terribly as to be left alone without a man . . ."'[41]

Many of the stories Katherine writes in Bad Wörishofen concern pregnancy and childbirth and the ignorance of young women about sexual matters. In 'At Lehmann's' the narrator is a servant girl who knows nothing of the realities of sex and childbirth. The whole household is waiting for the birth of her employer's child and Sabina finds it all mysterious and threatening. 'Frau Lehmann's bad time was approaching. Anna and her friends referred to it as her "journey to Rome", and Sabina longed to ask questions, yet, being ashamed of her ignorance, was silent, trying to puzzle it out for herself. She knew practically nothing except that the Frau had a baby inside her, which had to come out – very painful indeed.' The climax of the story, where a young guest tries forcibly to seduce Sabina is interrupted by 'a frightful, tearing shriek' followed by the 'thin wailing of a baby' from the room above, enabling the terrified Sabina to escape from his embrace.[42]

Two or three weeks after her arrival at the pension, Katherine is caught in a storm while walking barefoot in the woods as directed for the cure. The following day she becomes ill, feeling 'a terrible confusion' in her body 'and so cold'. She curls up in bed with a hot water bottle, shivering, and longs for her grandmother.

> The only adorable thing I can imagine is for my Grandmother to put me to bed – & bring me a bowl of hot bread & milk & standing, her hands folded – the left thumb over the right – and say in her adorable voice:– 'There darling – isn't that nice.' Oh what a miracle of happiness that would be. To wake later to find her turning down the bedclothes to see if your feet were cold – & wrapping them up in a little pink singlet softer than a cat's fur . . . Alas![43]

Katherine is not aware of it as she writes to Garnet, but she is in the early stages of labour – 'I think it is the pain that makes me shiver and feel dizzy'. It is 'a recurring pain' that 'seems to diminish and grow worse': Katherine knows nothing of contractions. It is a Sunday, Garnet's day off, 'yet another Sunday' full of memories 'of sweetness and anguish. Glasgow – Liverpool – Carlton Hill – Our Home.' Katherine goes downstairs to drink a little soup for her supper 'and the old Doctor next me – suddenly said "Please go to bed now"'. Katherine spends the next few hours in agony. 'When I felt morning was at last come I lighted a candle – looked at the watch & found it was just a quarter to twelve.' She is tempted to take a dose of Veronal, but manages to resist. 'Now I am up and dressed – propping . . .' The letter ends in mid-sentence.[44]

To lose a baby, after all the trauma of childbirth, is one of the worst things that can happen to any woman. For a young girl to endure this alone in a foreign country surrounded by strangers is unimaginable. Katherine allows Ida to believe that she has had a 'miscarriage', which she blames on lifting a heavy trunk from the top of a wardrobe. But at more than six months pregnant it is not a miscarriage. Katherine has to give birth to a child too immature to survive without modern technology, though too early to be recorded in the German register of still births. The parts that Veronal, and the chill she contracted walking in the woods, played in the premature birth and death of the baby are not calculable. It is a grief so deep Katherine has to struggle to survive the depression, and the strong feelings of guilt it brings with it. Two of her stories based on this period of her life feature the murders of children – in 'The Child who was Tired', a young servant girl smothers a baby so that she can get some rest, and in an unpublished fragment, a woman called Elena Bendall selfishly, knowingly, sings her sick little boy to death in a German pension, though his eyes implore her to stop. The death of Katherine's baby also brings back suppressed childhood memories of Gwen – a younger sister who died shortly after birth – and, in her journal, Katherine describes her grandmother cradling the dead baby in her arms. 'She lay in grandmother's arms, her eyes just open to show a line of blue, her face very white.'[45]

In her journal Katherine also allows her grief to write itself out in elegiac poems.

> So that mysterious mother faint with sleep
> Had given into her arms her new-born son,
> And felt upon her bosom the cherished one
> Breath and stiffen his tiny limbs and weep.
> Her arms became as wings, folding him over
> Into that lovely pleasance, and her heart
> Beat like a tiny bell: 'He is my lover,
> He is my son, and we shall never part –
> Never, never, never, never – but why?'
> And suddenly she bowed her head and began to cry.[46]

In German, on the flyleaf of her journal, she writes: 'I must fight to forget; I must fight to be able to respect myself again. I must do something so that I am able to believe in life again.'[47] Ida's answer to the tragic, distraught letters that are arriving from Bad Wörishofen is to consult her nursing friend, Miss Good. She mentions an eight-year-old boy, Charlie Walter, who is suffering from malnutrition and a bad chest. When Ida suggests that the boy 'convalesce with Katherine', she 'jump[s] at the idea'. A label is attached to his jacket and he is sent across to Germany for Katherine to collect at the station. She nurses him back to health at the spa, and he appears in one of the German stories as Karl who, taken for a walk, 'like a happy child, gambolled ahead, and cut down as many flowers as possible with the stick of his mother's parasol.' He also slithers down a chestnut tree 'very much the worse for twigs', and picks out the works of a watch with a hairpin – 'Do you mean to say, my dear Herr Langen, you did not stop the child! . . . 'Da, that child has such energy; never is his brain at peace. If he is not doing one thing, he is doing another.' Charlie is returned to England a couple of months later 'healthy and well' and Katherine never mentions him again.[48]

7

Coming of Age in Bavaria

Her genius . . . is difficult to define; it is so very elusive, evanescent. She has an extra-ordinary gift of satire. Her letters are full of wonderful thumbnail sketches of people and places. She seems to be able to absorb an atmosphere and to reproduce it in a sentence. She has the gift of realism with a dainty turn of caricature which I find immensely clever and unique . . .

R. A. ORAGE 'MRS FOISACRE',
NEW AGE, MAY 1912

Katherine does not go back to England with Charlie, though she is now free to do so and, though she tells Ida that she dislikes Germany and the Germans, she stays on in Bad Wörishofen. She moves out of the pension, with all its depressing associations, and rents a room above the post office, in the apartment of the woman who runs a small library there, and then, a few weeks later, moves in with the postman, Johann Brechenmacher, and his wife. Katherine's stay produces one of her most mature stories, 'Frau Brechenmacher Attends a Wedding'. The details, as in her other German stories, are taken directly from life. The postman's wife has four children under the age of nine in two cramped rooms with only the most primitive of toilet facilities. Frau Brechenmacher's black crocheted shawl and the brooch with the 'four medals to the Virgin dangling from it' – one for each child – are all faithfully described.[1] The crude humour of the German wedding party is also vividly evoked. The bride, who already has an illegitimate child, is handed a coffee pot by the bridegroom. Theresa 'lifted

116

the lid, peeped in, then shut it down with a little scream and sat biting her lips. The bridegroom wrenched the pot away from her and drew forth a baby's bottle and two little cradles holding china dolls. As he dandled these treasures before Theresa the hot room seemed to heave and sway with laughter. Frau Brechenmacher did not think it funny.'[2]

At the Brechenmachers' Katherine enjoys some celebrity as an author. She is still signing herself into the guest books as 'Käthe Beauchamp Bowden, Schriftstellerin [woman writer]' – though most people assume she is either Australian or English. She becomes part of an expatriate social group, and makes friends with an Austrian couple (not featured in her stories) and begins to spend a lot of time with a young Polish journalist, seven years older than herself, called Floryan Sobieniowski, who is in Bad Wörishofen for his health. He is attractive in a dark, east European fashion, a slender man with a dreamy face and drooping moustache and, like all Katherine's men, has a strong feminine side to his nature. She appears to find men with more forceful personalities – she calls them 'Pa men' – threatening. As a young married woman living alone, she is particularly vulnerable to predatory males. Katherine complains to Ida about an Austrian, a 'rough bully', who tries repeatedly to force his attentions on her. Floryan is at first a convenient shield who helps 'to keep bothers with other men away' but quickly becomes a friend and companion. They sing Slavic songs together round the piano and 'Katziana', as he affectionately calls her, takes up the bow again to play an accompaniment on the violin. Inevitably, Floryan falls in love with her. On the rebound from Garnet, still suffering from post-natal depression, Katherine believes herself in love with him and allows herself to be cherished. Ida thinks it is Floryan Katherine uses for the character of Casimir in a bitter story called 'The Swing of the Pendulum', written about this time. 'If she had been happy when they first met she never would have looked at him – but they had been like two patients in the same hospital ward – each finding comfort in the sickness of the other – sweet foundation for a love episode! Misfortune had knocked their heads together: they had looked at each other, stunned with the conflict and sympathised . . .'

Katherine begins to make plans for a new life and asks her sister Jeanne to buy her a Polish dictionary for her twenty-first birthday in October. She writes a poem, 'Floryan Nachdenklich' – literally 'Floryan Thoughtful', in which she describes him sitting 'in the black chintz chair/An Indian curtain behind his head', deep in contemplation. A graduate of Cracow

University, he speaks several languages, including Russian and German, and his interests are in literature and art. He shares with Katherine a love of Russian novels and introduces her to the Polish dramatic poet, Stanislaw Wyspianski. Wyspianski is a focus for those who want freedom from Russian domination in Poland and Katherine seems to identify herself with the poet's 'lawless and self-destructive energy'. She begins a long poem to Wyspianski, using a form borrowed from Walt Whitman, which runs to eight pages. It is a poem of rebirth and regeneration, lyrical and personal.

> From the other side of the world,
> From a little island cradled in the giant sea bosom,
> From a little land with no history,
> (Making its own history, slowly and clumsily
> Piecing together this and that, finding the pattern, solving the problem,
> Like a child with a box of bricks),
> I, a woman, with the taint of the pioneer in my blood,
> Full of a youthful strength that wars with itself and is lawless,
> I sing your praises, Magnificent warrior; I proclaim your triumphant battle.[3]

Floryan translates the poem into Polish for publication in Warsaw, and together they begin to translate one of Wyspianski's plays, The Judges, into English. Other translations are planned. Their letters to each other envisage a fruitful collaboration. It is in Floryan's company that Katherine begins to study Chekhov, in a German translation, borrowing one of his plots for a free adaptation later published with the title 'The Child who was Tired'. Poems and stories are spilling out of her, almost faster than she can write them down. Two of her poems are accepted for publication – a children's verse called 'A Day in Bed' appears, beautifully illustrated, in the Lone Hand in Sydney on 5 October 1909 and her 'October' poem, written at Beauchamp Lodge, is published in the London Daily News on 3 November.

Snow begins to fall. Winter is closing in and by the beginning of November, Bad Wörishofen is isolated by drifts. Katherine writes to Jeanne from the warmth of her room during the long winter evening. 'Last night, sitting working here, the great jug of scarlet blackberry wine threw a twisted shadow on the wall – rather, my lamplight, more than a little fascinated, stencilled for me the trailing garlands with a wizard finger, and so I thought of you.'[4] It is the only letter of Katherine's that survives from this period of her life and pictures a cosy solitude. But at some time during these months, Katherine and Floryan seem to have become lovers. Floryan plans to go to Paris to study, earning his living from reviews and articles, and he suggests that Katherine live with him there until she can be divorced from George Bowden. Katherine, being unusually cautious, writes to her older and more experienced friend Vere Bartrick-Baker, in London for advice. Vere is worried enough to send a long, frantic letter in reply.

> My dearest girl
>
> When I received your last letter I nearly collapsed, it seemed as though an icy hand had clutched my heart and rendered me inert for the space of a couple of seconds ... Childie, why should it have been difficult to make things clear to me, have I no intuition or knowledge of life, did you think I wouldn't understand or sympathise? Dear little woman, it was bound to come, and I saw it racing along the road of life carrying you away with the unexpectedness and sweetness of it all ... When a man, be he English or any other nationality meets a woman with your physical attractions, brilliant brains, half heart broken ... it is the nature of a man to plan to possess her — as his wife — or as his mistress.

Floryan, it seems, has argued that if they live together it will force George's hand and he will either have to divorce Katherine or be ridiculed by his friends. But this, Vere insists, could be fatal. Floryan might not keep his promises.

> If a man can possess a woman before he has the right to do so, why should he tie himself down when she is free to marry? Women are so constituted that if they love, they can't bear to refuse the beloved his heart's desire. I am telling you all this not because I consider it awfully weak-minded of you to place yourself so absolutely in the hands of a man, who knows you have no one in the world to look to for maintenance when you go away with him, or because I think its wrong ... there may be a bitter bitter cup for you to swallow, so bitter my darkling girl ... When a man can get what he wants, he tires, oh, so quickly.

Vere insists that Katherine give her 'a sacred, holy promise' that if, when her divorce comes through, Floryan does not immediately marry her, she will not hesitate, but come straight to Vere — 'we will together patch up your cloth of life somehow . . . money is not to weigh with you . . . Dearest little girl, promise me this. It is simply asked . . . I can say no more childie, you asked me to dive deep with you, I have to the best of my ability, if your man fails I am your trump card but don't tell him about me.' She signs the letter 'Your most loving friend Vere' and the postscript says: 'keep this letter at the bottom of your box, so that if things go crooked, you can take it out and remind yourself what you promised me'.[5]

At the end of November Floryan leaves Bad Wörishofen to travel to Munich, possibly accompanied by Katherine – Ida has hazy memories of Munich being mentioned – and then on to Cracow alone, talking to publishers about the projects he and Katherine have been discussing. He arranges to meet Katherine in Paris at the beginning of January. She writes him loving, happy letters while he is away, but at some time during December she becomes ill and this, too, is communicated to Floryan, who is very concerned when her daily letters fail to arrive. He writes to her in stilted, imperfect German. 'Kathleen, love! Will you not speak to me today – three times already the postman has been and brought nothing . . . You can't know how I long for you, how my thoughts are full of you all the time . . . I see all of Worishofen and no matter where I look, no matter what I think of, you are instantly with me . . . We are one!' The following day a letter from Katherine arrives assuring him that she loves him and how she dreams of them in Paris, smoking, talking, reading together – the shared life (and shared room) they have envisaged. Floryan is ecstatic. 'Goodnight, Kathleen, goodnight, and how will it be with that dream? The white forest, that I see in your room now, tells me, calls me to come to it. O Kathleen, perhaps in 18 days. Goodnight. Give me your hands. Your Floryan.'[6]

Katherine is once more worrying about her health. Despite her summer 'Wasserkur', her heart is behaving oddly, as it had in Wellington before she left for London and she is experiencing palpitations. 'Heaven knows I look well enough – like a Wienerin [Viennese] people say here and they could not say more – but I am not at all well – my heart is all wrong – and I have the most horrible attacks of too much heart – or far too little.' She again fears that she has inherited a heart condition from her mother and grandfather and has a premonition that she will not live long. 'When I am alone the böse or gute Geist [evil or good spirit] jogs my elbow and says – 'You'll have so much of this sort of thing later on – Make use of a short daylight.'[7] It may be anxiety that makes her heart race and jump, for after Floryan has left another health problem, more urgent and familiar, begins to give Katherine sleepless nights and in the third week of December she panics, cabling Ida to send her the money for a train fare to London. Ida immediately telegraphs £6, advising Katherine to arrive in the morning, on the same train that Charlie Walter had taken, so that Ida can meet her without Colonel Baker's knowledge. He does not approve of their continuing friendship.

At the end of December Katherine arrives back in London and takes a small, cheap room at the Strand Palace Hotel, but even the 11s. a day for bed and breakfast is more than she can afford and she must depend on Ida until she can find something more suitable. Ida is selling the bonds left to her by her mother but Ida does not begrudge Katherine and is anxious because she suspects that her friend is not eating and is making the hotel breakfast last all day.

Floryan arrives in Paris, finds a room and is worried to discover that Katherine has gone instead to London. 'I'm terribly tired, but happy to be in Paris at last. If only you were here already . . . But I will be very patient – but this uneasiness always. How are you? Are you well again, or still sick?' He pleads with her to write to him 'so I can be at ease'.[8] Katherine's anxieties about her health and about Floryan's dependability are weighing her down. Once more depressed and frantic, she makes what to those around her is an incomprehensible decision. George Bowden, at a house party in Lincolnshire, has his dinner interrupted by the butler bringing three telegrams to the table on a silver salver, each one more urgent than its predecessor, requesting his presence in London and signed 'Your Wife'. George is reluctant and wary, but still cares enough for Katherine to make the journey. When Katherine tells him that she wishes to live with him as his wife, and put the past behind them, he agrees, though he has no idea why she has suddenly reappeared in his life.[9] Katherine confides in no one, but the following week she moves into his new flat at 62 Gloucester Place and into his bed. Ida suspects that Katherine has been corresponding with George during her stay in Germany, but George preserves a dignified silence on the subject.

There are pressing reasons why Katherine might once again need George's protection. If she has become pregnant by the unreliable, impecunious Floryan,[10] and has serious doubts about the stability of their relationship, then she will need a husband to provide some kind of socially acceptable context for the child. And Katherine knows that if she has another child outside marriage she will be irretrievably lost in the eyes of the world. If she has lived with Bowden, however briefly, the child will appear to be his. Once more, Katherine's apparently irrational actions are motivated by fear.[11]

The physical side of the Bowdens' relationship is a failure. Katherine complains to Ida of George's 'lack of delicacy'. Soon she is a frigid body on the other side of the bed. But she now has a father for the child she believes she is carrying.[12] Katherine sings at one of George's musical evenings, attends social events with him and during the day, while he is giving singing lessons, she works on her stories in the empty flat. The *Idler* magazine accepts a New Zealand story called 'Mary' for the February edition. It is a nostalgic account of life in Wellington, featuring a child called Kass, and the Beauchamps' gardener Pat. The same issue also includes an intriguing story called 'En Famille in the Fatherland' by Cicely Wilmot. Katherine takes out her own German stories and shows one of them to George, who is very impressed. She also shows him a sonnet called 'Loneliness', describing what George calls one of her 'black humours'.

> Now it is Loneliness who comes at night
> Instead of Sleep to sit beside my bed.
> Like a tired child I lie and wait her tread.
> I watch her softly blowing out the light.
> Motionless sitting, neither left nor right
> She turns, and weary, weary, droops her head.
> She, too, is old; she, too, has fought the fight.
> So! With the laurel she is garlanded.
>
> Through the sad dark the slowly ebbing tide
> Breaks on a barren shore, unsatisfied.
> A strange wind flows ... then silence. I am fain
> To turn to Loneliness, to take her hand,
> Cling to her, waiting till the barren land
> Fills with the dreadful monotone of rain.[13]

George, shocked by the melancholic tone of the poem, suggests one or two alterations to make it lighter. The title, he says, should be altered to 'Solitude'. Katherine is incandescent with rage, particularly when he pedantically inserts a comma. There is a bitter quarrel. 'I know more about commas than you ever will!' she shouts.[14] But when the air has cleared,

George suggests that Katherine should send some of her work to an alternative literary magazine called the New Age, whose editor is an acquaintance he has met at the Saleebys'. The periodical, which declares itself to be 'A Weekly Review of Politics, Literature and Art', has a stylish front cover designed by typographer Eric Gill carrying a strong political cartoon in black and white. The editor is A. R. Orage, who insists on his name being pronounced in the French way and is deeply offended when people rhyme it with porridge. He is sensitive about his working class background, which he escaped by being sponsored through teachers' training college by a wealthy benefactor. He is also very touchy about the fact that he lost the chance to go to Oxford or Cambridge when he made an unwise early marriage. Now separated from his wife, Orage has embarked on an unconventional editorial career with the New Age, which is partially funded by George Bernard Shaw. The New Age is a periodical that perfectly represents the wide-ranging interests of its editor and has a sharp, satirical edge that suits Katherine's work, though it is unlikely to provide her with a living. It makes so little money, Orage jokes that it should be called the 'No Wage'.

Throughout January and February it carries a number of articles and letters on 'the German question'. War with Germany is already being freely discussed and is regarded by many as inevitable. In this context, Katherine's German stories are controversial and topical. When Herr Rat remarks at dinner, 'I suppose you are frightened of an invasion too, eh?', the narrator's spirited answer is certain to appeal to the English reader. 'I assure you we are not afraid.' As the dialogue continues, the contempt of the Germans for their English adversary is made satisfyingly clear.

'Well, then, you ought to be,' said the Herr Rat. 'You have got no army at all – a few little boys with their veins full of nicotine poisoning.'

'Don't be afraid,' Herr Hoffmann said. 'We don't want England. If we did we would have had her long ago. We really do not want you.'

Katherine recognises the suitability of the New Age for her own work and approves the eclectic mix of politics, art, literature and satire. Its challenging style is exactly what she likes. It has, writes Orage, 'had a rather stormy youth and sown a fair crop of . . . wild oats . . . We are not afraid to tell the truth, even when it goes against our inclinations and prejudices, and those of our readers. We are not always looking round the corner, fearful of being overheard by some malevolent fool. We do not tremble when angry letters reach us from subscribers.'[15] A typical letter from the editor responding to an author's complaint about one of the magazine's savagely critical reviews suggests that the author's only remedy is 'to write better novels'.

The *New Age* has an address in Cursitor Street, off Chancery Lane, and the office is at the top of a narrow stone staircase 'spiced with printer's ink', the walls shaking from the thudding of the presses on the floor above. Visitors have first to get past Miss Marks, a 'lady secretary of sombre appearance',[16] whose mission in life is to shield the editor from unwelcome callers. Katherine is shown to a crowded, smoky office, hardly bigger than a cubicle, where she is introduced to Orage – now in his late thirties, but still handsome in an unconventional way, despite the red birth mark on his cheek – rangy, dark, with a long, muscular face and penetrating eyes. His mistress, Beatrice Hastings, is also there. Born in South Africa and brought to England as a child, she is a free spirit who writes for the magazine under an almost unlimited number of pseudonyms. She is witty and sarcastic, a passionate suffragist and cares little what people think of her. In appearance there is a great similarity between Beatrice and Katherine – both slim and dark with lively eyes and a vividness of expression – but Beatrice is taller 'strange and really beautiful', Katherine records, with a 'fairy air about her and her pretty little head so fine'.[17] Beatrice has gold rings in her ears, upturned Turkish shoes and her hair is plaited like that of a gypsy. There is an instant rapport, not just between the women, but also with Orage himself. He is very impressed by Katherine's work and publishes 'Bavarian Babies: the Child who was Tired' on 24 February,[18] following it two weeks later with 'Germans at Meat'.

Katherine has finally found an outlet for her work and an editor who understands what she is trying to do. It is her first experience of editorial input and from Orage Katherine learns a great deal about editing and structuring her work. So far she has shaped things instinctively, or borrowed forms from other writers; now she writes with a greater awareness of technique, trusting her own voice. Orage also warns against falling into the trap of sentimentality – sentimentalists lie in thought and feeling; they are insincere and the reader will hear it as clearly as a flat note in music. The pursuit of truth is everything. 'Though the truth is brutal, it is tolerable.'[19] He also shows her how to edit the self-conscious narrator out of her stories, letting 'things speak for themselves'. In March Orage publishes 'The Baron' and 'The Luftbad'. Beatrice and another *New Age* writer, John M. Kennedy, try to stir up controversy with a series of spoof letters from contributors with names like 'He Visto' and 'M. Chessyre of Dresden', who pretend to be affronted by the content. 'I beg to state that, in my lowly opinion, I consider Miss K M has given quite a wrong impression of the home life of these people . . . Of course in some of the other German States the birch is greatly used, and it is no uncommon thing for a house wife to birch the bare back of her maidservant or daughter; but this does not apply to Bavaria.' Another asserts that, 'English people who can believe "Germans at Meat" to be a typical picture of the educated class in this country are surely on a level with the Herren Rat and Hoffman, and doubtless unconvincible.'[20] The lively correspondence runs to the end of March perhaps hoping to intrigue the readership and advertise the series of stories.

But for the next two months, Katherine is absent from its pages. Once again, her private life has threatened to subvert her career as an author.

In March, only a few weeks after moving in with George, Katherine becomes critically ill and is taken to hospital with peritonitis. An emergency operation is performed and her fallopian tube removed. Katherine doesn't tell anyone why, and it's possible that her doctors didn't explain it even to her, but one of the most common reasons for peritonitis and the removal of a fallopian tube in young women is ectopic pregnancy. In this condition, the fertilised egg lodges in the tube rather than the womb and, about three months into the pregnancy, grows large enough to rupture the tube and cause massive pelvic inflammation. This is a life-threatening event, requiring immediate surgery. Katherine hasn't told George that she's pregnant and, perhaps to prevent him discussing her condition with the surgeon she tells Ida that the doctor has been making improper advances to her and that she must be rescued straight away. Ida hires a large carriage called a 'growler' and collects Katherine – still with the stitches in the wound – from hospital. There is a painful journey over London cobbles before they reach the flat that Ida and her sister have been sharing since Colonel Baker emigrated to Rhodesia at the end of January. Here, Ida and her friend Miss Good nurse Katherine back to health.

Afterwards, thinking that some sea air will raise Katherine's spirits, Ida takes rooms in Sussex – first over a grocer's shop in Rottingdean, and then in a little cottage close to the ocean. Ida goes with her, abandoning her classes at the Academy of Music. Katherine's condition worsens and the doctor suspects that she has rheumatic fever. Her joints ache and she has a recurring high temperature. The local physician she sees knows nothing of pelvic tuberculosis – a rare complication of the disease – or the way the bacilli can invade the bloodstream, particularly after abdominal surgery, producing symptoms very like those of rheumatic fever. Katherine herself does not know what is wrong with her – only that she takes a long time to recover and is forced to send for Mr Kay to arrange with her father for payment of the doctor's bills.

The slow convalescence by the sea is a peaceful time. The two young women take in a stray dog, and go for rambling walks along the cliffs, filling the house with 'flowering grasses and large white daisies'. Ida makes excursions into Brighton and brings back library books – not always to Katherine's taste – and buys her presents, indulging Katherine's love of 'soft silk scarves'.[21] For the first time, Ida has Katherine all to herself, and revels in the fact that she is needed. She expresses her love for Katherine in small physical acts, caring for her like a mother with a child, and Katherine is ill enough in body and spirit to allow herself to be cherished without protest. Ida puts Katherine to bed when she faints during a dramatic thunderstorm directly overhead, calms her night fears, brushes her long, wavy hair to soothe her, and takes pleasure in preparing nourishing meals to build up her strength. She is horrified when Katherine decides to explore a ruined house at the top of a cliff 'railed off as dangerous . . . half of its garden already gone'. Katherine climbs inside the building, followed 'very reluctantly' by Ida, aware that the walls are trembling with the pounding of the waves on the rocks below. Ida can't rest until Katherine is safely back on the path. The incident is a metaphor for their whole lives: Katherine always takes the most dangerous road and Ida is always there waiting to rescue her.

At the cottage, she photographs Katherine on the daybed, wrapped in the Egyptian shawl that has such painful memories of Garnet, and it is here that Katherine finishes the poem begun at Carlton Hill, 'Sleeping Together'. Katherine is ill, physically and neurologically, and memories and dreams still have the power to reduce her to a state of collapse. Sheltered and cared for by Ida, she works her way through these feelings in her poems and stories, to the point where she can view them more objectively and reassure herself that the past no longer has any power to destroy her.

> Do not tremble so! There can be no harm
> In just remembering – that is all.

A perplexed George Bowden comes down once or perhaps twice, according to Ida. Katherine tells her that she doesn't want to go back to George. Ida loyally asks no questions. For Katherine, George has served his purpose. Now that there is no baby, she doesn't need a husband. Callously, unable to face him herself, she asks Ida to take him away on the pretext of showing him the village.

There are other, more welcome, visitors to the cottage. Orage and Beatrice come down to stay, as well as literary friends Katherine has made since she arrived in London. When the cottage becomes too crowded Ida goes back to her sister's flat to make room for them. She stoically allows Katherine to believe she doesn't mind, but she's beginning to feel threatened by these new friends. Katherine's belongings are retrieved from George's apartment, probably by Ida, but various bits and pieces are left behind, among them an ambiguous letter dated 1909, addressed to no particular recipient and wrapped inside another sheet of paper to serve as an envelope. When he reads it, George believes that it is meant for him and that the contents fully explain the failure of his marriage. His wife obviously has 'unnatural tendencies'.

> Did you ever read the life of Oscar Wilde – not only read it but think of Wilde – picture his exact decadence? And wherein lay his extra-ordinary weakness and failure? In New Zealand Wilde acted so strongly and terribly upon me that I was constantly subject to exactly the same fits of madness as those which caused his ruin and his mental decay. When I am miserable now – these recur . . . This is my secret from the world and from you . . .

She talks in the letter of sharing this secret with Kitty Mackenzie, and refers to the death of the Trowells' friend 'Rudolph' in Brussels, who shot himself. Katherine ends: 'I think my mind is morally unhinged and that is the reason – I know it is a degradation so unspeakable that – one perceives the dignity in pistols'.[22] The letter is melodramatic and ambiguous. The undisclosed secret vice to which Katherine confesses has been interpreted as forbidden homosexual desire, but the references to a sin that would render both herself and Kitty 'insane or paralytic' could also be to masturbation, the 'sin of Onan', which was one of Wilde's other vices. For George the note can have only one meaning and he keeps it as a salve to his pride.[23] Everything is explained. From now on his entire interpretation of their relationship will be coloured by it.

At the end of July, when Katherine is well enough to go back to London, Ida writes to Garnet, returning the ring he had once sent to Katherine and assuring him that her marriage is over – 'She will never join G. Bowden again'. Ida gives Garnet Katherine's new address (does Katherine hope that he will visit her there?) and tells him the name by which she wants to be known: 'now she is Katherine Mansfield . . . That is her writing name and she is taking it almost entirely now.'[24]

In her personal life, Katherine is still unsure what to call herself. Having left Kathleen Beauchamp behind when she married, she is now repudiating the name of Bowden, which is legally hers and which appears on her passport. Mansfield is her middle name, the surname of the grandmother with whom she had such a special relationship as a child, and as such has a significant identity. Her first name is more difficult. She answers to Kass and Katie when addressed by family and old friends. To new friends she is Katherine, the name she had used in Wellington for one of her first publications. For a few months she spells it with a C 'for religious reasons' and plays with Russian versions such as 'Katerina' or the German 'Käthe'. None of these names seem to fit the new identity she is trying to establish. 'Who am I?' is a question she asks frequently in her journal. She feels herself a permanent outsider, a little colonial, an exile from her country, no longer a New Zealander, but not English either, cast off by her family, a married woman not living with her husband – existing precariously outside the moral code of middle class society. She has become adept at acting different parts, inhabiting other characters, concealing, pretending. 'Which self? Which of my many – well, really, that's what it looks like coming to – hundreds of selves? . . . there are moments when I feel I am nothing but the small clerk of some hotel without a proprietor, who has all his work cut out to enter the names and hand the keys to the wilful guests.'[25] Katherine Mansfield is as good a name as any for this shape-shifter, though who K.M. really is, has still to emerge.

ABOVE: Katherine Mansfield, aged 10. *Alexander Turnbull Library, 1/4-015041-F*

ABOVE RIGHT: Margaret Mansfield Dyer, Katherine's beloved grandmother. *Conor Williamson, courtesy of the Katherine Mansfield Society, with kind permission*

BELOW: Katherine's birthplace, no. 11 Tinakori Road, Wellington. *Author collection*

ABOVE LEFT: The Beauchamp family in 1897, left–right: Chaddie, Harold Beauchamp, Leslie, Vera, Annie Beauchamp, Jeanne and Katherine. *Alexander Turnbull Library, 1/2-017396-F*

ABOVE RIGHT: Maata Mahupuku, Katherine's school friend in Wellington and the object of a teenage passion. *Alexander Turnbull Library, 1/2-049811-F (detail)*

BELOW LEFT: Ida Baker, the 'perfect friend' with whom Katherine had a love/hate relationship. *Alexander Turnbull Library, with kind permission of Peter Day*

BELOW RIGHT: Queen's College in London, where Katherine was educated between 1903 and 1906. *Alexander Turnbull Library, F-16235-1/4*

ABOVE: Arnold (left) and Garnet Trowell. *The Trowell Family*

TOP: George Bowden. *Harry Ransom Humanities Research Center, Austin, Texas*

ABOVE: The Pension Müller, Wörishofen. *Reinhard F. E. Wolf*

TOP: Katherine Mansfield in 1906. *Alexander Turnbull Library, 1/2-162827-F*

RIGHT: Floryan Sobieniowski, the Polish writer Katherine met in Wörishofen. *Casimir Wilkomirski, Rhythm, 1912*

M. Elizabeth Greenwood, Woodward St., Wellington.

your loving sister Jeanne - 1913.

TOP LEFT: Jeanne, Katherine's youngest sister, in 1913. _Janine Renshaw-Beauchamp, courtesy of the Katherine Mansfield Society, with kind permission_

TOP RIGHT: 'Chaddie', the middle sister. _Janine Renshaw-Beauchamp, courtesy of the Katherine Mansfield Society, with kind permission_

LEFT: Vera, the eldest of the Beauchamp siblings. _Janine Renshaw-Beauchamp, courtesy of the Katherine Mansfield Society, with kind permission_

ABOVE: Leslie Heron Beauchamp, Katherine's younger brother in his First World War uniform. She was devastated by his death in 1915. _Janine Renshaw-Beauchamp, courtesy of the Katherine Mansfield Society, with kind permission_

ABOVE: Zennor – Katherine's tower is on the left and the Lawrences' cottage on the right. *Author collection*

RIGHT: Francis Carco. *Alexander Turnbull Library, F-44569-1/2*

BELOW: D. H. Lawrence and Frieda at the beginning of their relationship with Katherine and John. *University of Nottingham*

LEFT: Garsington Manor, Oxfordshire home of Ottoline and Philip Morrell. *National Portrait Gallery*

BELOW: Katherine's great friend Samuel Koteliansky with Ottoline Morrell. *National Portrait Gallery*

BOTTOM: Virginia Woolf and Lytton Strachey a Garsington. *National Portrait Gallery*

8

In Search of Katherine Mansfield

By dint of hiding from others the self that is within us — we may end by being unable to find it ourselves.

KATHERINE MANSFIELD, NOTEBOOK 29, 1907

Two more of Katherine's German stories appear in the July 1910 issues of the *New Age*. Her health has improved dramatically over the summer and at the beginning of August she returns to London to stay with Beatrice and Orage at their apartment in Kensington. Katherine is introduced to a much more bohemian city than she had previously seen. She is taken to a party given by the poet and mystic, Aleister Crowley, where she smokes cannabis for the first time, hoping for some kind of psychic revelation. Instead, she gains an insight into her own character. While others are in lotus-land, she sits on the floor arranging matches in mathematical patterns.

Two other pension sketches are published during her first weeks with Beatrice and Orage, as well as letters on such diverse subjects as newspaper coverage of notorious murderer Dr Crippen's arrest (objecting to 'the scrapings of prison plates which the "Daily Mail" so obligingly heats up for breakfast each morning') and an attack on the popular novels of Elinor Glynn.[1] She and Beatrice collaborate on satirical reviews and spoofs.

They are both good at spotting the absurd or pretentious and sending it up mercilessly. In the five months since they first met, they have become very close. Like Katherine, Beatrice is a married woman who has left her husband. She has also lost a baby. Ten years older and much more cynical, Beatrice rails against the married state and considers child-bearing humiliating and beastly. When Katherine has her heroine protest, 'I consider child-bearing the most ignominious of all professions', it is Beatrice she is quoting.[2] Beatrice knows all about contraception and abortion, has had several affairs – with both men and women – is adept at concealing her past and encourages Katherine to disregard convention and pursue sexual freedom. She has a vicious tongue and in her company Katherine can give vent to her own biting wit. At first this liberation is exhilarating. They spend wild weekends together at Beatrice's cottage in Sussex, but after Katherine comes back to London she feels guilty for the things that she has done and said. In Beatrice's company she has drunk too much brandy and bitched about people of whom she is actually quite fond. She complains to Ida that Beatrice brings out the worst in her, confessing to another friend: 'It's terrible when two women get together. I don't know which of the two of us was the more disgusting'.[3] It's obvious to Ida that the relationship can't last. Both women are strong characters with defensive egos and by September they are beginning to be wary of each other. They are competitors, after all – and not just in the literary sense. Orage, always something of a womaniser, is as fascinated by Katherine's personality as he is by her talent, and Beatrice is not a woman to tolerate a rival in either sphere. The triad begins to show the strain and soon the apartment is not big enough for the three of them. At some point the disagreement becomes physical – a friend who comes to call walks in on two flushed, angry women and a bead necklace scattered across the floor – though the incident is lightly brushed over. The *New Age* ceases to publish Katherine's work and for eight months Beatrice has its pages all to herself.

Katherine moves into a flat on Cheyne Walk in Chelsea, overlooking the river, which has been temporarily vacated by Orage's friend, the painter Henry Bishop, who has gone away for five months to Morocco. For the first time since she left New Zealand, after living in a succession of hotels and hostels and bed and breakfast rooms, Katherine has a place of her own that she can arrange in her own style. As friends observe, she has an innate sense of theatre – 'a couple of candles stuck in a skull, another between the high windows, a lamp on the floor shining through yellow chrysanthemums, and herself accurately in the centre, in a patterned pink kimono and white flowered frock, the one cluster of primary brightness in the room'. Influenced by the Japan–British Exhibition held in London in September 1910, Katherine is experimenting with minimalism. She buys for her bedroom a Japanese doll, called Ribni after a character in an Aleksandr Kuprin short story called 'Captain Ribnikov'. One of Henry's paintings of 'a river flowing through reedy country' is on the living room wall, 'a stack of canvases and a bundle of tall dry rushes' left behind by him are arranged in a corner, and on the wall 'two crosspieces of a strainer up on a nail looking like a deserted crucifix'.⁴ A guitar, which Katherine – regretting the sale of her cello – has begun to use to accompany her singing, hangs behind the door. It is the kind of deliberately staged bohemian decor sent up in magazine articles railing against decadence.

Under the Japanese influence, Katherine has also changed her personal style to match her new identity. Her hair, though still worn up at the back, is combed forward into a fringe across her forehead, creating a frame for her face, Japanese fashion. Chronically short of money, she has found a clever, but cheap, dressmaker in Chelsea and begins to assemble a basic wardrobe of black and white – long skirts and blouses she can interchange, giving the impression that she has more clothes than she actually possesses. She adds striking touches of colour with taffeta waistcoats and velvet jackets in the vivid purples, reds and blues that she loves and brightly coloured striped French stockings.

The Japan–British Exhibition has opened Katherine's eyes to oriental literature and she has begun to read the work of Yone Noguchi, finding in him a 'true authentic voice' that thrills her. Noguchi's most widely published book is his first novel, *The American Diary of a Japanese Girl*. Bound in linen with Japanese mother-of-pearl fasteners and containing foldout illustrations on rice paper, the book is a beautiful object in itself. The experimental nature of the text fascinates Katherine. It is witty, poignant and vividly written. The central character speaks directly to the reader in an intimate and irreverent way; the narrative element of the story is pared down to a minimum; the plot often unfolds in dialogue; and the girl's character is fleshed out by interior monologue.

In Henry's bookcase there are books on painting that also lead Katherine in new directions and she begins to take an interest in the Imagist and Symbolist movements. She has loved the work of Walter Pater since she was a student at Queen's College and in 1910 his essays on the Renaissance are reprinted. Beginning to learn a new way of looking, she copies quotations from *Studies in Art and Poetry* into her journal, making Pater's philosophy her own. 'Every moment some form grows perfect in hand or face; some tone on the hills or the sea is choicer than the rest; some mood of passion or insight or intellectual excitement is irresistibly real and attractive to us – for that moment only. Not the fruit of experience, but experience itself, is the end . . . To burn always with this hard, gem-like flame, to maintain this ecstasy, is success in life.'[5]

But the defining moment in Katherine's writing life is the exhibition, *Manet and the Post-Impressionists*, mounted in London in November 1910 by Roger Fry. This features the work of Cezanne, whose paintings are familiar to some on this side of the English Channel, as well as canvases by the unrecognised Gauguin and Van Gogh. Fry tries to define the differences between these painters and the Impressionists by stating that they seek to portray not only the way that light falls on their subjects, but also 'the emotional significance which lies in things, and is the most important subject matter in art'.[6] The Impressionists had been concerned with surface realism; the Post-Impressionists explore deeper structures. The exhibition is a sensation. Katherine visits the Grafton Galleries with friends and returns again and again on her own until each picture is imprinted on her memory. As she stands in front of a Van Gogh she realises that these paintings can teach her about narrative structure. Just as the painter has distorted perspective and representation to be true to colour and emotion, taking the images towards abstraction, so his technique can be applied to literature. Like W. B. Yeats, Katherine has read Arthur Symons' seminal work on symbolism, which asserts that the writer must escape 'the old bondage of rhetoric . . . Description is banished that beautiful things may be evoked, magically' so that 'the soul of things can be made visible' and 'literature . . . may at last attain liberty.'[7] According to Symons, both the Impressionists and the Symbolists are seeking the same thing – the 'very essence of truth'. Katherine has a kind of epiphany, recording afterwards that Van Gogh's paintings, particularly the *Sunflowers* and a portrait of the postman, Joseph Roulin, had taught her 'something about writing, which was queer, a kind of freedom – or rather, a shaking free'.[8] For Katherine this search for a new means of expression is defined in Walter Pater's words: 'the passage and dissolution of impressions, images, sensations . . . that continual vanishing away, that strange, perpetual weaving and unweaving of ourselves'.[9]

Katherine loves living on Cheyne Walk. She can see the Thames from her windows and watch the light dappling the plane trees along the Embankment. Through the long evenings of an Indian summer she works in the front room, listening to the street sounds and the calls of the barge-men, floating through the open windows. There is a pub on the corner and Katherine listens to the buskers singing on the pavement.

> *Somebody loves me*
> *How do I know*
> *Somebody's eyes 'ave told me so-o.*[10]

Her days are filled with writing. She is working on her novel 'Maata', using it to exorcise her bitter experience with the Trowells. She constructs a chapter plan and calculates that if she can write twenty-four pages of her exercise book every day (5000 words) she can finish a 75,000-word novel in fifteen days. But Katherine is distracted by ideas for short stories. Having exhausted the German material, she is casting around for a new direction and experimenting with several different styles. Beatrice Hastings rejects most of this material as being too sentimental. The satirical pieces, which Katherine regards as ephemera, are, in Beatrice's words, 'balls better', but they are not a priority for their author. Without publication in the New Age to direct her output, Katherine is adrift in the highly competitive London literary marketplace. A collection of thirty-six poems, titled 'The Earth Child' is turned down,[11] and only one piece is published that autumn, a sentimental fairy story in a magazine called The Open Window. A few months later, a New Age review, in Beatrice's distinctive style, rubbishes the maga-zine and lampoons Katherine's contribution.

The wood-cutter read Grimm and Andersen, and was good-tempered: his wife read Ibsen and Shaw, and burnt his supper of fried onions when he brought home a little boy to be the playmate of his baby daughter. The waif increased in wisdom and stature, and in favour with the fairies; and the girl grew to love him and the works of Shakespeare, Milton, Dickens, Maeterlinck, Ibsen, Shaw, and Omar Khayyam. The boy wanted to find the world, and she wanted to find herself. When the parents died, the girl went to London, and became a great actress; 'but in her bed, at night, she thought of the Boy in the little hut on the hill, and cried.' He, dazed by solitude, prepared himself for . . . the world by reading Mudie's Library. 'One night, as he sat by the fireplace a great mountain of books, from the mantel-piece above, fell on him and killed him. It was very terrible.' Thus, learning killed the lad. The same afternoon the Girl refused an offer of marriage, and drove to Liverpool Street Station. 'Oh! I have been a fool,' she cried. 'I do not want myself, and I do not want the world, but just the Boy, the Boy.' She kissed his corpse, and her heart broke. Thus, woe killed the woman. They were buried together, and the green grass grew all round; but the golden buttercups were not allowed to decorate their grave, for 'a wind came and scattered the petals far and away over the world.' O, Shaw! where is thy sting? O, Grimm! where is thy victory?[12]

Katherine is devastated, but takes the message to heart and performs a ruthless exorcism on manuscripts she had previously cherished. The fairy story is ripped up and fed to the fire. 'I have a perfectly frantic desire to write something really fine, and an inability to do so which is infinitely distressing . . . But the difficulty is that I am not yet free enough to give myself uninterrupted hours.'[13]

This is largely her own fault. Katherine's life is very sociable. There are smoky afternoons in the basement of an ABC café across the road from the New Age offices, with other contributors, a select group of young intellectuals – almost exclusively men – who meet to discuss politics, philosophy, art and literature. Among them is John M. Kennedy, an overweight Irishman who writes on foreign affairs for the Daily Telegraph and is rumoured to be a spy; a young poet called Paul Selver who translates Slavic literature and is something of a Chekhov expert; and the nineteen-year-old Carl E. Bechhofer, another east European specialist with a gift for undergraduate style lampoons. Conversation ranges from the constitutional crisis that has just ended the House of Lords' right to block legislation, to Nietzsche and Schopenhauer.

As Katherine listens, she is very conscious of the gaps in her own education. Queen's College had provided much better instruction than most girls were given in the first decade of the twentieth century, but it was still an education designed for the future wives of educated men. Katherine has never been to university and knows little of the Greek and Latin texts being quoted around her and even less of philosophical concepts. Even her knowledge of literature is shallower and more patchy than she would like. She is aware that she lacks the critical grounding in logic needed to back up an argument. The opinions she does dare to put forward are quickly scorned: in the rarefied atmosphere of these discussions, women are not taken very seriously except as material for improvement. Orage, sending up Katherine's literary preferences, is happy to act as her mentor: 'Her taste is very uncertain and rather promiscuous. If she were not so quick to see that a thing is good when it is pointed out to her, I should be appalled by her state of mind. For instance, she likes Whitman and at the same time loves Milton. She plays Beethoven and yet finds relief in Sankey and Moody's hymns. Swinburne she thinks the greatest poet since Shelley . . . I tell her that her education has been shocking, and she always ends by confessing and deploring the fact, and appealing to me for guidance.'[14] Orage, making fun of Katherine's new habit of dressing in black and white, nicknames her 'the marmozet', sitting among them 'silent and furtive . . . picking up everything everyone said and did, grist for the sketch-mill'.[15]

As well as these new literary acquaintances, old friends from Queen's College are regular visitors to her flat – her cousin Sylvia Payne, Vere Bartrick-Baker and Gwen Rouse, who brings news of the Trowells. Katherine takes care to keep the two parts of her life separate. Orage observes that 'she trails a crowd of second-rate friends – the debris of her wrecked past – from whom she will gradually disembarrass herself'.[16] But Katherine, though she keeps her friends in separate compartments, is more loyal than either Orage or Beatrice is prepared to give her credit for.

The solitary nights are harder to endure. Alone in the flat, Katherine is once more affected by ugly dreams and fears so real she has to pile the furniture behind the door in order to feel secure. It is difficult to keep despair at bay, remembering the lost freedom of family life in New Zealand that she had taken so much for granted: 'the knowledge that an she would she could shake from her all the self-forged chains & banish all, & pillow her head in her Mother's lap. All that irretrievably gone now.'[17] Ida often sleeps in the spare room to keep Katherine company. If Katherine is having a bad attack of insomnia they get up in the small hours and have tea and eggs together in the tiny kitchen. Ida, who has given up her study of music, is constantly in the background to care for Katherine. During the day there are sometimes 'undesirable people' from whom she needs to be protected. A persistent man comes to the door and will not take no for an answer when Ida tells him that he can't come in. Ida steadfastly refuses, 'preparing to shut the door quickly'. Eventually he goes away.[18]

Katherine is having relationships with several young men: her old German teacher Walter Rippmann, the *New Age*'s John M. Kennedy (who may or may not have given her a fur coat), Francis Heinemann, son of the publisher (who presents her with a carved Russian village for Christmas), an Austrian journalist called Geza Silberer who writes under the pseudonym Sils Vara (another candidate for the fur coat) and, more seriously, William Orton. William is a grocer's son, educated as a scholarship boy and now a teacher and, like Katherine, an aspiring writer. He is the same age and feels an outsider, as she does. They meet at the house of a mutual friend, playing tennis. He, too, has had something published in the *New Age*. They both experience 'a sort of instant recognition'. Going home on the tube 'Katharina (she was being very Russian just then)', suddenly asks 'Do you believe in Pan?' and they spend the evening wandering around Euston discussing the question. Two nights later he is invited to Cheyne Walk. They talk about literature, the problems of their lives, 'laugh at them with genuine happy laughter; and then hug each other'. If either has any money they go out and eat. There is a wooden bowl on the shelf and 'whoever has a half-sovereign puts it in'. They discuss the symbolism of Chekhov 'in which things speak for themselves'. This is what Katherine is aiming for and William believes that it is 'the very essence of her genius'.[19]

They have both become excited by reading new work – listening for the true authentic voice that will speak to them. Katherine gives her copy of Yone Noguchi to William, taking his journal in exchange. From now on they write in it together, as she had once done with Garnet. Katherine often writes poetry – still heavily influenced by Whitman – and sometimes prose. She has started work on a new series of sketches, some of them, particularly 'How Pearl Button was Kidnapped', with a strong New Zealand theme. 'Pearl Button' is a reworking of a very early fragment Katherine had written before she left Wellington. All the stories are recognisably autobiographical. 'New Dresses' features a money-conscious father with a careless, tomboy daughter who is always getting into trouble and is constantly misunderstood. 'A Birthday', though the characters are given German names, is set in the first house on Tinakori Road, and describes the birth of a third child to a man remarkably like Harold Beauchamp.

William is awed by Katherine's single-mindedness, recording that she 'lives to write'. She is always 'the artist, subject always to art's pitiless demand for purity, clarity, and thoroughness'. Obedience to its discipline makes her happy, but he is aware of the fragile nature of Katherine's emotional balance, and her inability to manage her own life as carefully as it should be managed. He observes that she is not as tough as she likes to think and is playing 'fast and loose' with her own happiness and security. Her 'thirst for experience' is enormous – 'a genuine thing, indicating a genuine need'. They are both, in William's words, 'leading lives of passionate intensity . . . Coming together from time to time to share experiences.'

Both have other relationships. Katherine's are perhaps more casual but William is emotionally involved with another woman and has ambitions to go to university as a late entrant. He is in no position to make commitments. When William's girlfriend ends their affair because of his feelings for Katherine, they talk about marriage. But Katherine does not want to move out to Surrey and become a teacher's wife. William feels that he can't move to London and exist on what he can earn as a writer. He still wants to go to university. 'No bargaining is permitted.'[20]

When Henry Bishop returns at the beginning of 1911, Katherine has to leave the flat. Her father's allowance is almost the same amount that William is earning as a junior teacher, but he lives at the school and has his accommodation and meals paid for in addition to his earnings. Katherine has to pay for everything out of her allowance. Ida finds cheaper rooms on the top floor of what William Orton called a 'barrack-like block of flats' called Clovelly Mansions in the Grays Inn Road not far from the *New Age* office. William tells Katherine that it's a mistake – she should have tried harder to stay put. The windows look out across the wet roofs and smoking chimneys of East London. It's noisy, too, when the windows are open – there's a constant flow of traffic along the street below – and there are long flights of stairs to climb with no lift. The flat is unfurnished. Katherine covers the walls with brown paper and puts pale yellow bamboo matting and cushions on the floor, Japanese style. Ida scours London for travel posters to put up in the kitchen, making the walls so bright that the room seems 'to sail happily away'.[21] Almost the only furniture they possess is a grand piano Katherine had acquired in Cheyne Walk. Madame Alexandra, the opera singer who lived on the floor above, had heard Katherine singing with her guitar and offered to give her lessons. Anxious to get back to music, Katherine agreed, and was persuaded to buy the second-hand piano. Ida is a joint signatory on the agreement and has a half share in it.

The piano is placed in the centre of the main room. In the smaller of the two rooms Katherine puts a couple of divan sofas covered in black and a Buddha that had been brought back from Burma by Ida's mother on a low table. It's called the 'Buddha room' and the girls keep a bowl of water full of floating chrysanthemums in front of the statue.

Something of the flat's atmosphere is conveyed in a barbed skit by Orage, satirising Katherine as 'Mrs Foisacre', published in the New Age in May 1912:

> Her room was quaintly furnished, for all the world as if relays of minor poets had been each given a cubic yard to decorate. On this wall were the deposits of the French Symbolist school – drawings of spooks and of male and female figures shaped like vegetables. On that wall were photographic reproductions of the Parthenon friezes; the highwater mark, I suspected, of some pseudo-classic youth who yearned to be strong. The floor was covered with matting, and an earthenware fountain in the midst played by means of a pump. There was a piano and a host of divans. Oh, divans, I thought. Divans! What a lollipop life we are in for! Turkish delight, scented cigarettes, lotus-land, minor poetry, spooks – and where is the guitar? There, as I live, hanging behind the door![22]

Here, Katherine dreams vainly of 'achieving a firm spiritual peace, in the midst of a life that insists on being vivid and restless'.[23]

Her male escorts take her to the Vienna Café in Bloomsbury where all the beautiful people (and Sils Vara) go, she has dinner with John M. Kennedy at a favourite Italian restaurant on the corner of the Grays Inn Road, makes drinks last all evening at the Café Royal when not in the money, and she is also seen in the Cave of the Golden Calf, England's first 'Artists' Cabaret Club', just off Regent Street, newly opened by Frida Strindberg, a wealthy bohemian with a passion for the arts. Katherine's striking looks, talent for mimicry – particularly Irish and cockney accents – and her ability to turn a clever phrase mean that she gets invitations to 'arty' parties, particularly those thrown by Gwen Otter, a famous Chelsea hostess, where she meets all the 'in' people. Katherine can always be relied upon to entertain. But her literary social climbing creates enemies and she is afterwards satirised for being witty in order to cover her intellectual inadequacies. Katherine is now leading the life she has always wanted to live – a published writer, at the heart of literary London, independent and successful. But it is also a very artificial existence and Katherine is aware of a vacuum at the centre of it. She still has no one to share her life with – a need visible to all who know her, including Orage, who comments: 'If only she could find the friend, the companion, the intellectual comrade in a man, how happy she would be . . .'[24]

This is one need that can't be filled by Ida, who has become aware that Katherine has moved into another social sphere, where Ida can't follow. She realises that Katherine is 'meeting people with a mental capacity nearer to her own',[25] and they are growing apart. Katherine is also becoming irritated by Ida's possessive love, which has begun to demand, mutely, some form of response. She tells a cruel anecdote, alleging that Ida had opened the door of the bathroom in the flat one day and stood there, naked, hoping – desiring – that Katherine would turn and look at her and realise how beautiful she really was. Katherine says that she refused to turn round and look at Ida, but does not explain how she could otherwise possibly have known that Ida was naked.

In 'Maata', she writes about Ida under the name of Rhoda – an allusion to one of Ida's nicknames, the 'Rhodesian Mountain'. Katherine is aiming for a kind of 'song of songs', a psalm of love and longing from Rhoda to Maata, but the result is overwritten and sickeningly sentimental. She imagines Rhoda waking in the morning and kneeling in front of Maata's photograph, in an attitude of yearning: 'Maata has never kissed me on the mouth, but I know what her lips feel like – they feel like carnations. I can see them . . . Do not be sad, my darling. Let me keep away from you everything that is not beautiful and fitting. You are perfection. How can you help being hurt by this world, Maata. It is my destiny to serve you. I was dead when you found me and without you I am nothing. Let me serve . . . There is only one thing left that has any terror for me . . . it is that you have grown too strong to need me.' Rhoda, using the same phrase as Ida, sees herself as 'a strong, silent force of love'. The vignette cleverly portrays the earthy physicality of Ida, which at times revolts Katherine. She describes Rhoda's attitude to food. 'She cut some rounds of bread, buttered them thickly & spread them with jam, and ate, stuffing her mouth full, washing it down with milk. "Dare I go on, dare I?" The same battle was fought each morning between her violent bodily hunger & a wavering sense of shame.'[26] This is a struggle that the fastidious Katherine has witnessed often in Ida's company. In a letter to a friend, Katherine describes Ida eating a banana. 'She eats them so slowly, so terribly slowly. And they know it – somehow;

they realise what's in store for them when she reaches out her hand. I have seen bananas turn absolutely livid with terror on her plate . . .'[27]

There is also the suffocating quality of Ida's love, made doubly maddening by Katherine's awareness of how much she still relies on it. When Ida flies after Katherine on a chilly day to tell her that she's forgotten her coat and that it's too cold to go out without it, Katherine is furious and throws it back at her. But not far down the Grays Inn Road, in a bitter east wind, Katherine is frozen to the bone and forced to go back to the flat and admit that she's been wrong. Ida writes with understanding of Katherine's desire for independence and her own grief as she begins to know 'the almost physical ache that comes with the realisation of being inadequate'.[28]

Katherine's family write to tell her that they are coming over from New Zealand for the coronation of George V in June and Katherine looks forward to meeting them, particularly her mother, hoping that this time they will be proud of her. But in the spring of 1911, Katherine has a shock. Her period fails to arrive and she believes that she is pregnant again. After her initial horror, Katherine begins to take a more positive view of the situation. Her longing for a child overwhelms practical considerations. This time, she tells Ida, she is in a better position to have a baby – she has her own flat, she is more secure and mentally much stronger than she was even a year ago. But there is the problem of money, and the imminent arrival of her parents. However much she wants the baby, she can't bear to face her mother, pregnant again without a visible husband. Ida is sent round to the offices of Francis Heinemann to ask for help and believes that he is the father. John M. Kennedy proudly tells a mutual friend that the child is his. There's no mention of Geza Silberer and Katherine is silent on the subject of William Orton, who now wears the black opal ring she had once given to Garnet. But even if the unidentified father of her child had been willing to marry her, she is still officially married to George Bowden and divorce is not easy.

The problem is still unresolved in April when Ida goes off to Rhodesia to visit her father. She leaves some money in a bank account for Katherine and the baby. Ida feels guilty at deserting Katherine when she needs her most, but Katherine insists that she must go. As the taxi drives Ida away to the station, Katherine gives her a bouquet of carnations.

Many years later, Ida writes, 'I cannot imagine how I could have left her at that time; it was a foolish thing to do.'[29] After Ida's departure, Katherine revives her relationship with Beatrice Hastings, whom she nicknames

'Biggy B'. They go down to Sussex to stay at the cottage in Ditchling, where they drink a great deal, tramp down muddy country lanes, smoke too many cigarettes and are 'clever, amusing . . . bitter and cruel' together again,[30] composing a spoof on their favourite authors for the New Age.[31] Katherine is at her satirical best. The pregnancy mysteriously evaporates and when Ida returns she is convinced that Beatrice has persuaded Katherine to have an abortion. A story called 'A Birthday' appears in the 18 May edition of the New Age. It is an account of a birth rather than a termination, but another story surfaces later, describing a visit to a sleazy and ambiguous doctor who is able, for a fee, to 'remove complications' and set a woman's mind at rest. Whether it is written from personal experience is something only Katherine can know.

9

'The Model Boys-will-be-boys Pseudo Intellectual Magazine'

She was ready to go out, dressed in a tailored suit of dark blue serge, with a small cream-coloured straw-hat trimmed with a tiny bunch of gay flowers — there was something almost boyish about her. Perhaps it came from the little tailored coat, which hung straight from the shoulders. But no: it was more inward than that. She was not, somehow, primarily a woman. I was not conscious of her as a woman. She was a perfectly exquisite, perfectly simple human being, whose naturalness made me natural. With her there was no need to pretend.

JOHN MIDDLETON MURRY, *BETWEEN TWO WORLDS*

On 1 June 1911 the *New Age* publishes a letter by an Oxford undergraduate called John Middleton Murry. His friends call him Jack. He has been staying in Paris during the university vacation and has become entranced by the intellectual freedom of the city and the cosmopolitan group of young people he has met there. After an unhappy suburban childhood and a narrow, intense education, Paris has blown all his received ideas about art and life apart. Like many a product of all-male educational establishments, John is unsure of himself in the company of women. Sexually innocent when he arrived in Paris, within a few weeks he had become emotionally and physically entangled with a young woman on the fringes of the 'demi-mondaine', that group of not quite prostitutes who haunted the cafés looking for men to take them under their protection. Marguéritte had given John his first sexual experience. Wildly in love with her, he had proposed marriage and since then she has been his dependant. John, living on a small scholarship, is not in a position to support her and does not know what to do. He needs extra money and is seeking to earn it through

journalism. Through Marguéritte he has met the French writer and journalist Francis Carco. In the cafés frequented by artists and writers he has
also met the Scottish Colourist John Duncan Fergusson, who introduces
him to Picasso and two female painters – the legendary Parisian figure
Georges Banks and an American Fauvist called Anne Estelle Rice. Together
with Fergusson, and another Oxford undergraduate called Michael Sadler,
John has been discussing the possibility of starting up a small magazine dedicated to new ideas in art and literature. It is to be called Rhythm,
founded on their theories of harmony and balance in art, and influenced
by the work of the French philosopher Henri Bergson. Through his long,
well-argued letter in the New Age on 'Bergson in Paris' John Murry hopes to
raise his own profile and attract publicity. Few of the readers are aware that
the essay is the work of a twenty-one-year-old undergraduate.

Katherine's June contribution to the New Age is a satire on the coronation
of George V, 'with apologies to Theocritus', written as a dialogue between
two East End charwomen who go up to the West End, unsuccessfully, to
see the king. Annie Beauchamp arrives in London for the great social event
at the end of May with Katherine's sisters, Chaddie and Jeanne, and her
brother Leslie, or 'Chummie' as he is now known. Harold Beauchamp has
been detained in Wellington on business and, though he arrives at the end
of July, he is very disappointed to miss the coronation. On his previous
visit to England he had been presented to George when he was Prince of
Wales and is very proud that he had once shaken the future king's hand.

Although there is a loving reunion between Katherine and her family, her relations with her mother are cool. Meeting Annie for the first
time since the German experience, Katherine appraises her mother with
as much objectivity as she can. She sees the delicacy and the courage
she has always admired, but also the detachment. The memory of what
Katherine has lost is painful. Annie is never going to give her daughter the
unconditional love she seeks. And there are no signs of forgiveness, or of a
welcome back into the family fold. Katherine is aware that a considerable
distance is being placed between herself and her sisters. The family does
not spend a great deal of time in Katherine's company. Chaddie and Jeanne
are quickly swallowed back into the Beauchamp clan's social circle from
which Katherine has been exiled ever since she married George Bowden
and was sent to Germany. Katherine isn't the kind of young woman a
respectable Edwardian middle class parent would choose to introduce to
their daughters. There's an aura of undisclosed scandal, a woman living

alone with a reputation for being 'fast'. Her sisters are aware of undiscussed family traumas, a tightening of the lips whenever Katherine's name is mentioned, questions that must never be asked. Katherine has crossed a boundary; she has chosen the wild and dangerous territory beyond the family garden where her sisters still lead protected lives. When they are together their conversation is heavily rooted in New Zealand and Katherine keeps her current life hidden.

Her brother Chummie, now seventeen, is a particular delight. Katherine has always felt an affinity with her only brother and, although he was away at boarding school for long periods while she was at home in Wellington, she feels he understands her best. He, too, would like to be a writer, though his father has other ideas. Katherine sympathises. She gives him Ida's key to the flat so that he can come and go as he pleases. This requires some ingenuity on Katherine's part to keep Chummie ignorant of her private life. In the journal she shares with William Orton, she records an erotic, passionate encounter with someone she describes simply as 'The Man'. 'It grew dark. I crouched against him like a wild cat . . . We made love to each other like two wild beasts . . . I felt mad with passion – wanted to kill.'[1] Preserving a facade of respectability while living the life of an emancipated woman is not easy. Orage's satire on Katherine describes secret assignations, whispered conversations behind doors, bribes to doormen, hastily sent telegrams and complicated subterfuges that make her life seem like a Whitehall farce.

The first issue of Rhythm makes its appearance in the summer. Inside a thick grey paper cover decorated with one of John Fergusson's striking designs, there are bold black and white prints and the contents have a firmly continental feel. There is a study by Picasso – the first to be published in Britain – a story in French by Francis Carco, a drawing of Scheherazade by Anne Estelle Rice, studies by Samuel John Peploe (another Scottish Colourist) and articles by Frederick Goodyear and Michael Sadler. It is apparent from the beginning that Rhythm takes itself very seriously. There is no satire and no political lampoons. But the magazine's intention to cover art, literature and music is more attractive to Katherine than the Fabian character of the New Age. She has little interest in politics but is in sympathy with John Murry's exposition of his own beliefs, which are to be made flesh in the magazine – the idea of rhythm in art, propounded by Fergusson, and a definition of Modernism, the word that will come to be used to define both Katherine and the small group of contributors.

'Art is the true and only expression of reality . . .' The artist 'must return to the moment of pure perception to see the essential forms, the essential harmonies of line and colour, the essential music of the world. Modernism is not the capricious outburst of intellectual dipsomania. It penetrates beneath the outward surface of the world, and disengages the rhythms that lie at the heart of things, rhythms strange to the eye, unaccustomed to the ear, primitive harmonies of the world.'[2]

The magazine sells very well. The content is bold and at the leading edge of what is happening in art and literature – the stories address reality, the poetry does not always rhyme and the drawings drift towards abstraction. An older generation of critics is understandably scandalised, but the more contemporary New Age, Rhythm's main competitor, is also scathing about the judgement of the youthful editor: 'There is not a page that is not stupid or crazed or vulgar'.[3]

By the end of the summer, John's life is in turmoil. He has completely lost his bearings 'both intellectually and emotionally'. Oxford seems stale and unreal, and he has recently abandoned Marguéritte, after allowing her to believe that his mother, who is quite ignorant of John's involvement with a French girl, disapproves of their engagement. He feels profoundly guilty that, on his last visit to Paris, he had not seen Marguéritte as promised. 'I had not told her the train I should come by, and, after twenty-four hours of waiting in a Paris hotel to find the courage to meet her, I fled to England. I never wrote to her again; nor did I read the letters she wrote to me. After some months they ceased.' He quotes Thomas Hardy: 'Not a line of her writing have I;/Not a thread of her hair . . .'[4]

Friends decide that John needs more sexual experience to put his affair with Marguéritte in perspective and they take him to a brothel in Oxford. John finds the whole business repugnant, particularly when he later discovers that he has contracted gonorrhoea. His dreams of a pure romantic love are tarnished by the physical realities of the sexual act.

According to William Orton, Katherine's first 'serious illness of the lungs' develops in August 1911. Her fever is so high that she lies on her bed at Clovelly Mansions hallucinating. At times she feels herself levitating towards the ceiling, and sometimes 'the little red elephants on the edge of her Indian cotton bedspread' appear to wave their trunks, 'processing solemnly round and round their limited pathway'.[5] The doctor tells Katherine's mother that she has pleurisy and advises the family to send her south to the sun. No one asks why a healthy young woman of twenty-one with no history of susceptibility to lung disease should be suffering from pleurisy in the middle of the summer. Katherine's illness coincides with some kind of crisis in her relationship with William. Encouraged by her parents, but not financed by them, Katherine goes to Geneva via Paris alone; William, who describes his mental state as 'half demented', to the Isle of Wight and then St Malo.

Ida, on her way home from Rhodesia, tries to make contact with Katherine in Paris, but their telegrams cross and they miss each other. Chummie, concerned for his sister, goes to see Ida as soon as she gets back to London and gives her Katherine's address in Geneva. Despite being exhausted by her journey, Ida stays only long enough to change her clothes and 'scrape together £5' plus her train fare before she sets off again for Switzerland. She finds Katherine in a small pension with less than a pound in her purse to pay the bill. Her first desperate question to Ida as she opens the door is 'Have you brought any money with you?'[6]

For a week, the pair share a sunny room at the top of the house, with the 'sweet, clear air . . . from the distant mountains' blowing in through the open windows.[7] But then Katherine meets an Austrian family she had known in Bad Wörishofen and Ida, always hypersensitive, begins to feel superfluous. After a few days Ida returns to London, leaving Katherine enough money for the rest of her stay. Back at the flat, Ida discovers that in her absence Katherine has been unable to keep up the repayments on the piano, a bill that Ida – jointly liable – has to settle by selling more of her mother's bonds. Instead of blaming Katherine for her lack of ability to manage money, Ida feels very bitter about what she sees as Harold Beauchamp's meanness towards his daughter. Katherine has been brought up to take luxury for granted and there are still things she can't give up. She likes smart clothes and has a passion for French perfume in cut-glass atomisers. 'I can't explain but my spirit seems to need luxury,' she has one of her characters remark. 'I can only expand among beautiful things.'[8] Harold Beauchamp's allowance is only sufficient for the essentials. Perhaps he hopes that penury will drive his errant daughter back into the fold of family life.

Katherine returns at the end of August and a few days later William Orton comes back from France. Troubled and confused by his personal life, he returns to Katherine and as usual in her company 'everything falls into its allotted place' and he feels balanced and whole. Katherine writes in their shared journal, 'My love for [William] has changed; it is become more imperative and compelling. Sometimes I think hopelessly that we will never be together – yet if there is any truth left in me I know that only together shall we two create and be fulfilled the one in the other . . .' But the uncertainty of it all is making Katherine unhappy and affecting her health. 'I want to begin another life,' she confides to the journal, 'this one is worn to tearing point.' The next entry, on 6 September 1911, begins 'I am very lonely and ill today' and ends with a poem:

I lose my way down every path
I stumble over every stone
And every gate and every door
Is locked 'gainst me alone.[9]

As always when she is depressed, Katherine turns to her work: 'Do other artists feel as I do – the driving necessity – the crying need – the hounding desire that [will] never be satisfied – that knows no peace?'[10] The publisher Stephen Swift has offered to bring out a collected edition of her German pension stories. There are close links between Swift and the New Age: John M. Kennedy, Beatrice Hastings and several other contributors have also been published by him and any one of them may have made the introduction. The advance is only £15, less than two months' allowance from Katherine's father, but she will be published alongside such authors as Arthur Ransome, Wilfred Scawen Blunt and Hillaire Belloc. Advertisements for the forthcoming anthology appear in the October literary supplements of the New Age. On the strength of this, Katherine writes a short letter to the leading literary agent J. B. Pinker, asking for an interview. She sends him a story called 'Hide and Seek', a creature of 'abnormal size' which he returns, and Katherine destroys it in another editorial inferno.

By 29 October she and William are writing sentimentally inflated farewell messages to each other in the journal. 'It is late night – tomorrow I shall be far away . . . I live only, only in my imagination. All my feelings are there and my desires and my ambitions. It is not that I wish so much to renounce the world – it has gone.' On All Saints Day, 1 November, William writes back: 'The year is drawing to a close . . . From far away I reach out the arms of my soul to you. From far away I know you mine for ever and ever . . . I am sealed with your mark, and you are sealed with mine.'[11] Her love affair with him has been another dead end. Another man has failed her. Like her character Maata, she often feels completely alone: 'Standing there in the dark she drifted away to that shadowy loneliness which some-times seemed to her to be her only true life, the only changeless truth . . .'[12]

On 30 November 1911 John Middleton Murry is once more a contribu-tor to the New Age. His controversial article on the 'Art of Pablo Picasso' unleashes a storm of protest on the subject of contemporary art, which is good publicity for John's new magazine. The autumn issue of Rhythm is as much of a success as its predecessor and Katherine is persuaded to send some work to the editor by Walter L. George, a novelist and socio-political writer with strong feminist sympathies, who seems to see Katherine as his protégée. He sends John one of her 'fairy' stories, with an enthusiastic introductory note. Though the story 'puzzles and intrigues' John, he rejects it but is interested enough to ask for more of her work. This time Katherine, perhaps on Walter's advice, chooses one of her New Zealand stories, 'The Woman at the Store', a dark, brooding tale worked up from journal notes made during the Urewera camping trip just before she left for England. John is excited by it and sends an immediate acceptance, stating extrava-gantly that it is 'by far the best story' the magazine has ever received.[13]

It seems to Katherine that she is on the edge of real recognition. With its bright orange jacket, In a German Pension, published in December, is conspic-uously visible in the London bookshops. The Beauchamps, still in England, are apparently pleased, though there are no recorded comments. A review in the Spectator compares Katherine's sketches to the German stories of her cousin Elizabeth von Arnim and there are favourable reviews in the Daily Telegraph, the Athenaeum, the Pall Mall Gazette, the Times and the Morning Post. Beatrice Hastings reviews it for the New Age rather less sarcastically than usual, even though she is suffering some personal jealousy. Her own novel, set in South Africa and privately printed by Stephen Swift in 1911 after serialisation in the New Age, had attracted very little attention. Katherine, Beatrice writes patronisingly (but with absolute truth), must get 'quite clear of the lachrymose sentimentality that so often goes with the satirical gift' – if she can do that she will be 'one of the most promising of young writers'.[14] It is as close to a good review as the New Age ever gets.

John Murry buys a copy of Katherine's book and is even more intrigued by its author. 'The stories that made up In a German Pension seemed to express, with a power I envied, my own revulsion from life; and I conceived a strong desire to meet Katherine Mansfield.'[15] John has also been adopted as a protégé by Walter George. Given to labelling people, Walter refers to John as the 'brilliant young Bergsonian'; Katherine is 'a wayward and cynical Mongolian'. He tantalises John with descriptions of Katherine as a mysterious, formidable woman 'not only difficult to meet, but terribly clever'.[16]

Walter invites John to a dinner to celebrate the publication of Katherine's book. With a complete lack of social skill that makes him awkward in company, John is speechless with nerves and appears, even to himself, impossibly gauche. Walter's wife, a gentle, eccentric woman who smokes tobacco in a man's briar pipe, is kind to John and tries, unsuccessfully, to make him feel more comfortable. Katherine arrives late in a taxi with all the drama of the star performer. Ida has helped her to dress, putting Katherine's hair up for her and arranging a single red flower on the dove-grey evening dress with its matching gauze scarf. The effect is simple, but stunning. The introductions are made and the guests ushered into the dining room. Mrs George has placed John on the opposite side of the table, where he watches Katherine across the candles and flowers. He is particularly drawn to her hands, which are small and delicate. She holds them cupped, her long fingers curled inwards 'like a shell'. John, kept silent by shyness, observes the way in which Katherine carefully manipulates the conversation like an actress playing a part. Aware that she is 'on show', and wary of John Murry's reputation as a serious intellectual and Oxford scholar, at first she appears aloof and reserved. Walter calls her 'Yekaterina' and serves German red plum soup in honour of her book. He has portrayed her to John as a cynic, 'perpetually on the point of saying very bitter and witty things', but Katherine refuses to conform and John is amused to see her 'turn the tables' on her host so that he appears 'like a kindly, well-groomed, but not very quick-witted dog who must be humoured and allowed to do his trick: the chief of which was his obvious expectation that she should do hers'.

Katherine fascinates John but his first impressions are not entirely favourable. He is unable to penetrate her mask. She comes to life only when talking about writing and after dinner they become involved in a passionate discussion on the difficulties of simplicity. John confesses that his own attempts at fiction and poetry are 'dogged by a truly horrible emotional exaggeration'.[17] For the first time Katherine realises that he, too, is involved in the creative process of art, struggling to become a poet and a novelist. Her manner towards him becomes more sympathetic and by the end of the evening they are so deep in conversation that John forgets the time and is in danger of missing his train. Katherine offers to let him share her taxi, but he refuses because he does not have enough money in his pocket to pay for it. She invites him to 'come to tea sometime', but forgets to give him her address.[18]

Katherine does not record her first impressions of John in her journal, but she talks to Ida. 'She was much impressed by him: his mind, his looks, everything about him.'[19] In January, having not heard from him again, Katherine sends a postcard to remind John that he had promised to let her review something for Rhythm. He sends her a book of poetry and they begin a formal correspondence discussing the author. They still haven't met again when Katherine travels to Geneva in February. She sends a postcard of Lake Geneva to William Orton with an enigmatic message on the reverse, assuring him that she is 'quite alone'. The visit is without explanation; perhaps a search for the new life she has been craving, or possibly for her health. In the two stories she writes, set in Geneva – 'Violet' and 'Pension Seguin' – her female characters have been sent there either for their 'nerves' or in order to 'forget'. Whatever the reasons, Katherine writes to John from Geneva to invite him for 'brown bread and Russian cherry jam' when she returns.[20]

It's a rainy day at the end of February 1912 when John climbs the long flights of stairs at 69 Clovelly Mansions. He's surprised by the lack of furniture – Katherine offers him the only chair and sits on a cushion on the floor serving him tea in porcelain bowls. This time she is more friendly and soon John is confiding to her that he hates Oxford, has lost interest in his studies, is oppressed by the weight of that expected 'First' and doesn't know how to endure the months before his final exams. He wants more than anything to be a writer, yet to leave Oxford seems equally impossible since he is maintained by scholarships and bursaries.

Katherine listens gravely. There is no ideal solution, she tells him pragmatically: 'life is just like that'. It is an expression that Katherine has begun to use quite often. 'But,' she adds with complete conviction, 'Don't stay at Oxford, whatever you do. It's wrong.'[21] John runs back down the many stairs, feeling as if a weight has been lifted from his shoulders. As he stands in the street waving up to Katherine's window, John knows that he has found a woman he can talk to who shares his love of literature.

Only ten months younger than Katherine in age, John is years younger in maturity. His childhood, which he prefers not to discuss, is a story of emotional deprivation, physical and psychological abuse. John's father has always believed in Victorian discipline: when he was small, John, a sensitive and imaginative boy, had been beaten for every transgression, however minor. His mother, whom he loves, is a gentle, timid woman, dominated by her husband and helpless to defend her son. At one point in his childhood John, after months of begging, had been allowed to have a pet dog, but came home from school one day to find the animal cowering in a doorway, badly injured and refusing to go back to the house with him. His mother can give him no explanation. John believes for the rest of his life that his father had either kicked or beaten the dog until it was too afraid to return home.

As a young child John had been precociously intelligent, able to read *The Times* by age three, escaping domestic realities by plunging into the world of books. He realised at a very early age that his father was in awe of his son's intellect and that academic achievement earned approval. As long as he could sustain the high level of his grades, he was safe from his father's anger. When John wrote about his childhood, he described it as perpetually marred by fear. 'There was no sunlight in his memory at all. There was only gloom and grit and sordidness, amid which he had run like a drop of water in grey dust, complete and separate and hidden . . . Why had there been no relief from it all, not one lovely, calm, sunlit thing to look back upon? Why had he worked with terror in his soul at his grammar school when he had taken his scholarship? Why had he never [had] a moment's enjoyment of his own cleverness, even? Terror and darkness, terror and darkness . . .'[22]

During John's childhood Murry senior had worked as a civil servant at the Inland Revenue during the day and then in the evening as a clerk for the Penny Bank to earn the money for his son's education. His hard work was rewarded when John won scholarships first to Christ's Hospital, the Blue Coat School, and then to Brasenose College, Oxford. Despite the burden of obligation, John saw the scholarships as his only way out, though the slog of study involved 'the complete obliteration of [his] childhood'.[23] He has emerged a nervous, insecure, guilt-ridden young man with 'a devouring desire to love and be loved'.[24] It is this underlying damage, this sense that he is a hurt child, that is so appealing to women.

At the *New Age* offices, Katherine's new friendship with John is viewed as laughable. Relations between Katherine and the *New Age* have been cooling for several months. The first signs had appeared in October when a moody 'prose poem' by Katherine was published on the letter page, where it looked utterly ridiculous. Her former friends at the periodical have been alienated by her treatment of John M. Kennedy, who was apparently devastated when Katherine casually ended their relationship and had threatened to shoot himself. Beatrice describes Katherine as an uncaring, self-regarding bitch who slept with him and accepted expensive presents despite confessing that she didn't love him. Their animosity is also being fuelled by Beatrice's resentment of Katherine's literary success and Orage's attitude towards the undergraduate pretensions of Rhythm and its editor. Katherine is made aware that she must choose where her loyalties lie. She feels artistically more at home with Rhythm and is strongly drawn to John as a person. In February, while Katherine is in Geneva, the New Age prints the first of a series of attacks on Rhythm. John is personified as 'Forester' in one of Orage's 'Tales for Men Only':

> Forester's special and unique gift was undoubtedly his sense of form and rhythm of words. Poetry or prose, no matter which it was, he instantly diagnosed both as regards its rank in the order of verbal creation and in spiritual content by means of its rhythm alone. He would open any book one chose to offer him, and after reading a sentence or two to himself in an interior fashion he would deliver judgment on the whole work with a precision, insight and illumination that were pontifically magical.[25]

In the next issue of the New Age, Katherine makes an appearance as Forester's sister, a dominating influence equipped with sentimental literary tastes and a close knowledge of the epigrams of Oscar Wilde. Although the New Age prints one of Katherine's stories and a satirical piece on 7 March,[26] her relationship with Orage's publication is rapidly wearing out.

Rhythm prints 'The Woman at the Store' in its spring issue, with two Russian poems purporting to be by Boris Petrovsky and 'translated' by Katherine, but transparently hers. The attacks in the New Age become more personal. A skit, probably by Beatrice, portrays Rhythm as 'The Model Boys-will-be-boys Pseudo Intellectual Magazine' and includes 'Selections from "Phlegm". [With profuse apologies to "Rhythm"].' Katherine's story is accused of being 'wilfully defiant of the rules of art'; her poetry is 'a joke' avenging all the 'sickly versifiers' she had once satirised in the New Age. A spoof Mansfield poem written by Beatrice, 'Translated from the

Phlegmish', is viciously accurate.[27] John, shocked and wounded by the ferocity of the New Age's opposition, composes a bewildered but dignified rebuttal. Katherine, though hurt, is used to Beatrice's barbed nib, but she is outraged on John's behalf, and the attacks draw them closer together. Their letters become more intimate.

John has left Oxford and is living with his parents and his nine-year-old brother in Wandsworth until he can find a means of earning his living. They have given John a room of his own to turn into a kind of bed-sitting-room, but he still feels stifled by the atmosphere – 'the dark, thick cloth on the table, the dark Victorian furniture, the sunless rooms with no flowers'.[28] He writes to Katherine, asking for her opinion on some manuscripts that have been sent to Rhythm 'both under strong recommendation from people I believe in. One I think is rotten, the other quite good. Tell me what you think of them . . .'[29] He also encloses some poems of his own and promises some of his short stories as soon as the box arrives from Oxford. They have begun a literary dialogue, punctuated by visits to her flat where he lies on the floor with his manuscripts 'waving his legs in the air' like 'a little boy playing with his toys'.[30]

Katherine, vilified in the New Age and finding it difficult to work at Clovelly Mansions, now floats a plan to move into the country, where she feels she might find the peace and quiet she craves. 'You mustn't go on imagining all these places,' John writes, admitting that he, too, is 'simply dying for sea washed windy hills – and it can't be done for ages.'[31] Katherine has been offered the lease of Cherry Tree Cottage, which she fantasises about calling Heronsgate – Heron is her brother's middle name. Herons have a magical quality for her; they are always connected with homemaking and security. In a letter now lost she describes the wonderful garden at the cottage and a damp room she speculates might be suitable for a tramp. Will John come and visit her there? John makes a joke of it:

Your d–d house has got on my brain. I've just drawn a wonderful picture of it in words and told a friend of mine that I'm going to live there – you can run out naked in the long grass and roll, roll, right under the pine trees, and little winds creep about and pink your body all warm, and right over the wall on the right hand side is a deep place, all white nettle and convolvulus, and you don't dare jump down because there must be creepy things in the water, so you wriggle back under the tummocky grass right back to the Cherry Tree; and then you cry just out of pure joy because you know the world is made for you and you can do anything with it . . . I hate this bloody place. You'll be able to write masterpieces . . . and I won't . . . When you're swinging on Heron's Gate you must ask me down to the tramp room I am a goodish tramp . . .[32]

John's fortunes are improving. The editor of the *Westminster Gazette* has taken him on as a freelance, writing filler 'paragraphs' and reviews at 7s. 6d. a time. It is very good money and John is elated. At last he is liberated from both Oxford and his parents. He goes straight round to Katherine's flat with the news and there is a celebratory dinner with John's friend, Frederick Goodyear, who has been admiring Katherine's work for months and pestering John to introduce her. The meeting is a success. Goodyear delights Katherine with his descriptions of a new career in advertising, promoting the virtues of the Stepney Progressive Furnishing Company. 'In me the great twin streams of the Zeitgeist converge,' he tells Katherine. 'Advertising and Hire Purchase.' They laugh a great deal and after dinner they walk round the statue of Eros in Piccadilly Circus, gazing up at the pale spring moon and talking about John's new job. 'I shall begin hunting for a room tomorrow,' John says. 'Not more than ten shillings a week.' But then Katherine makes a suggestion. 'Why not take a room in my flat? There's the music-room. I hardly ever use it, and I certainly don't need it . . . Would seven-and-six be too much?' It is a very bold suggestion. For a woman alone, in Katherine's ambiguous position, to share a flat with a single man, is scandalous. But John cares as little for convention as she does. Encouraged by Goodyear – 'whatever you do, don't live at home' – he accepts with gratitude.[33]

Ida has not seen this coming. Since she returned from Rhodesia she has been preoccupied by the problem of how to earn a living. Her mother's inheritance has almost gone – quite a lot of it spent on Katherine – and her father's tiny annuity is not enough to keep her, though Ida lives in the flat he leases for her and her sister. She and a friend have rented a shop and are setting up a small hairdressing and beauty salon, which they hope will provide a livelihood. Ida arrives at Katherine's flat in early April, 'happily looking forward' to spending the whole weekend with Katherine and finds 'Alas!', on her arrival, that she has to spend it rearranging the flat for John's occupation, giving up her divan bed in the Buddha room and filling a cupboard with food for him. Katherine, knowing that he has no money, persuades Ida that they should hide a £5 note among the groceries. Then, before he arrives, Ida leaves 'forlornly' to go back to her sister's flat. Both realise that this is a significant moment in their relationship. Katherine goes with Ida for part of the way on the top of a London omnibus where they talk – something they rarely ever do – about their friendship and what it means to them. Katherine gives Ida a book of 'occult wisdom' inscribed with a poem, called 'The Secret', which she has written especially for her.[34]

> In the profoundest Ocean
> There is a rainbow shell,
> It is always there, shining most stilly
> Under the great storm waves
> And under the happy little waves
> That the old Greeks called 'ripples of laughter'.
> And you listen, the rainbow shell
> Sings – in the profoundest ocean.
> It is always there, singing most silently!

But Ida knows that there is a fatal inequality in their affections; she is only one strand of Katherine's life – Katherine is the whole of hers.

At the end of March the Beauchamps reluctantly prepare to return home: Annie remarks that she would rather live above a fish and chip shop in London than anywhere in New Zealand.[35] Katherine's brother Leslie had hoped to be allowed to remain, but Harold Beauchamp, having seen the consequences of Katherine's youthful experiment, is adamant that his other children are not going to be allowed to repeat that mistake. Katherine's life is changing. She has not yet realised the full significance of her action in taking in John like a stray cat. She sees him as a dreamer, like Garnet, an innocent at large in a harsh world, and this childlike quality attracts her. John seems to speak the same language and he shares the same attitudes to art and life. Could he be the soulmate she has always hoped for? Is this the new direction she has been searching for? At the beginning of 1912, Katherine is aware of subtle alterations within herself. She is becoming a different person, chastened and, if not cynical, then at least sobered. She has come through a scorching experience, inflicted on herself, and has acquired a dark self-knowledge (she calls it 'the snail under the leaf'), which will inform everything she does. But there is also optimism. As for her New Zealand character Rewa in the story she works on spasmodically,

'The Future is quite in darkness but I know now that I am on the road again, back again, and that [this] time I journey with a fuller knowledge – a child no longer'.[36]

PART III

The Two Katherines

It took Murry himself three years to ascertain that Violet
was not Katherine.

F. A. LEA, JOHN MIDDLETON MURRY: *A BIOGRAPHY*

10

Violet

It was summer. It was warm, but not too hot. She sat on the steps of the bungalow slicing up beans and putting them in a basin. On each side of the shingle path nasturtiums flamed, yellow and red. The gate was open, then came the road, the cliffs, the sunny glittering sea.

VIOLET LE MAISTRE, THE OLD COASTGUARD STATION, DORSET

By 1924, a year after Katherine's death, some readers were complaining that John had turned the *Adelphi* into her literary mausoleum. The February issue was further evidence of his continuing obsession. It contained an unpublished story, 'Something Childish but Very Natural', which she had written in 1913, a long translation from the Russian called the 'Reminiscences of Leonid Andreyev' (one of Katherine's collaborations with Koteliansky), and a 'verse fragment' from Katherine's journal beginning: 'So that mysterious mother faint with sleep/Had given into her arms her new-born son . . .' But there was also something new; alongside Katherine's tragic lines, was a short poem called 'The Watchers' by Violet le Maistre. It was romantic, abstract by comparison with the raw emotion of Katherine's, but metrically competent and in the Georgian tradition.

> *When full of tears I cried aloud*
>> *Under the wide and senseless sky*

> Was there some god behind a cloud
>> Watching with ancient friendly eye;
>
> And in the quiet unmoving trees
>> Was there a sprite with reedy hair
>> Shaken and torn from thoughtless ease
>>> Longing this human grief to share?

Born on 13 May 1901 at Shenfield, in Essex, Violet le Maistre was the eldest child of a wealthy upper middle class family who lived at Oxshott, near Epsom, in Surrey. On her mother's side the family was descended from the poet Cowper and distinctly artistic. Violet's mother, Jessie, came from a large landowning family, and she passed on to her children a share in the Paston Hall estate in Northamptonshire, which included 400 hectares of prime arable land, run as a family trust. Jessie's death, in the influenza epidemic after the Great War, affected Violet profoundly. Many of her poems, like 'The Watchers', have an undertow of sadness and loss.

Violet's father's family came from Jersey and though originally of Huguenot extraction, was by now solidly rooted in the British establishment; one of her uncles was a clergyman, and her father, an engineer by profession, had distinguished himself during the war and was now director of the British Standards Board. But on the le Maistre side of the family, too, there was a streak of quirky individualism – another uncle was a painter, Violet's father Charles and her sister Tina were committed Christian Scientists and her brother Wynyard was studying languages at the Sorbonne. Violet had been educated at expensive girls' boarding schools in Devon and had then chosen to go to drama school in London, though her ambitions were to write the scripts or produce the plays rather than tread the boards. When Violet left drama school at the age of twenty-one she had still not found what she was searching for. She was drawn to writing, but had no idea whether what she had written was any good. After much discussion with her best friend Alison, she decided to send some of her work to the editor of the *Adelphi*.

When she first walked into John Murry's office in the autumn of 1923 she appeared quite unsophisticated and much younger than her age – a slim figure with wavy chestnut hair, whose outward naivety and innocence hid quiet poise and determination. Her lack of guile and soft, low-pitched voice were immediately attractive to John, who was also impressed that 'there was, in the fragments of her writing, a lovely and incorrupt fidelity to the beauty seen which, though hesitant, belonged to the same order as Katherine Mansfield's'.[1] They exchanged letters and then on her second visit to John's office he took her out to tea in the Strand and they talked about the Chekhov John had recommended her to read. She was flattered and encouraged by his interest, especially when he accepted 'The Watchers' for the *Adelphi*.

Violet's life among the rich middle classes of Surrey was a hedonistic post-war existence of tennis parties, flappers in open-topped cars, and girls who took courses in flower arranging and interior design or had jobs they did not need, while they waited for the right man to arrive. Violet was as keen to escape this world as Katherine had been to leave New Zealand. But Violet was less adventurous than Katherine and more conventional, still a 'child woman' living, at home with her father and sister, a life of stultifying boredom and routine. She was restless for something new, had read Katherine's work and was awed by her talent. Violet had also read the *Adelphi* and had followed, with empathy, the path of John's grief at his wife's death. She loved his intimate, confessional writing and felt that through his books and articles she already knew their author. Her meetings with him and their sporadic correspondence confirmed her impressions of his character. John's isolation and obvious need moved Violet to pity and love. At some point during the winter she showed Alison his photograph in a magazine and said, 'That's the man I'm going to marry.'[2]

John was unaware of Violet's interest in himself as a person rather than as an editor and mentor. She was thirteen years younger – the same age as his brother Richard, who was currently studying at the Slade. John wondered whether Violet and Richard would get on. Richard was a painter, like Violet's uncle, and there were other consanguinities. 'She was the very girl for my brother . . . She was too good not to be kept in the family, so to speak, though obviously she was not for me: 35 and old and battered.' He introduced them to each other but, though Richard liked her a great deal, Violet did not seem particularly interested. Then, just before he was due to go on holiday with his brother, John invited Violet to dinner in his lodgings in Pond Street, intending to plead Richard's case.

It was only when he was waiting for Violet to arrive that John became aware of a strange note in his own feelings. He watched the clock. The time for her arrival came and went. John paced backwards and forwards from the kitchen to the window. The filet mignon he was cooking might be spoiled. But was it only the meal he was worried about? 'Why was I so anxious that this girl should come? Why was I feeling that, if she did not come, a spark would go out in my heart?'[3]

Violet had got lost in the unfamiliar maze of streets and eventually arrived, breathless and apologetic. Through an emotionally charged dinner they talked again of Chekhov and Constance Garnett's translations, as well as Violet's own work. She was delighted that John had accepted her poem for the *Adelphi*, but it was fiction that she most wanted to publish. Soon the conversation turned to more personal subjects and John was forced to realise that there was more between them than friendship. 'Something she said about my photograph made me feel that I had no right to keep quiet any more – it would be untrue, unjust and cruel.'[4] Always shy in love, it took John some time to find the courage to cross the room and embrace her. But as soon as they had kissed, Violet confessed her own feelings, asking John if he also loved her. 'I didn't know I did; but I do,' he told her. By the end of the evening they had agreed to marry as soon as possible. Violet met a need that had not been fulfilled by Brett, or Frieda, or Vere. 'It seemed to me very wonderful to be loved by one so young, for I did feel old. I felt that the kind of love she had for me, and which she had awakened in me, had passed out of my life thirteen years before, when I first fell in love with Katherine; and, even at that moment, it struck me as strange that precisely the same thing had happened again.'[5]

But even as John acknowledged his need for Violet, he was aware of the power that Katherine still had over him. He dreamed he saw her lying in her coffin, 'swathed in black and white . . . with her head lifted. She was not dead, and she had been struggling (for life?) below.' Katherine spoke to him in the dream, but was silenced by a woman (remarkably like Ida Baker) sitting beside the coffin. In John's waking life, everything reminded him of her. As he had seen the Lawrences and Brett off on the boat-train to America in early March he had thought 'How long we waved' and then remembered how Katherine had written that same phrase to him after he had seen her off on the train to Bandol four years earlier. 'There's no describing the dull pain of such a memory . . .' As he came out of the station and looked up at the circling gulls he could hear Katherine's voice describing them 'buttoned into tight little suet jackets'. And as he lay in bed he heard her voice singing the music hall airs she had always sung around the house – 'like the Mouse song and "My Pay was Forty Cents a Day" it tore my heart. This feeling of loss . . . grows steadily worse and worse.'[6]

The novel that John had begun the previous year was also haunted by Katherine. He called it *The Voyage*, a title also borne by a short story that she had written before she died. Like all John's novels, it is transparently auto-biographical. The characters are recognisable to anyone with the slightest knowledge of their originals. Even Koteliansky makes a cameo appearance as Kosmitch (a Russian with a large, distinctive head and wild hair) who suggests to the hero, Whickham, that 'they ought to publish a fat monthly as big as the telephone book' – exactly the words used by Murry of the *Adelphi* when he and Kot discussed it. Whickham is John himself – gifted, but indecisive, weak, romantic, desperately shy and impractical. Anne is Katherine, decisive and capable, a woman who takes taxis everywhere and lives with an unattractive female companion who loves music. The heroine has, like Katherine, been to Menton and is inordinately fond of the grand-mother who had brought her up. 'There's nobody like a grandmother, a real grandmother,' Anne remarks in Mansfield mode. Her rival for the soul of the hero is Emilia, who is a portrait of Elizabeth Bibesco. Married to one of Whickham's friends, she is exotic, seductive and manipulative. Even though he knows it will ruin his relationship with Anne, Whickham can't resist her wiles. It is all remarkably chaste, as John claimed that his affair with Elizabeth had been: there are a few indiscreet meetings at her house, some embraces in a taxi and a couple of letters. But Anne and Whickham, like Katherine and John, still see it as a betrayal; it is the deceit that mat-ters and there are long philosophical discussions on the nature of love and truth.[7] The novel was to have been a kind of catharsis, but it did little to relieve John's misery or his feelings of guilt and it had terrible reviews. 'This is the dullest book I have ever read,' said the *New Statesman*, and L. P. Hartley wrote, 'This kind of writing simply will not do.'[8]

The cure for John's unhappiness seemed to lie in the simple, unde-manding love that Violet le Maistre offered. The day after his proposal of marriage had been accepted, he set off on his long planned Easter holiday with Richard in Dorset, travelling in his new Trojan car. On the way down, 'puffing out of London . . . into the sardonic rain', they called at John's cot-tage and he retrieved Katherine's little pearl ring, posting it to Violet to seal their engagement. It was a potent symbol of the nature of their relationship, which would always involve the absent Katherine, and it said a lot about Violet's character that she was willing to accept another woman's relic.

John found Dorset ancient and numinous – he was awed and pro-foundly moved by the human history in the landscape around him, as well as the silence and the space. It was a religious experience 'to have sat on a barren upland by the embers of a wood fire with our foreheads touching the stars, musing on nothing to the cry of the sad and restless peewit and the droning of the ghostly snipe; to have listened with fitful interludes of sleep all through one night in the woodland to a nightingale trying her reluctant song in vain' and above all to have listened to 'the murmuring, caressing sound of the sea'.[9]

In Dorset John paid a second visit to Thomas Hardy. Hardy had been impressed by John's defence of his work in the *Adelphi* against hostile critics earlier in the year, and had written that if John were ever in the vicinity . . . John had called at Hardy's big, ugly house at Max Gate and formed an instant rapport with him and his second wife Florence. Now, once more in Dorset, John called again with his brother and was made equally welcome. After tea, Hardy recommended that John and Richard should drive further south to see the phenomenon of Chesil Bank.

Swimming off Chesil Beach John first saw the long, low outline of a white building looking out towards the sea. Flights of honking swans were passing overhead to their nests at the swannery in Abbotsbury, and he remembered the fantasy that he had shared with Katherine, almost from their first meeting, of living in a cottage in the country: 'Heron's gate – my god those herons just coming in on a wisp of wind and flickering over the pine tops'.[10] Swans, he thought, were 'the next best birds to herons'. Intrigued by the house, John and Richard went exploring down the 1.6-kilometre track that skirted the shore. It was an old coastguard station, a two-storey clapboard building in four separate cottages, standing on a plinth of pebbles in half a hectare of land. It was empty and uncared for, the garden uncultivated apart from a line of wind-blown tamarisks. The house caught John's imagination. Isolated, exposed to every battering Channel storm, it seemed to offer what he needed most – calm and space in which to write and the prospect of a home for Violet and the children he hoped to have, and had longed for in his first marriage: 'a little Katherine' and 'a little John'. He recalled the old nursery rhyme in his notebook: 'Now you're married I wish you joy/First a girl and then a boy'. It did not occur to him that Violet might have very different ambitions.

A week later, as he passed through Abbotsbury and Dorchester on the way back to London, John saw a notice in an estate agent's window stating that the Old Coastguard Station was to be sold by auction. Though he had only £200 in the bank at the time, John was determined to buy it. This was not as risky a proposition as he later allowed people to think. The *Adelphi* was a great success, his own work was earning money and there were royalties to come on Katherine's book sales. Without consulting Violet, he attended the auction and bid up to £925 on the property. This was a considerable sum in 1924, but Katherine's royalty cheque for *The Dove's Nest* in America alone was in excess of £1000 – more than enough to purchase a home for his new wife – and publishing contracts were already negotiated for the sale of another collection of stories, *Something Childish but Very Natural*, on both sides of the Atlantic. 'Even at that moment I was struck by the irony of it,' John wrote. 'In my half superstitious way (of one who seeks meanings in all things) I felt that Katherine's blessing was on our marriage.'

It was decided that the wedding should take place quickly. Perhaps worried about the reaction of his friends, John sent out some invitations at the last moment. 'This is to tell you that I am going to be married tomorrow (Tuesday) morning at 11.30 at St Stephens, Belsize Park . . . to a girl of 22 called Violet le Maistre, whom I met about 6 months ago, and six weeks ago suddenly decided that I wanted for my wife. I should have let you know before; but the whole thing happened so suddenly and unexpectedly that I have left undone all those things I ought to have done. A handful of my friends are coming – and I would be glad if you were with them, but I realise the notice is too appallingly short.'[11] Not surprisingly, the recipient of this somewhat reluctant invitation declined. There was a general lack of empathy with John's need for human love and companionship. Prudence Maufe's sentiments, expressed in a letter to a friend, were typical. 'I really could not see HOW he could bring himself to marry someone else after his intense passion for Katherine.'[12] Others were more understanding. Lawrence, informed by Brett of the impending marriage, wrote to him from Taos wishing him 'an acquiescent, peaceful happiness'.[13]

On 19 May, the night before the marriage, John made a long entry in his diary. 'Clothed and in my right mind and about to be married at 11.30 tomorrow. Not for a single moment have I felt doubt or misgiving since the Wednesday night when it happened six weeks ago; and for me that is astonishing.' He noted how his love for Violet had grown over the weeks, drawn out of him by her own affectionate personality. And then he came to what he described as 'the mystery'.

> I shall not be able to express it, I know; but I must put down some hint of it, even though for myself alone. I feel that Katherine smiles upon this thing

– that it has her blessing and fulfils her purpose. I know perfectly well that there is the simple and matter of fact explanation that I, being what I am, needed a woman to love and have for true companion, and looked until I found her. I won't deny it; but the truth I feel about it – and I am, if I ever was, calm and in my right mind – is different. If I were to say that Katherine sent Violet to me, I should shrink from my own words. Treat them as a gross symbol, however, and they contain my real feeling. Katherine had a hand – her divine and lovely little hand, curved like a shell holding some precious and invisible gift. Yes, with her hands Katherine gave me Violet . . .[14]

Despite a rational rejection of the Eastern concept of the transmigration of souls, John believed that Katherine's spirit lived on: 'It is a presence which incarnates itself; and it waits for the opportunity of incarnation . . . Violet was ready for me. We recognised each other; and Katherine's incarnation was accomplished – not in Violet, not in me, but in both of us together, and in the child that will be born. That sounds, I know, fantastic . . . But the belief, and the sweet and true reality of it is there. When I am with Violet I know, and I feel no possibility of illusion.'[15] But John's belief that Katherine was living on set the scene for a marriage based on the very illusions he was repudiating.

Unlike John's bleak register office marriage to Katherine, this was a conventional high church ceremony. Violet's uncle officiated, and she walked up the aisle on her father's arm accompanied by her sister and her best friend. Because of the short notice, few people were there to witness the marriage, and Violet never put on record her feelings about this hasty, secretive ceremony. There was no formal wedding breakfast – just a simple family meal – and no honeymoon. Violet moved immediately into John's cramped rented rooms in Pond Street – the ceilings were so low that he used to joke they lived on pancakes. Two months later, when the purchase of the Old Coastguard Station had been completed, Violet and John began the process of moving to Dorset.

Their arrival was inauspicious. It took all day for their steam-powered pantechnicon to reach Dorset and by the time it got to the village it was late evening and the light was beginning to fade. The farm workers and the horses they had engaged to unload their furniture and transport it from the main road down the shingle track to the house, had been haymaking all day in the fields and were too exhausted to do any more work. The furniture was put on the beach to wait until morning. ''Twill be all right, if only it doant rain,' the foreman said. But the following morning it did rain and one of the men, whom they suspected of sleeping in their house overnight, had a severe epileptic attack in the yard, which disturbed Violet considerably.[16]

But eventually all their furniture was carried inside and the cottage was habitable. Two of the other cottages were quickly let, one to John's friend Henry Tomlinson (who was working on a novel and a biography of Hardy) and the other to various family friends, though neither was occupied for more than a few weeks at a time – it was too far to London. A housekeeper was engaged and a gardener. John, determined to realise his ambition to grow things, bought several fruit trees to create an orchard behind the house. The gardener, more knowledgeable about the challenge of growing anything on the seashore, laughed and told John that when he left, he would be taking the trees with him. John optimistically dug them in and had a tennis court laid out. He also bought a small boat and a seine net, intending to learn to sail and go mackerel fishing. He wanted to spend as much time as he could at Abbotsbury. When he had first gone up to Oxford, John had spent some vacations living on a farm, rather than going back to his parents' bleak home in Wandsworth. Those rural months, learning to ride a horse, helping his landlord around the farm, had left him with a great longing to live in the country, which he now felt able to fulfil. Though he kept rooms in London in order to please Violet, the Old Coastguard Station was to be his main home. Violet, desperate to escape the stultifying existence of Surrey, would have preferred the stimulation of London to fuel her writing. She missed the theatre, in particular, but had to be content with fleeting winter visits.

But the main problem was that Violet did not feel that the house was really hers. She had had no part in choosing it, and it was furnished with the items that John had acquired during his life with Katherine – her writing desk, her chairs, her table linen. Katherine's photograph hung in his study, her books were on the shelves. For John it was as if nothing had changed; his life went on as usual, and he admitted later that it took him a long time to realise that the woman he shared it with was a different personality. 'It never struck me for a moment that there was a great difference between Katherine when I first met her, and Violet now.' Although the two women had been of a similar age when he met them, they could not have been more different in character. Katherine had been vastly experienced and very much in control of her own life; Violet had led a sheltered existence, much indulged by her autocratic father, and was by nature more dependent. Katherine had forged a mask of steel to protect her secret self; Violet was transparent and vulnerable.

Katherine 'continued to run like [a] mysterious river' through John's soul.[17] Like the fictional Rebecca, she was the third person in his relationship with Violet, who found it difficult to adjust to the reality of marriage. She and John had scarcely known each other beforehand and were pitched into intimacy too quickly. Not only was Violet sexually innocent; John, despite his marriage to Katherine and his love affairs, was still profoundly ignorant on sexual matters. He knew little or nothing about contraception, and nothing of the finer points of lovemaking, something that had greatly bothered the more knowledgeable Katherine. And before he and Violet could learn to enjoy their physical relationship, she became pregnant. 'I can see now, plainly enough,' John wrote later, 'how great was my failure in imagination. I can see now that, had I been a wiser man, I should gently have initiated her into all the infinite delights of physical love between a man and woman who truly love one another, and waited patiently until the positive desire for children was kindled in her. But in those days I did not know how, and I did not understand the need.'[18]

The power balance of this second marriage was very different from that of the first. Whereas Katherine had kept her independence and had often dominated John, taking the sexual initiative, Violet expected to assume a more submissive role. She anticipated that John, so much older, would take the lead in most things. His passivity surprised her. His fear of conflict, his need for absolute love and his own emotional blindness to the needs of others were a shock to Violet, as were his inhibitions. Essentially a kind and loving man, he was always worried about money, guilt-ridden, unable to commit himself fully to pleasure. The fear and darkness of his childhood made it impossible for him to be completely free – the repressive regime of the joyless bank clerk was permanently lodged in his soul. This was John's tragedy, but it was also Violet's. Katherine had longed for him to be passionate, to experience life as deeply and recklessly as she did, but he had never been able to do so. He had once confessed to her, by way of apology, that he had 'a very timid, girlish, love-seeking sort of soul'.[19] John had never been much of a risk taker, though he often wished that he was. Part of Violet's attraction was the childlike quality of her love, which spoke to the perennial child within himself. She called him 'Golly' and used the kind of baby-talk that new lovers adopt. Neither of them could remember who had first said, 'Don't let's ever be grown-up!'[20]

Not only was Violet's relationship with John still immature, she was also finding her feet as a housekeeper, and as a hostess to his friends, and trying to develop and establish herself as a writer. The Hardys were near neighbours in Dorset and often invited the Murrys to tea. Katherine had not been intimidated by social contact with the literary heavyweights that she and John had mixed with – a group that included the whole of 'Bloomsbury', as well as T. S. Eliot, Walter de la Mare, John Galsworthy, E. M. Forster and H. G. Wells – but Violet was still very young, and she was not welcomed into John's circle of friends as readily as she would have wished. Most of them had known Katherine and Violet was aware of comparisons being made that were not always favourable to her. John's rented rooms, with a shared bathroom, had been at the top of his friend Boris Anrep's house. Although Violet moved in with John after the wedding, the arrangement did not last. Soon Virginia Woolf was recording gleefully that 'Murry [is] married again to a woman who spends an hour in the W.C. & so the Anreps have turned them out'.[21] After advertising – or 'whining publicly' as Virginia put it – in the *Adelphi*, John was eventually offered rooms in Chelsea by another friend, but he and Violet were without a base in London for quite a while.

Violet's reason for spending so much time in the bathroom was quickly apparent. John was ecstatic about her pregnancy but Violet was devastated. At first John put her malaise down to morning sickness, so it came as a profound shock when Violet sought him out one day to say that she had something to confess which she was afraid would hurt him. Assured by John that nothing could lessen his love for her, she admitted the reason for her unhappiness. 'I don't really want this baby. I've tried to want it, but I can't, I only want you. And I'm afraid it will come between us. You won't love me so much.' Although John tried to comfort her, to assure her that the baby would be 'our own bond of love made incarnate, which, so far from coming between us, would only unite us the more', Violet did not believe him and John realised that 'the faint shadow that had fallen between us remained'.[22]

Violet was not only threatened by John's obvious longing for the child; she was afraid of being trapped by motherhood before she had had any life of her own. Her writing was important to her and she had scarcely had any time to develop it. Violet was also lonely at the Old Coastguard Station where they spent a large part of their time since the loss of their London rooms. Murry shut himself up in the study and read Katherine's papers, caught up in what his daughter later described as 'a preoccupation with worlds she [Violet] could not enter, that no living soul could penetrate'.[23] He fantasised about recreating the life he had had with Katherine, he writing at one table, Katherine at another, sharing cigarettes and reading their work aloud to each other. Violet's next poem in the *Adelphi* was tellingly entitled 'Ghost Hunters' and towards the end of the year she wrote a story called 'The Dream', about a man who lives in a dream world, far removed from reality, believing continually that everything will be all right – though his wife knows the truth. Even when he is sacked for incompetence, the reality still does not sink in: 'no more dinginess, no more office, no more London, no more grind. The open country now, blue sky and birds singing, hedges with flowers. Such an exquisite dream!'[24] John was living out his own dream at the Old Coastguard Station, but it was not Violet's. The story was published in the *Adelphi* in January 1925 under the name Mary Arden, a pseudonym John had chosen for her.

Throughout 1924 John was working on an edition of Katherine's poems, another collection of her stories and beginning the transcription of her notebooks and letters for publication, as well as producing a vast body of work of his own. He had finished *The Voyage*, and was working on a published edition of lectures delivered at Oxford on 'The Problems of Style', as well as editing the *Adelphi* and writing a variety of reviews and essays in other periodicals. Since the failure of his novel, he had vowed never to write another, intending to devote himself entirely to criticism and literary journalism.

He was studying Keats, having been invited to give the Clark lectures at Cambridge – a series eventually published as *Keats and Shakespeare*. John used his experience with Katherine to inform Keats' relationship with Fanny Brawne, claiming that to have 'known a writer of genius who suffered from consumption' gave him a special insight. However, he avoided exploring the analogy too deeply. Fanny was at fault, John asserted, for not loving Keats enough. 'The uncertainty of love fanned the spark of his disease into a devouring flame.'[25] If Fanny had loved him more, perhaps he would not have died so young. But John did not apply this argument to himself and Katherine. And if he had failed to love Katherine enough when she was alive, he was certainly atoning for it now.

John discovered many parallels between Katherine and Keats, apart from early death caused by tuberculosis, leaving work unfinished and genius unfulfilled. Both endured periods of 'creative sterility and inward despair'. Both believed in the importance of truth in art – expressed by Keats as 'Beauty is truth, truth beauty'. 'At the end,' Katherine had written, 'Truth is the one thing worth having.'[26] There was also that restless travelling in search of good health, which produced such a wealth of correspondence. Katherine's letters, John wrote in an essay, 'are essential to a real understanding of her work. They form a single whole with her stories; one naturally fulfils and completes the other. Indeed, there were moments when it seemed to me that her letters more completely expressed the nature of her genius than even the most remarkable of her stories. There have been moments when I have felt the same about the poetry and the letters of Keats.'[27]

John was so immersed in his relationship with the dead he was in danger of neglecting his living wife. Second marriages are always a minefield of memories and associations, but here there was another level of peril. Violet, fragile and all too human, had to contend with a legend that was daily being created in her husband's mind and put before the public. In a house bought with Katherine's money, surrounded by her possessions, her husband lost in a re-creation of his first wife, it was no wonder that Violet was soon deeply depressed. How do you contend with a ghost? In order to understand her husband, Violet read the work of her predecessor and tried to emulate Katherine's success. Desperate for John's love and attention, she began to turn herself into another version of Katherine. Her wavy chestnut hair was cropped into a shiny bob with a fringe, and her handwriting – which had always been similar in style to Katherine's – now became almost indistinguishable. Violet's relatives and her friend Alison were concerned at the changes they observed. Their visits to the Old Coastguard Station were fraught with tension as they witnessed her unhappiness but could do nothing to alleviate it. Richard Murry, who spent a lot of time there painting, and sailing his brother's boat, firmly believed that Violet had been 'possessed' by the spirit of Katherine Mansfield.

Acquaintances were often similarly confused. One young man who visited the Murrys in Dorset had known before his visit that John had been married to Katherine and had heard of her tragic death. 'I can still recall,' he wrote afterwards, 'how disconcerted I was when I found him sitting on the Chesil Beach alongside a young woman who looked astonishingly like K.M., and whose idiom, when she addressed him, evoked to an embarrassing degree the Wiggery-Tiggery idiom of K.M.'s Journal and Letters.

I lunched with them a couple of days later, and it did not ease my youthful diffidence to find the initials "K.M." neatly embroidered in a corner of my table napkin.'[28] John was blind to the transformation. Only afterwards, when it was too late, could he see what had happened. 'She wanted to be what she believed I would like her to be and thought she was. Which was darling in her, but tragic in its consequences, owing to my failure to understand. I was naive, ignorant.'[29]

It was not just Violet that John was neglecting; the *Adelphi* also suffered from his preoccupations. He was so immersed in his work that he more than once forgot the magazine's publishing deadline and had to be reminded by Henry Tomlinson. His partners were furious. John admitted that 'when I am absorbed into pursuing to some ultimate conclusion an idea that has come to me, I lose all sense of reality'.[30] His editorial policy was attracting increasing criticism. Packing the *Adelphi* with self-indulgent essays and editorials, his plans to serialise his own work on Keats and a projected 'Life of Jesus', as well as the repeated inclusion of his dead wife's work, had done the periodical no good at all. Readers were falling away and the sales figures, which had been over 15,000 initially,[31] were now down to about 5000. A crisis came when the income from the *Adelphi* dropped to £55 – enough to cover the £40 owed to contributors, but not enough to pay any salaries. Koteliansky, as the business manager, now faced the prospect of working for nothing, and was driven to protest. He blamed John for the magazine's decline. When they had founded the *Adelphi* they had agreed that it should have 'a life of its own, irrespective of the views, beliefs and convictions of any one of its contributors'.[32] But it had become the mouthpiece of its editor, who appeared to have lost touch with the readership.

Contributors and financial backers were soon drawn into the conflict between John and Koteliansky. Tomlinson and J. W. N. Sullivan, though uneasy about the direction the *Adelphi* was taking under John's editorship, felt bound to support him. Others agreed with Koteliansky that John had betrayed the ideals of the magazine and was using it as a vehicle for his own thoughts and opinions. One of them had to go – it was obvious that they could no longer work together. When Koteliansky threatened to resign, John reciprocated by offering to sell him his share, presumably to call his bluff, but Koteliansky promptly accepted. The offer was then withdrawn. Koteliansky, already incensed by John's behaviour towards Katherine while she was alive and his editorial scavenging after her death, decided that it was impossible to deal with him. John's actions drove others to protest. For Katherine's cousin Sydney Waterlow, John's treatment of Koteliansky was also the last straw. He wrote John a stiff but dignified letter, breaking off all contact. 'The falsity in our own relationship, for which you are responsible, can no longer be tolerated: so that until you can eliminate it, there can be no further communication.'[33]

By February Murry was appealing for subscribers and holding out a begging bowl to *Adelphi* readers. D. H. Lawrence wrote to John, almost relishing the 'absolutely prize sewer-mess' that he was in and advised him to 'drop the Christ stuff: it's putrescence'. He told John firmly that the cause of the failure of the *Adelphi* was in his own nature. 'Spunk is what one wants, not introspective sentiment. The last is your vice. You rot your own manhood at the roots with it. But apparently it's what you want.' He saw John facing a choice in his life. 'Either you go on wheeling a wheelbarrow and lecturing at Cambridge and going softer and softer inside, or you make a hard fight with yourself, pull yourself up, harden yourself, throw your feelings down the drain and face the world as a fighter. – You won't though.'[34]

On 19 April 1925 Violet gave birth to a baby girl. John, waiting anxiously downstairs, recorded the event in his diary. 'The sudden intense silence, like a lapse into the womb of all life, then out of the covering darkness, the tiny incredible cry, that sounded high and incommensurable above the steady boom of the great Atlantic waves; this was marvellous.' While John wrote of his delight, Violet, traumatised by the birth and still suffering from depression, turned her face to the wall when the nurse offered her the baby, as though she knew already that it could not belong to her. She had been a surrogate mother, bearing another woman's child. John was absolutely convinced that this infant was the inheritor of Katherine Mansfield's spiritual heritage. 'I . . . felt, quite simply, that Violet's daughter was Katherine's daughter, and I named her accordingly.' Not surprisingly, Violet continued to reject the baby, refusing to feed or hold her. Little Katherine Middleton Murry the second was delicate and did not thrive as she should have done. It was John who lavished his daughter with love, helping Nanny to feed her, spooning gruel out of a silver porringer. 'I loved my little daughter as Katherine would have loved her, with her love as well as my own . . .'[35] What Violet had feared happened: she had lost a large part of her husband's attention and affection to her daughter. John was also bitter that Violet refused to breast-feed her baby – it was against nature not to, he argued, it was 'shutting the door on the angel'.[36] But Violet would not, and for a short time she left both John and the baby, though where she went is unclear.

However, by the time the baby was three months old, Violet's feelings towards her daughter had begun to soften, though she confessed to Alison that she was still plagued by guilt about her inability to love the child as she felt she should. Violet nicknamed Katherine the 'egg-weg' because of her bald, downy head. The nickname, shortened to Weg, was how Katherine was known for the rest of her life – a name given to her by her real mother, one that belonged exclusively to her and not to the dead woman whose ghostly presence haunted their lives and would do so through three generations. The adult Weg wrote that 'the myth and the mysterious presence of Katherine Mansfield, of my father's love for her . . . determined the very landscape of the soul with which I was born.' She added savagely: 'about my own youthful nostrils floated the perfumed incense of genius, sweet and sickly, indescribable, unnameable, invisible, and yet for ever there'.[37]

11

The Failure of Love

How terrible are one's failures in love. They haunt the secretest places of one's soul for years and years — for ever.

JOHN MIDDLETON MURRY, DIARIES

It was a glorious summer. As Violet recovered her strength and emerged from depression, they walked along the headland, picnicked on Chesil Beach, John went mackerel fishing with Richard, dug a vegetable garden and in the evenings he and Violet wrote together at their separate desks, listening to the hushing — what Violet described as the 'Mmm — ssh — ah, ah' — of the waves on the pebbled shore. 'It was like the golden days at the Villa Pauline,' John wrote in his journal, 'when Katherine sat writing "Prelude" on one side of the kitchen-table, while I wrote 'Doestoevsky' on the other.'[1]

John had begun his *Life of Jesus Christ* — a curious choice for an agnostic — and was padding out the *Adelphi* with long extracts from it. His editorials, too, were full of discussions on the nature of religion and belief. John did not believe that Jesus Christ was God, though he was 'a hero of heroes'. Faith he saw as 'A beauty that cannot die', rising out of the ashes of despair like the obstinate Phoenix. 'Out of the chaos, the despair, the agony of this contemplation, rises a voice like the singing of a solitary bird after the terror of a storm.'[2] The finished book had a mixed reception, satisfying neither the committed agnostic nor the fervent Christian. *The Life of Jesus Christ* occupied roughly a quarter of the space in the *Adelphi* over eleven months. His obsessive, introspective editorials increased this percentage. Sales figures dropped even further, but there was no longer anyone on the editorial board to challenge his policy.

Violet was working on her short stories, still very much under the influence of Katherine Mansfield. 'A Charming Old Man' appeared in the June edition of the *Adelphi*. Viewed on its own terms, as an apprenticeship piece, the story was competently written and showed the very real promise of its author. It was quickly picked up by another publisher for an anthology and gave Violet's fragile ego a much-needed boost. 'A Charming Old Man' is a vignette with no plot and little character development, in the manner of Katherine's early work. But, though the atmosphere of the boarding house and the relationship between the old man and his daughter are well written, the story lacks magic and there is little sense of what is going on underneath the surface – something Katherine did superbly by concentrating on 'the essence of things', the complexity of consciousness, and the subtext of human relationships. Violet's stories are less abstract than Katherine's and have a much more conventional authorial voice, and linear narrative. To compare Violet's early work with Katherine's is grossly unfair, but the comparison was being made all the time, by the public, her friends, her husband and by Violet herself. There was one part of Katherine's 'The Married Man's Story' that Violet felt encapsulated the whole of life. When Katherine wrote how it felt to walk in the garden across the dew-soaked grass and 'a mournful, glorious voice' began to sing, Violet felt that voice singing inside herself. That, she told Alison, was how she wanted to write. Katherine had set the standard that Violet aimed for in life and art. The fact that it was unachievable gave Violet a constant sensation of failure which compounded her guilt about what she regarded as her maternal failures. She still resented the fact that Weg's birth had 'stolen her creativity' as well as her husband's attention. Was she simply unmaternal, she asked herself?[3]

When Weg was three months old, John went into the bathroom to help Violet read the weighing scales and the simple task developed into a spontaneous, loving, coming together – the first since the arrival of the baby. The shadow that had been between them for months was lifted by a mutual delight in intimacy. But John was worried afterwards, anxious that

Violet might conceive another child before she had recovered from the first. In September his fears were realised. Violet came into his study and told him that she was pregnant again. 'She wept as though her heart was broken and there was nothing I could say that would comfort her.'[4]

Throughout her second unwelcome pregnancy Violet struggled for creative space. She worked on her stories whenever she could, managing to complete and polish three more for publication in the *Adelphi* – 'The Casual Acquaintance', 'The Button' and 'The Idealist'. She was gradually developing her own distinctive style. Informed by her knowledge of drama, Violet's mature stories have well-crafted scenes and dialogue, and the narrator usually has a moral point of view – something absent from Katherine Mansfield's work. Violet was beginning to find her 'voice' as well as her subject matter. In 'The Idealist', as in 'The Dream', the subject is a man who is always in pursuit of the unattainable – in this case, the ideal relationship. He goes from woman to woman, searching for perfect understanding, but he is always disappointed. At first the reader sympathises with the hero, but he quickly shows himself to be selfish and shallow rather than sensitive and misunderstood. On one occasion, conscious that he has inadvertently hurt his wife, he asks her to play the piano, expecting her to play one of the little Chopin pieces that she usually preferred. They irritate him by their triviality, but he is prepared to endure them as a penance. 'But ah,' her choice is shocking; 'the Beethoven thing she played was desperately, so terribly tragic that wretched Harold began to feel it was the wailing of his own tormented soul. Or no, not only his own perhaps, but the wailings of all poor, wretched men who thought they had found the ideal woman and instead were disappointed, miserable and lonely.'[5] Harold keeps commenting on himself as 'a rum chap, a rum chap' and it is hard for the reader not to make a parallel with John's habit of describing himself as 'a queer fish, a queer fish'. The moral of the story is neatly tied up when Harold is manipulated into marriage by what was then called 'a designing woman' and gets his just reward.

In October 1925 Lawrence came to England for a visit. He was only forty, but already in the end stages of tuberculosis. The dry Mexican summers had helped to prolong his life, but the winters were a struggle and he confessed that he had 'almost fallen into the Styx' the previous year.[6] John was anxious that Lawrence and Frieda should come down to Dorset to stay at the Old Coastguard Station – he wanted them to meet Violet and Weg – but the timing did not work out. In the end he went to London alone, there was a brief, intense meeting and Lawrence invited the Murrys to join him and Frieda in Italy in January. But the reunion never took place. John was reluctant to leave his pregnant wife and baby daughter and Violet was too unwell to travel. Lawrence was furious. Part of his anger was to do with the *Adelphi* – John had asked him if he could publish some of his work without payment and Lawrence was offended. He wrote to Brett that 'he's got plenty of money, really, property and investments – richer than all of us put together'.[7] It was true. With Katherine's royalties still flooding in, John's own income (about £800) from journalism, as well as Violet's generous annuity, he was banking about £2500 a year – a large amount at the time. Yet John was always convinced that he was on the verge of poverty – another legacy of his childhood. Bitter letters passed between the two men. Each felt let down by the other.

When John Middleton Murry junior was born, on 9 May 1926, Violet was still only twenty-four and had two children with a year and three weeks between them. Lawrence, when he received the news in Italy, was prompted to write: 'Another John Middleton – ye Gods!'[8] Like his sister Weg, the little boy was never known by his birth name, but was always called Colin, later shortened to Col. This time John failed to feel the same kind of elation and joy that he had experienced at Weg's birth. He had established such a strong emotional bond with his daughter that, without realising it, he took much less interest in his newborn son. Violet found it just as difficult to love her second baby. Colin seemed to absorb the atmosphere by osmosis even before he was old enough to analyse it. 'Perhaps I divined,' he wrote later, 'that I was not getting what I considered to be my fair share of love and attention. Obstinately I declined to thrive.'[9] Always 'second in the love queue', he remained a delicate, sickly baby, despite the attentions of a full-time nanny, sea air and summer sunshine. Violet found it much harder to recover after Col's birth. Two pregnancies in less than eighteen months and an enormous amount of guilt had left her exhausted and depressed. She began to lose weight. Her health, as well as the baby's, became a cause for concern.

Throughout 1926 John was totally immersed in his transcription of extracts from Katherine's notebooks, which he intended to publish the following year. He was ploughing his way through the motley collection of fifty-three notebooks and diaries and loose manuscript drafts that Katherine had left behind among her possessions. Her almost illegible handwriting was a major challenge – even when Katherine was alive, friends and family had complained that they could not decipher sections of her letters. Her notebooks were even worse – filled with hasty scribbles pencilled on trains, at garden tables, even on horse-drawn buses, as well as drafts and descriptions scrambled onto the page as her pen raced to keep pace with her imagination. There were a few early exercise books covering her time in Wellington and at Queen's College, and then a three-year gap; apart from a few random entries and loose pages, Katherine had destroyed all the grief-laden notebooks from the period of her love affairs with Garnet and Floryan between 1909 and 1912. Most of the notebooks were dated after 1912, the year in which John and Katherine had first lived together. It was a fragmentary, disorganised collection and far from the orderly record of a writer's mind that John wanted to put before the public. His intention was to publish a small volume of selections that would be representative of the whole and form a credible 'writer's journal'. He took a creative approach to the editing of the notebooks, cutting and pasting for maximum emotional impact and narrative effect, guessing at words he could not read and rewriting some sentences to make passages link together better. They were to tell a story of Katherine's life and character, that, while not wholly false, was not entirely truthful either. Katherine, who had cared so much for truth in art, was not there to object to what she might well have described as 'a lie in the soul'.

In John's mind Katherine had undergone a kind of sanctification in the two and a half years since her death. Her work, he told a friend, was 'sacred' to him. The Saint Katherine he was putting before the public was a very different person from the complex woman who had shared his life, who could at her best be charismatic, funny and profoundly compassionate, but at her worst became a 'castatrix triumphans', a raging fury, a savage satirist, and an extremely deceitful manipulator. The 'real' Katherine Mansfield was so intensely private and well defended, that not even she had been sure of her own identity.

Katherine's unexpurgated notebooks and journals have been described by Angela Carter as 'a fabulous (using the word in its true sense) autobiography of the soul'.[10] Their pages contain the entire range of Katherine's life and work, her development from schoolgirl to mature author, from reckless child to driven woman. John discovered much that Katherine had never told him – a phrase written on a train 'when shall I sit and read to my little son', and then later in France a reference to 'the baby of

Garnet's love'.[11] Katherine had given him, as she gave everyone, a strictly edited account of her early life. There were also painful revelations about her affair with his friend Francis Carco, which he had condoned without knowing the details, and searing comments on their own relationship that he had never read before. He was forcing himself to relive and reassess his memories of their time together. He came to the conclusion that Katherine had kept details of her past from him because she 'was enchanted by my innocence, and wanted to preserve it, and . . . to put away her own "experience", which was considerable and much of it an unhappy memory. She wanted to annihilate her past.'[12] But he also castigated himself for not asking more questions, because he sensed, dimly, that it might have been a relief for Katherine to tell him everything.

There was a great deal in the notebooks that did not fit the view of Katherine he wanted to put forward, and much that – at a time when publishing was still censored – could not be printed. Many of the participants were still alive and capable of litigation, so it was hardly surprising that John, who had been chief censor at the War Office during the war, put his blue pencil to good use. The Katherine he wanted his readers to know was high-minded and 'pure'. 'It is as though the glass through which she looked upon life were crystal-clear. And this quality of her work corresponds to a quality in her life.' The agony of her last years, when she raged against the sentence of death and had to fight for every breath, was rarefied into a kind of literary martyrdom. 'She suffered greatly, she delighted greatly: but her suffering and her delight were never partial, they filled the whole of her.'[13]

Those who had known Katherine well read John's introduction to the book with incomprehension and derision. Others were surprised to find that he claimed such a big influence on the direction of her work. He gave the impression that it was only his influence that allowed her to be published in the magazines he edited. 'When the *Blue Review* died . . . Katherine Mansfield had no place to write in . . . the *Signature* died within two months, and again Katherine Mansfield had nowhere to write, until I became editor of *The Athenaeum*.' Although he and Katherine had lived apart for much of their relationship, he told readers that he had 'worked with her during the greater part of her career as a writer . . . copied and punctuated and criticised her stories as they were written . . .'[14] Katherine would not have been pleased.

But, in John's defence, by publishing these extracts from her notebooks, he allowed the public to read some of the best of Katherine's writing – observations, character sketches, autobiographical vignettes that were utterly personal and direct and full of her own particular brand of wit. Koteliansky complained that John had left out all the jokes, which was true. But still the journal captivated readers from its first publication in 1927 and became one of her best-selling works. John placed a dedication on the title page – not to Katherine, or his wife Violet, but to the fictional 'Mary Arden'.

The journal was followed by a selection of Katherine's letters, equally censored, which involved John in another intensive bout of transcription and the reading of unpalatable material. Both Lawrence and Koteliansky were outraged by John's exposure of Katherine's private papers and Ida, too, was upset by his revelations. Sydney Waterlow observed that there was a 'stern Katherine' somewhere up there who would be judging it all.[15] Koteliansky wrote to Ida to say that it was the absolute end of his relationship with John – he would never have anything to do with him again. Lawrence speculated that John had added things into Katherine's letters – Ottoline Morrell made the same accusation – to make them more moving for readers. They were both wrong. John altered the character of the letters by subtraction rather than addition, by removing the caustic wit and the self-parody that often accompanied her saddest pronouncements.

While John continued his painful journey through Katherine's life that summer, both his wife's and his son's health deteriorated. Violet's temperature fluctuation, her weight loss and the stubborn cough she had developed could no longer be ignored and John took his family to London partly in the hope that the diversion would lift Violet's spirits but also to be closer to expert medical opinion. He had taken a flat in Hampstead, in the area known as the 'Vale of Health', not far from the house he had lived in with Katherine. One of the doctors John consulted was the psychiatrist James Young, who had held Katherine while she haemorrhaged to death at Fontainebleau and who was now back in London, thoroughly disillusioned with Gurdjieff. James saw Violet and, like her physician, suspected tuberculosis, but the main drain on her health, in the opinion of all the doctors John consulted, was a calamitous third pregnancy. In early January, Violet was taken into a private clinic for a termination. The infant Col was also suspected of having tuberculosis, and admitted to a children's hospital. John, as he often did when under stress, became ill with pneumonia.

January and February 1927 were bleak, with Col in hospital and Violet often too ill to get out of bed. James, now familiarly referred to as Jimmy, with his earthy humour and colourful scatological language, became a frequent visitor to the flat and a close friend. His visits made Violet laugh. The stimulation of London also suited her and when she was well enough she began reviewing books and plays for the *Adelphi*. But at the beginning of March the physician did a sputum analysis, which confirmed what both he and James had suspected. Violet, he told John, had active tuberculosis. John was shattered. How could this happen to him twice? 'Had I to be taught, in this terrible fashion, that the love of the soul was indeed an illusion which led to death? . . . If that was the meaning, then to learn it would kill me.' Everything was 'darkness and desolation'.[16]

John was even more stunned by Violet's words when he summoned up the nerve to give her the doctors' verdict. Her response chilled him to the bone.

> 'O, I'm so glad!' she said. 'I wanted this to happen.'
>
> I stared into her shining eyes. 'You wanted this to happen', I repeated, slowly and dully, while my world turned upside down.
>
> 'You see Golly!' she explained. 'I wanted you to love me as much as you loved Katherine – and how could you, without this?'[17]

Violet later explained this in her letters and notebooks. Since she had first read Katherine's work she had felt that, if the price of writing like Katherine was to suffer tuberculosis, she would willingly do so in order to become a great writer.

John vowed that Violet would be cured. With Katherine he had lacked not only love, but courage and patience. 'Now, God helping me, I would fail in neither . . . I had failed Katherine; Violet I would not fail. The very whole of me would be cast into the struggle for her life.'[18] He insisted that she go to a sanatorium – something Katherine had always refused. Though she would have liked to stay at home with her husband and children, on 14 May a defeated Violet went to the Edward VII sanatorium at Midhurst for a regime of rest, healthy schoolroom food and fresh air – all that could be offered to a TB patient until the discovery of antibiotics. As Violet left, Col was discharged from hospital into the care of his father and his nanny. He was now a year old, but Violet had been with her baby son for only a few months of his life and had lost the opportunity to bond with him.

At Midhirst she spent her time resting as much as she could and polishing a group of stories for publication. *Luck and Other Stories* appeared in September 1927. The title story, 'Luck', is a modern fable and typical of the style that Violet had developed. Two girls, rather like herself and Alison, dream of being famous but are afraid it will never happen. Georgie seems to be the one with the most talent and the one most likely to succeed. She is going to be a pianist and needs to practise, but she ignores the boring exercises, playing only the pieces she likes, and then wonders why her fingers will not work properly. She gives up music and takes up secretarial school instead, but loses jobs because she has no application. She envies her friend Cassie for getting good jobs and a fiancé, believing it is all down to luck.

One of the most interesting stories in the collection features a woman who is paying a family visit for the funeral of her aunt. It gives an insight into the kind of torture that Violet must have endured after the birth of Weg. An elderly woman questions Madeline about her baby, who is nine months old.

'Such a nice age! Boy or girl?'

'Girl.'

'Oh. Did you feed it yourself?'

'No, as a matter of fact, I didn't.'

'My dear,' said Mrs Rickworth, looking towards the ceiling in consternation, 'you don't know what you've missed! . . . Those little hands!' She said in a sort of wail. 'That little face!'

'Oh well, you see,' said Madeline rather coldly, 'I couldn't, as it happened.'[19]

In another story, Eva, bored and cynical, thinks that men use women, consuming them 'like a piece of food' and then pushing them away,[20] but the whole moral of the narrative is that Eva, because she has no life of her own and is completely passive, allows herself to be consumed.

John arranged to have the collection reviewed in the *Adelphi* by a close friend, who contrasted it rather oddly with Virginia Woolf's novel, *To the Lighthouse*. Virginia's masterpiece was unappreciated by the reviewer, who was unashamedly biased: 'Mrs Woolf's pudding is sent to the table halfcooked and indigestible', while Mary Arden, on the other hand, had produced something much easier to swallow. The extravagant praise was not unqualified, however: 'She makes her mistakes – this is her first book – and at times her touch is uncertain, and, feeling her way, she tentatively strikes a wrong note. But as long as she is in her depth, she is completely mistress of her art, and when she is out of it, she gives a vivid and satisfying glimpse of what she will be doing as time goes on.' The reviewer comes to the odd conclusion that Mrs Woolf is 'not a writer of creative fiction' but 'Miss Arden decidedly is'.[21] The review, though it gave Violet encouragement, only increased Virginia Woolf's contempt for John Murry.

In another bizarre juxtaposition, the same issue of the magazine featured Henry Tomlinson's review of the *Journal of Katherine Mansfield*, which celebrated Katherine's 'calm acceptance' of her death sentence – the misleading impression that John had given by his choice of quotations. For Violet in her sanatorium, facing a similar fate, this saintly, fictional figure was still her role model and – unaware that the mirror image was a grotesque distortion – she tried to be as little trouble as possible and emulate her predecessor's attitudes. 'She submitted implicitly to every prescription, never rebelled, never complained.'[22] But beneath the surface Violet was less compliant. In a letter to John she confessed that 'Under the meekness of "If you don't mind", there's a fighting spirit lurking'. Violet disliked the matron intensely. On her imperious ward rounds she would pause beside Violet's bed and ask, '"Well, how are you?" "Oh, all right, I think," I'd reply. But my irony was quite lost on her. "You can't have much the matter with you if you have to think about it," she would reply' and then she would walk on. The nurses were equally insensitive. '"Well, you're only a kiddy really, aren't you?" they'd say. "And got all your life before you."' Violet was left to observe wryly, 'That's a good-natured exaggeration . . .'[23] Thinking about the waste, and comparing present suffering with past ecstasy, Violet misquoted two lines from Wordsworth's 'Intimations of Immortality' in her letter to John: 'Who shall bring back the hour/Of splendour in the grass and glory in the flower?' John would have known by heart the lines that follow: 'We will grieve not, rather find/Strength in what remains behind'.

In a terrible irony, while John was celebrating Katherine's life in print and Violet was trying to come to terms with tuberculosis, a New Zealand fan visited Katherine's grave in Avon and was horrified to discover that her coffin had been moved into the communal part of the cemetery because the bill for her exclusive plot had never been paid. Harold Beauchamp was told of it immediately and, without consulting John, sent Jeanne's husband, Charles Renshaw, to France to put things right. Katherine's coffin was dug up and moved again, this time to a more permanent situation.

In the same month that Violet was admitted to Midhurst, John informed his readers that 'owing to domestic circumstances I have been unable to write the usual editorial. I regret still more that, owing to these same circumstances, I must bring the *Adelphi* to an end with the next number.'[24] In Violet's absence he needed more time to look after his children and finish the books he was working on, including the selected edition of Katherine's letters. He was also in a state of nervous collapse. The ideal existence that he had envisioned for himself and Violet in their 'Heronsgate' beside the sea had proved illusory. As though haunted by the terrible repetition of his past, the final numbers of the *Adelphi* contained not only the 'Last Words' of Katherine Mansfield, but also a lengthy article by James Young on the Gurdjieff regime at Fontainebleau. The magazine itself was about to experience a renaissance. After a few uncertain months, the *Adelphi* was relaunched as a quarterly periodical, renamed the *New Adelphi*. It featured several new writers, including Max Plowman and Sir Richard Rees, two influential men who became friends as well as contributors and who would eventually take over the editorship of the magazine.

By the end of the summer it was clear that Violet's treatment had been ineffective and the doctors told John that it was now only a matter of time. When Violet returned from the sanatorium to the clear sea air of Abbotsbury in the autumn, his joy at seeing her again was tempered by the knowledge that he could not once more endure the experience of losing someone he loved. 'The pain is too fearful, the loneliness too terrible. No power on earth can assuage that pain.'[25] He was unable to work. Violet's medical bills were enormous and friends were concerned about the Murrys' finances. The Royal Literary Fund became a benefactor and Edmund Gosse applied to the prime minister for a special grant of £250. When Florence Hardy visited the Murrys to deliver the cheque she observed the fragile state of Violet's health and the depression of 'the hapless pair', commenting that 'Murry now believes that she is going to get better and she thinks so too, but I am afraid there is not the slightest hope of that'.[26]

The bleakness of that winter, isolated at the Old Coastguard Station, with the constant sound of the sea pounding on the shingle below the house, affected all their spirits. Violet's father and her sister Tina visited and tried to persuade Violet to follow the approach of Christian Science, but she refused, not because she did not think the practitioner (the 'witch-doctor', as she put it) would do her good, but because she would despise herself for giving in to their persuasion. In the spring Colin was back in hospital again with suspected TB and it was a long way to drive for the weekly visit – all that was allowed for children at the time. Violet was too weak to go. John confessed in a letter to a friend that she had not been out of bed since her diagnosis. Colin firmly believed, until he was an adult, that his mother had died when he was two because he had only one memory of her. John's friends began to urge him to consider moving closer to civilisation. Among them was Max Plowman, who, like Lawrence, was one of the few men ever to form an intense friendship with John. Pathologically shy, John related to very few people and always more easily to women. In 1928 he was so depressed and introverted that he avoided personal contact more determinedly than usual, but Max persevered, attracted by John's obvious need.

Max was a well-established poet of the Great War who had served in the trenches and become a conscientious objector. He and his wife were deeply religious, with a strong mystical dimension to their faith. Both were working on William Blake when they met John – Dorothy preparing an edition of The Book of Urizen, and Max writing a book on Blake's life and work. Max believed in the power of love to work miracles. 'Our great difference,' he wrote to John shortly after they met, 'lies in my belief in the efficacy of faith.' John's problem was that he was too rational. 'To rationalise it is to kill it.'[27] The Plowmans' twelve-year-old son had recently died from meningitis and Max felt he could understand John's feelings of grief and bewilderment and believed that he and Dorothy could help the Murrys to deal with their own tragedy. Max did not call it 'faith healing' and there was no laying on of hands, but he did believe that love and faith were all powerful.

The Old Coastguard Station was sold and John found a brand-new bungalow surrounded by large gardens at Yately, about 50 kilometres from London. There were no stairs for Violet to struggle up and the large airy rooms opened directly out into the garden. Two other close friends, including James Young, lived nearby and Richard Rees rented a cottage there shortly afterwards. Col, whose condition had not improved in hospital, was rescued by James, who said that to keep the sensitive little boy in a sanatorium was 'tantamount to a death sentence'. Col was brought home to Yately, but had a recurrent nightmare, which lasted into adulthood, 'of being trapped and abandoned inside a white-barred cage from which there was no escape'.[28] He was also conscious of an underlying resentment towards the father who had put him there, and who, so evidently, preferred his sister Weg.

John's literary life had now to be lived around a framework of nurses and housekeepers, many of whom were completely unsuitable for their jobs. Violet was too ill and John too inexperienced to select the right people.[29] An elderly nanny looked after the children, who were often too lively for her to control. When they escaped and ran away into the garden she could not run fast enough to catch them and would burst into tears. The extremely efficient nurse that John employed to look after Violet and oversee the nursery, turned out to be autocratic and cruel. Sister Verity caned the children for small offences and both Weg and Col, who suffered from night terrors, were refused night lights and punished for wetting their beds. Old Nanny was terrified of her and so was Violet. A fragment of notebook, later sold to the Alexander Turnbull Library by John and thought at first to be one of Katherine's, records Violet's feelings of being under surveillance and needing to escape. She was trying desperately to write a 'gay, young story – excited impetuous (written so it is closely woven)' but feeling 'Miserable and wretched' and wanting to go to London. 'But no, no, how can I get on? Misery and bitterness keep coming between. How can I have bright pictures who can't move from this one place month after month? There is no stimulus . . .'[30] Worse still, was the inhibiting presence of Sister Verity. On one occasion Violet lost her self-control completely and hurled a book at her, admitting afterwards that it was 'a useless extravagance and weakening'. 'Just now I'm so full of loathing for her – that it's like a rotting of the soul. How can one work?' The relationship that Violet had with John was by now so poor that she couldn't ask him to remove her. She found, as Katherine had done, that she could not talk to John, or anyone close to her about her illness and its prognosis, though this silence was sometimes comforting. 'If a very terrifying thing is going to happen – not just yet, tho' quite soon – it has a way of seeming much less real if you don't talk about it to anyone. Then it becomes far-off, part of another world, and there is the feeling that almost anything may happen before hand to prevent it altogether.'[31] The house, she wrote, had become a house of death.

A certain amount of responsibility for looking after Violet rested on John, particularly at night – carrying her to the toilet, cleaning up when she was sick, giving her medicine, providing her with the conversation and company she craved. Anyone who has ever nursed a terminally ill relative will understand the emotional desperation John had to deal with. There were times when he lost his temper and suffered agonies of guilt. Violet was all too aware of the burden that was being placed on him and it had a negative effect on her health. 'Violet has gone steadily downhill. Tonight for the first time, I felt that she was really giving up hope. "She didn't mind dying so much," she said, "though that was bitter enough, but she couldn't bear the thought of the pain it would be to me." I lay there helpless and hopeless beside her, trying to be still inside . . . I don't know, never shall know, why Love leads to this inevitable disaster.'[32]

It was an unbearable ordeal. 'How tired I am of listening to that cough of Violet's!'[33] Its 'dull hammering' upon his spine, with all its echoes of his last years with Katherine, was insupportable. There were times when he longed for Violet to die quickly, but these were followed by feelings of guilt. He loved Violet desperately, but began to withdraw from her, in anticipation of the inevitable loss that was to come. 'It struck me while I was sitting by her fire after supper that I have been completely worn out by the stress of loving her; something has been worn clean away.' There was a tremendous sense of injustice, of being the pawn of an arbitrary universe. 'What I notice, with a sort of dismay, is that the weariness and resentment begins to lift its head again in me. When she was in extremis, I could forget myself and think only of helping her; but when that tension is over, I slip back to the old condition. It's no use either condemning or excusing myself. I am weary of it all . . . Has any man had quite such an unspeakably bloody life as I?'[34]

His friends were worried that he might commit suicide. James Young did his best to take John out of himself. A keen golfer, he introduced John to the sport and they often spent the weekends on the golf course, where James cursed and swore his way from hole to hole. Golf became a drug for John, a physical release from his torments, and, always competitive, he quickly acquired a better handicap than James. Max and Dorothy Plowman dedicated themselves to helping both John and Violet in every way they could. Max made it his business to begin the task of saving Violet through faith and love. She was, he wrote, 'a radiantly beautiful person, absolutely honest, straight, direct as an arrow, brilliantly intelligent, humorous, and of the most exquisite sensibility'.[35] John was pulling her down because he could not believe in the possibility of her recovery. Dorothy tackled the domestic situation. Old Nanny was replaced by the younger Maud Hogben and the sadistic Sister Verity was replaced by a twenty-eight-year-old farmer's daughter called Betty Cockbayne – practical, hardworking and ruthlessly cheerful. She swept through the house like a spring gale, singing, laughing and banishing Violet's depression like winter cobwebs. First impressions were good, but Betty was also highly strung and given to violent temper tantrums, though these qualities were not initially apparent. She had had little education and John found her down-to-earth practical approach to life refreshing. 'You people,' she once said, after an evening listening to the tortuous metaphysical discussion John was having with Max and James, 'take life too damn seriously.'[36] John was deeply attracted by Betty's 'earth-mother' characteristics, particularly her glowing physical health. He admitted being 'travailed by a longing for physical love'. For a while he fantasised about his first love, Marguéritte, and even considered putting an advertisement in the French newspapers. He was very close to a complete breakdown. When James took John away for a holiday to Brittany he slept with a prostitute, but once again regretted it. For John sex without love was sordid and comfortless. What he wanted was the experience of 'lying with the beloved in my arms'.[37]

Lawrence wrote to John from the Hotel Beau Rivage in Bandol, on the French Riviera, having just found out that Katherine had stayed in the same hotel during her search for health. The discovery that he was following in her footsteps rattled him. Though Lawrence was 'distressed' to hear of Violet's illness, he no longer felt much sympathy with John. Their strange 'blood-brotherhood' was over. Katherine, he declared, had been worth a thousand Johns. His letter to John was abrupt. 'I know well that we "missed it," as you put it. I don't understand you, your workings are beyond me. And you don't get me. You said in your review of my poems: "this is not life, life is not like that." And you have the same attitude to the real me. Life is not like that – ergo, there is no such animal . . . am tired of being told there is no such animal, by animals who are merely different . . . We don't know one another – if you knew how little we know one another! And let's not pretend. By pretending a bit, we had some jolly times, in the past. But we all had to pretend a bit – and we could none of us keep it up.'[38]

Lawrence died of tuberculosis at Vence in the Alpes Maritimes on 2 March 1930. He was only forty-four. As soon as John heard of his death he went out to Vence to offer advice and comfort to Frieda, leaving Violet in the care of Max and Dorothy Plowman. The inevitable happened – with Lawrence no longer alive to inhibit them, John went to bed with Frieda. 'With her, and with her for the first time in my life, I knew what fulfilment in love really meant.'[39] Violet was momentarily forgotten as John contemplated the future with Frieda. After Katherine's death they had talked of marriage, even though Lawrence was still alive. Now he proposed to Frieda and was surprised when she asked for time to think about it. The answer when it came was 'No'. Frieda, though she still felt great affection for John, had regretted the episode 'almost immediately'.[40]

Lawrence's death left John with a sense of unreality – a whole part of his life was over, another link with Katherine broken. 'I am beginning to feel old – definitely not strong, a bit wispy, as though the roots had been loosened – a new feeling.'[41] He passed over the editorship of the New Adelphi to Max Plowman and Richard Rees and poured much of his energy into writing a book about his relationship with Lawrence. It was not a biography, but a personal memoir that became the ultimate betrayal of their friendship. This was the moment that he became Judas to Lawrence's Christ. There was also, perhaps, an element of revenge. Lawrence had used John's character in a number of short stories as well as Women in Love, and one story in particular, 'Smile', about the death of Katherine and John's reaction to it, had been particularly hurtful. The controversial Son of Woman was finished on 30 October 1930 and published in the spring to a barrage of protest. Frieda was particularly vocal. His book was 'miserable'. John was 'A sanctimonious little whipper-snapper sitting in the judgement seat! You, taking the shine out of Lawrence! . . . You made a fairy tale out of our life, but a sordid personal one! No, you are horrid! . . . You wrote that book out of a nasty spirit and you want to make money out of it – you won't make as much as you think, pandering to the vile in people, his enemies. And in such bad slimy taste! God help anybody that cares for you!'[42]

Violet had deteriorated throughout the summer and by the beginning of December the doctors told John that her lungs were almost consumed by the bacteria, 'the last bolt had been shot' medically, and she had very little time left. John lacked the courage to tell her their prognosis, taking refuge in comforting 'white lies'. He confided his grief to his diary afterwards. 'O, my sweetheart! Sweetheart – that is the only word. Oh, you who come after me, don't let a woman become your sweetheart. It's unbearable

– unbearable; just unbearable. For she will die, and the world will stand still, and your heart will burst. I have had two sweethearts. And my heart is breaking again, but oh, more terribly. Katherine had her life, but Violet has had nothing – nothing.'[43] The Plowmans were concerned that John's desolation did little to support Violet.

At the end of December he went to Margate with James for a much-needed rest and once again the Plowmans took charge of Violet's well-being. Max was convinced that 'love could conquer all' and wanted to put it to the test. But his battle for Violet's spiritual and physical health had consequences that neither he nor John had foreseen. When John came back from Margate, Violet was transformed by happiness and she had something important to tell him. 'I know it will hurt you. But I must tell you . . . I don't love you any more. I am in love with Max.'[44] For John it was the story of his first marriage all over again. Violet, too, was thinking a great deal about Katherine and Fontainebleau. She understood now much that had been mysterious to her when she married John. He had withdrawn himself from Katherine when things became too much, just as he had withdrawn from her. Katherine had gone to Fontainebleau seeking the loving support John had been unable to give, and Violet, too, was now having to find it elsewhere. When Max and Dorothy proposed that Violet should come to their house in Golders Green to be nursed she agreed at once.

On his return to Yately, John recorded in his diary that he was glad to see Betty Cockbayne again 'according to the law, rather too glad. She looked the picture of health.' The contrast with Violet, shrunk to a wraith, lying on her bed surrounded by the paraphernalia of sickness, was striking. 'What's the use of denying it?' he wrote. 'At this moment, I should like [Betty] for my mistress. That, in a simple sense, would do me good: and I should have more "virtue" to give V. I believe. The only reason not to try this is that "V would know and be hurt" . . . For myself alone, I haven't a scruple in the matter.'[45]

Violet departed from Yately on 18 February, leaving John alone in the bungalow with Betty, the children and their nanny Maud. It was a dangerous situation. Violet, caught up in her own battle for survival, was oblivious. The change of scene had altered her state of mind: she had achieved a level of serenity she had never thought possible. A week or so after Violet arrived, Dorothy forwarded a letter to John, full of Violet's spontaneous sweetness.

I must just write a note to sing to you a minute of this marvellous certainty, this joy, this relief . . . I had breakfast this morning consisting not of coffee and toast and butter and marmalade, but nectar and food of Paradise . . .The rough seas are behind. The water is calm and sunny and clear. I lie in bed and listen to the birds singing. I know why you are reading Blake. Isn't the Book of Thel beautiful? Life is punctuated here by reading of poetry aloud. Oh dear me, heavenly things I had never heard before. I believe even the bed must feel thrilled. And then there are talks with Max when it is as tho' doors in life were being opened and veils lifted. I didn't begin to go to sleep last night till 11, but that didn't matter a bit. There, I expect I scandalise you. So be scandalised. Now I must stop to sit on the jerry, so farewell.[46]

John went up to London to visit her and came back feeling that 'it was wrong for me to be there . . . I have no place near V. any more'. The distance between John and his wife was now much more than the drive from Yately to Golders Green. He had lost her to the Plowmans and was worried that Max was 'hurrying V. to physical death – to spiritual beatitude and physical death . . . Is Max putting a beautiful, but illusory belief to a supreme test: or is he a wise brave man making a dying girl happy? . . . Or, again, is he bearing my burden – loving Violet for me?' The situation became even more bizarre when Dorothy became jealous of the relationship and made approaches to John. Could he not love her – spiritually of course – as Max was loving Violet? John recoiled, but the encounter made him realise how sexually and emotionally deprived he was. When he came home to Yately he found Betty sitting in her nightdress with Maud at the kitchen table and the desire he felt for her became too great to ignore. That night he dreamed about her, 'and, alas, woke up and could not sleep again. So in the morning I told her. And she said she had dreamed of me. But she didn't tell me her dream.' And he was too afraid to enquire. But the following night when she brought his bedtime milk he called her back into the room and asked her. 'She put her arms round me. "I want to sleep with you," she said. And she did.'[47]

The children were taken to see their mother at the Plowmans'. Col remembered the pale March sunshine slanting through the windows and a plate of dark blue grapes on the bedside table. His mother's eyes seemed as dark as the grapes. With thin, translucent fingers she broke off a little bunch and held them out to him, but as he went to take them she began 'a sort of dry, hiccupping cough' and the children were bundled quickly out of the room.[48] It was Col's only memory of his mother. For Weg, a year older, Violet was 'a shadow with a low voice, gentle, absent. She moved, a vague presence. I cannot ever remember her embracing me nor ever remember her laugh.'[49]

It was the last week of Violet's life. John reported that her breathing was now very bad and her mouth had become 'crooked'. Nevertheless the homoeopathic doctor the Plowmans had called in told her that his test showed that 'she was building up'. Such deceptions made John angry. It was one thing to withhold information from her; quite another to tell her lies.

John was living in a kind of limbo. During the day he tried to work, played with the children and went up to London every three or four days to see Violet. His nights were spent with Betty Cockbayne, who proved to be a revelation of physical love. She was the earth mother of his dreams. John began to wonder whether all his views of love and male-female relationships had been wrong. Perhaps the 'spiritual love' he had craved was a mistake – perhaps it just led to the kind of disaster he had experienced with Katherine and Violet? Would a relationship on purely physical terms be better because it was simpler? While he tried to work this out in his diary, his children were dancing round the water pump in the yard outside chanting:

Old Ada Co'bayne,
Old Ada Co'bayne,
Go, go go to Spain,
Never come back to us again![50]

A few days later the inevitable happened: Weg saw John and Betty in an intimate embrace out in the rose garden. John was horrified and then began to be afraid that Weg might tell Violet on their next visit. Should he tell her himself? That exactly the same thing had happened with Katherine was never mentioned. With Katherine he had made the decision that she had the right to know – she had always insisted on the truth. Should he not do the same with Violet? Other things preyed on John's mind. It did not seem right that she had not been told the truth about her condition. Max was 'cheating her' into health. In his emotional confusion, John seemed unaware that Violet had only days to live. When he visited her on 26 March she 'seemed to be definitely much "farther away". Her eyes dull, and scarcely focussed, her mouth drooping.'[51] The only food she could eat was boiled rice in very small quantities. John had a long talk with Max, during which he confessed that he and Betty had become lovers. Max was disgusted. He told John that 'Violet must never know'. Dorothy was less surprised. On a previous visit to Yately to see John and the children she had observed Betty: 'The woman, in all her paraphernalia, sleek and glossy, waiting. An absolutely natural force; awful, and yet in its own way, grand. I seemed to understand everything at that moment . . .' Dorothy was less inclined to blame John for what happened. 'He could no more help playing that part in that drama than a fly, once caught, can get out of a spider's web. She had him.'[52]

On Saturday the 28th, Max went up to Violet's room in the afternoon and found her holding a letter from John and 'weeping bitterly'. Her chest and throat were terribly painful. Max summoned the doctor, who came straight away and gave Violet an injection of morphine. By Sunday evening she was in extremis and begged the doctor to 'put her out of her pain' – she looked up at Max and begged jokingly 'Just cut my throat, will you?' The doctor gave her another huge injection and shortly afterwards she fell asleep. The nurse called Max at 3 a.m. and he saw immediately that it would soon be over. 'She lay on her right side. Her head high on the pillows. She drew three great sighs and then her head dropped.'[53] After helping the nurse to lay Violet out, Max walked the empty streets. When he returned to the house, he rang John, who recorded his wife's death in his diary. 'March 30th 1931. Weg is watching at my elbow while I write this, before breakfast.' He arrived at the Plowmans' house at midday. Alone in the room, John kissed the lips of a dead wife for the second time in his life and slipped Katherine's little pearl ring from Violet's finger to keep for his daughter. Afterwards he confided to his diary that 'Death was cruel to her darling face as it was to Katherine's'.[54]

Dorothy had been away for the weekend when Violet died. When she returned and heard the story, she was furious. The letter John had sent Violet on that last day preyed on her mind. He had taken it away with him, among her other possessions. The nurse had told Dorothy that it had made Violet 'cry and cry and cry'. 'What was in that letter? Why had he sent it then? There was no doubt in Dorothy's mind that John had killed Violet.'[55] Years later she spoke her doubts to an older, adult Weg and the question burned in her mind too.

John did not tell the children until 1 April. Their mother had been a shadowy figure in their lives for some time and he did not expect them to feel a great deal. 'Weg thought a little while and said, "It's a good thing you didn't die, Dadda. Then we should only have had Maud and Miss Cockbayne . . ." Col, as usual going to extremes, said, "If Maud and Miss Cockbayne had died too . . ." "I expect," said Weg, "that we should have found another house to go in." '[56]

The funeral was a bleak occasion. Violet's family were there and close friends, and most of them, but particularly the Plowmans, were horrified to see that Betty came to the funeral with John. He had already told Max that he was going to marry her. Her period was late and she believed that she might be pregnant. Marrying her seemed to be the solution to John's predicament – it would provide continuity for the children; it would be a simple, uncomplicated relationship built on physical relations; there would be no messy emotions. 'Probably I couldn't love anyone but a girl. Katherine was a girl. I don't know what Woman is; and never shall.' But a week later he was having second thoughts. Betty was depressed. The Plowmans had been to visit and had snubbed her. Her period had arrived and 'the disappointment of no baby . . . made Wednesday night rather painful'. Betty's father had also warned John against her and he began to wonder whether he was doing the right thing. 'Perhaps it was all stupid and mistaken; perhaps I had better go away and live with the children alone, and put up with the horror of "well meaning", scheming, sympathetic females.'[57]

Returning to Yately, John was plagued by recollection: 'Her room – darling Violet!' When, in the evening, he looked at 'one of the frocks which V bought and never wore – a beige silk frock with a little brown bow; the very dress of the very girl I loved; my little sweetheart – the sadness came over me; and later, when I listened to Richard Tauber singing . . . I was engulfed in it. One mustn't think; it's too sad.' His grief for Violet brought back more forcefully images from his life with Katherine. 'In the kitchen, with the green lamp without a shade. Tiddlums asleep in the Brett armchair, writing at the table which was my desk when I began the *Adelphi*, the black clock wheezily striking – that Katherine and I swopped for the marble time piece at Hollanders. Everything, if I dare to read its language, is full of memories . . .'[58]

Within a month, unable to live with the memories it contained, he had sold the house at Yately and bought an eighteenth-century former rectory at Larling in Suffolk. On 23 May he and Betty were married in the local register office. His witnesses were James Young, Betty's sister Molly and the children's nanny, Maud Hogben.

Afterwards, Weg recalled, her mother Violet 'took her place among the photographs, a grave profile. Mamma. Her name was rarely mentioned . . . Violet? Who spoke of Violet? It was Katherine who came, strong and striding, from beyond and occupied quite naturally the throne of honour, saying, "I am here".'[59]

PART IV

The Member of a Wandering Tribe

How hard it is to escape from places. However carefully one
goes they hold you – you leave little bits of yourself fluttering on the fences – little rags and shreds of your very life.
KATHERINE MANSFIELD TO IDA BAKER, MARCH 1922

PART IV

The Member of a Vanishing Tribe

12

Tig and Wig

Once upon a time a young man and a young woman loved each other and poetry so much that they decided to devote their lives together to the furtherance and encouragement of English poetry — especially the poetry of young and unknown writers like themselves . . .

PALL MALL GAZETTE, 23 OCTOBER 1912

It is Friday 12 April 1912. John Murry wakes for the first time in the Buddha room at 69 Clovelly Mansions. Katherine is knocking on the door. 'I've finished with the bathroom,' she calls. 'And your breakfast is in the kitchen.' She has left the table laid for him, and the kettle boiling on the gas ring. There is brown bread and butter and honey, and a large brown egg in an egg-cup. Half a sheet of blue notepaper is tucked underneath with some words printed on it. 'This is your egg. You must boil it. K.M.'[1]

Katherine is often out and John works on his journalistic commissions for the *Westminster Gazette* late into the night. When Katherine is at home they make tea and sit in front of the fire in her small sitting-room talking. At first their conversations centre on literature and the submissions for *Rhythm* that John shows her. He values Katherine's judgement because of her experience on the *New Age* and soon proposes that she becomes an assistant editor alongside Michael Sadler, though he has not thought through the politics of introducing a female into an all-male editorial team. This is a time when artists and writers are universally referred to as 'he'; women do not have the right to vote and are expected, like children, to be seen but not heard in polite society. Katherine comes from a young country where everything is freer and more entrepreneurial; her character is confrontational and her language is too colourful for a well-brought up young lady. Gossip has it that she has been turned off a London omnibus for calling a woman a whore, because she had abused the suffragette movement.[2] Whoever Katherine is working with, there are bound to be clashes.

The first joint decision from Clovelly Mansions is that Rhythm should be published monthly. But before the next issue appears there is a financial crisis. Though sales have been running at four or five hundred per quarter, the printers have been printing 3000 copies of each edition on a sale or return basis and the order has never been changed. John, totally inexperienced in financial dealings or the management of a magazine, finds that he is now liable for the debt. Katherine talks to her publisher Stephen Swift and he agrees to take over financial responsibility for the magazine and pay Katherine and John £10 each as editors, though John will still have to pay the £100 owing to the printers. There will be no more money from Michael Sadler and his father: it is John's mistake and he must pay. But he is earning enough to make this seem feasible – his editorial fee from Swift will cover it comfortably. In June the first edition appears, with a new blue cover naming Katherine Mansfield and Michael Sadler as assistant editors. It is significant that Katherine's name comes first. The editorial, 'On the Meaning of Rhythm', is signed by John and Katherine – not Michael – and it is clear from the content that this partnership is the future direction of the magazine. The following month Michael's name is missing from the editorial listing.

The first evidence of Katherine's involvement is the inclusion of work by authors such as Yone Noguchi, as well as stories and poems with a definite Russian flavour, but her main influence is the introduction of satire. Katherine brings to Rhythm her own acerbic style of reviewing. On a volume of poems by novelist John Galsworthy she concludes by saying: 'Mr Galsworthy is wise in that he avoids all mention of the word "poetry" in connection with his verses'.[3] Despite the fact that Beatrice and Orage taught her this technique, the New Age sneers at it. They both think that Rhythm does Katherine's work no good at all, since she can publish what she likes without firm editorial input. Orage has already given Katherine an ultimatum – either the New Age or Rhythm – but they still hold some of her material and in the same month, perhaps as a comment on her actual review, they publish Katherine's hilarious spoof analysis of 'Professor Rattyscum's lavishly illustrated book of travel "From Sewer to Cathedral Spire" . . . illustrated by his wife'. It is a masterpiece of derision. 'There is something of a divine swoop in the Professor's immediate grip of you: in the way he leads you from the figure of Mrs Rattyscum painting, perhaps, some intimate corner of the Sahara, to the dining-table, to the roasted bird or the willow pattern dish set in a little mat of pale yellow straw.'[4] But it seems designed to ridicule Katherine's more serious literary persona.

Relations between Clovelly Mansions and Chancery Lane are made more turbulent in May when Orage satirises Katherine as 'Marcia Foisacre' in one of his 'Tales for Men Only', published in five instalments in the *New Age*. Mrs Foisacre is married but separated from her husband, about whom she is rather vague. She has a flat, as 'all such ladies have', with a doorman who can be tipped to turn a blind eye to her gentleman callers. 'On the way to Mrs. Foisacre's flat she warned us that she could not invite us in. We're very respectable, and we keeps ourselves to ourselves in these flats, she mimicked. We married ladies have to be very particular – with the hall-porter about . . . He requires such large tips!' 'Marcia' (a snide reference to Maata?) is intellectually weak, secretly preferring the music hall to the opera house, and is continually affecting poses that reflect the character of the company she keeps. Orage even attacks Katherine's most intimate life. Mrs Foisacre is apparently no longer interested in sex, 'as coldly logical as you could be', but this is dismissed by the narrator as yet another pose. It ends with a crushing summary of her character. 'Mrs. Foisacre is an empty husk, as promiscuous as a rabbit, as responsible as a bubble and as deceitful as a cat.'[5] The fact that this attack comes from Orage's pen makes it even more bitter for Katherine. This is more than just a literary feud.

Rhythm continues to be controversial, though not always in the right way. John is a classicist and his knowledge of contemporary English literature is narrow. He makes editorial gaffes that appal more serious critics and damage the magazine's reputation. In June, reviewing a dull, derivative collection of poetry by a little-known poet, he states that 'James Stephen is the greatest poet of our day. With this book he has stepped at once into the company of those whom we consider the greatest poets the world has ever known.'[6] The following month he asserts that Frank Harris, a notorious amorist who once declared that Casanova was not good enough to tie his bootlaces, is the greatest writer since Shakespeare. When John, dimly aware that by expressing such deeply felt but naive opinions he has laid himself open to ridicule, is challenged by an outraged reader in a bookshop, he humiliates himself even further by bursting into tears and 'rushing blindly out of the shop'.[7] The New Age takes full advantage of his embarrassment. Katherine's last satire, a pastiche of Gogol called 'Green Goggles', appears a week later, but after that the breach is complete. She tells Orage that it is all over.

Katherine has chosen Rhythm and John, who, on the surface of things, seems the perfect soulmate: a writer and editor, deeply committed to literature, sharing her ideals of truth and beauty, a gentle, sensitive man as battered by life as she has been. Her dream of the perfect relationship is spelled out in her story 'Psychology'. 'The special thrilling quality of their friendship was in their complete surrender. Like two open cities in the midst of some vast plain their two minds lay open to each other . . . They were eager, serious travellers, absorbed in understanding what was to be seen and discovering what was hidden – making the most of this extraordinary absolute chance which made it possible for him to be utterly truthful to her and for her to be utterly sincere with him.'[8]

There is a delicate distinction between being 'truthful' and being 'sincere'. John is perfectly frank about Marguéritte and the episode with the Oxford prostitute, the horrors of his home life and his ambitions for the future. Katherine, however, tells a carefully edited story of her past – her love for Garnet, but not his child; the marriage to George Bowden; her alienation from her family; some of her failed love affairs, but not all. Though she finds John easy to talk to, she keeps part of herself back, fearing that the full details of her life would disgust him. There are still things about John that puzzle her. His sexual timidity is one of them. Does he find her as attractive as she finds him?

After about three weeks of sharing a roof, confident of her own feelings for John, Katherine asks one evening as they are about to go to their separate beds, 'Why don't you make me your mistress?' John, taken by surprise, responds, 'Because I feel it would spoil everything.' Katherine, with a bitter inflection that is lost on John, replies, 'So do I!' John is afraid that sex would ruin his relationship with Katherine, just as it had his affair with Marguéritte. Katherine feels rejected and fears that John does not care for her. Even when she says, 'Murry, I love you. Doesn't that make any difference?', he continues to refuse her.[9] Katherine tells Ida that there are 'dark, turbulent, unresolved problems' within him that could be cured by love,[10] if only he would allow himself to be loved. John remembers afterwards, with regret, that he was held back by a 'cold ghostly fear. An icy wind from nowhere would blow upon my soul, against which I was powerless.'[11]

But a couple of weeks later, there is an incident that brings them together. In the pub where they sometimes go for a drink, they see a middle-aged prostitute looking at herself in the mirror 'with terrible self-knowledge'. It is an image of sadness and wasted life that is significant for both of them. 'Against that vision – and all its meaning – we knew we must hold together for ever.'[12] That night they share a bed for the first time as lovers and giggle over John's former reluctance. Katherine tells a friend, 'We laughed and we laughed and we laughed without stopping.'[13]

Although John is sharing Katherine's flat, an illusion of respectability has to be preserved for the landlord, the other tenants and the world in general. When Katherine invites people round for tea, John either goes out or stays in his bedroom until they have gone. He also has to be careful not to be seen by the doorman and the neighbours when entering or leaving the flat late at night or early in the morning. Their life together begins to resemble the subterfuges of Mrs Foisacre in Orage's brutal sketch. Katherine's friend Gordon Campbell, an Irish barrister, poet, playwright and critic she met at W. L. George's house, is one of the few trusted to know the truth. Katherine is very fond of Gordon. He is a wonderful conversationalist, gossiping about people with a particular Irish humour – a mixture of 'fantasy and mockery but done without malice' which his friends call 'Campbelling'.[14] One afternoon, when he and Katherine are having tea in her flat, she suddenly calls, 'You can come out, Tiger!', and John emerges from his room to be introduced. Gordon realises that he is privileged to be admitted to the secret. But he quickly becomes John's friend rather than Katherine's and this intimate male alliance is a source of jealousy. Gordon's own marriage that summer to Beatrice Elvery, a young Irish painter from the Slade, is another factor in their changing relationship.

John and Katherine can't get married, but they can at least have a honeymoon. John takes Katherine to Paris and introduces her to 'the Rhythm circle'. In the main *rendezvous* of the Rotonde, the Dome and the more dubious Café Harcourt, Katherine catches tantalising glimpses of Marcel Proust, 'a tall, slim man in black with a sickly yellow face'. She meets the androgynous Georges Banks, 'a big woman who wore men's clothes and looked like Oscar Wilde and was always weeping'.[15] Georges, who has a soft spot for John, repels Katherine, but she particularly likes 'Johnny'

Fergusson and his mistress Anne Estelle Rice. They make a striking pair – the tall Fergusson in his tailored businessman's overcoat, and Anne by his side, shorter, plump and 'bronze-coloured', with animated blue eyes. She and Katherine are attracted to each other straight away. Anne is fascinated by Katherine's 'compelling and vivid' personality. Most arresting are Katherine's 'beautiful eyes, dark, sombre and questioning', sending out 'a penetrating beam into the crannies and recesses of one's nature'. Anne is also intrigued by Katherine's chameleon-like incarnations. She can be 'a femme fatale' in a long black dress with a sequin scarf around her head, or 'Katoushka in a Russian peasant's costume of brilliant colour', and once she appears in a black cloak, and a black turban with a white fez on top.[16] Anne is working on a series of gigantic murals for an American department store and when Katherine visits her studio she is so overwhelmed by them that she bursts into tears and has to rush out of the room. Katherine's friends think it is one of her 'stunts', put on for show, but Anne is touched.

And then there is John's journalist friend Francis Carco. Katherine initially suspends judgement. He is handsome in the French fashion, small, plump, 'with an olive skin, black eyes with long lashes, black silky hair cut short, tiny square teeth'. His hands are supple and small, almost like a girl's, and he wears 'a thin gold bracelet' above his left elbow.[17] Carco is sardonic, clever, sexually predatory and definitely dangerous.

When they return to England, John takes Katherine to meet his parents in Wandsworth. It does not occur to him that they might be hostile towards his choice of partner. He is, in his own words, 'naive and deluded'. From their point of view Katherine is a married woman, so the relationship is scandalous. They also blame her for their brilliant son leaving Oxford and abandoning a certain first class degree and the glittering civil service career that lay ahead. She has ruined him. Katherine, with her fur coat, her French perfume, coloured stockings and make-up, belongs to a world they do not understand; she is alien and unwelcome. The atmosphere in the parlour at Nicosia Road is rigid with disgust – if John had brought a harlot in off the street the reception could not have been cooler. John's nine-year-old brother crouches in a corner of the room 'bewildered and frightened'. Katherine feels humiliated. The Murrys' reaction strips away much of the self-respect she has carefully built up since the birth of Garnet's baby and forces her to see their relationship as the outside world would regard it if they knew the truth. To live together outside marriage is to be excluded from respectable society. Katherine experiences a deep sense of shame, that the most personal (the most truthful) details of her life – her illegitimate child, her mistaken marriage and her love affairs – are sordid and unclean in others' eyes. The only answer is to conceal them.[18]

On 23 May Katherine receives a letter from George Bowden, which had been given to Mr Kay. George is going to the United States and wants to talk to her about a discreet American divorce. Katherine sends him a friendly letter inviting him to the flat to discuss it. 'I think it is in every way the wisest plan for us both.'[19] There is a surreal evening, with everyone being very civilised, which ends when George – at Katherine's request – accompanies himself in a couple of songs on her piano. As he is leaving he asks Katherine whether she and John intend to marry. She turns to John, eyebrows raised quizzically, and asks, 'Do we, J.M.?' George has the feeling that marriage is not really important to her and this puzzles him. On paper Katherine likes the idea of being free to marry John, and she hates the name Bowden, but the idea of divorce with all its sordid associations – photographs in seedy hotels, the public admission of adultery – is repugnant to her, as it is to George. He is already suffering, psychologically and emotionally, from the trauma of their relationship. A quiet American divorce would save them both from further humiliation and George, a gentleman to the end, tells Katherine that he will take care of everything, including the costs. Katherine, too, seems prepared to co-operate. George conveniently comes into possession of a number of papers that clearly incriminate her. Not only does he have the anonymous letter confessing to sexually deviant desires, but two love letters from Floryan Sobieniowski, a letter from Ida about Katherine's return from Germany, a letter from Ida to Garnet Trowell stating Katherine's intention not to return to her husband, and Vere Bartrick-Baker's long letter advising Katherine about her affair with Floryan.[20] It is difficult to see how he could have obtained such a portfolio of evidence unless Katherine had given it to him.

Shortly afterwards Katherine goes to answer the door bell and finds John's mother and aunt, 'frantic and hysterical', intent upon forcing their way into the flat to 'rescue' John from her influence. John hears a scuffle in the hallway, then Katherine calling, 'Jack!' He comes running out of the sitting-room to help, and has to use physical force to push his mother out of the door. When he has locked and bolted it, he discovers that Katherine has collapsed on the floor, shaking with fear, her face chalk-white. John, too, feels physically sick. He carries Katherine into the sitting-room and tucks her up on the sofa under a rug, holding her hand as they both listen to the barrage of abuse outside on the landing – audible to everyone on the stairwell. John is so angry about the incident and the distress it has caused Katherine that he tells his parents he is breaking off all contact with them. Shortly after the disturbance, the neighbours, already suspicious about the comings and goings from the flat, complain, and threaten to inform the landlord. Katherine and John will have to move. They decide to leave London and find a cottage in the country where they can write, edit Rhythm and live a quiet, private existence together.

But before they can do so, an unwelcome figure from Katherine's past arrives in London. Floryan has decided that he would rather be there than in Paris. Katherine is relatively easy to find, as they move in the same circles, and it is possible, and thoroughly in character, for her to have been in contact with him during the intervening years. She may even have met him accidentally when she and John were in Paris. She tells John very little about Floryan and at first he seems a useful addition to the pan-European mix of Rhythm. His name appears on the title page of the July edition as the foreign correspondent from Poland.

The momentum of Rhythm is now thoroughly exciting. The magazine is printing work by established writers and such newcomers as H. G. Wells, Hugh Walpole, Ford Madox Hueffer (later Ford Madox Ford), Rupert Brooke and W. H. Davies, and the artwork is cutting edge, including Cezanne, Picasso and Orthon Friesz as well as the Fauves. One of John's friends, novelist and critic Gilbert Cannan, jokingly christens John and Katherine the 'Two Tigers', after a design that appears in the magazine of a tiger treading on a monkey's tail, and this becomes their pseudonym for reviews and editorials. John is so untigerlike that his nickname is soon dropped, but Katherine is still referred to as 'Tiger' by friends and acquaintances. Eventually John shortens it to 'Tig', which then becomes 'Wig' and for a while Katherine answers to both. In the summer of 1912 the future looks good for the Tigers. The debt to the printer will soon be paid off, John is earning good money as a journalist, Stephen Swift is paying them £10 each as editors, and Katherine's German pension stories are selling well. She hopes to have 'Maata' ready to offer Swift by the end of the year. Their joint income is around £450, more than enough to finance the lease of a cottage in the country where rents are cheaper, and they begin to visit house agents.

Rhythm now has several foreign correspondents (all unpaid) representing the United States, Spain, France, Germany, Italy and Poland, and is regularly attracting new visual artists as well as writers. Henri Gaudier-Brzeska is in London and sends *Rhythm* some drawings that greatly impress the Two Tigers. Henri is invited to supper and he asks whether he can bring his 'sister' Sophie. He is rather younger than John, barely twenty-one – a gaunt Frenchman, with hollow eyes and broad cheekbones, long dark hair falling over his face, full of nervous energy and 'passionate simplicity', and very protective towards his female companion. Sophie Brzeska, highly strung and visibly unstable, is about twenty years older and Polish. It is obvious that they are not brother and sister and they quickly confess that they are living together – making it possible for John and Katherine to admit their own situation. But though Henri and Sophie love each other and have shared a bed, Sophie declares that their relationship is completely platonic, which Katherine finds very strange. She questions Henri obliquely about his 'passions', mentioning a certain 'English writer', and he, having had brief liaisons with men, knows exactly what she is asking, though he declines to be drawn on it. Despite Katherine's reservations about the couple, there is instant empathy between the two men and very soon the Gaudier-Brzeskas have told their hosts the whole story of their lives. Sophie in particular is eager for Katherine to know what she had been through before she met Henri. Katherine is suspicious of such instant intimacy. She senses 'something hungry and avid' about Sophie, a void 'incessantly seeking to be filled'.[21] Sophie holds onto Katherine's arm and talks close to her face, forcing her to draw back. She seems to expect Katherine to be equally confessional, but Katherine pulls her hand away; the mask comes down.

On that first evening they spend so much time talking that the 'pot au feu' Katherine had cooked is forgotten until they smell burning. It is too far gone to be rescued so they have to make do with bread and cheese. Katherine is mortified, but the atmosphere is so casual that no one really minds. Henri seems fascinated by John's strong body and his 'magnificent head like a Greek god'.[22] When they leave, he tells John that he wants to make a clay model of his head, then he suddenly takes him in his arms in a ferocious embrace.

When John goes round to the Gaudier-Brzeskas' room in Chelsea for the first sitting, he is horrified by the starkness of their existence. There is an old bed, 'a couple of seedy deck-chairs, and a scrap of matting on the floor'. Sophie is curled up on the bed smoking and writing in a notebook. Henri tells him that she is writing a novel about her life. While

Henri works, he repeatedly comes to stand beside his model, running his hands over John's face and hair in a way that makes him extremely uncomfortable. 'I had the uneasy feeling that I had unwittingly awakened in Gaudier a kind of passion that was incomprehensible to me, and therefore alarming.'[23] Katherine is quite sure there is something homo-erotic in their relationship – in fact there is a sexual ambivalence about both the Gaudier-Brzeskas that she finds disturbing. Further meetings are arranged, but Katherine makes excuses and only John goes. Katherine tells John that though she pities Sophie, she is afraid of her, believing that she is the kind of woman who will 'fasten her tentacles round her and suck her dry'.[24] Katherine's reaction is one that Sophie is used to. Men are fascinated by her, but women find her neurotic, 'treacherous, suspicious, easily affronted, violently hurt'.[25] When John invites the Gaudier-Brzeskas to dinner again and Katherine sends a telegram cancelling because she is unwell, Sophie begins to suspect that Katherine does not like her. Henri, more innocent, thinks that they have made a lasting friendship.

In August Katherine and John find a pretty period house – 'a "cottage" in the Jane Austen sense of the word'[26] – at Runcton near Chichester, for only £40 a year, and for the first time Katherine is able to set up home properly. She refers to the cottage in letters as 'our first house, our wedding house'. They buy furniture from a London store, Maples, on hire purchase and on 4 September 1912 'Mr and Mrs John Middleton Murry' move in. It is a great comfort to Katherine to have a settled relationship. 'To have another person with you – who goes to bed when you do & is there when you wake up – who turns to you & to whom you turn.'[27] The view from the bedroom window is also a source of delight. She writes to her cousin Sylvia of her love for the country landscape. 'I don't care any more for cities. There's no time to grow in them or to discover the dusk and feel the rain cloud and hear the wind rise and fall.'[28] But from the beginning their idyllic existence feels somehow unreal. It is as if they are 'dream children' pretending to be married; the beautiful house 'with its sun-dappled rooms, its walled garden, and its medlar trees' seems to be 'a kind of stage scenery that might be removed in the twinkling of an eye'.[29] And almost immediately the 'snail under the leaf' manifests itself. The ex-soldier Katherine has employed as a 'man of all work' is not only dirty but also a drunk and is discovered stealing from them. When her period is late and Katherine longs for a child to complete her relationship with John, her hopes come to nothing.

As she becomes increasingly secure with John, she begins to share more of her past. She tells him about her affair with Geza Silberer and allows John to read his letters, which she afterwards burns. He is shocked by some of the physical details they contain, which give him a glimpse of Katherine's more sophisticated sexual past. When Sils Vara writes of kissing her breasts, John realises that it has never occurred to him to do so. The act of sexual intercourse for John is exactly that – he knows nothing of lovemaking and foreplay. There are 'no caresses, no preliminaries', only 'a climax without a crescendo'.[30] The more experienced Katherine has been careful not to take too much of the initiative and reveal a knowledge she feels ashamed of. But John realises after reading Sils' letters that he must seem a rather inadequate lover. Katherine, who has registered John's reaction to her revelation, decides to burn all her 'huge complaining' letters and diaries from 1909 to the present day. The truth about Bad Wörishofen, Garnet's baby and her marriage to George, must remain secret. A few precious, innocent, communications are kept, sketches for stories and notebook fragments. Everything else is consigned to the fire, wiping out her past. Ida knows, but Katherine is certain that Ida will never tell.

The peace and quiet Katherine and John had hoped for fails to materialise. As soon as Henri and Sophie hear about the cottage they begin to talk about coming down to visit them frequently – perhaps even to live with them, sharing expenses. When John tells them that the cottage is a long way from London and quite difficult to get to, Henri is undaunted. He will stay in London and come down at weekends; Sophie will come and live with them – London does not suit her and she needs somewhere more congenial to write her life story. Katherine is devastated. She does not want to share her new home with anyone other than John and particularly not with Sophie. John doesn't see why not and they have their first real quarrel. John thinks Sophie should be invited: 'There's plenty of room'. Katherine is adamant. 'I don't want to see her here – she's too violent – I won't have her.' John continues to try to persuade Katherine – 'She's not like that – I don't see why'– but Katherine explodes: 'Leave me alone, I don't like her and I don't want to see her'.[31] Unfortunately the quarrel is overheard by Henri, who has come down to Runcton unannounced, and he reports back to Sophie. From London he writes a letter to John referring to the 'wickedness of

Katherine Mansfield' and her 'fiendish jealousy'. Their friendship has been false. 'Your acquaintance has been for me one long suffering – not only for me but also for the object of my love, which is twice worse.'[32]

It is an ugly episode that leaves Katherine emotionally bruised. Before she has recovered, there is a more sinister arrival. Floryan turns up on the doorstep with 'two big black trunks full of books and manuscripts', and a reluctant Katherine can't force him to leave. He appears, even to John, to regard himself as their 'dependent for life',[33] and wanders through the rooms like the ghost of Hamlet's father. The house echoes with his 'forlorn Slavic songs'. He borrows money from Katherine and doesn't pay his way, but she can't refuse him because he knows too much about her. John has not been told about their relationship. It's a precarious situation.

But towards the middle of October, before they are even properly settled into the cottage, there is another crisis. Stephen Swift disappears from London overnight, having cleared his bank account and taken the cashbox, leaving bills unpaid and a large debt for Rhythm. It gradually emerges that his real name is actually Charles Hosken, also known as Charles Granville and Henry Charos James, a fraudster and bigamist who had married and abandoned no fewer than three women and jumped bail on an earlier prosecution. Not only is Rhythm in trouble, but there can be no royalties for Katherine's book of short stories, which has recently gone into a third edition. Financially things are extremely bleak. Katherine pledges her allowance to pay off the debt, the cottage has to be given up and the furniture, so lovingly chosen eight weeks earlier, is repossessed. The writ server wears hideous yellow gloves and leans on the grand piano 'making it thereby indescribably his own'.[34] Some of John's books have to be sold, but the piano is eventually saved, together with the Buddha and other items that had belonged to Ida's mother.

Within weeks, Katherine and John are back in London, in Chancery Lane, sharing a tiny kitchen, a bedroom and a living room that doubles as the offices for Rhythm. The disadvantages are many: it is only a few doors down from the New Age offices, the windows 'keep out more light than they let in' and the bedroom looks out onto a row of 'gloomy houses'.[35] There is no furniture and they have to make do with a chair lent by Ida, a single bed and a couple of packing cases. Even more depressing is the fact that Floryan is camping out on the living-room floor. John gives him even more money to make him go away, but his efforts are unsuccessful. Floryan now owes them about £40.

Throughout the winter Katherine is desperately unhappy and often ill. Both she and John have pleurisy. The rooms are dirty, cramped and cold and they have no money at all. The amount owed on *Rhythm* is enormous, but it doesn't occur to them that the debt should be Stephen Swift's, not theirs. There are fears that the bailiffs will appear again and Ida is instructed to rescue her mother's chair, carrying it down the fire escape at the back. Neither John nor Katherine is very good at economising. They eat jellied eels from a street stall and penny pies from a meat pie shop, but then have to go into a pub and buy drinks to take the taste away. The landlady, thinking they are out of work actors, stands them free beers. Sardines and eggs and bread fill the cupboard at home and John, remembering his mother's economies at Nicosia Road, shows Katherine how to buy ham bones to make into soup – one saucepan full can last for days. Floryan is a constant drain on their resources. He is supposed to pay them 10s. a week board and lodging, but instead borrows money from them at the rate of a pound a week. John is too timid to get rid of him and Katherine is too afraid of what he might reveal to John if she tries. Ida is also in difficult circumstances. Her sister has gone to Rhodesia to live with their father, so the flat that they had shared has been given up. All Ida's possessions are in storage and she is living in an attic on Baker Street. Despite regular advertisements in *Rhythm*, the hair brushing and beauty salon that she and her friend had opened often does not make enough to pay them a wage. Sometimes they are so hungry that they have to eat the porridge oats they use for face-packs.

Katherine can't write under such conditions. She is so desperate to work that it is as though 'some insidious & terrible worm ate & ate at my heart – a frightful & intolerable agony overcomes me. I feel that I must be alone or die, that a book has got to be conceived & written.'[36] But *Rhythm* drains all her spare energy. Their friends have clubbed together to provide some money for the magazine to continue with Martin Secker as the publisher. Winston Churchill's secretary Eddie Marsh, a well-known patron of the arts, is also pledging money and giving them moral support. They owe money to all their friends. John is advised to petition for bankruptcy, though he refuses to take the advice and prefers to stumble on. A friend writes an upbeat article in the *Pall Mall Gazette*, which is a clear plea for subscribers. Katherine writes letters to a number of writers, including D. H. Lawrence, asking if they will contribute material free of charge to help *Rhythm* stay alive. Lawrence is in Italy, having just eloped with Frieda

Weekley, and responds with a story, 'The Soiled Rose', waiving a fee. 'I am as poor as a church mouse, so feel quite grand giving something away.' He offers to review German books for Rhythm and adds, 'I shall probably be in London at the end of March – immediately after Easter – and then, if your tea-kettle is still hot, I shall be glad to ask you for the cup you offered me.'[37]

As well as soliciting copy, Katherine walks long distances almost every day, canvassing shops and offices for advertisements, carefully writing up the results in a notebook.[38] Very few commercial enterprises want to appear in such a small magazine with a limited circulation. Heal's is one of the few who feel that the Art Deco style of Rhythm is suitable. Katherine is also looking for theatrical work to supplement their income, but though she is talented, there is little space for an amateur. Katherine has a depressing interview with an agent about walk-on parts and fails the audition. Rebecca West sees Katherine at The Cave of the Golden Calf, where she introduces the acts and performs one of her own sketches. But these opportunities are rare. She keeps meticulous accounts, recording every penny spent. The notebook entries are interspersed with light-hearted verses.

> Tea, the chemist & marmalade
> Far indeed today I've strayed
> Through paths untrodden, shops unbeaten
> And now the bloody stuff is eaten
> The chemist the marmalade & tea
> Lord how nice & cheap they be![39]

The strain starts to tell and Katherine's heart begins to 'flutter' as it has always done when she is under extreme stress. She has several bouts of illness during the winter – Ida describes her as 'fading away' – and her relationship with John is suffering. Friends witness angry scenes. On one occasion she storms into the bookshop in St Martins Court where John spends quite a lot of his time, bangs the door key down on the counter and shouts, 'Tell him I've left!'[40] Eventually Gilbert Cannan suggests a cheap Victorian red-brick semi-detached house in the Buckinghamshire village of Cholesbury, close to the old windmill he shares with his wife Mary. Katherine rents it furnished and lives there alone during the week. John comes down at weekends with Gordon Campbell, who has agreed to share the rent while his wife is away in Ireland having their first baby.

Katherine is trying to finish 'Maata', but she can't get the plot to work. She admits that 'the plots of my stories leave me perfectly cold'.[41] She has taught herself the technique of the impressionistic short story – capturing a moment in time, multi-layered and complex, but she has problems with the structure of a longer narrative. 'This story seems to me to lack coherence and sharpness. That's the principal thing: it's not at all sharp. It's like eating a bunch of grapes instead of a grain of caviare . . . I have a pretty bad habit of spreading myself at times, of overwriting and understating – it's just carelessness.'[42] Because the material of the novel is so intimately connected with the Trowell family and her memories of Garnet, it is difficult to order objectively. A long and detailed synopsis is worked out in her notebook and some draft chapters written, but she's unable to finish it, even though the house provides the space she needs. 'To be without books and to be alone are the 2 essentials to my writing – endless time no fires to attend to, no-one to wait for – days and nights on end.'[43] But though she loves the country and needs the quiet and the creative space it offers her, the lonely nights are an ordeal. The cottage is old and full of noises: 'last night the wind howled and I gloomed and shivered – and heard locks being filed and ladders balanced against windows & footsteps padding up-stairs . . . mon Dieu! by midnight the whole world has turned into a butcher!'[44]

At the weekends, their friends come down from London: Gordon Campbell, Gilbert Cannan, Rupert Brooke, Frederick Goodyear and Ida Baker. There are riotous nights when they play poker for pennies. But without proper domestic help, entertaining puts a great strain on Katherine's resources. She finds herself excluded from their literary discussions, confined to the kitchen, scrubbing congealed mutton fat off a sinkful of plates and pans, simmering with resentment that eventually boils over into a terrible quarrel with John. He goes back to London without speaking to her and she has to write a letter immediately to try to explain how she feels: 'when I have to clean up twice over or wash up extra unnecessary things I get frightfully impatient and want to be working. So often, this week, I've heard you and Gordon talking while I washed dishes. Well, someone's got to wash dishes & get food . . . Yes, I hate hate HATE doing these things that you accept just as all men accept of their women. I can only play the servant with very bad grace indeed . . . I walk about with a mind full of ghosts of saucepans & primus stoves & "will there be enough to go round" . . . & you calling (whatever I am doing Tig – isn't there going to be tea. Its five o'clock.) As though I were a dilatory housemaid!' But even as she complains, she loathes herself for doing so. 'I am disgusted & repelled by the creature who shouts at you "you might at least empty the pail & wash out the tea leaves!"' It is, she reflects, all because they lack enough money to employ anyone other than the occasional cleaning lady to do the heaviest and dirtiest domestic tasks. Other women of Katherine's class have cooks and maids.[45]

Katherine confides in Ida that, though she loves him, she is having doubts about John. She has overheard him talking to Frederick Goodyear after she had gone to bed, saying that what he really wants is a woman who could keep him. Does he just want her for her money? Without her allowance, Rhythm would be impossible. There is also his solipsism – a blindness to the people around him that isolates John emotionally. Katherine finds him 'lonely and difficult for me to understand'.[46] Ida has already noted his detachment, his lack of awareness of others' sensibilities. Out on a walk in the marshes, he had borrowed a carved stick she had brought back from Rhodesia and of which she was very fond. John absent-mindedly swung it into the reeds, making no attempt to find it again, and did not apologise for the loss. In company he scarcely notices her; Ida says it is as though she is invisible to him.

John is becoming increasingly dependent on Katherine's presence and finds the imposed separation from her 'hard to bear'. He confesses that he feels 'like a naked outpost in an enemy country'.[47] Ida observes that 'he must always have a woman to lean upon who would encourage him and keep up his morale'.[48] But his attachment to Katherine is even more fundamental than that. John is a self-made man who, through education, has risen from a lower middle class background into the upper strata of society. He has friends like Gordon Campbell, heir to a title and estates, as well as some of the biggest names in literature and art. But he feels a fraud; that he does not belong. Katherine, also an outsider, understands his insecurity. With her he feels 'free and careless, gay and confident, as though the immense accumulation of an artificial self, which had been gathering about me ever since I could remember, were suddenly lifted from me'. He is 'real with her, and with no one else.'[49]

Since their quarrel with the Gaudier-Brzeskas in October, threatening letters have been arriving at Chancery Lane demanding money for the drawings John had published in Rhythm, though it had always been clearly understood that publication was gratis. On several occasions the

Gaudier-Brzeskas had come to the flat, shouting abuse through the door, which John declined to open. Knowing Henri's physical strength, John was afraid of what he might do. At the beginning of May, John, without thinking, answers a knock on the door in the middle of the afternoon. Henri is standing outside with Georges Banks: 'Now, we've got you'. John is roughly pushed aside as they rush into the room and begin tearing drawings off the wall and rifling through papers on his desk, looking for Georges' submissions as well as Henri's, overturning furniture 'in an outburst of insane hatred'. When John again declines to pay and reminds Henri of their agreement, he is hit across the face. I should like to murder you, says Henri, 'squeezing his fingers together round an imaginary throat . . . "But you're not worth murdering."'[50] The crime is accomplished by proxy. John learns later that Henri, Sophie and one of their friends had put the clay model of his head against a wall and smashed it. The experience devastates John.

It is a very stressful week. Floryan appears in Cholesbury looking for some possessions he has left behind. Katherine sends him back to London, instructing Ida to go to the flat and reclaim Floryan's belongings, as though she does not trust John to deal with him. Despite her warning that Floryan is 'a rather dangerous fraud',[51] he manages to borrow another £15 from John before he leaves, promising to pay it back. There is also a letter from George Bowden informing Katherine that divorce papers are going to be served in a few days' time. But the papers never materialise and the prospect of divorce evaporates. Because Katherine and George were married in Britain and are living there, an American divorce would not be valid. She remains Mrs George Bowden on her passport and all official documents.

The new incarnation of *Rhythm* is fading as sales dwindle. John resurrects it briefly as the *Blue Review*, but after three issues that, too, is abandoned to avoid piling up even more debt. The house in Cholesbury has to be given up and Katherine wearily moves back to London. The Chancery Lane flat is replaced with a pleasanter apartment in Barons Court, which is larger and cheaper, but further from the centre. Ida lends them her mother's furniture, which saves her the costs of storage. John, as the professional man of letters, has one of the rooms for his office, while Katherine has to write on the table in the living room. It is the first sign of inequality in the way their work is regarded. Katherine sees it as directly related to money. 'John would think me important if I brought him L.S.D. [pounds, shillings and pence]. He thinks he's far and away the first fiddle.'[52] John is now earning

£12 a week from critical articles and reviewing and is ambitious for the future. Literary journalism is not what he wants to do – he has an idea for a novel, if only he could get the time to write it. He is jealous of what he sees as Katherine's freedom; she is jealous that his 'work' is taken more seriously than hers, and envies his steady output – she is still unable to write anything that satisfies her. There is tension and Ida senses that things are 'not all they should be'. Katherine sometimes goes to Ida's rented room 'in order to have some time to herself'. There she can 'work or dream, remote and safe from everyone'.[53]

In the summer D. H. Lawrence and Frieda make their promised visit to London. Katherine and John are familiar with Lawrence's published work, but the physical realities are a surprise – Lawrence is a cross between 'a plumber's mate' and an Old Testament prophet.[54] He talks as bluntly as the Derbyshire miner's son he still is. Frieda is a plump, blonde, green-eyed German Frau, who dresses extravagantly in frills and lace, has unlimited vitality and an aristocratic carelessness of what people think about her. She laughs when Lawrence tells them how she had thrown a perfectly good (and expensive) pair of shoes into the river because the heel came off one of them, shouting, 'Things are there for me and not I for them.'[55] That kind of disregard for possessions offends Lawrence's working class sensibilities, yet everyone can see that he is proud of her status as a daughter of Baron von Richthofen.

A spontaneous friendship immediately develops between the four of them. Frieda loves Katherine 'like a younger sister';[56] a more reserved Katherine admires Frieda's unconventionality. Between Lawrence and John there is a deeper, more complicated attraction, beyond a shared passion for literature. John loves and admires the older man with what he sees as a 'pure' affection. Lawrence turns John into a fictional hero who, though heterosexual, is able to experience an erotic 'manly love' that is superior to the merely sexual relations between man and woman. There are dangerous cross-currents between the two couples. Lawrence and Katherine are the dominant personalities, both gifted, both attracted and repelled by each other; John is fascinated by Frieda's expansive sensuality; Frieda, a natural giver, is enchanted by the 'I am really only a little boy, be good to me' look in John's eyes.[57]

The Murrys are invited to visit the Lawrences at Broadstairs in Kent and, though at first too short of money to afford the train fare, they eventually make the trip with their mutual friend Gordon Campbell, spending a golden afternoon drinking wine on the beach and swimming naked in the sea. During the afternoon, John and Katherine discuss their predicament. Lawrence has no sympathy with the Murrys' depression at the failure of the *Blue Review* and *Rhythm*. What they need, he insists is 'a thorough rest'. They have been working themselves threadbare, 'all for nothing'. He tries to persuade them to come to Italy, where he has rented a small house near Lerici. The prospect is appealing. Under Lawrence's influence, they can both believe that 'once across the Channel, inspiration will run free, thought be profound, and words come back to the speechless'.[58] Lawrence gives John a copy of his newly published novel, *Sons and Lovers*, which they read on the train and which only increases John's determination to write his own novel.

Money is a continual problem. Although they still have Katherine's income to live on, as well as John's earnings from journalism, their joint income is not enough to repay what is owed. John's creditors, offered 7 shillings in the pound, refuse to accept a composition. Katherine's allowance remains safe because it can't be 'attached' to pay the debt without the Beauchamps and Mr Kay becoming involved and Katherine's father would never have sanctioned such an action. And legally, as Gordon Campbell advises them, the debt is John's responsibility as editor of the magazine. John still finds the idea of bankruptcy repugnant and eventually persuades the printer to accept payment in quarterly instalments. Martin Secker agrees to waive the £30 owed to him if John will write a book on Dostoevsky. Katherine suggests that, now they are no longer tied by the monthly editions of *Rhythm*, they should go to Paris, out of reach of the bailiffs, where they can live more cheaply and write. Paris might also be better for her health. In London she has developed eczema, followed by an attack of flu 'and then – familiar ailment – a touch of congestion'. Katherine sees herself as a normally healthy twenty-four-year-old and never seeks medical advice about the lung trouble that 'clings so fond' through the winter.[59] It is her heart she worries about – it has raced and pounded irregularly since she was a child and she is convinced that it will kill her.

In the middle of December they do a dramatic 'flit' across the Channel to Paris, taking Ida's mother's furniture, though it costs them £25 to have it packed and transported, which they pay for by selling the piano. Ida has decided to go out to Rhodesia to look after her father and it makes sense for 'Katie' to have the furniture rather than pay to keep it in storage. It is not a particularly good time to go – Katherine's sister Vera is about to arrive in London to give birth to her second child and Katherine had been looking forward to seeing her again and spending time with the little nephew she has never seen.

Finding an affordable apartment in Paris is much more difficult than Katherine had expected and they are stuck in two tiny rooms on the top floor of a cheap hotel. She writes to her sister Chaddie, now married to a professional soldier out in India, thanking her for the gift of a rug for the anticipated flat: 'We are both wretched without a home & without our own particular creature comforts'.[60] But by Christmas they have signed the lease for 31 Rue de Tournon in the Sixth Arrondissement and just before new year Thomas Cook's deliver the furniture. The flowers are bought, the kettle is boiling on the gas stove and Katherine gives a sigh of relief. Her love of Paris is obvious to everyone. Friends 'remember her gaiety, the way she would flounce into a restaurant and sweep her wide black hat from her bobbed head and hang it among the men's hats on the rack'.[61] The actress in her enjoys the ripple of interest that her entrance causes, particularly among the men. Paris, Katherine observes, is vibrantly 'human' and has a grace and nobility that sets it apart from other cities.[62] But it is an odd time to be in the French capital. Although there is no sense of threat in the city, the possibility of war is being discussed in the cafés and some artists are already preparing to leave.

The social life is very much to Katherine's taste and she has plenty of time to get to know John's friends. Despite a ten-year age difference, she and Anne Estelle Rice find they have much in common – both female creative artists, both from the colonies (Anne is American) and both living unconventional lives. Anne's six-year affair with J. D. Fergusson is in trouble because, to Anne's great distress, he has met a young English dancer, Margaret Morris. Anne is being ardently pursued by O. Raymond Drey, a journalist and art critic whom Katherine finds 'a silly fellow'. The relationship between the two women is free of the complications that mark some of Katherine's other female friendships – there is the mutual respect of fellow artists and a developing, sisterly affection. They have been conducting a dialogue on art, music and literature through the pages of Rhythm, but now they have a chance to get to know each other intimately. Anne likes Katherine's New Zealand stories and encourages her to go back to her childhood for material. Katherine's story, 'Ole Underwood', is dedicated to Anne.

Katherine also finds herself spending a lot of time in the company of Francis Carco, ostensibly to improve her French. Though he had been one of John's first contacts in Paris, John now feels that he is being used by Carco to get work in England and does not trust him. Carco, whose real name is François Carcopino, has already established himself as a poet and novelist in France. His first novel, *Instincts*, had been published in 1911 and he's in the process of finishing *Jésus-la-Caille*. He lives in Montmartre and his lifestyle, among prostitutes and artists, is as Bohemian as any of the characters in his stories. Katherine is fascinated by him. He generates excitement, is 'rich and careless'[63] and seems to be all the things that John is not – strong-willed, self-sufficient, motivated. Carco notes that he and Katherine share a 'natural taste' for 'absurd and dangerous existences . . . a kind of plaintive romanticism where the exotic mingles with the marvellous, not without a touch of humour, of disillusion'.[64] There is a noticeable physical attraction between Katherine and Carco, which, for the moment, she can ignore.

There is another man in the picture too. Frederick Goodyear has arrived in Paris, having thrown up his job in London in order to work on a novel, and it is apparent to everyone, even John, that he is in love with Katherine, though she regards him only as a friend. Goodyear is a kind man, intelligent and full of integrity. She jokes that he is the very model of a 'Pa-man', like her father. Katherine rarely falls for conventional men.

In January, beginning to settle into her new life, Katherine writes a long ambitious story called 'Something Childish but Very Natural', which takes its essence from her time at Carlton Hill with the Trowells. It is about innocence and longing – a teenage romance told from the boy's point of view and full of mistaken assumptions and dreams that are never going to be fulfilled. There's a cottage that seems like the Garden of Eden, but the snake in the apple tree is sex. The story's title is that of a Coleridge poem. Katherine is reading the Romantic poets and the diary of Dorothy Wordsworth, but her sense of humour is never far from the surface and she can't resist sending the Wordsworths up, though she no longer has an outlet for witty parodies and has to write them for her own amusement.

William (P.G.) Is very well
And gravely blithe – you know his way

Talking with woodruff or harebell
And idling all the summer day
As he can well afford to do.
P.G. for that again. For who
Is more Divinely Entitled to . . .

My dear, you hardly would believe
That William could so sigh and grieve
over a simple childish tale
How 'Mary Trod Upon the Snail'
Or 'Little Ernie Lost his Pail'
And then perhaps a good half mile
He walks to get an appetite
For supper which we take at night
In the substantial country style . . .
And so on ad.lib.What a Pa-man![65]

To John's surprise, though he had fallen in love with the city as a student, he now finds himself unable to work in Paris. His novel is going badly and he does not have the reference materials for the book on Dostoevsky. Above all he misses the contact with other literary men. 'I need an audience. Here I haven't the half dozen intelligent people that I have in England who believe that there's something in me and listen to what I have to say. I lose a valuable stimulus . . . My real place is in England . . . In Paris I should always be a stranger in a strange city.'[66] John feels his social ineptitude more in France: he can't even strike up a relationship with the man who sells him cigarettes. He is also earning much less than he could in London. He has arranged to review for The Times, but there is not enough of this work. They could live, very simply, on Katherine's income, but – whatever he had previously said to Goodyear – John now maintains that he hates the thought and that in any case it would not pay the Rhythm debts. The quarterly payment is due at the beginning of January, but there is not enough money to make it. John is told that bankruptcy proceedings are being taken against him in London and that unless he goes there in person and explains the position, things may turn out badly.

At the end of January he goes back to England, to stay with Gordon Campbell and appear before the official receiver. Despite his dread, he is well treated and it is accepted that the debt is not morally his. Nevertheless he is declared bankrupt, though without fault, and no attachment of his earnings is made. He is now free of the debt, but must live with the restrictions of bankruptcy and its stigma. While he is in England, reconnecting with his friends, the *Westminster Gazette* offers him the position of art critic at £5 a week. It is a kind of ultimatum – if he goes back to Paris, his job will not be kept open. John knows exactly what he wants to do, but does not know how Katherine will react.

Although Katherine finds Paris much more stimulating than London, she is sympathetic to John's predicament and resigned to reality. 'If we cannot live over here on £10 a month (and we can't) there's an end of this place for the present.' She advises him to take the Westminster job for the time being 'and feel the security of a regular £5 a week'.[67] Inwardly Katherine is desperately unhappy at the prospect of yet another upheaval. She has already moved six times in less than a year. 'It is as though God opened his hand and let you dance on it a little and then shut it up tight – so tight that you could not even cry.'[68] Worse still, there is no money to ship their belongings back to England. She writes to Ida, asking for help, but Ida is herself in dire financial straits, having just paid for her passage to Rhodesia. All she can raise is a £5 note, which she tears in half and sends in two separate envelopes because she does not trust the French post. The two halves arrive on different days, rendering Katherine incredulous. The money is enough for their train fares, but not for the furniture, most of which is Ida's, left to her by her mother. John and Carco wander round the hotels and bordellos of the poorer quarters of Paris trying to find someone to buy it. Eventually, the owner of a brothel offers £4 – a fraction of what it is worth. No thought is given to Ida's feelings.

On 24 February, Katherine writes to Ida, heading her letter 'last moments'. All their personal belongings are packed and she is waiting for the men to come and take away the furniture. Katherine's guitar has gone and John has even sold the bedding. The flat already has an air of abandonment, 'grimy and draughty and smelling of dust, tea leaves and senna leaves and match ends in the sink – cigaret ash on the floor'. Even the ticking of the clock seems desperate. Katherine is tired of 'this disgusting atmosphere & of eating hardboiled eggs out of my hand and drinking milk out of a bottle . . . What we shall do until the train goes I can't think.' Leaving the apartment is like a little death – 'to change habitations is to die to them'. She writes an obituary in her notebook: 'To KMM & JMM of a flat 31 Rue de Tournon – stillborn –'. When Katherine arrives back in London she discovers that the 'femme de menage' who had been so 'gushing and grateful' has stolen her fur coat.[69]

Like a nomad, Katherine now camps out in a borrowed flat at Beaufort Mansions in Chelsea. The rent is being paid by Gordon Campbell. Katherine's optimism about the future is almost eroded. Ida's departure for Rhodesia is only a couple of weeks away. Katherine writes about Ida in her notebook, using the old euphemism 'toothache' to describe the emotional pain she is feeling. 'Have I ruined her happy life – am I to blame? When I see her pale and so tired that she shuffles her feet as she walks when she comes to me – drenched after tears – when I see the buttons hanging off her coats & her skirt torn – why do I call myself to account for all this, & feel that I am responsible for her. She gave me the gift of her self.' Katherine blames herself for taking Ida too much for granted, for using her and giving far too little in return. 'Sometimes I excuse myself. "We were too much of an age. I was experimenting & being hurt when she leaned upon me. I couldn't have stopped the sacrifice if I'd wanted to –" but its all prevarication.'[70]

Katherine has begun to have nightmares again and is overcome with a terrible sense of foreboding. She dreams she is walking down a road in New Zealand, on the edge of a deep ravine, with her little sister Jeanne. They are both terrified, but Katherine has to hide her fear to comfort her sister. There is the noise of horses and chariots rushing towards them and they have nowhere to go except the road. At the last moment, though, nothing passes but a sinister black horse with a black rider, 'as tall as a house . . . gliding past them like a ship through dark water'. In the dream Katherine shouts and screams and struggles to wake up, until at last she surfaces on the bed, sweating with terror. The feeling persists even in daylight. 'Today the world is cracking. I'm waiting for Jack & Ida. I have been sewing as Mother used to with one's heart pushing in the needle. Horrible! But is there really something far more horrible than ever could resolve itself into reality and is it that something which terrifies me so?'[71] Something has begun to trouble Katherine – something she can't talk about to anyone. Katherine confesses in her notebook that she is 'frightened in private'.[72] Ida comes round to say goodbye, already late for the boat-train, and at the last moment finds herself unable to say the words. She takes her violin and runs out into the rain without looking back.

13

Rananim

'They were neither of them quite enough in love to imagine that £350 a year would supply them with all the comforts of life.' Jane Austen's Elinor and Edward. My god! Say I.

KATHERINE MANSFIELD, 31 RUE DE TOURNON, PARIS, 19 FEBRUARY 1914

'Why haven't I got a real "home" – a real life'? Katherine has been watching children playing in the park with their Chinese nurse. 'Why haven't I got a Chinese nurse with green trousers and two babies who rush at me and clasp my knees – I'm not a girl – I'm a woman. I want things. Shall I ever have them?'[1] Katherine continues to be homeless. At £2 a week the borrowed flat in Chelsea is too expensive and they can't keep taking money from Gordon Campbell indefinitely. She and John move into 10s. rented rooms that are unbearably squalid. They have only two tables, two chairs and a double mattress on the floor. When Lawrence and Frieda come to visit, Katherine breaks down and confesses her feelings of horror at the shared toilet, the rubbish on the stairs, the smell of urine and rotting vegetables. John listens tight-lipped and when the Lawrences leave there is a terrible row that goes on until one in the morning. Katherine has hurt his pride – why did she have to complain so publicly? It's part of his guilt that he can't provide for her. They move again, into a beautiful flat with large windows and a view over a garden, but Katherine discovers, only after they have signed the lease, that it's infested with cockroaches. She pays for fumigation, but it doesn't work. As soon as the light is turned out the kitchen floor is heaving with brown bodies, and in the bedroom the bugs crawl onto the mattress as they sleep.

Shortly after they move in, John develops pleurisy and a week later Katherine suddenly 'collapses into a chair, white and unable to speak', her heart galloping so much that she can't move. John thinks she is having a heart attack and rushes out into the street to summon a doctor. On the way he meets the Campbells, who go to sit with Katherine until medical help arrives. She is distraught and appears to be in the grip of some kind of panic, gasping, 'The death jacket! The death jacket!' The doctor administers brandy – the standard treatment for hysteria – and leaves. When she becomes calmer, Katherine explains to Beatrice that she is wearing a silk jacket that had belonged to W. L. George's wife, who has recently died – possibly wearing the jacket. When Katherine's heart had begun to gallop, she had believed that she too was going to die.[2]

Just after her panic attack, Katherine is seriously ill with pleurisy again. The doctor who treats both her and John is horrified by their living conditions and refuses to charge them. Katherine's recovery is delayed by the fact that her congested lungs are constantly inhaling the fumes of the paraffin and sulphur they are using to deter the cockroaches. Katherine feels permanently unclean and longs to go back to Paris. London has too many associations for her now. She goes to a concert with Beatrice Campbell, but the violinist's hair grows in just the way that Garnet's had and memories of the Trowells plunge her into melancholy. 'I ought to be able to write about them wonderfully.'[3] But she can't. The past is constantly with her. Early crocuses in Battersea Park remind her of autumn in Bavaria. She keeps dreaming about New Zealand. On her mother's birthday she wakes at 2 a.m. and sits on the windowseat thinking about her. 'I would love to see her again & the little frown between her brows and to hear her voice. But I don't think I will.'[4] The memory of the past is always there between Katherine and the ideal relationship she longs for with John. 'Ah, how I long to talk about It, sometimes – not for a moment but until I am tired out and I have got rid of the burden of memory.'[5] John is not a good listener and Katherine is 'dreadfully wretched' when he appears bored or far away. But even if he did listen, Katherine doesn't feel able to take the risk. In any relationship, she writes, there is always just one secret that can never be told. She still doesn't trust John enough to tell him everything.

Katherine is sleeping badly and unable to write. 'I have decided to tear up everything that I've written and start again.' Every time she tries to develop an idea, it dissolves under her pen. The beautiful becomes 'pretty pretty', and the satire becomes mockery. 'If I could write with my old fluency for one day the spell would be broken.'[6] It doesn't help that John is working steadily on his first novel, aptly titled *Still Life*. The plot is autobiographical and the characters taken from the people around him – 'Anne' is Katherine, Carco is the cynical Frenchman 'Dupont', there is a Scottish painter based on J. D. Fergusson called 'Ramsay', and John himself is 'Temple'. The character of 'Dennis Beauchamp', who falls in love with the heroine, Anne, and gives up his job to follow her and her husband to Paris, is based on Frederick Goodyear. John says, in discussions with Lawrence, that he wants to write a novel like Stendhal, but the result is cluttered and dull and the dialogue is stilted. When he shows the first draft to Katherine she is as tactful as she can be without hurting his feelings, though it is the kind of pretentious manuscript she used to enjoy sending up in the *New Age*, infected with 'a kind of melodramatic intellectual sentimentality'. In her journal she writes, '"I'm afraid you are too psychological, Mr Temple." Then I went off and bought the bacon.' Nevertheless, John has managed to finish a novel. Katherine has nothing. 'The book to be written is still unwritten.'[7] There has been a complete reversal of their fortunes. When they first met, Katherine was the literary star, John merely the editor of a little magazine. Now John is the man of letters of whom great things are expected, and Katherine a writer of amusing sketches who has not published anything serious for years. When an acquaintance in the Café Royal asks her, 'Do you still write?', it's as though he had scorched her soul with his words.[8]

Naomi Royde Smith, the influential literary editor of the *Westminster Gazette*, invites Katherine to a 'women only' event at her house, but the evening is not a success. The guests talk about 'ghosts and childbeds' and gossip among themselves. Katherine hates this kind of female society, which increases her sense of isolation. 'Pretty room & pretty people, pretty coffee & cigarettes out of a silver tankard. A sort of sham Meredith atmosphere lurking ... I was wretched. I have nothing to say to "charming" women. I feel like a cat among tigers.'[9] She is deeply depressed and feels 'terribly lonely ... Nothing helps or could help me except a person who could guess. And Jack is far too absorbed in his own affairs poor dear to ever do so.'[10] Her love for him can no longer disguise the reality of their relationship. Not only has their partnership failed to benefit her writing, she knows now that John will never be able to return her feelings, or fill her needs, as she would like. His childhood has made him emotionally illiterate, unable to empathise with the feelings of others or to give a great deal. It is something he realises himself. 'I have noticed in myself a never-ending desire to be a child. I want to lose myself in another, to resign my personality, to be protected . . . and almost physically to be mothered like a child.'[11] Katherine does not want John to be her child: 'Ah, I wish I had a lover to nurse me – love me – hold me – comfort me – to stop me thinking.'[12] John is completely unaware that when they make love she sometimes fakes orgasm. She writes in her notebook: 'J x K W L [*John and Katherine Were Lovers*] last night and I deceived'.[13]

The Lawrences are back in England, D. H. looking thin and ill. He has begun to notice blood on the handkerchiefs he coughs into, though he tells no one about his condition, denying it even to himself. Frieda's divorce has come through and, on 13 July 1914, she and Lawrence are finally free to marry at the Kensington register office. Katherine, John, and Gordon Campbell are asked to be their witnesses. On the way to the office, Lawrence, having forgotten to buy a ring, suddenly stops the taxi outside a jeweller's shop and dashes in. Frieda takes off the wedding ring that had been given to her by her first husband, Ernest Weekley, and hands it to Katherine. To John's surprise, Katherine places it on her wedding finger. This symbol of a broken marriage seems to have a significance for Katherine that John can't understand.

The Lawrences are only a few years older than the Murrys but from the beginning Lawrence assumes the role of mentor, directing not only John's personal life but also his writing. He tells John that he is 'the best critic in England',[14] and has definite opinions on the quality of his fiction. 'Stick to criticism', he advises him in one letter, 'don't try a novel.'[15] Lawrence's relationship with Katherine is ambivalent. If they had both been men, they might have been friends, but Lawrence believes that friendship between a man and a woman is impossible. There is always the sexual element. He regards her as a talented writer of satirical sketches rather than a serious writer of fiction, and thinks that John might do better if free from his emotional dependency on her. Katherine is growing more wary of Lawrence's influence on John. Katherine thinks Lawrence is a combination of three people; 'the black devil', whom she hates, 'the preacher' she does not believe in, and 'the artist' she loves and values. Her understanding of his personality comes from a recognition of shared traits – 'I am more like L than anybody. We are unthinkably alike'.[16]

Frieda and Katherine are also developing reservations about each other. Katherine had originally been sympathetic to Frieda and had carried messages and presents to the three children she is forbidden to see, but now she is beginning to find her fits of weeping tiresome. She thinks Frieda is shallow and trivial and an unsuitable wife for Lawrence. Frieda thinks Katherine presents a false impression of herself and is a bit of a self-dramatist.

There are intense conversations about literature. Lawrence defends the explicit nature of his work – he has a mission to 'rescue the fallen angel of sex'.[17] The two couples talk incessantly about sex, and Freud's theories. The Campbells join them for Thursday evening discussions on the new science of the unconscious. Psychoanalysts have pounced on Lawrence's novel *Sons and Lovers* and begun to dissect it. Lawrence is a great deal more knowledgeable about Freud than any of the others, though Katherine is quick to begin reading the texts and to highlight points on which she disagrees. There are lively debates. Lawrence is utterly frank about his own sexual intercourse with Frieda and asks the others probing questions about theirs. John can't see anything wrong with his physical relationship with Katherine, which he regards as completely normal. He is 'quite incurious' about his 'complexes and repressions' and quite happy to remain so.[18] Katherine will not be drawn on the subject. She is happy to discuss Lawrence and Frieda's sex life, but not her own, and has little patience with the notion that sex is all important and underlies everything. Beatrice Campbell also thinks Lawrence's habit of asking intimate questions is impertinent and is very much in sympathy with Katherine's feelings, expressed in a letter to Beatrice: 'I shall never see sex in trees, sex in running brooks, sex in stones and sex in everything. The number of things that are really phallic, from fountain pens onwards!'[19]

On 4 August 1914 the long-expected war with Germany is declared. Katherine's German pension stories are suddenly topical, but she turns down an offer to republish them. It isn't just that she has matured in the way she writes, or that one of the stories is a juvenile copy of Chekhov

– there is something repugnant in the idea of cashing in on the jingoism of war. She writes to Laura Bright, the woman she regards as her god-mother in Wellington, about the changes in London – all the stations full of trains crowded with troops on their way to France, singing and cheering. At night the street lamps and electric signs are darkened, 'and huge searchlights sweep the sky and the hundreds of London newspaper boys run up and down the streets like little black crows shouting: "War! Latest news of the War! War!!"' Katherine repeats the moral obligation that is the justification for war, that 'England is fighting for something beyond mere worldly gain and power'. By the middle of September, the realities of the war are beginning to appear in the city, 'Last week I saw some of the poor Belgian refugees arriving in London, one an old lady of 93, who had walked miles to escape the soldiers. Her house had been burned down and all her possessions were gone, but she stepped out of the train in a black dress and white muslin cap, calm, her hands folded as though she were walking into a friend's house.'[20]

John is at first caught up in the exuberance of other young men towards the conflict. Francis Carco enlists, as do William Orton, Frederick Goodyear, Rupert Brooke and Henri Gaudier. John and a friend from Oxford join a territorial battalion on the spur of the moment, but as soon as he gets home to Katherine John regrets what he has done. He goes to see the doctor who has recently treated them both and is given a certificate of exemption for military service that says 'Pleurisy. Query TB'. It is the first time the word has been mentioned. John insists that the certificate has been written out of sympathy, but it is a chilling diagnosis. It must have occurred to both of them that it might be true, but they don't discuss the possibility that either of them might have the disease and Katherine doesn't ask any questions in her notebook.

Spared the prospect of military service, John and Katherine begin house hunting. Their recent experience has convinced them that cheap properties in London are uninhabitable, so they decide to look in the country again. It is a dreary business on a limited budget, but Katherine keeps her sense of humour in a poem called 'The Deaf House Agent'.

> . . . He said 'I can't hear'
> He muttered 'Don't shout
> I can hear very well!'
> He mumbled: 'I can't catch a word

I can't follow.'
Then Jack with a voice like a Protestant bell
Roared 'Particulars. Farmhouse. At 10 quid a year!'
'I dunno wot place you are talking about.'
Said the deaf old man.
Said Jack 'What the HELL'
But the deaf old man took a pin from his desk, picked a piece of wool the size of a
hen's egg from his ear, had a good look at it, decided in its favour & replaced it in the
aforementioned organ.[21]

At the end of August they take a holiday in a borrowed cottage in Cornwall, then go to stay in Sussex with the Lawrences. There is also a holiday on Gordon Campbell's estate in Ireland. Katherine insists that Ida should come too but, since she is not invited, Ida has to stay in a bed and breakfast in the neighbouring village. Every afternoon Katherine clambers along the rocks to meet and talk to Ida, though at first she is not introduced to the others. Beatrice Campbell thinks this is very strange behaviour and offers to provide a room for Ida, which Katherine refuses, explaining that Ida would feel awkward, as the uninvited guest, because she is so very shy. Ida later says that Katherine had wanted her to go to Ireland 'because she did not want me to be lonely during the holiday, but also because she was glad to have an excuse to leave the party and come to me where she could be "alone" and herself'.[22] The Campbells compromise by inviting Ida to tea on several afternoons, but Beatrice notices that Katherine does not look pleased.

At the end of September, the Murrys are back in London again looking for somewhere to live. There is very little that they can afford. In the end they take Rose Tree Cottage, at The Lee, near Great Missenden in Buckinghamshire, not far from the house where the Lawrences are living in Chesham. The roof leaks, it has an outside toilet at the bottom of the garden, cold water only and no electricity, but it is cheap and Katherine also has a servant to do the heavy work – scrubbing floors, cleaning and laying the fires, cleaning the oil lamps and doing the heavy washing once a week in the outside wash-house. The other advantage is that the cottage is in the country, away from the London smogs. Katherine is still enthusiastic about living in the country. When she stands in the garden watching a huge harvest moon low in the sky, she is, for the moment, 'deeply happy'. 'Out of the front door a field of big turnips and beyond a spiky wood with red bands of light behind it. Out of the back door an old tree with just a leaf or two remaining & a moon perched in the branches . . . I feel my own self awake and stretching.' Katherine hopes to write some of the stories that are taking shape in her mind, which is 'full of embroidery' just waiting to be stitched together. She knows that she is now 'streets ahead' of writers like Gorky in the matter of technique, but what is the point of that if she can't put the words on the page?[23]

For John there is the prospect of a closer dialogue with D. H. Lawrence. John is hoping to finish his novel and Lawrence is working on *The Rainbow*. Lawrence has an idea: he wants to gather 'about twenty souls and sail away from this world of war and squalor and found a little colony where there shall be no money but a sort of communism as far as necessaries of life go, and some real decency'.[24] It is to be called Rananim. The name comes from a walking holiday Lawrence had taken in the Lake District after his wedding the previous summer. He and his three companions had crouched behind a dry stone wall while 'the rain flew by in streams, and the wind came rushing through the chinks in the wall' and the Russian, Koteliansky, had intoned psalms in Hebrew: 'Ranani Sadekim Bandanoi'. Lawrence's Rananim is to be on an island, somewhere warm. Katherine and John are to be among the desired recruits, but Katherine is less than enthusiastic. Although the idea sounds interesting, 'some part of me is blind to it'.[25] She suspects that it's a dream rather than a reality – an island of the mind rather than the earth. Katherine notices that when she suggests particular islands that might be suitable or starts producing maps and ferry timetables, partly to tease Lawrence, the atmosphere changes.

Relations between the newly married Lawrences are not good. Frieda is suffering grief at the loss of her three children. Under the terms of her divorce settlement, as an adulteress she is forbidden to have any contact with them. Lawrence refers to it as 'this drawn sword of the children between us',[26] and is callously impatient with her because he feels Frieda's son and two daughters are more important than he is. 'When a woman has got children, she thinks the whole world wags only for them and her.'[27] One wet afternoon in November there is a terrible quarrel and Frieda arrives at Rose Tree Cottage saying that she has left Lawrence for good. While John comforts Frieda in front of the fire Katherine is given the task of tramping across the fields with a message for her husband. When she arrives at the house, Lawrence is not alone. The Russian friend he had met on holiday is staying with him. Though Katherine scarcely notices the man, the visitor is very impressed when the door opens and a young woman 'with her skirt tucked up in wellington boots, soaking wet' tells Lawrence that Frieda is never coming back. 'Tell her I never want to see her again',[28] Lawrence shouts and Katherine disappears back into the rain. It is her first meeting with Samuel Solomonovich Koteliansky. Later, when the Lawrences' quarrel has been made up, the Murrys are invited to the cottage and Katherine and Kot, as everyone calls him, embark on one of the most important friendships of their lives.

Koteliansky is a Ukrainian Jew who had come to England to escape persecution, after graduating from Kiev University, and then remained to work as a translator at the Russian Law Bureau. He tells Katherine that he had organised 'a revolution against the Czarist regime' in Kiev, but only he had had the courage to turn up, so he had started walking and did not stop until he reached London. Kot is an eccentric character, plump, with a liking for English tweeds, a strong, east European face with wild black hair that stands straight up on his head, and eyes that have a 'desperate and yet resigned intensity' behind the gold pince nez perched on his nose.[29] To John and Lawrence he looks like 'Sennacherib on a bas-relief; a Semitic King of Kings, a monumental Rabbi, a Moses . . .'[30] His temperament is romantic but easily plunged into what his friends call 'Hebraic gloom'. He says that he had taught himself to howl like a dog in order to keep wolves at bay in the Ukrainian wilderness and it has become his party trick. Katherine, already fascinated by all things Russian, begins an impassioned debate on Russian literature. Kot falls in love with her non-conformist spirit: from the first he worships and idealises her. 'I love her too well to judge her fairly and tolerantly,' he writes to a friend.[31] He calls her Kissienka and begins to send her presents – a Russian skirt, cigarettes, books and chocolates. Katherine writes back: 'Koteliansky, it is my turn to give presents, I am beginning to feel. Tell me – what shall I give? One thing if you want it is yours to keep.' She signs it, 'your loving friend'.[32] What Kot writes in reply dismays and saddens her. 'No dear Koteliansky, my letter did not "mean that".' She realises that she must cool the situation. 'Let us meet perhaps, quite by chance, tomorrow or months or years hence. That is best.'[33]

Kot has perhaps sensed that all is not well with the Murrys' relationship. Katherine is disillusioned about her life with John and beginning to think of Carco and Paris. When she reads Carco's letters to John she feels as if 'I want to laugh and run into the road'. 'His confidence and his warm sensational life' contrast strongly with John's emotional timidity. Carco also understands the 'enamelled spoon' – Katherine's name for those unnecessary luxuries, or gestures, that put the gloss on ordinary experience.[34] She writes to Carco and gets a reply that makes her hopeful. 'I have not told Jack that I have heard again from Francis . . . he told me that all the while we had been in Paris he had loved me.' Carco talks of taking her in his arms to fill the emptiness of his life, I want only you, he writes in French, you are and you will be 'toute de ma vie'.[35] Katherine is sure that these are love letters. She tentatively shows one to John, who only laughs. Katherine takes one to Beatrice Campbell for her advice, but Beatrice is not sure either. She feels that Katherine is 'trying to convince herself as well as me'.[36] Carco invites Katherine to France if she can get permission to travel. He is serving as a postman-corporal with a cavalry regiment stationed near the front at Gray, south-east of Paris, not far from Dijon. The temptation to go into the war zone is irresistible for Katherine, looking for new experiences that might kick-start her writing, and Carco's invitation comes at a time of maximum disillusionment with John. In her journal she writes, without explanation, 'I do not trust Jack . . .'[37]

She has just overheard a conversation with Gordon Campbell that has made her reassess their relationship. The two men were discussing their sex lives, under the influence of Lawrence and Freud, and John had commented that he found it odd that Katherine 'always submitted' to him now, no longer taking the initiative as she once had. Worried by what John says, Katherine ignores the taboo they have imposed on each other's notebooks and opens John's, finding a passage where he speculates whether Katherine is anything 'more than a gratification' or a comfort to him. Sex for John is nothing to do with erotic pleasure, but a childlike comfort mechanism; he needs to be cuddled and comforted. He has also been discussing it with Lawrence, who is of the opinion that 'When a man takes a woman, he is merely repeating a known reaction upon himself . . . And this is like self-abuse or masturbation.'[38] In his notebook John wonders whether it is fair to 'use' Katherine in this way. John's sexual impulses are deeply suppressed. He confesses that as an adolescent he had managed, by rigid discipline of thought and action, to overcome the urge to masturbate. Sex for John is always underlain by guilt.

The diary entry makes Katherine wretched, but it also brings her to a decision. 'That decides me – frees me. I'll play this game no longer. I created the situation – very well – I'll do the other thing with moderate care,

& before it is too late . . . For him I am hardly anything except a gratification & a comfort . . .' She admits that she is passive, submitting to John's
desire for sex, because she has not been feeling 'the strength' of her own
desires towards him. Now she does feel desire, but for Carco, not John.
'Jack – Jack – we are not going to stay together. I know that as well as you
do. Don't be afraid of hurting me. What we have got each to kill is my
you & your me. That's all. Let's do it nicely & go to the funeral in the same
carriage & hold hands hard over the new grave & smile & wish each other
luck. I can. And so can you.'[39]

Although restless and fed up, not only with John, but with being
stranded in a country cottage far from the main action of the war, publicly
Katherine keeps up the front of being in love with John and committed to a permanent relationship. He suspects nothing. Katherine finds this
strange, writing in her notebook: 'As long as one's mood isn't directed
towards or against him he's quite unconscious and unsuspicious'.[40] At
Christmas her father sends her 5 guineas, which she spends on the servant's wages. Writing extravagant letters of thanks back to Wellington, she
tells her family that she has been reading the French 'yellow book', which
The Times is publishing – an account of the development of the war from
France's point of view – and hopes to go to France in January to 'write
some human documents for a newspaper syndicate'. She's fascinated by
the farcical and tragic reports that are already emerging from the front,
telling her father the story of a young man who 'got his foot wounded
while being reproved by his colonel for not having shaved that morning.
"Why haven't you shaved sir," he roared. "When a shell whistled over
our heads and exploded in the market square and caught me in the foot."
(Whereupon I heard you saying – "I suppose that was about the closest
shave you ever had in your life".)'[41] Her letters to her father are full of
black humour, but those to her mother are very different. Annie has been
'severely ill' and Katherine writes her a letter full of yearning and love,
ending it 'I am always your own devoted child'.[42]

By Christmas it is clear that the conflict is not going to be over soon. On
Christmas Eve Katherine and John go to the Lawrences, where John gets
drunk and insults D. H. by implying that he can't create living characters
in his novels – they are merely mouthpieces for his ideas. Katherine, 'with
a long, ridiculous face,' sings some music hall songs which Frieda loves,
but Lawrence condemns as 'too fast'.[43] Then on Christmas Day they are all
invited to Gilbert and Mary Cannan's converted windmill for a big party.

The Cannans are an odd couple. Gilbert is excitable, ebullient and rather edgy – already in the early stages of megalomania. His wife Mary is an actress who had formerly been in a platonic marriage with the author J. M. Barrie. She still has the sheepdog that inspired Nana in *Peter Pan*. The Cannans have a large social circle, most of whom are present at the party, including the young Slade artist Mark Gertler and Koteliansky. Everyone drinks too much, but particularly Katherine, who has made up her mind to leave John and is feeling reckless and miserable. John has written a play for entertainment that closely resembles the actual situation; an unhappy wife (Katherine), is attracted to a romantic foreigner (Koteliansky), who commits suicide when he's rejected. The wife then falls in love with someone else (Gertler), but comes to her senses and goes back to her loyal husband. Either through drink or intention, however, no one but Kot sticks to the script. Mark Gertler and Katherine, both gifted mimics, act out the love scene rather too realistically for the nerves of the audience. John cries out, 'You're supposed to come back to me' and Katherine says, 'But I don't want to.' Lawrence storms onto the improvised stage, shouting at John for 'exposing himself'. Gertler is found crying outside because he has kissed another man's woman and betrayed the painter Dora Carrington, whom he really loves. Frieda tells him that Katherine is a bad woman and she should not have tempted him. The Murrys lie in bed together afterwards, bewildered, exhausted and hung over.

The Murrys see in 1915 at Rose Tree Cottage and Katherine thinks of absent friends. 'The ghost of Lesley [Ida] ran through my heart her hair flying – very pale, with dark startled eyes. And I thought of Francis.' Her secret life is like an underground river 'that only I can hear'.[44] It seems more real to her than her present life with John. Her new year wishes are to do with publication and money – John wants to cut down on journalism in order to write his novel. If he will not earn money then Katherine must. She writes a list of ideas for stories in her notebook. One of them is 'Farkey Anderson', a convicted murderer from the New Zealand backblocks who had fascinated her as a child. The other, just beginning to germinate in her mind, is 'The Aloe'. She is also working on 'Brave Love', a story about choice. The central argument is whether the characters are able to make choices about their lives or whether they are driven by natural forces outside their power to control. Mitka, the innocent east European sailor who is the object of a married woman's predatory fascination, says that 'If you really look yourself in the open face and say what you want to do you can do it', while Valerie believes that 'You get caught in a wheel and round and round you go'.[45] She is more pragmatic than Mitka, and though she goes to her lover, she is so revolted by his dirty, sordid room that she flies back to her wealthy husband of convenience, called – as in 'Maata' – Mr Evershed. The narrative is a window into Katherine's state of mind, though she confesses that she has no idea what the story is about, or whether it is any good. She has set herself a deadline to finish it before the end of the month.[46] There is a strong conviction that she is working against the clock: 'I am getting old . . . At times the fear of death is dreadful.'[47]

January is punctuated by letters to and from Carco. Her moods swing according to the postman's visits. Even when she goes up to London to have her hair done and collect her allowance from Mr Kay, her mind is in France. 'He has haunted me all day . . . I longed for him so, & yet I dare not push my thoughts as far as they will go . . . had my photograph taken for him.' She analyses her feelings constantly. 'I love Jack, but all the while my heart says Too late Too late. Adieu. I know I shall go.' John is insecure and unusually demanding sexually – in her room after supper, they make love on a fur rug in front of the fire, as well as in bed. Katherine almost 'cuts through his line of male' by talking about Carco.[48] Katherine, despite her desire for another man, continues to submit to John, but now 'it is always under a sort of protest which I call an adieu submission. It always may be the last time.'[49] Katherine sometimes feels 'bitterly ashamed', but at the same time feels that she betrays Carco when she makes love with John. 'My anxious heart is eating up my body, eating up my nerves, eating up my brain . . . Yes love like this is a malady, a fever, a storm. It is almost like hate, one is so hot with it & never, never calm – never for an instant.'[50] Sometimes she tries to talk to John about it, but he does not seem to realise the significance of what she is saying or, if he does, does not allow her to say it. Eventually Katherine makes him understand that, though she still loves him, she can no longer live with him. She wants to be free: she is going to take a room on her own in London. She has worked out that she can furnish it with the bare essentials for less than £5. They lie in bed discussing it. 'We gave each other our freedom in a strange way.'[51]

In London, Katherine stays with Anne Estelle Rice, newly married to O. Raymond Drey after a painful breach with J. D. Fergusson, who is now deeply involved with Margaret Morris. Anne tells Katherine that she had agreed to marry Drey, even though she did not love him, because she felt that their friendship would provide a good basis for marriage. They have all left Paris because of the war. Katherine would like to join them in London, but she can't find any suitable lodgings. Her search for a new outlet for her work is also abortive. A meeting with the agent Curtis Brown comes to nothing. Her work is not yet commercial enough, and she doesn't have a novel to offer him. Back in Great Missenden, Katherine is ill with a bout of flu that leaves a lingering cough and acute depression. The Lawrences have moved to Sussex into another borrowed cottage, and John has quarrelled with Gordon Campbell, so there is not even the distraction of convivial evenings with friends. 'Life is like sawdust and sand.' Finally, on 6 February, she gets the letter she has been waiting for: Carco 'wants me to come immediately'. John thinks she is going to Paris for 'ten days self-restoration' – Katherine does not tell him her real intentions.[52]

In London Katherine, collects another month's allowance, and bumps into her brother Chummie at the bank. He has come to England on impulse with the intention of joining the British army to fight in France and is about to go to Oxford's Balliol College on an officers' training course. Katherine is delighted to see him. They have lunch and she gives him the impression that everything is perfect in her relationship – 'she is more in love with him than ever'[53] – and Chummie thinks that John is accompanying her to France, where they are both going to write about the war. He 'lends' her £10 for the trip. By 16 February Katherine is in Paris. Carco is letting her use his flat on the Quai aux Fleurs until she can get the permission she needs to enter the war zone. In stilted French she writes to him at the front: 'Darling, I intend in a few days to leave Paris and come to you at Besancon. I am in the little café downstairs on the quai. The weather is delightful and I feel close to you. I kiss you.'[54] They are still addressing each other as 'vous', rather than the intimate 'tu'. And even now, Katherine has second thoughts and sits crying in the park.

Beatrice Hastings is also in Paris. Her relationship with Orage had broken up a year earlier and she has settled in Paris to write a column for the New Age under the pseudonym of 'Alice Morning'. She tells Katherine that she had left Orage because he wasn't passionate enough. Almost since her arrival Beatrice has been the mistress of the artist Amedeo Modigliani and their violent, drunken brawls have become legendary. Independent again, separated from their male partners, Katherine and Beatrice make up their quarrel – now it is Orage 'who wants kicking'. Beatrice is well on the way to becoming an alcoholic, breezily declaring that when she is in company, 'I go to the cupboard and nip cognacs till it's all over for me, my dear.'[55] Her flat in Montparnasse has recently been set on fire – possibly by Modi after an argument – and in her smoke-blackened rooms she and Katherine get drunk together and offer mutual commiserations. Beatrice, no friend of John Murry's, encourages Katherine to go to Carco. Together they concoct a story about a terminally ill aunt in the little town of Gray, who must be visited. Carco sends her a letter signed Marguerite Bombard, clearly designed to be used to secure a pass. Katherine hopes that this and her persuasive charm with men will get her through. She has her hair fashionably cropped at a Paris salon and borrows a military-style overcoat.

Three days later she writes in her notebook 'Came to Gray', followed by the words 'One night' heavily underlined. Katherine has had a long, cold and difficult journey on French trains overloaded with troops. The gruesome scale of the European conflict is hard to take in. 'Are all these laughing voices really going to the war?' The platforms on the opposite side are crowded with wounded men waiting to be taken away from the front, 'waving their bandages' at the train as it passes through. There are terrible sights – carriages packed with German prisoners, a man who looks as though he has '2 red carnations over his ears, one man as though his hand was covered in black sealing wax'. Katherine's train passes cemeteries that seem to be 'full of corn-flowers and poppies and daisies'. Then she realises that, in the dim February light, 'they are not flowers at all. They are bunches of ribbons tied onto the soldiers' graves.'[56]

But it is only at the end of the journey that Katherine is really frightened. In the large room in the Gray station all travel passes have to be inspected by two colonels, God I and God II, 'like colonels in comic opera', wearing black 'tea-cosy' hats with golden tassels and smoking Egyptian cigarettes. Katherine presents her passport, her ticket and the letter from her sick aunt. One colonel, his eyes 'like 2 little grey stones', says 'it won't do at all', but the other intervenes and allows her through to where Carco is waiting outside the station, 'terribly pale'. They have to pretend that they are not together, since he is on duty, so she follows him down the street to the tollhouse on the bridge where Carco has hired a rather decrepit horse-drawn cab and they tear away, 'both doors flapping and banging'. It is 'like an elopement'. He takes her to a lodging house where he has taken a square, white room, 'furnished with a bed, a wax apple and an immense flowery clock'. Here at last they can be natural with each other. 'Laughing & trembling we pressed against each other a long long kiss.' They have dinner in a restaurant nearby and then back to bed. When Katherine asks if it's cold, Carco replies, 'No, not at all cold. Viens ma bebe, don't be frightened. The waves are quite small.' With his 'laughing face & his pretty hair, one hand with a bangle over the sheets', he looks like a girl. After so much longing, 'the act of love [is] somehow quite incidental'.[57]

The following morning she writes in her notebook while waiting for her breakfast. Carco's belt and sword are beside her on the chair and she worries that her little escapade may result in him being put in a military prison. There is another, more disturbing, feeling, 'very profound, that he does not love me at all'. With great courage, Katherine admits that she has made a mistake about her own emotions too – 'I don't really love him now I know him'. She realises that she has romanticised her feelings for Carco: it has been sex, not love. She describes their night together, how she watched him 'quite naked making up the fire with a tiny brass poker' and how she has just seen him get dressed 'brushing his hair with my ivory hair brush, & then just for a moment I saw him passing the window – & then he was gone. That is a terrible moment for a woman.' She drafts letters to Frieda Lawrence, and one to 'Jaggle dearest' that describes her meeting with Carco, but not their night together.[58]

In Katherine's absence John, who has just been rejected by the two people closest to him, is beginning to develop flu symptoms. He is lonely and apprehensive in the empty cottage, a 'going-in-to-examination feeling'. Devastated when Gordon Campbell failed to arrive for a weekend visit, John writes him a long, tortured letter, which he is too afraid to post. In it he confesses what Gordon has meant to him. 'I can't throw myself into an abyss . . . It will be an effort for me to keep away from you. I don't delude myself about that. I'm not one of the strong men. Besides my love for you grew quietly and in secret. I never knew that it was there until it snapped, at about 8 o'clock of the night of last Saturday week, if you would know. It took two years. I can't get rid of it in a day.' His feelings for Gordon are something of a shock to him. They are not sexual: John's love demonstrates a much deeper need than the purely physical. Because of his looks, he is often the object of homosexual desire, but the men he loves are always older father-figures. 'It seems to me now that I asked too much of you – but then, I wonder, can I ask too much – I of you . . . There was some stupid mistake

– some romantic imagination of my own, it may have been. Whatever it was, it was a good thing, for now I can see that I must have loved you as one man seldom loves another. I look back at myself and find that I would have given you anything . . .'[59]

John, utterly miserable, decides to go to the Lawrences at Pullborough in Sussex, where they have borrowed a converted long barn. He arrives with raging influenza and Lawrence bundles him straight into bed, 'looking after me as though I were a child'. Friends believe that this episode of 'fond care'[60] appears in chapter IX of *Aaron's Rod*, where Lawrence describes how Rawdon Lilly massages Aaron's body with camphorated oil 'as mothers do their babies when their bowels don't work', in order to cure him of influenza and constipation: 'Every speck of the man's lower body – the abdomen, the buttocks, the thighs and knees, down to his feet . . .' When John is well enough to get up, he pours out his anxieties about Katherine and Gordon, and Lawrence castigates him for his 'inertia' in letting Katherine go. He has got too close to Gordon and 'left Katherine out in the cold'. He accuses John of lacking a sensual nature. John, now better informed about Freudian psychology, acknowledges that there is some truth in it. 'I feel certain that that part of me was terribly stunted by my father. It worries me profoundly that it may have been irreparable.'[61] Lawrence is also fictionalising John and Katherine's relationship, beginning the process of turning Katherine into Gudrun and John into Gerald for *Women in Love*. John is conscious of nothing but their intellectual debate and Lawrence's confidence in his powers. In Lawrence's opinion, John is the 'coming man' in literature – his natural successor. In his friend's company John can believe that he will achieve great things.

Katherine returns to Paris and Beatrice. She stays in Carco's flat again and writes up her experience in her notebook. It becomes 'An Indiscreet Journey', a verbatim account of her visit to Gray. Katherine is unaware that Carco is doing something similar. His notes and memories of their brief affair, and her letters to him, are to be woven into his next novel, *Les Innocents*, with Katherine as the heroine, Winnie, a journalist avid for copy, who murders a character based on Beatrice Hastings. In Paris Katherine also writes a story called 'The Little Governess', which she sends to Kot, asking him to submit it to a magazine for her. It is a completely new departure, based on someone she has seen on the train, it concerns an innocent young woman, betrayed into indiscretion and 'ruined'. Katherine realises that she has written something special. 'I've written such different things just lately – much much better – and I'm going on writing them.' Katherine has found a new direction in her writing but, in her personal life, nothing is solved. A little voice at the back of her mind is saying, 'This has happened to you before and will happen again and again and again.'[62]

A defeated Katherine returns to London on 28 February. John goes straight from the Lawrences to Victoria and records the meeting in his diary before he goes to bed. 'Tig and I were constrained and miserable when we met, above all when I heard she had been to Gray to see C[arc]o.'[63] Katherine's letters from France to 'Dearest Jaggle' have been lively and affectionate, but face to face she is cold and distant. 'She was strange, her hair was cut short and she was aggressively defensive. I was not to imagine that she had returned to me. She had come simply because there was nowhere else to go . . . I felt sorry and longed to comfort her. But I did not know how.'[64]

Back in Great Missenden, in the cold, damp cottage, Katherine immediately goes down with a severe attack of rheumatism in her hip, and is so crippled by it that she can't even turn over in bed without crying out in pain. To make matters worse, she is sleeping on the camp bed, since she and John are still not reconciled. She longs for 'hot weather and happy love and broad bands of sunlight and cafes – all the things that make life to me'.[65] Kot sends Katherine chocolates and whisky and cigarettes. She has, he tells her, 'a special disease', not necessarily physical,[66] and Katherine agrees. Lying in agony, listening to the rain dripping through the cottage roof, she is forced to allow John to look after her and his stubborn concern and refusal to be alienated begin to bridge the gap between them. It is 'a strange, nightmarish time' and John writes a poem in his notebook to express his feelings, which contains a telling line 'the hemlock eyes of love's grim loyalty'.

> . . . what is love on this late afternoon –
> a warm word whispered to a mocking moon,
> a child gazing forlornly through the window-pane
> at the relentless rain.[67]

Katherine begins to talk about why she had decided to leave him – the overheard conversations, the entry in his notebook, the obsession with Gordon Campbell, her feeling that she means nothing more to him than physical comfort and a housekeeper. John tries to explain, but gets lost in the very intellectualisation of his own emotions of which Katherine accuses him. But eventually they achieve a truce. The miserable cottage will be given up. Katherine agrees to help John look for rooms in London, but is adamant about 'the necessity of Paris' for herself: it is the only place where she feels certain she can write – 'my work is snapping at my heels but I have to down rover it'.[68] Her return to England has been the *reculer pour mieux sauter*' of the French proverb – a retreat in order to make a better move forward. By 18 March John is renting two rooms in Notting Hill and Katherine is back in Carco's apartment on the Quai aux Fleurs overlooking the Seine, savouring her solitude.

> It is morning. I lie in the empty bed, the huge bed – big as a field and as cold and unsheltered. Through the shutters the sunlight comes up from the river and flows over the ceiling in trembling waves. From outside comes the noise of a hammer tapping and down below in the house a door opens and shuts. But all about me I hear the solitude spinning her web. Is this my room. Are these my clothes folded over the arm chair. Under the pillow – sign and seal of a lonely woman – ticks my watch.[69]

She writes to Kot, trying to explain why she had fled back across the Channel, referring to her 'special disease' – 'the illness that I had in England and longed to be cured of – is quite gone for ever – I believe it was my "heart" after all, you know, but not the kind of heart that Dr Eder punches.'[70]

Beatrice has moved from her fire-damaged flat to another in Montmartre, which Katherine envies. Two of the rooms open onto a garden and there is a big porcelain stove to heat the flat. Beatrice has a grey carpet, 'lamps in bowls with Chinese shades – a piano – 2 divans 2 armchairs – books – flowers a bright fire'. It is just what Katherine would like for herself and could afford in Paris if she were not committed to living with John. Beatrice and Modigliani are estranged after he hurled her out of the window into the garden at one of her parties. She is having brief liaisons with Picasso, and two other artists. Saddened to see what Beatrice has become through drink and drugs, Katherine fears for her future. 'I love her, but take an intense cold interest in noting the signs.'[71] Katherine, remembering how they had got drunk together, very publicly, on her last visit to Paris, stays sober on soda water.

The atmosphere of Paris is good for Katherine, even though most of her former friends have left. She can open the windows of Carco's flat and lean out over the quay, watching the boats on the water, inhaling the beach smell of wet sand from the barges at the wharf, listening to the voices in the street below, just as she had done in Cheyne Walk. It feels magical, but the war has come very close to Paris and one evening Katherine experiences her first Zeppelin raid: 'there was a sharp quick sound of running and then the trumpets from all sides flaring "garde a vous" . . . in a minute every light went out except one point on the bridges. The night was bright with stars . . . & then there came a loud noise like doo-da-doo-da repeated hundreds of times . . . I saw the rush of heads & bodies turning upwards as the Ultimate Fish . . . passed by, flying high with fins of silky grey.'[72] Her relationship with John seems more attractive from a distance. In letters she can talk herself back into love with him. From Paris she writes: 'my dearest dear – I love you utterly – utterly beyond words – & I will not be sad. I will not take our staying in our own rooms for a little as anything serious.'[73]

There are cold wet days with 'a wind like a carving knife'. Katherine complains that her 'lung hates this weather'. She takes refuge in a little café with her hands around a hot cup of black coffee, watching flakes of snow drift past the window, and suddenly experiences 'that strange silence that falls upon your heart . . . a kind of dying before the new breath is blown into you'; the creative pause that presages a story. 'I felt that – & I knew that I should write here.' A few days later she records that she has fallen 'into the open arms' of her first novel. 'Juliet' and 'Maata' were only juvenile attempts compared with this. Memories of Wellington come tumbling out onto the pages of her notebook.

Our house in Tinakori Road stood far back from the road. It was a big white painted square house with a slender pillared verandah and balcony running all the way round. In the front from the verandah edge the garden sloped away in terraces & flights of concrete steps – down – until you reached the stone wall covered with nasturtiums . . . and a huge pair of old iron gates that were never used and clashed and clamoured when Bogey [Leslie] & I tried to swing on them.[74]

'The Aloe', 'commencé March 12th', is an account of childhood in New Zealand – but also something else. The flowering of the aloe is a symbol of creativity itself – of 'otherness' – taken from one of Walter Pater's essays: 'A certain strangeness, something of the blossoming of the Aloe, is indeed an element in all true works of art'.[75] As she leans over a bridge on the Seine watching the boats float past underneath her, Katherine glimpses a possible form for the novel: 'I suddenly discovered that one of those boats was exactly what I want my novel to be – Not big, almost "grotesque" in shape I mean perhaps heavy – with people rather dark and seen strangely as they move in the sharp light and shadow and I want bright shivering lights in it and the sound of water.'[76]

John's letters to Katherine are all about his difficulties in furnishing the two rooms in Notting Hill and how much it is costing him. Gone are the days of ordering furniture from Maples: John spends all his spare time searching the second-hand shops of Kensington and Bayswater for bargains. He is tetchy and irritable. 'It just seems like a great waste, of energy & money & time . . . I'm dog-tired.'[77] Some kitchen cupboards are bought for shillings in a junk shop and enamelled blue with Ripolin paint. But he can't find anyone to sew loose covers and curtains: 'I hunted all over Baker St. for a couple of hours in vain. Please give me some directions that will do.' It is complete role reversal. At one point his letters fail to arrive and Katherine fears the worst, until she realises that he is addressing them to Mrs G. Bowden and the concierge knows her only as Katherine Mansfield. In reality John is missing Katherine dreadfully. 'I do want you . . . not just desire, or wickedness, or excitement, but the being of two good souls and bodies together & making suddenly a better thing. Now I would have you back.' And he is certain that, if she comes, Katherine will 'stick to him'.[78]

For Katherine, life on her own in Paris is becoming much less fun. Her relationship with Beatrice does not long survive close proximity. At one of 'Biggy B's' parties, Katherine provokes a quarrel by flirting and dancing with a very attractive 'blonde and passionate' young woman who has already taken Beatrice's fancy. Then Katherine refuses to stay the night as she had promised because Beatrice has drunk almost a whole bottle of brandy and become 'impossible'. There is an ugly row – Beatrice flares up 'in a fury' and calls Katherine a '*femme publique*' (prostitute) in front of the other guests. Katherine tells Beatrice that she has finished with her forever and storms out of the flat. Now that she is completely alone, Katherine's mind turns towards John and his patient affection. Her letters become increasingly passionate. 'Life is too short for our love even though we stayed together every moment of all the years . . . Tig is a tired girl and she is crying. I want you – I want you. Without you life is nothing. Your woman. Tig.'[79] On impulse, she returns to London, but realises her mistake immediately, confiding to Kot: 'I cannot write my book living in these two rooms. It is impossible – and if I do not write this book I shall die.' She tells him that she is returning to Paris and Carco's flat to work on 'The Aloe'. 'Jack wonderfully understands.'[80]

In Paris, once more writing the novel, Katherine has to confront her dilemma, which seems insoluble: John can't work out of London, she can't work in it – at least in the circumstances they can afford to live in. Her left hip is hurting badly and she longs for comfort with John, imagining an ideal life together. 'To write all the morning and then to get lunch over quickly and to write again in the afternoon & have supper and one cigarette together and then to be alone again until bed-time.' Instead, she feels 'all this life drying up, like milk, in an old breast'. She wants 'friends and people and a house'.[81] The war accentuates the feeling that there is no time to lose. She dreams of Rupert Brooke, who has been killed on 23 April, and then comes the news that Henri Gaudier, too, is dead. In England there is talk of conscription and Katherine is afraid for John and dreams of him in khaki. The Lawrences are making John anxious by telling him that Katherine has gone to Carco again. Katherine is very angry and calls Frieda 'a great fat sod'. She assures John that Carco 'doesn't exist for me',[82] and allows him to think that the Frenchman is not even aware that she is borrowing his flat. But Katherine is writing to Carco all the time, and the letters are very like those she is writing to John.

Food is scarce in Paris. Katherine is tired of eating in cheap cafés and being given strange meals made from anonymous animals – 'hairs feathers and all – and a hoof thrown in for make weight'.[83] John forwards a letter from Ida in Rhodesia, who writes of 'grass and birds and little animals and herself and our friendship'. At the end of her letter she asks, 'Katie, dearie – what is Eternity?' All their quarrels and irritations are forgotten and Katherine recalls only their 'careless, very intimate joy' and wishes that Ida were there with her. 'There is something quite absolute in Lesley . . . She's about the nearest thing to 'eternal' that I could ever imagine. I wish she were not so far away.'[84] Katherine tries to analyse what John can't give her that is fulfilled by Ida. Is it because Ida needs her more? 'Somehow I do always have to be "needed" to be happy.' And John does not like doing many of the things that Katherine enjoys, such as going out for a walk on a Saturday afternoon or visiting the music hall. 'I do wish my tall, pale friend were here to walk with and sit with. You're not the slightest use – for it doesn't come natural for you to desire to do such things with me.'[85]

Katherine's anxieties for John, and her fear of being alone at night, force her to consider going back to London. Now it is John who is not sure, frightened that Katherine will 'make a scene'. She vacillates, sending tortured letters to London – she is torn between needing to write and needing John. She is suffering mentally and physically. The mysterious rheumatic pains in her hip are 'simply dreadful'. One of the most common secondary sites for tuberculosis is the hip socket: the bacilli in her lungs and abdomen have now migrated to her bones. Katherine feels 'ill and alone'. When she hears the concierge describing her as 'la maitresse de Francis Carco' and learns that he is coming back shortly, Katherine writes to John telling him that she is returning on the following Wednesday. 'If I stay they will 1. cut the gas off 2. arrest me as a spy 3. F C is coming to Paris at the end of next week.'[86] Her work is finished in rough draft and she hopes that, even if she can't write, she can edit the manuscript in London. Though she keeps John guessing until the very last moment, she arrives on the boat-train at Victoria on 19 May.

One of Katherine's stipulations for living in London with John is that they find somewhere more congenial to rent. Her father has just raised her allowance by another £30 a year, so it is possible to look at more expensive properties. To entertain Kot, Katherine turns house hunting into a play for three characters.

Scene II

K[atherine]: Tell me frankly. Does it not feel damp to you?

Visionary Caretaker: I've had fires in all the rooms, m'm. Beautiful fires they were too. It seemed a pity to let them out; they burned that lovely.

M. Or N.[the initials used to denote the bride and groom in the traditional Anglican marriage service]: It feels as dry as bone to me, I must say.

The Visionary Caretaker beams at M. or N. Her little girl puts her head round the door. In her pinafore she has rather a wet kitten.

Visionary C.: And if you should like a chicken at any time, m'm, or a few greens I'm sure my husband and I would be only too pleased etc etc etc etc etc . . .'[87]

The 'gracious stucco house' at 5 Acacia Road, in St John's Wood – the same neighbourhood as the Trowells – is only five minutes' walk from where Beatrice and Gordon are now living. The landlord is properly theatrical and the house has been inhabited by an opera singer. The 'aspecks', as Katherine calls them, are excellent.[88] It has a garden with a pear tree and a small sunny attic where Katherine can write. John is friends again with Gordon and there are lively Sunday evening discussions at their house with Kot and Gertler and the Lawrences. Needing a female friend and having little in common with Frieda, Katherine forms a closer friendship with Beatrice Campbell, who is a talented painter and a former student of the Slade. At first Beatrice finds Katherine 'a difficult person to know . . . very complex, very self-critical and self-centred, struggling to make herself different, to get rid of what she considered the bad parts of herself . . . terribly private and sometimes hard to approach'.[89] But Katherine gradually lets down her guard in Beatrice's company, admiring her gaiety and quiet poise, and sharing her love of conversation – particularly gossip – about the people they know. Beatrice, in full flight from her conventional upbringing, loves Katherine's gift for mimicry, her 'delicate taste in bawdy'. There is one memorable party where Katherine has too much to drink, and does impressions of Hollywood actresses, one of which involves sliding down an ironing board assisted by D. H. Lawrence.[90]

For the Lawrences, too, are living in Hampstead. Lawrence and John agree to collaborate on a new periodical, to be called *Signature*. It is to be a mouthpiece for Lawrence's philosophy, with John as his disciple. Lawrence is to be 'the preacher, John will be the revealer of the individual soul with respect to the big questions', Bertrand Russell 'will do something serious' and Gilbert Cannan will 'flounder pre-historically'.[91] In the end neither of the latter can be persuaded to join them and the magazine features only Lawrence, John and Katherine. The two men are the intellectual heavyweights; Katherine is to provide the light relief by contributing some of her satirical sketches. Her contributions – in the middle between Lawrence and John's metaphysical sermons – are printed under a new pseudonym, 'Matilda Berry', and they are neither sketches nor satirical pieces. Her first contribution is called 'Autumns', a trilogy of memories from New Zealand narrated in the first person: her father's forbidden apple tree at the house in Tinakori Road, followed by two sections that later become 'The Wind Blows'. In the next issues, Katherine's story 'The Little Governess', which has never found a home, is published in two parts.

Signature is sold by subscription only, and the difficult job of advertising it and persuading people to subscribe is given to Kot, as the 'business manager'. He and John have also embarked on a project to translate Russian texts. They are working on a collection of Chekhov stories, extracts from Dostoevsky's journal and the work of Aleksandr Kuprin. In addition, John has a contract as a book reviewer as well as his post as an art critic. His future looks promising and he is hopeful that publication of his novel, *Still Life*, will establish him as a serious writer in the mind of the public and his friends. But no one wants to publish it and John's hopes of a lucrative career as a novelist begin to fade. Eventually his old friend Michael Sadler agrees to bring it out, though the amount of money he offers is less than the bill John has just paid for having it typed. He abandons fiction for the moment and begins to work hard on the Dostoevsky book, discussing it furiously with Lawrence and Kot.

Everyone's lives are overshadowed by the war. As conscription seems to be a real possibility, John is becoming more and more ardently pacifist. Almost every week, a friend, an acquaintance, a member of the family, is killed or wounded at the front. The Lawrences are in a very difficult position because of Frieda's German origins and all their friends are under suspicion as a result. Walking across Hampstead Heath one evening, the Murrys and Lawrences look up at a Zeppelin buzzing uncertainly among the clouds. Frieda realises that inside it 'are perhaps men I have danced with when I was a girl, boys I have played with'.[92] Lawrence puts their feelings into words: 'if we are all going to be rushed down to extinction . . . one must speak for life and growth, amid all this mass of destruction and disintegration'.[93]

Katherine's brother Chummie, based in Aldershot, visits when he can get leave, and in these heightened emotional times she makes him the focus of her nostalgia for home and family. They sit in the garden on summer evenings playing games of 'Do you remember?', vividly reconstructing their shared childhood. The story she writes for *Signature* describes how she and Chummie used to run down to the quay to watch the ships depart and fantasise about their own departures. 'We are on board, leaning over the rail arm in arm . . . brother and sister . . . goodbye, little island, goodbye.'[94] The siblings are very alike. Chummie has a strong feminine side to his personality and the same delicate sensibility as his sister. On a route march with his platoon he had been distressed to see how the soldiers trampled swathes of 'primroses, violets and snowdrops' into the mud. Contemporaries regard him as slightly effeminate, and Katherine is very protective. Chummie is being trained as an instructor, rather than being sent to the front, so Katherine feels there is a good chance that he will survive the war. He spends a week on holiday in London with her, before being mobilised. On 25 August, after seeing him off on the train to Aldershot, she writes him a note in Selfridge's reading room: 'It meant a tremendous lot, seeing you and being with you again and I was so frightfully proud of you . . .' It ends: 'This is not a letter. It is only my arms round you for a quick minute.'[95] Chummie takes it with him when he leaves for France on 22 September.

On 11 October 1915, four days after the publication of the first issue of Signature, Katherine receives a telegram informing her that her brother is dead. She is too shocked to cry and at first can't believe that it is true. She rushes off to see Mr Kay at the bank, who assures her that it is. A grenade that Chummie was demonstrating blew up in his hand, killing both him and his sergeant. A few days later a letter arrives from someone who was there telling Katherine that he had bled to death, saying, over and over, 'God forgive me for all I have done'. His last words had been 'Lift my head, I can't breathe'. In a note to Kot, Katherine quotes the letter, adding her own name: 'Lift my head, Katie, I can't breathe'.[96] She wants passionately to feel that her brother's last thoughts had been of her.

At first Katherine tells no one else. Her grief is too deep and too private. The Murrys are invited to the Campbells for dinner and Katherine insists on going, asking John and Kot not to tell anyone what has happened. She is gay and lively as usual and nobody suspects that anything is wrong. Three days later, when Beatrice Campbell casually enquires about her brother, Katherine looks at her 'in a queer, wild, hard way', then tells her grimly that he has been 'Blown to bits!'[97] The details are not for discussion. In her journal Katherine goes over and over the last time Chummie visited Acacia Road, their last conversation. They had been walking up and down the garden in the dusk, 'the Michaelmas daisies bright as feathers', listening to the familiar sound of pears dropping from the tree into the grass, as at Tinakori Road.

'Did you hear that Katie? Can you find it?' . . . He puts his arms round her. They pace up and down. A thin round moon shines over the pear tree & the ivy walls of the garden glitter like metal. The air smells chill, heavy, very cold.

We shall go back there one day, when it's all over.
We'll go back together.
And find everything.
Everything.

Leslie had been absolutely confident that he would survive the war. 'I feel it's as certain as this pear . . . I couldn't not come back, you know that feeling. Its awfully mysterious.'

And then he had put his arms around her and kissed her.

'Goodbye darling.
Ah, why do you say that!
Darling goodbye – good bye –'[98]

Lawrence's novel, *The Rainbow*, published at the end of September, is attracting a hostile response. One reviewer calls it 'a monstrous wilderness of phallicism'; others regard it as vicious or obscene. As Katherine mourns her brother through another black October, police arrive at the publisher's offices to seize all remaining copies of the book. The publisher is charged with an obscene publication and the court orders the book to be burnt. Though the Murrys are outraged on Lawrence's behalf, Katherine and John do not like the novel at all. Katherine in particular hates the scene where the pregnant Anna dances naked in front of a mirror. She condemns the book as 'female', using the word in its pejorative sense, though she feels strongly that Lawrence does not truthfully convey the motivation or the psychology of his female characters. John is repelled by the 'warm, close, heavy promiscuity of flesh'.[99]

Lawrence has been taken up by Lady Ottoline Morrell, sister of the Duke of Portland, wife of Liberal MP Philip Morrell and a great collector of human curiosities from the diverse worlds of art and politics. For several months Lawrence has been trying to persuade her to invite the Murrys to one of her salons: 'Murry has a genuine side to his nature: so has Mrs Murry. Don't mistrust them. They are valuable, I know.'[100] As a result Katherine and

John are invited to one of Ottoline's London salons with the Lawrences and the Campbells. John is very impressed by Bloomsbury and aware of the value of contacts such as Bertrand Russell; Katherine is more sceptical. The grand setting brings out the worst in her and she spends the evening mentally pretending to be a prostitute who has wandered in from the street, trying to see everything through the eyes of a street walker. Beatrice Campbell is shocked by this side of Katherine – 'she could be so false and unreal that you shrank from her' – but on reflection concludes that it is 'a sort of armour, something to protect her intense hypersensitiveness'.[101]

Signature is given up and Lawrence makes up his mind to go to America, where *The Rainbow* is expected to be given a warmer reception. 'I am so sick in body and soul, that if I don't go away I shall die.'[102] Katherine feels exactly the same. Her return to England has not been a happy experience. The house in Acacia Road now has too many ghosts and she is desperate to escape. John unwillingly agrees to accompany her to the south of France, which is still untouched by the war. Katherine arranges for the house to be taken over by a Russian couple from the translation bureau, with Kot as a sub-tenant.

One of Lawrence's Bloomsbury acquaintances, the Honourable Dorothy Brett, decides to throw a farewell party for him on the night before he is supposed to leave for America. It is to be a small, select dinner at her studio with his closest friends. The atmosphere is gloomy. Lawrence, still agonising over *The Rainbow*, arrives looking 'pathetic, miserable, ill and obviously devoured by internal distresses'. Katherine and John, about to leave for France, are also in turmoil, though they hide it well. Brett, as she is known, is profoundly deaf and used to recording images to paint. She notes Katherine, whose 'dark eyes glance about like a birds, the pale face is a quiet mask, full of hidden laughter, wit and gaiety'. Then John 'rolls in with the gait of a sailor, his dark curly hair is getting a bit thin on top. He is nervous, shy, a small man. The eyes are large and hazel with a strange unseeing look.' Koteliansky is there and Gertler with his girlfriend Dora Carrington, 'dressed like an Augustus John girl'. They are all playing charades when Lytton Strachey arrives late with a crowd of gatecrashers carrying bottles. The party becomes wild. Lawrence is talking to one of the uninvited guests in Italian, Katherine is on the sofa 'clasped in some man's arms', Gertler and Carrington are quarrelling, Kot singing one of his mournful Hebrew dirges on the balcony, Brett is playing the pianola and people are dancing – everyone is drunk. John, propped up against the wall by his friends, has to be carried back to their flat.[103]

Things are not good between John and Katherine. Chummie's death has destroyed the delicate equilibrium of their relationship, which had been gradually re-established over the summer. Katherine's grief isolates her from John, who has no idea how to comfort her. She feels numb inside, as though something of herself had died with Chummie. 'Yes, though he is lying in the middle of a little wood in France and I am still walking upright ... I am just as much dead as he is.' Katherine can't bear John to touch her and confides to her journal: 'You know I can never be Jack's lover again'.[104]

14

Prelude

It is going to be a splendid summer . . .

I shall be correcting the proofs of my novel
(third in a trilogy − simultaneous publication
in four continents) . . .

And Poems? Yes, there will certainly be Poems.
They sing in my head, they tingle along my nerves.
It is all magnificently about to begin.

FLEUR ADOCK, 'FUTURE WORK'

Travelling in wartime is never simple − there are permits and passports and visas to be obtained and a scramble for oversubscribed train and boat tickets. Katherine and John leave England hurriedly on 15 November, cancelling dinner engagements at the last moment. Katherine writes from Marseilles to tell Kot that, in the rush, she has left behind several of her treasured possessions: the fur rug (on which she and John had once made love in front of the fire), which she wants Kot to have, and her brother's cap − returned to her by his commanding officer. France is already accentuating the differences between John and Katherine. She insists that Kot should not believe the conjugal 'we' John uses in his letters. What it implies about her own feelings and attitudes 'is not really true of me − never'.[1]

Marseilles is almost too vivid for Katherine to describe. The city is full of troops, 'French, African, Indian, English', and the narrow streets are choked with people, painted carriages, pack-mules and traders. Katherine notes sardonically that everybody cheats John on sight. 'Even before he bought anything they put up the price.'[2] The weather is bitterly cold and Marseilles is noisier than they had expected. They are staying in the Hotel Oasis on one of the busy main roads and the clattering of horses' hooves on the cobbles and the clanging of the trams keeps them both awake. In a fit of severe depression, Katherine writes a sorrowful letter about her brother to the Beauchamps in New Zealand. This upsets her father, who has been devastated by the loss of his only son, but her mother is pleased by this demonstration of feeling on Katherine's part and tells a friend that Leslie's death has brought 'poor old Kass right into the [family] fold again'.[3]

Marseilles is in the full bite of a vicious mistral; Katherine becomes chilled and develops a fever so severe that the lilies on the wallpaper come out and bow to her as she lies in bed. After they suffer a terrible bout of food poisoning, caught from eating mussels in a cheap café, the city loses its charm completely and they move on in search of a quiet place to work, spending two weeks in Cassis, between the mountains and the sea. The resort appeals to Katherine, but not to John, who is hankering for London, despite a stern note from Lawrence, sent care of Thomas Cook's – 'You are a miserable devil – always *lamentoso*. You feel sick at being ejected from your habitual surroundings – it is natural. But do look on the bright side!! . . . London is vile beyond words; a fog that hurts one's inside . . . Don't come back to London – be advised – it is so wretched.'[4]

The mistral is also blowing in Cassis, stirring up a fine dust that penetrates the gauze shutters on the windows, and the Murrys feel obliged to move on again. Bandol, further along the coast and less fashionable, seems promising and Katherine takes a room at the Hotel Beau Rivage. The rooms are spacious, with views over the sea, and there's a terrace shaded by palm trees with steps down to the promenade where boats are moored and the men play boules. The bay is sheltered from the wind and even though it is December the weather is warm – there are oranges on the trees and the jonquils are already in bloom. Katherine is enchanted. On her first day alone there she walks round the bay 'which is very beautiful & wild & like my NZ', coming home by 'little lanes & crooked ways bordered with olive trees – past the flower farms'.[5] She can feel the warm sun on her skin, smell the waxy scent of the jonquils and the 'wild spicy scent of the rosemary' growing among the rocks. Below the window of her room she can hear the fishermen shouting and whistling to each other as they bring in their boats and the waves thudding against the breakwater.

The sound of the sea, 'after such a long silence is almost unbearable'.[6]

Bandol would have been ideal if John had been able to stay with her. But on 8 December Katherine writes to tell Anne Estelle Rice that her 'little John Bull Murry' had gone back to London two days after they arrived. 'Perhaps that will tell you a little what kind of time we have had.'[7] Sitting on the rocks at Cassis, watching Katherine weep from grief and depression, John had suddenly burst 'into a fury of anger against her'. John feels that his place in her heart has been taken by Chummie, writing afterwards that Katherine's brother 'though dead was far more real and near to her than I was now; and that was anguish to me'.[8] But Katherine will not go back to England with John because she is convinced that she can't write there. France has given her back 'her power of detailed vision'. As she explains in a letter to Kot, it's the details that matter – they are 'the life in the life', recalled in vivid waking dreams. She explains what she means, describing a dinner they had all had together in the damp cottage at Great Missenden. 'The queer thing is that, dreaming like that I can't help living it all, down to the smallest details – down to the very dampness of the salt at supper that night and the way it came out on your plate, the exact shape of the salt spoon . . .'[9]

Left to herself at the hotel, Katherine plans solitary walks on the pine-clad hills above the town and along the coast to the little village of Sanary, but after a few days she has a return visit of the Marseilles fever, 'with all its symptoms – loss of appetite, shivering fits, dysentery' and a sore throat. 'What on earth can it be?' The following day she has a severe attack of rheumatism in her left hip, which prevents her from putting on her stockings, or walking more than a few steps. Katherine spends several days in bed, describing herself as 'a ragged creature'. The maid supplies her with hot water bottles and lime flower tea, massaging her limbs with '*alcool camphre*'. An English guest at the hotel – the head of Guy's dental hospital – sends her his remedy for sciatica, made up by a local pharmacist, which is far more effective. Katherine is overcome by the kindness of those around her and frustrated at her condition. 'I turned to the wall & cried bitterly . . . I think mostly from rage.' Much of her anger is because she has had no letter from John since he returned to England. 'You will write to me every day', she had begged when he left. 'Once a day really isn't too often & its my only dear signal that you are well.'[10] John, in England, is complaining to everyone that he has had 'a dreadful time' in France. He is overwhelmed by a backlog of work and the search for lodgings, and preoccupied by renewed social contact with his circle of friends. Frederick Goodyear, now a corporal meteorologist with the Royal Engineers, is on leave from France for five days. He and John do the rounds of the Campbells and the Lawrences, go out for dinner together and Goodyear spends the night on the floor in John's room, assuring him that he can sleep 'even on a dirty floor, with the greatest satisfaction'. He tells funny stories of life in France and seems full of humour, but in fact is close to a breakdown – 'sick of the war and desperately anxious to be a free man again'.[11] When Goodyear expresses sadness at the death of Katherine's brother, John urges him to write and gives him her address. The Lawrences are still in London, having had to cancel their booked passage to America because Lawrence is unable to get a visa, and the lawsuit over The Rainbow is still dragging on. Many who had taken Lawrence up after Sons and Lovers have now drifted away and his relationship with those who remain has intensified. John is one of the most faithful and Lawrence is rapidly taking the place in his affections previously occupied by Gordon Campbell.

But in spite of his busy life, John does manage to write Katherine frequent letters, increasingly concerned when he doesn't receive a reply. 'Either you are too ill to write, or you have been so terribly hurt that you don't want to write to me any more.'[12] The postal service between England and France is not good at the best of times and the war has disrupted communications even further. Katherine and John become locked into a cycle of action and reaction. By the time letters have arrived and been replied to the mood of the sender has swung in the opposite direction. John, in the middle of his hectic social life, is unable to picture Katherine lying alone in her room, with only his letters to wait for, fretting about her life and situation, grieving for the brother whose photograph sits on the mantelpiece, convinced that John has abandoned her. 'Oh Jack,' she scrawls across the bottom of her letter – 'I appeal even to your imagination as a novelist – do not leave me like this without news. It is so cruel – cruel . . .' In another letter she again attacks him for what she regards as his neglect of her. 'You have hurt me terribly. You were so SURE I would be lonely in this quiet room – but once away I suppose you "forgot".'[13]

Her emotions fluctuate. Since Katherine left England her monthly period, 'Tante Marthe', has been absent. Katherine has wild hopes which are crushed by the 'shock' of its eventual arrival. She thinks often of the child she had conceived with Garnet. In her dreams, and perhaps deep in her subconscious, the deaths of her baby and her 'baby' brother have become closely linked. She has a particularly vivid and disturbing dream that she describes to John, choosing her words carefully.

> I dreamed that I had a baby (Virtue always rewards me with this elfin child) and Grandmother was alive. I had been to sleep after it was born & when I woke it was night & I saw all the people in the house lying on their backs asleep too. And I was sure my baby was dead. For a long time I was too frightened to call anyone – but finally called to Grandmother & she came in and said nonsense, child he's getting on beautifully (as though 'he' were a cake in the oven.) She brought him in to reassure me – a charming little creature in a flannel gown with a tuft of hair. So I got up and kissed Grandmother who handed me the baby and I went downstairs & met you in the street.[14]

Katherine often dreams of her grandmother and her brother – so vividly that when she wakes she can still feel Chummie's hand in hers. She is beginning to come to terms with his death by immersing herself totally in her memories of him – what she calls 'entering into her loss'.[15] She writes obsessively to Chummie in her journal, long melodramatic passages of eulogy, and thinks of him constantly.

> To L.H.B.
> Last night for the first time since you were dead
> I walked with you, my brother, in a dream.
> We were at home again beside the stream
> Fringed with tall berry bushes, white and red.
> 'Don't touch them: they are poisonous,' I said
> But your hand hovered, and I saw a beam
> Of strange bright laughter flying round your head
> And as you stopped I saw the berries gleam
> 'Don't you remember? We called them Dead Man's Bread!'
> I woke and heard the wind moan and the roar
> Of the dark water tumbling on the shore.
> Where – where is the path of my dream for my eager feet
> By the remembered stream my brother stands
> Waiting for me with berries in his hands
> 'These are my body. Sister, take and eat.'[16]

As she rests in the absolute quiet of her room, 'so still you could hear a spider spin', words are beginning to write themselves in her mind. 'I am now so tied and bound so caged that I know I'll sing. I'm just on the point of writing something awfully good.'[17] But she is paralysed by inaction. 'To do things, even to write, absolutely for myself and by myself is awfully hard for me. God knows why when my desire is so strong?' The idea of writing for someone else, for her dead brother, begins to take hold. 'I see you opposite to me, I see your thoughtful seeing eyes. Yes, it is to you . . .'[18]

One of the most comforting letters that she receives is from Lawrence. 'Do not be sad,' he tells her. 'It is one life which is passing away from us, one "I" is dying; but there is another coming into being, which is the happy, creative you.' In Lawrence's opinion, she has had to die with her brother in order to be reborn into 'a clean life to begin from the start, new, and happy. Don't be afraid, don't doubt it, it is so.' He tells her that she has more courage than John: 'He runs away . . . he is not a man yet'. Lawrence confesses that he is not sure he can give John the relationship he wants. 'I am tired of this insistence on the personal element; personal truth, personal reality . . . I want relations which are not purely personal, based on purely personal qualities; but relations based upon some unanimous accord in truth or belief, and a harmony of purpose, rather than of personality. I am weary of personality.'[19] Lawrence has cancelled another reservation to travel to America and is now planning to stay with his sister in Derbyshire before going down to a borrowed cottage in Cornwall. He still hopes to get to Florida eventually and continues to think about Rananim. 'When you come back, I want you and Murry to live with us, or near us, in unanimity; not these separations. Let us all live together and create a new world . . . I want so much that we should create a life in common, a new spirit, a spirit of unanimity between a few of us who are desirous in spirit, that we should add our lives together, to make one tree, each of us free and producing in his separate fashion, but all of us together forming one spring, a unanimous blossoming . . . Let us make some plans for March.'[20] Katherine has no intention of living with the Lawrences, writing a negative letter to John on the subject, though she is more tactful in her reply to Lawrence.

In London, without Katherine. John is more miserable than he had imagined he could be. 'Fed up with the world', he has failed to find congenial lodgings and is still in a rented room; Christmas is approaching; Lawrence,

Kot and Campbell are all preoccupied with their own affairs and have little time to spend with him. A scheme to buy a private printing press to bring out their own work and sell it by subscription comes to nothing because the money can't be raised. There are estrangements and misunderstandings. John becomes anxious about his relationship with Katherine and begins to reassess the priorities in his life. When Lawrence will not show him one of Katherine's letters (a 'wild kind of letter' written in 'a fit of positive despair'),[21] John begins to wonder whether, by refusing to remain with her in France, he has lost her for good. 'Why did I leave you? I keep on asking myself the question, and I find no answer. I can remember nothing of what urged me back. It must have been strong and overwhelming – but it is all gone.'[22]

Katherine, slowly recovering in the warm Mediterranean sun, is free of rheumatism for the first time in a year. When she wakes in the morning and opens the shutters the sun is glittering on the sea, filling her with optimism. She is beginning to love this wild and beautiful stretch of coast. 'When the wind blows I go to the windiest possible place and I feel the cold come flying under my arms – When the sea is high I go down among the rocks where the spray reaches and I have games with the sea.'[23] She wanders through the streets and back lanes of Bandol, peering through gates at empty summer villas – some with 'a louer' ('to rent') on the gate – and mentally moving in. She imagines herself and John on the terrace, a glass of wine and cigarette in hand, looking out over the sea after a day of hard work together, in perfect accord. Even if John does not come, it may be cheaper to rent a villa than stay in the hotel. For 88 F she can get four rooms, with electric light, heating and a sheltered garden. She writes letters to John full of regret for his absence. 'When I go for my walks and scramble on the rocks there is no Bogey somewhere with a little worn Homer in his hand – that when I fly round a particularly lovely corner I do not see – coming to meet me . . . you, careless, whistling frightfully out of tune.' This image of John is 'too sweet and too painful to imagine even in play. I can never be completely happy without you and the nearer I feel to life and to being myself the greater is my longing to have you with me.'[24]

John is feeling something similar and over Christmas at Garsington Manor – invited there at last by Ottoline Morrell – he writes to Katherine telling her that, if she will not return to England, he is thinking of coming out to join her and work on his Dostoevsky book. Katherine sends him the telegram he had requested stating that she is ill and that he must come at once, so that he can get permission to travel to France under wartime regulations, but by the time it arrives he has changed his mind again. Katherine is bewildered by his indecision. She receives his 'happy' letters from Garsington, then his next telling her to forget he ever said 'find a villa'. 'I had a most terrible feeling that you did not want to leave England and that it were better for you not to come again . . . I want you to do what you please . . . I shall be glad when this is all settled.' But just as she sends him a telegram 'IMPLORE DON'T COME DON'T WANT UNDERSTAND PERFECTLY',[25] he makes up his mind. 'It seemed suddenly so childish – not childish, but criminal – to stay away from you a day longer.'[26] This sudden decision is the result of a push from Ottoline. During a long chat in her dressing room John pours out his feelings for Katherine and gives a nostalgic account of what he believes to be 'their transcendental union of soul and body'. Ottoline feels that John is 'lost and unhappy without her'. She gives him £5 and tells him to go to France at once: 'I knew he was longing for me to give him this advice, and in an hour or two I was waving him off at the gates'.[27]

Meanwhile, Katherine has found the Villa Pauline – a tiny two-up two-down furnished holiday home up one of the back lanes of Bandol, perched on the hillside above the shore facing out across another bay. The verandah has the sun all day and there's 'a little round table where we can sit & eat or work. A charming tiny kitchen with pots & pans & big coffee pot, you know. Electric light, water downstairs & upstairs too in the cabinet de toilette. A most refined "water closet" . . . The salle a manger is small & square with the light low over the table – It leads on to the verandah & overlooks the sea. So does the chambre a coucher.'[28] The house situated in the garden of a larger house owned by Monsieur and Madame Allegre and may once have been a servant's lodge. By 31 December Katherine has the windows and doors open, the beds aired, and is standing in the market 'in a state of lively terrified joy', buying three dozen rosebuds and six bunches of violets for the house.[29] On 1 January, having borrowed £10 from Lawrence, John arrives in Bandol by train.

Lawrence has often told John that he should agree to go away with Katherine and live on her money and write, but he has always resisted Lawrence's advice. Even now, John insists that it is only temporary – when his book on Dostoevsky is finished he must go back to London, to his friends and his literary life. It is clear he expects Katherine to return with him at the beginning of the summer. But for the moment she has the stability she needs – warm sun, sea air, healthy food, companionship and no stress. And for two months she is well and happy.

She and John quickly establish a routine. They get up at 6.30 a.m., light the fire, wash and dress, then walk down the lane into town, buying their food at the small shops whose awnings line the street behind the seafront – bakers and butchers and fishmongers and vegetable stalls and cantinas selling local wine. They have a strict budget, dictated by Katherine's income, but there's enough – £3 a week – to pay the rent and a 'femme' to do the cleaning, and some left over for small luxuries such as cigarettes, wine and flowers and some new clothes for John. They live on omelettes and oranges, dates, salad, and baguettes spread with honey. Onion soup is on the menu quite often. Back at the villa they make coffee and have a simple French breakfast before beginning to write. From 8.30 to midday they work – at first together on the table in the little 'salon' that looks out across their landlord's kitchen garden towards the sea. Katherine has to struggle with her appetite – from 11 a.m. she is often so hungry she puts the clock forward surreptitiously. She mutters 'Beefsteak and fried potatoes!', raises her eyes to heaven and scribbles in the margin of her manuscript, 'I'm so hungry, simply empty'.[30] She fantasises about huge English roast dinners '& an armchair in front of the fire to boaconstrict in afterwards'.[31] After lunch, if the weather is fine, they go for a walk before coming home for supper. In the evening they sit on either side of the kitchen table, warmed by the fire, writing and occasionally discussing what they are doing. Sometimes, for fun, they set each other the task of writing a daily poem on a particular theme. Then to bed before ten, after washing in the bidet, with all the intimacy of a couple in a settled relationship – 'we soap each others backs & hop about in the tops of our pyjamas and scrabble into bed winking our toes'. For John it's a time 'of simple happiness . . . When every day [is] pure delight.'[32]

But Katherine's feelings are more complicated. While John works industriously on Dostoevsky, she finds it hard to 'blaze and burn'. For her, the joint endeavours in the petit salon are not productive. She is also having trouble sleeping, often coming downstairs in the night to sit beside the embers of the fire and watch the stars from the window. 'I was terribly sad. The night before when I lay in bed I felt suddenly passionate. I wanted Jack to embrace me. But as I turned to speak to him or to kiss him I saw my brother lying fast asleep – and I got cold. That happens nearly always.'[33] She has begun to transfer some of her feelings for her brother to John: she has started to call him by Leslie's childhood nickname of Bogey. Given the unresolved problems in their relationship, Katherine is incredulous at the degree of harmony they have managed to achieve.

> Outside the sky is light with stars;
> There's a hollow roaring from the sea,
> And, alas for the little almond-flowers,
> The wind is shaking the almond tree,
> How little I thought, a year ago,
> In that horrible cottage upon the Lee,
> That he and I should be sitting so
> And sipping a cup of camomile tea.[34]

Katherine's immersion in her memories of her brother and their childhood has convinced her that this is where her direction as a writer lies. 'Now I want to write recollections of my own country.' This is her territory, and she can make her brother live again in her stories. In her memory she ranges with Chummie 'over all the remembered places. I am never far away from them. I long to renew them in writing . . . Oh, I want for one moment to make our undiscovered country leap into the eyes of the old world. It must be mysterious, as though floating – it must take the breath . . . all must be told with a sense of mystery, a radiance, an after glow because you, my little sun of it, are set. You have dropped over the dazzling brim of the world.' She leans out of her window and dreams, feeling 'always trembling on the brink of poetry'. Katherine wants 'to write a kind of long elegy to you – perhaps not in poetry. No, perhaps in Prose – almost certainly in a kind of special prose.' She envisages stories and a 'minute note book to be published some day'. There will be 'no novels, no problem stories, nothing that is not simple, open. Any of this I may start at any moment.'[35]

She is still working on 'The Aloe', making it the vehicle for her unstructured memories, but has no clear idea where it is going and is toying with other concepts. There are a number of false beginnings, and by the first week of February she is in despair. 'I have written practically nothing yet & now again the time is getting short. There is nothing done. I am no nearer my achievement than I was 2 months ago & I keep half doubting my will to perform anything . . . if I went back to England without a book finished I should give myself up. I should know that, whatever I said, I was not really a writer & had no claim to "a table in my room".' She asks herself why she hesitates? Is it idleness? Or lack of willpower? She feels the need to assert herself, to re-establish her self-belief. Working at the same table as John is not a good idea. 'Jack's application is a perpetual reminder to me.'[36] She moves a table up into the bedroom, looking out over the almond tree. She can hear the sea and it is 'so quiet and so high . . . I feel I shall be able to write here'.[37] She must earn money – to finance her own lifestyle, to provide for Ida in order to assuage her guilt and also to pay John's debts, which still hang over them and are the subject of bitter disputes.

In the petit salon at Villa Pauline there is a great deal of discussion of Dostoevsky. Katherine is reading all the novels again and making notes for John, which are scattered through her notebook interspersed with her drafts for 'The Aloe'. 'Having read the whole of the Idiot through again, & fairly carefully, I feel slightly more bewildered than I did before as regards Nastasya Philippovna's character. She's really not well done – she's badly done, & there goes up as one reads on a kind of irritation, a balked fascination which almost succeeds finally in blotting out those first & really marvellous impressions of her. What was Dostoevsky really aiming at?'[38] Katherine's knowledge of Russian literature and her understanding of narrative technique are very useful to John. She is also reading the Bible in a detailed way, for the first time in her life, and her prose style begins to take on the cadences of the King James version. As with her desire to reread Shakespeare, she is curious about the historical context, whether 'Lot followed close on Noah', and what the people were like in appearance and character. It is human history and motivation that interest her, not academic theory.[39]

Throughout January and February, Katherine is receiving letters from a lonely Frederick Goodyear back in France: 'I greatly miss your talent for double entendre, which made conversation with you one of the consolations of life'. He is perfectly frank about his feelings, talking to her as if she were another man. His sexual experience has been confined to '5 whores, 1 engagement, several interminable sentimental friendships. Like the hedgehog, I've never been buggered at all.' In France he has become an expert in masturbation to the extent that he wonders whether there will be 'anything left worth having'. Katherine writes flirtatiously to him about French furniture – 'never one comfortable chair. If you want to talk the only possible thing to do is go to bed . . . I quite understand the reason for what is called french moral laxity – you're simply forced into bed – no matter with whom – there's no other place for you.' Goodyear, with a light, ironic touch, confesses his feelings for her. 'All the time I have known you you have been fixt up with Murry, & that's been final so far as I am concerned, though it has made things very awkward between us . . . If love is only love when it is resistless, I don't love you. But if it is a relative emotion, I do. Personally, I think everything everywhere is bunkum.' Katherine writes back assuring him that 'I did not, swayed by a resistless passion say that I loved you. Nevertheless I'm prepared to say it again looking at this pound of onions that hangs in a string kit from a saucepan nail.' She signs her letter 'with my strictly relative love', asking him to write again 'when everything is not too bunkum'. The effect is one of great familiarity and affection.[40]

In her notebook, alongside her letter to Goodyear, is an interesting paragraph. 'My head is full of only one thing. I can't begin writing or even thinking because all my thoughts revolve round le seul sujet. It is a real vice avec moi au present. I keep thinking round and round it, beating up and down it and still it stays in my head and wont let me be. I keep figuring it out, making other plans, feeling sure I still haven't got enough wits. How maddening it is!'[41] And earlier, as she waits for the postman, she breaks off from 'The Aloe' to ask, 'Who is he whom I seek?' The answer does not seem to be John Murry. 'It is a warm, loving, eager companion in whose Love there are no horrible dark gulfs, none of those terribly beetling cliffs and thick peaks that frighten me in my dreams. Neither shall he shut at evening like a jealous flower. He will be open all night long to me – but he is not.'[42]

On 15 February Katherine records that she has 'broken the silence' and begun to write. It is the breakthrough she has been looking for. On the following day she says that she has 'found The Aloe', finally got to 'the truth of it'. Addressing her brother, she writes that after rereading it she can see that 'The Aloe is right. The Aloe is lovely. It simply fascinates me, and I know that it is what you would wish me to write.' She has a clear idea suddenly of the shape of the story and the last chapter: 'It is your birth – your coming in the autumn'. This is to be tied in with the flowering of the aloe in the garden, for the only time in a hundred years. 'Oh I want this book to be written. It must be done.'[43] Other ideas are abandoned.

The central event that Katherine has chosen from her childhood is the Beauchamps' removal from the house in Tinakori Road to Chesney Wold in the village of Karori, just outside Wellington, when she was five years old. Although the family lived there for only a few years before returning to Tinakori Road, the house in the country, called Tarana in the story, has remained fixed in Katherine's imagination as an image of pure happiness. She describes the child Kezia's first glimpse of the house by moonlight: 'The soft white bulk of it lay stretched upon the green garden like a sleeping beast – and now one and now another of the windows leaped into light – Some one was walking through the empty rooms carrying a lighted candle. From a window downstairs the light of a fire flickered – a strange beautiful excitement seemed to stream from the house in quivering ripples. Over its roofs the verandah poles, the window sashes the moon swung her silver lantern.' In the garden is an aloe that is just about to flower. Kezia is fascinated by 'the fat swelling plant with its cruel leaves its towering fleshy stem. High above them, as though becalmed in the air, and yet holding so fast to the earth it grew from it might have had claws and not roots. The curving leaves seemed to be hiding something; the big blind stem cut into the air as if no wind could ever shake it.'[44]

The Burnell family, like the Beauchamps, consists of a grandmother who takes care of the family, a 'Pa-man' father who has business in the city, a 'delicate' mother very like Annie Beauchamp about to give birth to her fourth child, her sister Beryl who lives with them, three small daughters and a handyman called Pat. The names of the characters are taken from Katherine's family members – Burnell is Annie's middle name, Isabella is Katherine's grandmother's middle name, Aunt Belle becomes Beryl Fairfield – a rough translation of Beauchamp, one of the children is called Charlotte, abbreviated to Lottie, and Pat is Patrick Sheehan, who worked for the Beauchamps at Karori. The story belongs to Kezia, the youngest daughter, who provides a 'child's-eye view' of the events unfolding around her, but the point of view also floats in and out of the minds of the other characters. The story begins on the evening of removal day and the reader is pitched straight into the action, like a scene from a film.

> There was not an inch of room for Lottie and Kezia in the buggy. When Pat swung them on top of the luggage they wobbled; the Grandmother's lap was full and Linda Burnell could not possibly have held a lump of a child on hers for such a distance. Isabel, very superior perched beside Pat on the driver's seat. Hold-alls, bags and band boxes were piled upon the floor.
>
> 'These are absolute necessities that I will not let out of my sight for one instant,' said Linda Burnell, her voice trembling with fatigue and over excitement.

Lottie and Kezia stood on the patch of lawn just inside the gate all ready for the fray in their reefer coats with brass anchor buttons and little round caps with battle ship ribbons. Hand in hand. They stared with round inquiring eyes first at the 'absolute necessities' and then at their Mother.

'We shall simply have to leave them. That is all. We shall simply have to cast them off,' said Linda Burnell. A strange little laugh flew from her lips; she leaned back upon the buttoned leather cushions and shut her eyes . . . laughing silently.[45]

Katherine's mother flies from her pen in the guise of Linda, and her father is drawn from life as the pompous, rather spoilt Stanley Burnell, whose presence as the only male in a family of women does not ensure the kind of respect he feels is his due. But it is the character of Beryl Fairfield that gives Katherine the most trouble. She is loosely based on her aunt, though there are also elements of Katherine's own personality in the character – two selves in opposition.

Katherine's concentration is disturbed when she gets upsetting letters from her family telling her that Harold Beauchamp is paying for her mother and sisters to go to see Vera in Canada. Katherine writes to Vera, barely concealing her hurt. 'I envy you indeed with the lovely prospect of a visit from Mother and Jeanne. Unfortunately I am rather in the dark about their plans for Father has only mentioned the idea of their voyage to me once & that was in his last letter and he has never breathed a word that I should come – Yet, if he had offered the trip to Chaddie [in India] that means he could afford it – doesn't it?' Katherine feels excluded, but is too proud to take the matter up with her father, though she makes it clear to Vera that she would come if the fare was paid: 'We have not the money and I should not ask Father for it . . . I feel it simply isn't my place to do so.'[46]

But almost at the same time, Mr Kay writes to say that Harold has raised Katherine's allowance again – to £13 a month. This is not the time to be ungracious, or to ask for more. Katherine writes a long loving letter to her father, saying 'how much I love and admire and how very much you mean to me. Forgive my childish faults, my generous darling Daddy, and keep me in your heart.'[47]

Towards the end of February, Lawrence's letters begin to threaten Katherine's solitude. He has been ill with congestion of the lungs throughout January, 'in a sort of "all gone but my cap" state', but is now recovering and he and

Frieda are going to live at a tiny hamlet called Zennor, near St Ives, where houses are extremely cheap. 'You will come at the end of April,' he writes confidently, 'when it will be warm.'[48] John, who has never envisaged staying at the Villa Pauline for more than a few months, responds sympathetically. A telegram is sent to Lawrence agreeing to the proposition in principle. But Katherine does not want to leave just as she has begun to find her way into 'The Aloe', and hates the idea of living anywhere near the Lawrences and distrusts the idea of a community. She tells John, 'you know we are not made to do that kind of thing ever.'[49] Cornwall does not appeal either. On holiday there the previous year, Katherine had seen a woman torturing a cat and the cruelty has been fused with the landscape in her memory.

By the beginning of March Lawrence's letters are more importunate. He has found a cottage for £5 a year and at right angles to it – only 'twelve strides' away – three cottages converted into a long house for only £16 a year, with kitchen, dining room and study on the ground floor, three bedrooms above the main house and a tower over the study. Lawrence includes a detailed drawing in his letter.

The tower room, accessible only from the study, would be perfect for Katherine. It has big windows and panelled walls and a terracotta ceiling. 'I call it already Katherine's house, Katherine's tower. There is something very attractive about it. It is very old, native to the earth, like rock, yet dry and all in the light of the hills and the sea.' John raises anxieties about a man called Heseltine, whom Lawrence has also invited to Zennor, and about past misunderstandings over the printing press. Lawrence dismisses them all. 'No more quarrels and quibbles. Let it be agreed for ever. I am *Blutbruder* [blood brother]; a *Blutbruderschaft* between us all. Tell K. not to be so queasy.' Frieda adds her own exhortations in a postscript, assuring Katherine that they will live 'like the lilies in the fields'; there will be no more 'soul harassing', no more 'deep things'.[50]

There seems no way out of it. John is determined to go to Lawrence, though he has misgivings about whether Katherine will be able to endure it. She reluctantly agrees to spend the summer with them in Cornwall, leaving Bandol at the end of April. She tells a friend that her book 'won't be old enough to travel until then'.[51] 'The Aloe' seems doomed to be stunted by transplantation, just as it has begun to grow and flourish.

Living in New Zealand has not protected the Beauchamp family from the effects of the war in Europe. Chummie had been killed in October 1915 and on 28 February 1916 there is another death. Katherine's sister Chaddie is in India, where her husband, Lieutenant-Colonel John Perkins has been posted but, just before she embarks on the journey to Europe for the promised visit to Vera, he dies suddenly and at the age of twenty-nine Chaddie is a widow. Her ship, the *Sardinia*, is due to call at Marseilles on its way back to England and Katherine plans to meet her there, spending the week before in a fever of anxiety – fearing that the ship might be sunk by German U-boats, worrying about the trip to Marseilles and 'wondering what I shall do if the boat arrives in the middle of the night or what shall I do if someone robs me while I am there . . . And what she will say & if she will expect me. These things fly through my head like mad things. They never finish and then there is always the idea that I may by some awful error miss her. It isn't possible. And what we shall do when we do meet.'[52] Some of Katherine's fears are justified. She stays in the Hotel Oasis again and during the night is woken by someone rattling the handle of her bedroom door. 'Then came a KNOCK.' Katherine leaps out of bed, puts on her kimono, arms herself with a pair of scissors and opens the door. 'There stood a horrid creature in his night shirt who began mumbling something about the wrong door – but he leered.'[53] Katherine slams the door and walks up and down in a fury, surprised to find herself more angry than frightened.

After four years of separation, Katherine's reunion with Chaddie is very emotional. There is grief for the deaths of a husband and a brother; and a shared childhood to be remembered. Katherine cherishes happy memories of Chaddie – the most sweet-natured of her sisters – and remembers an earthquake in New Zealand when their father had rushed into their bedroom to carry them out into the garden. 'I can see Chaddie now, who was very "weedy" at the time and only had a wisp of hair tied up with a piece of pink wool for the night.'[54] But there is little real sympathy and understanding between the two women. Their lives have taken different directions. Chaddie goes on her way to England and Canada; Katherine returns to the Villa Pauline.

Katherine had hoped to stay in Bandol until the end of April but, by the end of March, John has decided that they must leave. The war in France is intensifying – the Battle of Verdun had begun on 21 February, widely reported in the French papers – and the price of food is going up every day. In England a conscription bill has been introduced, requiring military service of some kind from every man of military age and John is not enough of a pacifist to hide away abroad. Katherine doesn't want to stay in France without John, but Bandol is still peaceful and sunny and it is with extreme reluctance, and tears of disappointment, that Katherine hands the keys back to Madame Allegre and pulls the little iron gate shut for the last time. She knows that she can never really be part of Lawrence's dream. A few weeks earlier John had scribbled a prophetic postscript on one of her letters: 'We are going to stay with the Lawrences for ever and ever as perhaps you know; I daresay eternity will last the whole of the summer.'[55]

The journey from London to Cornwall by train is not only expensive but interminable. As lush fields and woods give way to bare moors, Katherine grows more and more depressed. When they finally reach the railway station at St Ives, there's still an 8-kilometre carriage ride along the clifftops to the tiny granite village of Zennor. The Lawrences watch eagerly as John and Katherine rattle down the lane towards them. Frieda thinks that the travel-weary Katherine looks like 'an emigrant' perched on top of a cart-load of luggage and belongings collected from 5 Acacia Road. Neither of the Murrys appear to be in good health, despite the winter in Bandol. John had fallen ill as soon as he arrived back in England and Katherine, too, is thin and pale.

They have arranged to stay at the Tinners Arms in Zennor while they decorate and furnish the cottage and Katherine finds the small pub with its flagged floors and draughty rooms as comfortless as the landscape. The sky is a steely grey, almost the same colour as the sea, and a constant wind blows rain off the North Atlantic. Turning away from the window of their room, Katherine tells John, 'I shall never like this place.' She writes to her friends that 'everything seems to be made of boulders – We shall have to eat off stones as well as have them for our pillows.'[56] Things are little better when they move into the cottage across the moor at Higher Tregerthen. It is incurably damp, which is bad for Katherine's health. Rain not only drips through the flat roof of the tower, it leaks down one of the chimneys and runs down the dining room wall. To make matters even worse, the earth closet they have to share with the Lawrences is in full view of the cottage door, which offends Katherine's fastidious nature.

But John is thoroughly enjoying the renewed relationship with Lawrence, who surrounds him with 'warm and irresistible intimacy'. On fine days they shoulder their rucksacks like two boys and march together over the hill for brisk country walks, or go 'clowning' into St Ives, where they buy cheap Victorian furniture in Benney's sale rooms. There's a frenzy 'of painting chairs and polishing brass and mending old clocks, putting plates on dressers . . .'[57] The Lawrences' cottage has pink walls and blue cupboards; the Murrys' has white walls and black furniture. It is, John writes in his diary, a reflection of his state of mind, influenced by what he senses of Katherine's thoughts and feelings.

At first there is a superficial harmony between the couples – Katherine enjoys the combative discussions with Lawrence; she walks to Zennor with Frieda for the shopping. There are companionable evenings in front of the fire talking about their childhoods, and trips out to sea in a dinghy where they laugh hysterically and sing endless rounds of 'Row, row, row your boat'.

But it lasts less than a month. The atmosphere at Higher Tregerthen is electrically charged. Even John is aware of the emotional politics. He observes that Lawrence's non-intellectual, 'earth mother' relationship with Frieda leaves room 'and perhaps need, for a relation with a man of something of the kind and quality of my relation with Katherine'. The man Lawrence has chosen for this special friendship is John. Instinctively withdrawing from Lawrence's powerful need, John is terrified when he talks of 'some inviolable sacrament between us – some pre-Christian blood-rite in keeping with the primeval rocks about us'.[58]

Katherine, too, is appalled by these suggestions. Lawrence does not seem to be the person she had known before. He has taken up sewing, and there are abrupt changes of personality. 'He simply raves, roars, beats the table, abuses everybody.' Afterwards he has attacks of fever, appearing 'haggard and broken'. Living with the Lawrences is like 'sitting on a railway station' with his temper 'like a big black engine puffing and snorting', ready at any moment to take off with a shriek of steam. 'It's impossible,' Katherine writes, 'to be anything to him but a kind of playful acquaintance.'[59] She is also shocked by the relationship between Lawrence and Frieda, now observed at close quarters: his insistence that a couple must fight a battle until each dies to the other before they can become one; his declared preference for sexual intercourse – 'taking her as a dog does a bitch'. Katherine thinks that Frieda is a bad influence on Lawrence, not only because her literary views are simplistic, but because she is too volatile. Their explosive quarrels do not make for a peaceful existence and

Katherine tells Beatrice Campbell that 'They are both too rough for me to enjoy playing with'.[60] The situation between Lawrence and Frieda is too sordid for Katherine – 'it offends ones soul beyond words. I don't know which disgusts one worse – when they are very loving and playing with each other or when they are roaring at each other and he is pulling out Frieda's hair and saying "I'll cut your bloody throat, you bitch" and Frieda is running up and down the road screaming for "Jack" to save her!!'[61] The trigger points of these scenes are usually to do with Frieda's misery at being separated from her children, which at times becomes insupportable. Frieda confesses that she feels 'a deep rage' when she thinks of the injustice of the situation, 'that this is the law of man; and if I were a prostitute the children would be mine and a man would be obliged to pay me'.[62] Katherine should understand and empathise, but with cruel detachment she refuses to acknowledge Frieda's suffering – perhaps reluctant to revisit long suppressed emotions and desires.

Day after day, Katherine lies on her bed in the tower room, listening to rain dripping into buckets, chain smoking, mentally constructing a story set in Marseilles and rereading 'The Aloe', which now seems totally unreal. Across the garden, Lawrence and Frieda are alternately fighting or making love with equal violence, and, downstairs in the study, John is correcting the proofs of *Still Life* and *Dostoevsky* and endlessly analysing his own emotions in his journal. The maid, nicknamed 'the Cornish Pasty' because she is stolid and has thick ankles, is stumping about in the kitchen, and Katherine is longing to be somewhere else. She hates the grey stone walls, the grey sea, the grey clouds, the cold, grass-levelling wind. Even as the English winter edges into spring and the late sun glitters on the water, Katherine feels alien here. The second-hand chairs, enamelled black, sit in the dining room like a funeral procession. The view across the moors is unrelievedly bleak. There are few trees and the ones that survive are contorted by the wind into grotesque shapes. Sometimes the wind is so strong that it howls over the roof and forces open the door, allowing the rain to pour into the kitchen.

In a letter to Beatrice Campbell Katherine is nostalgic for the sound of 'Sunday afternoon pianos' but there isn't 'even the ghost of a pianner here. Nothing but the clock and the fire and sometimes a gust of wind breaking over the house. This house is very like a house left high and dry. It has the same "hollow" feeling – the same big beams and narrow doors and passages that only a fish could swim through without touching and the little round windows at the back are just like port-holes ...' If her own house feels like a shipwreck, Katherine tells Beatrice that she is going to call Lawrences' cottage 'The Phallus'.[63]

Lawrence is writing *Women in Love* at such a great pace that Frieda thinks the title should be 'Dies Irae'. A great deal of Katherine goes into Gudrun, who is 'very beautiful' and wears distinctive clothes 'a dress of dark-blue silky stuff, with ruches of blue silk lace in the neck and sleeves; and ... cherry-coloured stockings'. Lawrence captures Katherine's mixture of 'confidence and diffidence' and her effect on other people – many of them intimidated by her 'perfect sang-froid and simple bareness of manner' but those close to her finding her 'charming, so infinitely charming, in her softness and her fine, exquisite richness of texture and delicacy of line. There was a certain playfulness about her too, such a piquancy of ironic suggestion, an untouched reserve.' Gudrun's emphasis is always on experience, experience, experience, whatever the cost. Lawrence also describes what he most dislikes in Katherine – the way she observes people 'closely, with objective curiosity'. Gudrun sees everyone 'as a complete figure, like a character in a book, or a subject in a picture, or a marionette in a theatre, a finished creation', and imagines lives and situations for them. She knows them, and they are 'sealed and stamped and finished with', added up and crossed out, like a mathematical problem that has been solved.[64] Gudrun is a painter, not a writer, but still a creative artist, though the larger canvases are not her territory. She must always work on small things – 'little things ... that one can put between one's hands ... full of instinctive passion'. Gudrun is also a feminist: 'The freedom, the liberty, the mobility!' she cries, in Katherine's voice, 'strangely flushed and brilliant. "You're a man, you want to do a thing, you do it. You haven't the *thousand* obstacles a woman has in front of her."'[65]

John admits that 'Lawrence found the germ of Gerald in me' and that 'a few of the episodes between Rupert and Gerald [are] taken from conversations between Lawrence and me'.[66] When Lawrence has Rupert say, 'I believe in the additional perfect relationship between man and man – additional to marriage', it is Lawrence speaking about himself and John, putting into Rupert's mouth his own belief that a man needs two kinds of love to be fully satisfied – the love of a woman and the love of a man. This kind of bisexual ethic, which Lawrence calls 'manly love', is superior to the purely heterosexual kind. John states unequivocally that the 'queer wrestling-match between the two [Gerald and Rupert] is more or less what he [Lawrence] meant by the "blood sacrament" between us at which he hinted'. This is a reference to the extraordinary passage in the novel where Rupert and Gerald wrestle naked behind locked doors, described in the manner of a passionate sexual encounter: 'The two men began to struggle together ... They stopped, they discussed methods, they practised grips and throws, they became more accustomed to each other, to each other's rhythm, they got a kind of mutual physical understanding. And then again they had a real struggle. They seemed to drive their white flesh deeper and deeper against each other, as if they would fuse it into a oneness ... Birkin ... seemed to penetrate into Gerald's heavier, riper bulk, to interfuse his body through the body of the other, as if to bring it subtly into his influence, always seizing with some rapid sensuous fore-knowledge every motion of the other body, converting and counteracting it, playing upon the limbs and frame of Gerald like some strong wind.'[67]

The suppressed first chapter of *Women in Love* is even more explicit about the nature of Birkin's interest in Gerald: 'although he was always terribly intimate with at least one woman, and practically never intimate with a man, yet the male physique had a fascination for him, and for the female physique he felt only a fondness, a sort of sacred love, as for a sister.

In the street, it was the men who roused him by their flesh and their manly, vigorous movement, quite apart from all the individual character, whilst he studied the women as sisters, knowing their meaning and their intents ... This was the one and only secret he kept to himself, this secret of his passionate and sudden, spasmodic affinity for men he saw. He kept this secret even from himself. He knew what he felt, but he always kept the knowledge at bay.'[68]

When John eventually reads the novel he realises the nature of the ambiguities that made him uncomfortable in Lawrence's presence. At the time, John's instincts sense the dangerous sub-text of their conversations and cause him to withdraw from the intimacy that has been established between them. 'What he really wanted of me he never put into words, and to this day I am doubtful whether he ever knew. But what he imagined he wanted is stated clearly enough in the novel.'[69] John's rejection of the 'higher union' with Lawrence affects the older man profoundly.

Katherine is fed up with the Lawrences – the quarrels, the constant analysis of sex, the endless navel gazing. 'Am I wrong in not being able to accept these people just as they are – laughing when they laugh and going away from them when they fight?' she asks Kot on 11 May. 'Tell me ... It seems to me so degraded – so horrible to see I can't stand it. And I feel so furiously angry; I hate them for it.' She can't work under these conditions and is already beginning to formulate a plan for her escape. 'I am making preparations for changing everything.'[70]

She writes a similar letter to Goodyear, and receives a stern reply. Since the break with Orage, Goodyear, himself a promising writer, is the only friend to discuss work with her in a frank and constructive way. He recommends a more active life to steady her 'over-twanged inelastic literary nerve'. She must stop living so much in the past – 'It is a case of burning your boats, mentally, every morning, when you get up'. And she must somehow get over her dislike of 'human beings in their social compacts . . . You seem to live happily and egalitarianly enough in a republic of sounds and scents and grasses and dews and cafe-mirrors and odd things and appearances generally. I don't see why you should draw the line at man, only another phase of nature.' Goodyear has no illusions about Katherine's character and does not allow her to have any either. He scolds her about her untruthfulness, though she is 'an old darling' in spite of it, and her sentimentality, asking her to 'send a further sample of water (spiritually speaking) for analysis'.[71]

But by the third week of May the Cornish idyll is over. A policeman arrives at the door, telling both John and Lawrence that they must register for military service, just as relations between the two couples reach a new low. Katherine and John have been drawn into a quarrel between Frieda and Ottoline. Ottoline thinks both Frieda's mind and personality are vulgar and has asked Lawrence not to bring her to Garsington. Her feelings about Frieda, expressed in letters to those close to her, are quite extreme: 'If only we could put her in a sack and drown her!'[72] But gossiping friends have leaked the contents of private letters to those never intended to receive them. A letter from Ottoline to John is steamed open in the Lawrences' kitchen and precipitates a tremendous row. Frieda and Katherine are no longer speaking to each other and John overhears Lawrence referring to him as 'an obscene bug' who is sucking all his vital energies away. Officially, Katherine and John are leaving because Katherine doesn't like the landscape. As Lawrence writes scornfully to Ottoline, 'Unfortunately the Murrys do not like the country – it is too rocky and bleak for them. They should have a soft valley, with leaves and the ring-dove cooing.'[73] Katherine is keen to go to London and back to France as soon as possible. John still wants to stay in Cornwall and hankers after a boat and a garden. There's a compromise. Katherine has an idea that the southern coast, near Marazion, where they had once had a picnic on a beach of pure white sand, might have a kinder climate. They find a pleasant, double-fronted cottage at Mylor at the mouth of the Truro River for £18 a year and arrange to move in the second week of June. Katherine goes ahead by train while John stays behind to pack up their furniture. He calls goodbye to the Lawrences as he leaves and Frieda gaily wishes him well. Lawrence says nothing and John fears that their relationship is over for ever.

Throughout June Katherine and John are at the Mylor cottage. Services are fairly primitive and fresh water has to be taken from a pump shared with a neighbour, but the front garden runs down to the sea, and Katherine has a maid who brings them fresh raspberries wrapped in a rhubarb leaf and a small black and white kitten. John hires a sailing dinghy and messes about in the water. He is managing to earn enough money by writing reviews for literary periodicals and his two books are just about to be published. There is a truce with Lawrence, who has accepted an invitation to visit them at Mylor. John is happy; Katherine is not. She is still unable to write, still mourning the Villa Pauline and constantly irritated by village women who call at the cottage to invite her to sales of work 'on behalf of the Seamen's Mission' or the Red Cross. This is not the life she wants to live and she is overcome with a violent restlessness that refuses to go away. She tells Kot that she is too sad to write: 'Life is so hateful just now that I am quite numb'.[74]

Goodyear, on leave from France, comes down to Cornwall to spend a few days with them. He is in a reckless, cynical frame of mind – bored by his clerical job with the meteorological unit and feeling that perhaps he should do something more active in the war. The offensive on the Somme begins while he is at Mylor, and it is apparent from the beginning that there are massive casualties. Goodyear decides that he will get a transfer to a front-line regiment as soon as his leave is over. He tells Katherine and John that he doesn't care if he dies or not – he probably will, but if he can't have his freedom he might as well do the thing properly. Everything, everywhere, is still bunkum. The atmosphere at the cottage is difficult. The frank letters Katherine and Goodyear have been exchanging make for an intimacy between them that can't be shared with John. What happens at Mylor is never openly discussed, but Goodyear's presence precipitates a crisis in the Murrys' relationship, already worn threadbare by living with the Lawrences. After a few days, John takes Goodyear, who is very keen to see Lawrence, over to Zennor on a visit, sleeping overnight on the floor of the tower. While they are there, John confides to Lawrence that he and Katherine have negotiated a contract whereby each of them is free to go in whatever direction they choose. Lawrence writes to his friends that Katherine is very dissatisfied with John.[75]

On 8 July Katherine takes the train to London, intending to stay for a few days with Beatrice and Gordon Campbell so that she can look for rooms. She has an invitation from Ottoline to spend a weekend at Garsington Manor, where she hopes to make useful contacts among the Bloomsbury élite. John has already been to Garsington but, though Katherine has been corresponding with Ottoline, this is the first time she has been invited. It seems significant to her friends that she is going alone. Katherine also talks to Kot about the possibility of visiting Denmark in September – where Goodyear has connections – and tells him that she and John are no longer together. 'Life feels wonderful and different for at last I am free again.'[76]

15

The 'Blooms Berries'

As the horse pulling the dogcart trots up the drive, bringing Katherine from the station, Garsington is lovely in the July sunlight, with its 'untidy, romantic, haunted grange appearance'.[1] It is a home rather than a stately showpiece — the kind of place that Katherine has imagined for herself. Outside, it is a Tudor house of dignified pale stone, mellowed by weather; inside, the decor is flamboyant, reflecting the character of its chatelaine. The seventeenth-century panelling in the dining room has been painted scarlet and there are yellow curtains at the mullioned windows and Turkish rugs on the polished oak floor. The Morrells have only recently moved to Garsington and the house is still being restored, resulting in some interesting contrasts. Ottoline's own apartments are exquisite, but the guest bedrooms are a lottery — some of them in farm workers' cottages and barns outside — and in the drawing-room priceless furniture that has been in the family for generations stands beside armchairs covered in faded chintz sagging comfortably onto the threadbare Aubusson rugs. The whole

276

effect is 'patched, gilded and preposterous'.[2] The facilities are equally ram-shackle. Guests are astonished to find that there is no hot water in the solitary bathroom and only one toilet for the whole house as well as the outbuildings. The result is one of Katherine's horrors – overflowing 'jer-ries' of urine (and worse) under beds and in commodes, for the servants to empty every morning.

Katherine's hostess greets her in the hall. Ottoline is an original. She is very tall, with striking, rather masculine, features that include a long, equine nose, and she avoids ugliness by dressing extravagantly – in huge feathered hats, velvet cloaks, sumptuous dresses, all in brilliant colours – like a medieval grande dame. She surrounds herself with people to fill the gap in her life left by her unsatisfactory 'open' marriage to Philip Morrell, who is described by one of her friends as 'very well-meaning' but 'a dreary old death's head'.[3] Ottoline has just had a long, disastrous affair with the socialist philosopher Bertrand Russell, which has left her emotionally damaged. She is greedy for love and friendship and unbelievably generous to her friends, but often depressed by the way in which her hospitality is taken for granted, or even abused. The young people, she complains, look on her not as a person, but as the 'kind manageress of a hotel'. Ottoline is afraid that Katherine has come to Garsington only to 'gather copy for her novels'.[4] And she is right to be worried about the use that writers are mak-ing of her patronage. As Katherine arrives, Aldous Huxley is curled up on a chair in the library already taking notes for his cruel satire Chrome Yellow, and D. H. Lawrence, the recipient of both money and gifts, is in Zennor, encouraged by a vengeful Frieda, busily writing Ottoline into Women in Love as Hermione Roddice, with little attempt at disguise and a complete disregard for the consequences.

Katherine is very nervous about this visit. The letters she has already written to Ottoline show the 'false' side of her character. They are fawning and reverent, with a 'we are so grateful you have decided to notice us' tone, designed to make Ottoline feel appreciated. Katherine has worked hard to get her invitation to Garsington on the back of Lawrence's introduction and knows she must make the most of the opportunity. Katherine has always been good at networking but here, among the aristocracy, she feels even more of a 'little barbarian from the colonies' than usual. She already knows Dora Carrington – the object of Mark Gertler's hopeless passion – but the other guests are either strangers or mere acquaintances. Katherine had met Bertrand Russell only once, when Lawrence had brought him to a Signature magazine meeting with herself, John and Kot at an office in Holborn. He had made his dislike of them all quite plain at the time – 'I thought Murry *beastly* and the whole atmosphere of the three dead and putrefying'[5] – but he is now a relative by marriage: Katherine's cousin Elizabeth von Arnim has recently married Bertrand's brother, the Earl Russell. Lytton Strachey had been one of the gate-crashers at Brett's farewell party for Lawrence, but the rest of the 'Blooms Berries', as Katherine calls them, are known to her only by reputation. Their complicated, incestuous relationships are difficult for an outsider to fathom. Virginia Woolf's sister, the painter Vanessa Bell, is there with her lover Duncan Grant, and his lover David 'Bunny' Garnett. Vanessa's husband, Clive Bell, and his bi-sexual mistress Mary Hutchinson are also guests.

Brett, who currently has a passionate crush on Ottoline and is painting her portrait, has been an acquaintance for over a year, though Brett and Katherine have never talked properly. Brett, who met Katherine very briefly at the farewell party for Lawrence, is nervous of closer contact, terrified by her 'reputation of brilliancy, of a sort of ironic ruthlessness toward small minds and less agile brains'. But Katherine is so intimidated by the atmosphere that at dinner that evening, sitting next to Brett at the long refectory table, she is 'watchful, cold, withdrawn into herself', silently observing the others and listening to the conversation that 'roars up and down', punctuated by 'Bertrand Russell's horse-like laugh'. Brett, in an agony of shyness, cut off from the general conversation by her deafness, begins to drop tiny pellets of bread into Katherine's jacket pocket. Back in her bedroom, Katherine finds the bread and knows who has put it there. Touched by this mute act of communication, she goes up to Brett's room for a long, intimate chat. The following day Katherine accepts an invitation to Brett's studio and recognises, in her work, a fellow artist, worthy of respect. Brett, on her part, finds the private Katherine more sympathetic and approachable than she could possibly have imagined. Like two girls at boarding school they 'make a secret pact of friendship'.[6]

Katherine knows she is being observed and judged by the Garsington set and remains on her best behaviour. She gets on well with Mary Hutchinson, who invites her for a weekend visit, and with Lytton Strachey. They discuss Dorothy Wordsworth's *Journals*, which Katherine had read in Paris, and Lytton, intrigued by Katherine's enigmatic persona, decides that she is 'decidedly an interesting creature', though she has 'a sharp and slightly vulgarly-fanciful intellect'.[7] Katherine sees little of Aldous Huxley, who spends his time either trawling through Ottoline's library or in the company of a young Belgian refugee called Maria Nys, with whom he has fallen in love. Bertrand Russell, very much the lion of the pride, is rather warmer towards Katherine on this second meeting, but she knows that he is someone to be wary of, with his reputation for intellectual savagery, firmly expressed in his own pronouncements: 'I find it difficult to talk to the ordinary mortal, for the language they use is so inaccurate that to me it seems absurd. The ordinary view of life is too immature to be tolerable to me.'[8] He is also sexually predatory – a breed of men Katherine is very familiar with – but he has just taken another mistress, a secret he is keeping from Ottoline.

As the weekend progresses, Katherine and Ottoline begin to relax with each other. They both love Russian music and literature and they both disapprove of Frieda Lawrence's influence on her husband. Katherine, like Ottoline, believes that Frieda's natural vitality and force of personality dominate Lawrence to his detriment, and tells her that 'The "dear man" . . . whom we all loved is hidden away, absorbed, completely lost, like a little gold ring in that immense German Christmas pudding which is Frieda.'[9]

During the day guests entertain themselves by reading, talking or walking in the grounds. On warm days swimming costumes and towels can be borrowed for a dip in the old fish pond. After dinner the company provide their own entertainment, by playing charades, parlour games, dancing, singing, acting plays – all of which are very much to Katherine's taste. One evening, 'after much persuasion', she consents to sing, accompanying herself on the guitar. Not music hall jingles this time, but folk songs, and Negro spirituals, sung 'in a low whispering voice, all caution momentarily forgotten, her quick expressive face [rippling] with light and fun, her humour bubbling over'.[10] But there is a murmur somewhere in the audience, a laugh in the wrong place and suddenly Katherine, sensing criticism, stops. Everyone pleads with her to continue, but her guard has gone up and her face is once more inscrutable. The audience feels uncomfortable and the evening ends in a minor key.

Ottoline is aware of Katherine's unease among her guests, confiding her impressions to the journal she writes every night before she goes to bed. 'I think Katherine feels unsure of her position, partly because she is a New Zealander and is not as yet very easy or natural in England and she is constantly playing different parts.' When she is feeling insecure her lively face becomes like that of a Japanese doll, 'as if she kept it still and impassive to hide behind, as anyone else might hold up a fan or an eighteenth-century mask. Does she I wonder take it off when she is alone with Murry?'[11]

Katherine is addressing just this aspect of herself in 'The Aloe', developing the character of Beryl Fairfield and trying to resolve the problem of Beryl's two selves, of her double or 'sosie'. 'What is it that I'm getting at?' Katherine asks in her notebook, supplying the answer straight away. 'The fact that for a long time now, she really hasn't been even able to control her second self; its her second self who now controls her.' In order for the character to have unity, Katherine decides she must 'merge her into herself'.[12] Katherine constructs a scene where Beryl sits in her room writing a bright, superficial letter to a friend, aware that her 'other self', standing behind her shoulder, is guiding the pen. This false self had originally been useful in social interaction, 'to get her out of awkward positions – to glide her over hateful moments – to help her to bear the stupid ugly sometimes beastly things that happened', but it is beginning to dominate: 'days, weeks at a time passed without her ever for a moment ceasing to act a part'. Perhaps, Beryl speculates, this is because she is not leading the life she wants to, and her 'real self' only makes her wretchedly aware of that. The real moments are rare and come most often when she is alone – 'certain nights when the wind blew with a forlorn cry and she lay cold in her bed wakeful and listening certain lovely evenings when she passed down a road where there were houses and big gardens and the sound of a piano came from one of the houses' – moments when she feels 'life is wonderful – life is rich and mysterious'.[13] Only at these moments is she truly herself.

On the train going back to London, early on Monday morning, Katherine reads Virginia Woolf's first novel, The Voyage Out, which Ottoline has lent her. It had been published the previous year, and everyone had been talking about it at Garsington. The book, with its occasional glimmerings of a new direction in literature, fuels Katherine's paranoia about her own lack of productivity and her awareness that 'The Aloe' is still only a collection of rough drafts. Through Sydney Waterlow, who is a friend of the Woolf's, Katherine has heard about Virginia's struggle to write, her recent breakdown and the extraordinary delicacy of her mind. Katherine is both intrigued by Virginia and jealous of her achievement.

Almost as soon as Katherine has left Garsington, Lytton is writing to Virginia about her. 'She spoke with great enthusiasm about The Voyage Out, and said she wanted to make your acquaintance more than anyone else's. So I said I thought it might be managed. Was I rash? I really believe you'd find her entertaining.'[14] Virginia is similarly aware of Katherine's reputation and her writing. 'Katherine Mansfield has dogged my steps for three years,' she replies to Lytton, 'I'm always on the point of meeting her, or of reading her stories, and I have never managed to do either. But once Sydney Waterlow produced Middleton Murry instead of her – a moon calf looking youth – her husband?' Virginia had not been impressed with John but she is intrigued enough on the subject of Katherine to tell Lytton, 'Do arrange a meeting.'[15]

Katherine leaves Garsington with a number of invitations, including one from Ottoline, begging her to come again later in the summer. Ottoline has been impressed by Katherine: 'I love her vivid awareness of the trembling beauty of life'.[16] Katherine is equally impressed by Ottoline and writes Kot a letter telling him that Garsington was not what she had imagined at all. She had gone to mock and realises now that there is something 'real and sympathetic' there.[17] The door is open for a new era of creative stimulation and collaboration – Lytton has already asked her if she will contribute to the Garsington Chronicle, the house newspaper recently suggested by Dora Carrington. But instead of staying in London as her friends expect, Katherine goes straight back to Cornwall for a reunion with John. Although Kot is amazed because he had thought the Murrys' relationship at an end, others are not surprised. Gertler, who has no romantic illusions about Katherine, had already predicted it. Ottoline discusses Katherine with Brett, who understands her dilemma perfectly: 'Poor Katherine is torn in two I believe – Pity for the shy gentle clinging man she lives with and the passionate desire for freedom . . . behind her if she goes a knife left buried in Murry's heart, the loss (possibly) of valued friends – that I believe to be her particular Hell.'[18]

John is suffering from one of his black depressions. The prospect of losing Katherine terrifies him; he finds the thought of communal army life repugnant and the recent publication of Still Life has been greeted by a polite silence. Doestoevsky receives muted reviews, but Lawrence, the man whose opinion he values most, doesn't even bother to read it. He tells John that he has 'looked in it here and there' and found it unable to transcend the mundane and give new revelations of Doestoevsky's art.[19] John feels wounded by all these rejections.

The knowledge that John is about to be called up for military service of some kind seems to makes Katherine possessive. Though his eyesight is too poor for combat, his future is very uncertain. Katherine writes to

Mary Hutchinson, postponing their weekend, because 'Murry is, at this moment, hovering too dreadfully between the Ministry of Munitions, the latrines of India, the flies of Aden & a certain Bureau Internationale in the Haymarket . . . Until I know which it is and when it is to be I don't feel that I can even unreasonably leave him.'[20] On the recommendation of well-placed friends, John goes up to London to look for war work at the Home Office, in order to avoid conscription, and with no one else in the house, Katherine is lonely and fearful. During the day she reads the novels of Georges Sand in French, bought for a shilling in a local sale room. Sand's passion for writing and her love of independence make her a role model. Katherine is haunted by an image of Sand 'getting up very early in the morning and putting a little white shawl round her shoulders and creeping down to the room where she wrote, kneeling down to light the fire and start her writing before anyone was awake'.[21]

The days are easily disposed of but at night Katherine is unable to sleep, even with a hammer on the table beside the bed, and jokes about it to Ottoline: 'I feel that to come upon a woman armed with a hammer might be damping to the spirits of the most Hardened Fiend'. She has come to hate the house at Mylor, with its frightening air of 'smugness – an eternal, a kind of Jesus-Christ-yesterday-today-and-forever quality of smugness which is most sinister. It is a perfect setting for a De Quincey murder.'[22] As usual when they are apart, her relationship with John becomes idealised and his shortcomings forgotten. 'I love you tonight beyond measure. Have I ever told you how I love your shoulders? When I hold you by your shoulders – put my arm round you & feel your fine delicious skin – warm & yet cool, like milk – and your slender bones – the bones of your shoulders . . . Good night, my heart. I am your own girl.'[23]

Chaddie returns to England in August and goes down to stay with Katherine and John in Cornwall. It's her first real encounter with Katherine's partner and she reports to the family that she finds him 'very easy, buoyant and gay . . . Very bohemian!'[24] Chaddie is the first member of the family, apart from Chummie, to meet John; the rest of the Beauchamps being unable to reconcile themselves completely to their daughter living with a man outside marriage. Katherine's alienation from her family is partly the result of having to keep so much of her life secret. Vera complains that Katherine is 'very selfish' because she never lets her family know what she's doing or where she is. It is 'very hurtful'.[25] But Katherine has no alternative if she wants to avoid their disapproval. Further deceits are being practised with

John's family. He has been reunited with his parents, whom he allows to think that he and Katherine are now a married couple. They are still far from accepting her, but the estrangement is over.

John, through his friend Eddie Marsh and other contacts he has made at Garsington, is offered a job in the War Office as a translator and moves to London permanently at the end of August, renting a room at a small hotel in Bloomsbury. The work suits John's temperament, even though the hours are long. In this very masculine, intellectual environment he meets many useful people, including the scientist and author J. W. N. Sullivan, who becomes a close friend and literary collaborator. Katherine feels abandoned after John leaves and she finds the Cornish house insupportable. Brett, who is spending almost all her time at Garsington or her parents' house in Kensington, in order to save money, suggests that Katherine should borrow her empty studio in Logan Place. So, at the beginning of September, Katherine goes up to London just in time to nurse John through a bout of influenza. 'Poor child! I kept him in bed all yesterday & fed him on milk and Oxo and this morning he has crept to the War Office – wispy and wan – like a moth after a shower of rain.'[26] But as soon as John is well enough, he is sent back to the hotel. Katherine can't work without her own space and she is determined to finish 'The Aloe'.

Throughout September, relations between the Murrys and the Lawrences are extremely volatile: echoes of the Cornish schism still reverberate between them. 'Frieda sent Murry a tremendous "biff" yesterday,' Katherine writes to Ottoline on the 12th, adding that she's tired of listening to Frieda's endless refrain, churned out like an organ grinder for anyone who will listen. But Katherine's growing dislike for Frieda and the coolness that has developed between herself and Lawrence doesn't prevent her from admiring his skill as a novelist and poet. An incident on 30 August had demonstrated her complete loyalty to him – a dramatic event that Lawrence writes into Women in Love as 'Gudrun at the Pompadour'. Katherine had gone with Gertler and Kot to the Café Royal and, because it was packed, they had sat at one end of a table already occupied by another group – a 'rather common' woman with dyed red hair, who had some connection with Lawrence's friend Heseltine, and two Indian students from Oxford contemptuously referred to by Gertler as 'University Blacks'. One of them was a Bengali Muslim called Surhawaddy who, with Heseltine and Kouyoumdjian, had been among those Lawrence had hoped to interest in Rananim. Surhawaddy is also a friend of Aldous Huxley's, and they had all been at Garsington the previous year with Lawrence, though Ottoline had difficulty relating to them – particularly Surhawaddy, whom she had thought 'extremely anti-English . . . foreign and remote'.[27] Katherine hadn't liked them either, writing disparagingly to Ottoline that it was a pity 'that dear Lorenzo sees rainbows round so many dull people and pots of gold in so many mean hearts'.[28]

Those at the table had been reading the latest volume of Lawrence's poems, Amores, and discussing it among themselves using, in Gertler's phrase, 'carefully picked, long words'. As Gertler had reported to Ottoline the following day, 'We had been ragging them all the time, but now we knew something drastic must be done. We sat and thought. Suddenly Katherine leant towards them and with a sweet smile said "Will you let me have that Book a moment?" "Certainly" they all beamed back – even more sweetly. Imagine their horror and utter amazement when Katharine without out a word more, Rose from the table, Book and all, we following most calmly – most calmly we walked out of the Café!!!'[29] Katherine hailed a taxi and they disappeared into the evening traffic, leaving the 'red-haired piece of dung' incredulous on the pavement. It had been a marvellous piece of theatre, but apart from its overt racism, the incident revealed an élitist view of art. Katherine, as she explains to a bewildered Ottoline, believes that artists belong 'to some sacred order . . . superior and apart from ordinary people'.[30]

Towards the middle of September Brett offers a more permanent solution to the Murrys' accommodation problems. She has decided to give up her studio and rent Maynard Keynes' house in Gower Street, living on the first floor herself and renting the attics to Carrington. Why don't John and Katherine rent the two rooms on the ground floor? That way they can live under the same roof, but still have their own space. Katherine agrees and in late September they move in. The house, which becomes known as the 'Ark', is like a student commune, with people popping in and out all the time. Lytton Strachey, Mark Gertler, Aldous Huxley, Ottoline Morrell and Bertrand Russell are frequent visitors. Katherine is suddenly at the heart of 'the Garsington set'.

It is October, Katherine's 'Black month'. There are leaves on the London pavements and barrel organs on the corners of the streets that bring back memories she would rather keep hidden. Soon she is in the grip of a depression deeper than any she has suffered since Bad Wörishofen, 'just living on a kind of quaking crust with blackness underneath which has paralysed – paralysed me – I have known this state of mind before but never as "violent a melancholy" as this and the diabolical thing about it is that I can't break through and tell the one whom I want to tell'.[31] Brett speculates that Katherine is in love with 'some man [who] has risen like the dawn on her horizon like they all will all her life – the Call of the Wild is in her and she can no more resist the call when it comes than any other wild animal'.[32] But Katherine's depression has more to do with the fact that everyone around her, including John, is publishing novels, stories and articles while all she has published since 1914 is one satirical sketch in the *New Age*, and two short pieces for *Signature*. She has nothing else to show for her years with John either, no settled home and no child. Knowing that she has conceived babies in the past with other men, she blames John for this too.

At the end of September, Ida reluctantly accompanies her father back to England. Though she wants to see her beloved Katherine again, she is very sad to leave Africa. She loves 'the lazy yet vibrant life of the untouched land with its few people and miles and miles of peace,' and writes nostalgically of watching the dawn from her bedroom window. 'In the moonlight the plantations of eucalyptus trees shone like still moonstones: in the early dawn the tall grasses swayed in the light breeze, heavy with dewdrops, till suddenly the sun rose and in one half hour the world was once more a hard, dry gold.'[33] As she and her father travel home on a troopship she forms a tentative friendship with an army officer, though she is too shy to pursue it. At twenty-nine, Ida's sexuality is still dormant and her affections still focused on Katherine. All too soon she is standing apprehensively on a station platform in grey English weather, waiting for Katherine to collect her and wondering whether Chummie's death and the two-year separation have changed their relationship. Ida's father checks into the Strand Palace Hotel, but Ida can't afford such luxury. She had assumed that she would be able to stay with Katherine, but when she arrives the welcome is decidedly lukewarm. The atmosphere at the 'Ark' is uncomfortable and there are no spare rooms. After a night on Katherine's sofa, Ida goes to stay with a married childhood friend in Chiswick and registers for war work.

By the time Ida arrives, Katherine has been at the Ark little more than a week, but it is already clear that the arrangement is not going to work.

In September Carrington had written excitedly, 'I shall like living with Katherine I am sure', and Brett had been equally enthusiastic. But within a few days Carrington is accusing Katherine of being 'double-faced' and Brett is complaining that Katherine waylays all their guests. 'No one gets further than Katherine! . . . Bertie, Lytton, etc. all disappear like magic.' She jokes about having her ear trumpet 'trained on the cracks in the floor'. By the end of October, Brett is writing to Ottoline asking her to 'just drop a hint that her flight into the unknown from the Ark would not offend me – a consideration I doubt ever entering her mind.' One possible explanation for Brett's desire to get rid of Katherine is her growing attachment to John, who is spending more and more time in her company, as she gaily informs Ottoline. 'Murry has been here this evening, making love to me all evening!'[34] John is clearly looking for love: he has already written to Ottoline, declaring that he believes himself to be in love with her.

Bloomsbury gossip speculates that Katherine is having an affair with Bertrand Russell. They meet frequently and letters fly backwards and forwards. But they are not love letters. Katherine's have a respectful reserve, and the slightly flirtatious quality of a young woman flattering the vanity of an older, and distinguished, man. 'I have just re-read your letter and now my head aches with a kind of sweet excitement. Do you know what I mean? It is what a little girl feels when she has been put to bed at the end of a long sunny day and still sees upon her closed eyelids the image of dancing boughs and flowery bushes. To work – to work! It is such infinite delight to know that we still have the best things to do and that we shall be comrades in the doing of them.'[35] Bertrand is to be a 'comrade'. Katherine always gets on better with men than women, preferring their conversation, hoping always for dialogue on equal terms.

> I tried to write to you yesterday but there were so many interruptions. Life seemed to rush in and out of my door like the teller of the tale in a Dostoevsky novel. But I thought of you. I re-read your letter, sitting on a bench at the top of the steps outside the British Museum . . . Your friendship was delightful, so delightful to me then that I sat there for a long time with the sun on my hands, almost too happy to move, and I began to call the pigeons to me with all kinds of little endearing names . . . Which left them quite cold . . . To feel that we are going to be truthful with each other, quite without reservation – that promises so great an adventure that it is difficult to remain calm. Do please talk to me about your work if you can.[36]

Bertrand is immensely impressed by Katherine. He tells Ottoline that he admires her passionately. Her conversation is 'marvellous, much better than her writing', but he is repelled by the dark side of her personality – what he calls her 'dark hatreds'. When she talks about people she is 'envious, dark, and full of alarming penetration' in discovering their secrets.[37] Bertrand is still married, though estranged from his wife, and romantically involved with two other women, apart from his continuing loyalty to Ottoline. His relationship with Katherine is limited by a need to be circumspect in the eyes of a gossiping world and it is fraught with misunderstandings. He is also very needy. He requires from women their undivided attention and admiration, and this is one aspect of the traditional male-female relationship that is anathema to Katherine. 'I meant to write to you immediately after you left me on Friday night to say how sorry I was to have been such cold comfort and so useless to lift even ever so little the cloud of your fatigue. For a long time I sat before the fire after you had gone feeling that your goodbye had been quite final – was it? And I did not explain myself as I wished to – I left unsaid so much that perhaps you were misled.' The next sentences make it clear, however, that their conversations are intellectual rather than corporeal. 'Its true that my desire is to bring all that I see and feel into harmony with that rare "vision" of life of which we spoke, and that if I do not achieve this I shall feel that my life has been a fault at last, and its my God terribly true that I don't see the means yet – I don't in the least know definitely how to live. But its equally true that life never bores me.'[38]

Throughout the autumn of 1916 there are further visits to Garsington, where Katherine is invited to Ottoline's personal sanctuary for intimate chats. Ottoline confides the misery of her relationship with Bertrand – how controlling and egotistical he had been. She had once told him that she wanted to spend her afternoons reading in order to educate herself and he had told her that it was a waste of time – she would learn far more from listening to him instead. In return Katherine tells Ottoline the story of her own life. Much of what Katherine reveals is outside Ottoline's experience and she is both shocked and fascinated.

She told me of the strange life she had led, of the opera company that she had found and after various adventures, of her marriage to a man called Bowden, who married her 'to protect' her. I didn't quite understand what the real position was, but she said that he took advantage of her and wanted to live with her which she had not bargained for, but I don't really know what is the truth of all this; obviously she disliked him and refused to live with him. She told me, too, of her meeting with Murry while he was still an undergraduate, and of his leaving Oxford to live with her, feeling that no sacrifice could be too great for the joy of her companionship. How they worked together on a magazine called Rhythm. This came to an end and they went to Paris for a time; but this is all rather vague in my mind, except that they enjoyed their life together and lived an adventurous and scampish life, such as taking a large house in the country, living in it for some months, going every Sunday to church where Murry would read the lessons, with the villagers touching their hats to them, enjoying the fun of being Landlord and Landlady, and then decamping leaving rent and trades-men and gardeners unpaid; and another time they had a piano on the three years hire purchase system, having partly paid for it they grew weary and poor and sold it, and then disappeared.

Although horrified by these revelations of irresponsibility, rather than the sexual adventures, Ottoline records perceptively that Katherine 'has had a very hard life, and that puts her on the defensive'. In these long conversa-tions Katherine also reveals the other side of her character, describing her childhood in New Zealand with such passion that Ottoline can actually see the aloe blossoming 'once in a fairy year'. It inspires Ottoline to wonder 'what she had been really like in those days which she loved to describe . . . I should love to have known this beautiful, secretive but impulsive and emotional woman before she had been hurt and bruised by life, and per-haps before the ambition of being an artist and a great writer, and of using people for that end had become such an absorbing game.'[39]

Despite Lytton's letter, Katherine has still not met Virginia Woolf. Though both women want a meeting, they are wary. A period of court-ship begins. Mutual friends go backwards and forwards with encouraging messages. There are a few tentative exchanges and then an invitation to dinner. Katherine is attracted to the 'strange, trembling, glinting quality' of Virginia's mind and to her physical beauty – a delicate, almost transparent skin stretched over fine bones, enormous eyes that sit deep in their sock-ets, watching everything, the whole framed by a confusion of silky hair escaping the control of combs and pins. Her manner is quiet, tremulous, visibly unstable, yet with a core of steel. She has an incisive wit and can be very funny and mischievous, earning her the family nickname of 'Goat'.

Virginia's impressions of Katherine are quite the opposite: she tells her sister Vanessa that Katherine is 'a forcible and utterly unscrupulous character'.[40] There is too much of the flesh and her manners are too 'forward' to please someone who has been brought up to value English reserve. Leonard Woolf likes Katherine because she makes him laugh, but Virginia looks down her patrician nose and wishes that her 'first impression of K.M. was not that she stinks like a – well civet cat that had taken to street walking. In truth, I'm a little shocked by her commonness at first sight; lines so hard & cheap.' But she is perceptive enough to admit that once the first impression has been put aside, 'she is so intelligent & inscrutable that she repays friendship'.[41]

Katherine's relationship with Virginia is marred by class differences. Virginia belongs to the upper classes of English society and has absorbed their strict conventions of speech and behaviour. To talk about a mirror, rather than a looking glass, is vulgar, as is discussing money, or the body. One writes letters on writing paper, not notepaper, and, at least in public, is polite to one's social inferiors. 'Ladies' do not wear make-up or perfume, though a little light 'toilet water' might be permitted. Clothes are bespoke, or purchased at exclusive shops, not bought off the peg at department stores such as Swan & Edgar. Among these people, Katherine is a foreigner in a country with strange tribal customs that she constantly infringes and, as the daughter of a colonial entrepreneur, she can never hope to belong. Her immediate circle is made up of people whose talents have lifted them out of the circumstances of their birth: Koteliansky is a Russian refugee, Mark Gertler is the son of immigrant Jewish fur sewers, Dora Carrington is the daughter of a Liverpool merchant, D. H. Lawrence's father had been a Nottinghamshire miner, and John Murry's father is a clerk in the civil service. At Garsington who you are is supposed to be more important than where you come from, but it is a turbulent mixture of people who are never entirely able to surmount their inherent class attitudes.

Some of the 'Blooms Berries' are repulsed by Katherine's directness, her earthiness and her ability to mock people's idiosyncrasies, including their own. When she uses New Zealand slang such as 'cross my heart and straight dinkum' or the ordinary swear words used in conversation by men, she is accused of having a mouth 'like a fish-wife from Wapping'. When she comes to a tea party and gives an entertaining account of a retail foray, acting the part of the shop assistant brilliantly, well-bred eyebrows are raised. When she goes to a balalaika concert with Ottoline, they are both enraptured by the music but, as they leave, Katherine ruins the evening for her companion by remarking, as she bids her goodnight, 'My corns are hurting. I must go to my old corn-cutter tomorrow.'[42]

Katherine's new friendship with Ottoline, her dislike of Frieda and her loyalty to Lawrence have drawn her into correspondence that could be regarded as either diplomatic or devious. The habit of circulating letters freely among the Garsington set means that private sentiments are very quickly made public. Frieda is bewildered that Katherine could be so nice to her face when they had lived together at Zennor and yet so cruel in letters to other people. Katherine's caustic tongue is not made for diplomacy, as Ottoline observes in her diary. When describing people she 'is certainly not kind or charitable'.[43] Frieda is having a terrible time in Cornwall. Lawrence has been in a black humour since the Murrys left and is spending much of his time at Tregerthen Farm, in the company of the local farmer, William Henry. When he comes back, often late at night, he is angry and quarrelsome and violent towards Frieda. At one point she breaks a heavy dish over his head in an attack that could easily have been fatal. During the day their cottage is liable to sudden visits from the local police, who are convinced that they are spying for the Germans. Frieda feels 'utterly alone', surrounded by 'creeping foulness'.[44] Desperately in need of friends, she can't understand why everyone seems to hate her and comes up to London to see her children and talk to Kot. A man of complete integrity, he is the one person who manages to stay above the back-biting, double standards and gossip. His friends say that telling a lie in Kot's company is impossible because the power of his honesty shames everyone into truth. He is horrified by what Frieda tells him about the Murrys – that they have been reviling Frieda to Ottoline, while at the same time writing friendly letters to Zennor. Kot breaks off his relationship with Katherine, accusing her of mendacity, and the Murrys decide to end all communication with the Lawrences. 'This is just as well,' Lawrence writes to Gertler, 'for I don't want it to go on. One gets too sick of all these twists and falsities.'[45]

The Murrys are invited to spend Christmas at Garsington. The guests have great fun decorating the house with Chinese lanterns, coloured paper garlands and evergreen swags. There is a fancy dress dinner and Katherine invents a very clever game where everyone must write an anonymous letter addressed to someone in the room, the names being drawn out of a hat. The results are hilarious and even libellous. Then someone suggests a variant where people are described by symbols, such as pictures and flow-ers and scents, and everyone has to guess who it is. Katherine is described 'by some rather exotic scent such as stephanotis or patchouli'. The meta-phor is not intended to be complimentary, and though her name is not mentioned everyone knows who is referred to. Ottoline is mortified by the atmosphere, confiding her feelings to her diary afterwards. 'The spite that was in the company maliciously flared out against her and hurt her. We all filed out of the drawing room to bed very silently. I knew that Katherine and Murry would have much to say about it when alone.'[46] It is not all they have to discuss. There is a great deal of gossip during the week about the way in which Bertrand Russell and Katherine have been sitting up late into the night in the red-lacquered dining room, talking and smoking. Ottoline, who suspects that they are talking about her, complains that they are keeping her awake and hints that she has overheard some of their con-versation. Bertrand, who has been asking Katherine's advice on how to break free from Ottoline, aggravates the situation by telling Ottoline that Katherine is 'a very jealous woman' who would like to poison her mind against other people so as to be her exclusive friend.

The highlight of the holiday is the play that Katherine scribbles out in pencil to entertain everyone: 'The Laurels' is a skit on Chekhov that sends up almost every convention of Russian literature. Lytton Strachey plays the 'wicked' Dr Keit, wearing a fur coat and a paper mask with a red worsted beard made by Carrington, who plays his grandchild, the illegiti-mate Muriel Dash, abandoned under the laurel hedge as a baby. Katherine is Muriel's mother, Florence Kaziany, who makes a dramatic return in time to prevent her daughter repeating her own mistake by falling fatally in love with the lodger – a Dostoevsky character called Ivan Tchek, played by John. Does it give Katherine a frisson to write and then play the part of an unmarried mother? 'Don't you know, Miss, that's the reason what young girls like me jump off buses & in front of trains and eat rat poison & swoller acids & often murder themselves?'[47] The play is, in Aldous Huxley's words, 'superb . . . a huge success'.[48] Katherine has finally earned her place in the *Garsington Chronicle*.

January 1917 is a difficult month – 'crisis after crisis'.[49] Ida has a skilled job as a tool setter in an aeroplane factory and just after Christmas is involved in an accident there. Katherine, knowing that Ida is living alone in lodgings, cancels a planned return to Garsington and devotes a lot of time taking Ida to hospital and nursing her back to health. Then Katherine herself is ill again with congestion of the lungs after getting chilled at a film studio where she had to walk about in 'a big bare studio in what the American producer calls "slap up evening dress"'.[50] John is rarely there, having been swallowed up by the war machine. Katherine realises that her position at the Ark has become untenable. She feels she is being spied on by Carrington, who writes bitchily to Bloomsbury friends about Katherine getting dressed up strangely (her film career?) and going out at night to walk the streets – something Katherine often does when she can't sleep. Carrington, in the grip of an obsession with Lytton, can't bear the fact that when he comes to call at the Ark, it is Katherine he wants to see. Katherine is tired of communal life and the lack of privacy makes it difficult to write. She would love to have a proper apartment in a desirable part of London, shared with John, but her heart sinks at the thought of trying to find one. Her past experiences 'have absolutely robbed me of my courage in that respect. When I am really faced with the practical prospect I draw back and shiver. Do you remember as vividly as I do ALL those houses ALL those flats ALL those rooms we have taken and withdrawn from [?] My valiant little warrior have you forgotten the horrors?'[51] Having to 'climb flights of dirty stairs & shiver past pails containing dead tea leaves & bitten ends of bread and marmalade outside other people's doors – the trace of those places seems to cling round the hem of ones skirt for ever'.[52]

Then there is the money problem. 'I'd far rather sit in a furnished room in an hotel & work than have a lovely flat & feel that the strain of money was crippling us again.'[53] Rents are only £60 to £65 a year, which Murry could easily afford out of his current salary of £260, with money over to keep both himself and Katherine but, under the conventions of their relationship, they each pay their own expenses and Katherine can't afford half the costs of such a property on her £156 allowance. She is also adamant that she must have a separate studio. There are other obstacles too. Landlords of quality apartments in London want references to make sure that their tenants are respectable. Katherine asks St John Hutchinson, Mary's husband, but he declines on the grounds that she and John are unmarried and living publicly 'in sin'. He politely avoids mention of the fact that John is also an undischarged bankrupt. Bertrand Russell steps in with an offer, but his reputation is tarnished since he is about to be tried in court for his activities as a pacifist. Finally Ottoline is asked for a character reference.

It is not a good time to ask. Lawrence's manuscript of *Women in Love* had arrived on Ottoline's doorstep just after her Christmas guests had left. She had begun to read it with great anticipation but turned absolutely 'pale with horror' finding herself called 'every name from an "old hag" obsessed by sex-mania, to a corrupt Sapphist'. There is an accurate description of Garsington in the novel, but, most annoying of all, 'the worst parts of it [are] written in Frieda's handwriting'.[54] Ottoline is terribly upset and her husband Philip goes to Lawrence's agent, J. B. Pinker, and tells him that if the novel is published in its present form they will sue for libel. Katherine has not yet seen the manuscript but has been told that two of the characters are based on her and John. Brett is also indignant and Katherine repeats her opinions to Ottoline: 'Left to himself, Lawrence goes mad'.[55] Frieda, of course, is at the bottom of it all. Katherine is adamant that the book should not be published, despite her belief in Lawrence as an author. 'He must be stopped. I think it is really fatal that such books should be published.'[56] The Morrells do not need to worry, however. After the débâcle of *The Rainbow* no one cares to take the risk with another novel and the manuscript is refused by every publisher in London. To compound Lawrence's troubles, he is also refused a passport to America because he is a man of military age.

Katherine's search for accommodation is complicated by the fact that George Bowden has been in touch again. He is now in America and has met a woman he wants to marry. Divorce proceedings are to be initiated. Neither John nor Katherine has forgotten that when Professor Ernest Weekley divorced Frieda, Lawrence was cited as co-respondent and ordered to pay punitive compensation to her husband. John must be protected from that, even if they have to live apart for a while. Katherine decides to rent a studio apartment, which means that John will either have to stay at the Ark or take rooms for himself somewhere else. The first place Katherine finds is snatched from her by a 'perfidious pole' (who may or may not have been Floryan, who keeps reappearing in her life when she least wants him). But eventually she finds the perfect studio apartment in Church Street, Chelsea. A rectangular room, built between two adjacent houses, it has a kitchen and balcony on a mezzanine level jutting out over the main room and, high above the door, a huge window that Katherine refers to as her 'Thou-God-Seest-Me' window. At the back, glass doors open onto a sunny communal garden and during the day the room is flooded with light. Katherine signs the lease at the end of January and her Cornish furniture is delivered the following week. Her Japanese doll, Ribni, sits on the mantelpiece beside her treasured Dresden clock, and the sofa bought at an auction in St Ives – so uncomfortable Katherine calls it 'the stickle-back' – is placed across the corner of the room facing the fire. A bowl of anemones is arranged on the black and yellow chest containing Katherine's clothes and her writing table is against the wall behind the door, giving her a view out into the garden.

The peace and privacy have an immediate effect on her ability to work. 'I am a recluse at present & do nothing but write & read & read & write – seeing nobody & going nowhere.' She turns down invitations to Garsington and is working on 'God knows how many long short stories and notes and sketches' as well as a play she calls 'Toots' or 'the Ship in the Harbour'.[57] Katherine has always been interested in the theatre and the walk-on roles she has been getting in the film industry have also begun to influence the way she writes. In an experimental story called 'The Black Cap', the action unrolls in cinematic scenes as though seen through the lens of a camera. Many of the sketches are either monologues or short playlets of the kind that she had once written for the New Age and some time in February or March she has a reunion with Orage. He has finally broken with an increasingly unstable Beatrice and, though a few of her 'Alice Morning' pieces appear sporadically, she is no longer a regular contributor. A selection of Katherine's fragments, written in Church Street, is published in the New Age in April 1917. Among them is an evocation of her solitary life.

Late in the evening, after you have cleared away your supper, blown the crumbs out of the book that you were reading, lighted the lamp, and curled up in front of the fire – that is the moment to beware of the rain. You are conscious of a sudden hush. You open your eyes wide. What's that? Hullo, it's raining! Reluctant at first, and then faster and faster, tapping against the window, beating on the door, comes the rain. The air seems to change; you are so aware of the dark flowing water that your hands and cheeks grow cold. You begin to walk up and down. How loud the rain sounds! You catch sight of yourself in the mirror, and you think that you look very plain. You say to that plain creature in the wavy glass: 'I am twenty-eight, and I have chosen, but absolutely deliberately chosen, to live quite alone for ever.' The creature in the glass gives a short laugh and says: 'C'est pour rire, ça. [That's laughable.]' But you reply severely: 'Don't speak French if you're English; it's a vulgar habit.' Now there are quick steps coming up the garden path, stopping at the door. Someone is coming. But nobody knocks. Again there are steps and again that pause as though someone felt for the wet door-knocker in the dark. You are sure that somebody is there. Nobody. You remember that the kitchen window is wide open. Is the rain coming in? No, not really. You lean out a moment. Two little roof gutters flow into the garden. In the dark they sound like two women sobbing and laughing, talking together and complaining and laughing, out in the wet garden. One says: 'Life is not gay, Katherine. No, life is not gay.' But now the rain is over. The lamp-post outside, yellow in the light, with a spray of shining tree across it, looks like a very bad illustration out of a Dickens novel. Yes, it is quite over. You make up the fire and squat before it, spreading out your hands, as though you had been rescued, from a shipwreck, and just to be alive and safe were bliss enough.[58]

In February 1917, Ida moves into the Church Street studio to keep Katherine company and also to be closer to the factory for the 7 a.m. start. In the *New Age* there's a short sketch of an evening with L.M., which gives a less than complimentary verbatim account of Ida's conversation and her relationship with Katherine, but Ida, content to know she is still needed, seems oblivious of this use of their friendship. She's thoroughly enjoying the practical work and the all-girls-together camaraderie of the shop floor and is making other friends among her co-workers, many of whom are debutantes and upper middle class girls like herself, cheerfully roughing it for the war effort. Ida's presence at Church Street gives Katherine a feeling of security. Ida sleeps on a bed on a little curtained balcony on the mezzanine level, beside the kitchen and when Katherine has visitors, she lies on her bed so quietly many of them don't even know she's there. After a while, she has an agreement with Katherine that she will stay out until 9 p.m., allowing Katherine private time with John. On the nights that Ida can't be there, Katherine, 'after a struggle to be "sensible"', walks the streets from midnight 'till early dawn' because she is too afraid to be alone in the flat.[59] Her night terrors are sudden and 'so violent, so dreadful' that they are uncontrollable. On one occasion she runs out of the studio and through the streets to John's room in Fulham. He is at Garsington, but his landlady lets Katherine in. She sits in front of John's gas fire until the fear subsides, wrapped in his overcoat, surrounded by his familiar possessions, writing a love letter in his private notebook.[60]

Katherine and John are leading separate lives – he comments in his diary that they have 'gone beyond the personal'. He goes to see her almost every evening and allows her to cook him some supper, and occasionally even spends the night when Ida is away, but declares that 'life with her [is] no part of the texture of my life any more'.[61] His wartime experiences have deadened his sensibilities and he is losing 'all belief in love'. News of the death of Frederick Goodyear in France on 23 May, affects them both deeply in different ways. For John it is just one more confirmation of the senseless horror of the war. For Katherine the loss is more personal. Any hopes she may have had about a relationship with Goodyear after the war are now gone. Two of the men she has most loved, her brother and Goodyear, are both dead and she commits herself even more strongly to her work. On 30 May Katherine writes in her notebook, 'To be alive and to be a "writer" is enough . . . There is nothing like it.'[62]

In May a school friend from Wellington, Marion Ruddick, visits London on leave from France where she is serving as a nurse aide with the Voluntary Aid Detachment. She has been given Katherine's address by Chaddie, who is working at the War Graves Registry. Marion finds it hard to believe that the Katherine she had known in New Zealand is the 'slight young woman' who opens the door. Katherine has lost weight, her hair is 'short and straight' and her eyes seem enormous, accentuated by 'the pallor of her now oval face'. Marion notices that Katherine moves around the room 'slowly and with slight difficulty'.

Katherine has been ignoring the deterioration in her physical health. Over the winter she has been troubled by a 'disastrous' cough, and by arthritis. Every now and then her hip flares up, preventing her from walking very far. Her spine has begun to ache and she has pain in her arm and hand. Marion and Katherine sit outside the studio doors under the laburnum tree, drinking tea and reminiscing, before going out to lunch in Soho. Marion notices that when it is time to go, Katherine gets up from the chair, carefully, 'with the brave little laugh she gave when in pain or discomfort'. Katherine's lack of concern for her own physical well-being worries Marion. At Le Petit Savoyard in Greek Street, one of Katherine's favourite restaurants, she smokes cheap cigarettes known as 'Yellow Perils' during the meal and drinks cup after cup of coffee.[63]

Throughout the spring and summer of 1917 Katherine's life becomes more sociable again. There are invitations to Bloomsbury parties and new friendships with Siegfried Sassoon and T. S. Eliot. Katherine records walking home from a party with Tom Eliot on a moonlit night, 'past rows of little ugly houses hiding behind bitter smelling privet hedges' while 'a great number of amorous black cats looped across the road'.[64] Anne Estelle Rice and J. D. Fergusson have been living in London since the beginning of the war, and Katherine is often at the theatre founded by Fergusson's mistress, the dancer Margaret Morris, to promote her particular style of modern dance. Virginia Woolf comes to tea and a delicate intimacy is gradually established. They discuss literature, finding common ground – 'Virginia . . . pray consider how rare is it to find someone with the same passion for writing that you have, who desires to be scrupulously truthful with you'.[65] Katherine is not so scrupulous when she gives Virginia an account of her early history that exaggerates her sexual adventures and expands the short period with Garnet in Scotland into a more prolonged episode, travelling with the chorus of the opera company, cooking kippers over gas rings and living on porridge. 'I had an odd talk with K. Mansfield last night,' Virginia writes to her sister Vanessa. 'She seems to have gone every sort of hog since she was 17.' But Virginia thinks Katherine has 'a much better idea of writing than most'.[66] Her sister agrees. On the twin subjects of art and literature, there is no one except 'KM or Forster even with whom its worth discussing one's business'.[67]

When Virginia and Leonard buy a printing press, Katherine is the first person to be asked for a story, to be printed after their own joint publication, *Two Stories*, containing Leonard's 'Two Jews' and Virginia's 'The Mark on the Wall'. The obvious choice for the Hogarth Press is 'The Aloe', but it is too unwieldy in its present form and Katherine begins to edit it down under a new title, 'Prelude', suggested by John. In June Virginia invites Katherine to dine with her alone and Katherine confesses that ever since their last meeting she has been a bit 'haunted' by her, adding 'I long to see you again'. Virginia is the first woman with whom Katherine can talk about writing on the same level. They share an absolute commitment to their work; both are searching for a new way of 'showing and telling', and both are trying to succeed in what is viewed as a man's world. 'I love to think of you, Virginia, as my friend. Don't cry me an ardent creature or say, with your head a little on one side, smiling as though you knew some enchanting secret: "Well, Katherine, we shall see".'[68]

Apart from encouraging Katherine to edit 'The Aloe' into 'Prelude', the conversations with Virginia help Katherine to crystallise her own ideas about fictional technique. As she tells Dorothy Brett, in order for art to make 'that divine spring into the bounding outlines of things' it must first pass through the process of trying 'to become these things'. She explains that when she writes about apples or ducks she becomes that object: 'this whole process of becoming the duck (what Lawrence would, perhaps call this "consummation with the duck or the apple") is so thrilling that I can hardly breathe, only to think about it. For although that is as far as most people can get, it is really only the "prelude". There follows the moment when you are more duck, more apple or more Natasha than any of these objects could ever possibly be.'[69] Her use of the word 'prelude' in this context gives a clue to her enigmatic title for the revised 'Aloe'.

Virginia has not yet been to Garsington, but Katherine waxes lyrical on its virtues, describing a recent visit to her. The weather had been stunning, with long, hot, dry summer days and warm summer nights with the scent of flowers blowing in through the open windows. Katherine and Ottoline had cut lavender, sweet geranium, verbena, rose leaves and rosemary to make pot-pourri and, in the evening, Katherine had wandered alone in the garden among the beds of nicotiana and night-scented stock. Carrington and some of her friends 'danced a wild and lovely ballet on the lawn, their white limbs shining in the moonlight' and then all stripped off to go skinny-dipping in the pond.

> The big dark house hid secretly
> Behind the magnolia and the spreading pear-tree,
> But there was a sound of music – music rippled and ran
> Like a lady laughing behind her fan,' . . .

> 'I can't dance to that Hungarian stuff,
> The rhythm in it is not passionate enough,'
> Said somebody. 'I absolutely refuse . . .'
> But he took off his socks and his shoes . . .

> 'Is the moon a virgin or is she a harlot?'
> Asked somebody. Nobody would tell.
> The faces and the hands moved in a pattern
> As the music rose and fell,
> In a dancing, mysterious, moon-bright pattern
> Like flowers nodding under the sea . . .[70]

The garden at Garsington fascinates Katherine. It reminds her of the one in Tolstoy's story 'Family Happiness', which she has read so often she knows it almost by heart. When she returns to London an idea for another story begins to grow. 'Who,' she asks in a letter, 'is going to write about that flower garden. It might be so wonderful – do you see how I mean? There would be people walking in the garden – several pairs of people – their conversation their slow pacing – their glances as they pass one another – the pauses as the flowers 'come in' as it were – as a bright dazzle, an exquisite haunting scent, a shape so formal and fine, so much a flower of the mind . . . The "pairs" of people must be very different and there must be a slight touch of enchantment . . . A kind of, musically speaking – conversation set to flowers.'[71] This 'glimpse of the garden, all flying green and gold', stirs something in Virginia's mind that is distilled into the story she calls 'Kew Gardens', written within a week or so of receiving Katherine's letter. When Virginia shows it to her, Katherine accepts with a good grace that her idea has been 'stolen'. The 'Flower Bed', she writes, 'is very good. 'There's a still, quivering, changing light over it all and a sense of those couples dissolving in the bright air which fascinates me.'[72]

Katherine's own work has been increasingly hampered by pain and rheumatism in her right hand. On 31 July she goes to visit the Beauchamp family doctor and spends half the day 'being thumped and banged & held up by the heels'. The doctor tells her very firmly that if she spends another winter in England she will 'bend and bow under my rheumatism until I [become] a sort of permanent croquet hoop'.[73] After the hip and the spine, the joints of the wrist and hand are most commonly affected as tuberculosis progresses, but no one has made the connection. Katherine is now having to employ a typist to type out her stories because her hand is too painful to copy them.

She has been a regular contributor to the New Age since April. It is the usual mix of actresses in hard times falling into prostitution, charwomen and dissatisfied wives. But among them are some of her mature stories, such as 'Mr Reginald Peacock's Day', 'A Dill Pickle' and 'Monsieur Seguin's Goat' – a translation from Alphonse Daudet. Some of her contributions express her growing cynicism about the world of art and letters, and for the gossiping, back-stabbing, amoral people she meets in it. There is a cruel satire of the kind of conversation she overhears from the serious young men at Garsington and, in the same piece, an indictment of friendship between women. 'Why are we so shy of each other?' the female narrator asks, and answers herself straight away: 'Women are such traitors to one another, aren't they? One can feel that one is everything to another woman, her dearest friend – her closest – and the most commonplace little man has only to come along and lift a finger for her to betray you, to let you down!'[74]

This is perhaps a reference to what Katherine regards as Ottoline's betrayal of their friendship. She now believes that Ottoline is trying to take John away from her. On their last visit, Ottoline had offered them both a cottage in the grounds, which they could have as a weekend retreat. Katherine is initially delighted. John, who has begun to write a long verse play called 'Cinnamon and Angelica', stays on at Garsington in July after Katherine leaves to go back to London. Ottoline is aware that things are fragile between the Murrys. During her stay, Katherine had been very impatient with John's absorption in his work, complaining that every time she went near him she felt like an interruption. She had shocked Ottoline by telling her that she 'would like to shake him' and calling him 'a little mole hung out on a string to dry'. She had also said that she would like to find John 'a sweet gentle "Muriel", who would give no trouble, but would pet him, look after him and mend his clothes'.[75]

John feels estranged from Katherine. In the five years they have been together, she has pushed him away and pulled him towards her until he scarcely knows what their relationship is meant to be. His feelings are expressed in a poem called 'The Return'.

> An hour and I shall see you. Delicately
> A light will pass across your wakening eyes;
> They will be smiling, steady, saying to me;
> 'There was no parting, all those days were lies.
> I left you on the instant.' I will hesitate
> Whether to kiss you, but a second gone
> Since last we kissed; decide when all too late;
> Then wonder would a year of love atone.
>
> You, knowing my mind, will smile and touch my hand.
> Or did you touch it then? . . . Ah, no, an hour,
> A leaden hour, that will not understand,
> But moon-faced mocks me from the tall clock-tower

And will not lock the door upon the band
Of devil doubts that hold me in their power.[76]

In the first months of their relationship he had asked her to marry him, and refers to her everywhere as his wife but, now that their marriage is on the brink of becoming a reality, he is suffering second thoughts. Does he really want to be tied irrevocably to this mercurial woman? There are unpleasant memories of how she left him for Carco, resurrected by Carco's latest novel, *Les Innocents*, which John is asked to review for the *Times Literary Supplement*. Katherine is recognisably portrayed as the main female character and there are quotations from her letters that reveal far more of their relationship than John had been aware of at the time. It is a significant blow to realise that Katherine had not told him the truth. John is now more socially confident and aware that other women find him attractive.

Perhaps subconsciously looking for a way of escape and desperately looking for uncritical love, he naively pursues a relationship with Ottoline, who is on the rebound from Bertrand Russell and vulnerable. He tells her the tragic story of his childhood, and persuades Ottoline to offer a place on the farm to his younger brother Richard, who is a conscientious objector. They sit up late into the night discussing poetry and literature. Ottoline is unwittingly drawn into intimacy. Suddenly, late one evening in the red room, John makes what could be construed as a pass at Ottoline and asks her outright whether he can 'come into her heart'. Startled, she gives a noncommittal answer and goes up to bed. But later, unable to sleep, she gets up and goes out into the garden. John hears her, opens his window and she calls him down. They walk in the moonlit garden and talk. Nothing happens and Ottoline believes that she has successfully defused the situation. But when John returns to London he is so distraught and wretched that Katherine presses him until, like a scene from a melodrama, he shows her a handkerchief Ottoline had given him and tells her that Ottoline has fallen passionately in love with him. Katherine is devastated. John, at her insistence, writes a formal letter refusing the cottage and Katherine's previously enthusiastic correspondence with Ottoline becomes noticeably cool. 'There are three unfinished letters to you in my writing case,' she writes on 11 August, 'one is even five pages long. I could not re-read them but I know why they were not sent . . . I heard my own little mocking, mechanical voice, loathed it, and chose silence.'[77]

Ottoline is bewildered, but aware that she is being used in some kind of emotional game. She comes up to London to confront Katherine and try to explain what had happened. The only way to disabuse Katherine of her impression is to say what Ottoline feels is the truth: 'What a mean liar Murry is'. Understanding more of John's emotional make-up than anyone else, Katherine realises that Ottoline is not entirely to blame and assures her that the crisis between them is over – 'for my part, my friendship couldn't end'. Ottoline is less sure. Brett then tells Ottoline that Katherine is fiercely jealous and talking about her in the bitter, cruel way that Ottoline recognises. 'She enjoys mocking,' Ottoline writes, 'and I recoil from it.'[78]

Towards the end of August, Katherine makes a much anticipated visit to the Woolfs at Asheham House, in Sussex. Lytton Strachey is there too and there are long walks over the downs hunting for mushrooms, and evenings in the garden talking about literature and discussing mutual friends. Virginia is quick to relay Garsington gossip about Katherine passed on by her brother-in-law Clive Bell, relating to Bertrand Russell – there's even a rumour she's been sleeping with Mark Gertler. Katherine refutes this: '. . . don't let THEM ever persuade you that I spend any of my precious time swapping hats or committing adultery – I'm far too arrogant & proud. However, let them think what they like.'[79] To Ottoline she is even more vehement. 'To Hell with the Blooms Berries.'[80]

Though their letters are superficially affectionate, the rift between Katherine and Ottoline is not fully healed and neither completely trusts the other. The people around them make the most of the situation, sharpening their teeth on the 'old Gossip Bone', and labelling it 'The Mansfield Intrigue'.[81] Stories spread like Chinese Whispers. A light-hearted sentence about a visit to the theatre in one of Katherine's letters to Ottoline – 'the Bangos were only really lovely once and last time I felt that I was playing Cook to your Duchess in Alice in Wonderland'[82] – reaches Virginia as 'You shan't play the Countess to my Cook any more'.[83] Katherine is furious, blaming Clive Bell again, and there is an awkward dinner party with Virginia at Hogarth House in Richmond, where 'delicate things' are discussed and smoothed over.

Katherine is particularly sensitive to gossip during the autumn, since her divorce from George Bowden is to be heard shortly. Few people in Bloomsbury know that Katherine is Mrs George Bowden and secrecy is imperative. George is granted a decree nisi against Katherine on 17 October on the grounds of adultery, but it will be six months before the decree becomes absolute and she is free to marry John. She makes plans for a new apartment. There are dreams of a cottage in the country with some land for John. It will be called The Heron, in memory of her brother, Leslie Heron Beauchamp.

John has recently been promoted, with a doubling of his salary: he is now the editor of a publication called the *Daily Review of the Foreign Press* and shortly to become chief censor. He is still working on his verse play, 'Cinnamon and Angelica', perhaps as an antidote to the dull grind of his war work. The plot of the play is extraordinary. Two warring kingdoms are ruled by star-crossed lovers, Cinnamon Prince of the Peppercorns, and Angelica Princess of the Cloves, who are doomed never to be together. Among the other 'spice' characters are Colonel Mace and a housekeeper called Vanilla Bean. It is an antique thing, which might have had relevance a hundred, or even two hundred years earlier, but it sounds stale and melodramatic in 1917. Beautiful lines drown in seas of sentimental abstraction and the language is contorted and archaic. Prince Cinnamon is described as being

> Sick like Endymion of the wondrous story
> In converse with Paeona; till he flings
> His thought-o'erwearied body on a bed
> Of poppies . . .

John shows the early drafts to Katherine, who always struggles to tell him frankly what she feels about his work. She often makes encouraging noises face to face, then writes a letter afterwards with the unpalatable facts concealed, like a pill wrapped up in bleached linen. His poetry contains 'beautiful things', she tells him, but he has a tendency in his writing to expose himself. 'What is it? Is it your desire to torture yourself or to pity yourself or something far subtler?' He should be less confessional in his work, particularly his journalism and hide his inner self as she does, whatever the cost. 'Don't lower your mask until you have another mask prepared beneath – As terrible as you like – but a mask.'[84]

The strain of leading a double life as a civil servant and a writer is beginning to tell on John, who is more fragile mentally and physically than anyone guesses. Overworking, anxious about the future, emotionally confused about his personal life, he neglects himself and by the end of October weighs less than 50 kilograms. One morning he wakes in his room and feels too weak to get out of bed and go to the office. His land-lady sends a note to Katherine, who summons the doctor. John is having a severe breakdown and the doctor also tells Katherine that his weight loss indicates he is at risk from TB. Complete rest is prescribed, preferably in the country. Katherine has to swallow her pride and write to Ottoline. 'Murry is VERY ill. The doctor says he must go away for at least five weeks and perhaps for longer . . . He has been really WASTING AWAY. I simply turn to you.'[85] Ottoline, generous to the last, sends an immediate telegram: 'OF COURSE DELIGHTED HAVE YOU BOTH DEAREST KATHERINE COME SOON WHY NOT TODAY'.[86] Leave of absence is arranged from the War Office and John goes down to Garsington, without Katherine, whose own health is far from robust, though John has failed to notice her deteriora-tion and, characteristically, she always makes light of her ailments.

A fortnight after John goes to Garsington, Katherine comes down for a weekend visit. The November weather is bitterly cold and Katherine arrives almost frozen from the ride in the dogcart. The following day she feels unwell and has to stay in bed. She tells Ottoline that it is only a 'bit of a chill', but she is still feeling ill when she takes the train back to London and shortly after arriving develops a high fever, cough and the familiar chest pains – 'as though I had been shot in the wing' – that Katherine associates with pleurisy. 'It's nothing,' she tells Ida, 'I've had it before, it will go.'[87] The doctor, called by Ida, confirms the diagnosis and insists that Katherine 'lie low' for at least a week. She promises to stay in bed and tells Ida that 'Ma Parker', the 'daily' she shares with Anne Estelle Rice, will come in and 'see to everything'. Ida is horrified to discover that this is a lie and that Katherine has been coping alone while she has been at work. It is not only Katherine's chest that is the trouble – as usual, when the hidden bacilli flare up in her lungs, their compatriots riot in her bones. 'My bloody rheu-matism has ramped and raged – When it really descends on me – I become a crawling thing without the power of doing anything except cursing my fate . . . I am so down in the depths that I can't imagine anything ever fish-ing me up again.'[88] There's also a new symptom. As Katherine lies sleepless in the middle of the night she's aware of a heightened state of mind she calls 'furious bliss'.[89] She can feel her blood buzzing in her veins. Katherine refuses to accept the verdict of the Beauchamps' doctor, and her neigh-bour, Prudence Maufe, recommends another Harley Street specialist, Dr Ainger. He is a New Zealander, loves Tolstoy and is much more congenial, but his diagnosis is as depressing as his colleague's. Dr Ainger forbids her to travel 'even in a car from this door to that',[90] and she reluctantly has to cancel an invitation to Garsington for Christmas. J. D. Fergusson calls and makes Katherine laugh too much by talking of 'one foot in the grave and the other on a banana skin'. Her sister Chaddie and Aunt Belle arrive, bringing hampers of food, warm rugs and a quilted housecoat big enough 'for at least three Wigs great with child'. It is an indicator of how much weight Katherine has lost. She tells John that Ida, Chaddie and Belle 'have stuffed this place with food for me'. But, though she eats 'like a warrior', everything goes into a sort of 'Dead Letter Office'.[91] Ida is doing her best to make sure that Katherine has a nourishing diet and it infuriates and exhausts Katherine to argue against the implacable will of 'the Rhodesian Mountain', a nickname that refers to Ida's immovability as well as her height and her large feet.

She: Which would you rather have. Hot milk or Oxo.
Me: Oxo please.
She: Oh, don't you think you'd rather have hot milk?
Me: No thanks. Oxo, please.
She: But don't you think hot milk is more nourishing.
Me: Oxo, please.
She: I wish you would have hot milk, just to please me.
Me: Oxo, please.
She: Very well dear. But what about having Oxo in the hot milk. Isn't that a good idea?
Me: Plain Oxo, please.
She: (from the kitchen) Oh, Katya dear, I find there isn't any Oxo left. Will you have milk?
Me: !!!!!!!![92]

John comes up to London briefly to see Katherine and finds her 'thin and bright-eyed in her little bed',[93] insisting that she's mending fast. Knowing that her doctors have recommended that she stay out of England for the winter, John suggests she returns to the south of France, but Katherine refuses to consider it. She doesn't want to be parted from John again, she has a lively circle of friends, and her work is going well. The interruption is not to be considered. 'Please don't mention it . . . I just couldn't. I am really not the least seriously ill.'[94] She has found a flat near John's room in Redcliffe Road. It's big enough for both of them, when they are able to live together again, and, at 11s a week, not too expensive. John is shocked by Katherine's appearance. She is still taking an optimistic view of her doctor's opinion, but John senses that she's not telling him everything and that things are much more serious. He leaves for Garsington with a horrible sense of foreboding. 'Deep in my heart,' he writes later, 'was the black stone of unbelief.'[95]

Although all Katherine wants to do is stay in England and move into her new flat, she is not to be given the chance. On his next visit Dr Ainger spells out the reality of tuberculosis.[96] She writes to John at Garsington, telling him the worst without ever mentioning the word. Her left lung has a 'loud deafening creak', there is a spot on her right lung and unless she takes sensible measures it will develop. 'It is *evidement* rather a bad'un of its kind.' There is only one course open to her. 'The doctor says I must never stay in England for another winter but must leave in September & not come back until April, and at present as soon as I am well enough he has given me a medical certificate for the South of France, and I hope to be able to leave in January.' She asks John to write to the Hotel Beau Rivage to book a room with a view of the sea, 'But don't mention LUNGS or they will take fright. You know the french. They'd imagine I had come there to gallop away.' The prospect of the journey is daunting, and neither John nor Ida can get leave from their war work to accompany her – Ida's factory is willing to release her but her visa application is refused. Katherine is gripped by fear. 'I feel that life has changed so and it has all happened so quickly – all my plans are altered – all my future is touched by this, all our future rather. It's like suddenly mounting a very fresh, very unfamiliar horse – a *queer queer* feeling . . . I wish we could have been married before I go.'[97]

John spends Christmas at Garsington with Ottoline and Brett; Katherine alone in London with Ida. On 7 January 1918, Ida dresses Katherine in her warmest clothes, 'with a large fur muff owned by one or other of us', and she and John take Katherine to the station, anxiously watching her walk down the platform to the boat-train, frail and very alone, 'swaying a little with weakness' as she walks.[98]

PART V

Betty

When she was in full spate Betty was awe-inspiring — a
truly elemental fury. To attempt to reason with her was
impossible. She despised reason. To try to follow her line of
thought when she was working herself up into a rage was
to risk permanent dislocation of the intellect. Not only
that, at such times she exuded a sort of black, demonic
force of pure annihilation like a psychic miasma.

COLIN MIDDLETON MURRY, ONE HAND CLAPPING

16

In Limbo

Wandering between two worlds, one dead,
The other powerless to be born ...

MATTHEW ARNOLD, *STANZAS FROM THE GRANDE CHARTREUSE*

When John moved to Norfolk in July 1931 he was almost forty-two and had not yet found the settled relationship and secure family life he craved. He wrote in his journal: 'I have a longing to take root and to abide in one place. I have had this longing now for so many years; but it has never been fulfilled.'[1] Eight weeks after the death of his young wife Violet he had married his housekeeper, Betty Cockbayne, to provide continuity for himself and his two small children. She was already pregnant. Still in a catatonic emotional state, John sublimated his grief in writing, physical exercise and an intense attachment to his daughter, Weg, who was the image of her mother and whom he believed to embody the spirit of Katherine Mansfield. His son, Colin, was constantly overlooked, observing silently as Weg sat in a privileged position on his father's knee, watching from the staircase as Weg was welcomed into his father's study, too young to fathom the particular emotional blindness that caused his father, when challenged, to deny favouritism.

John was now quite a wealthy man. Apart from his own earnings from literature, there was the annuity from Violet's trust fund, and Katherine's royalties formed a substantial part of his income – at least £500 a year. Her stories were selling well on both sides of the Atlantic, the *Journal of Katherine Mansfield*, published in 1927, had been particularly popular and a compilation of her book reviews, *Novels and Novelists*, published in 1930, was also paying its way. The days of country cottages and timber-clad bungalows were gone. Larling was a gentleman's residence, a large and graceful Georgian rectory with a walled garden, set in over 3.5 hectares of meadowland, hidden from the road by mature trees. After the restrictions of the bungalow at Yateley, where everything had been geared to nurse a dying Violet, the children found the freedom wonderful. John, a recent convert to socialism, enrolled them both in the village school and set about reclaiming the land. He planted fruit trees, dug vegetable beds and kept bees, just as he and Katherine had always dreamed when they talked about 'The Heron'. There was only one flaw in this idyllic existence – his wife Betty.

John had been warned by her family that she had an ungovernable temper but, while Violet was alive, he had never seen evidence of it. The dark side of Betty's nature began to reveal itself after their marriage. Her circumstances were unenviable. The position of any woman promoted from servant to wife in such a class-ridden age was difficult. Betty was a farmer's daughter, practical and hardworking, but with little education: she was barely able to read and write. She constantly felt inferior among John's intellectual friends. Suspecting that she had caught John on the rebound, she also felt insecure in his affections. She was in her late twenties, big boned, and nobody had ever called her beautiful. She was jealous of every woman who entered John's orbit, and of every woman he had ever known; rivals, alive or dead, could not be tolerated. After Frieda Lawrence came to stay, Betty smashed a Dresden candlestick over John's head. She sacked female servants if she thought they were a threat to her authority, and was rude to the wives of John's friends if she caught a whiff of condescension.

Reminders of Violet's memory were swept into cupboards and drawers, her children beaten into line. Col, a shy four-year-old, was no threat – he could even make her laugh – but Weg, a delicate beauty adored by her father, was another matter. Betty told her repeatedly that she was 'lazy and ugly' and punished her without justification. She called Weg a 'sly little bitch' and told her it was no wonder her mother hadn't wanted her. Col watched, helpless, as his sister was humiliated, smacked and bullied daily, though Betty was careful not to pick on Weg when John was there. And when her own child, Mary, was born, things became even worse. 'Betty acquired a new strength . . . The tap-tap of her wedding ring on the sides of the pastry bowl on baking day was subtly indicative of new authority in her.'² Col and Weg were not allowed to go up the front staircase of the house: they had to go up the servants' stairs at the back. This rule did not apply to Mary, who had to be put first in everything, to have the best of everything. If challenged, Betty would explode in a ferocious tirade that left spectators shaken to the core. It was pointless for John to remind her that Mary was his child too. Betty would shout, 'Mary is mine. She came out of me and she's part of me!'³ John, desperate for peace, escaped to his study and locked the door.

The dead made quieter companions. Violet's ashes were in a brown paper parcel in the corner cupboard and Katherine's photograph hung above the desk. As well as his continued involvement in the *Adelphi*, John was working on an account of his socialist conversion called *The Necessity of Communism*, and the first chapters of his autobiography, *Between Two Worlds*, which told the story of his childhood and his early life with Katherine. It was intended to be the first of two volumes but the second was never completed. He was also engaged in the arduous task of transcribing Katherine's papers for a new biography that he had recently authorised, and another instalment of her journal. His retreat into the world of literature drove Betty to an even greater pitch of fury. She knew that she would never be able to compete with Katherine for John's attention. Even John's leather blotter, a gift from Katherine, still displayed the doodle scrawled in one corner in Katherine's handwriting – a red heart with an arrow through it and the legend 'KM/JM *the bes' of all*'.⁴ Only in bed was John wholly Betty's as she introduced him to an animalistic sensuality (what John called 'the Earth-mother') he had once glimpsed with Frieda Lawrence, but never experienced in any of his other relationships, held back by his 'fearful shyness of sex'. He wrote sadly in his journal: 'How I must have wanted to make love to Katherine & to Violet: yet it was so suppressed that even now I have to write: "how I must have wanted" rather than "how I wanted".'⁵

Within weeks John's marriage with Betty had fallen into a pattern of extremes, swinging from open warfare, through domestic truce to sexual release. But Betty seems to have understood long before her husband that things were not going to work out. Only a couple of months after they moved to Larling she went into John's study and pleaded with him to give her £20 for the child she was expecting and let her go. 'She would get a room, and go to work as soon as her baby was born . . . "Let me go out of your life – for ever. Please! Please!"' John was utterly bewildered. 'We were not unhappy. And anyhow the baby was mine as much as hers . . . We had made a home for it . . . The whole thing was incomprehensible.' He refused to even consider it. But the next day she tried to run away. She was halfway to the railway station when John caught up with her and brought her back. 'She came neither willingly nor reluctantly, as one submitting to Fate.'[6]

When their daughter Mary, always called Mêh, was born in January 1932, ten months after Violet's death, John once more fell in love with the baby. Weg joined Col at the bottom of the love queue and she felt it intensely. Not only did she have to do battle with a new stepmother and a baby sister, but also with the memory of her namesake. Her father even referred to her in his diary as 'Katherine-Violet's child'. Weg often felt that she was living someone else's life. When her father gave her a new suit-case as a present, he put the initials KMM on it, which, as he was quick to remind her, were also those of that other Katherine Murry. Every time she looked at it, she was aware of the burden of expectation.

In 1932 John was thinking a great deal about Katherine. His life with her seemed so long ago, and yet she was still fundamental to him. On her birthday he wrote: 'Katherine is complete, immortal – not personally mine. She gave me myself by leaving me. The shock of that bereavement was the one crucial happening of my life. Everything afterwards grows out of that. And if I go down to posterity simply as the husband of Katherine Mansfield – well, it won't be far from the truth.'[7] He had just written to Stanford University in America about a young academic called Ruth Mantz, who in 1931 had published a critical bibliography of Katherine's work for which he had written the introduction. Would it be possible for her to help him with the transcription and editing of Katherine's papers? John was ploughing through her notebooks with the intention of publishing another selection, to be called 'The Scrapbook of Katherine Mansfield'. Stanford obliged, sending Ruth to England on the Charlotte Ashley Felton Memorial Fellowship. Having done so much work on Katherine already, Ruth was very keen to write her biography, and John agreed. It was supposed to be a collaboration, and his name appeared on the book spine in front of hers, but it was a very unequal split. Most of the work was Ruth's;

the editorial hand was John's, though the blue pencil that he had wielded as chief censor at the War Office was visible only to those who knew the wider story.

Ruth initially found John charming and very helpful, willing to be teased about his editorial oversights – 'I always had a very bad memory' – and to admit that his relationship with Katherine had often been difficult and that they had been completely happy only in Bandol. Otherwise Ruth recorded that 'our conversations and working sessions were devoted only to the deciphering of KM's handwriting, to collating and assessing the facts then available, and of course to agreeing on the data I had assembled during my research in New Zealand'. A lot of time was spent dating Katherine's letters and notebook entries and Ruth did not always agree with John's decisions. She also noted that he changed words in some of Katherine's letters, either to obscure the meaning, or to make them seem less accusatory towards himself. Some important letters were missing; some had pieces torn off. The editorial process seemed designed to soften and smooth, for public consumption, a relationship that had often been anything but. Ruth had already identified what she regarded as 'the Mansfield Myth', which she dated from the publication of *The Dove's Nest* in 1923, and she was troubled by it. In his introduction to this volume of stories John had 'developed the theme of "purity" at the expense of other qualities that had endeared Katherine to her few real friends'. Similarly, in his edition of the journal, 'KM the mimic, the cynic, the mystic, the flirt who had to try her charm on every man, was ignored'. John had also edited out 'the "masked" pretender' and the entertainer capable of 'merciless parody'. Ruth was particularly critical of his arrangement of material from Katherine's notebooks. 'Certain of the diary jottings no doubt give an insight into the mood and manner of the workings of KM's mind, but arranged as they are in the Journal the result is biographically inaccurate.'[8] She was later even more scathing, writing that 'As a source for autobiographical reference it might as well be classified as fiction', so much so that it invalidated all biographies written with reference to it.[9] But when Ruth challenged John about this, his reaction was 'immediate and left no doubt that he knew what he was doing. He recoiled and said angrily, "There is no 'myth'!"'[10]

John's introduction sets the tone of the biography – Katherine's work and life are discussed in the context of Blake, Keats and Jesus, John's major preoccupations since her death. There is a reverence, a playing down of the grittier episodes in her life, of her whole existence as a woman; her mistakes are admitted only to provide a dark contrast so that her art can blaze more fiercely. Her suffering, too, is seen as a bar that great artists must cross in order to purify their art. Ruth is permitted no independent view – John insists that the opinions expressed in the book are his. In the last chapter, a brief narrative of Katherine's life after she met John is taken word for word from his account of it in *Between Two Worlds*.

It could have been very different. Ruth researched Katherine's life in New Zealand meticulously, interviewing family members (Harold Beauchamp was still alive) and friends John had never met. She quoted extensively from Katherine's juvenile journals, including excerpts from her early novel 'Juliet', charting her progress as a developing writer in a way that illuminates her work. Ruth talked to all Katherine's friends, including Ida Baker, Koteliansky, Beatrice Campbell and Anne Estelle Rice. They trusted Ruth and told her a great deal that John would have preferred her not to have known. Ruth met A. R. Orage in a little Italian café in Soho and heard all about Katherine's first involvement with the *New Age* and its contributors, long before she met John. Orage told her that Beatrice Hastings was once again living in North London, in a precarious mental condition, and had become a 'spiritualist painter'. Ruth went to see Beatrice, 'up dark narrow stairs', across a landing littered with old gin bottles. There, in a filthy, cluttered room 'a small dishevelled woman stood before one of the easels', painting 'incoherent vague pale abstractions. Jealousy of Katherine Mansfield still seemed to devour her.'[11]

Ruth's conversations with those who had known Katherine in her early days in London began to uncover a great deal that John had either not known or wanted to suppress: the details of her love affair with Garnet Trowell and the subsequent pregnancy, as well as her mysterious pregnancy when living at Clovelly Mansions with Ida. Ruth also talked to others and later told another biographer that Katherine had become pregnant with Floryan Sobieniowski, though there was a misunderstanding about the date, which Ruth allowed to pass without further comment. Worst of all, tucked into the back of one of Katherine's journals, Ruth found a medical report from a Dr Bouchage, referring to Dr Sorapure's diagnosis and mentioning the word gonorrhoea. John was horrified by Ruth's discoveries, particularly the latter, not just for the sake of Katherine's reputation, but partly because he (and some of his friends) knew that he had had gonorrhoea just before he and Katherine met. John did not believe that he had infected her – he preferred to think she had caught the disease from

Francis Carco. There was a great deal that could not be said. A compromise was reached. Ruth would write about Katherine's youth, stopping the narrative at the point where she and John met and began to live together. The biography ended when their relationship began, with the explanation that 'The rest of Katherine Mansfield's life – a bare eleven years – is written by her own hand in her Journal and her Letters'. Anything else, said the last page, in one of the most blatant of literary lies, 'will add little that is essential to the picture of herself'.[12]

Any disagreement between John and Ruth was carefully concealed. It would have been an unequal struggle. She was young and had not yet established her reputation; he was one of the leading men of letters in the English-speaking world. He also possessed most of the relevant manuscript material. John quite literally 'owned' Katherine's reputation. Ruth returned to America and continued to write the second volume of Katherine's life, subtitled 'The Garsington Gate', presumably hoping to be able to publish it at some point. She never did. John rarely mentioned her. And in John's biography, written by his friend Frank Lea in 1959, shortly after John's death, despite a detailed account of the writing of *Between Two Worlds* and that particular period at Larling, there is no mention of either Ruth or the biography. Nor is it listed among John's publications, both individual and collaborative, in the bibliography.

Life at Larling was not all misery. It was much more sociable than the bungalow at Yateley had ever been. Sir Richard Rees rented one of the empty wings of the house and came down from London most weekends. The Plowmans came to stay. Frank Lea was a frequent visitor and became a kind of unofficial secretary. John's brother Richard was also at Larling a great deal, though Betty hated him. Richard, still single, was now trying to earn a living as a painter. The children loved him, and he had a very close relationship with John: in the afternoons they dug the garden together, planting trees and rose bushes. In the mornings John wrote while Richard painted. He had been commissioned by John to paint a portrait of Violet from photographs and memory. When finished it was hung in John's study next to Katherine's and the likeness was so striking that most visitors thought both depicted the same woman.

In June 1932, Dr James Young bought a property near Larling and moved in with his new American wife Helen, also a doctor, and her two daughters from two previous marriages. The Youngs' relationship was almost as stormy as the Murrys'. James was a hyperactive workaholic whose temperament was quite unsuited to the married state and Helen, John noted in his journal, was so profoundly neurotic 'as to be quite unmanageable'.[13] Nevertheless John, who had always liked James, now became good friends with Helen. Betty could hardly bear Helen in the house, but James was one of the few people who could deal with Betty. When she threw a tantrum during a lunch party, he launched into an impressive tirade that silenced her: 'if you don't shut your foul mouth woman – and keep it shut! – I swear to God that I'll break this log over your bloody, stupid, ignorant head!'[14] But Betty's instincts were right. There was a strong attraction between John and Helen.

In the middle of this situation, completely unconsidered, were the children, traumatised by the loss of their mother and unable to understand what was going on around them. Weg had, from the beginning, gained a special place in her father's heart even if it had been temporarily usurped by Mêh, but Col, who had spent a year of his childhood in a TB hospital, was the most neglected. 'A firm pattern had already become established for me. Life, I understood, was to be full of quite appalling experiences and there was absolutely nothing I could do to avoid them. I was out on my own.'[15] His father, he had already observed, had a 'quality of remoteness' that made him unapproachable. John's experience with his own father had left him without any idea of how to be a father himself. Though he was by nature kind and loving, his ordinary sense of natural justice deserted him when he had to deal with his children. On one occasion, flush with money from an American lecture tour, he asked the children what they would really like to have. Weg asked for a piano and Col said that he would like the dog he had always longed for. Both were firmly promised, but only the piano ever materialised. Weg was jubilant; Col bitter. The dog had, apparently, been overruled by Betty. Incidents like these coloured the children's attitudes to their father as they grew up. Weg would refer to John as a 'beloved Quixote'; Col described him as 'brilliant, remote and unloving'. He believed that his father blamed him for Violet's death and punished him subconsciously.

On 16 April 1934, Col was sent to Brighton to stay with his Murry grandparents, who had retired there. Col was left there for three months while his father went away, though this was never explained to him. Weg and Mary were both allowed to stay at home, which mystified Col even further. In Brighton, despite his grandmother's attempts to protect him, Col experienced the full force of his grandfather's brutality. He had brought his cherished teddy bear with him but his grandfather removed it from his bed on the first night, saying 'Boys don't need dolls'. Col sobbed his heart out into the pillow. On another occasion, a severe abscess on a tooth was dismissed as imaginary and not worth paying for a visit to the dentist. His grandmother had to take him secretly after finding him almost unconscious with pain under the hearthrug in the parlour. Petty cruelties Col was used to, but when he was beaten black and blue for finding a coin down a crack in the floorboards and spending it on sweets, and then again for a minor disobedience, he encountered a grimmer reality. His grandfather knocked him to the ground with his fist, then proceeded to kick him, knocking his head into the banisters so hard that the imprint was left on his face. Despite his visible injuries, Col was still not sent back to Larling by his grandmother, whose own will had long since been defeated by her unreasonable husband. This experience helped Col to understand his own father much more – the 'imagined horror of having Grandpa for a father made me shudder' – but 'it could not explain why he had condemned me to Brighton in the first place'.[16] John seemed intent on forcing his son to endure the same sufferings he had experienced in his own bleak childhood, which had rendered him intellectually precocious but emotionally illiterate. When eight-year-old Col was finally taken back home in July, it was only to be told that, from September, he would be attending the local grammar school as a weekly boarder. As Thetford was only 15 kilometres from Larling and other village children caught the train there every day, Col did not understand why he, too, could not come home. The bullying and abuse he suffered at that school had a lasting effect: it 'numbed some growing point in me; convinced me that I was no good'.[17]

Weg was not having an easy time either. Her whole life was now over-shadowed by fear. 'It hung upon the air like a perpetual storm, perpetually on-coming, perpetually menacing . . . I learned how to tiptoe up the back stairs without a single one creaking. I knew on which board to creep along the landing to my bedroom . . . I learned how to become a shadow, almost invisible.'[18] The Larling rectory echoed with raised voices and the sound of breaking china: a pair of Chinese vases, Katherine's Dresden clock . . . The silences were ominous, like the eerie interval before a hurricane. The adult Weg could still remember the terrible scenes she witnessed. John's work, the one area that Betty could neither understand nor control, was usually the focus of her anger, which soon went beyond words into physical abuse.

> 'Jesus Christ himself . . . wouldn't put up with you as I have done!' Voices rise, crashes and shrieks. Little Mary is screaming: 'Mummy! Dadda!'
>
> My father, white as parchment, his head bleeding, collapses on a chair.
>
> I am cold, frozen with horror. She is killing him.
>
> 'Dadda, Dadda! It's all right. It will be all right.' My heart turns to fury, white hot . . .
>
> Betty, who has broken a tea-table on his head, comes towards us with fantastic physical strength, shrieking and shaking.'

At the last moment the gardener, Bodge, comes into the room and Weg remembers her father shouting, 'Get the woman out of here. Get her out!'[19]

Betty's anger fed John's masochism and desire for punishment. 'Am I attracted only by two kinds of women – one that I kill, the other that kills me?'[20] It was not the first time that he had thought about this. Lines in The Voyage, spoken by his autobiographical main character, describe the same desire: 'I thought you might be diabolically clever and determined and cruel. And that fascinated me. I should like to be destroyed by someone, some woman, you know. Really annihilated. The moth in the candle-flame.'[21] There were also, in John's interaction with Betty, echoes of Lawrence's philosophy – that in a perfect relationship the man and the woman should fight each other almost to the death until they break through to true harmony, beyond dominance.

In September Weg, like Col, was sent to boarding school. Both were miserable. Both made poor academic progress. John seemed oblivious to it all. 'The thing I know nearest to personal love now is love of my children . . . I think that if circumstances would allow I should go on cheerfully having more and more babies for ever. After all, I feel that I am a fit and proper person to give little children a real start in life.'[22] His son Col later agreed that John had had it in him to be a perfect father and husband; the problem was his inability to choose the right woman and, having made the mistake, his inability to extricate himself from the situation.

By 1934 the violence between himself and Betty had escalated. The children could hear the rows from their bedrooms – 'screams and footsteps running along the landing, then sobs and Betty shouting: "You take your two children and I'll take mine!"' Then John's weary voice: 'Oh shut up, woman! Shut up or I'll kill you!'[23] John felt that Betty would not respect him if he simply allowed her to beat him, so, following Lawrence's example, he began to retaliate. 'I was lost in an utterly new world of unknown experience: where I beat her, and was completely unashamed for beating her – where at moments I seemed to come within a hair's breadth of killing her.'[24] They were locked into a terrible cycle of domestic violence.

Intellectually, John knew the consequences of this for his children. He and James Young, whose own relationship was now disintegrating, were writing a treatise on modern marriage. In it they quoted Nietzsche: 'The unresolved discords in the relation of the parents' characters and sentiments survive in the nature of the child and make up the history of its inner sufferings'. In his journals, the only reason John could give for staying with Betty was that he could not bear to be parted from Mêh. For her sake, he would have to endure whatever Betty handed out and find some way of living with her. His experience of marriage, either as a participant or an observer, did not help him at all. His own parents' marriage had been violent; the Lawrences' relationship had been as turbulent as his own; James and Helen, both intelligent human beings, were tearing each other apart. Perhaps the malaise went deeper? John was always tempted to intellectualise personal situations: 'The old social order of which marriage was an integral part is collapsing'.[25] He followed the rise of Fascism in Europe closely and was convinced that only a new vision of society could save humanity. He became more and more committed to putting his new political philosophy into practice. As a 'born again' socialist, he had become close to H. G. Wells and renewed his friendship with Max Plowman. He wrote to his friends about the necessity of a community project, as a demonstration of the superiority of socialism. The Adelphi Centre was to be partly a fusion of Lawrence's vision of Rananim, socialist ideology and the 'Heron' dreams John had once shared with Katherine. 'If one could get Lumley's farm, and four or five congenial people to work it, we could surely hammer out a livelihood of some sort . . . It should be a centre of study, propaganda, and above all a place for the formation of a revolutionary elite: where equality was always lived.' Perversely, now that John was living the life of a literary gentleman, with servants and gardeners, he longed for 'the simple life'. 'Why not mugs and platters for meals? Why more than one clean shirt a week, one pair of socks? Why not take turns at cooking simple meals? Why not clean your room and make your bed yourself?'[26]

Throughout his struggles with Betty, John had increasingly sought refuge in a religion he had once repudiated. He went to the local church, had theological conversations with the vicar and even considered being ordained himself. It did not seem to John that Marxism and Christianity should be incompatible and he was prepared to go through all kinds of intellectual gymnastics to defend his position. He was now a member, not of the Labour Party, but of a splinter group called the Independent Labour Party, which looked to him for some kind of ideological leadership. All John's years of studying Russian literature and, more recently, the work of Karl Marx, had convinced him of Marx's rightness. He also read and reread Lawrence's *Fantasia of the Unconscious*, published in 1922, and was profoundly inspired by its arguments. As he had in *Psychoanalysis and the Unconscious* (1921), Lawrence used these essays to suggest an alternative to the Freudian psychoanalytic theory of the unconscious and the incest motive and developed his ideas about raising and educating children, about marriage and about social and political action.

It was out of this eccentric mixture of ideas that the Adelphi Centre was created. It was to be 'a sort of religious brotherhood'. They would be 'bound to one another' to serve the common cause and those better off would be expected to live on the same level as the others.[27] For John this meant that he had to consider giving up his home, his family and his children, just as Lawrence had directed in *Fantasia*: 'He may not pause to remember that he has a life to lose, or a wife and children to leave. He must carry forward the banner of life, though seven worlds perish.'[28] John's father solved one problem by writing a bitter letter of repudiation after reading a review of John's *The Necessity of Communism*, which had been published in 1932. He was disgusted with his son: 'You have denied God; now you will deny your country'.[29] Many others felt the same. John's views were out of step with national sentiment and he was increasingly unpopular with the literary establishment – a figure to be mocked and satirised. William Gerhardi wrote in a review that 'Middleton Murry has a faculty of estranging you by a manner which suggests that you are in a stage of development from which he has just emerged, and is watching your progress with hope from a point further along the road'.[30] John's credibility was in decline, and even his close friends were against him. Richard Rees predicted that the Adelphi Centre would be a focus for 'proletarian scroungers' and 'bourgeois escapers'; Max Plowman referred to it as 'a home for stray dogs'.[31]

But John's brother Richard remained supportive and, on 10 September 1934, they found just what they were looking for – a large farmhouse with cottage, outbuildings and two large fields at Langham near Colchester. John put forward £1000 of the purchase price and the other £1475 was raised by subscription. It was to be run as a limited company and its objectives were 'to promote the education of children and adults of any age, whether male or female, and whether separately or by way of co-education in accordance with the philosophy, principles and methods heretofore set forth or hereafter to be set forth in the published writings of John Middleton Murry and Professor John MacMurray'.[32] The stage was set for John Murry to become a new political messiah, propounding Lawrence's ideas as well as his own.

Betty was the one problem in this carefully worked-out plan. A staunch conservative, she had no intention of living by socialist principles and threatened to wreck the Adelphi Centre. During the autumn, an already stormy relationship became untenable. In December John escaped on another lecture tour to America. He also had another, more personal, invitation. Helen Young had left her husband and was living in New York. She and John had been corresponding and had planned a reunion without the knowledge of their partners.

John found America vast and bewildering. Brought up in a rigid English social and academic straitjacket, he was among people who thought and behaved very differently. He was there to lecture on Keats, but had also been asked to give a talk about Katherine Mansfield, following publication of *Between Two Worlds* and the Ruth Mantz biography. Oddly, there is not a single reference in that lecture to the account of Katherine's life that also bears John's name as co-author. The full story, John asserts, 'is told in the first volume of my autobiography, *Between Two Worlds*, and in her *Journal* and *Letters*'. Although the lecture added nothing to what was already in the public domain, it was a unique account of John's current view of Katherine's literary standing and significance. His opinion seemed, in 1936, to have come closer to Lawrence's original assessment of her talent. 'In scope,' said John, 'Katherine Mansfield was a tiny artist; but because she was a perfectly pure, and perfectly submissive, artist she was a great one'. It was the perfect male put-down. Nevertheless, John goes on to say, this was the essence of her genius – 'simplicity in complexity', great art in miniature.

John claimed that 'the distinguishing mark' of Katherine's genius was 'spontaneity', which he defined by saying that 'her art was not really distinct from her life'. She was 'a person who responded . . . to her experience of Life'. This, too, was an argument frequently used against female creative artists – that their art was instinctive and intuitive rather than intellectual. John also asserted that 'she was never what we understand by a professional writer', though Katherine had never thought of herself as anything else. As it was for Virginia Woolf, writing was 'a job', 'business'; one's whole life was directed towards 'being a writer'. Katherine was not a professional writer only in the sense that she did not have to earn her entire living from her work. In John's view, the 'nature of her genius' lay in her 'simplicity', a simplicity that was not, despite all Katherine's journal entries attesting to the contrary, 'a technical achievement'. This simplicity was purified by 'a long travail of soul' – the old cliché of art being rendered sublime by suffering. 'Katherine could look back on her life, with all its miseries and all its brevity, and declare that "in spite of all" it was good: that "in spite of all" suffering was a privilege, pain the gateway to a deeper joy, sorrow the birth-pang of a new beauty. "In spite of all" – the phrase, mysterious and simple as life, contains the secret of herself and her art.'[33]

While many of his listeners were enthralled by John's account of Katherine's life and his interpretation of her work, others were disgusted by the personal details of their relationship – very reticent by today's standards – that John had included. One distinguished academic 'was so disturbed that he cancelled his reservation for the faculty dinner with Murry that evening'.[34]

The strain of the tour was beginning to tell. It was one of the worst winters anyone could remember and John battled from city to city through blizzards and ice storms. 'The trains are never on time – because there's always a fresh blizzard – so I find myself stranded at wayside stations at 3 am, having neatly missed the connection.'[35] He caught flu and lay shivering and depressed in a succession of New England hotels. At the end of March he returned to New York and a reunion with Helen Young, whose letters had followed him around America, since their brief meeting there at the end of December. She already believed herself to be in love with him and had pleaded with him to respond. 'Tired and beaten' by his struggle with Betty and the arduous American journey, John was now perfectly willing to fall in love with her. On 1 April, a date that should perhaps have inspired more scepticism, John wrote in his journal of his love for Helen.

'Complete mutual surrender, complete acceptance, complete simplicity, complete faith – what has this been all my life long but a dream – in which I had ceased to believe, because I *dared* not believe in it.' They were together for two weeks and John made up his mind that when he returned to England he would leave Betty and make a new relationship with Helen, who became 'Nehale' in his journal to protect her identity. But this fictionalisation of her name was also symbolic of John's desire to see in 'Nehale' all that he needed. Her neuroses were forgotten. Helen offered him, or so he thought, the sanctuary of peace and love he craved: 'after 46 years of a life as bitter as most men have lived, only one thing matters; and that is *tenderness*'.[36] When he returned to Larling, John found Betty about to depart for a Mediterranean cruise. Focused on her own, much-needed holiday, she reacted to the information that he was leaving her to live at the Adelphi Centre with both rage and a considerable amount of scepticism.

In the three and a half months that John had been away, Betty had been completely in control at Larling, with no one to stand as a buffer between her and the two older children. Weg had become 'a tired and mouse-like creature', reduced to the status of 'an unpaid drudge, scrubbing and polishing to Betty's directions'. She was desperate for Betty's approval, but nothing she did was ever good enough and her efforts were despised. One day, when things had been particularly bad, Weg ran away to a neighbour, begging not to be taken back. She was, of course, and thereafter, according to her brother, believed herself to be 'in Hell indeed'.[37] Col survived by using the tactics he had learnt at school – keeping quiet and out of the way. As a boy, he was not required to do housework, so was able to spend his holidays out in the garden with Bodge. When it rained, he explored the extensive attics and storerooms of the rectory. It was there one day, searching a discarded chest of drawers, that he found one of his father's old diaries, lodged behind a drawer. In it were entries relating to his father's marriage to Violet and an account of Col's own conception, which he read with considerable interest. Further on was a record of Violet's reaction to the news that she was pregnant again. The knowledge that he, like his sister Weg, had been unwanted, came like a lightning strike. Col was enveloped in 'a sort of smothering misery'. 'I think I realised then that nothing could ever be quite the same again.'[38]

17

'The Last Hell'

Four hundred miles away as the crow flies and almost forty years. The invisible thread of memory trembles, plunges into darkness, a darkness of the soul that seemingly no human can uncover. Voices cry from the past. But how can they be heard from those depths where the being foundered, struggling desperately to breathe, to understand, to survive?

KATHERINE MIDDLETON MURRY, BELOVED QUIXOTE

On 28 May 1936, while Betty was away, John left Larling to live at the Adelphi Centre at Langham. After five years of struggling to make his appalling marriage work, he believed that he was leaving for good. Weg and Col were away at boarding school, so only Mêh was left at home with her nanny. John found the parting almost unbearable: 'nothing will ever take this pain away'.[1] When, a few days later, Betty returned from her cruise to discover that her husband had left her for another woman, her anger was unleashed in an orgy of destruction. Precious belongings John had left behind, including books and valuable works of art, were smashed or burnt. As Colin remembered, 'Had Bodge not had the forethought to lock up the petrol cans in the generator house she would in all probability have razed Larling to the ground'.[2] When the fury had abated she tried emotional blackmail against John, using his love for Mêh as a weapon. One of her tactics was to ring Langham and then put her sobbing daughter on the phone to beg her father to come home. Betty refused to recognise the separation, or to countenance a divorce. 'The result was a phantasmagoria of comings and going, negotiations, altercations, raids, kidnappings and settlements that settled nothing.'[3] Pages have been torn out of John's journal for this period and for the next four years his notebooks are a mutilated patchwork of scissored pages, brown paper pasted over passages that could not be cut out, the remaining entries spattered with blue-pencilled words and phrases. Some notebooks and letters went missing altogether, including material relating to both Violet and Katherine. John believed that Betty had burnt them.

Helen came over for a week at the end of May. John took Weg to meet her at a hotel in Norwich and Weg, sensing the meeting was important, refused to be charmed by Helen, whom she had heard Betty refer to as 'that fucken whore'. Col was also less than enthusiastic at the thought of Helen as a stepmother. There was awkwardness all round. But it was agreed that when things had settled down Helen would travel to England and live at Langham in the cottage with John. Weg and Col came to Langham for their summer holidays. Weg, relieved to be free of Betty, had a 'new freedom and gaiety'.[4] She was at last able to make her father see how much she had suffered by being systematically rejected by her stepmother. Col enjoyed Langham, but felt no closer to his father and was actually homesick for Larling and his little sister Mêh.

The Adelphi Centre was an odd community of men and women of varying ages that included an out-of-work architect, a sculptor from London and his Canadian fiancée, a free-loading young writer and a secretary from Scotland who was a fan of John's books. It was, as Max Plowman had predicted, very middle class and the proletariat that John had hoped for never arrived. Hardly any work went on, but there was a great deal of talking round tables and a lot of sex, followed inevitably by friction. John was a theorist, not a manager of people. Placed in a community of conflicting egos and incompatible personalities, he was lost. The high-minded discussions he had envisaged degenerated into arguments over the washing-up. In July, the outbreak of civil war in Spain created a further sense of unease and several of John's friends left to fight against Franco's Fascism.

One of the most disruptive elements at Langham was the turbulence of John's personal life. The 'Adelphi brotherhood' had a ringside seat for the duel between Betty and Helen for possession of John. Mêh was the main battleground. Betty made it very difficult for John to have any contact with her whatsoever. On one occasion John actually kidnapped Mêh, with the agreement of his solicitor, and refused to give her back. Legally at the time, children 'belonged' to their father and women had fewer rights in a divorce. John had anticipated that the transition from Betty to Helen would be stormy. He arranged for Weg to go to Belgium for a year, ostensibly to improve her French, with a young woman who was writing a thesis on Katherine Mansfield. After the kidnapping episode, he also agreed with Betty that Mêh would go to London during the week with her nanny, to attend a kindergarten there; she was to stay with friends who would allow John access to his daughter on neutral territory. Col, a weekly boarder at a local school, became the only witness of events at Langham. John sent a telegram urging Helen to come to England to stay with him and arranged to meet her ship in Southampton. After four months of celibacy and conflict, he was longing to be with her, writing in his journal: 'I am just simply "in love" with a youthful, incredible love, such as I had twenty five years ago'.[5] The analogy was with Marguéritte rather than Katherine. But John had scarcely spent one night with Helen in the hotel before he realised that once more he had pinned all his hopes on the wrong woman.

Physically the reunion was not a success and John's feelings for Helen, face to face, were not as strong as he had believed them to be. Helen's were much more urgent and demanding and he shrank from her raw need: 'I feel that I am in an *impossible* situation'. She came back to Langham with him, but their relationship did not improve. John offered to pay her fare back to America, but then Helen told him that she was pregnant. The pregnancy was fictional and John blamed Helen for trying to blackmail him into staying with her. There were hysterical scenes. John felt he was being 'disembowelled alive'. Eventually, desperate for Mêh, John had a meeting in London with Betty on 7 October and, to the bewilderment of everyone who knew him, agreed to go back to Larling. Betty had promised him that she would make an effort to change. John stipulated that he wanted to be free to spend his weekends with Helen at Langham. Betty agreed. Even more surprisingly, Helen took the news 'quite peacefully, as I believed she would'. John told his diary that 'The rebirth of love in me through Helen has enabled me to love Betty again'.[6]

On 14 October he wrote to Max Plowman, with extraordinary naivety: 'isn't it wonderful that the day I go back to Larling is Katherine's birthday. Ah, dear Max, darling Max, these last days have been terrible and wonderful . . . Helen is through. Last night she gave me up: sent me back to Betty with joy. Love has conquered. I have – we have – been through the last

Hell. Henceforward there is nothing but Love and Joy.'[7] But whatever John believed, neither Helen nor Betty was willing to tolerate the other. Helen did not want him to resume sexual relations with his wife: 'It would hurt me if you slept with Betty again . . .' But sex with Betty was inevitable. And within a fortnight of the new arrangement Betty found herself unable to tolerate his weekends with Helen. John returned from Langham to endure 'one of the grimmest nights I have ever spent . . . I felt that something at last was broken in me; the life and the virtue seemed to have left me for ever . . .'[8]

All this left the occupants of the Adelphi Centre rocking 'like a harbour of canoes in the wake of a whale'.[9] And when John, who had initially supported the communist cause in Spain, suddenly joined the Peace Pledge Union, swearing the oath, 'I renounce war, and I will never support or sanction another', his conversion to pacifism swamped the project completely. Some members left; financial support was withdrawn. The Independent Labour Party, who had looked to John for ideological leadership, also felt betrayed. Just as Hitler was preparing to invade Austria and European politics accelerated towards war, John began to write The Necessity of Pacifism.

There was no pacifism in his private life. Part of his agreement with Betty was that they would have another baby to 'cement their union' and if it was a boy it would be named for D. H. Lawrence. David was enthusiastically conceived, but by the time he was born his parents' relationship had descended to a level of conflict that defied belief. Betty had declared herself willing to be 're-educated' and John began the task straight away. 'I do not think I set about it clumsily or condescendingly. I began quite simply as I should have done with a backward child. I tried to interest her in improving her own handwriting and spelling, which was that of an illiterate; I persuaded her to learn a few good but simple poems and to copy them out carefully in a handsome leather book which I bought for her . . . I knew I must have infinite patience.'[10] But it was futile and patronising. Betty had little interest in these things and his attempts to change her nature soon provoked a 'fury of hatred'.

John had also begun to think again about joining the priesthood. He was assured by the Bishop of Chichester that his lack of orthodox belief in the dogmas of the church would not be a bar to ordination. Col, home from boarding school, was astonished when his father produced a prayer book and read a psalm every morning over breakfast. Betty was also expected to get down on her knees and pray with him before going to bed. She refused. In his journal, John confided his own doubts about his religious vocation. 'How could I honestly become a priest when I had made so absolute a failure of Christian marriage?' He had to face the fact that his reasons for entering the priesthood had a great deal to do with Betty. 'I wanted to run away from my marriage.'[11] John's programme of education for Betty had failed and she taunted him continually about his affair with Helen. 'You're a fool – a fool. Don't you know that women are all bitches – *all* of them?' He was finally forced to admit that the compromise he had hoped to achieve was not possible. 'Then I knew that there was indeed an impassable gulf between us.' He went to sleep in a separate room. Weg, now back from a wonderful year in Belgium and enrolled at the local grammar school as a day girl, was utterly miserable. Sometimes John would creep into his daughter's room, 'where she lay silently weeping in the dark. We hardly ever spoke. There was nothing to say. But we held each other tight; and we comforted each other – she in her suffering, I in my despair.'[12]

John's physical and mental deterioration was visible to everyone who knew him. One friend had a vivid memory of him 'slumped in a deck-chair, head bent, as though all the cares of the world were on his shoulders: and the poignancy of his suffering moved me'.[13] John had begun to suffer numbness and cramp in his right leg and was unable to walk more than a few metres without pain. Burger's Disease was diagnosed – the nerves of his legs were affected, and there was narrowing of the arteries and veins caused by heavy smoking. He had always smoked 'like a prairie fire'.[14] But his illness meant a reconciliation with James Young, and John confided that the stress of the previous two years had been unbearable 'judged even by my standards'.[15] James told John bluntly that he would have to reduce his workload and advised John to go into hospital for 'diathermy and massage' in an attempt to alleviate the condition without surgery. While he was in hospital in May 1938 his fourth child, David, was born – another hostage to chain John to a destructive marriage.

Through all of this, John had been steadily working on a new compilation of extracts from Katherine's notebooks. It was an arduous task, given the amount of material, its fragmentary nature and the difficulty of Katherine's handwriting. Margaret Scott, who eventually transcribed all Katherine's letters and notebooks, regards his achievement as astonishing. 'Only another transcriber, coming after him, can perceive the quiet dogged hard labour he put into these volumes. He commands a respect and an admiration that no amount of disapproval of his editorial methods can diminish.'[16] This editorially dubious compilation was published in 1939 as The Scrapbook of Katherine Mansfield. Since he had given the impression that the 1927 Journal was definitive, some explanation of this extra material was required. The Scrapbook, he explained, was a collection of 'unpublished fragments' – uncollected stories and 'new journal entries' – which had been overlooked when he put the first volume together, partly because of time constraints and partly 'because her handwriting is very difficult'. For the first time he admitted the nature of the source material. 'This seemingly haphazard arrangement, though on a larger scale, is singularly like that of one of her own notebooks – ordinary French school cahiers mostly – in which finished and unfinished stories, quotations, odd observations, intimate confessions, unposted letters, and stray sentences are crammed up like some rich thievery. Except in point of legibility this scrapbook is, in fact, more like one of her own notebooks even than her published journal.' This introduction, written at Larling in June 1939, also promised another edition of Katherine's letters, if his 'power of work' was restored to him the following year.[17] John was desperately tired and disillusioned. As he told a friend, 'Love does not work miracles. It did not save Katherine or Violet from death; it did not save Betty from wanting to kill me.'[18] And it could not save his children.

Life at Larling was bleak and hopeless. 'Even now, nearly twenty years later,' wrote Col, 'I can still be drawn back in dreams to those appalling scenes and awake in the grip of the old familiar terror. It was as though we were all under some terrible sentence – so terrible in fact that we hardly dared to speak of it even among ourselves. Fear crept into us like a cold fog . . . Gradually it dawned on all of us that there was no way out. This was to be our life and we must make the best of it.'[19]

John's emotional confusion and sense of despair were made worse by the fact that he had recently met a woman with whom he felt a complete rapport. Mary Gamble, the daughter of a wealthy Lincoln architect, had been educated at Queen's College – the same school that Katherine had attended. She was a prominent member of the Peace Pledge Union, an intelligent, independent woman who had published three volumes of poetry when she was younger and had been a parliamentary candidate for the Independent Labour Party. Mary was much more complex than she appeared. She had lived with her close friend Ruth Baker for the past

ten years in a relationship that was highly ambiguous and had given rise
to unpleasant gossip outside the family. Mary had also had several sexual
liaisons with men and beneath her plain, conventional exterior, was something of an adventuress. She had read John's articles and books and believed
in his ideas absolutely. They had been corresponding intermittently since
1932, but met for the first time only when she shared a platform with
him at a PPU rally. Afterwards she and her friend Ruth went to a café with
John and another speaker. 'I sat next to John and, as we talked and smoked,
an extraordinary feeling of harmony and belonging came over me. Later
John told me he had had exactly the same experience.'[20] The relationship
remained impersonal; not only was John married, but Mary was involved
with another man and her integrity was absolute. They were both members of the PPU executive committee and a few weeks later John invited
Mary to lunch before a meeting. They talked so much, however, that John
forgot to give her any food and she forgot to ask. Afterwards she almost
fainted from hunger. But she had become aware during that conversation
that they shared something unique. 'Perhaps,' Mary wrote later, 'it is always
the same when lovers first recognize the beloved in each other.'[21] John saw
in Mary a calm intelligence and a commitment to the same ideals. In her
company he felt secure and at peace. The contrast with his marriage was
bitter.

Reminders of his 'failures in love' were everywhere. Frieda Lawrence,
now living in Taos with a young Italian called Angelo Ravagli, came to
Larling. They had been drawn together again by a legal dispute over
Lawrence's will in which John gave evidence for Frieda, and by the publication of a book on Lawrence, *A Savage Pilgrimage*, written by an old friend,
Catherine Carswell, who accused John of 'telling lies about Lawrence' in
his *Son of Woman*. Privately he admitted that she had caught him out 'in
an evasion',[22] but took exception to her other revelations. Supported by
Frieda, John publicly accused her of inaccuracy and threatened a libel
action. The book was withdrawn and parts of it rewritten. In the spring
there was a visit from Brett, who recovered the letters Katherine had
sent her and which John had borrowed. There was also a meeting with
Elizabeth Bibesco, for whom he felt 'all the old tenderness', provoking
explosions of jealousy from Betty. For John it brought back memories of
his guilt towards Katherine. One evening he picked up Katherine's copy
of Chekhov's story 'The Peasant' and found that she had underlined a passage: 'Whenever there is someone in a family who has long been ill, and

hopelessly ill, there come painful moments when all timidly, secretly, at the bottom of their hearts long for his death'. In the margin she had written contemptuously 'and even write poems'! Katherine was referring to a poem she had found in John's notebook shortly after the diagnosis of her tuberculosis, anticipating her death. The discovery of Katherine's comments forced John to reconsider his supposedly 'ideal' relationship with her. 'Last night as I was going to bed, I looked hard at her photograph – with her sad eyes, in the portrait taken at Mentone; and I said aloud to her; "there's something always so sad in your eyes when I look at you – as though you had been let down. But I don't think I let you down." Nor do I think it. But maybe another would think my finding of that underlining and that note was the answer.'[23]

In April 1939, John was forced to go into hospital for an operation on his leg, which the surgeon botched, causing massive pain that could not be relieved even by morphine. For six weeks John was without sleep. Once out of hospital, he went to friends in Wales to convalesce and while there had a complete nervous breakdown. 'It began in the middle of tea-time. Suddenly, I felt very queer indeed . . . As my consciousness translated the extraordinary and terrible sensation, it was that I was certainly going mad . . . It seemed to me that I was on the brink of a spiritual abyss, some vast internal void.' James Young was summoned, gave John a powerful sedative and put him to bed in his own house, where he cared for John himself. After two weeks of intense psychological anguish, numbed by opiates, John began to recover, only to realise that something quite fundamental had changed within his mind. His feelings for Betty had vanished. 'I felt an immense pity for her, but no love. That had been finally killed.'[24]

In July, back at Larling, wondering what to do, John received a letter from Mary Gamble asking his advice about the man she was involved with. She told John that 'Tom' loved her deeply and was begging her to go away with him, but, though she had only friendly affection for him, she did not want to hurt him. Mary valued John's opinion 'more than any man alive'. What should she do? John's reply was profoundly disconcerting. He urged her not to give in to this man out of pity, but to be honest about her feelings. Then he added:

The sense of your destiny and mine, or mine and yours, being somehow entwined, has visited me at intervals since we both sat in that cafe after the meeting at Oxford. I have tried to put you out of my mind, but always something has happened to bring you back again. I have done nothing, remained quite passive, in my heart of hearts more hoping that nothing would happen to bring us closer than fearing it. But with a slow and to me frightening inevitability something always has happened. And at last the time came when my heart began to beat faster at seeing your handwriting on an envelope . . .

It's no good; I cannot be a father confessor to you in these matters; my heart is too much involved. I don't want to fall in love with you . . . But it is no use pretending; my hunger for a woman who will be gentle towards me grows month by month. And destiny has determined that the woman is you. I don't know what I want with you. I think no more than to be with you for a day now and then – to be assured that my dream of love between a man and woman is not only a dream. God knows that the anguish of love is all too familiar to me . . . As far as I know, I don't want to be your lover. If I were younger I should desire this tenderly, passionately. But I think that that is gone from me. Maybe it is only that I am tired, tired, tired. But that is what I want from you – rest from my weariness; the beating of my heart tells me that you are capable of the tenderness of love, and that you have this wonderful and precious thing to give me – and that you will. I want you to take me in your arms, to let me sleep in peace with you, to reassure me of the eternity of human love. I want, I need terribly, to believe in love between a man and woman again. Now that I know you have suffered the anguish of love, I am not afraid to speak.[25]

Mary realised very quickly that she did indeed want to give John the tenderness he needed. They arranged to meet on 1 August at Cambridge railway station. It was a glorious summer's day and as Mary drove to the station she 'was in a panic of nervousness'. She had no illusions about herself. She was plain, middle-aged and knew that John was surrounded by women much more attractive than herself. When he arrived they shook hands formally and he got into the car. 'I don't remember that we said anything. I drove back along the Huntingdon road because it was the way I knew. After a few miles he said, "Couldn't we turn off?" I took the next road on the left and very soon he said, "Please stop the car." I did so, and he took me in his arms.'[26] They had a picnic lunch in a field and talked for the first time about their complicated private lives and their hopes for the future. There were several other similar meetings during August and by the time war was declared on 3 September, they were both committed to a relationship that went deeper than either sex or love. It was the union of mind and body John had always dreamed of. When Weg came home from school, one evening in December, she found Betty in her father's wrecked office, waving a letter at her and shouting, 'Your father's gone off with another woman! . . . off with another whore!'[27]

PART VI

The Dark Katherine

Oh God, I do get black . . . I simply go dark. God knows,
my 'blackness' does not come from anything in your letters.
Truthfully, I think it comes from my health; it's part of
my illness — just that. I feel 'ill' and I feel a longing, longing for you: for our home, our life, and for a little baby.
A very dark, obscure, frightening thing seems to rise up in
my soul and threaten these desires . . . that is all.

KATHERINE MANSFIELD TO JOHN MURRY, 8 JUNE 1918

18

Facing Oblivion

Suppose I were to die now quite suddenly, seized by some illness; perhaps I should not know of my danger ... Soon afterwards nothing would remain of me – nothing ... nothing ... nothing! ... It is this which has always terrified me. To live, to have so much ambition, to suffer, weep, struggle – and then oblivion! ... oblivion ... as if I had never been.

MARIE BASHKIRTSEFF, PARIS, 1 MAY 1884

January 1918 is bitterly cold. London is frozen: 'Lord knows how many degrees of frost, and a wind that [is] simply unspeakable'.[1] John and Ida hope that Katherine is warmer in France, but she arrives at Le Havre on the 8th in a blizzard and the boat lies at anchor, 'tossing & pitching & rolling' for hours before the passengers are able to disembark. The next train to Paris does not leave until 5 p.m. After waiting all day, Katherine finds herself in a filthy unheated carriage with a broken window and so many people that she is unable to lie down as she has been instructed to do. Hampered by the weather, the train arrives at the Gare St Lazare four-and-a-half hours late. Having left London early on Monday afternoon, it has taken Katherine until 2 a.m. on Wednesday just to get to Paris. There is a blizzard there too, and the streets – pitch dark because of the war – are so slippery with ice that 'qu'on marche comme un poulet malade [one walks like a sick chicken]'. But Katherine, though exhausted, is invigorated by the city. She writes gaily to John that there is 'a wonderful spirit here – so

337

much humour, life, gaiety, sorrow, one cannot see it all & not think with amazement of the strange cement-like state of England'.[2]

But by the time she reaches Bandol, her optimism has vanished. The train to Marseilles, unheated and without a restaurant car, delayed by the weather, crawls through blizzards, arrives late yet again. The journey is made even more of a trial by two women, dressed like mourners at a funeral, talking about illness and death. 'I sat in the corner feeling damned ill myself. The big one, rolling about in the shaking train, said what a fatal place this coast is for anyone who is even threatened with lung trouble . . . This recital, in that dark moving train, told by that big woman swathed in black had an effect on me that I couldn't own and never mentioned. I knew the woman was a fool, hysterical, morbid, but I believed her; and her voice has gone on somewhere echoing in me ever since.'[3]

At Marseilles Katherine is hustled by a pimp, given the wrong information and unable to get a meal at a crowded restaurant. She queues for a train, only to be told it has come in on another platform. Katherine describes for John how 'the people swarmed in just like apes climbing into bushes – & I had just thrown my rugs into it when it was stated that it was only for permissionaires and did not stop before Toulon . . . I staggered out, & got in another train on another platform, asked 3 people if it was the right one who did not know – & sat down in the corner – completely dished.' The carriage was occupied by eight Serbian officers and their dogs and shortly afterwards there was a riot in the station and a group of French soldiers, 'furious – very ugly, & vile', tried to seize the train and evict all civilians and the Serbians. 'They banged on the windows, wrenched open the doors & threw out the people & their luggage after them. They came to our carriage swarmed in – told the officers they too must go and one caught hold of me as though I were a sort of packet of rugs – I never said a word for I was far too tired and vague to care about anything except I was determined not to cry.' Katherine is saved by one of the Serbian officers who claims that she is his wife. They let their dogs off the leashes and barricade the carriage doors.[4]

The train arrives in Bandol late at night with a strong mistral blowing. Katherine's final shock, when the cab reaches the hotel, is to find that the Beau Rivage has never received John's letter reserving her a room, it's under new management and there's no heating. Fortunately they have rooms free so Katherine takes the cheapest and goes straight to bed with a hot water bottle and some soup. The journey has consumed the last vestiges of her strength: she has a high fever and her bad lung is burning 'like a flat iron' in her chest.

The following morning she's revived by glimpses of the 'hyacinth blue sea' glittering under the sun, the palm trees flashing in the wind, 'and the mountains, violet in the shadow, and jade green in the sun'. Everything will be all right, she tells John, though 'it has been a bit of a bang . . . And I'll tell you exactly what I feel like. I feel like a fly who has been dropped into the milk jug & fished out again.' When she has the energy she walks along the promenade to the shops and finds that hardly anyone remembers her; Madame Allegre at the Villa Pauline knows Katherine only by her voice; even Madame Gamel, one of the shopkeepers with whom they had been particularly friendly, doesn't recognise Katherine until she explains who she is. 'Ah! you have changed a lot because you've been very ill, haven't you? You no longer look like a young girl.'[5] Katherine has lost almost 13 kilograms and a lightness has gone out of her face. When she looks in the mirror she finds two grey hairs at her temples. She is barely twenty-nine but in the space of a year she has turned into an old woman. This change is hard to accept.

The town has changed too – everything has doubled in price since the war began, the only cigarettes to be had are foul 'camel droppings' and the fields of jonquils have vanished. The hotel flowerbeds, once full of geraniums, have degenerated into rubbish pits with 'little scrubby bushes . . . broken bottles & bits of lead piping chucked among them'. There are soldiers everywhere, urinating and defecating on the beach underneath Katherine's window and once she sees them playing football with what she speculates might be a dead animal. Many of them are from French North Africa – 'coal black nigger soldiers in full french uniform'. Katherine confesses the prejudice, common in her generation among white colonials, that had informed her seizure of Lawrence's poetry in the Café Royal. 'I have a horror of black men . . . And the sight of these particular ones in their spruce European clothes gives me an unpleasant turn. If I were queen they would never be allowed to escape from their cotton fields and coconuts.'[6] The girl who once had such respect for Maori seems to be unable to extend it to other ethnic groups.

The hotel is at least quiet and after a few days of rest, Katherine begins to feel that she might be able to work. She stays in bed late in the morning, gets up for lunch, takes a short walk if the weather is warm enough and then sits at a little table in front of the fire, wrapped up in her warmest clothes and the furs that Chaddie had given her for Christmas. The room is cold and Katherine has to buy her own firewood. The grate doesn't draw well and Katherine finds herself wishing for Ida. Her back is 'hurting horribly' and she's coughing all the time. 'My left lung aches & aches.'[7] But it's not her own health that concerns her most. By 17 January she's beginning to be anxious about John, still not fully recovered from his breakdown, and there are accounts in the newspapers of air raids in London. She has received only one letter from him since she left and she begins to wonder what has happened to him. She can't bear the thought of losing one more person she loves.

Used to living apart from her, surrounded by his friends, preoccupied with his work at the War Office, trying to write poetry and essays in the evening, John has not yet realised that this is a different kind of separation. But when Katherine sends a panicky telegram he responds quickly, promising to write every day in future. A few years earlier he had written prophetically: 'We seem to be fated to suffer because of letters when we are away from each other'. The problem with letters is the three-day time lapse: the cycle of action and reaction creates false crises.

The letters that are reaching John in London are creating great anxiety for him and Ida. It's obvious that Katherine is very ill. She's unable to sleep, plagued by the night sweats that are a feature of TB. 'I had to keep sponging my face & kept thinking "it must be five o clock" and finding it was only a quarter past one. Oh, these long, lonely nights when one is ill!' The fear of death is a constant companion in the dark and she is haunted by her childlessness. 'I really did, at one or two times, think I would "peg out" here, never having had a heron or a heronette and that simply horrified me.'[8] John urges her to see a doctor in Bandol, and to get a medical certificate so that he can organise a visa for Ida. 'I don't think there's any doubt that she'll be able to come to you if you can get a medical certificate signed by a British Consul . . . But then I don't know whether you really want L.M. . . . She is urgent to go.' John is well aware of the delicacy of it. 'On the one hand, it would lift an enormous, incessant load from my mind if I knew she was with you; on the other hand, I don't know whether, if she came now, you wouldn't be angry.'[9] Katherine is angry. Her mood has changed. She remembers how much she detests the way that Ida takes her over and just now she's feeling too weak to resist. In spite of her illness, she's finding the solitude creative. 'Dead quiet and spinning away',[10] she doesn't want to be interrupted.

On 24 January she writes a letter to Fergusson, vividly describing the town with colours and sounds and scents – she writes to him as she does to no one else, painting scenes with words. 'I have begun to work . . . and shall keep at it all I know.'[11] A few days later she tells John that she is 'fully launched, right out in the deep sea',[12] though she refuses to tell him what she is working on. It is a story called 'Je ne parle pas Francais' and it comes from Katherine's present mood of extreme hopelessness, which she admits is one of her two main 'kick-offs' in the writing game. The story is 'a cry against corruption' in the widest sense, portraying a cynical, tainted world where innocence is crushed and even friendship counts for nothing. The characters of Dick Harmon and the unreliable and corrupt narrator Raoul Duquette are based recognisably on John Murry and Francis Carco ('& Gertler & God knows who', as Katherine tells John), though it is impossible not to see a shadow of Garnet Trowell in Dick, buckling under his mother's pressure. Mouse, the timid, helpless English girl who can't speak French, is created from what John has told Katherine about his first love, Marguéritte. Dick Harmon abandons Mouse, just as John had once abandoned Marguéritte, ostensibly because he can't betray his mother. Katherine is anxious that John should not identify too closely with these associations: 'I hope you'll see (of course you will) that I am not writing with a sting. I'm not, indeed!'[13] The story has even more of a poisoned bite in the character of Raoul Duquette. It is difficult not to discern an element of revenge, since Carco had used Katherine's character and her letters in his novel *Les Innocents*. The description of Raoul is a good physical portrait of Carco, even down to the inference of sexual ambiguity, and the salacious African laundress supposedly based on what Carco had told Katherine of his own childhood in the French colonies.

But what Katherine makes of all these impressions and experiences is something unique. 'Is it good? I am frightened. For I stand or fall by it. It's as far as I can get at present and I have gone for it, bitten deeper & deeper & deeper than ever I have before.'[14] John's reply is reassuring. He compares her story to Dostoevsky's 'Letters from the Underworld' and tells her that it's different to anything else she has previously written: 'I mean in scope & skeleton & structure, the exquisite exactness – the "this & nothing else" – of your vision in the detail is there just as before. How can I put it? This is the only writing of yours I know that seems to be *dangerous*.'[15] But John is upset by 'Je ne parle pas Francais'. 'The second part which she sent me . . . struck me dumb and numb with pain. It hurt too much.' He doesn't associate it with Marguéritte, but thinks that Katherine has made a deliberate parallel between the abandonment of Mouse by Dick, and his own abandonment of Katherine alone in France. 'The fate of the Mouse, caught in the toils of the world's evil, abandoned by her lover, is Katherine's fate.'[16] John feels he is being accused.

John and Ida are becoming increasingly alarmed by Katherine's letters, mentioning 'homesickness & anxiety & panic'. 'I suffer so frightfully from insomnia here and from night terrors.' She feels terribly isolated; she longs for 'human contact . . . & that of course I don't have at all. I miss it very much . . . I must have a two legged person to talk to . . . Not to sleep and to be alone is a very neat example of HELL.'[17] She begins to talk about coming home in March instead of staying until April. There are rumours that the Germans are planning a new offensive and she is afraid that it might block her return to England. John is encouraging Ida to go to France: 'I am all for her going,' he tells Katherine. 'She could bring you back safely.'[18] It would ease his mind – and assuage his guilt – to know that Katherine had someone with her.

On 10 February, Katherine records that she has received 'A MOST MYSTERIOUS TELEGRAM which so horrifies and bewilders me that I don't dare to let myself think of it. I must wait. It says am coming Leave this afternoon Baker!!!' Katherine's first thought is that something has happened to John, since she has not been receiving regular letters from him. But there are also two letters from Ida – '2 hysterical mad screams – "Oh my darling make the doctor let me come" – "Oh my darling eat"'. It is too late to do anything: Ida is on her way. Katherine is aghast.[19] The night before Ida's telegram, Katherine had dreamt a story completely 'even down to its name which was "Sun & Moon" . . . I didn't dream that I read it. No I was in it, part of it & it played round invisible me.' She writes it out from her 3 a.m. notes during the afternoon, driven by the knowledge that at any moment Ida will arrive. 'Every sound from outside is her – she. What the HELL does it mean.' After she has finished the story she writes a furious letter to John. 'Bogey I have done with her. I asked her not to come; said I didn't want her & then she wired me "leaving" – That ends it. She's a revolting hysterical ghoul.'[20]

About six o'clock on 12 February, Katherine hears that 'special knock!!!'[21] on her door and the familiar – dreaded – voice saying, 'May I come in?' And there is Ida, desperately worried, clutching a bag of rather squashed babas au rhum bought in Paris. She allows Katherine to vent her feelings, with only a small protest: 'I thought you were very ill'. Privately Ida is devastated by her hostile reception. 'My heart sank to the uttermost depths. All that struggle and effort and anguish of mind and body was wasted – thrown away – and useless. I was not welcome.[22] Ida agrees to a daily routine: Katherine will work in the mornings uninterrupted; they will have meals together and a short walk in the afternoon between two and five. In the evening Katherine will write for two hours until dinner, then sit in her room and read. Ida, glad to be there in case she is needed, understands Katherine's attitude despite her own disappointment. Katherine has always been the independent one, reckless for her own safety, hating anyone who tries to curb her, hating anyone she depends on. To admit that she needs Ida, would be to admit that she is ill, and to admit that might be fatal. When Katherine has calmed down, she goes for a walk alone, and lies down under a pine tree looking out over the bay. At first she laments that she won't be able to write with Ida there – 'the wells and the springs are poisoned'– then realises that, already, a new story, 'Bliss', is taking shape in her mind.[23]

But Katherine is more gravely ill than she knows. Pain and exhaustion make her irascible and Ida's presence grates on her nerves. Her non-stop trivial conversation at meals 'nearly makes me die with fury'. Ida rattles on about people at the factory where she is now supervisor: 'oh dear me, I wonder what my little foreman is doing'. Her lack of literary understanding exasperates Katherine, who reproduces Ida's voice in her letters and notebooks with a cruel nib: 'Katie mine who is Wordsworth. Must I like him? It's no good looking cross because I love you my angel from the little tip of that cross eyebrow to the all of you. When am I going to brush your hair again?' Ida's concern for Katherines's health is equally unwelcome. But under it all, when Katherine is honest, she is glad that Ida will be there to travel back with her. 'Frankly that is a relief – to feel I would have someone to help me. I am not much good at this travelling alone.'[24]

On 18 February, Katherine insists on taking Ida for a long uphill walk that had been a favourite in the days when she stayed at the Villa Pauline. But, getting tired, she takes what she thinks is a short cut and loses her way. She's barely able to put one foot in front of the other by the time they get back to the hotel. The following morning Katherine wakes just after dawn, gets up to open the shutters and then jumps back into bed. The movement makes her cough. Her mouth tastes strange – she spits and there in her hand is bright red arterial blood. Tuberculosis is no longer just a pain in her chest when she breathes; she is staring at the reality of it. Now, every time she coughs she spits more blood. Her handkerchiefs look like those of 'a pork butcher'. 'Oh, yes, of course I am frightened,' she writes in her notebook. 'I don't want to be ill, I mean "seriously" away from Jack . . . 2nd I don't want to find this is real consumption, perhaps it's going to gallop – who knows – and I shan't have my work written. That's what matters. How unbearable it would be to die, leave "scraps", "bits", nothing real finished.'[25] Ida goes instantly for an English doctor, who examines Katherine and reads her a series of stern warnings. She has lost weight since she arrived in Bandol, and she has a fever. There must be no walks, no sitting in draughty cold rooms; she must be kept warm, have plenty of rest and good food. Above all she must not think of going back to England until the spring. Though they had promised each other that they would always write the truth, Katherine's letter to John is a triumph of economy. 'I have not been so well these last few days. Today I saw a doctor . . . I've got a bit of a temperature & I am not so fat as I was when I came – & Bogey, this is NOT serious does NOT keep me in bed is absolutely easily curable, but I have been spitting a bit of blood.' John is not to worry. Katherine quotes the example of Lawrence and her own Aunt Belle, who had had TB some years earlier and recovered.[26]

Despite, or perhaps because of, this serious development of her disease, Katherine is even more desperate to go back to England. She knows she needs rest, sunshine, the kind of food – butter, meat, fish, sugar – that is readily available in France, but not in cold, beleaguered England where everything is rationed, and above all she must avoid any kind of stress. But Katherine has become completely focused on returning to England to marry John as soon as her divorce becomes absolute in April. 'I feel that it will make things so easy, all sorts of things, & the feeling will be quite quite different . . . Apart from thousands of other things I know I shall take the most childish delight in speaking of you as my husband after you really are . . .' She can't wait to get rid of the 'loathed and abominated' name Bowden that stares up at her from her official papers, and is desperate to avoid 'the Human Snigger' she is subjected to as a woman living in sin. Once they are married, everything will come right – they will buy a printing press like the Woolfs, to be called 'The Heron Press'; they will live in 'a real cottage' and sup on 'honey dew and milk of Paradise; we will be happy and free immediately'.[27] Katherine has even begun to cherish hopes of 'a heron or a heronette'. She and John had made love in his flat on the

Sunday before she left England and since then her period has been absent. It is another reason for wanting to get back to John as soon as possible.[28] But the other reason, which John understands, though it remains publicly unacknowledged, is that she is afraid of dying before she sees John again.

In the meantime she tries to control her irritation with Ida and concentrate on her new story. By 28 February she has finished 'Bliss', and confesses, as she sends it off to John, that she is 'an absolute rag'. The story, written so quickly, is a clever parody of the literary dinner parties Katherine has attended so often. The character of Eddie is a caricature of Aldous Huxley, 'a fish out of the Garsington pond (which gives me joy)', and Bertha's husband Harry, Katherine admits, is 'touched with' her old friend W. L. George. Only the women spring to life as themselves: Bertha the model wife, the Nanny who controls the children (and Bertha) and Miss Fulton, the 'bright young thing' who goes everywhere in taxis, is a danger to men and somehow reminds the reader of Katherine herself.[29] All the subtle nuances and intuitions of female relationships are laid on the page to be interpreted. Bertha's sudden awareness of sensual – and sexual – pleasures is written in lyrical prose and the final moments of disillusion, when she discovers that her newly desired husband is having an affair with the woman responsible for her arousal, is handled with delicate skill. It is a romantic story, told with the simplicity and understatement that had been the subject of her first conversation with John at the Georges' dinner party. John's verdict, eagerly awaited, is that it is 'very very good', but there are things that jar – a surname 'Wangle', which is 'ever so slightly discordant', and the fact that she has put some of Bertha's dialogue in inverted commas. John recommends cutting the words altogether: 'her clumsy phrases are at the heart of her. But I think that, being what she is, she would avoid the phrases and, however impatiently, prefer her own dumbness.'[30] The surname is changed, the inverted commas removed, but the words remain.

Getting back to England is not as simple as Katherine had imagined. Ida can return at any time, but Katherine, having obtained special medical permission to be there, will require the same to return. John tries the ruse of sending a telegram, 'Mother worse, operation necessary', but that has been attempted so often that the authorities will not allow it. Nor are the doctors willing to agree that it is in Katherine's best interests to leave France. So she sets out to persuade the rather shady English doctor – 'a little sot with poached eyes who bites his fingers' – who has taken up residence in Bandol. Katherine imagines morbidly that he has had to leave England because 'he has killed some poor girl with a dirty buttonhook'. When the doctor arrives at the hotel, smelling of drink, Katherine, dressed in her red dress, made up, smiles at him, flirts with him, lets him talk and eventually gets the chit. But the experience sickens her. 'An old dead sad wretched self blows about . . . how hideous human beings are – how loathsome it was to catch this toad as I did . . . I kept hearing him say, very thick "any trouble is a pleasure for a lovely woman".'[31] The following day Ida and Katherine go to the consulate in Marseilles to get the necessary permissions. Ida is in her element: queuing for tickets, going backwards and forwards to the police for visas and to Cook's arranging baggage and hotels. In the end Katherine can get permission only to travel as far as Paris, but 'I don't think – having got so far & pleading as I shall – they can withhold their consent to my going further'.[32]

On 21 March Katherine is on the train at Marseilles, feeling 'so bloody ill – such a bellyache & a backache and a headache', but armed with sleeping tablets and painkillers, and a suitcase full of chocolate, nougat, butter and French perfume. Ida loses her suitcase in the chaos and has to buy essential belongings and a rucksack. After another weary train journey Katherine's arrival in Paris is a shock. The city is in a state of siege. She is refused permission to travel on, until the authorities receive a letter of authorisation from London. This means she will have to stay for a week in Paris and this, too, requires police permission. The hotels are full and Katherine almost collapses with the exhaustion of 'the journey and getting about – and the disappointment and fatigue of this looking for rooms'. She adds a sentence that seems to sum up the present nature of her life with John: 'This journey – it never never ends – I seem to have been trying to get back from that moment we stopped waving'.[33] John gets Sydney Waterlow to pull strings with the military authorities but by that time the German bombardment of Paris has begun. All civilian travel is suspended and Katherine is trapped.

Katherine and Ida trawl the hotels – Ida tries to insist that they should do it in a taxi – and there are arguments about how much they can afford, but eventually Katherine sees a quiet hotel in a corner of the Place de la Sorbonne, next to a bookshop. It is clean and affordable, at 6 F per night, though the rooms offered are on the sixth floor and there is no lift. Wearily, she and Ida trail up the stairs behind the bellboy, carrying their bags. 'I seem to spend half my life arriving at strange hotels. And asking if I may go to bed immediately. "And would you mind filling my hot water bottle? . . . Thank you; that is delicious. No; I shan't require anything more." The strange door shuts upon the stranger, and then I slip down in the sheets. Waiting for the shadows to come out of the corners and spin their slow, slow web over the Ugliest Wallpaper of All.'[34]

Katherine refuses to be daunted: 'until they let me come home I shall stay here and write'. She and Ida eat out in a cheap restaurant chain called Duvals, and spend the first week going backwards and forwards to the air-raid shelters in the cellar to avoid the bombs being dropped by the German aircraft overhead. Apart from the struggle up and down seven flights of stairs, the shelters are cold and damp 'like tombs'. Katherine describes sitting there at one o'clock in the morning, trembling with cold, 'in a heap of coal on an old upturned box – listening to the bloody Poles & Russians – it all seemed a sort of endless dream'.[35] The lack of sleep and the physical effort sap all Katherine's energy and she decides that she would rather risk death in her room. Every night after that, Ida brings her pillows and blankets to sleep on the floor under Katherine's bed. Sometimes she massages Katherine's back to relieve the pain in her spine and one day she finds 'a slight swelling'. Katherine is filled with panic. Is this some kind of spinal disease? A growth?

The Germans begin to pound Paris with their heaviest artillery. Big Bertha, or 'Long-sighted Lizzie', is firing every eighteen minutes. Katherine is aware that the troops are very near. A church crowded with people is shelled on Good Friday and then on 2 April a house opposite the hotel is hit, the roof and windows gone, the street piled with rubble, the occupants' clothes hanging from the trees in the street. It is impossible to leave, but their prolonged stay is beginning to cause financial problems. Katherine's mother had sent money from her own account to buy a wedding dress – 'she said I was not even to tell Chaddie, as it was her "secret funds" . . . To make myself a lovely girl the day I was married'[36] – and Katherine is prepared to spend this to keep herself and Ida. But no letters are getting through and Mr Kay can't get money to Katherine either. Ida goes to the British Consulate to see whether she can get any paid work and is sent to 'an underground *cantine* for soldiers & refugees'. Katherine goes too, but is forced to give it up after the first day. 'I couldn't do it . . . It was too hard work.' Ida suspects that she goes to visit Carco to borrow money. But on 6 April, the necessary permission arrives from England and Katherine spends her days 'rushing from office to photographer to police station to Commissaire & Consul, Cooks & and M.P.O.' in vile icy weather, to get the necessary bookings and visas. Mr Kay's money arrives at last and Katherine and Ida celebrate with a drink. Ida, who has no head for alcohol, is reduced to helpless giggles on only one Dubonnet. The ticket offices are besieged by people wanting to leave, but on 10 April Katherine and Ida manage to be among the lucky two hundred allowed onto the boat at Le Havre.

John is appalled at Katherine's condition when she arrives in London the following day. Since she went to Bandol she has lost another 6 kilograms and now weighs only just under 45. Three months of nervous anxiety and the ravages of tuberculosis have reduced her to a wraith. 'I feel horribly weak & rocky now that the strain is over – blissfully happy – incredibly happy – but really ill.' She writes ecstatically of the joy of 'ones OWN fire – and lighting the gas & making tea, and oh! The hot bath which really was hot – & Jack & Jack and Jack.' Even Ida is no longer the 'fiend guardian' but 'dearest Jones' and there are oblique apologies (as Ida had known there would be) for what 'that sad sick Katie whose back ached in her brain' has said and done.[37]

Katherine's decree absolute has still not been pronounced by the court and plans for the wedding have to be postponed. John must urgently get Katherine to a doctor. Ainger, her first choice, is away and she is seen by one of his assistants, who diagnoses the swelling on her spine as a tubercular gland and recommends complete rest and plenty of nourishing food. When Ainger returns he reinforces his assistant's advice, but tells Katherine plainly that her haemorrhage, fever and weight loss are symptoms of phthisis – the last and most serious stage of tuberculosis – and recommends that she should go to a sanatorium. Katherine is horrified: 'It's a 2nd lunatic asylum to me'. She had seen enough of such institutions in Bad Wörishofen. Eventually she persuades Ainger that it 'would kill me much faster than cure me'. Ainger insists that she must then have a sanatorium lifestyle at home: 'Must live in a summer house . . . eat & drink milk and not get excited or run or leap or worry about anything'. There are more dire warnings about the infectious nature of her illness: 'I must not borrow a handkerchief . . . Or drink out of loving cups or eat the little bear's porridge with his spoon.'[38] Katherine feels contaminated. John is determined to follow the doctor's advice and get her out of London. Anne

Estelle Rice, now living in Cornwall with her husband, recommends a hotel in Looe, a small fishing village on the southern coast. It's the warmest and sunniest part of the British Isles and John hopes that it might work.

Katherine is finding time and energy to see her friends. Virginia Woolf invites her to lunch and is taken aback by her appearance, even though she has been told that Katherine has been 'dangerously ill . . . with haemorrhage from the lungs'. The lunch is rather stiff – too much time has elapsed since they last met – but by the end of it, they are back on solid ground, as Virginia records in her diary. 'My theory is that I get down to what is true rock in her, through the numerous vapours & pores which sicken or bewilder most of our friends. It's her love of writing I think.'[39] The Woolfs are still printing 'Prelude', battling with their own inexperience and untrained part-time help, but they hope to have it on sale by the end of June. Virginia dislikes the woodblock that J. D. Fergusson has designed for the cover and, to make matters worse, the title has mistakenly been printed as 'The Prelude'. But it is too late to change.

Katherine has been corresponding constantly with Fergusson and he is one of the first people to come to the flat. Over the years he's become Katherine's friend rather than John's. They call each other Fergusson and Mansfield, as if they were both men. With him Katherine can talk about 'this art business' and 'what is honesty',[40] and they understand, in a way that John does not, about creative interpretation of the world they inhabit and which they see in a very similar way. Something of their relationship is captured in a description Katherine writes in her notebook of a morning spent at his studio. It is a still life in words.

'Well sit down Mansfield, and reposez-vous' said Fergusson, 'and I'll get on with my dressing.'

So he went into his bedroom & shut the door between, and I sat on the end of the sofa. The sun came full through the two windows. Dividing the studio into four – two quarters of light and two of shadow . . . Very beautiful, oh God is a blue teapot with two white cups attending, a red apple among oranges addeth fire to flame – in the white bookcases the books fly up and down in scales of colour, with pink and lilac notes recurring until nothing remains but them, sounding over and over.

There are a number of frames, some painted and some plain, leaning against the wall, and the picture of a naked woman with her arms raised, languid, as though her heavy flowering beauty were almost too great to

bear. There are two sticks and an umbrella in one corner, and in the fireplace
– a kettle, curiously like a bird.

White net curtains hang over the windows. For all the sun it is raining
outside. The gas in the middle of the room has a pale yellow paper shade
and as Fergusson dresses he keeps up a constant whistling.

Reposez-vous.

Oui, je me repose . . .[41]

Fergusson is to be 'best man' at Katherine's long-awaited wedding.
'Darling Brett' is to be Katherine's witness. Ida can't get any more leave
from the factory and there may also be an element of superstition, left
over from Katherine's first marriage, which Ida had witnessed. This one
is scarcely better. No church ceremony, since Katherine is a divorcee; no
publicity, since some important people – including John's parents – think
they are already married; and no fuss, since Katherine is too ill for much
celebration. Brett will collect John from his office and meet Katherine and
Fergusson at the Kensington register office. Nevertheless, Katherine is bubbling over with anticipation. 'It will be Great Fun, Larks and Jollifications.
I am wearing, of course, a simple Robe of White Crepe de Chine and
Pearl Butterfly presented by our dear Queen. Murry, naturally, top hat and
carnation buttonhole.'[42] Afterwards there will be a wedding breakfast at
a restaurant. But Katherine's decree is delayed yet again and the wedding
has to be postponed for another day. Finally, on Friday 3 May, John places
Frieda's wedding ring on Katherine's finger, this time officially, and they
are pronounced man and wife. There are no photographs; no crowd of
congratulatory friends, many of whom are offended that they have not
been invited – particularly Ottoline.

But it's John's actions that are the subject of recriminations for the rest
of Katherine's life. Instead of reacting joyfully to the moment, John kisses
Katherine reluctantly, then turns away to wipe his mouth with a handkerchief. She is devastated. 'Our marriage. You cannot imagine what that was
to have meant to me. It's fantastic, I suppose. It was to have shone apart
from all else in my life. And really it was only part of the nightmare after
all. You never once held me in your arms and called me your wife.'[43] John's
state of mind is one of horror and fear, as he tries to explain to her later.
'The only thing I want to say is that perhaps you didn't quite know how
afraid I was: how my soul was struck dumb with terror at your illness. I
seemed neither to be able to speak nor to breathe, I could never say what I

wanted to say to you . . . My longing to hold you in my arms was terrible; but more terrible was the thought which held me back. "No, I mustn't; I shall hurt her." At that moment the knowledge of your illness blinded me like a flash of lightning – tore right through my heart.'[44]

The wedding that Katherine describes in her notebook shortly afterwards seems to be grounded in memories of her own. The girl putting on her hat in front of the mirror who 'fastens on a white veil and hardly knows herself. Is it becoming or is it not? . . . Two dark bold eyes stare through the mesh – surely not hers.' And then the champagne tastes bitter: 'I had to drink it because it was there, but there was something positively malicious in the way the little bubbles hurled themselves to the rim, danced, broke – they seemed to be jeering at me'.[45]

19

At the Bottom of the Sea

There is no limit to human suffering. When one thinks: 'now I have touched the bottom of the sea, now I can go no deeper' – one goes deeper. And so it is for ever . . .

KATHERINE MANSFIELD, UNBOUND PAPERS, 1920

The Headland Hotel in Looe is a huge Victorian building, standing on the edge of a spit of land, staring out to sea, separated from the waves by the width of the road. At ground level there is a glass verandah for cold days – an indoor garden 'hung between the sun and the sea'. Katherine's first-floor room, booked by Anne Estelle Rice, has three windows facing the sun and she can lie in bed and listen to the sound of the waves on the rocks, no longer joyous, only sad. 'It makes me feel what a blind, dreadful – losing & finding affair our life has been.'[1] Katherine is still fighting off an attack of pleurisy contracted just before she left London. Her lung is acutely painful, but she has nothing to do but eat and rest. She is reading Dorothy Wordsworth's journals for the second time, spending most of the day in bed, being dosed on cod liver oil and iron tonic, fed with porridge and mackerel and milk puddings. Everyone at the hotel is 'amazingly kind', Anne calls frequently with flowers and food, and the young doctor who comes to see her every day seems to know exactly what he is doing. Katherine can't write yet. 'I can't get into touch with my mind. I am standing gasping in one of those disgusting telephone boxes and I can't "get through". "Sorry. There's no reply" tinkles out the little voice . . . Then I suppose there is nobody in the building – nobody at all.'[2]

Appalling scenarios of suffering and death play themselves out in her imagination – spinal disease, a paralytic stroke, heart failure, being crippled, 'My face all deformed'. Sometimes the pain is unendurable and she has to 'pace from corner to corner, then up and down, up and down the pain racked me like a curse and I could hardly breathe'. If she goes down to the verandah, the effort leaves her exhausted – 'in a daze of fatigue . . . I can barely walk, can't think, don't dare to go to sleep because if I do I know I'll lie awake through the night and that is my horror . . . But these are, Hard Lines.'[3] The nights are an ordeal. Katherine describes them in a journal entry headed Pulmonary Tuberculosis, which she then reorganises into a poem called 'Malade'.

> The man in the room next to mine
> Has the same complaint as I.
> When I wake in the night I hear him turning.
> And then he coughs.
> And I cough.
> And after a silence I cough.
> And he coughs again –
> This goes on for a long time
> Until I feel we are like two roosters
> Calling to each other at false dawn
> From far-away hidden farms.[4]

She tells Ida, 'It seems a mockery to be 29 . . . when there is so much that one longs to do and be and have'.[5] Katherine cares about writing, above everything else, but so far she has accomplished very little. What happened to all the promise of the girl who published In a German Pension? What has she done with all the wasted years in between? To make matters worse, she has only just begun to realise what she can do. When she had written 'Je ne parle pas Francais', she had felt 'a sort of authority', that she had 'in a way grown up as a writer'. And there's a much more personal grief. Anne Estelle Rice, at the age of forty, is pregnant, glowing with maternity, while the hope that Katherine had cherished in Bandol has come to nothing. Her period, unusually heavy and debilitating, arrives on 2 June for the first time since Christmas. Will there ever be a child?

Katherine's desperation spills over into angry letters to John. 'I feel "ill" and I feel a longing, longing for you: for our home, our life, and for a little baby. A very dark, obscure, frightening thing seems to rise up in my soul and threaten these desires'.[6] She accuses him of neglect, of not believing in their future together, of not loving her enough. John, struggling to come to terms with the knowledge that he has just married someone who may not have very long to live, is as desperate as she is. 'I've been rather depressed to-day. I started it by weeping over your letter . . . Do you think that when I'm away from you I am happy? Do you think I live at all? . . . Surely you know how I hunger to be with you . . . So much you say & write hurts me.'[7] John is very close to another nervous collapse and so miserable he sometimes wishes that he could die too. He walks the empty streets at night, ignoring the air raids, 'In the superstitious hope that a merciful bomb would drop near me'.

He proposes that, if Katherine won't go to a sanatorium, they should take a house in one of the healthier parts of London – Hampstead, the old Vale of Health – with Ida to run it for them and servants to do the rough work. He worries about money, but he is earning enough while the war lasts – more than enough – and surely, afterwards, they can both earn from their writing and there is still Katherine's allowance. Initially, Katherine welcomes the idea, then turns against it, leaving John bewildered and angry. He writes later, when it's too late, with more understanding:

The last thread of connection between herself and the world frayed and snapped. She felt 'utterly homeless, just uprooted', an atom of flotsam 'tossed about on any old strange tide'. She woke in the dark she dreaded and heard the wail of the sea, and 'her little watch raced round and round, and the watch was like a symbol of imbecile existence'. This was the bottom-less pit, into which she fell, apart and alone. In such a moment she would, with a single gesture, scatter all my laborious plans for bringing us together again. She did not want a home, she wanted only to wander from place to place till the end came. What had she to do with houses and lands? She was by nature homeless and vagrant. Just as I was struggling to conclude some sort of bargain with the exorbitant landlord, 'Don't let's have the Monster (she wrote). I hate the idea. I don't want it at all. Don't let's ever have a house in London. I am sure the whole idea is wrong. It is idiotic, I think, for

us to be together when I am in the least ill. Waste of energy. I realize that.'
And then she would announce her intention of leaving the hotel, because it
was too expensive or too respectable, and in the same breath refuse to take
any money from me.[8]

Money is a problem. Katherine is now getting £4 a week from her
father, but the hotel costs more than £5. Since their marriage, even though
John now earns more than three times Katherine's allowance, their financial arrangements have not changed. Katherine still pays her own expenses
and hates having to ask John for money. 'I dare not.' She prefers to ask Ida,
who is much less able to afford it. In June Katherine quarrels with Ida
too, her demanding letters provoking Ida to protest that she is being used.
Katherine responds icily:

You're not just an agency to which I apply for pills and cigarettes, free of
charge, though your whole letter was concerned with trying to make me
believe that's what I've brought our 'relationship' to. However if it pleases
you to feel it, my dear, you must feel it. Lord knows I deserve it enough,
according to the WORLD. I thought you were the person I flew to with bad
tempers, worries, depressions, money troubles, wants, rages, silence, enfin
– but the little bottles, boxes and postal orders, though God knows welcome, seemed to me to be only the trimmings – and not the feast. However
you think otherwise – which is humiliating to us both.[9]

Ida is in an agony of doubt about the proposal John has just put to
her. She enjoys her job at the factory, loves the atmosphere at the hostel
where she is living, has made friends and has a life of her own where she
is valued. She knows that to go with Katherine will be difficult. Ida has no
illusions about her own limitations as a housekeeper: she will be exposing
herself to criticism and there will be no chance to make her own decisions
or live as she pleases. It will be Katherine's home, and everything will have
to be done Katherine's way. But in the end there is no question about Ida's
final decision: 'Nothing else would have been possible.' And then there is
the inevitable apology and explanation from Katherine: 'The truth is that
for the time being my nature is quite changed by illness'. She blames the
pain and the sleepless nights. 'I turn into a fiend.'[10]

Katherine can't cope alone with the psychological effects of suffering
and the fear of death. At one point she writes a letter to John in which she

tries to explain how she feels. 'Nearly every night at 11 o'clock I begin wishing it were 11 a.m. I walk up and down – look at the bed – look at the writing-table – look in the glass and am frightened of that girl with the burning eyes – think "will my candle last until it's light?" – and then sit for a long time staring at the carpet – so long that it's only a fluke that one ever looks up again. And, oh God! this terrifying idea that one must die, and may be going to die . . .' She ends with a plea: 'I MUST NOT BE LEFT ALONE'.[11] But as soon as Katherine writes the letter, she realises that it is too harrowing for John to read. She seals the envelope and tucks it into the back of her notebook as 'interesting evidence'.

By the end of July Katherine is back in London with John, enduring the air raids and the food queues as the war drags on through its fourth year. She is still frail, but the country cooking, the rest and the sunshine have had some effect and she now weighs a little more than she did before she went to Cornwall. She has also managed to bring back some writing – a number of notebook sketches and the complex and bitter 'A Married Man's Story' about a man who poisons his wife, though this remains unfinished. Katherine's fortunes as a published writer are about to change. Her problem, she believes, is her own lack of confidence, her fear of rejection – 'my timidity before closed doors. My debate as to whether I shall ring too loud or not laugh enough . . . it's deep deep deep: in fact it is the "explanation" of the failure of K.M. as a writer up to the present.'[12] Now she's driven by a greater fear – that time will run out before she has accomplished anything. The slim blue edition of 'Prelude' is published on 10 July, but attracts little attention. The general opinion in Bloomsbury is that it won't 'set the Thames on fire'.[13] The Hogarth Press is still a rather amateur undertaking and Virginia does not expect to sell more than a hundred copies. Katherine feels sensitive about it. 'I am thankful people are buying a copy or two of Prelude,'[14] she tells Virginia. 'I have felt guilty towards you on its account, as a matter of fact, for I thought it had been a Bad Failure & you cursed the day.'[15]

One of the vignettes that Katherine had written in Cornwall – 'Carnation', a portrait of emotional intensity between two girls at a ladies' college – is taken by the *Nation* and, to Katherine's surprise, one of her *New Age* pieces, 'A Pic-nic', has been 'stolen' by a German magazine, and appears in the July issue of the *Continental Times* subtitled 'A Study of the Middle Class Mind'. 'Isn't it surprising!' Katherine writes to Ida, 'really, to see my work taking up a whole page gave me a huge thrill.'[16] The most exciting development is that one of the 'heavy' literary periodicals, the *English Review*, has decided to accept 'Bliss', for their August edition for a fee of 6 guineas. Virginia Woolf, just coming to the end of her unsatisfactory novel *Night and Day* and plagued by her own insecurities, observes that 'I suppose a great many tongues are now busy with K.M.'. She can't resist some spiteful comments. 'Prelude' is full of 'cheap realities', though she grudgingly admits that it at least has 'living power; the detached existence of a work of art'. 'Bliss', however, is rooted in shallow soil and never gets beyond 'superficial smartness' and that, Virginia declares, will be the ruin of Katherine. 'I don't see how much faith in her as woman or writer can survive that sort of story . . . She'll go on doing this sort of thing, perfectly to her & Murry's satisfaction.'[17] But Katherine is already aware of the dangers that lie in facility and reliance on writerly tricks. She has put her own reservations into the mouth of Raoul Duquette in 'Je ne parle pas Francais', when he admires his own technique as a writer: 'It comes from the pen so gently; it has such a "dying fall". . . One never knows when a little tag like that may come in useful to round off a paragraph.'

Katherine is beginning to think about another collection: she already has 'Prelude', 'Bliss', 'Je ne parle pas Francais', 'The Little Governess', 'Sun and Moon' and her *New Age* pieces from the previous year – 'A Dill Pickle' and 'Mr Reginald Peacock's Day'. Her main reservation is that none of it is good enough: 'I begin to wish to God I could destroy all that I have written & start again'. She uses her experience as a cellist to describe why it fails: none of it is 'in the middle of the note',[18] but shaded into the quarter tones. Only someone with equally perfect pitch can know.

Before Katherine has been back a month, John's work as a reviewer plunges them both into controversy. The Morrells, who have taken up Siegfried Sassoon as a protégé, had forwarded his new book of poems to John, hoping for a favourable press. John, however, dislikes the poetry and feels unable to deliver anything but an honest assessment. His highly critical review offends the Morrells and leads to a very public counter-attack on John in the *Nation*. To Katherine's exasperation, John is standing on his principles: 'Must you make of everything an affair of Life & Death?'[19] Katherine's relationship with Ottoline, already strained, becomes more distant.

In the middle of all this, Katherine receives news from New Zealand that her mother has died on 8 August after a major operation. The exact state of Annie's health has been kept from her children – she has never been strong and much less so after the death of her son – but in the last few months she has been very ill indeed. Her letters to or about Katherine are generally censorious, describing all Katherine's troubles as self-inflicted, but her attitude towards the prodigal daughter has gradually been changing. When Annie had heard of Katherine's diagnosis in January, she had told a friend that she wanted to get on a boat straight away, if only she had been well enough to make the trip. 'It seems that nothing much can be done for her now,' Annie had written, 'but make the remainder of her life as happy and comfy as possible.'[20] Knowing that her daughter might have only a short time to live, Annie decided against reinstating Katherine in her will, since the money would then go to John. She had sent loving, concerned letters to Katherine, instructed Mr Kay to pay her medical bills and sent Katherine money for her wedding. Annie had also written generous letters to John, welcoming him into the family, concealing both her reservations about his character and the state of her own health. Katherine hasn't seen her mother for so many years and the memory of the grief they have caused each other – all those undiscussed, unforgiven things – make Annie Beauchamp's death difficult to come to terms with. It is 'a blow on the heart'.[21]

While Katherine was in Cornwall, John had taken the lease of 2 Portland Villas in Hampstead – a lovely tall Georgian building full of sunlight, with beautiful views across London from the upstairs windows. After arguments with the landlord about the shared cost, the whole house has been redecorated to Katherine's instructions. It is to be an unconventional vision in grey and yellow. The staircase has grey walls and carpet; the banisters and the edges of the stairs are lacquered black, the bathroom and Ida's room are yellow with grey cupboards and curtains patterned in orange, blue and green; only the kitchen is white and turquoise. There is so much grey that Katherine christens it 'the Elephant'. They move in at the end of August. Ida is the paid housekeeper at £2 a week, nominally in charge of the cook and maid, but she is so nervous about the arrangement that they are soon taking their orders directly from Katherine. Ida scrapes vegetables, waits on tables, does the shopping, cleans, polishes, lights fires and nurses her beloved Katie. She changes the hot water bottles 'so marvelously often' that Katherine complains she hardly ever has one. They are 'always being taken or brought back'.[22] Ida does her best, but is too anxious to please and so afraid of making mistakes that she's unable to make decisions. Everything – what to have for lunch, a pattern for a blouse, whether to order one ton of coal or two of anthracite – must be referred to Katherine, who does not treat her well. 'I loathe female, virgin love.'[23] Ida's friends are supposed to be welcome but Katherine and John are rude to the two young men she invites to tea and they never call again. Katherine makes Ida burn the treasured box of letters that she has kept – some dating back to 1906 – all through the period of Katherine's relationship with Garnet Trowell. 'Pages and pages of her early girlish enthusiasms, hopes and visions – pictures of her own land and the England of her dreams.' Ida shows them to Katherine, wondering if they might provide material for her work, but after glancing at one or two, Katherine says, 'What dreadful rubbish – burn them *all*!'[24]

Katherine is blinded by pain and fear. 'Health seems to me now more remote than anything – unattainable. Best to stay in bed and be horrid from there.'[25] When she comes downstairs she is obsessively controlling, adjusting cushions, moving chairs that are an inch out of place: 'My house is rather a joy when I can forget that the tooth glass is out of proportion with the lotion bottle'.[26] She is desperate for a normal existence, to be treated as a woman rather than an invalid, but Ida is 'too immature, too emotionally involved and insecure',[27] and John is simply unable to play the game. He feels that his life is 'one long lie – of Love. To have no faith, and pretend one; to have no hope and pretend it; to watch day by day the circle round Katherine growing narrower and to feign not to see it . . . my life with Katherine [has] become one complete pretence.'[28] Just as he had done as a child, John escapes from his misery in work. When he comes home from the War Office, he shuts himself in his room and writes. He has given himself a phenomenal workload. He is still writing articles and reviews for the *Nation*, working on a book to be called *The Evolution of an Intellectual* as well as a long poem called *The Critic in Judgement*, promised to the Hogarth Press, and his verse play 'Cinnamon and Angelica'. Katherine describes in her journal how she goes up to John's room and opens the door. All is 'in indescribable disorder' and the air is thick with cigarette smoke. John lifts his head, with that curious blind gaze of his, and holds out a hand, but Katherine, sensing that she is unwelcome, silently goes away again. 'It [is] not my place.'[29]

During the first months at the Elephant John and Katherine are still sharing a bedroom, though John finds it difficult to sleep while Katherine lies awake coughing all night. But she finds the intimacy comforting, lying talking in the dark, reading poetry out of the same book, and the physical joy of touch: 'when they got into bed together her feet rushed to greet his like little puppies that had been separated all day from their brothers'.[30] Cuddling is almost all there is left. Katherine is too ill for sex, though she still desires it, and John is afraid of contagion.

The only person who seems able to remain outside the bitter circle, is John's younger brother Arthur, who is now studying at the London school of printing and design. Katherine hates the name and always calls him Richard, until eventually he keeps it. Richard adores Katherine. When he helps John to dig the garden, Katherine stands at the window of the Elephant, with opera floating out into the air from the gramophone, miming all the actions, making him laugh. He becomes her honorary brother, filling the gap left by Chummie. Richard is helping John with his printing project and the Heron Press is thumping away in the basement. They are printing a collection of John's poems, written between 1916 and 1917, and a pamphlet edition of Katherine's story 'Je ne parle pas Francais'.

Katherine is very unwell but still fighting. Her doctors have prescribed a series of 'Electricity Treatments' for her rheumatic pain but she finds the regular electric shocks extremely debilitating. There are constant public humiliations when she overtaxes herself. She goes to a photographic exhibition and faints, carried out by 'two WAACS and a Wren',[31] who are not impressed. An expedition to the Woolfs' at Asheham is planned, but Katherine is not well enough to go on the day, which offends Virginia. Dinner parties are different, since Katherine can slip quietly from sofa to table and back again. Koteliansky, still at 5 Acacia Road, is startled to receive a telegram that simply says, 'Come tonight, Katherine'. The Campbells have also received one and all three arrive on the doorstep expecting some dire emergency, only to find that they have been invited to a convivial dinner party where all past quarrels and differences are to be put to one side and friendships renewed. Katherine and Kot plan a collaboration, translating Chekhov's letters and suddenly their relationship is back on the old footing again. The Elephant becomes very sociable. Ottoline calls when she is in London, Virginia Woolf comes almost every week for lunch or tea and Brett, already 'more than half in love' with John, has rented a house nearby and is there so often she regards herself as one of the family.

Lawrence is another visitor, while John is at the War Office. The Lawrences are in London, having been driven out of Cornwall, and Katherine, warned

by Gertler, dreads bumping into them. Frieda is in bed with the influenza
that is raging throughout Britain, and Lawrence comes to visit the Murrys
at the Elephant as if nothing had ever happened between them. Katherine
is astonished. 'He was just his old merry, rich self, laughing, describing
things, giving you pictures, full of enthusiasm and joy in a future where
we were all "vagabonds" – we simply did not talk about people. We kept to
things like nuts and cowslips & fires in woods, and his black self was not.'[32]
But it's different when John is there. There is a coldness between the two
men that neither seems willing to thaw. 'They are both too proud & M. is
too jealous.'[33] As soon as John comes home, Lawrence leaves.

Walter de la Mare also becomes a frequent caller and after one of his
visits writes a poem for Katherine which he calls 'Horse in a Field'.

> We sat and talked. It was June, and the summer light
> Lay fair upon ceiling and wall as the day took flight.
> Tranquil the room – with its colours and shadows wan,
> Cherries, and china, and flowers: and the hour slid on.
> Dark hair, dark eye, slim fingers – you made the tea,
> Pausing with spoon uplifted, to speak to me.
> Lulled by our thoughts and our voices, happy were we!

They play an old riddle game where each has to contribute a line from
a given image, and then develop it, batting the lines between them.
'Supposing I just say, "Horse in a field?" I said, "What do you see?"'
Katherine's quick mind responds, constructing the scene and creating the
horse's pedigree: 'Peace out of Storm' or 'Beauty – of Jeopardy'. The name
of the horse, de la Mare concludes, 'is Genius'.[34]

On the surface, Katherine now has everything she desires – friends, a
husband, a beautiful house, a cat and kittens tumbling down the stairs,
servants, enough money to pay for it all. But there is a canker at the heart
of the rose. Her illness makes her feel very temporary and she has no sense
of being at home in Hampstead. Even the flowers outside seem to be saying
'and what are you doing in a London garden?' She is the 'little Colonial'
who doesn't belong. 'Look at her,' the plants shout, 'lying on our grass, pretending she lives here, pretending this is her garden & that tall back of the

house with the windows open & the coloured curtains lifting is her house. She is a stranger – an alien.' And sometimes she feels even further removed. 'She is nothing but a little girl sitting on the Tinakori hills & dreaming.'[35]

Throughout September Katherine's condition deteriorates. John, spurred on by the Beauchamp family, is anxious to consult the best medical opinions that can be found. A colleague at the War Office recommends a famous TB specialist, who examines Katherine. Then Katherine's father sends Sydney Beauchamp, who arrives on her thirtieth birthday. Both medical men patronise Katherine, telling her incomplete things, using euphemisms. The specialist allows her to believe that she is 'serious but recoverable', though her cousin is much more honest and tells her, 'Well, dear, of course, you won't make old bones'.[36] Downstairs they tell John the truth, man to man. If Katherine won't submit to the strict discipline of a sanatorium, she may have only two or three years to live – four at the outside. Katherine is absolutely against the idea of a sanatorium and John can't persuade her. She refuses to believe that her case is hopeless. When Katherine asks John if he really believes that she can get well again, he lies and tells her that he does. But Katherine reads his notebook and finds a poem that seems to anticipate her death.

> Thou has made love all thy religion
> Thy life is built on its foundation stone
> Nothing remains to thee [when] it is gone
> And thou be left in desert lands alone:
> Thy love is built on her life: it is frail
> Even as her pained breath.
>
> . . . love's own light put out untimely
> [That] on a labour'd breath shall bear her soul away
> To where her voice shall never reach to me . . .[37]

John has crossed out 'when' and substituted 'if', but the original word is clearly visible. Katherine scrawls across the page: 'I don't think one ought to cultivate these flowers. The first page has lovely things in it, but why waste [such] flowers in journals? Oh I do think it is so wrong. Please don't lay me out. How can you!'[38]

Katherine continues to go from doctor to doctor, hoping that someone will offer her hope. Dr Ainger has been sent to France, so she consults

John's own doctor, Croft-Hill, and another recommended by Virginia Woolf, the local Dr Stonham in Hampstead. They are all unanimous on the subject of tuberculosis – it is in her spine and her lungs, and has penetrated her entire system, though no one explains it to her properly.[39] They talk about spots and cavities and this and that being 'badly affected'. All the doctors Katherine sees withhold information from her: they believe she has probably had TB since at least 1911 if not earlier. All Katherine wants, or thinks she wants, is someone to be straight with her, but she doesn't believe even the small truths they offer. 'Why are doctors so preposterous? I see them in their hundreds, moving among sham Jacobean furniture, warming their large pink hands at little gas fires and asking the poor visitor if this will come off or pull down – curse em.'[40]

If she had been able to ask, and they had been willing to tell, she would also have found out that TB is one of the significant causes of female infertility. Katherine is still puzzled by her gynaecological symptoms – the irregular menstruation, sometimes as heavy as if she is having a miscarriage, the strange discharges, and the failure to conceive. Anne Estelle Rice recommends her own gynaecologist, Dr Victor Sorapure, who is working at the Hampstead Hospital. He was a foundling, who had been abandoned on a convent doorstep in Paris with 'nothing but a shawl on and a paper pinned on his poor little chest with SORAPURE written on it'.[41] Katherine is fascinated by his story and likes him at once – he makes her feel comfortable and has a spiritual dimension to his personality that echoes Katherine's own sensibility. From the beginning he tells her exactly what she has been longing to hear. 'As he stood at the door he said quietly, "Nothing is incurable. It is all a question of time . . . what seems so useless today may just be that link that will make all plain to a future generation" . . . I had a sense – of the larger breath of the mysterious lives within lives.'[42] His greatest service is to tell her that quality of life is vitally important. 'Tubercular patients ought to enjoy themselves.' He agrees with her that institutional life would preserve the body a little longer but kill something vital in her. She would have no privacy. She would be unable to write. Katherine is delighted to find someone who understands her, but she confuses sympathetic human understanding with a similar depth of medical understanding about her condition.

Sorapure is not a TB specialist. He approaches Katherine's symptoms from his own experience of general surgery and pathology, and some of them seem familiar. He asks her about her medical history and she tells him the secret things she can't tell the important doctors summoned by the Beauchamp family or John – about her operation (but not, it seems, the baby), her strange symptoms afterwards and particularly her 'rheumatism', which Katherine still regards as separate from her 'lung trouble'. Sorapure, faced with a young woman who has had multiple sexual partners, one of whom (John Murry) is known to have been infected, suspects gonorrhoea, which in its late stages can produce peritonitis and septic inflammation of the joints, particularly those in the wrist and ankle. These symptoms are 'very likely', he tells her, to be 'of gonococcal origin'.[43] Sorapure is noted for making intuitive and often inspired diagnoses. He does not appear to consider that Katherine has none of the other symptoms that might be expected in a patient who has had a sexually transmitted disease for nearly ten years. There are no laboratory tests. Sorapure's diagnosis is retrospective and extremely dangerous, since there is no evidence except his own assumptions and circumstantial information volunteered by Katherine. Every one of her symptoms fits the classic profile of tuberculosis and none of her specialist doctors has ever suggested otherwise.

When Sorapure tells her what he suspects, Katherine is devastated. But his catastrophic diagnosis seems to fit with her own thoughts on the relationship between moral and physical well-being and anxiety about her unconventional past. 'Am I ever free from the sense of guilt, even? Never.'[44] She had joked once with Gertler and Beatrice Campbell about being 'a soiled woman'; Sorapure has just confirmed this and that knowledge drives a further wedge between herself and John. For she could have caught gonorrhoea from him, but there was also her affair with Carco – a casual lover of women and frequenter of the brothels of Montmartre. Has he cursed her with this? But if Sorapure is right, the infection dates much further back, to Bad Wörishofen or even earlier. In her journal she writes, 'Often I reproach myself for my "private" life – which after all, were I to die, would astonish those nearest to me. Then, (as yesterday) I realise how little Jack shares with me.'[45] Sorapure's diagnosis, which Katherine feels she deserves, also puts an end to her hopes of a family. She thinks wistfully of the time, almost six years ago, when they had moved to the cottage at Runcton and she had believed herself pregnant. 'Any children? he asked, taking out his stethoscope as I struggled with my nightgown. No, no children. But what would he have said if I'd told him that until a few days ago I had had a little child, aged five & 3/4 – of – indeterminate sex. Some days it was a boy. For two years now it had often been a little girl . . .'[46]

Tuberculosis also affects the nervous system as toxins clog the blood-stream. Katherine becomes prey to terrible rages, of the kind that Lawrence used to have. 'My fits of temper are really terrifying. I had one this morn-ing & tore a page up of the book I was reading – and absolutely lost my head. Very significant. When it was over J. came in and stared. What is the matter? What have you done? "Why?" You look all dark. He drew back the curtains and called it an effect of light but when I came into my studio to dress I saw it was not that. I was a deep earthy colour, & was green with pinched eyes . . . I am more like L. than anybody.'[47]

The war ends on 11 November and for a short time Katherine is joy-ful. 'I opened the window and it really did seem – just in those first few moments that a wonderful change happened – not in human creatures' hearts – no – but in the air – there seemed just for a breath of time – a silence.'[48] She thinks of the people who have died, particularly her brother, and is aware that nothing can be same again. John is out of a job, but is quickly offered editorship of the *Athenaeum*, a prestigious literary peri-odical, at the phenomenal salary of £800 a year. He will also be earning another £250 from other work, though he does not tell Katherine this initially. He is now properly launched into the world of literature and this widens the gap between him and Katherine.

The English winter is hard for her to endure, though she manages a facade of black humour for her friends. The weather, she writes to Virginia, 'sets up ponds & pools in my Left Lung where the Germs and the Toxins – two families I detest', bathe and refresh themselves and flourish and multiply.[49] She tells Kot that her cough 'is like a big wild dog who fol-lowed me home one day & has taken a most unpleasant fancy to me'.[50] But by December Katherine has reached an impasse in her fight against 'the enemy'. 'I feel in my heart as though I have died – as far as personal life goes.'[51] By Christmas she is too ill to leave the house, often too weak to go downstairs. She gives in to her doctors and decides to live a sanatorium regime at home: separate bedrooms, a shelter in the garden to lie in on fine days, and a rigid diet. She also agrees to go abroad again the following year, to Switzerland, with Ida in attendance.

John is more and more detached. He brings home books but no longer talks to her about them, and is emotionally inscrutable. Katherine feels he's cutting her off because he can't bear it. Ida contemptuously accuses him of drowning in self-pity.[52] Katherine uses the same analogy. Rather than pulling the fly out of the milk and drying it off, 'He is so inclined to cast himself into the milk jug after the fly'. She thinks he is too English – 'I do lament that he is not warm, ardent, eager, full of quick response, careless, spendthrift of himself, vividly alive, high spirited. But it makes no difference to my love. But the lack of these qualities in his country I HATE.'[53]

Katherine is determined to make what might be her last Christmas in her own home memorable for everyone. The huge traditional lunch gradually gives way, 'under the influence of wine & Chinese mottoes', to a party, which she describes to Brett. Kot, Gertler and the Campbells play charades: 'The red chairs became a pirate ship. Koteliansky wore a muff on his head & Campbell a doormat tied under the chin'. Katherine has hung little gifts on the tree for everyone and she hands them out with great ceremony. 'I wanted to say to everybody – Let us stay forever just as we are – Don't let us ever wake up & find it is all over.'[54] But with the new year comes a resurgence of depression. There is no one to stand with Katherine at the window to listen to the bells at midnight. John is in bed and Ida has retreated to her room, overwhelmed by the tragedies of her own life. Having lost her mother to illness at the age of thirteen, she has recently lost her father who, in a fit of depression, has had an 'accident' with a gun in Rhodesia.

Alone in the dark, Katherine has no optimism as she lies awake looking into the future, seeing herself once more as the unfortunate fly. 'Oh, the times when she had walked upside down on the ceiling, run up glittering panes, floated on a lake of light, flashed through a shining beam!' Now she is being punished for her temerity. 'And God looked upon the fly fallen into the jug of milk and saw that it was good. And the smallest Cherubims & Seraphims of all who delight in misfortune struck their silver harps & shrilled: How is the fly fallen, fallen.'[55]

20

The Perfect Friend

In spite of what I have said — and shall say — you have been a 'perfect' friend to me.

KATHERINE MANSFIELD TO IDA BAKER, 1920

I have never questioned my love for Katherine — questioning that was unimportant . . . because I loved her — all those years and still do . . . [it is] as true and shining and as near as I, as a human being, can get to the Love of God.

IDA BAKER, 'RANDOM THOUGHTS', 1974

On 9 September 1919, three days before she is due to leave England for the Mediterranean, Katherine sits down to write a letter for John.

My Darling Boy,
I am leaving this letter with Mr Kay just in case I should pop off suddenly and not have the opportunity or the chance of talking over these things.

If I were you I'd sell off all the furniture and go off on a long sea voyage on a cargo boat, say. Don't stay in London. Cut right away to some lovely place.

Any money I have is yours, of course. I expect there will be enough to bury me. I don't want to be cremated and I don't want a tombstone or anything like that. If it's possible to choose a quiet place — please do. You know how I hate noise . . . All my MSS I simply leave to you . . . That's all. But don't let anybody mourn me. It can't be helped. I think you ought to marry again and have children. If you do give your little girl the pearl ring.

Yours for ever. Wig.

She is beginning to face the inevitability of her own death. In her notebook, Katherine begs for more time to complete her work: 'Then I don't mind dying. I live to write: the lovely world (God how lovely the external world is!) is there and I bathe in it and am refreshed. But I feel as though I had a DUTY, someone has set me a task which I am bound to finish. Let me finish it: let me finish it without hurrying, leaving all as fair as I can.'[1]

Katherine has endured eight months of struggle with the British climate. 'Life on a Sofa is just hell.'[2] She now weighs only 44 kilograms and has become, in Lytton Strachey's words, a gaunt, 'virulent . . . broomstick of a creature'.[3] In January Sorapure had put her through a series of injections to cure her supposed gonorrhoea, which had given her a high fever and made her worse, but Katherine still has absolute confidence in him. When, in August, she had agreed to go into a sanatorium for six months, Sorapure had persuaded her to change her mind. It was only her 'indomitable will' that has kept her alive so far, he had told her. A sanatorium would be 'a highly dangerous experiment' that would kill her because it would keep her from her work. Instead she should head for the Italian Riviera and stay there for at least two years. To Katherine his words are 'breath, life – healing, everything'. He had given her permission to do what she prefers to do. 'Being ill, & bearing all the depression of those round me had, I think, almost made me insane. I just gave up hope. Now I am full of hope again'.[4]

As Katherine prepares to leave, her father is in London, having brought Jeanne from New Zealand to keep Chaddie company. The two sisters are going to live together in a country house bought for them by Harold Beauchamp. Katherine is delighted to see her father again, to be enveloped in his arms, inhaling against his shoulder the aura of success – the fine cloth of his handmade suits, the smell of cigars and expensive soap. But she is disappointed that his generosity towards her sisters does not extend to her. He is now an extremely rich man (he carries John Murry's entire annual salary around in his wallet) and Katherine had hoped for extra help with her large medical bills, which she has not been able to pay (she feels particularly guilty about Sorapure). But though Harold raises her allowance by a few pounds, nothing else is volunteered. His feelings towards Katherine's husband may have had something to do with this. His long-awaited meeting with John is a disaster. John is even more shy than usual – 'in one of his moods' – and can't be prompted to talk to his father-in-law or even to look him in the eye. It is 'dreadful mizery' for Katherine, but John tells her that she can't expect him to change. He is as he is.[5] John is unable to go away with her – his editorship of the *Athenaeum* means he is tied to London, and he has just been asked to give a series of lectures at Oxford on 'the Problem of Style'. His literary career is flourishing and he does not want to give it up. Ida is going with her instead and John accompanies them to San Remo, where he has booked rooms in a small hotel run by an Englishman. The journey is long and exhausting, but the hotel seems clean and quiet, though it gives Katherine an unpleasant sense of *déjà vu*. 'Oh – how I loathe hotels. I know I shall die in one. I shall stand in front of a crochet dressing-table cover, pick up a long invisible hairpin left by the last "lady" and die with disgust.'[6]

But before Ida can unpack Katherine's suitcase, the hotel manager apologetically asks John to remove her. Under Italian regulations, tuberculosis is a notifiable disease and there are complaints from other guests about Katherine's cough and the risk of infection. The manager tactfully offers a small villa in the hills above Ospedaletti, a small town with 'nothing but a laundry, a flower market and wine shop'. There is no running water, but the landlord promises that it will be fixed. Katherine takes the house for the winter and suffers the humiliation of having to pay for the fumigation of her hotel room. The Casetta Deerholm, apart from its isolation, is beautiful at first glance – 'in the sun's eye and the sea's eye – It is built on the slope of a wild hill covered with figs, olives, and tamarisk trees and a thick small shrubbery – and herbs like lavender and thyme and rosemary' overlooking the Mediterranean.[7] There are two small bedrooms upstairs, a sitting room and kitchen downstairs, and a wide verandah where Katherine can work, shaded from the autumn sun.

Initially, she's emotionally stable and soon establishes a routine of rest and work. There's a 'long story' tugging away at the back of her mind, but she doesn't yet have the energy to tackle it. She wonders whether the *Athenaeum* would take a column from her – extracts from her notebook recording impressions and observations – 'A certain light or a fragment of talk over a table or workmen going home in the evening' – but John doesn't take the idea up.[8] Katherine has been reviewing fiction for the *Athenaeum* since February and has agreed to continue while she's abroad. John pays her £10 a month for this work, bringing her total monthly income up to £35, of which £5 is paid to Ida. The books are sent out to her from England. She finds it 'a thousand times harder' to write reviews in Italy, because she has no one to discuss them with critically: 'I'm "out of it" and see so few papers & never hear talk'. She worries incessantly that her reviews are not good enough, or that they are not what John wants,[9] or that she does not measure up intellectually. John's literary erudition awes her. 'You've always such a vast choice of sticks in the hall-stand for when you want to go walking and [an] even vaster choice of umbrellas – while I go all unprotected and exposed with only a fearful sense of the heavens lowering.'[10] But the work is a lifesaver because it prevents her thinking too much about her situation. She begs John to send her newspapers and magazines and promises to pay for them. 'I cannot exist without mental stimulants.'[11]

Katherine's reviews contain some of her most interesting writing, because they discuss the nature of writing itself. She is highly critical of the 'stream of consciousness' technique employed by Dorothy Richardson. 'There is no plot no beginning, middle or end. Things just "happen" one after another with incredible rapidity and at break-neck speed. There is Miss Richardson, holding out her mind, as it were, and there is Life hurling objects into it as fast as she can throw.' And 'she has no memory' – essential if the characters are 'to be truly alive'. Katherine sets out her ideas on experimental fiction. 'Having decided on the novel form, one cannot lightly throw one's story over the mill without replacing it with another story which is, in its way, obedient to the rules of that discarded one. There must be the same setting out upon a voyage of discovery (but through unknown seas instead of charted waters), the same difficulties and dangers must be encountered, and there must be an ever-increasing sense of the greatness of the adventure and an ever more passionate desire to possess and explore the mysterious country. There must be given the crisis when the great final attempt is made which succeeds – or does not succeed.' Without this 'central point of significance', 'the form of the novel, as we see it, is lost'. The purpose of great fiction is not to entertain, but 'to reveal a little of the mystery of life'.

She is most illuminating on the difference between writing short stories and novels. 'In the case of the short story it is possible to give orders that, unless the house is on fire – and even then, not until the front staircase is well alight – one must not be disturbed; but a novel is an affair of weeks, of months; time after time the author is forced to leave what he has written today exposed to what may happen before tomorrow. How can one measure the influence of the interruptions and distractions that come between?'[12]

For Katherine's thirty-first birthday on 14 October John sends her a silver spoon and Ida has squandered a large part of her monthly allowance on a bottle of Katherine's favourite perfume, Genêt Fleuri. Chaddie and Jeanne have sent her 'an ordinary small 1d matchbox' enamelled yellow and painted with an 'ugly' Chinaman, 'Oriental department, 1/11¾'. The note with it says 'to our darling Katie with our united love & best wishes'. Katherine tells John that she will keep it forever 'and remember the size of their hearts by it'.[13] There's a letter from her father that doesn't even mention her birthday and Katherine remembers sadly that he has just sent her sister Chaddie £10 for hers. In her dreams, it's her father beside her on the ship back to New Zealand, her father's warehouse that she's trapped in, unable to write. Money would make such a difference to her life.

The Casetta Deerholm doesn't seem so ideal as the autumn deepens towards winter. The water supply has still not been connected and on warm days the house is invaded by mosquitoes and biting gnats so small that they sneak through the finest nets. When the sun doesn't shine, the hillside is bitterly cold and the small stove in the kitchen proves totally inadequate to heat the villa. Katherine has been told she must keep warm, but she gets chilled easily in the draughty house and has to go to bed. There are also problems trying to exchange money – Italian banks have their own systems and Mr Kay can't just telegraph funds. In the village, laundry, firewood and food are all much more expensive than they had been led to expect. Ida, who doesn't understand the currency, is often cheated when trying to calculate prices in lire. The local Italians, living at subsistence level, have no qualms about trying to fleece expatriate visitors. There are also problems with security. The front door doesn't lock properly and there has been a surge of anti-British feeling in Italy since the end of the war, that occasionally erupts into violence. The owner gives Katherine a gun for protection, which she and Ida practise using. But only once are they troubled by unexplained noises in the night: 'Some men very late, ringing and ringing the bell' until Ida, calling 'Qui va la?' from the bedroom window, fires several pistol shots into the darkness.[14]

Katherine and Ida, living together in such a small place, are soon quarrelling. Katherine wants – needs – Ida to be everything she's not. They can't get a maid because the local girls are all afraid of catching TB, so Ida has to cope alone with their domestic affairs. She's stubborn, clumsy and inept; her appetite for food revolts Katherine, and her terror of offending or doing the wrong thing drives her to a frenzy of irritation. Ida is also impractical: she breaks dishes, glasses, thermometers, wastes money on fuel because she doesn't know how to operate the chimney flue and burns the meals. There are times when Katherine hates Ida so much she's almost consumed by it. Ida, aware of her feelings, does her best to remain in the background and wait until the fit is over. But there are times when even she is driven to protest. 'L.M. and I reached a crise at tea-time and after that the frightful urgency of our feelings died down a bit . . . It ruined yesterday and made me so tired that I felt I could have slept days and nights away.'[15] Ida knows that she irritates Katherine, admitting that she is 'quite unable to provide her with the mental support' she needs.[16] This makes Ida feel powerless and inadequate. Katherine hates, above all, the lack of independence; being told what she may or may not do; being watched all the time; being too weak to resist. Exhaustion is now her greatest enemy and the energy she has must be rationed. 'I have discovered that I cannot burn the candle at one end & write a book with the other.'[17] She is constantly fighting, 'the most overwhelming depression', which the doctors tell her is the result of the toxins in her bloodstream. Katherine wonders whether it is anything to do with the opium in the cough mixture she's been taking for the past two years, and which she feels increases her 'nervous sensitiveness'.[18]

Within weeks, Katherine's tuberculosis has flared up again and Ida has to summon the local doctors. One, Foster, is straightforward and brusque, but his bedside manner is 'frank and rather on the brutal side'. The other, Ansaldi, is more encouraging. Her lungs are showing some improvement, but she is not warm enough – 'a chill or influenza might mean disaster' and she must avoid mental stress. Ansaldi is entirely optimistic about her prognosis, but Katherine discovers quite quickly that he is offering her false hope because he thinks she needs 'cheering up'. She is furious.[19]

Katherine's father is in France, visiting his elderly cousin, Connie Beauchamp, and her friend and companion Jinnie Fullerton. Both women are ardent Catholics, dedicated to nursing. They already have a nursing home in Hampstead and are currently running a much more exclusive private clinic in Menton, across the French border, only a short drive away from Ospedaletti, catering for rich invalids. Harold Beauchamp has planned to visit Katherine with them during his stay there. They all arrive on 12 November in a large, chauffeur-driven car and take Katherine out for a drive to San Remo. She admits to being 'just a little corrupted . . . That big soft purring motor, the rugs & cushions – the warmth and delicacy . . .

It was thrilling for me.' Ida cooks lunch, trying not to burn anything, while Katherine's guests express their reservations about the villa. 'They were horrified by the cold.' Connie assures Katherine that Menton is much warmer and more sheltered. The climate there would be much better suited to Katherine's health. They try very hard to persuade her to come, but Katherine can't face being uprooted again. Harold hugs her emotionally when they leave saying, 'Get better you little wonder. You're your mother over again,' which touches Katherine deeply. But he offers no creature comforts, leaving only five cigarettes and a small bunch of wild flowers tied with a piece of grass.[20] But Harold Beauchamp is very concerned about his daughter, writing an anguished letter from Menton: 'My heart aches when I think of you in that lonely little villa on the hillside'.[21]

In the aftermath of his visit, Katherine is overtaken by feelings of isolation and the sense of being unloved. It doesn't help that John can only find time to write a couple of times a week, that his letters are full of his activities, lively meetings with Brett – 'she's not ill she can run, she can play tennis with Murry'[22] – lunches and dinners with the Woolfs and Tom Eliot. The domestic details he includes and descriptions of the delightful antics of Katherine's kitten Wingley are guaranteed to make her homesick. Sydney Waterlow and his wife have moved temporarily into Katherine's house with John and she can't bear the thought of another woman running her home. There are arguments and misunderstandings about money. He spends £11 on a small table for her room in England when her letters reveal that she needs money for firewood and warm clothes. Katherine feels that John should be more generous towards her; he counts pennies and is unable to see that her physical and emotional needs require something more. It frustrates her that he is still living in the future rather than the inconvenient, painful, 'now'. John is saving money to buy a house in the country, the 'Heron' of which they have always dreamed, in the naive hope that Katherine might be able to live in it the following year. Her present comfort, and health, are being jeopardised by a dream she no longer shares. 'Shall we really have such a house? It's not too late? . . . I get overwhelmed at times that it is all over.'[23]

But though John is often blind to her needs, Katherine's jealous, accusing letters show little appreciation of his position. He is as lonely and unhappy as she is and it is not his fault that he is in London and she is in Ospedaletti. Sometimes his longing for her spills over in his letters. 'You and I together – lovers . . . something in me faints at the thought of feeling your wonderful body beneath mine again, of kissing your breasts as I used to, going from your breasts to your lips & to your breasts again, till the whole of me melted away into you and I became a pulse of your heart. My God, to be lovers again.'[24] His letter distresses Katherine, who is suffering her own agonies of sexual frustration. 'It is all memories now – radiant marvellous faraway memories of happiness. Ah, how terrible life can be!'[25]

Eventually she crashes, sending John a series of desperate letters and some extremely painful poems written under the pseudonym 'Elizabeth Stanley'. In one poem a woman embittered by love contemplates throwing her wedding ring into the sea. Another is addressed to 'The New Husband' and written in the style of the old English ballad.

> Some one came to me and said
> Forget, forget that you've been wed
> Who's your man to leave you be
> Ill and cold in a far country
> Who's the husband – who's the stone
> Could leave a child like you alone.

It seems directed against John personally.

> I had received that very day
> A letter from the Other to say
> That in six months – he hoped – no longer
> I would be so much better and stronger
> That he would close his books and come
> With radiant looks to bear me home.

> Ha! Ha! Six months, six weeks, six hours
> Among these glittering palms and flowers
> With Melancholy at my side
> For my old nurse and for my guide
> Despair – and for my footman Pain –
> I'll never see my home again.[26]

John, distraught, hardly knows what to believe as her moods swing wildly from one letter to the next. 'Don't say one day "I can ignore L.M." & the next "she is killing me".' He adds perceptively a few weeks later, 'I begin to feel from your letters that I'm only a kind of ghost to you . . . Your idea of me seems to get a long way from the reality.'[27] Katherine has cast John in a role for which he is totally unfitted and he is unable to transform himself into her ideal husband. She takes up several pages of her notebook trying to analyse their relationship. John has become more and more depressed in response to her letters, 'but not for me'. John writes about 'the suffering I caused him: his suffering, his nerves, he wasn't made of whipcord or steel, the fruit was bitter for him'. She double underlines all the 'I's' in his letter as if to emphasise his egoism. His lack of generosity with money is particularly hurtful: he expects her to pay for the warm scarves, medicines and books he sends. But the real problem is that her illness has altered the dynamic of their relationship. 'Before that I had been the man and he had been the woman and he had been called upon to make no real efforts. He'd never really "supported" me. When we first met, in fact, it was I who kept him, and afterwards we'd always acted (more or less) like men-friends. Then this illness – getting worse and worse, and turning me into a woman and asking him to put himself away and bear things for me.' She still loves him passionately, but this latest crisis has 'cut through something'.[28]

John's immediate reaction is to drop everything and come out to Ospedaletti for Christmas. Five days after receiving Katherine's letter, he is there with her. For two weeks there is a semblance of domestic happiness. 'But,' Katherine's journal records, 'something is wrong.' They play cards in the evening, read poetry and discuss books as usual, though John sleeps in the spare room and Ida on a sofa at the bottom of Katherine's bed. There are futile, difficult conversations in an attempt to resolve their misunderstandings. Katherine tells John that there is something in him that denies 'fertility'. He tells her that he will never change. This is a hard truth. Although she sends him letters with drawings of their hoped for little boy and girl, Katherine knows that they will 'never have children' together, either real or metaphorical. After he leaves on 2 January, Katherine's health takes another downward turn. Her heart is pounding erratically and she can't sleep. The feelings of abandonment are very similar to those she had experienced in Bad Wörishofen. Katherine's journal is the barometer of her state of mind – 'Heart attack 8am. Awful day . . . I did not sleep . . . BLACK . . . a day spent in hell . . . Help me God! . . . appalling night of misery deciding that J. had no more need of our love . . . I cannot sleep. I lie retracing my steps – going over all the old life before . . . The baby of

Garnet's love.'[29] Ida does what she can to comfort Katherine and her devotion at last wins through. 'It is not only that the hatred is gone – something positive is there which is very like love for her. She has convinced me at last, against all my opposition that she is trying to do all in her power for me – and that she is devoted to the one idea which is (please forgive my egoism) to see me well again. This time she has fed me, helped me, got up in the middle of the night to make me hot milk and rub my feet, brought me flowers, *served* me as one could not be served if one were not loved. All silently and gently too, even after all my bitter ravings at her and railing against her. She has simply shown me that she understands and I feel that she does.'[30]

Unknown to Katherine, Ida is writing to John, because she wants him to confront Katherine's suffering. Too ill to go out and not only homesick, she is also 'mind-lonely'. Katherine 'has spent all the long 24 hours of night and day in that little depressing bedroom with the continual thundering of the sea outside and the dismal patter of the rain and the grey muffled light of storm clouds . . . Many times I have found her just quietly crying and crying.' Ida can't understand why John doesn't do something to help.[31]

Finally Katherine, unable to bear her illness in isolation any more, writes to her cousin Connie and asks if she can come to stay with her at Menton. She also begins a new story, though the pen feels 'like a walking stick' because she is so weak. 'The Man without a Temperament' is thought out on the same night she lies awake deciding that John no longer needs her, and Katherine writes it out very quickly the following day, between 9.30 a.m. and midnight, stopping only to eat. Born out of depression and desperation, it is a poignant, sensitive account, written from the man's point of view, about a couple staying in a Riviera hotel because of the woman's health. The husband is outwardly devoted to his wife's needs, but their whole relationship is warped by her fear of 'being a drag on him' and his dutiful acceptance and the necessity to hide his regrets from her. Any love he has had for her has evaporated and the story ends with a lie.

> 'Boogles, listen. Come closer. I sometimes wonder – do you mind awfully being out here with me?'
>
> He bends down. He kisses her. He tucks her in, he smooths the pillow.
>
> 'Rot!' he whispers.'

After the story is finished, she lies awake until 5.30 a.m. in a heightened state of mental anguish. 'I love him but he rejects my living love . . . These are the worst days of my whole life.'[32] Katherine sends the story to John two days later, perhaps hoping that its message will get through. But though he acknowledges receipt of the manuscript, and tells Katherine the story 'is curiously beautiful', he says very little about the content and when he does, he believes it to be a sensitive and loving portrait of a sensitive and loving man.[33]

Menton is less frequented by tourists than its next-door neighbour Monte Carlo, crammed against the Mediterranean by the bare rocky slopes of the mountains that rise steeply behind it. It's clean, quiet, with a few imposing public buildings and the villas of the gently rich occupying the lower slopes looking out over the sea. There isn't a great deal to do. Apart from a short stroll along the seafront, anything further afield requires good lungs and a strong heart. But it's warm all year round and the sunlight glares from the sea and the pale grey rocks winter and summer.

Katherine is hurt to discover that she won't be staying in Connie's house because a wealthy patient from London might object to sharing her space with a TB sufferer. Connie has booked Katherine into the Clinique l'Hermitage, founded by members of the Russian royal family in 1882 when they needed somewhere to recuperate, and still treating a lot of Russian patients. Menton has dozens of clinics and hospitals that have been used throughout the war to house the wounded and to treat the victims of tuberculosis. The climate is ideal for convalescence – warm even in February and sheltered from the bitter winds of the mistral.

The Hermitage costs 30 F a day, and is quite luxurious. It is 'almost supernaturally' clean, and has four windows 'overlooking great gardens & mountains – wonderful flowers – tea with toast & honey & butter, a charming maid'. But within a few days the 'brilliant' doctors are 'an ass and an ass'.[34] Now that Katherine is in a clinic, Ida becomes surplus to requirements. She had originally intended to go to Rhodesia to visit her sister in May while Katherine went back to England with John, but this plan, too, has fallen through. Ida stays at the Pension Anglaise, near the Hermitage, and takes a job as a nurse at another clinic so that she can spend time in the evenings with Katherine, who still needs her support and continues to pay her an allowance.

Inevitably, after the first impressions have worn off, Katherine finds the clinic noisy, full of 'uglies' with disgusting habits, and is relieved when, with the permission of the rich patient and a doctor who is prepared to sign that she is not 'actively' infectious, Connie and Jinnie move her into the Villa Flora. Katherine's bedroom is a vision in grey and silver, with a balcony overlooking the bay. She can sit in the garden under the lemon trees in a bath chair, with a little table carefully arranged beside her, and write. Katherine asks John to forward her collection of short stories, turned down by Heinemann in the autumn, to two other publishers. Her first choice is Grant Richards, with whom she's been corresponding, but John annoys her by arranging a deal with Michael Sadler – now calling himself Sadleir – at Constable. John finally convinces Katherine that it is the best deal she can hope for, with an advance of £40. She's worried that John will keep the advance to repay money he believes she owes him for sending her a coat and paying one or two bills, but Katherine needs the money for her medical expenses, her rent to Connie for the room and Ida's allowance.

Katherine's bitterness towards John increases. In the New Year's honours list he has been given an OBE for his war work and is at the height of his literary career. When he refuses to contribute even £10 a month towards Katherine's expenses, sending her pages and pages of accounts to justify his position, it hardens her heart even more. She resents the fact that he is spending money on life insurance policies for himself, a new suit and bric-à-brac for the house, rather than trying to alleviate her miserable situation. The contrast with Ida's generosity is stark. There are other blows. On 5 January Harold Beauchamp had married Laura Bright, Annie Beauchamp's best friend, who had come to live next door when she was widowed a few years earlier. And in February there's a letter from D. H. Lawrence, whose friendship had so recently been renewed, that strikes like a knife. 'He spat in my face & threw filth at me and said "I loathe you. You revolt me stewing in your consumption".' Lawrence refers to John, who has recently rejected several of his pieces for the *Athenaeum*, as 'a dirty little worm'.[35]

The two doctors Katherine detests for their French 'flatterie and galanterie',[36] X-ray her lungs to find out the extent of the disease and propose a strict regime of rest for three months, good food and massage. The X-rays reveal that her left lung has been almost completely destroyed by the TB bacilli and the right one is also affected. They explain to her that her heart trouble occurs because, since she has only one working lung, it is having to pump twice as hard to get the oxygen into her system. The warmth of Menton suits Katherine and, providing she doesn't exert herself too much, she is as well there as she can ever hope to be. But Connie and Jinnie have taken it upon themselves not only to try to cure Katherine's body, but also her soul. She is, as they know, acutely vulnerable. Full of guilt and the fear of death, Katherine finds Catholicism and the certainties it offers of absolution and everlasting life very attractive. She almost succumbs, writing a letter to Ida confiding what she can't say face to face in case Ida laughs at her. 'This afternoon when we were lying on the hills . . . I knew there was a God.' Katherine tells Ida that she intends to be received into the Catholic church. 'I want to make life wonderful if I can.'[37]

On the advice of the doctors, who are adamant that she must spend at least two years out of England, and her own experience of the climate, Katherine has decided that she will come back to Menton in the autumn, spending only the brief summer months with John. She writes, begging him to give up the idea of buying a country house because she won't be able to live there. For the few months she will be in England she wants to be in the centre of activity. The Elephant is her home; he must not give it up. Ida is looking for a flat or a villa in Menton where Katherine can spend the winter. Connie and Jinnie are also looking for another, smaller, property and when they find two adjoining flats in Menton, they persuade Katherine to take the other. There are three bedrooms, a maid's room, a sitting room and breakfast room, a kitchen and bathroom and a dressing room for John. It has been beautifully decorated by an Italian contessa. Katherine pays the deposit and returns to England with Ida on 27 April. She leaves the warmth with regret. 'I'll never leave here another year before the end of May. It's too perfect.'[38]

London is unbearably cold and damp. 'It is simply tragic to meet this reluctant painful England again,'[39] Katherine's lungs and her tubercular arthritis are immediately worse and Dorothy Brett sends her a stove as a present, to keep her warm. There is more significance in this gift than Katherine realises.

The gap between John's perception of Katherine's capabilities and her actual state of health is huge. She tries to warn him, but he responds: 'I didn't a bit like what you said about your coughing still. Does that only happen on a bad day? . . . good God, don't think I shall be disappointed if you have to go slow, and don't imagine that I've got in my head that you're coming back perfectly fit.' He imagines 'a Wig who is beginning painfully & slowly to mend',[40] not a Wig who is painfully and slowly progressing towards death.

He has planned a holiday at a hotel in Devon, but it's obvious as soon as Katherine arrives that she is too weak and needs far more rest and nursing than could be provided there. Public transport is impossible – she can only travel door-to-door in a car. In his diary John acknowledges his own capacity for self-delusion. 'How I clutch at straws! How I persuade myself that that which I want to be is! Two letters from Tig and I am ready to believe that she is getting better.'[41] In false optimism, John has just bought a longed-for cottage in the country, to which he had hoped to go at weekends with Katherine. Broomies, in Sussex, has been purchased for £400 with a mortgage in Katherine's name because John is still an undischarged bankrupt. She has no objection to the project, but she knows that it's no longer a realistic possibility for her. She isn't even well enough to go down to look at the cottage. Katherine would prefer to stay in the south of France, if only John were able to go too, but he is living in a separate world.

A visit to John's office at the *Athenaeum* reveals to Katherine how far apart they have become. Hoping to find 'life and literature', she discovers only 'unthinkable disorder and ugliness'. Aldous Huxley, Maurice Forster and John Sullivan are engaged in conversations that seem contaminated by 'a smell of stone and dust'. This is not her world. 'I heard myself speaking of lemon trees . . . nobody cared, nobody wanted to know.' In the car on the way to buy a coffee pot to celebrate their wedding anniversary, Katherine and John stare out of opposite windows. He is sure the shop will be shut; she remembers 'how blue the lavender was'. She regards it as a lesson. 'One must live alone and work & put away one's passion – one's passion for Life. It must all go into work.'[42]

What she craves most from her stay in London is intellectual stimulation. A week after she arrives, Tom Eliot and his wife are invited to dinner. Katherine hates Vivien because her neuroses repel her, but she is very fond of Tom. After they leave, John and Katherine have an argument over Vivien, whom John finds quite attractive. The dinner has not been a success. Eliot writes afterwards to Ezra Pound, who has known Katherine since her *New Age* days, 'I must say that [Murry] is much more difficult to deal with when K.M. is about, and I have an impression that she terrorizes him . . . I believe her to be a dangerous WOMAN; and of course two sentimentalists together are more than two times as noxious as one.'[43]

Katherine sends a note to Virginia, asking her to call and apologising for not writing to her before. Virginia looks back on the progress of their friendship which, she judges, has been 'almost entirely founded on quick-sands. It has been marked by curious slides & arrests . . . We have been intimate, intense perhaps rather than open.'[44] There has been a coolness between them – Katherine fears a breach – since her review of Virginia's novel *Night and Day* in the *Athenaeum* back in November. Katherine had implied that the book was 'old fashioned' and disappointing and Virginia has been hurt. Privately Katherine believes that the book is 'a lie in the soul' because it ignores the war.[45] But, motivated by affection and curios-ity, Virginia goes to Hampstead, and is shocked by Katherine's physical frailty when she is shown up to her room. Katherine 'gets up, very slowly, from her writing table', looking very ill, moving 'languidly, drawing her-self across the room, like some suffering animal'.[46] Katherine reassures Virginia about her novel, though Virginia had been 'determined not to speak of it'. Katherine, choosing her words carefully, tells her that it was 'An amazing achievement'. Once the difficult ground has been navigated, they have '2 hours of priceless talk'.[47] Throughout the summer, Virginia goes back to Portland Villas whenever Katherine is well enough to see her. She notices a new quality in Katherine. 'I said "You've changed. Got through something" indeed there's a sort of self command about her as if having mastered something . . . she told me of her terrific experiences last winter – experience of loneliness chiefly.' Katherine tells her how John had arrived at Christmas with a 'Now I'm here it's all right' kind of attitude; how she had gone to him for assurance but 'didn't get it; & will never look for that particular quality again'.[48]

There are new visitors to Portland Villas too. Katherine had met Sydney and Violet Schiff in the south of France, where they have a house at Roquebrune. Sydney is the financial backer of a periodical called *Art and Letters*, which has just published 'The Man without a Temperament'. He had antagonised Katherine initially by offering unwelcome editorial advice. In person, Katherine finds him much more congenial and makes a good friend of his wife, who buys clothes for Katherine and tries to make life comfortable for her in small ways. Another visitor is Katherine's cousin Elizabeth von Arnim, now Countess Russell, but recently separated from

Bertrand Russell's brother. The two cousins have had very little to do with each other in the past, but Elizabeth is pleased with Katherine's review of her latest book and curious enough to call. Elizabeth is in her early fifties, short, slim, dark and still very attractive. Her public facade is of a smart, rather brittle socialite with a reputation for witty backchat. When told that a male acquaintance had been wounded in seventeen places, she had remarked, 'I didn't know a man had seventeen places'. Men are terrified of her 'powerful and possessive' personality. Katherine finds her rather artificial, and observes that her 'claw like hands covered in jewels' are vulgar, on a par with her mind. Behind the facade Elizabeth is intimidated by Katherine's intelligence, which turns her 'spiritual fingers into thumbs'.[49] But they have a lively conversation on the subject of sex, which Elizabeth has decided she can live without.

Much of Katherine's time in London is taken up with the details of her new collection, *Bliss and other Stories*, to be published in the autumn. Michael Sadleir wants to include some of the old stories from *Rhythm*, but Katherine disagrees. They are simply not good enough. He also wants her to make some changes to 'Je ne parle pas Francais', which is sexually explicit in places and likely to offend. In the aftermath of Lawrence's experience, publishers are treading carefully. John adds his editorial voice to Michael's and, in the end, Katherine deletes the offending words and phrases, as well as the last few lines, which she initially thinks are essential, but is persuaded are unnecessary.[50]

It becomes clear to Katherine, within a few weeks of her arrival, that John is spending too much time with her friend Dorothy Brett. Brett has been painting John's portrait, and they often play tennis together on the Hampstead courts. It's obvious that John finds her easier company than Katherine. Brett is bouncing with health, uncritical, down to earth and above all listens to John with admiration when he talks. While Katherine was in France there had been a confessional letter from Brett mentioning 'orgies', which involved John, and where Brett had got so drunk she had fallen into a toilet. There had also been a romantic expedition to the country, while Brett was helping John with his house hunting, which Brett felt was significant. John had protested his innocence. The orgies 'consisted in me rather gloomy with rather too much to drink gradually getting gloomier & gloomier'.[51] The animosity of Katherine's reply to Brett (the only one of Katherine's letters she doesn't keep) suggests that Katherine is not convinced by John's denials.

In July Katherine finds letters from Brett to John that upset her even more. John has apparently 'awakened' Brett's physical feelings towards men. 'When she wrote how she wanted to rush into the cornfield – horrified me. And then he must smack her hand and she threatens to cry over him until he's all wet.' Her first thought is that of every woman whose husband is in love with another woman – 'how can he?' Brett is '37, hysterical, unbalanced . . . And then the bitten nails – the dirty neck – the film on the teeth!'[52] John denies any involvement or responsibility for Brett's feelings. Katherine summons Brett from her house, which is conveniently round the corner. Brett is very much afraid of Katherine's tongue, which she states 'can cut the heart out of you like a knife'. Over the tea table Katherine accuses Brett, not just of being in love with him, but of having an affair with John. 'I was appalled! It had never entered my head . . . she upset the boiling water from the tea kettle onto her legs. She was crying and miserable. I did all I could, but I don't think I convinced her.'[53] Katherine asks for her letters back. She feels doubly hurt that Brett has betrayed her, since she had been a witness at their wedding, adding bitterly 'but that was great nonsense – such ceremonies are no more binding than tea parties'.[54] Apparently the liaison had begun at Garsington, the first Christmas that Katherine had been too ill to go there. John had kissed Brett under the mistletoe and then written a poem for her called 'The Wakened Dryad', putting it under her pillow with a note telling her she 'was a darling and hoping they would spend every Christmas together and every Christmas Eve kissing'.[55] It is easy for John to pass this off as a romantic misunderstanding, but what Brett can't tell Katherine is that recently John has been pressing her for a sexual relationship, which, he assures her, can only be beneficial to them both. Brett has so far drawn back, partly because she is afraid of losing her virginity, but mainly because she doesn't want to hurt Katherine.

A couple of weeks later, John tells Katherine that he's considering lodging at Brett's house with Mark Gertler that winter while she's away. 'The lack of sensitiveness as far as I am concerned – the selfishness of this staggers me.' Katherine confronts him with her fears and insists that he tell her the whole truth. John confesses that he has held hands with Brett, kissed her and that they are 'on the brink of something deeper and more hazardous'. Katherine's devastation and pain are too great even to be recorded in her journal. Only one entry seems to refer to it. 'I should like to have a secret code to put on "record" what I feel today. If I forget it may my right hand forget its cunning.' Later she adds the following lines in the margin: 'I wrote this because there is a real danger of forgetting that kind of intensity, & it won't do.' And then again, 'No, there is no danger of forgetting'.[56]

Under severe emotional stress, Katherine's health has deteriorated rapidly through the summer. She has lost another 2 kilograms in weight. 'I cough and cough and at each breath a dragging boiling bubbling sound is heard. I feel that my whole chest is boiling . . . I can't expand my chest – it's as though the chest has collapsed. Life is – getting a new breath.' There are times when she needs oxygen. It is obvious that John finds her disgusting. He 'is silent, hangs his head, hides his face with his fingers as though it were unendurable. "This is what she is doing to me."'[57] Katherine decides that she must go back to the south of France sooner than she had planned. John is relieved, but at least one friend is saddened at the thought of Katherine leaving. For Virginia it is the 'blankness of not having her to talk to' that is the greatest loss. 'A woman caring as I care for writing is rare enough I suppose to give me the queerest sense of echo coming back to me from her mind the second after I've spoken. Then, too, there's something in what she says of our being the only women, at this moment . . . With gift enough to make talk of writing interesting.'[58]

Connie Beauchamp and Jinnie Fullerton have bought a large house called the Villa Louise in Garavan at the Italian end of the town, a few hundred metres inside the French border. At the bottom of the garden is a small house rather like a gardener's cottage, or a gatehouse, called the Villa Isola Bella. 'A dolls house with a verandah, garden, everything complete.' The idea of the flat is given up and Katherine accepts the offer of the cottage from the beginning of September. Ida is once more to go with her. She is the one person on whom Katherine can depend, her 'sworn friend'. 'Jones, I am not at all well yet – terribly nervous and exacting and always in pain – But I'll get over it – But I need you and I rely on you – I lean hard on you – yet I can't thank you or give you anything in return – except my love. You have that always.'[59]

LEFT: The Beau Rivage Hotel, Bandol, where Katherine had her first haemorrhage. *Author collection*

LEFT: The Villa Pauline, Bandol. *Author collection*

LEFT: The Villa Isola Bella, Menton. *Author collection*

LEFT: Katherine on the steps at the Villa Isola Bella. *Alexander Turnbull Library, 1/2-011916-F*

ABOVE: Katherine's bedroom at Villa Isola Bella. *Alexander Turnbull Library, 1/2-011918-F*

BELOW: Dorothy Brett, Katherine and Ida Baker in the hotel garden at Sierre. *Alexander Turnbull Library, 1/2-011925-F*

ABOVE: Katherine Mansfield's passport from 1918 to 1923. *Alexander Turnbull Library, 1/2-028694-F*

LEFT: Katherine's last photograph. *Alexander Turnbull Library, PAColl-6826-1-15-1*

BELOW: One of the final entries in Katherine's notebook for 1922. Alexander Turnbull Library, qMS-1282

ABOVE: John Middleton Murry at his desk. *Private collection*

RIGHT: Katherine's grave in the cemetery at Avon, near Fontainebleau. *Author collection*

BELOW RIGHT: George Gurdjieff. *Gurdjieff Foundation*

BELOW: Violet le Maistre at the time of her marriage to John Middleton. *Private collection*

ABOVE: John, Violet and their two young children – Katherine, always known as 'Weg', and John, always known as 'Col'. *Private collection*

ABOVE RIGHT: Richard Murry. *Alexander Turnbull Library, 1/4-009908-F (detail)*

BELOW: The Old Coastguard Station, Dorset, Violet's first home, bought with Katherine Mansfield's royalties and furnished with her belongings. *Private collection*

LEFT: Violet Middleton Murry, aged 27, bedridden and suffering from tuberculosis. Drawing by Richard Murry. *Private collection*

BELOW: Max Plowman, poet and journalist, friend of John Middleton Murry. *Private collection*

LEFT: Betty Cockbayne, John Middleton Murry's third wife. *Private collection*

ABOVE: The Old Vicarage, Larling, where John Middleton Murry lived with his family during the 1930s.
Private collection

BELOW LEFT: Dr James Young, Katherine Mansfield's doctor at Fontainebleau, with John Middleton Murry's children, Weg and Col. *Private collection*

BELOW RIGHT: Violet's daughter, the young Katherine Middleton Murry, always known as 'Weg'.
Private collection

ABOVE LEFT: John Middleton Murry with his youngest son, David, at Larling. *Private collection*

ABOVE RIGHT: Mary Middleton Murry, always known as 'Mêh', at Larling. *Private collection*

BELOW LEFT: Violet's son, the young John Middleton Murry, known as 'Col'. *Private collection*

BELOW RIGHT: Mary Gamble, John Middleton Murry's fourth wife. *Private collection*

21

'A Writer First and a Woman After'

Almighty Father of all and Most Celestial Giver
Who has granted to us thy children a Heart & Lungs & a Liver
If upon me should descend thy beautiful gift of tongues
Incline not thine Omnipotent ear to my remarks on Lungs.

KATHERINE MANSFIELD, 'VERSES WRIT IN A FOREIGN BED', 16 SEPTEMBER 1920

In Katherine's passport photograph she looks haggard and haunted and unfit to travel, but the journey to Menton is less of an ordeal with Ida to look after her. Then, after long hours in the train, there is the bliss of arrival at the Villa Isola Bella. She stands beside Ida on the terrace and falls in love with the Mediterranean all over again. The only drawback is that the house lacks a proper bathroom and they have to bathe in a portable douche. The house is also right next to the railway line, but the station at Garavan is tiny and there are very few trains.

Within two days of Katherine's arrival there's a communication from John, who has opened a letter addressed to her at the Elephant. It's from Floryan Sobieniowski, who has seen advance notices for *Bliss*, and is asking for money to suppress certain letters that Katherine had written to him years earlier. He also hints threateningly about 'the Chelsea period and good received'. Katherine tells John she doesn't know what he means by that, but 'it is true that he does possess letters written during my

385

acquaintance with him which I would give any money to recover'. Having talked it over with Ida, who is well aware of the threat posed to Katherine's reputation, Ida is willing to lend Katherine £40 to buy him off. 'It's not a waste of £40. . . As to the letters, needless to say they are yours. I'd like them destroyed as they are, but that's for you to say darling.'[1] In the end John agrees to send them out to Katherine, with a signed declaration from Floryan that he won't bother them again. There is great concern when the letters are lost in the post somewhere between London and Menton, but they do eventually arrive.

Katherine has made a vow, since leaving England, that she will make fewer demands on John. 'I'm a writer first & a woman after; I can't give you all you want – above all a kind of easy relaxation which is essential to you . . . I was blind not to have understood it in the Brett affair.' She has realised, since that episode, that to hold on too tightly is to risk losing him altogether. 'I have a perfect horror of demanding help, of asking you to – hold my hand. You're as free as can be again.'[2] But it is easier to promise, than to keep. Katherine's illness and its prognosis have forced her to dig very deep into her own resources. Now she is conscious of a barrier between herself and other people, because she has a knowledge they lack. Facing her own death has given her a new vision. 'Suffering – bodily suffering such as I've known for three years. It has changed forever everything – even the appearance of the world is not the same – there is something added. Everything has its shadow . . .'[3] Sorapure has helped her to come to terms with it. He had told her in London that suffering is a repairing process. 'I really think I should have just died in that room upstairs if he had not taken me by the hand, like you take a little girl who is frightened of a dog & led me up to my pain & showed it to me & proved that it wasn't going to eat me.'[4]

She explains that she is writing more profoundly and consciously from within herself, and she uses the aloe as a symbol of the 'true' immortal self, struggling to become free.

Is it not possible that the rage for confession, autobiography, especially for memories of earliest childhood is explained by our persistent yet mysterious belief in a self which is continuous and permanent, which, untouched by all we acquire and all we shed, pushes a green spear through the leaves and through the mould, thrusts a sealed bud through years of darkness until, one day, the light discovers it and shakes the flower free and – we are alive – we are flowering for our moment upon the earth. This is the moment which, after all, we live for, the moment of direct feeling when we are most ourselves and least personal.[5]

Her journals record an intensity of experience that produces some of her greatest writing, surpassing anything in the stories and give a taste of what might have been achieved if she had lived. 'And yet one has these "glimpses" before which all that one ever has written (what has one written) all (yes, all) that one ever has read, pales . . . The waves, as I drove home this afternoon – and the high foam, how it was suspended in the air before it fell . . . What is it that happens in that moment of suspension? It is timeless. In that moment (what do I mean) the whole life of the soul is contained. One is flung up – out of life – one is "held" – and then, down, bright, broken, glittering on to the rocks, tossed back – part of the ebb and flow.'[6] She seems to be thinking of Lawrence, and of a particular piece he had written for Signature, just after Chummie's death. Death 'is neither here nor there. Death is a temporal, relative fact' in the ebbing and flowing of the tides of the universe. 'The wave of earth flung up in spray, a lark, a cloud of larks, against the white wave of the sun. The spray of earth and the foam of heaven are one, consummated, a rainbow mid-way, a song. The larks return to earth, the rays go back to heaven. But these are only the shuttles that weave the iris, the song, mid-way, in absoluteness, timelessness.'[7]

Publishers Methuen are keen for Katherine to write a 'journal' for publication the following Christmas, but after agreeing, Katherine has insufficient energy to follow the project through. The privately printed edition of 'Je ne parle pas Francais' has been well reviewed by friends, but not everyone likes the story. Katherine's father is disgusted by what he sees as its tawdry theme and throws it into the fireplace; Jinnie Fullerton finds it offensive to her religion: 'But how could you say that about the Blessed Virgin! It must have hurt Our Lady so terribly. And I saw the B.V. throwing away her copy . . . & saying "Really this K.M. is all that her friends say [of] her to me".'[8] Katherine has had plenty of time away from her cousin to rethink the idea of conversion to Catholicism. Before Katherine left for England, Jinnie had given her a copy of The Imitation of Christ by Thomas à Kempis, and Katherine had struck an angry pencil through the paragraphs instructing absolute obedience to the will of God. She doesn't want the discipline of religion, only its reassurance. She believes that Jinnie and

Connie may be 'offended with me for not giving in about the Church . . . It's in their eyes every time they look at me.' Katherine is forced to adopt 'a kind of No Popery manner'.[9]

She confides her feelings about her father's lack of generosity to Connie and is surprised at the reaction. The two older women are quite clear that Katherine's father has no obligation to provide her with any money at all – that he gives her anything is out of the goodness of his heart. It's her husband's responsibility to support her and this is how Harold Beauchamp sees it. Katherine suddenly becomes racked with anxiety that he may cut off her allowance at any time, expecting John to pay for everything. When she hears that Mr Kay has sent her bank pass book out to New Zealand for her father to see, she panics. The £40 advance for *Bliss* has just been paid into her account. If he sees that she is actually earning money . . . Katherine is so upset that when a letter comes from Mr Kay she dare not open it and sends it to John to read for her. She need not have worried; Harold Beauchamp has no intention of cutting off Katherine's allowance – unknown to her, he pays her sisters an equal amount.

Katherine is working very hard to earn money. As well as reviewing every week for the *Athenaeum*, she is also writing commercial stories for a number of magazines. Her work is now sought after and she has decided that she needs a proper agent, rather than relying on John to submit her stories and manage her literary affairs. This decision is made more urgent when John supplies Constable with the wrong photograph for the cover of *Bliss*, sending the 1914 one of a younger, plumper Katherine with fluffy hair – a photograph she had had taken for Carco. Katherine is absolutely furious. John has also forgotten her birthday for the first time in their relationship. He is the recipient of several angry letters, followed by an apology. She is overtired and unwell. Everything gets blown up out of proportion. Two weeks later her doctor, a French specialist called Bouchage, tells her that she must give up journalism – the stress of meeting deadlines is putting a strain on her heart and shortening her life. Katherine hopes that an agent like J. B. Pinker will be able to sell her stories in a wider market so that she can still earn the money she needs. Freed from the grind of churning out reviews, she hopes to be able to return to serious work.

She is trying to get further with her embryo novel, 'Karori', but it eludes her. There are mornings when she looks out of the window at the mountains and wonders why she bothers at all. 'Short stories seem unreal & not worth doing. I don't want to write; I want to Live.'[10] Other ideas come to nothing. Personal problems intervene. 'I thought, a few minutes ago that I could have written a whole novel about a Liar. A man who was devoted to his wife but who lied. But I couldn't. I couldn't write a whole novel about anything. I suppose I shall write stories about it. But at this moment I can't get through to anything. There's something like a great wall of sand between me and the whole of my "world". I feel as though I am dirty or disgusted or both . . . Everything I think of seems false.'[11]

The Garsington and Bloomsbury gossip mills are loud with whispers about Katherine's husband. Alarmed by how much everyone seems to know, John decides to 'come clean' in a letter to Katherine; he should, he admits, have told her the whole truth from the beginning. He tries to make Katherine realise how much 'married chastity' is costing him, how desperately he needs to be 'comforted'. He tells her that he had even picked up a prostitute in Leicester Square, though he hadn't been able to take it any further. He had invited her for dinner at Maltzy's in the Tottenham Court Road, spent the evening talking to her and afterwards paid her 30s. Then he describes how he had gone to see Brett, feeling miserable and lonely, and taken her in his arms and caressed her, until suddenly 'a great loathing of myself & her came over me . . . I was more miserable than ever'. Shortly afterwards he had been invited to dinner with friends and he tells Katherine how Elizabeth Bibesco had been nice to him. In the taxi going home he had kissed her. Then she had invited him to dinner, but when he arrived she was unwell and he was shown up to her bedroom, where the meal was to be served. 'I ate at a little table at the foot of her bed and after dinner sat in a chair by her side.' Nothing happened, he assures Katherine, but Elizabeth Bibesco seems to be in love with him and she has sent him a short story to look at, which he unwisely sends to Katherine for an opinion.[12] Elizabeth is young – only twenty-three – and very beautiful. She is the daughter of the former prime minister, Herbert Asquith, and the wife of Prince Antoine Bibesco, a minor European nobleman. John is dazzled by the fact that she seems to want him. Katherine has met her and knows the kind of woman that Elizabeth is. 'She has a quick rapacious look – in fact she made me think of a gull with an absolutely insatiable appetite for bread, and all her vitality, her cries, her movements, her wheelings depend upon the person on the bridge who carries the loaf.'[13]

Katherine is more deeply hurt than she can ever disclose to John. Her first response is a telegram: 'STOP TORMENTING ME WITH THESE FALSE

DEPRESSING LETTERS AT ONCE BE A MAN OR DON'T WRITE ME'.[14] The letter that follows is courageous and bitter and not entirely truthful. 'I told you to be free – because I meant it. What happens in your personal life does NOT affect me. I have of you what I want – a relationship which is unique but it is not what the world understands by marriage.'[15] In her journal, she records that this is some of the worst suffering she has ever experienced – far worse than physical pain. It 'is boundless – it is eternity . . . Physical suffering is – child's play.' She knows she is unreasonable to expect John to live like a monk – it is the falling in love with women she knows that hurts most. Her whole life seems to be pain, but she refuses to be defeated by it. 'I do not want to die without leaving a record of my belief that suffering can be overcome. For I do believe it. What must one do? There is no question of what Jack calls passing beyond it; this is false. One must submit. Do not resist. Take it. Be overwhelmed. Accept it fully – make it part of Life.' The pain must be transmuted into something else. 'Life is a mystery. The fearful pain of these letters – of the knowledge that Jack wishes me dead – and of his killing me – will fade. I must turn to work. I must put my agony into something – change it . . .' As for John, 'I must not blame him any more and I must not go back. Thus was it. Let it be.'[16]

A few days later John arrives in Menton for Christmas, embarrassed, guilty, but penitent. Whatever he has done or said, Katherine loves him and needs him. There can be no separation. 'We are . . . two sides of the medal – separate, distinct, and yet making one.'[17] John assures Katherine that it is all over with Elizabeth Bibesco – 'I swear on my honour' – but Katherine suspects she is still writing to him. 'The letters disappear. All the other letters are left on the table but not those. Why? I am to forget everything – to behave as though everything has not been. But I can't.'[18]

Talking it through in Menton, John decides to make a radical change in his life. It is obvious that Katherine is never going to be well enough to live in England again and separation hasn't worked for either of them. He had been intending to leave the *Athenaeum* anyway – probably in the spring – so now he will go rather earlier and, instead of moving into Broomies, come out to join Katherine here. The Villa Isola Bella can be leased for another year, the Elephant will be given up, the cottage sold and they will live simply and cheaply in the sun. This is not really the sacrifice that John allows Katherine (and the rest of the world) to think. He can now earn as much freelance as he was earning as editor of the periodical and he wants to work on some personal projects – a novel, and a collection of essays and his lectures on style. Through a lecture agent he can now earn 10 guineas for a single talk, plus travel expenses. When he returns to London he arranges for the *Athenaeum*, the sales of which have been declining since he became editor, to be merged with the *Nation*, a much more political publication that employs John to write editorials and reviews. He leaves behind a letter for Katherine to read after he has gone, telling her that despite 'the horrors' of the past three weeks, being with her means more to him than anything else. He urges her to 'trust me as though I were part of your own heart. I am part of your heart' and he promises her that 'all things are quite straight & plain in front of me'.[19]

The first copy of *Bliss and other Stories* arrives in time for Christmas 1920 and the reviews are better than Katherine could ever have hoped for. 'There is every sign that it is a biggish success.'[20] Even Virginia writes to congratulate her, though privately she tells her sister that she had found it 'so brilliant, – so hard, and so shallow, and so sentimental that I had to rush to the bookcase for something to drink. Shakespeare, Conrad . . .'[21] Like Virginia, not all the reviewers are on Katherine's side. One in particular remarks on her ability to portray brittle women who live on their nerves.

> Those figures which she draws in most carefully are women; they are selfish, weak, cultured, irritable, and conceited. *Bliss* in one sense is a book of neurotics; a literary corridor of the psychopathic ward. But with what a vigour does she depict these neurotics. Typical of them is Monica Tyrrell, who suffered from nerves every morning from eight o'clock till about half-past eleven, 'suffered so terribly that these hours were – agonising, simply.' . . . Most horrible of all is the woman in 'The Escape', with her refrain of: 'Oh, why am I made to bear these things? . . . Oh, to care as I care – to feel as I feel, and never to be saved anything – never to know for one moment what it was to . . . to . . .' From this treatment of Katherine Mansfield one might think that she was no more than a literary specialist in nervous disorders. The idea is mistaken; only about a third of the stories in her volume deal specifically with neurotics. It is simply that her handling of them is so vivid that they overshadow most of the other characters.[22]

But even those who dislike her work are in no doubt about Katherine's talent. She has 'got hold of [a] new and necessary form. So far she has used it only in a short story, but there is no reason why she should not meet with the same success if she applied it to a full-length novel.'[23] Alfred Knopf, in

America, have now decided to publish Bliss in February and Constable are already talking about another book. Katherine promises to let her publisher have her new work the following month. 'It will be long short stories: I'll never write a real live novel.'[24] Bliss brings a flurry of letters from people who have read it with admiration. John Galsworthy is particularly appreciative. 'It seemed to me that in "Prelude" you really achieved that new form which has been so hopelessly fumbled for by practically everybody but TTchehov (Oh! bother! The man has not two Ts). Indeed, you out-tchehoved Tchehov in that story – a very beautiful piece of work.'[25] One of the letter-writers is Orage and Katherine replies with a short note that is almost a farewell: 'I want to tell you how sensible I am of your wonderful unfailing kindness to me in the "old days". And to thank you for all you let me learn from you . . . You taught me to write, you taught me to think; you showed me what there was to be done and what not to do . . . Thank you for everything. If only one day I might write a book of stories good enough to "offer" you . . . If I don't succeed in keeping the coffin from the door you will know this was my ambition.'[26] Other letters have a similar ring of finality. 'Goodbye, dear Ottoline,' and to Koteliansky (who has been angry with her for losing some of his Chekhov transcripts), 'Dear friend – do not think evil of me – forgive me. Kissienka.'[27]

The success of Bliss comes as Katherine's health has taken another sudden downturn – serious enough to bring John back from England only days after he had arrived. Katherine jokes that her health is so precarious 'it seems the only way to make sure he won't be late for the funeral!'[28] The tuberculosis has flared up all over her body: she is coughing blood again, her heart is fluttering badly and a tubercular gland in her neck has become enlarged, pressing on an artery and making one side of her head numb and painful. There are days when Katherine can't even talk and has to write what she wants to say in her notebook. She is back in bed, enduring the burden of Ida's care. Katherine hates to be watched. 'If I sigh I know that her head lifts – I know that those grave large eyes solemnly fix on me . . . if I turn she suggests a cushion or another rug. If I turn again then it is my back. Might she try to rub it for me? There is no escape. All night a faint rustle, the smallest cough and her soft voice asks did you speak. Can I do anything. If I do absolutely nothing then she discovers my fatigue under my eyes.'[29] It is hard, but Katherine can't do without Ida.

It's the middle of February before she's well enough to get up and March before she can go out into the garden. But in the weeks that she has been confined to her room, Katherine has finished one of her most important stories, 'The Daughters of the Late Colonel'. One of the sisters, Jug-jug, is based on her cousin Sylvia Payne. Ida, whose second name is Constance, is the model for Constantia. Katherine is afraid the readers will not understand what she is trying to do with her characters, and think she is 'poking fun at the poor old things', but though she had begun with the idea that they were amusing, 'the moment I looked deeper . . . I bowed down to the beauty that was hidden in their lives'.[30] Katherine completes the final draft of the story through yet another sleepless night and she and Ida celebrate at 3 a.m. over a cup of tea, 'with the pale morning light gleaming through the golden sprays of the mimosa trees' outside.[31]

By the middle of February John has wound up the *Athenaeum* and comes out to Menton so that Ida can go back to England – partly to have a much-needed holiday and partly to pack up the Elephant and put the furniture into storage. Katherine's infected gland has to be punctured surgically as soon as she's well enough to be driven to the hospital. Though she makes light of it in her letters, she dreads the wait for the surgeon 'in a huge, grim ante-chamber', before being taken through 'dark little doorways, down underground passages' that end 'in one of those white tiled rooms, with glass shelves, a fine display of delicate steel, too many wash basins, a frosted windy glass & a narrow little black sofa with steel grips for the patient to cling to'.[32] It is a very painful procedure that has to be repeated several times. Katherine is insulted afterwards when John asks her to pay half the taxi fare and the driver's tip. 'Fancy not paying for your wife's carriage to & from the surgery!' she writes to Ida. 'I really am staggered . . . I suppose if one fainted he would make one pay 3d for a 6d glass of sal volatile.'[33] She has also intercepted another hysterical letter from Elizabeth Bibesco, urging John to break free from Katherine. 'You have withstood her so gallantly so far how can you give way now . . . You swore nothing on earth should ever come between us.'[34] There's also a letter from Elizabeth Bibesco to Katherine, accusing her of treating John callously by holding onto him when she is too sick 'to make any kind of life or happiness for him'.[35] Katherine should free him for a healthy relationship with someone else. Katherine writes a scathing, patronising letter to Elizabeth, instructing her to stop sending letters to John, and she makes Ida promise that she will never forget, and never forgive John for what he has done.

The tapping of the gland is unsuccessful and another swelling is discovered in Katherine's right lung, pressing on her bronchial tube. As the air temperature rises towards a Mediterranean summer, Katherine's constant fever makes the heat unbearable and she begins to feel suffocated: 'Throttling strangling by the throat a helpless exhausted little black silk bag ... Frail – Frail – I felt Life was no more than this.'[36] Bouchage tells her that her only hope is to go to Switzerland to see a specialist called Henry Spahlinger, whose vaccine treatments for advanced tuberculosis are rumoured to be very successful. Katherine decides that she must try them, even if it means entering a sanatorium. She wants desperately to live, and any possible cure must be attempted. So, just as she seems settled in one 'dear perpetual place', she moves on again.[37]

Letters are burnt – her own to Floryan, Lawrence's soul-searing denunciation, almost all John's depressing letters from September 1919 to January 1920 – and unsatisfactory manuscripts are also destroyed. Katherine confesses that every time she moves it's as though she's preparing for a death. Ida has arranged hotels and *wagons-lits* tickets and by 5 May Katherine is talking 'German to a German' for the first time since she was in Geneva in 1912. She is staying at the Hotel Beau Site at Clarens-Montreux near Lausanne – two rooms and a balcony all to herself, with views of the mountains and Lake Geneva – and Ida is at a pension nearby. Katherine is posing as 'a lady with a weak heart & lungs of Spanish leather-o', but though she finds the cool dry air a relief after the summer heat of Menton, she isn't sure about the Swiss: 'the people are so UGLY; ... all the women have pear shaped derrieres, ugly heads, awful feet. All the men wear ready-made check flannelette suits, six sizes too small and felt hats another six sizes too small with a little pre-war feather sticking up behind.' The food also does not come up to French standards. 'It seems to lie down and wait for you ... you are not attracted. You don't feel that keenness to meet it and know more of it and get on very intimate terms. The asparagus is always stone dead. As to the *puree de pommes de terre* you feel inclined to call it "uncle".'[38] But the hygiene is faultless. 'The cleanliness of Switzerland! Darling, it is frightening. The chastity of my lily-white bed! The waxy-fine floors! The huge bouquet of white lilac, fresh crisp from the laundry in my little salon! Every daisy in the grass below has a starched frill – the very bird droppings are dazzling.'[39]

John is in Oxford delivering his lectures on style. He is not a natural public speaker and worries about having to read the scripts rather than talk from notes, but the content is not in question – Tom Eliot, having dinner with Virginia Woolf, predicts that his new career will be very successful. As Lawrence had once told him, 'The Crown' is there for John to take. But going back to Oxford is a strange experience. John realises that he would have made a very good don, but is glad that he has taken a different course. 'I love Oxford; but in the way I love my father. We're utterly strange to each other.' The atmosphere is unreal, as though he has stepped out of life into another world, hearing and seeing everything 'from an incredible distance'.[40] John is still coping with almost unbearable sexual frustration and writes to Katherine about an embarrassing wet dream – the 'accusing splotches' on a friend's guest bed.[41] While in England John is also trying to arrange a future for his brother Richard, who has been living with, and being taught by, Brett. John's father is utterly opposed to Richard studying art and even though a Slade scholarship is a distinct possibility, refuses to sign the necessary papers. John has decided that he will have to finance Richard himself.

Katherine can't find a good doctor in Montreux and has to take a train to Sierre to consult Dr Stephani, the most eminent TB specialist in Switzerland. Sierre, in the Rhône Valley, is so beautiful it captures Katherine's imagination. 'There are ancient tiny castles on small round wooded knolls, and . . . there are deep, deep meadows. Little herd boys lie on their backs or their bellies & their tiny white goats spring about on the mountain slopes. These mountains have little lawns set with trees, little glades & miniature woods & torrents on the lower slopes . . . You meet tiny girls all alone with flocks of black sheep or herds of huge yellow cows . . . And houses are so few, so remote.' Above all there are no tourists. Katherine begins to think of a chalet up here, where she can be treated by the best doctors without having to go into a sanatorium. Stephani is 'extremely nice', but he can only tell her that she 'has a chance' – not even a good chance. It's a disappointment. 'I always expect these doctor men to say – "Get better? Of course you will! We'll put you right in no time. Six months at the very most & you'll be fit as a fiddle again."'[42] Enquiries made to local doctors and a letter written to Sorapure, reveal that the Spahlinger treatment she had hoped for is a myth. 'There is no serum . . . its purely experimental & very terrifying in its results at present.'[43] Stephani wants to put Katherine into a sanatorium in Montana, but she decides that an institution, however luxurious, is still not for her. She stays only one night at a clinic called the Palace Hotel and agrees to be treated as an outpatient by a local TB specialist, Dr Hudson.

At the end of May the winners of the Hawthornden Prize are announced. It had been widely expected that Katherine would be given it for *Bliss*, but she has been 'robbed', in Virginia's words, by a young novelist called Romer Wilson, for *The Death of Society*. Although Virginia is bitchily glad that Katherine has not won, she sums up the decision accurately in her diary: 'I assure you, when Virginia's old, no one will be talking of Romer Wilson'.[44] Katherine tries not to mind the loss of the £100 prize money, or the literary validation. She is struggling to meet her magazine deadlines in a series of hotel rooms in Sierre. But, despite the disruption of constant relocation, the atmosphere of endless journeying and anonymous rooms is fruitful. Katherine always writes well on trains and in strange locations, taken out of familiar terrain, functioning as an observer. These places of transition provide a creative space for observation and memory to collide. She writes to Brett about staircases: 'One is somehow suspended. One is on neutral ground – not in ones own world nor in a strange one. They are an almost perfect meeting place.'[45]

When she hears that Brett wants to come out for a holiday, Katherine replies straight away, 'I'm working . . . I sound horribly ungracious. I cannot help it. I am determined to finish something before my time is up. Perhaps Murry explained to you that the specialist only gives me a chance – no more. This makes a great difference, you know. It makes one want to hurry in case one is caught. Work to me is more important than anything, I fear, and I'm working against time.'[46]

By the end of June John is there with her and shortly afterwards they take the lease of the Chalet Les Sapins near Montana, which is owned by Dr Hudson's mother. It's in the middle of the forest: 'there's not even a fence or a bar between it and the trees. So you picture the wolves breathing under the front door, the bears looking through our keyhole and bright tigers dashing at the lighted window panes.'[47] The chalet is substantial, built on three floors, with verandahs on each level facing the valley. The kitchen and bathroom are on the lower floor, the living and dining rooms on the first floor and the bedrooms at the top. The air in Montana is clear and dry, but it is over 1500 metres above sea level and the altitude challenges Katherine's already weakened heart. She is rarely able to manage the two flights of stairs down to the bathroom. The problem is solved by carrying a tin bath up to her room and cans of heated water from the kitchen. Ida bathes her like a baby, pouring hot water over her and wrapping her in a towel to dry, just as her grandmother had done when she was a small child.

By chance Katherine's cousin Elizabeth has a house not far away, 'a half hour scramble down the mountain' at Randogne, where she is staying with a much younger companion and lover called Frere. Katherine feels guilty because she has been out of touch for so long, but Elizabeth is very happy to have congenial neighbours. Dressed in her black cloak and 'bishop's gaiters', clutching bouquets of flowers, she is a frequent caller in the afternoon if Katherine is well enough to see her, though their relationship is still tricky because they exist on such different planes. Elizabeth is content to be a commercial writer; Katherine is not. The older woman is in awe of Katherine's intellect. Conversation is inhibited because Elizabeth feels that she must choose her words carefully. When she calls one of Katherine's stories 'pretty', meaning it as a compliment, Katherine is insulted. But they share the same family history, and both are fastidious, delighting in beautiful things.

Throughout July Katherine is working with phenomenal speed and concentration. She writes a story called 'Mr and Mrs Dove', but isn't happy with it. 'It's not quite the kind of truth I'm after.' She wants to be 'nearer, far, far nearer than that. I want to use all my force even when I am tracing a fine line.' The following week she completes 'An Ideal Family', which is 'better than the Doves' but still not good enough. She is beginning to be dissatisfied with her technique. 'I feel again that this kind of knowledge is too easy for me; it's even a kind of trickery. I know so much more. This looks & smells like a story but I wouldn't buy it. I don't want to possess it – to live with it. NO.'[48] Towards the end of July Katherine receives a letter from Marion Ruddick's family, who have also sent her some old photographs of the girls as children in New Zealand. She writes them a nostalgic letter about Marion, remembering excursions to Island Bay and how they bathed their dolls in the rock pools. A few days later Katherine tells Brett that she is working on a new story 'called "At the Bay" & it's (I hope) full of sand and seaweed and bathing dresses hanging over verandahs & sandshoes on window sills, and little pink "sea" convolvulus, and rather gritty sandwiches and the tide coming in'.[49] The sixty-page story is 'a continuation of Prelude', giving more intimate glimpses of the Burnell family. 'It is so strange to bring the dead to life again. There's my grandmother, back in her chair with her pink knitting, there stalks my uncle over the grass. I feel as I write "you are not dead my darlings. All is remembered."' . . . And one feels possessed.' She has tried 'to make it as familiar to "you" as it is to me . . . And, too, one tries to go deep – to speak to the secret self we all have.'[50]

'Going deep' in the story, the young Kezia confronts death. She is with her grandmother, who is thinking of a son who died in the Australian gold fields.

> 'Does everybody have to die?' asked Kezia.
>   'Everybody!'
>   'Me?' Kezia sounded fearfully incredulous.
>   'Some day, my darling.'
>   'But, Grandma.' Kezia waved her left leg and waggled the toes. They felt sandy. 'What if I just won't?'
>   The old woman sighed again and drew a long thread from the ball. 'We're not asked, Kezia,' she said sadly. 'It happens to all of us sooner or later.'

Kezia asks her grandmother to promise that she will never die. 'Say never . . . say never . . . say never – .' But the old woman tickles her to make her laugh until 'both of them had forgotten what the "never" was about'.

Katherine has found a housekeeper called Ernestine, so, feeling very much like the third person in the relationship, Ida moves out into a local pension and decides to take a job in a local clinic. Believing that Katherine is being well looked after by Ernestine and John, Ida returns to England in August to see her sister, who has just had a son, also intending to bring back Katherine's much-loved cat Wingley to complete the family. While Ida is away, the Furies descend on Katherine, bringing 'high fever, deadly sickness and weakness'. She is ill with dysentery – another unpleasant feature of advanced tuberculosis – and her swollen gland has to be punctured every week. 'It holds up my work so. Just when I am busy.' There is, in Ida's letters from England, some talk of her going to India to work with children in a mission orphanage – something she would really like to do. And she tells Katherine that she has accepted the task of chaperoning a young English girl back to France. This makes Katherine very jealous. She senses that she might lose Ida to someone else and accuses her of being a flirt. 'I am not going to flirt back, Miss, and say how I want you as part of my life and can't really imagine being without you. The ties that bind us! Heavens, they are so strong that you'd bleed to death if you really cut away. But don't. Oh please don't make me have to protest. Accept! Take your place! Be my friend! Don't pay me out for what has been . . . You can, in spite of my rages, read as much love as you like into this letter. You won't read more than is there.'[51]

Ida decides against India, not without some regrets, and goes back to her job at the clinic as soon as she returns. She enjoys the nursing and the independence, though she calls at the chalet every day before going home. She is still incurably accident prone and causes an explosion in the chalet kitchen by leaving a warming pan on the kitchen stove all night until it boils dry. About 2 a.m. it bursts, bringing down a shelf, part of the ceiling and cracking the top of the stove. But despite Ida's annoying faults, Katherine has realised once again that she is indispensable. Ernestine is unreliable, an appalling cook and 'as mad as a sober Swiss can be'.[52] John is too wrapped up in his work to attend to Katherine's personal needs. On 7 September she writes Ida a letter, formally offering her a job 'to manage things for me as if I were a man'. She will pay Ida £10–12 a month to look after the house and her clothes, 'to do just simply what is necessary – i.e. what I should do if I hadn't a profession', so that Katherine is free to write. This is to be much more than a commercial arrangement: 'The truth is friendship is to me every bit as sacred and eternal as marriage. I want to know from you if you think the same.'[53] So once more Ida comes back to the chalet to manage Katherine's life, though she still sleeps at the pension down the road.

By now there is a chill in the air and already summer is slipping south over the mountains. Katherine is working as fast as she can, writing commercial stories for the *Sphere* and the *Mercury* – sometimes one a week – in order to pay her medical bills, as well as several longer, more complex stories for her collection. She sometimes writes for nine hours a day. Katherine finishes 'At the Bay' late at night on 11 September, writing 'Thanks be to God' under the last line. She sends it straight to Pinker, asking him to include it in the collection and make it the title story. At the end of the month she accepts Constable's offer for the book – this time a more substantial £100. Katherine's imagination is still rooted in New Zealand and she has already begun another long story, 'The Garden Party', based on the parties her parents used to give at home in Tinakori Road, but also incorporating memories of the one she had been given by the prime minister's wife when she left Wellington. But she can't find a way into the story. It takes her nearly a month to 'recover' from 'At the Bay'. She is haunted by images and memories: 'the sound of the sea and Beryl fanning her hair at the window'.

Katherine is struggling for simplicity – the exact words that will convey to the reader what it is she sees and hears. 'To be "simple" enough as one would be simple before God.'[54] In the finished story, her technique is dazzling, the opening sentence phrased as if the reader is coming in on a conversation – continuing a narrative that has begun a long time ago. 'And after all the weather was ideal. They could not have had a more perfect day for a garden-party if they had ordered it.' It is not the weather, though, but death that interrupts the celebrations. A carter who lives in the labourers' cottages along the lane below the garden has been killed in an accident, and his body is carried past the house just as the children are sampling the cream puffs and the men are erecting the marquee. The child Laura insists that 'we can't possibly have a garden-party with a man dead just outside the front gate' and can't understand why the adults don't see her point of view. The party must go on. '"You are being very absurd, Laura," her mother says coldly. "People like that don't expect sacrifices from us. And it's not very sympathetic to spoil everybody's enjoyment as you're doing now."' Laura is asked by her mother to take a basket of food to the cottage and the terrified girl is taken in to see the young man, lying on the bed. 'Fast asleep – sleeping so soundly, so deeply . . . His head was sunk in the pillow, his eyes were closed; they were blind under the closed eyelids. He was given up to his dream. What did garden-parties and baskets and lace frocks matter to him? He was far from all those things. He was wonderful, beautiful . . . Happy . . . happy . . . All is well, said that sleeping face. This is just as it should be. I am content.' The story is finished only three weeks later, on her birthday, and Katherine sends it to Pinker and to Constable, asking them to include it in the collection and call it The Garden Party. 'At the Bay', she now realises, is too vague and unmemorable for a title.

Snow has fallen, which makes it difficult for Katherine to take even short walks, though on fine days she is able to take a ride in a horse and trap. She hates snow – 'all that whiteness has a mock mystery about it that I dislike very much' – and longs for a glimpse of the 'fertile, fertile earth!'[55] John, who is an excellent sportsman, is learning to ski and Katherine watches him enviously out of the window. John is working hard on his novel, The Things We Are. The critics have panned his Collected Poems 1916–20, published on 21 October. 'Most of the reviewers seized the book only to whack him on the head with it.'[56] He is also working on a collection of essays, Countries of the Mind, and a book on Shakespeare. In the evenings, Katherine enjoys reading and discussing the plays with John – this is the mental stimulation that was lacking in Menton. Her cat, Wingley, purrs on her lap and sleeps at night on her bed. She and John find relief in fantasy as they lie in their separate beds in adjacent rooms. They will have a farm and John will go off and mow the meadows. There will be a beautiful country house. 'We are both most fearful dreamers, especially when it's late & we lie staring at the ceiling. It begins with me. M. declares he won't talk. Its too late. Then I hear "Certainly not more than two floors & a large open fireplace." A long pause. K: "What about bees?" J.M.M.: "Most certainly bees and I aspire to a goat."'[57]

Katherine is more than ever conscious of the passage of time. As she writes to a friend, 'the beauty of the world is a kind of anguish; it is almost too much to bear. It is such a strange way to live; it is like being a child again – but all glorified. The light shakes through the grass, and the wind whispers over, and one's heart trembles . . . But it is the silence which is so different. It's as though the silence became your old nurse who said: "Very well, you may play a little longer if you are so happy and not tired (tired!), but remember I have called you." But the sun goes down so fast, so terribly fast. Now it is shining through the top-most branches of the thinning tree – now there is only a rim of gold to the hill.'[58]

When he's not skiing or skating on the lake, John is spending a lot of his time down at Elizabeth's. He goes there for lively entertainment and sometimes for dinner with the house guests. Under the influence of wine and female sympathy, he reveals very personal things about his relationship with Katherine. Elizabeth's lover Frere overhears John telling her that, during the war, Katherine had once, in a fit of self-destruction, gone down to the front and contracted a venereal disease from one of the soldiers. Elizabeth presumes this is syphilis and, though she has previously been critical of John's attitude to Katherine, begins to realise why John can't sleep with his wife and why their relationship is so difficult.

Katherine is trying, for a second time, to complete 'A Married Man's Story', but a letter from Brett about a 'dolls' still life' she is painting, arrests her imagination. 'There is a kind of smugness & rakishness combined in dolls & heaven knows how much else that's exquisite & the only word I can think of is precious. What a life one leads with them. How complete. Their hats – how perfect – and their shoes, or even minute boots. And the pose of a dolls hand – very dimpled with spreading fingers. Female dolls in their nakedness are the most female things on earth . . .'[59] Dolls, like her own Ribni, have a fascination for Katherine, as mute companions, as surrogate children. And then there is the piece she had written in her journal, years ago, remembering her dead baby sister on Grandmother's lap and the photographer taking the picture that hung on the nursery wall, with the dolls' house – a whole world of childhood exploration – permanently visible in the background. Four weeks later, Katherine is writing to Pinker asking if he can find a home for a story called 'The Dolls House', though it is too late to include it in her new collection.

By November, after the long summer bout of writing, Katherine is feeling tired and unable to work. She accuses herself of wasting time. 'There the work is, there the stories wait for me, grow tired, wilt, fade, because I will not come . . . What is to be done.'[60] A great deal of Katherine's lethargy is caused by the codeine mixture she is being given six times a day for her pain; it makes her feel at one remove from reality during the day and gives her vivid dreams at night. She jokes about her physical condition, composing a variant on 'Mary, Mary quite contrary'. In Katie's garden the only things that grow are

> Doctor's bills
> And chemist's pills
> And hot bottils all in a row . . .[61]

But she is actually better in herself than she has been for a long time. Ida's presence means she can rest and conserve all her energy for writing, and having John beside her gives her the mental peace and emotional stability she needs. Then a letter arrives from Kot telling Katherine about a Russian physician in Paris, Ivan Manoukhin, Gorky's doctor, who claims to have discovered a new cure for tuberculosis, using radiation. Katherine writes to Kot for his address. 'If there was a chance of seeing him and if he was not too expensive I would go to Paris in the Spring and ask him to treat me.'[62] There is no hurry. But on 29 November, Katherine learns that her second cousin, Sir Sydney Beauchamp, who had examined her in London, has been killed in an accident. It gives Katherine a terrible jolt. The same day she writes again, this time more urgently to Kot, asking for information. 'I want to stop this illness, as soon as possible.' At the beginning of December, she writes in French to Manoukhin that she would like to try his treatment. 'I have been ill for four years. Both lungs have been attacked and my heart is also affected. All the same, I am not seriously ill.'[63]

She does not want to be uprooted from her quiet life at the chalet, but she longs, more than anything else, to be cured, to be able to fulfil herself as a writer. Elizabeth disturbs her by suggesting that if she does recover, she may no longer write.

In December the bitter cold of the mountains has settled around the chalet. John is shivering as he sits with Katherine in her room and she is so ill that she is confined to bed. 'The cold is terrifying . . . One can't work: one's brain is frozen hard & I can't breathe better than a fish in an empty tank . . . I would leave here tomorrow but where can one go? One begins the wandering of a consumptive – fatal! Everybody does it and dies.'[64] But while Katherine is still bed-bound over Christmas, a letter from Manoukhin arrives. The treatment takes fifteen weeks and is effective, providing the tuberculosis is not too far advanced. Katherine is determined, as soon as she is well enough, to go to Paris and ask if she can be treated. If he agrees she will return to Paris in May. There are terrible arguments with John, who does not want her to go. He feels that the alpine air has improved her health, though it is actually the domestic peace and tranquillity that have made the difference. The latest relapse has reminded Katherine just how sick she is. 'Why am I haunted every single day of my life by the nearness of death and its inevitability! . . . And I can't speak of it. If I tell J. it makes him unhappy. If I don't tell him it leaves me to fight it. I am tired of the battle. No one knows how tired.'[65] She dare not ignore any possible cure. Only a miracle can help her now and Manoukhin promises just that. She tells Elizabeth that this is her last chance.

John is very reluctant to accompany Katherine to Paris, despite her frailty. He disapproves of what she is doing and wants to stay at the chalet to work. Katherine says nothing, but privately she feels that it is yet another example of his lack of regard for her. It's Ida who helps Katherine down to the front entrance, who picks her up when she slips trying to get into the sleigh, Ida who carries the bags and the fur rugs and organises hotels and train tickets. But John does go to the station at Sierre to say goodbye, with a 'quick but not hurried kiss'.[66]

On 31 January Katherine writes to John from Paris to report that she has already seen Manoukhin. Each treatment will cost 300 F – as much as her weekly allowance – but he has said, 'I can promise to cure you – to make you as though you never had this disease.' His partner, Dr Donat, has also told her that there are 'absolutely no cavities' in her lungs and therefore she is 'absolutely curable'.[67]

PART VII

A Religion of Love

Love does not work miracles. It did not save
Katherine or Violet from death. It did not save Betty from
wanting to kill me.

JOHN MIDDLETON MURRY, 26 MARCH 1940

22

Keeping Faith

I ask myself: 'have I kept faith with my darling?' And I feel deep in my soul a great joy, because I know that I have. And then I feel strangely that I am in touch with her . . . it is as though she gazed into my soul . . .

JOHN MIDDLETON MURRY, DIARY, 1947

By 1940, John was more exhausted and emotionally bankrupt than he had ever been. He was also at his most unpopular as a critic and author. His alignment with the pacifist Peace Pledge Union at the outbreak of war in 1939 meant his views were out of step with the mood of the country, and his romantic and intuitive approach to criticism meant that he was regarded as outmoded by the literary establishment. Katherine had upbraided him frequently for being unable to get beyond 'the personal' in his writing. John read Katherine's terse analysis of his style again as he transcribed the letters she had written to him towards the end of her life. 'I think as a critic that me or us is superfluous. If they must be there then you must write a poem or a story . . .' She felt that there was too much self-consciousness in his work. 'When you know you are a voice crying in the wilderness cry but don't say "I am a voice crying in the wilderness." To my thinking (and I am as you know so infinitely incomparably nearer the public than you) the force of either the blow you strike or the

407

praise you want to sing is broken by this.'[1]

There were too many memories in John's life now. 'The possibility of life lies in forgetting, not in remembering,' he had written after Violet's death. 'For who, consciously remembering the agonies and disasters of the past, would dare to hope and be brave again? Consciousness would make cowards of us all.'[2] In editing Katherine's work, John coped by subtly altering the significance of past events, and by being selective in what he remembered. It was the only way he could go on.

The approach of war was ominous for those who had experienced 1914. The whole world seemed to be undergoing a painful dislocation. John listened to Prime Minister Neville Chamberlain's broadcast on 3 September 1939 with increasing sadness. 'The news today is so grim it fills me with foreboding – bringing back memories of the days, the months rather – when Katherine and I were parted from one-another and held apart.'[3] Now, his public and private lives were again in turmoil. John was reluctantly realising that, for the sake of his health and sanity, he must separate from Betty, even though this would mean leaving the children he loved profoundly. Although passionately in love with Mary Gamble, he veered between conviction, doubt and despair.

This time, however, John had fallen in love with a strong woman, whose personality contained not a flicker of neurosis, and who was prepared to dedicate her life to loving him. Soon after they met, Mary told a woman friend that if John wanted a permanent relationship, 'I should not mind in the least if I never spoke at another meeting, or wrote another article, or sat on another committee. I should be utterly happy mending his socks, and doing his washing, and cooking for him.'[4] It surprised everyone that Mary, who had always been independent and single-minded, could so willingly contemplate subsuming her life into John's. But their compatibility and sense of 'oneness' made for intense happiness. John wrote in his diary: 'Mary is the woman part and I the man part of a single being . . .We live in an uninterrupted communion with each other.'[5] Their growing emotional closeness was not harmed by John's initial impotence. His physical health and the recent nervous breakdown meant he was unable to be Mary's lover on the first occasions they spent the night together. But mutual trust had a healing effect. By the autumn Mary was able to write of 'the sheer delight of his love-making. The magic of his touch which sent thrill after thrill through my body. The look in his eyes when he fell in love with me as he put it, "over and over again". The exquisite moment when I lay waiting for him to join me. Passionately, tenderly, I loved my lover.'[6] She gave John what he had always needed – absolute, unconditional love and this time, it was not an illusion. His relief and happiness were recorded in his journal. 'During the last war I was starved of physical love. This war has been my slow and gentle entrance into greater riches of physical love than I had ever dreamed: it is as though the extremity of inhuman destruction were matched, and somehow denied, by the perfection of human joy . . . I cannot help, at least, thinking sometimes that the entire blissfulness of our love must have some meaning beyond itself. At any rate, I am convinced that love such as ours is the one complete and simple reply to the war.'[7] John had learnt a great deal from his previous relationships, particularly with Katherine. He wrote to Mary, 'A little while after you had gone, I found myself saying to myself aloud: "Well, she is lovely." I caught myself saying it, and I vowed to myself that I would remember to tell you. I remember Katherine once said to me: "I know you think all sorts of nice things about me, but why don't you say them sometimes? A woman does so love to hear them." So, I've let you overhear that simple one.'[8]

After a year of brief meetings, snatching days and nights whenever they could, against the background of air raids, the evacuation of Dunkirk and bleak newspaper headlines, the security provided by Mary's love gave John the courage to make a partial break with Betty, though he still could not bring himself to leave his children. Mary had to accept that they could live together for only part of the week, and this meant moving from Lincolnshire to Norfolk to be nearer to John. Mary's only stipulation was that her friend Ruth Baker, who had been her companion for more than ten years, should be included in their household. 'The possibility of causing unhappiness to [Ruth] had been a constant fear at the back of my mind. We had been friends for a very long time, and had shared a flat together in London for ten years before we moved to Grey Garth. Rooted in love and trust our friendship was indeed surpassing. The inevitable separation, which my relation with John involved must, I knew, cause her suffering.' John apparently groaned, 'Oh God, not another Baker!', but gave in gracefully because he liked Ruth.[9]

Ruth and Mary rented out their cottage in Lincolnshire and moved to the Adelphi Centre at Langham in June 1940. The centre's focus had subtly changed since its foundation. Max Plowman, a close friend of Mary's before she had met John, had been living there with a group of young Basque refugees displaced by the Spanish Civil War. The children had gradually been repatriated as the war came to an end and in 1939 the centre had become a home for elderly evacuees from the east end of London. Max had put together a team of conscientious objectors to repair the house and buildings, and this group now also wanted to stay, with a view to establishing a community working on the land. This was a project very close to Max's heart. But these two diverse groups of different ages and with very different needs had become problematic for Max to manage. In the end the evacuees occupied the main centre building, and the young volunteers moved into an adjacent cottage. Their self-styled leader, a twenty-four-year-old Quaker called Geoff, caused problems for both Max and John because of his tendency to dominate the others. Mary, a born organiser, brought an infusion of common sense to this conflict of male egos. Ruth Baker was also a valuable addition: tactful, self-effacing and willing to work hard, she quickly took over secretarial and administrative roles at the centre. John sometimes came to stay at Langham for one or two nights and Mary rented a cottage nearby at Dedham where they could have more privacy.

In June 1940 John was asked to be the editor of *Peace News*. This meant that he had to be in London two or three days a week. He and Mary took a small bed-sit in Finsbury Park, which they hoped was far enough from the city centre to avoid the bombing, and John began to re-establish his literary career. The BBC asked him to do a series of radio talks on 'Europe in Travail'. John believed that the roots of this war lay in the mistakes made by the Treaty of Versailles in 1919, as well as subsequent government policy, which had caused massive unemployment. 'Modern society has found no way of keeping its machines moving and its members at work, save by preparing for war.'[10] Mary sat at home listening to 'the strange intriguing music'[11] of John's voice delivering ideas that he feared would be anathema to those caught up in the first enthusiasm of the conflict with Hitler. The broadcasts brought John an avalanche of fan mail but also provoked questions in the House of Commons, where an embarrassed Harold Nicolson found himself defending the government against a charge that they had allowed a known communist and active pacifist a public platform during a period of national emergency.[12] It was a criminal offence to do or say anything that might cause 'alarm and despondency' in the country. John, who had censored others during the Great War, now found himself censored. Fear of a 'sixth column' of informers and spies was rife in Britain. Detectives came to the Adelphi Centre and also searched Larling, while the village policeman kept an eye on John in the workshop. They found nothing, but John knew he was constantly under surveillance.

John was never good at keeping secrets. Betty quickly found out that he was living with Mary for part of the week. She could not accept his sleeping with another woman, even though he no longer slept with her. There were violent public scenes witnessed by the neighbours. 'I die daily,'[13] John confessed to a friend. The children were inevitably drawn into the conflict and John asked Weg to post letters to Mary, hiding them in her school books until she passed the letter box. Weg noticed the name on the envelope but never asked any questions. It was enough that her father thought it important: 'A life-line, any life-line for him'.[14] But the risks for her, if Betty had found out, were very great. Betty was now so jealous of Weg that she was forbidden to sit with John on the train when he left for London: Weg had to travel in the school compartment, her father in another. But on the way home Weg would join him secretly for the first part of the journey, transferring back to her own compartment before they reached Thetford, where Betty would be waiting with the car.

By the end of 1940 the contrast between the domestic hell at Larling and John's tranquil, constructive relationship with Mary was extreme. It was obvious to everyone that he could not continue to live in two places at once. The dilemma, as always, was his children. He believed implicitly that Weg and Col, now fifteen and fourteen, would come to live with him if he required them to do so, but he also knew that Betty would never allow John access to Mêh and David, and would prevent Weg and Col from seeing them too. 'You keep your children and I'll keep mine,' was Betty's constant refrain. If John left, he would be splitting up the family, and his two younger children would be entirely exposed to their mother's vindictive temper. David was now 'an angelic, utterly adorable little boy of three . . . hopelessly bewildered by his mother's extraordinary alternations of mood' and his father's absences. David followed his older siblings around, gaining from them 'the love that was denied him elsewhere'.[15] As John noted, 'The children here, through a common suffering, have learned to live a strange and wonderful close-knit life of their own'.[16] They were also very attached to their nanny, Ruby, who had been looking after them since they first moved to Larling and was the one secure and reliable human being in their lives. But Ruby was about to be recruited into the war effort, leaving the children completely unprotected.

Larling just had to be endured, as Weg later wrote in her diary – 'Its subterfuge, its trickeries, its obscenities . . . The destructiveness of it.'[17] The general consensus was that Betty was mad: in Col's words, 'we should, all four, have been ruined for life'.[18] Weg observed that 'the brains of his children were almost paralysed by their suffering'.[19] Col was struggling at boarding school, unable to concentrate on his academic work, and feeling as if he was 'swimming desperately for my life in three feet of water'.[20] He was saved by the discovery that he could write, spilling his feelings into stories and poems. Weg, who also had a gift for words, had not yet discovered that she could do the same. Everything was internalised: 'The psychological wounds I suffered were too deep ever to be healed.'[21] Mêh kept her own counsel throughout her life, but David became a damaged, unhappy young adult whose life ended tragically in his twenties. 'In the debacle when all was broken up at Larling,' Weg wrote, 'David was sacrificed.'[22]

The death of Max Plowman in the summer of 1941 altered the balance of John's priorities. Max had been ill for some time with an unspecified complaint. Friends noticed that he looked tired and had grown thin and grey. In June he developed pneumonia and was dead within a few days. His death, a terrible shock for friends and family, also meant that John had to take a much higher profile role at the Adelphi Centre, and he was soon spending more and more time at Langham and less at Larling. He and Mary bought a row of labourers' cottages and converted them into a house for themselves and Ruth to live in.

The strain of leading a double life with so many commitments began to tell on John. Once more on the brink of nervous collapse, he even speculated in his diary on the moral justification for murdering Betty. He arranged a meeting between the two women, though it was not clear what he hoped to achieve by it and the result was predictably disastrous. There were violent scenes and Betty scrawled across John's journal, 'Mary Gamble is just a rotten dirty woman & so is Middleton Mury rotten'.[23] In the end, John decided that, while he was going through his own particular Gethsemane, it was necessary to separate from Mary in order to shield her from Betty's wrath, and also to prevent his love for her influencing his judgement. Only he alone could make this decision, in what Mary described as a kind of 'knightly vigil'.[24] She went through torture, but clung to the belief that the separation would be temporary, that their bond was too strong to be broken.

At first it was a relief 'to be alone and to be in love', and inevitably his thoughts went back to his life with Katherine, who had said 'that was exactly what I liked; to be alone and in love with her. When she was actually there it "complicated" things. Oh, oh! There was more than a grain of truth in it, I fear.'[25] For several weeks, John wrestled with despair and loneliness, fending off Betty's rages and trying to come to some sort of legal settlement for the good of the children. Betty's terms were simple: she would keep Larling and the children and John could bugger off with his mistress. Betty stole his private diaries and letters and gave them to her own solicitor as evidence of his adultery, even though she was refusing to divorce him, and the situation deteriorated into a messy and undignified fight over children and property. Betty also tried to reassert the powerful pull of sexuality, but this time it failed. She referred to Mary as 'the old drunk' and could not understand why John should prefer a woman she described as a dried-up spinster with a face like a monkey. John was advised that he could get a divorce on the grounds of mental cruelty, but he was still trying to hold everything together. He failed to persuade Betty that he could spend half the week with Mary – the kind of compromise she had agreed to with Helen Young – and the prospect of a life without Mary seemed insupportable.

Eventually John's nerve gave way. The following week he telephoned Mary and left Larling with only a suitcase. 'That's over,' John told her when she met him at the station. 'I shall never go back again.'[26] Mary was horrified by his physical condition. He had lost a great deal of weight and looked ten years older than he actually was, but he was finally convinced that he had taken the only course open to him. 'We have to be together; and though I have no idea what will finally happen about the children and Larling, I must stick to the one certainty I have.'[27] Friends could not understand how he could leave his children behind – one commented, 'I would not have left my dog, even for a day'.[28] Some thought that John was still following Lawrence's theory of '"male purpose". . . The man had to forge ahead, the woman and children coming after him.' But Lawrence had had no children and did not understand the bond. 'He never had to alter his course because of the woman and children.'[29]

The first few weeks were desperate, as John grieved for the children Betty refused to allow him to see. At one point, he begged Mary to have a child for him. It was a terrible moment for her. She had often, passionately, wanted to have a child by John, but she feared that their unmarried status would cause too much offence to her family and friends – who had only just accepted her relationship – and illegitimacy would be a problem for the child. There was also her age: she was forty-one. Afterwards Mary always told people that she had refused John because it was wrong to conceive a child simply to be a sticking plaster for a parent's grief. But her diaries tell another story. For a while it seems that they both hoped for a child – she consulted a doctor who told her there was no reason why she should not have a 'beautiful baby' – but nothing happened.[30]

They set up home together at Langham in the converted cottages. At Larling, things were quieter without John. Betty took to her bed, 'the scrubbing and the cleaning were abandoned'.[31] Because Weg was no longer a rival for John's attention, Betty's attitude towards her softened. But it did not last for long. Weg went for a few days' holiday with a friend in London and on the way back to Norfolk she met her father at Liverpool Street Station. John took her to the café for tea and introduced her to an unknown woman sitting at the table, saying simply, 'This is Mary'. Weg observed that she was wearing black, which contrasted strangely with her white skin. Under the black hat with its dark veil, 'her blue eyes were very extraordinary: they were extremely pale, as near to being transparent as eyes could possibly be yet clouded: like little blue pools of water troubled by clouds overhead'.[32] Back at Larling that evening, Betty guessed, by uncanny intuition, that Weg had met Mary while she was in London and when Weg denied it, Betty came at her with a knife in the kitchen and had to be restrained by the gardener.

Through December and January, Weg lodged during the week near her school and went back to Larling only at weekends. Her love for David continued to keep her there and she still hoped, somehow, that one day her father would come back, Betty would be calm and reasonable and everything would be perfect. But on 31 January, Weg suddenly realised that she could not face going home again. Constantly in pain, she was experiencing upsurges 'of fear and agony, a kind of crucifixion'.[33] On Friday afternoon, instead of going to the station, she went to the home of her headmistress, Miss Wood, and asked for asylum. John was summoned from Langham and Mary drove him over to Thetford, Weg's belongings were collected from Larling by John and Miss Wood, while Betty was out, and arrangements were made for Weg to stay with the headmistress temporarily. But there was one more scene to be played out. When Betty returned and realised what had happened she went straight to the school. Weg was on stage for the dress rehearsal of the school play when Betty, dragging Mêh behind her, burst into the hall, shouting obscenities. Weg ran for the safety of the headmistress's door with Betty in pursuit and Mêh crying 'Mummy! Mummy!' John was in the sitting-room talking to the headmistress about Weg's future and Mary was also there, waiting to drive him home. Betty attacked Mary, pulling her hair out by the roots. Eventually, Betty was persuaded to leave and Weg went back to Langham with John.

To Mary's relief, Weg appeared to accept her as a stepmother, but Weg suppressed her real feelings out of love for her father: '. . . he never knew of my misgivings, or of the strange sadness within me'.[34] Weg's anger was confided to her diaries. As she grew older she wrote of the 'sick relationship' between Mary and Ruth, which she could hardly tolerate, and 'the old, old fear of pain, of confrontation' that still afflicted her, as well as the sense of being used rather than valued – 'I am a SKIVVY for D's wives – that is all'.[35] But she also recorded the terrible ambivalence of her feelings: 'How I have loved those step-mothers . . . how I have curried their favour! . . . I longed for them to love me.'[36]

John assumed that, as Weg was now living with him, that Col would prefer to do so too. But Col wanted to spend his school holidays with his siblings at Larling and was very angry when his father 'simply took it for granted that I must wish to do what Weg had done . . . God knows, it wasn't as if he *needed* me with him. He had Weg and the woman he loved, surely they were enough. Yet here he was appealing to *my* loyalty to him. It was unfair – monstrously unfair. Why, he wasn't thinking of *me* at all, but of *himself*, of *his* happiness.' Col felt that if he went back to Larling he would forfeit his father's love, and run the risk of being thrown out by Betty anyway, but if he joined his father at Langham, he 'would be damned as a traitor in Betty's eyes and would forfeit all chance of ever living at Larling again'.[37] He loved Larling and he loved Mêh and David; his father was a much more remote figure who had always preferred Weg. But Col knew that he would have to obey his father. His only hope, he realised, was to make Mary like him so that life at Langham was at least bearable.

On Monday 30 March Col went from school to Paddington Station where he had arranged to rendezvous with his father, only to find that he was expected to travel up to Norfolk alone. He was met by Mary at the station, without any introduction. She was terrified that she would make a bad impression and let John down by alienating his son, but Col, the perfect diplomat, was charming and helpful. Back at Adelphi Cottages,

Col was introduced to Ruth Baker and took to her immediately. It was all easier than anyone had hoped, and more than John deserved. To Mary's relief, John's children accepted her presence in their lives, and treated her politely. The reservations they had about yet another stepmother and the grief they felt at being parted from their siblings at Larling was kept private. As Col had anticipated, Betty made it clear that he could not have a foot in both camps: if he chose to live with John he could not visit Larling. Col was devastated by the separation from his younger siblings.

John, still only fifty-two and looking for a new start, was thinking more and more about farming as a career. He had always enjoyed growing things and cultivating the garden had made him feel close to the natural order of the world. Katherine had often joked that when John dug a vegetable bed he dug as deep and as earnestly as if he was digging a grave. Just before she died, Katherine had written him a letter about his future. He was too intellectual, she told him; he should get nearer to the earth. 'Grow things. Plant. Dig up. Garden. I feel with all the force of my being that "happiness" is in these things . . . Do anything to work with your hands in contact with the earth.' He should also have animals. 'Birds – rabbits – a goat – anything, and live through it or them . . . I am trying to tell you what I feel deep down is your way of escape . . .'[38] The war had made John think about different ways of living and he wanted to try the same kind of experiment that he had begun at the Adelphi Centre, but this time with a farm – a proper farm rather than the desultory collection of scattered fields at Langham that was barely a smallholding. Would it be possible for a diverse group of people to buy a run-down farm and make it into a profitable enterprise, while living as a community? He envisaged a group of pacifists, engaged in work on the land, in the way that Ottoline Morrell and her husband had run Garsington in 1917. He and Mary were discussing the possibility in the kitchen at Adelphi Cottages on the same February day that the Air Ministry decided to requisition the centre for the war effort. This meant that the residents would be homeless. The evacuees could be relocated, but what would happen to the Farm Group? Suddenly it seemed to be meant.

John quickly found Lodge Farm at Thelnetham in Norfolk, not far from Larling. It had 73 hectares of neglected land and a huge house that could accommodate the volunteers. John bought it for £3325 and moved in on 2 October 1942. It was a big purchase for someone whose capital was still tied up in Larling and the Adelphi Centre, and who was now supporting two families, but John had always been a hoarder, squirrelling money away against the future, and – as well as his editorial salaries and earnings from his books – he was still receiving Katherine's royalties and Violet's allowance. To make up the shortfall, John sold some of Katherine's manuscripts. 'It is Katherine who has bought this farm for us,' John wrote in his journal a few days later, 'and Violet who has stocked it.'[39]

John now had to run a large agricultural business with only his instincts and a few theoretical books to guide him. He kept meticulous records, listing every field in his notebooks and writing down the amount of fertiliser, method of cultivation and yield. He bought a small number of pedigree red poll cattle, to be called the Adelphi Herd, a pregnant sow, and four Suffolk Punch horses, as well as an assortment of second-hand farm machinery. The volunteers – ten men and two women – were transferred from Langham. Geoff, hated by most but liked by John, was still nominally in charge of this assortment of young, enthusiastic people with little experience of farm work. One of their first tasks was to repair the farmhouse, which was almost as neglected as the land. There was no bathroom or indoor toilet and only well water. Cooking facilities were also primitive – Mary initially had to cater for fifteen people on an open range. But within a year there was an Aga in the kitchen, bathrooms were installed, an artesian well had been drilled, a domestic rota had been established for cooking and cleaning and life at Lodge Farm settled down.

The project was flawed from the beginning. There was no real definition of what the 'community' was, no articulated common aims and ideals and no agreement on remuneration. John wanted only a return on the capital he had invested in the farm, in the form of interest at 3½ per cent, but even this small amount upset the socialist sensitivities of the volunteers. Their income was also a thorny subject. At the centre, they had all drawn money for their needs from a common pot, financed by the Adelphi organisation, which had been run at a loss. Now the money was coming from John's own pocket and a loss could not be contemplated. John immediately laid down rules: each individual could draw a maximum of 10s. as an allowance, though bed and board was free in return for their physical labour. The members of the community objected, because they felt that these terms relegated them to the status of hired farm labourers.

John then offered to provide the purchase cost of the farm as a loan to the community, which, if they made it sufficiently profitable, could be paid off in a few years. They would then own it outright. But the more militant members of the group saw this as blatant capitalism and did not want the responsibility. The matter of responsibility became a battleground between John and the volunteers. The group was careless about implements they had never had to pay for, and about their working hours. The hay might need to be brought in before the rain, but it mattered little to some members whether this was accomplished or not, since they were not financially liable for the consequences. John called the group together and gave them a lecture on the mutual obligations of community members and the problems of communally owned possessions. What he wanted to foster was 'a continual increase in personal responsibility. That is essential if we are to have due respect for persons and things.'[40] His fundamental mistake, he realised afterwards, was that he had forgotten what it was like to be young.

John and Mary found communal living difficult. The other members never felt quite comfortable under the same roof as 'the Big Three', as they called Mary, Ruth and John. Conversations came to a halt when they walked into a room and occasionally there was outright hostility, particularly to Mary. The other women found her 'school-mistressy' and they called her 'Milady' behind her back. Ruth coped better, but John simply did not enjoy living with a houseful of young people, even though he and Mary spent three days a week in London. But when Weg and Col were home from school it was impossible to create any semblance of home life for them and Col hated being expected to work on the farm with the others. Things became even more complicated when Geoff fell in love with Weg, now seventeen and growing into a beautiful young woman. For Weg, this was a new experience. 'Until I was 17 I didn't know what the sensation happiness was. I remember my surprise when I first experienced it. Instead I had a knowledge of human suffering, was homeless and had always been an outcast, craved love and affection and belonging.'[41] Urged by Mary, it became clear to John that separate accommodation would have to be found for the family. A derelict cottage on the farm was renovated and sold to Ruth Baker, and when a nearby house that John and Mary had always admired came onto the market, they bought it immediately changing its name to Lower Lodge. It was close enough to allow John to oversee the management of the farm, but far enough away to maintain their independence. Ruth remained in the cottage, but came to the house daily to act as John's secretary.

Having recently written an attack on the church's support for the war – *The Betrayal of Christ by the Churches*, published in 1940 – John was at work on a book called *Adam and Eve*, in which he tackled the complex relations between men and women. In a strange juxtaposition of texts, the draft chapters were written on the back of page proofs of his edition of Katherine's 'Scrapbook'. In *Adam and Eve*, John declared that Lawrence had been wrong to say that physical and spiritual love were incompatible. His own experience – of spiritual love for Katherine and Violet, physical love for Betty and finally both for Mary – had shown that each was necessary for a perfect relationship. This kind of complete human love was also essential for society and the church was making a great mistake to ignore it, treating sex as a sin and insisting on duty and the institution of marriage at the expense of love. 'This is a matter in which my whole religious belief, my whole integrity as a man, is utterly involved.'[42] Weg later thought that John's account of 'Love, Fear and Resurrection' in the book was of primary importance for anyone trying to understand his psyche. It was written out of his own personal suffering: 'at Larling I witnessed his crucifixion as no-one else did'.[43]

John was also writing books and pamphlets that were more political, though just as personal.[44] He looked forward to the re-establishment of socialism after the war, aware, unlike other commentators, of the difficulties that the centralised power created by the war machine would present to a peacetime society. The problems of capitalist economics and the move towards globalisation threatened democracy itself. This, John argued, could thrive only in 'communities of such a size that men can grasp and understand them as a whole, and be continually conscious of their obligations to one another within them'.[45] His writings made him new friendships, notably with novelist Henry Williamson, author of *Tarka the Otter*, who was farming nearby and who became a frequent visitor to Lower Lodge. John was conscious of an intensity of feeling. 'There was between us (perhaps) somewhat the same relation as there was between me and Lawrence at Greatham – in Viola Meynell's cottage – in 1915 ... certainly ... I have not had a comparable feeling for a man since Lawrence.'[46] He defended Williamson, whose fiction, centred on nature and social history, had become unfashionable, in a series of essays, and offered to read and comment on his manuscripts.

At the end of the war, John sold his interest in the *Adelphi*, resigned as editor of *Peace News* and threw himself into life as a landowner and member of the local community. He and Mary both became parish councillors, formed a village hall committee and with Ruth Baker started the amateur Lodge Farm Theatre Company. John wrote some of the plays and toured them round local villages. Management of the farm and its personnel, which had become very contentious, took up more and more of his time. The experiment failed in the end, because it was John's community, his vision, his money. In order to belong, the members had to believe in and be totally loyal to him, rather than to the collective. Old members left after quarrelling with each other, or with John; new members arrived who were totally unsuitable. They included an alcoholic, a homeless ex-priest, three rather insular Glaswegians and a tramp with mental health problems. The public perception was that the farm was run by 'conchies, cranks and queers'.[47] At the end of the war, the conscientious objectors wandered off; two couples loyal to John remained and the farm had now to be worked with employed labour. The whole basis of the enterprise changed: John owned the farm and directed its operations through a manager and hired workers, some of them local, but he also made use of displaced persons or prisoners of war. It was now overtly what it had been all along – the fiction of a 'co-operative' or self-sustaining community had gone.

Lower Lodge was also depleted. The children had both been recruited for military service. Col had been called up into the armed forces as soon as he left school and Weg had elected to train as a nurse in London, though her career was cut short when she was suspected of having a tubercular kidney. Thankfully it was a false alarm, but her kidney was removed as a safeguard. In the final years of the war, Weg had fallen in love with a Polish refugee working at the farm and, like that other Katherine, bought a Polish dictionary and began to learn the language. The relationship foundered when he was repatriated after the war, but Weg had discovered a talent for languages. In 1946 she went first to Exeter University to study French and then in 1949 to Paris to study at the Sorbonne. It was at this point that Weg suddenly decided not to return to Thelnetham and to leave England altogether. The reasons she gave her father for this abrupt departure were not the ones she discussed with her brother Col. Her relationship with Mary had deteriorated and there had been a scene on the staircase at Lodge Farm, where John had made it clear that Mary came first in his life now. Weg, feeling completely betrayed by the father she adored, was consumed by 'the blind desire to run away from England the home of my misery, run away from those step-mothers who would annihilate me with their jealousy'.[48]

In 1946, with both children gone, Mary and John were alone together for the first time. John wrote, 'I live – we live – in a quite new dimension of experience, in which the ordinary is magical.'[49] Their happiness seemed like a miracle, and many of their friends thought that it was well deserved.

Since Ruth Mantz's 1933 biography, there had been several enquiries from other scholars and biographers wanting to write about Katherine's life, including an intriguing letter from a 'Mrs Wharton', but John had turned them all away. After the war there was a new atmosphere of academic democracy and John's role as guardian of Katherine's reputation could no longer be sustained. In 1947 a letter arrived at Lower Lodge from a young New Zealand scholar already working on a biography of Katherine Mansfield. Antony Alpers asked for John's co-operation and was cautiously given it, after John realised that the book would be written whether he wanted it or not. Alpers' intention at the time was to write a new account of Katherine's childhood in New Zealand and her development as a writer, because he felt that Ruth Mantz's book had been unsatisfactory – leaving a great deal unsaid and containing a number of inaccuracies. Many of the people he contacted had been angered by it, including Katherine's first husband, George Bowden, who called it 'an exploitation' and sent Alpers a copy of the letter he had sent to John Murry. Ruth Mantz's account, George wrote, had been 'so lacking in accuracy of circumstance and suggestion as to compel me to take active exception . . . There is a gross violation of fact and a degree of malicious construction to which the reader is invited, which amount to perfidy to one possessing first hand knowledge.' The letter went even further. 'One must doubt if there exists such a tissue of misleading statements purporting to be an authentic record in the whole of British Biography.'[50]

The Beauchamp family had also been incensed by the Mantz biography, and particularly by the impression it gave that Harold Beauchamp had been mean and penny pinching. They backed Alpers. Only a New Zealander could really write about what the country of her birth had meant to Katherine and how it had influenced her work. The New Zealand government officially supported the project and an American scholar, Joan Corbett, who had just arrived in Auckland on a research fellowship for another new biography of Katherine, was forced to abandon her work. She felt very bitter about it, but issued a warning note. 'Murry still holds the bulk of the manuscripts and it is to be doubted that a truly sympathetic and understanding biography can be written during his lifetime.'[51]

Alpers was young and inexperienced, but he was persistent and fired with enthusiasm. He talked to most of Katherine's friends and family and was often told things which he 'didn't understand or didn't believe, at least with sufficient confidence to print them'.[52] As Joan Corbett had predicted, he was hampered by the fact that John was still alive and Alpers feared that he would not be given permission to publish some of the more controversial material he had uncovered. Very few of Katherine's letters or her notebooks were in the public domain – only the selections edited by John – and many other people were reluctant to show Alpers the letters they possessed. Katherine's 'purity' was still being protected. To add to his problems, Alpers quickly realised that, if the biography appeared to be authorised by John, it would be badly received by the critics. He had to tread a very fine line between obtaining John's co-operation and maintaining objectivity.

This task required endless diplomacy: despite the polite exchanges there was a deeply felt antagonism between the two men. And, as Alpers tried to pursue the truth, some of John's friends and former colleagues closed ranks around him. In August 1948 Alpers wrote of his frustration to J. D. Fergusson: 'it encourages me to know that you stand by Murry still. I gather one has to admire him secretly here, if at all; but I can't raise any moral indignation against his conduct to Katherine Mansfield either before or after her death. I hope to have the guts when the time comes to say what I think about him. Meanwhile there is some awkwardness. He is quite naturally distant, knowing that the job takes me into the presence of many people who dislike him. I wish you were here to tell me how to handle it.'[53]

The resulting biography was cautious, but at least it was independent. Some of the information it contained caused John considerable pain. After talking to George Bowden, Alpers had uncovered details of Katherine's marriage that were new to John. He had not known, either, about Katherine's affair with William Orton, who had subsequently become a widely respected historian at an American university. Unnoticed by John, he had published, in 1937, a novel called *The Last Romantic*, which was an autobiographical account of his relationship with Katherine and included excerpts from their letters and the journal they had jointly kept. John's ignorance surprised Alpers, but John told him: 'I knew nothing of Katherine's past . . . it was not for me to pry',[54] though he admitted that it might have been a relief for Katherine if he had at least asked. Unlike Ruth Mantz, Alpers was quite prepared to reveal his findings in print, and for the first time, Katherine's illegitimate baby by Garnet Trowell, her pregnancy at Cheyne Walk and her affair with Francis Carco were all made public. The book did not please everyone who had helped the author. Ida Baker felt betrayed by it, since Alpers had failed to believe some of the things she had told him, even though they were true, and she felt he had portrayed Katherine as a serious and tragic figure: 'Alpers never caught her gaiety – sense of humour – joy at the tiny things of life'. Also deeply offensive was Alpers' portrait of herself as 'a weakly adoring parasite'.[55]

Alpers' research prompted John to return to Katherine's manuscripts and finish the task of editing the rest of her letters and notebooks. He could also refuse access to Alpers, on the pretext that he was working on them himself. On 15 June 1948, John recorded in his diary that he was 'pegging away with the preparations for the new edition of Katherine's letters . . . I have had this on my conscience a long while . . . no one, I believe will ever be able to read Katherine's letters as well as I can. Therefore, before I die, I must produce as complete an edition as I can.' But it was a laborious task, 'settling the order of undated letters, deciphering and transcribing, and it puts a heavy strain on my eyes. Besides, I suppose I am still too implicated in them not to feel a psychological strain also.'[56] He was particularly hurt by the 'disloyalty' of her confidences about their relationship in letters to Sydney Schiff and Koteliansky during the final year of her life. In the end, only Katherine's letters to John found their way into the volume. It was to be a portrait of a relationship, the record of a unique love affair that survived adversity and prospered 'in spite of all'.

On Katherine's birthday he received royalties from Michael Sadleir on the new edition of her stories, which had been published just after the war. He had expected £1000, and was disappointed to find only £277. He imagined Katherine smiling ironically at him, as he wrote the complaint in his diary. The money, he 'told' her, would be put to practical use straight away: 'the £277 will just about pay for the new tractor. This farm is as much yours as anybody.'[57] He admitted to feelings of guilt for having 'capitalized' her work.

Reliving old experiences brought other painful admissions, particularly regret at his love affair with Elizabeth Bibesco. 'Reading Katherine's letters of November 1920 is not a pleasant business. I read them with a kind of sickening apprehension of what is coming . . .'[58] Many of them were included in this edition, giving the impression that he was being absolutely frank. The omissions were subtle. Names were deleted, rendering some passages meaningless. Katherine's poem 'The New Husband' was there, but not the despairing poems that accompanied it. Her horror at the wrong photograph having been sent to Constable for the cover of her book was recorded, but not the story of Elizabeth Bibesco, who appeared only in passing reference as 'A'. There were no letters at all between 11 December 1920 and 11 January 1921, a period not wholly accounted for by John's two-week holiday in Menton. It is possible that these letters, like others, were destroyed. But, in the main, a large number of Katherine's letters to John were published, even those that accused him of meanness and neglect. John held little back, though the negative letters seem by implication – and the assistance of editorial notes – to arise out of the effects of Katherine's illness, rather than his own behaviour. 'The truth was that she was hypersensitive and it was probably a direct consequence of her disease.'[59]

By January 1949 he had completed the task, but he still continued to deliberate on 'past sins'. 'I think I failed in many ways, but I never failed in the essential. K's love for me, my love for her was incommensurable with anything else in my life. Whatever the hesitations, everything gave way before it. And it determined the whole pattern of my life. All that was to come after grew out of that. And though re-reading her letters is in many ways a terrible experience; tempting me to measure myself against perfection and to believe that I might have had the power to ward off the inevitable, – I think it is good.'[60]

In 1949 there were more changes for the family. Betty decided that Larling was too much to cope with on her own and moved to a smaller house near Winchester. Larling was put up for sale. John visited the house on the day of the auction and felt no regrets at letting it go. 'Each room has its own particular memory of horror.'[61] The experience of Larling had left scars on the whole family. Mêh, who had seen her father only once since he left, was shy and fragile. She had failed her matriculation exams and the school had recommended that she take a secretarial course, which she hated. David, now eleven, claimed to have no memory of the first four years of his life and barely remembered John at all. He had failed the 'simple' entrance exam for Christ's Hospital and was struggling academically. There were brief meetings with his father, on neutral territory, for special coaching to get him through the exam. It mattered very much to John that his son should go to his former school, and David was trapped in his father's expectations. The older children had not fared well either. John's intense relationship with Weg had been compromised by his abandonment of her for Mary, and his relationship with Col – despite efforts on both sides to bridge the gap – had become more distant than ever. John did not understand his son and failed to see the damage done by his preference for Weg. 'I am now acutely conscious that Col has an unconquerable resentment towards me, and jealousy of me . . . I agree that it was hard on him that my leaving Betty & Larling should have caused him to be separated from [Mêh] and David. I have admitted too, that at a much earlier age, I rather neglected him, because I was preoccupied with Violet's illness. But these two things together, even if they were immensely magnified, would hardly amount to a justification of his attitude to me.'[62] Col, while conscious that he loved his father in some fundamental unalterable way, swung between extremes of hatred and admiration. As Larling went under the auctioneer's hammer, Col, who had passed the entrance exams for his father's old Oxford college only at the third attempt, became engaged to a young Jewish science student called Ruth Jezierski. John grudgingly admitted that he had become 'a son of whom I can be proud'.[63] In July 1949 Weg married a young Belgian actor and playwright called Jean De Coninck, whom she had met while studying at the Sorbonne. Weg settled in Belgium; Col in Brighton. From now on their lives would diverge.

In 1951, John's edition of *The Letters of Katherine Mansfield to John Middleton Murry* was published and further interest in her life was generated by the publication of a new and totally unauthorised American literary biography of Katherine written by Sylvia Berkman and published by Yale University Press. It was the first serious critical study of Katherine's work and identified her, alongside James Joyce, at 'the head of the broad stream of development in the modern short story'.[64] Sylvia had not relied on John Murry's editions, but had been assisted by a New Zealand collector and members of the Beauchamp family as well as Frieda Lawrence and Dorothy Brett, both now living in America. She had also been allowed to read Antony Alpers' manuscript in draft, which resulted in the revision of some biographical details. This sudden publicity, following a recent reprint of the Constable edition of the stories, focused attention on Katherine for a whole new generation of readers and writers. Then, on 19 October 1951, a lengthy letter appeared in the *Times Literary Supplement* accusing Katherine of plagiarism.

E. M. Almedingen, a British novelist, biographer and children's author of Russian descent, made a detailed case – by quoting parallel passages – for Katherine's story 'The Child who was Tired' being a plagiarised version of a story by Chekhov called 'Spat Kotcheska' (translated as 'Sleepy Head'). This was not the first time such an allegation had been made. As early as 1930 Elizabeth Schneider had pointed out in the *Spectator* that the similarity between the two stories 'is too great for us to suppose them entirely independent'.[65] Immediately John wrote to the *Times Literary Supplement*, refuting the suggestion that Katherine had 'lifted' the plot from Chekhov and arguing that she could not possibly have read an English translation before she wrote her story. Miss Almedingen wrote back, triumphantly citing an English version in 1903. At this point both Sylvia Berkman and Antony Alpers stepped in to argue that Katherine could have seen the story in a German version while at Bad Wörishofen and used it as an exercise in adaptation. They both agreed that, though there were similarities in the plot, Katherine's story was quite different to that of Chekhov.

It is, however, incontrovertible that Katherine 'used' Chekhov's characters and plot as a template. Whether this constitutes plagiarism would take a team of skilled lawyers to unravel and, since both authors are dead, Katherine's story is best regarded as a 'homage' to Chekhov, in the same way that the young John Constable used Claude Lorrain's *Landscape with Hagar and the Angel* as a template for his *Dedham Vale*, copying the composition, the perspective and the balance of light and shade. The structure and the composition were the same, but the landscape Constable painted was his own.

Katherine called the process 'absorbtion' in a letter she wrote to a young writer called Arnold Gibbons in July 1922. 'Perhaps you will agree that we all, as writers, to a certain extent, absorb each other when we love. (I am presuming that you love Tchekhov.) Anatole France would say we eat each other, but perhaps nourish is the better word. For instance Tchekhov's talent was nourished by Tolstoi's *Death of Ivan Ilyvitch*. It is very possible he never would have written as he did if he had not read that story ... All I felt about your stories was that you had not yet made the "gift" you had received from Tchekhov your own. You had not yet, finally made free with it & turned it to your own account.'[66]

In 1951 John went abroad for the first time since the war, and was struck by the differences across the Channel – the food was good and plentiful, if expensive, and the shops were full of goods unobtainable in Britain. The streets were lined with American cars. En route for Switzerland, he went to visit Weg in Belgium, where she and her husband had a new baby boy, also called John. Weg had been quite ill after the birth, spending some months at Lower Lodge before returning to her husband. For John, his first grand-child was another manifestation of Katherine's love. 'I feel that she has watched and is watching my life; that my communion with her through love is so simple and direct and intense at such a moment that all my life is subsumed under it . . . And this heritage of love I saw, renewed, incarnate, in Weg's little baby boy. I am convinced . . . that Katherine's spiritual herit-age has been passed on.'[67] Col was also now married, to Ruth Jezierski, and teaching English at a Jewish school in Sussex. He had just finished his first novel, which was not good enough to find a publisher, but his second, *The Golden Valley*, was in a very different class. It was an account of the years at Larling – minus Betty's brutality. Although the book was good, John did not like it and condemned it for being too autobiographical, afraid that he himself would be identified and his conduct criticised. The book was published in 1953, under the name Colin Middleton Murry, establishing Col as an author in his own right, but it created a further distance between himself and his father.

For John there was also a reunion with the Campbells in Ireland, and to Gordon and Beatrice's consternation, John sent them the letter he had written to Gordon in London thirty-seven years earlier. Gordon never commented on this overt declaration of love from the past, but offered to return the letter. He and Beatrice were very amused when John brought up the subject of the money that he still owed them from the days when he and Katherine had been penniless. 'He said he had not forgotten about it, but for him the debt seemed like a bond between himself and Gordon. He felt that if he paid the debt the bond would be broken.'[68]

John was now tackling what he believed to be his last editorial task – producing another edition of Katherine's manuscripts, which combined the 1927 *Journal* and the 1939 *Scrapbook* into one supposedly definitive edition. Given that he had allowed readers to believe that two distinctly different manuscripts existed, John's new version required a lot of explanation. In the introduction he gave a fuller account of the chaotic nature of Katherine's notebooks and their contents, but still tried to justify his earlier editions. The 'diligence' of both Ruth Mantz and Antony Alpers was acknowledged, as well as the material published by William Orton, which John incorporated into the new edition. But it was still, as critics were quick to point out, 'a brilliant piece of literary synthesis and editorial patchwork'.[69]

When, on 6 February 1954, Betty died suddenly, in the Royal County Hospital at Winchester, from a cerebral haemorrhage caused by high blood pressure, it was something of a shock. Mêh was pursuing a successful career as a nurse, and had been aware of her mother's illness, but David was still only sixteen, a student at Christ's Hospital, hopelessly out of his depth and struggling with depression. There was 'a great growing blank in his mind that there was no way out of'.[70] He would now have to live with a father he had seen only a few times since he was four. The funeral was a melancholy affair, but it was quickly followed by a wedding. Four weeks later, Mary and John were married at the register office in Bury St Edmunds, in a brief ceremony witnessed by a small group of close friends and family. Of the children, Col alone was absent because his daughter was born on the same day. Shortly afterwards, John arranged a family reunion in Brighton, where Col was living. He believed that at last all his children were gathered around him and Mary in complete happiness, but the serenity existed for him alone. Col observed that 'at least three of his children knew otherwise. Above the surface all seemed well enough but in the shadowy depths below, the currents and the counter-currents were running chill. We knew too much, and too much of what we knew we dared not speak about.'[71]

Conflict continued between Weg and Mary, still battling for ascendancy in John's affections. 'I called her "a pig",' Weg wrote. To which Mary retorted, 'You would never talk like that in front of your father. In front of him you always keep so quiet'.[72] But even as she recorded the incident in her diary, Weg also acknowledged the difficulty Mary faced. 'But what an awful step-daughter too to inherit! Moody, secretive "dreary" she once called me, emotionally strung taut, adoring Dadda (no man or woman could hope to be a patch on him!) And with of course a whopping I. [inferiority] C. [complex].'[73]

There was a spate of obituaries in *The Times*. In 1955, Kot died. In recent years he had suffered from heart disease and 'despair in the human condition and about himself'. Kot's depression had been so deep he had even tried to cut his own throat. John's publication of Katherine's letters and journals had upset him greatly. He told a friend: 'If you don't want to suffer pain, don't read the book'.[74] His animosity towards John had remained as strong as ever. But John's own health was also deteriorating. A lifetime of stress, British cuisine and chain smoking had been eating away at his reserves of health since his mid-forties, and John had been describing himself as 'a semi-invalid' since he was fifty. His legs had required several operations to relieve circulatory problems and now, at sixty-six, he walked with a severe limp, was too breathless to walk for more than a hundred metres or so and had begun to suffer from angina.

The following year Frieda Lawrence died and the news left John saddened and nostalgic. He filled pages and pages of his journal with memories of Lawrence and a revaluation of his work. The novels and stories in which Lawrence had used John as a character – *Women in Love*, 'Smile', 'The Last Laugh' – continued to trouble him. Lawrence had, John wrote, killed him off three times. Why? Frieda, too, had been thinking about the complex emotional politics of their relationship before she died. In one of her most recent letters she had written: 'I always told you – and you did not or could not believe me – that L. loved you . . . It never impressed me when he raved at you. Hadn't I known so absolutely that he cared for you? Maybe love does not care so much for male or female, but the ultimate very individual you. People are always shocked when the wife falls in love with the husband's best friend. It is almost inevitable and natural. I think my nose was a bit out of joint when you stayed with us and L. was more interested in you than in me.'[75]

In 1956, the French voted 'The Garden Party' one of the twelve best short stories ever written, and in October that year erected a memorial plaque to Katherine on the Villa Isola Bella at Menton. John and Mary went to Bandol and stayed at the Hotel Beau Rivage. It was the first time he had been there since Katherine died. He limped up the back lanes to look at the Villa Pauline, which had become a benchmark of happiness in his life, and it was as if, in a strange way, he was saying goodbye to Katherine. His children had conflicting views on Katherine. Weg – whose life had been most affected by her – thought that she had had a 'powerful and not necessarily benign influence' on John.[76] She had been the family curse – like

Daphne du Maurier's fictional Rebecca, the third person in all his relationships. John was also beginning to count the cost, writing in his journal: 'I have made of Love all of my religion . . . To this search for integrity – the reconciliation of Heart, Mind, Emotion and Intellect – I have sacrificed whatever talent for art I possessed.'[77]

On the night of 23 February 1957, John began to experience severe chest pain and the doctor told Mary that he was having a heart attack. He recovered from this, but two weeks later there was another, more serious, attack and John was taken into hospital. Mary hoped that he would recover from this too, but John himself was pessimistic. He felt worn out by fighting. When Mary urged him to go on living, John told her, 'I should not have asked Katherine to go on . . . I should be so happy to die tonight.'[78] He asked Mary to let him go peacefully and shortly afterwards lost consciousness. He died soon after midnight. Weg and Mêh were both there, but Col had gone back to Brighton, thinking the crisis was over, and David, who had joined the Merchant Navy, was at sea.

John's will came as a great surprise to many when it appeared in *The Times*. Apart from the property he had owned, he left almost £32,000. Anne Estelle Rice commented that she had always suspected he had a secret 'flair for the Stock Exchange'.[79] Katherine's letters were to be offered to the British Museum for £1000 and, failing that, to the Alexander Turnbull Library in Wellington. His own literary estate, as well as Katherine's, including all manuscript material, passed into the control of Mary, whom John trusted to dispose of everything according to his wishes. In reality, he left a legacy of conflict between his children and their stepmother.

After his funeral at Thelnetham, Mary could hardly believe that he would not 'at any moment, walk through the slender trees by the hedge, in his old grey flannel trousers and his golden jerkin with the zip, and the felt hat with the hole in which he loved to wear for croquet'.[80] Mary comforted herself by reading Katherine's journals and letters, which she was now, with Ruth Baker's help, sorting out for dispersal.

'Last night I came across these words of Katherine Mansfield. "Honesty is the only thing one seems to prize beyond life, love, death everything. O, you who come after me, will you believe it? At the end Truth is the only thing worth having; it is more thrilling than love, more joyful, and more passionate." And as I read them I remembered how much John and I owed to Katherine. O Katherine, Katherine, I never knew you, but so often I feel eternal gratitude for what you were. You and John knew more of the anguish of love than the happiness. You were young, and ill, and a genius. So often you experienced the agony of parting, and the misery of misunderstanding. Then finally your *acceptance* of suffering made you crystal clear for the truth to flow through you, and love was triumphant in "spite of all".'[81]

Weg, who knew more of the truth about 'the Mansfield myth', was sceptical of Mary's sentiments. Weg blamed Katherine for her own deep sense of alienation. 'I always felt, knew indeed, that I had come from somewhere far back, that I belonged not to Larling but elsewhere, I knew not what place.' The sense that she was 'Katherine's child', fostered by John, had haunted her childhood and she blamed all her sufferings upon it. 'My step-mothers were jealous not because I was Dadda's daughter of a previous marriage . . . but because I was the embodiment of Dadda's and Katherine's undying love.' Even now that she was a rational adult, the feeling of kinship persisted. Katherine's suffering and death were more real to Weg than those of her own mother. 'The appalling pain I felt and have always felt at reading Katherine and Between Two Worlds when K becomes ill and dies as compared with Violet's death . . . indicates something very deep and true.' After a lifetime of analysis and rationalisation, in which the influences of her birth mother and her two stepmothers were carefully considered, Weg could write only this admission: 'I can now say to myself (and to anyone else interested) K was my spiritual mother'.[82]

PART VIII

'The Levantine Psychic Shark'

I believe the greatest failing of all is to be frightened.
Perfect Love casteth out Fear. When I look back on my life
all my mistakes have been because I was afraid . . .Was
that why I had to look on death? Would nothing less cure
me? You know, one can't help wondering, sometimes . . . No,
not a personal god or any such nonsense. Much more likely
— the soul's desperate choice . . .

KATHERINE MANSFIELD TO JOHN MURRY, 18 OCTOBER 1920

23

The Soul's Desperate Choice

[T]hrough the mental fog that envelops me I see realities more clearly; such hard and bitter reali-
ties that to write them down will make me cry. But I can't even write them down. What's the
good of it? What's the good of anything? To have passed six years in working ten hours a day to
reach what? The beginning of talent and a mortal illness? . . . If I persist in thinking that 'fame'
is to repay me for everything, I must live, and in order to live I must take care of myself. What
an outlook, what frightful realities.

MARIE BASHKIRTSEFF, PARIS, 24 MARCH 1884

In February 1922, as Katherine takes the train from Switzerland to Paris to consult Gorky's physician Manoukhin, another Russian arrives in Europe from the east on a refugee passport. George Ivanovich Gurdjieff's origins are mysterious. Born more than forty years earlier in the shifting border-lands of Russia and Turkey, to a Greek father and an Armenian mother, his real name, nationality and date of birth are all uncertain. He has travelled to Egypt, India, Persia and Tibet, serviced sewing machines, sold carpets, corsets and cage birds, even practised hypnosis, in order to earn a living. His father had been a bardic poet, or ashokh, and Gurdjieff has been famil-iar with shamanic dancing and the mystic rituals of the east since he was young. He has gained a great reputation in Russia as a teacher of alternative wisdom. Some of his disciples, such as the philosopher P. D. Ouspensky, have become famous in their own right.

Since she was a very young girl, new directions in Katherine's life have been influenced by the books she was reading. As a teenager in Wellington it had been Oscar Wilde and Marie Bashkirtseff; in London it was Walter Pater and Yone Noguchi. At the beginning of 1922 it is a strange text called *Cosmic Anatomy and the Structure of the Ego* by an obscure author called Lewis Wallace, identified on the cover only as 'MB Oxon'. It had been sent to John Murry by Katherine's old mentor Orage, who hoped that he would review it for the *New Age*, but it didn't interest John at all, so he put it aside. Katherine, confined to bed in the Chalet des Sapins by the freezing winter weather, and in the grip of a depression deeper than any she has ever suffered, picks it up and, out of curiosity, begins to read.

The contents are an eccentric mixture of occult philosophy, the theosophical notions held by the followers of Madame Helena Blavatsky, and Gurdjieff's Eastern Gnosticism. Wallace propounds the 'personal time equation' that exhorts us all to 'live in the moment' – something Katherine has always felt to be essential – but it's only when he begins to examine the nature of consciousness and the identity of the self that she becomes fascinated. 'What is the universal mind?' she asks in her notebook. The notion that everything is linked together in one gigantic biosphere seems sensible, and the aims set out by Wallace echo her own longings. She copies them onto the flyleaf of her 1922 diary like New Year's resolutions: 'to escape from the prison of the flesh – of matter. To make the body an instrument, a servant . . . to act and not to dream.'[1] Katherine has always felt that she is too much at the mercy of her own emotions: 'My mind is not controlled. I idle, I give way, I sink into despair . . . I am not as complete as I must be.'[2] It's the concept of wholeness that attracts her most. Katherine has always struggled with her fractured self and as she has grown older the list of selves has grown longer: the cruel satirist, the actress, the clever intellectual, the independent feminist, the neurotic woman, the intense spirit . . . All the Katherines – the romantic and the dark – combine to form a multi-faceted and complex personality she longs to merge into a single, knowable, whole. Towards the end of January, as she travels to Paris to try yet another cure, *Cosmic Anatomy* goes with her on the train. She writes in her notebook: 'I have a suspicion like a certainty that the real cause of my illness is not my lungs at all, but something else. And if this were found and cured, all the rest would heal . . . I must heal my Self before I will be well.'[3]

In Paris Katherine checks herself and Ida into a hotel recommended by Anne Estelle Rice and makes an appointment with the doctor she has heard so much about. Manoukhin is disappointingly ordinary – 'a tall formal rather dry man . . . who speaks scarcely any French and has a lame Russian girl for his interpreter'. He examines Katherine and tells her that, as she only has TB in the 'second degree' he can certainly cure her. It will take fifteen 'seances' at the price of 300 F each, then she must spend the summer months in the mountains and then have another ten seances to prevent a recurrence of the disease. He insists that, rather than go back to Montana and begin the treatment in the spring, she should start now – travelling is very bad for her health. Katherine hesitates, but Manoukhin's secretary tells her that the doctor has already cured almost 8000 people in Moscow – some of them much worse than Katherine – and she should not wait.[4] This little speech is obviously designed to persuade her to sign up for the treatment, and in her notebook that evening Katherine records her immediate reaction: 'I did not believe it'.[5]

But despite her doubts about Manoukhin's credibility, Katherine's rational mind is telling her to stay, to give herself every possible chance of a cure, and this presents a dilemma. She has promised John that she will return after her interview and that they will come back to Paris together in the spring. If she stays she will upset John and destroy the delicate balance of their newly established relationship. He is adamant that he wants to remain at the chalet and work on his new novel – to break off now would be fatal. The following evening Katherine goes back to Manoukhin's flat for more information about the nature of the treatment, its risks and whether there would be any adverse effect on her heart. 'I told him . . . that I could not afford an experiment.' She is examined by his partner Dr Donat, 'an elderly man, rather like Anatole France in style, wearing a white coat and skull cap', and given an impressive lecture, with diagrams, about the way the spleen is blasted with radiation and the effect of this on the blood. 'The whole thing is new. That I realized keenly. It is the latest thing in science . . . One felt in the presence of real scientists – not doctors.' They offer her the hope, the 'real hope', that Katherine has been longing for.[6] But her instincts are still urging caution. She confesses her reservations to John in a letter, asking his advice. 'I hear, I see. I feel a great confidence in Manoukine – very great, and yet . . . I am absolutely divided . . . A dark secret unbelief holds me back. I see myself, after 15 goes, apologising to them for not being cured, so to speak.'[7] In her notebook she is even more frank. 'I have also a sneaking feeling – I used that word sneaking advisedly – that is he is a kind of unscrupulous imposter.'[8]

But Katherine wants desperately to live and dare not turn down any chance of a cure, however remote. Constable have just given her a big advance for her new collection, The Garden Party, which will pay some of the medical bills. She decides to stay and begin treatment at once. John's relief at being on his own, without the strain of anxiety about her health, is audible in the subtext of his letters. Katherine is scathing about it. '[He] talks of coming to "fetch" me in May. Well, if I am any better there will never be any more fetching. Of that I'm determined.'[9] Cosmic Anatomy has given Katherine a new way of looking at John. 'He is absolutely entangled in himself as usual.' She refers to him as 'the shellfish', a reference to his introverted personality and a dig at his self-involvement.[10]

Katherine's first 'seance' is more unpleasant than she had expected. Donat shouts at her and asks 'indecent questions' about bodily functions. Katherine cringes at the humiliation of her illness, the loss of control it brings, the way it reduces the patient to a level of infantile dependency.

The radiation gives Katherine palpitations and makes her feel nauseous as she tries to work in her hotel room afterwards. 'At night I had one of my terrible fits of temper over a pencil.'[11] But part of her black mood is generated by feelings of abandonment. John takes another two weeks before he realises that he should be in Paris with Katherine and, after some reluctant letters, and protests from Katherine that he must not, absolutely must not, alter his plans just because she seems to need him, he appears at the Victoria Palace hotel with a suitcase and a box of books. They take adjacent rooms – 'I am number 134 and Murry is number 135'[12] – and Katherine begins a story based around the paradox of their physical proximity and emotional distance: 'if a fire had broken out & we had been unable to move and only our charred bodies found, it would have been the most natural thing in the world for people to suppose we were – together'.[13]

Ida goes back to the chalet at Montana to pack up their belongings and try to find a tenant for the remainder of the lease and a new home for Wingley. Letters fly backwards and forwards, generating intense misunderstanding. Katherine is irritated by Ida's inability to deal with the closing up of the chalet and the posting of clothes and other essentials to Paris. Ida does her best, wanting to be able to say, 'There darling, it's all quite all right; I'm doing a job, I can manage, you don't need to worry',[14] but she has no talent for this kind of organisation. She dithers, and then, afraid of doing the wrong thing, does just that. Ida is also hampered by her poor command of the French language. 'How could I find out about the cheapest way of sending Katherine her belongings? How to sort out the distracting Swiss and French laws and customs? . . . How to get goods to the station, the post?'[15] There are several sharp letters from Katherine that elicit an emotional protest from Ida. Katherine's response is caustic. 'I don't believe in your shivering and shaking because of my barks. That's fantastic. If you don't yet know the dog I keep you never will.' But then she is more penitent. 'You mustn't be so silly as to imagine because I am such a horrible creature I don't love you. I am a kind of person under a curse . . . I can't say "nice" things to you. In fact I behave like a fiend. But ignore all that. Remember that through it all I love you and understand. That is always true.'[16]

Since John is determined to stay with Katherine in Paris and there is, theoretically, no need for Ida's help if they are living in a hotel, Ida plans to go back to England once she has packed up the chalet, and set up a tea shop on the south coast with a friend. Katherine sends her money and promises her £10 a month until the shop is earning enough to keep her. Katherine has supported Ida from her own income for the last few years and this has more than repaid the financial assistance Ida gave Katherine when she first came to England and again at intervals since. Ida's generosity has always been in stark contrast to John's penny-pinching instincts. Katherine is also familiar with Ida's capacity for self-sacrifice: 'I am sure you are being too careful about money. There's a false carefulness in your letters. I therefore send you £2.2.0 which I don't want to hear of again . . . also – are you having enough food? I mean by that decent meals – not bread or pudding.'[17]

The Garden Party is published at the end of February to ecstatic reviews that bring a jealous, snobbish, reaction from Virginia Woolf: 'So what does it matter if K.M. soars in the newspapers, runs up sales sky-high? Ah I have found a fine way of putting her in her place. The more she is praised, the more I am convinced she is bad. After all, there's some truth in this. She touches the spot too universally for that spot to be of the bluest blood.'[18] Leonard agrees and blames John for encouraging the sentimental streak in Katherine's work which threatens to weaken its fabric. John has 'corrupted and perverted and destroyed Katherine both as a person and a writer'.[19] Rebecca West admires what the Woolfs despise, contending that Katherine's stories are prose poems, validating her avowed aim to write 'not in poetry' but in a 'kind of special prose'.[20] William Orton had recognised, as far back as 1910, that all Katherine's writing 'was a kind of poetry, not so much in respect to form or content as in its extreme intensity and accuracy of realisation'.[21]

But it is another reviewer who touches the exposed nerve in Katherine's divided psyche, observing that all her characters are versions of her own, complicated self:

> ... we perceive too clearly that it is all a beautiful, an exquisite, a diabolically clever masquerade, with the protean Miss Mansfield taking now the part of Beryl, now that of 'The Young Girl', now that of both 'Daughters of the Late Colonel', now that of Miss Brill; achieving quite extraordinary ventriloquistic feats as Mr. Neave or Mr. Hammond – though she seldom attempts the masculine; and shining out beautifully, with not even the pretence of a mask, as Kezia. Yes, these people are all Miss Mansfield, all speak with her voice, think as she thinks, are rapidly, ecstatically aware, as she is aware; share her gestures and her genius; and represent, in short, not so many people or lives, but so many projections of Miss Mansfield's mind and personality into other people's bodies and houses. How exciting to disguise oneself, for a morning, as Ma Parker, or, for an afternoon, as the singing teacher![22]

Michael Sadleir has entered the collection for the Prix Femina-Vie Heureuse, a French prize for a book written by a woman and published in English. Katherine has no expectations – 'I don't win prizes' she tells him – and is not surprised to come third, the first prize going to Rose Macaulay. Katherine is dissatisfied by all the work she has done so far: 'all that I have written up till now seems to me to have been only . . . opening the window, pulling back the shutters'.[23] John Galsworthy sends her an admiring letter about the collection and asks 'What now?' but Katherine doesn't know. She has a glimpse, only a glimpse, of the kind of 'absolute truth' she is after. A review she had written a year earlier called 'Wanted a New World', had proposed a riddle:

> I am neither a short story, nor a sketch, nor an impression, nor a tale. I am written in prose. I am a great deal shorter than a novel; I may be only one page long, but, on the other hand, there is no reason why I should not be thirty. I have a special quality – a something, a something which is

immediately, perfectly recognisable. It belongs to me; it is of my essence. In fact I am often given away in the first sentence. I seem almost to stand or fall by it. It is to me what the first phrase of the song is to the singer. Those who know me feel, 'Yes, that is it.' And they are from that moment prepared for what is to follow.[24]

John's novel *The Things we Are* is published three weeks after *The Garden Party*, to reserved praise from the various friends he has persuaded to review it. His collection of essays, *Countries of the Mind*, scheduled for publication in the summer, now has an impressive list of 'works also by . . .' on the inside cover, including two novels, three volumes of poetry and four collections of essays. Although Katherine is aware of the limitations of John's fiction, she refrains from saying anything because previous comments have been so badly received, driving her to protest, 'You don't want criticism, you want flattery!'[25] This restraint widens the gap between them by limiting creative discussion.

In Paris Katherine is working on a new story called 'The Fly'. It is cruel and cynical, without sentiment or romance. A successful businessman, forced to think of the death of his only son in the war, tortures a fly to see how often it can be drowned in ink before it dies. It is not a comfortable story to read. Nor is her next, 'The Canary', written for a magazine contract and dedicated to Dorothy Brett. Both involve the fear of being forgotten after death. In 'The Fly', the father finds that, after suppressing the memory of his son for so long, he can no longer remember him clearly. The elderly woman in 'The Canary' – based on one of the hotel's permanent residents – is glad that the nail in the doorpost will remind others that her canary's cage had once hung there because, long after she is gone, the bird will be remembered when she is forgotten. It is hard not to see the story as a metaphor.

Katherine's creative energies are low, but she has to keep producing stories to pay her expenses. Her struggles with 'The Canary' are still fresh in her mind when she writes to her cousin Elizabeth that she is 'sick of my little stories bred in cages'.[26] She blames the inability to write on her inner chaos. Katherine increasingly feels that not until she can correct the faults in herself, as Frederick Goodyear had once told her, will she be able to write in the pure way that she wants to. How, she asks, do you drink clean water out of a dirty glass? She is more and more attracted to the ideas in *Cosmic Anatomy*. Katherine has always been emotionally drawn to all things

Russian – the vast sweep of landscape, the tragedy of its history reflected in those gigantic novels and passionate symphonies. Her favourite authors are Dostoevsky, Tolstoy, Chekhov, Turgenev, and Kuprin. She loves Russian music, loves dressing up in the Russian costumes Kot had given her, has even called herself Katoushka, Kissienka, Katrina, Catharine; part of her soul resonates with Russian culture. She is delighted when Manoukhin invites her to his home to meet Kuprin and some other Russian emigrés.

Katherine's weekly treatments continue. Her frail body is bombarded with powerful X-rays. At first she puts on a few grams in weight, feels better and hardly dares to believe that it will work – the thought that it might not fills her with terror. In a letter she confides to her cousin Elizabeth what ill health has meant to her. 'It is bitter to be ill. And the idea of being well – haunts me. Ever since I have realised this possibility I dream of it at night – dream I am alone – crossing streams or climbing hills or just walking. To be alone again. That is what health means to me; that is freedom. To be invisible, not to be offered chairs or given arms!'[27]

But soon Katherine begins to suffer from the effects of radiation sickness – pounding headaches, neuralgia, and for days afterwards her body burns as though it's being heated in a furnace until her bones seem about to melt. She quickly becomes sicker than she has ever been. 'The pain in my back and so on, makes my prison almost unendurable. I manage to get up, to dress, to make a show [of] getting to the restaurant & back without being discovered . . . The rest is rather like being a beetle shut in a book, so shackled that one can do nothing but lie down – and even to lie down becomes a kind of agony. The worst of it is I have again lost hope.'[28] Katherine is thin, hollow eyed and all her natural vivacity has vanished. Francis Carco, who bumps into Katherine and John on the pavement outside the hotel as she is being helped into a car to be taken for a drive, is shocked at the change in her.

Manoukhin assures Katherine that this is the 'grande reaction' experienced by everyone, and that it's the prelude to the cure. She wants to believe in Manoukhin because he is her only hope, but her doubts in his veracity are growing. On Katherine's next visit there is a distinct sense that things are not going well at the clinic. Manoukhin is 'distrait and a little angry'. The apparatus breaks down and doors are banged in frustration. Donat and Manoukhin aren't speaking to each other and the latter is so agitated that he can't remember any French at all.[29] It's very disturbing.

But life in Paris is not all gloom and suffering. Katherine has become reconciled with her father. In March she had plucked up enough courage to write to him for the first time in over a year, calling herself his 'undeserving little black sheep of a child', and admitting that she has completely misunderstood him. 'You have been – you are – the soul of generosity to us all.' There is also regret for the distance that has been allowed to develop between them. 'I sometimes wish that we could have been nearer to each other since I have been grown up and not the intolerant girl who returned to New Zealand with you years ago.' Katherine tells Harold in her letters about her latest book and its popularity. 'I have certainly been most fortunate as a writer. It is strange to remember buying a copy of the *Native Companion* on Lambton Quay and standing under a lamp post with darling Leslie to see if my story had been printed.'[30] She describes her treatment, at first enthusiastically, but later admitting that it has been 'on the whole successful [though] not quite as miraculous as depicted by the doctor'.[31] Delighted for her, Harold responds warmly. Katherine remarks dryly to Ida what a difference success has made to the way her father regards her, but much of the change is due to the new understanding Katherine now has of the relationship between parent and child.

Dorothy Brett also has a difficult relationship with her father, but Brett's approach is confrontational and for much of the time they are scarcely on speaking terms. Katherine advises her to take a more conciliatory line. 'There is nothing on earth like an appearance of discontent and failure to harden the hearts of men like your father.' Brett must not harbour grudges based on childhood memories and experiences. 'Ah Brett, we can't plead them – We simply can't! It means the end of all personal freedom if we do. We have to simply get over them, stifle them, no – root them out and fling them over the wall like weeds so that our own flowers can grow.'[32]

Katherine's friends Sydney and Violet Schiff are in Paris and take her out to a *thé dansant* at their expensive hotel. There are strawberry tartlets and lemon tea in cups as thin as eggshell and Katherine enjoys being cosseted. 'I do like luxury – just for a dip in and out of.'[33] Sydney brings James Joyce along because John is about to review *Ulysses* for the *Nation and Athenaeum*. Katherine is fascinated, having read the novel in manuscript and discussed it endlessly with Virginia Woolf. Her first instinct had been to ridicule, then, as she read it out loud she had suddenly admitted to Virginia that there was something in it – something powerful and new. When Brett asks whether she should read it, Katherine warns that *Ulysses* is 'fearfully difficult and obscure', but adds that she thinks 'Marian Bloom & Bloom are superbly seen at times' and there is 'many a "ripple of laughter" in it', though the coarseness often seems gratuitous.[34]

Katherine has already confided her inability to embrace the novel wholeheartedly to Sydney Schiff in letters. 'I have been perhaps unfair and captious . . . I can't get over the feeling of wet linoleum and unemptied pails and far worse horrors in the house of his mind.' Katherine prefers Proust's descriptions of 'flowering apple trees in the spring rain' to Joyce's detailed accounts of bodily functions.[35] Over tea Joyce proves a much more difficult personality than they had expected and Sydney leaves early. As usual in the company of male authors, Katherine finds herself overlooked. The classically educated Joyce and John race away discussing the references to the *Odyssey* in the novel – 'code words that must be picked up in each paragraph and so on'. Marian Bloom, Katherine now realises, is supposed to be Penelope, and 'she is also the night and the day, she is also an image of the teeming earth – full of seed, rolling round and round'. Katherine feels intellectually inferior, but afterwards Joyce tells the Schiffs that she had understood his novel better than her husband.[36]

John's brother Richard is a welcome visitor to Paris; Katherine's sisters and the talkative Brett less so. Soon Katherine becomes worn down by socialising and longs for privacy and space to complete her work. 'Doors that bang, voices raised, smells of cooking, even steps on the stairs are nothing short of anguish to me at times. There is an inner calm necessary to writing, a sense of equilibrium which is impossible to reach if it hasn't its outward semblance.'[37] It's a continual balancing act. Katherine needs the stimulation of human contact in order to generate ideas, but at the same time 'parties and literary society' are a distraction and the 'life of the head' only a 'half existence'. 'It seems to me one can't write anything worth the name unless one lives – really lives. Talk and all that kind of thing is a kind of frittering away.'[38] Her notebook is full of scraps and beginnings. Brett is a particular problem. She is Katherine's friend, but her attachment to John is a continuing source of concern. Katherine confides to Ida that she thinks Brett may marry John after she is dead and tries to persuade herself that it would be the right thing. On good days Katherine can acknowledge how 'hellish' it must be to live with a sick woman and admit that she can never be a proper wife to John again. 'He ought to divorce me, marry a really gay young healthy creature, have children and ask me to be godmother.'[39] On bad days she can't bear the thought of him with someone else.

John chafes in Paris. He is so close to England and he misses the intellectual life of London. There is also his continual anxiety for Katherine, which has to be hidden from her, and the strain this imposes becomes intolerable. He writes to a friend in March, 'When one is looking after one's wife who is ill, it becomes exceedingly difficult to write to anybody.' It is 'impossible to be detached . . . There's nothing you can say . . . you daren't say "I feel she is better" in case she instantly gets worse. And you can't say, "There's no improvement", because you can't even bear to say such a thing to yourself in silence.'[40] Although Katherine tells him that she is getting better, John can't always see it. There are moments of crazy optimism followed by despair. His diary entry for Thursday 20 April is typical: 'A bloody depressing day, even though the weather was beautiful and we drove in the Bois de Boulogne. The heavenly green of the trees . . . Tig has been really ill this week – pains in her lungs continually – intense pains in the abdomen. She says she feels weaker than she has felt for months – and her cough to my ear seems to have taken on the deep lung-tearing sound . . . and we were madly happy on Friday – absolutely confident. Oh for an end to the doubts!'[41]

In the confident moments they plan a life together – John wants to spend six months in England in a cottage during the summer, and then Katherine will spend the winters on the Mediterranean with Ida. Meanwhile, John tries to look after Katherine, in his own inept fashion. 'He even brushed my hair last night. It was rather queer brushing but there it was.'[42] John is no nurse; living in a world of his own and barely able to take care of himself, he is unable to anticipate her needs. She wastes precious energy organising her clothes and cleaning shoes, and John sometimes goes out to dinner and forgets that Katherine is alone and hungry in her room. Nevertheless, Katherine can see the funny side of his temperament. In a letter to Ida she describes going shopping with John to buy a hat. After the comical saga of 'the lost cheque book', they take a taxi to a huge department store. 'It was exactly like being in hell. The hats were loathsome. Jack as usual on such occasions would not speak to me and became furious. If I said "do you like that?" He replied "No. Horribly vulgar!" If I timidly stretched out a hand he hissed "Good God!" in my ear.' Outside the store again, a woman 'tried to commit suicide by flinging herself at his umbrella'. While they waited for a taxi, Katherine went to look at a stall 'where a man was selling Easter chickens that cheeped when you blew a whistle. The taxi came and Jack had by this time lost me. Finally, both of us raging, we got in drove to the hotel got out, got in again, and drove to another hat shop. "Get this damned thing over!" was Jack's excuse. There was a quiet shop we both knew . . . My one stipulation was that I didn't mind what kind of hat I bought but it must have no feathers. And I finally decided on a little fir cone with 2 whole birds on it!'[43]

Katherine is missing Ida desperately. 'I had better end this letter quickly for the old feeling is coming back – an ache, a longing – a feeling that I can't be satisfied unless I know you are near. Not on my account; not because I need you – but because in my horrid odious, intolerable way I love you and am yours ever K.M.'[44]

Ida is now in England, cycling along the south coast looking for the perfect place to open a tea shop. Brett is still in Paris and she helps Katherine pack up for the return to Switzerland. John, intent on saving money and wanting to be near Elizabeth in Randogne, has persuaded Katherine to stay in the Hotel Angleterre in Montana, rather than any of its more luxurious neighbours; Ida had booked rooms for them before she left. The journey from Paris to Switzerland is disastrous. Katherine is too weak to do anything for herself, and has to rely on John to organise tickets, reserve seats, luggage, passports and food for the journey. He has bought the tickets without realising that it is the Whitsun public holiday and the trains are all packed to bursting. In the chaos he gives the porter a 500 F note instead of a 50. On board there is no 'couchette' for Katherine, and no food. At the changeover in Sierre, he wanders off to the post office and they almost miss the next train. Some of their baggage is lost, including Katherine's favourite travelling clock and John's fountain pen. Katherine, exhausted by rushing around the station to find him, then has to endure a long, cold journey in an open cart to the hotel in icy rain that soaks her to the skin. At the Hotel Angleterre, which has only the most basic facilities, Katherine immediately goes down with a fierce attack of pleurisy. She is forced to admit what she had already realised in Paris, that without Ida to look after her, she can no longer manage with only John to help. 'Ida if you are not finally fixed up for the summer, listen to me. It's no go. I am almost as ill as ever I was, in every way . . . That journey nearly killed me literally. He had no idea I suffered at all, and could not understand why I looked "so awful" and why everybody seemed to think I was terribly ill. Jack can never understand. That is obvious.' But how to protect John's pride? She drafts a letter for Ida to send, saying that her plans have fallen through, suggesting herself as a 'companion secretary'.[45]

But however it is managed, there is a breach with John. Ida arrives towards the end of June and she and Katherine take the funicular railway down to Sierre and book into the Chateau Belle Vue hotel, making the excuse that Montana is too high for Katherine's heart. John goes further up the mountain to stay with Elizabeth in Randogne. The Belle Vue is much more welcoming than the Angleterre and there is 'an atmosphere of graciousness' and peace that is exactly what Katherine needs.[46] Like a symbol of the regeneration she seeks, there is a wonderful aloe in full flower in the garden beneath her window. Katherine sleeps a lot, and spends her afternoons sitting in the sunny garden writing and trying to recover her energies. In all her thought processes and her dreams, the ideas in *Cosmic Anatomy* have begun to run through everything. John declares that it is utter rubbish that defies rational analysis. Katherine, too, had once thought so, writing for *Rhythm* in 1912 that: 'Mysticism is perverted sensuality; it is "passionate admiration" for that which has no reality at all. It leads to the annihilation of any true artistic effort.'[47] But now she has begun to regard Gurdjieff's philosophy, as expounded by his disciples, as the one last hope. The power of the mind to heal the body is worth investigating. There are increasingly heated arguments when John comes down to Sierre for the weekend. Katherine feels that since Manoukhin's miracle has not happened, it is perhaps time to look for a miracle of another kind. John is still pinning his hopes on Manoukhin and urges her to return. Kot and Orage are talking about Gurdjieff and his disciple Ouspensky, both of whom are now in London, in their letters. Gurdjieff seems a gigantic figure – everyone describes him as 'extraordinary' – and he has just founded an institute to teach his ideas in Hampstead, funded by the fabulously rich socialite Lady Rothermere. Orage is already committed and other old names from the *New Age*, like Carl Bechhofer, are enthusiastically involved too. Some of John's friends, J. W. N. Sullivan and writer J. D. Beresford have also become converts.

Brett arrives in Sierre to stay at the hotel and Ida is incensed by her lack of sensitivity towards Katherine. Brett wanders into her room whenever she feels inclined and stays for hours, leaving Katherine exhausted. 'Brett is very very chastening. God has sent her to me as a Trial. I shall fail. It serves him right.'[48] After a few days, Katherine asks Ida to intervene, but when Ida comes into the room and suggests that Brett should leave Katherine to rest, Brett interprets it as jealousy. Brett is rude to Ida's face and scathing behind her back. John is also often at the hotel during Brett's visit and the atmosphere is tense.

July and August are unusually hot and the trees in the garden droop listlessly from lack of rain. There are days when Katherine does not even have the energy to pick up her pen. 'The Dove's Nest', a long story she describes as a 'short novel' and hopes to submit in instalments, to fulfil her contract for the magazine stories, remains unfinished – a patchwork of episodes. Katherine is increasingly concerned about her inability to write more than a few paragraphs at a time, but links it to her spiritual and moral state rather than to the exhaustion of her fight against terminal illness. Ida watches, unable to do anything to help, sensing that every day is a challenge for Katherine. At night, alone in the wide double bed, watching the flowers and leaves on the wallpaper 'gently weaving in the darkness', Katherine, who always talks of her lungs as her 'wings', no longer sees herself as the drowned, unfortunate fly in the poem she writes in her notebook, but as a bird whose wings have been broken.

> She is like a wounded bird resting on a pool . . .
> Timidly, timidly she lifts her head from her wing.
> In the sky there are two stars
> Floating, shining . . .
> O waters – do not cover me!
> I would look long and long at those beautiful stars!
> O my wings – lift me – lift me!
> I am not so dreadfully hurt.[49]

At the beginning of August, after Brett has gone, Katherine calls Ida into her room for a discussion about the deposition of her property after her death. Katherine is intensely matter of fact, though it causes Ida great distress – 'I could not face the thought of her dying'.[50] After the discussion Katherine writes a personal letter to John to be left with Mr Kay, then draws up a formal will in her room, witnessed by two of the hotel staff, before making arrangements to go back to London. She borrows £100 from her cousin Elizabeth to finance the trip and tells everyone, including John, that she is going back to see Sorapure about her heart, to get confirmation that Manoukhin's treatment has worked. But Ida suspects that Katherine has another agenda.

John surprises everyone by abandoning a proposed trip to Italy to travel back to England with Katherine and Ida but, when they arrive in London, Katherine goes to stay with Brett in Pond Street, Hampstead, and John lodges in the attic of the house next door with his friend, Boris Anrep. Katherine has made Brett promise not to tell anyone that she's in town, because she doesn't want to be inundated with visitors. She confesses in a letter to her cousin Elizabeth that she is going through a spiritual crisis, feeling disillusioned, flat – emotionally, spiritually and creatively bankrupt.[51] In a letter of apology to Ottoline Morrell, explaining why she can't see her, Katherine describes 'this poignant, almost unbearable feeling that all is passing. People who are well do not and cannot understand what it is . . .'[52]

The first people Katherine contacts are Orage and Koteliansky. Orage comes round to Brett's with a bottle of white wine. Now forty-nine, greyer and more untidy than ever, he greets her affectionately, 'embracing her and calling her "darling"'.[53] When they begin to talk he elaborates on Gurdjieff's theories with missionary zeal. He had first encountered these ideas in 1912, when Ouspensky published a book called Tertium Organum, and since then he has been a follower. But, he tells Katherine, even though Ouspensky is formidable, as soon as he met Gurdjieff he had realised that he was the master and Ouspensky only the pupil. Katherine is at last able to talk freely about their ideas without fearing the scorn that John pours on them. She tells Orage how dissatisfied she has become with 'the idea that Life must be a lesser thing' than she could imagine. If she cannot continue to grow, then she can see her life and vital energies dissipating like 'that of a river flowing away in countless little trickles over a dark swamp'. Katherine tells him that her life until now has been false but, in the ideas of Ouspensky, she has glimpsed 'the possibility of something quite other'.[54] Like Katherine, Orage has been feeling for some time that his whole life has been a lie. 'I may find that all I have regarded as the real "me", the literary man, the artist, the philosopher, all is artificial. Perhaps my real bent is cobbling old boots.'[55] He confesses that he is thinking of selling the New Age and going out to join Gurdjieff, who has been refused a visa to remain in Britain and gone to France, where Lady Rothermere is going to fund another institute. Orage also confirms that Ouspensky is giving a series of lectures in London and tells Katherine that he will arrange for them to go together; it might also be possible for her to meet Ouspensky.

Katherine's next visitor is Kot. He stands 'in the doorway,

broad-shouldered in the neat, worn, navy blue serge suit, holding himself back shyly. The immense broad brimmed, dark felt hat that she had given him "because it will become you" . . . held in his left hand.' Katherine makes tea for them and they discuss D. H. Lawrence's latest novel *Aaron's Rod*, which John has just reviewed. Katherine is deeply critical of the book, though she still believes in Lawrence as a writer. Kot is one of Lawrence's most passionate supporters and they are soon arguing. They talk briefly about Mark Gertler, who is also suffering from TB but, unlike Katherine, has chosen to be treated in a sanatorium. Before Kot leaves Katherine tells him something of her spiritual crisis. Kot tells her bluntly that she must 'become a simple person', give up the pretending, the acting, and all the little 'falsities' he hates in her. She needs to become an adult and leave the child world of John behind. He also says that, in order to mature and become an adult, 'one must be solitary and alone'. But that is the one thing Katherine finds unendurable. John, she tells Kot, 'is like a man under a curse' and though she is deeply sorry for him, and they are no longer officially together, she is 'determined to remain his friend'.[56] It's her first public admission that there's a rift between them.

Kot and Katherine begin work together on a series of Russian translations – Gorky's *Reminiscences of Leonid Andreyev* and Dostoevsky's letters to his wife.[57] It makes Katherine much happier to be working again. Her misery concerns Kot deeply because he doesn't fully understand it. But one day when he is in Katherine's room at Pond Street, discussing Dostoevsky's notebooks, Katherine suddenly stops talking and turns away.

Kot asks, 'What is the matter Kat'run?'

'Listen!' She puts her hand on his arm, something she rarely does.

Concerned and moved, Kot is at a loss to discover what she could have heard in that quiet Hampstead street. Then, from the room above, he hears 'Brett's crisp insistent voice in her familiar emphatic staccato, and then Murry's slurred tones' raised to reach Brett's ear trumpet. Katherine's eyes are full of tears. 'Will you promise me something, Koteliansky?' She tries to hide her face, struggling for composure.

'What is it, Kat'run?' Kot replaces his spectacles and grasps the arms of his chair as he leans forward.

'Will you promise me, Koteliansky,' Katherine asks, 'will you promise me that when I am dead, Murry will never marry Brett?'

They can still hear Brett and John talking above. Kot, who now understands a great deal, promises that he will do whatever he can.[58]

Katherine is still looking for reassurance about her physical condition. She goes to see Sorapure, whom she has always trusted. This time he tells her that she is much improved under Manoukhin and that, if she wants to carry on with the radiation treatment, there is a doctor in London who can give it to her. But as Katherine leaves, he takes Ida to one side and cautions her to take great care of her friend, because she is so fragile that even something as mild as a cold could be disastrous, and any sudden shock could precipitate a fatal haemorrhage.[59] Although Ida won't tell her what was said, Katherine is not entirely fooled by Sorapure's manner. She has one or two radiation sessions in London, but quickly discontinues them on the pretext that they do not have the same benefit that she had experienced in Paris. Katherine tells Brett afterwards that she no longer has faith in any kind of medical treatment.

Katherine's diary records the date of her first visit to one of Ouspensky's lectures in a modest house in Warwick Gardens, an experience documented by the friends who go with her. A Russian woman sits in the hallway ticking names off a list. In the drawing-room rows of chairs are arranged facing a blackboard and the speaker's table. The largely middle-aged audience members whisper, shuffle in their chairs. There's an air of expectancy. Then a thick-set man, with short silver hair and thick glasses, enters the room and stands behind the table. Without any introduction, he takes a minute piece of paper from his pocket, holds it only centimetres from his face and begins to talk about the nature of the self as if he is talking directly to Katherine: 'the principal mistake we make about ourselves is that we consider ourselves one'. When we use the word 'I', 'we suppose that we refer to the same thing all the time, when in reality we are divided into hundreds and hundreds of different "I's" . . . These "I's" change all the time; one suppresses another, one replaces another, and all this struggle makes up our inner life.' Ouspensky chalks a diagram on the board that resembles the multiple divisions of an insect's eye, then goes on to outline the four states of consciousness. 'We do not use even a small part of our powers and our forces . . . We have in us a large house full of beautiful furniture, with a library and many other rooms, but we live in the basement and the kitchen and cannot get out of them.' By observation and meditation, 'the study of oneself', it is possible for everyone to know their true nature and acquire power over their consciousness, their emotions and their imagination. Man is a machine, like a car or a train. Once we learn how it works, we can control it. Self-knowledge is the way to power.[60]

Katherine feels as if someone has suddenly opened a door in front of her.

At Brett's, Katherine is trying to finish polishing Kot's rough translations and has a large notice pinned to her door that says 'Working' in order to keep Brett at bay. Ida, who is staying with her friend Dolly Sutton in West London, comes every day to look after Katherine, and sits quietly in a corner of the room until a visitor arrives or Katherine sends her away. Even John has to make an appointment to see his wife when he's in town. John has gone to stay at Selsfield in Sussex with his friend Vivian Locke-Ellis, looking for the peace and quiet he needs to finish his novel, and he comes up to London only very occasionally. He is there on 7 September when Harold Beauchamp comes to tea, trying perhaps to make a better impression than he had done on the last occasion they had met. Katherine's father has been in London for some weeks, partly for business reasons and partly because Jeanne is to be married at the beginning of October. Katherine has not been particularly welcoming to any of her family, telling them that Brett's is not a suitable place to entertain – it's too untidy and she doesn't have her own cups and saucers. But there are lunches and tea parties in good hotels with her father and sisters. Marion Ruddick is also in London for a visit. In these surroundings, Katherine is able to present herself as healthier than she actually is and to make them believe that her medical treatment is working. Her father takes her statements at face value, and her sisters are too caught up in preparations for the wedding to notice how thin and ill Katherine really is, or how alien she feels among members of her family. They no longer have anything in common – it's as if they are travelling on the same train, but in separate carriages. Katherine is not impressed by Jeanne's fiancé and has no intention of going to the wedding, though she writes to John, asking him if he will go instead. His parting from Katherine is chilly. She writes to him at Selsfield, 'Our good bye reminded me of the goodbye of a brother and sister who aren't each other's favourites . . . but it didn't matter a little bit.'[61]

A postcard from Lawrence arrives at Brett's, forwarded from Garsington. It's an olive branch. This is typical of their relationship – the insults, the dramatic quarrels, the silences, and then a communication as if nothing has ever happened. Lawrence had once made Katherine swear a 'solemn pact' of friendship, insisting that it was, 'as binding, as solemn as marriage. We take each other for life, through everything – for ever.'[62] Now he is in Wellington and he and Frieda send Katherine a card showing two Maori greeting each other. 'We thought so hard of you here,' Frieda scribbles along the bottom. Lawrence is more abrupt. Does Katherine remember, he asks? He uses the Italian imperative form 'Ricordi?' Katherine does. She is homesick for New Zealand and at night she repeatedly dreams of going back, of taking a little pony carriage out to Karori with John, showing him all the 'remembered places'. In one of her letters she makes an important admission: 'Really, I am sure it does a writer no good to be transplanted – it does harm. One reaps the glittering top of the field, but there are no sheaves to bind . . . I think the only way to live as a writer is to draw upon one's real familiar life . . . Our secret life, the life we return to over and over again, the "do you remember" life is always the past.'[63]

Katherine is eking out her energy, rationing her social life in order to have time to work, seeing only those people she really wants to see. Virginia Woolf is not one of them. Their friendship has cooled because of a misunderstanding. Virginia is still offended that Katherine has not kept in touch while in Switzerland. At the end of their last meeting two years earlier, Katherine had promised 'never never to forget' and looked at Virginia 'as if (is this sentiment?) her eyes would like always to be faithful'. She had vowed to send Virginia her diary to read, and that she would write regularly, agreeing that their friendship was 'a real thing',[64] but Virginia has received nothing and doesn't realise that her own letter to Katherine had gone astray in the post. Now, when she hears that Sydney Waterlow has had a telephone call from Katherine while she herself has not even had a postcard, she is deeply hurt. Like most other people, Virginia fails to understand how ill Katherine is.

One of the most important of Katherine's friends is Anne Estelle Rice. Anne has seen Katherine recently in Paris and has an intuition that this will be their last meeting. On 22 September, Katherine is invited to lunch and Anne is determined to make it memorable. The whole household enters into the spirit of it. Anne's cook has prepared a wonderful meal and the cook's husband, Wagner, puts on a waistcoat and becomes the butler. After the main course, even though it's a warm day, Wagner, with great dignity, draws the dining room curtains, plunging them into darkness. Then the doors are flung open and Wagner makes a dramatic entrance carrying an early Christmas pudding, 'drenched in brandy', and 'lit up alarmingly'.

Anne tells Katherine about the 'puffers' she has painted on the nursery walls for her son, 'a mural of trains going through jungles, over bridges, through cities'. Katherine desperately wants to see them and climbs Anne's stairs, slowly, so slowly, 'clinging to the banisters'. She has to stop, panting, at every landing. Anne feels guilty, but Katherine is very determined.[65] Anne can't help contrasting this occasion with earlier days, recalling how they used to sit in the Café d'Harcourt in Paris where respectable women were not supposed to go, remembering the hotel in Cornwall where they had shared a summer, and Katherine at her studio in Chelsea, chain smoking, the box of cigarettes 'rarely out of her thin hands' and how, even in 'a fit of coughing, she could still say, "It's a queer world, darling, but in spite of everything, it's a rare, rare joy to be alive."'[66] Now Katherine tells her of her decision to go back to Paris and Anne senses a 'new serenity'. There has been a change – in place of struggle, there is 'a surrender, the supreme acceptance', as if Katherine has suddenly said, 'It's time to go'.[67]

On the 27th, Katherine arranges a meeting, through Orage, at Ouspensky's house. She has decided that she would like to find out more about Gurdjieff's teachings. Katherine explains that she is going to Paris to continue treatment with Manoukhin and that she wants to continue exploring the ideas she has been introduced to in his lectures. Ouspensky, who believes that Katherine is already 'halfway to death' and fully aware of it, writes afterwards that during their interview he was 'struck by the striving in her to make the best use even of these last days, to find the truth whose pressure she clearly felt but which she was unable to touch . . . I could not refuse when she asked me for the address of my friends in Paris.'[68] The same evening Katherine writes a letter to John, telling him only that she is going back to Paris to see Manoukhin immediately. 'I have changed my plans and am going to Paris on Monday for the treatment . . . Do you care to come up for Sunday night – say? There is no need to.'[69]

Five days later, in John's diary for Monday 2 October, under the caption *Pheasant shooting begins*, he writes the words, 'Tig left for Paris by the 11 o'clock from Victoria'.

24

'A Child of the Sun'

You know that I have long since looked upon all of us without exception as people who have suffered shipwreck and have been cast upon an uninhabited island, but who do not yet know of it. But these people here know it. The others, there, in life, still think that a steamer will come for them and that everything will go on in the old way. These already know that there will be no more of the old way. I am so glad that I can be here.

KATHERINE MANSFIELD TO P. D. OUSPENSKY, FONTAINEBLEAU,
THE DIARY OF JOHN MIDDLETON MURRY, 7 APRIL 1946

All the comfortable hotels are full, and after an exhausting search Katherine finds herself in 'A perfectly FEARFUL room that looked like the scene of a long line of murders. The water in the pipes sobbed and gurgled and argued all night and in the morning it sounded as though people broke open the shutters with hatchets.'[1] In the morning, she and Ida take a taxi to the little Select Hotel near the Sorbonne, where, just as in 1918, they are put into cheap, but quiet, attic rooms on the sixth floor. Katherine goes back to Manoukhin but, after two sessions, she is too ill to climb the stairs and has to descend to something 'less lofty, more expensive, but warmer'. She confesses in a letter that she is now simply 'a living, walking or lying down cough'.[2] Her voice is also affected and she can speak only in a strange whisper that seems 'to come from the void'.[3] Being ill does not improve her temper and she confesses that she is 'a perfect torment' to Ida. Katherine is still trying to follow Ouspensky's teachings, writing to John that 'a new way of being is not an easy thing to live . . . I have to

455

die to so much; I have to make such big changes . . . with all my soul I do long for a real life, for truth, and for real strength. It's simply incredible, watching K.M., to see how little causes a panic. She's a perfect corker at toppling over.'[4]

But Katherine is already making enquiries about what she needs to do to join Gurdjieff. There are three categories of people at the institute – his tribe of Russian followers, students who pay to be there and patients who have come to be cured. Katherine will have to be assessed and she will also have to pass a medical. A doctor will be sent from Fontainebleau to examine her. This is Katherine's first meeting with James Young, a physician and Jungian psychologist who has just abandoned a lucrative London practice to join Gurdjieff and is going to be sharing a room with Orage at the institute. There is instant rapport between Katherine and James and the interview lasts for more than two hours. He tells Katherine that he had once fasted for four days after reading Ouspensky, in order to experience the effects for himself; now he wants to explore Gurdjieff's theories about the power that the mind can exert to heal the body.

He explains Gurdjieff's 'method' to her. It is based on the premise that civilisation has taken man out of his 'natural' condition and developed certain aspects of his nature to the detriment of others. Powers and faculties have been lost, particularly those of mind and spirit. In order to encourage 'self development of the will', Gurdjieff takes the individual out of their comfort zone and puts them in 'radically new postures, both physical and psychological' in order to alter their perceptions of themselves.[5] Intellectuals are made to dig trenches, the rich have to become servants, everyone is made to give up whatever seems dearest to them in order to discover their true selves. Katherine comments that 'it all sounds wonderfully good & simple and what one needs'.[6] Gurdjieff also uses a system of disorientation. James tells Katherine that one is never sure when the next meal is going to be served, or when one is going to be allowed to go to bed. Routine is death to the spirit. They do exercises in mental arithmetic and Morse code in the evening, even though they are exhausted by a day's manual labour. It is called the 'Path of Development'. Everyone has to be lifted completely out of their normal lives in order to be remade and find themselves again. Then there are the sacred dances, which Gurdjieff choreographs: 'rhythmic exercises to music, dervish dances . . . the study of different ways of breathing, and so on'.[7] It all appeals to the old Katherine who has been buried for years by layers of cynicism and a hard defensive carapace; the Katherine that William Orton had known, who had been 'idealistic and deeply religious' and had once written in their shared notebook: 'It is not the coffin which is the shell, it is my body which is the shell'.[8]

In her notebook Katherine ignores her own instructions written a year earlier to 'Leave no sign' and keep her journal free from confessional analysis and emotional 'wallowing'. On 14 October, her thirty-fourth birthday, she covers pages and pages, analysing her relationship with John, her state of mind and her hopes for the future. The reasons for going to Gurdjieff are strong. She is at the end of her spiritual and physical resources. 'My spirit is nearly dead. My spring of life is so starved that it's just not dry.' Gurdjieff offers a single glimmer of hope, that in restoring her mind to health, it might be possible to heal her body. 'It seems to me childish and ridiculous to suppose one can be cured like a cow if one is not a cow . . . why hesitate?' Katherine admits that she is utterly terrified of the step she is about to take. The main reason is her fear of losing John. 'Face things. What have you of him now! What is your relationship. He talks to you – sometimes – and then goes off. He thinks of you tenderly. He dreams of a life with you some day when the miracle has happened. You are important to him as a dream. Not as a living reality. For you are not one. What do you share? Almost nothing. Yet there is a deep sweet tender flooding of feeling in my heart which is love for him and longing for him. But what is the good of it as things stand? Life together, with me ill, is simply torture with happy moments. But it's not life.'

At the bottom of the page she writes, like the old Katherine, 'Risk! Risk anything! Care no more for the opinions of others, for those voices. Do the hardest thing on earth for you. Act for yourself. Face the truth.' Standing alone to face death is the most difficult choice to make. 'But perhaps to people who are not ill all this is nonsense. They have never travelled this road. How can they see where I am? All the more reason to go boldly forward alone.' Across the top of the page she scribbles a comment for posterity. 'These pages from my journal. Don't let them distress you. The story has a happy ending – really & truly.'[9]

Encouraged by Orage, Katherine goes to Manoukhin's clinic and tells him that she is discontinuing the treatment and going to Fontainebleau to try Gurdjieff's method. In a letter to John she explains that she can't go on with the seances: 'almost immediately my heart began to play up, and after two applications I could hardly move at all'. Manoukhin is aware of the 'intimate drama' surrounding Katherine's decision. He goes to her hotel, with his wife as an interpreter, and begs her to reconsider. He refers to Gurdjieff with contempt as 'some Caucasian' and his wife exclaims 'If you go you will kill yourself'. But Katherine won't listen. 'I have had enough of life in hotels . . .' It is 'living the life of a corpse . . . a parasite'. In her journal she records how she 'sat in the Luxembourg Gardens. Cold, wretchedly unhappy . . . everything horrid.'[10]

John is bewildered and devastated by Katherine's new intention. 'Your going to Gurdjieff's institute may be everything that you think: I'm sure you know & I don't. But to give up Manoukin, as you evidently are doing, though you don't say so, seems to me criminal. I really mean wrong, utterly wrong . . . I simply don't understand what you are doing . . . You've passed clean out of my range & understanding: and so suddenly, Wig . . . I feel our ships are sailing away from each other, & that we're just waving.'[11]

John's protests are dismissed. In joining Gurdjieff Katherine is acknowledging that she has given up on conventional medicine. 'No treatment is any good to me, really,' she writes to John. 'It's all pretence. Manoukhin did make me heavier and a little stronger. But that was all if I really face the facts. The miracle never came near happening. It couldn't, Boge. And as for my spirit – well, as a result of that life at the Victoria Palace I stopped being a writer. I have only written long or short scraps since The Fly. If I had gone on with my old life I never would have written again, for I was dying of poverty of life.'[12] Reading, too, has become impossible. 'I am sick and tired of books and that's a dreadful fact. They are to me like sanwiches out of the Hatter's bag.'[13] Her reasons for going to Gurdjieff are simple: 'I want to learn something that no books can teach me, and I want to try and escape from my terrible illness'.[14]

Having made the decision, Katherine is aware that she is now on her own and must part with both John and Ida, who will have to learn to live without her now. Katherine is desperate for love and comfort, but also knows intuitively that, for their own sakes, she must loosen her ties with the very people who can provide it. Ida in particular has sacrificed her life for Katherine, who writes long letters of consolation to her. 'The part of you that lived through me has to die . . . do you see that our relationship was absolutely wrong now? You were identified with me. I prevented you from living at all. Now you have to learn and it's terribly hard.'[15] Katherine writes to John, telling him exactly the same thing. He can't possibly live through her; he must live for himself. 'Be true to one's own self – not to what anyone else on earth thinks one is.'[16]

In her notebook she writes of her own hopes. Not death and darkness and the paraphernalia of sickness: she wants to feel that she is walking towards life and light. She wants 'the power to live a full, adult, living breathing life in close contact [with] what I love – the earth and the wonders thereof, the sea, the sun. All that we mean when we speak of the external world . . . I want, by understanding myself, to understand others. I want to be all that I am capable of becoming so that I may be – (and here I have stopped and waited and waited and it's no good – there's only one phrase that will do) a child of the sun.' And then there is her work. In this ideal future, 'I want a garden, a small house, grass, animals, books, pictures, music. And out of this – the expression of this – I want to be writing. (Though I may write about cabmen. That's no matter.) But warm, eager living life – to be rooted in life – to learn, to desire, to know, to feel, to think, to act. That is what I want. And nothing less. That is what I must try for.'[17]

Two days after her thirty-fourth birthday, on a crisp October day, Katherine travels with Ida to Fontainebleau. They are met at the station by James Young and driven in a carriage up the impressive driveway of the chateau, between avenues of lime trees, each one standing in its own golden reflection of fallen leaves. The house, long and low, is mellow in the autumn sunshine; there's a fountain playing in the courtyard and beds full of newly planted crimson flowers. James tells Katherine something of the history of the house, still known locally as La Prieuré des Basses Loges, which had originally been a Carmelite monastery before it was bought by the Sun King, Louis XIV, for his mistress Madame de Maintenon. Before the war it had been owned by a wealthy Parisian lawyer, famous for defending Alfred Dreyfus during the great political scandal that had divided France some years earlier. He had installed electricity and central heating on some floors, but since then ten years of dilapidation have taken their toll. Gurdjieff's 'tribe' has only been in residence for a few weeks and there is renovation and alteration going on everywhere, but the food at lunch is wonderful, 'like a Gogol feast', the rooms are comfortable enough and there are three resident doctors to look after the health of the guests.[18] In the evening there is music and dance in front of a gigantic fire and Katherine and Ida are given tambourines so that they can join in.

Gurdjieff is the necromancer at the centre of Fontainebleau, holding it all together by his immense personality. Katherine has an interview with him the day after her arrival and sketches his character afterwards in her notebook. There is something slightly oriental about his dark, piercing eyes and wide cheekbones. His head is shaved under the astrakhan cap and he wears a full, Russian moustache. Katherine thinks 'he looks exactly like a Desert Chief. I kept thinking of Doughty's Arabia.'[19] Gurdjieff has been described by his supporters as a shaman and messiah; a charlatan and by his detractors as 'the Levantine psychic shark'.[20] He speaks no English or French, so Katherine can talk to him only through an interpreter. Gurdjieff often has to deal with the terminally ill who come to him as a last resort. He has heard about Katherine from Manoukhin, who has written a letter begging Gurdjieff not to take her, as well as from James Young. Gurdjieff's personal assessment, like Ouspensky's, is that she is one of those ready for 'a speedy departure from this world'. He also knows that if Katherine dies at La Prieuré, her reputation will attract massive negative publicity for his community. At first he tries hard to persuade her that the South of France would be a kinder environment than La Prieuré, where physical privation is part of the programme. 'And how much longer would I live?' Katherine asks. Her aim is 'not to be cured of my disease', but to make her mind and spirit whole. 'If you will let me, I will come and live the rest of my life at the Prieuré.'[21] Gurdjieff, won over by her passionate sincerity, tells her that she can stay for two weeks 'on approval'.

Katherine had intended only to stay overnight before returning to Paris to await Gurdjieff's verdict, but having been accepted she decides to stay on. Ida is to go back to the hotel and pack everything up. As she leaves on Thursday morning, Ida records in her diary that her 'emotional centres [are] entirely out of control'. She stays for one night at a hotel in Fontainebleau, 'dazed with grief' at having to say goodbye to Katherine. Ida fears that her 'earthly relationship with Katherine' is already at an end and that she may never see her again.[22] But Ida, knowing Katherine's propensity for changing her mind, is determined to stay close at hand in case she is needed and decides to get a job locally. When Katherine's stay is extended after the two weeks are up, Ida finds work on a farm at Lisieux, owned by a French feminist.

At the institute, Katherine is at first put into a sumptuous room − a kind of 'glorified Garsington' − in a section of the chateau christened 'the Ritz' by the others, where honoured guests stay when they arrive. She is ordered to 'eat, walk in the garden, pick the flowers and rest much'.[23] It is a great joy for Katherine not to be treated as an invalid. There is no one hovering over her, urging her to take care. She tells Ida she is learning how to look after cows, and how to make rugs from straw. One morning she watches the carpenters in the joiners' workshop, and it seems not impossible that she might learn how to do that too. The dancing is a revelation. Katherine has never cared particularly for dancing before 'but this – seems to be the key to the new world within me'.[24] The ancient Assyrian group dance has particular significance for her: 'To see it seems to change one's whole being for the time'. Another dance seems to contain 'the whole life of a woman'.[25] Even when Gurdjieff moves Katherine to a small, comfortless room as part of her 'Path of Development', so cold she has to live in her fur coat, she remains convinced of the rightness of her decision.

Katherine finds that being without John or Ida is not as arduous as she had expected. Their love and grief had become a burden rather than a support. In a letter Katherine writes of a different kind of loneliness and isolation here, and her 'desire to learn to work in the right way and to live as a conscious human being'.[26] Gurdjieff assigns a Russian girl named Olga Ivanovna, known as Olgivanna, who speaks good English, to befriend Katherine. She visits Katherine in her room for long talks, and asks her about her writing. 'Do you write dramas? . . . Do you write tragedies, novels, romances?' The questions seem to distress Katherine, who replies, 'No . . . only short stories; just short stories.' She tells Olgivanna afterwards that she had felt so wretched, 'she would have given anything if she could have answered at least one "yes" to the "big" things'.[27] Katherine is still raw from an immense put-down in London. Sydney and Violet Schiff had invited her to lunch just before she left England and Katherine had made a special effort to be there. But they had also invited the painter and author Wyndham Lewis, whose attitude to Katherine was contemptuous. He had described her in letters as 'nothing but a writer of 2 books of short stories' whose work was 'vulgar, dull and unpleasant'[28] and whose reputation had been inflated out of all proportion to its merits. Katherine's views on literature and Gurdjieff had been savaged across the Schiffs' dining table, leaving her quivering with rage and humiliation for days.

Katherine had arrived at Fontainebleau mentally and emotionally exhausted, but she is soon recording that 'there are things I long to write! Oh, how I long to!',[29] though she has made up her mind not to begin anything serious until after the winter. But she takes her notebook with her every day when she goes to the cowshed, where Gurdjieff has built her a platform above the cows where she can sit perched aloft like 'a great

Pa-woman'.[30] She writes beginnings, scraps, most of which she tears up. For the moment it is more important to learn to live. 'Oh Bogey, how I love this place!' Katherine exclaims in a letter. 'It is like a dream – or a miracle.'[31] But when John suggests coming for Christmas, she makes excuses, then tells him directly that she does not want to see him until the spring, until 'the old Wig has disappeared'.[32]

She sees James and Orage almost every day and they discuss what they are learning and the impact that it will have on their lives. While she patches the knees of James' trousers, Katherine tells Orage that she knows now that art, great art, can change people's lives – the greatest literature has a purpose. That is the kind of thing she wants to write, though nothing didactic. Literature that is didactic or desires only to please is minor literature. To observe and reflect reality is not enough. It is the internal purpose of the writer that must colour the text in a much more organic way. This is the source of all her inadequacy. 'I've been not only a mere camera, but I've been a selective camera and a camera without a creative principle.'[33]

In their last conversation she gives Orage an example of what she wants to write. 'Two people fall in love and marry.' They are both writers, 'competing for the laurel . . . One, or perhaps both of them has had previous affairs, the remains of which still linger like ghosts in the home. Both wish to forget, but the ghosts still walk.' Some authors, Katherine says, would turn the story into a moral tale, 'others would treat it pathetically, or solemnly or psychologically or melodramatically or humorously'. 'The late lamented Katherine Mansfield', as she describes herself, would have written 'one of her famous satiric sketches'. But the new Katherine would present it simply as 'a common adventure in ghost-laying'.

'And will this have a happy ending?' Orage asks. Katherine shakes her head. 'The problems might be too big.' The hero and the heroine must not be measured by their failures or achievements, she insists, but by their courage and inventiveness as they struggle to lay the ghosts in themselves and in each other.[34]

The ghost of John refuses to be banished. He is still in Sussex, working on his novel, The Voyage, reinventing Katherine as Anne, the vibrant, forceful, young woman his autobiographical hero is destined always to betray. Katherine's novel about her relationship with John remains in the Library of Unwritten Books.[35] As usual when they are apart, she has relented towards him, writing letters in the old way, tightening the threads that bind them together. 'Oh, my dearest Bogey, just wait and see how you and

I will live one day – so happily – so splendidly – But in the meantime, love, please never take what I say for "absolute". I do not take what you say for "final". I try & see it as relative. Essentially, you and I are together. I love you & I feel you are my man. It's that I want to build on and realise and really live in one of these days.'[36]

John and Ida are among the few people to whom Katherine still writes. She has little energy to spare for letters and the world beyond La Prieuré has become more and more distant. Her cousin Elizabeth is among those who feel the loss of both her company and her correspondence. 'Dearest cousin,' she writes to Katherine on 1 January 1923, 'I miss you so. Won't you send me one little line? I like to imagine that you are suddenly going to walk in, radiant and well and that is what you've been saving up for and that is why you haven't written . . . I miss you so!'[37]

Katherine's habit of using several notebooks at once, and the fact that her work is not always dated, makes it impossible to be certain what she was working on in those last weeks. But in the notebook she uses at Fontainebleau for her Russian vocabulary, she is making notes for a story called 'The New Baby', set in New Zealand. It begins with a voyage on the 'Duco', a Wellington steamer that serves the isolated communities in the bays around the harbour. There is an indomitable grandmother, like Granny Dyer – 'a little old woman, nearing seventy perhaps, very spry, with a piece of lilac in her bonnet & pale lilac strings' – who carries a tiny baby in her arms and teases the baby's mother by refusing to give up the infant until the girl is almost beside herself. It's an optimistic story, full of humour, followed by pages of phonetic transcription from the Russian language Katherine is trying to learn.[38]

On the very last page of her notebook, Katherine is conjugating the past tense of the verb 'to be' in Russian: 'I was, she was, we were'. She moves on to the negative and then into the interrogative: 'He was not, you were not, they were not. Was he? Was not she? We were not. Were you not? Was he not?'[39] And then there is a pause, as if Katherine has just put down her pen for a moment and turned away.

Endnotes

Abbreviations

ATL – Alexander Turnbull Library, Wellington
BR – Bertrand Russell
DB – Dorothy Brett
FL – Frieda Lawrence
GB – George Bowden
GT – Garnet Trowell
HB – Harold Beauchamp
IB – Ida Baker
JDF – John D. Fergusson
JMM – John Middleton Murry
Letters of KM – Vincent O' Sullivan and Margaret Scott (eds), The Collected Letters of Katherine
    Mansfield, Vols I, II, III, IV, V, Clarendon Press, Oxford, 1984, 1987, 1993,1996, 2008.
Memories of LM – Ida Baker, Katherine Mansfield: The Memories of LM, Virago, London, 1985.
Notebooks – Margaret Scott (ed.), The Katherine Mansfield Notebooks, Vols. 1 & 2, Lincoln University
    Press & Daphne Brasell Associates Ltd, Lincoln, 1997.
OM – Ottoline Morrell
VW – Virginia Woolf

INTRODUCTION

1. Notebooks, Vol. 1, p. 196.
2. Katherine Mansfield, 'In the Botanical Gardens', Native Companion, December 1907.
3. Marion Ruddick, Incidents in the childhood of Katherine Mansfield, MS-Papers-1339, ATL.
4. The High School Reporter, Wellington Girls' High School, Vol. 23, No. 20, 1898, ATL.
5. Letters of KM, Vol. I, to Vera Beauchamp, [April/May?] 1908.
6. Frances Porter, Born to New Zealand: A Biography of Jane Maria Atkinson, Bridget Williams Books, Wellington, 1995, p. 355.
7. Notebooks, Vol. 1, p. 196; p. 67, 'Juliet'.
8. Notebooks, Vol. 1, p. 196; p. 77, 'Summer Idylle'.
9. Katherine Mansfield, 'The Voyage', Sphere, 24 December 1921.
10. Margaret Scott, Recollecting Mansfield, Random House, Auckland, 2001, p. 76.
11. Katherine Mansfield, 'In the Botanical Gardens'.
12. Eileen Duggan, The Artists' Journal, New Zealand, 1931; Beauchamp Scrapbook, Vol. 2, ATL.

PART I – LEAVING ALL FAIR

CHAPTER 1: FONTAINEBLEAU

1. Last words in the printed edition of Katherine's notebooks. Also published as Katherine's 'last words' by JMM in the *Adelphi*, 1924, but probably written in 1922.
2. *Letters of KM*, Vol. V, to Charlotte Perkins and Jeanne Renshaw, 31 December 1922.
3. *Letters of KM*, Vol. V, to JMM, June 1922 (undated).
4. Ibid., to JMM, 11 October 1922.
5. *Notebooks*, Vol. 2, Notebook 42, p. 161.
6. Hermione Lee, Review of 'The Journal of Katherine Mansfield', Persephone Books, *Guardian*, 2 December 2006.
7. *Notebooks*, Vol. 2, Notebook 30, p. 288.
8. *Letters of KM*, Vol. V, to JMM, 26 December 1922.
9. James Moore, *Gurdjieff and Mansfield*, Routledge & Kegan Paul, London, 1980.
10. 'Lesley Moore'– Katherine's nickname for her.
11. Ida Baker, Diary, 1922, MS-Group-2365, ATL.
12. *Letters of KM*, Vol. V, to IB, 7 March 1922.
13. Ibid., to IB, 10 November 1922, 15 December 1922, January 1923 (undated).
14. Ida Baker, Diary, year?, MS-Group-2365, ATL.
15. Olgivanna, 'The Last Days of Katherine Mansfield', *The Bookman*, March 1931.
16. A. R. Orage, 'Talks with Katherine Mansfield at Fontainebleau', *The Century*, November 1924.
17. *Letters of KM*, Vol. V, to JMM, 31 December 1922.
18. Letter, H. M. Tomlinson to H. E. Herring, 8 December 1945, MS-Papers-0340, ATL.
19. JMM, autobiographical fragment, Diaries and notebooks, 1936–1947, MS-Group-0411, MSX-4162, MSX-4163, ATL.
20. Olgivanna, 'The Last Days of Katherine Mansfield'.
21. *Memories of LM*, p. 229.
22. *Letters of KM*, Vol. V, to IB, 24 October 1922.
23. *Memories of LM*, p. 229.
24. *Letters of KM*, Vol. II, to JMM, 9 September 1919.
25. Claire Tomalin, *Katherine Mansfield: A Secret Life*, Penguin, London, 1988, p. 103.
26. *Memories of LM*, p. 230.
27. Ibid.
28. The Diaries of DB, Charles Deering McCormick Library of Special Collections, Northwestern University Library, quoted Sean Hignett, *Brett: From Bloomsbury to New Mexico, A Biography*, Hodder & Stoughton, London, 1984.
29. *Memories of LM*, p. 231.

CHAPTER 2: THE HUSBAND'S STORY

1. John Middleton Murry, *God: An Introduction to the Science of Metabiology*, Jonathan Cape, London, 1929, p. 36.
2. Katherine Middleton Murry, *Beloved Quixote*, Souvenir Press, London, 1986, p. 35.
3. JMM to J. B. Pinker, 1 February 1923, MS-Papers-3981-106, ATL.
4. Ibid.
5. Letter, JMM to Prudence Maufe, MS-Papers-3995, Folder 1, ATL.
6. The Will of Katherine Middleton Murry, MS-Papers-7224-06, ATL.
7. *Letters of KM*, Vol. V, to JMM, 7 August 1922.
8. *Letters of KM*, Vol. IV, to OM, May 1921 (undated).
9. Sylvia Lynd, quote from Moira Lynd in Claire Tomalin, *Katherine Mansfield*, p. 241.
10. Anne Olivier Bell (ed.), assisted by Andrew McNeillie, *The Diary of Virginia Woolf, Volume Two, 1920–1924*, Hogarth Press, London, 1978, 16 January 1923.

11. Ida Baker, 'Random Thoughts', Peter Day, Papers relating to Ida Baker, MS-Group-1137, MSX-6303, ATL.
12. Diaries of DB, 1923, Charles Deering McCormick Library of Special Collections, Northwestern University Library.
13. Unpublished notebooks of JMM, private collection.
14. Diaries of DB, 1923, Charles Deering McCormick Library of Special Collections, Northwestern University Library.
15. Ibid.
16. JMM, Diaries and notebooks, Diary 20 Jun3–4 July 1938, MS-Group-0411, MSX-4154, ATL.
17. Letters of JMM to KM, December 1918, MS-Papers-4003, ATL.
18. JMM, [1 December 1937?], Diaries and notebooks, Diary 20 June 1937–4 June 1938, MS-Group-0411, MSX-4154, ATL.
19. Ibid.
20. Letter, JMM to DB, 4 April 1923, Charles Deering McCormick Library of Special Collections, Northwestern University Library.
21. Letter, JMM to Vere Bartrick-Baker, 11 March 1923, quoted F. A. Lea, John Middleton Murry: A Biography, Methuen, London, 1959, pp. 115–16.
22. Aldous Huxley (ed.), The Letters of D. H. Lawrence, Heinemann, London, 1932, to JMM, 27 April 1923, p. 566.
23. Aldous Huxley, Point Counter Point, HarperCollins, London, 1928.
24. Huxley (ed.), Letters of D. H. Lawrence, 2 February 1923, p. 562.
25. Warren Roberts, James T. Boulton and Elizabeth Mansfield (eds), The Letters of D. H. Lawrence, Volume IV, June 1921–March 1924, Cambridge University Press, Cambridge, 1987 to S. Koteliansky, April 1924 (undated); also see discussion in Edward Nehls, D.H. Lawrence: A Composite Biography, Vol. 2, University of Wisconsin Press, Madison, 1957.
26. Huxley (ed.), Letters of D. H. Lawrence, to Catherine Carswell, 29 September 1922, p. 556.
27. Ibid., to JMM, 25 October 1923, p. 582.
28. JMM, 18 December 1955, Diaries and notebooks, MS-Group-0411, MSX-4160, ATL.
29. Letters of FL to JMM, 1955–56, private collection. Frieda states explicitly that she was sad that they did not come together at this time, and she refers to their intimacy at Vence, after Lawrence's death. See also Letters of JMM to FL, 9 December 1951; FL to JMM, 19 December 1951; and FL to JMM, 10 December 1955; E. W. Tedlock (ed.), Frieda Lawrence, The Memoirs and Correspondence, Heinemann, London, 1961.
30. Diaries of DB, October 1923, Charles Deering McCormick Library of Special Collections, Northwestern University Library.
31. Janet Byrne, A Genius for Living: The Life of Frieda Lawrence, Bloomsbury, London, 1995, p. 193.
32. Boulton, J. T. & Vasey, L., The Letters of D.H. Lawrence, Vol.V, to R. Gardiner, 9 August 1924, p. 94.
33. Beloved Quixote, p. 23.
34. Huxley (ed.), Letters of D. H. Lawrence, to JMM, [28] January 1925, p. 628.
35. Roberts, Boulton and Mansfield (eds), Letters of D. H. Lawrence, to JMM, December 1923 (undated).
36. Letter, JMM to Sydney Waterlow, 27 November 1924, MS-Papers-1157, Folder 7, ATL.
37. Olivier Bell (ed.), Diary of Virginia Woolf, Volume Two, 6 March 1923.
38. Quoted Jeffrey Meyers, 'Murry's Cult of Mansfield', Journal of Modern Literature, Vol. 7, 1979.
39. Nigel Nicolson (ed.), The Letters of Virginia Woolf, Volume Two, 1912–1922, Chatto & Windus, London, 1976, to Vanessa Bell, 27 June 1917.

40. Huxley (ed.), *Letters of D. H. Lawrence*, to JMM, from Germany, 7 February 1924, p. 593.
41. Diaries of DB, 2 March 1924, Charles Deering McCormick Library of Special Collections, Northwestern University Library.
42. Pierre Sichel, *Modigliani*, Dutton, London, 1967.
43. JMM to Vere Bartrick-Baker, 2 June 1933, property of the Sullivan family.
44. *Beloved Quixote*, pp. 44–5.

CHAPTER 3: IDA'S STORY

1. Ida Baker, Katherine Mansfield: Memoirs of LM, MS-Group-0035, ALT; see also MS-Papers-3989-06, ATL.
2. Jeffrey Meyers, 'The Quest for Katherine Mansfield', *Biography: An Interdisciplinary Quarterly*, 1.3 (Summer 1978). Further information was given to me by Ida's executor, Peter Day, who claimed that he and Meyers had almost come to blows over the incident.
3. 'Introduction' by A. L. Barker, *The Memories of LM*, p. ix, and the author's conversations with Peter Day, July 2008.
4. Ida Baker, Katherine Mansfield: Memoirs of LM, MS-Group-0035, ATL.
5. *Letters of KM*, Vol. I, to Sylvia Payne, 25 August 1903.
6. Memoirs of LM, MS-Group-0035, ATL.
7. *Memories of LM*, p. 29.
8. Ibid., p. 235.
9. Ibid., p. xxix.
10. Ibid., p. 235.
11. *Letters of KM*, Vol. I, to Sylvia Payne, 23 December 1903.
12. *Memories of LM*, p. 235 .
13. Ibid., pp. 22–3.
14. Ibid., p. xxix.
15. *Notebooks*, Vol. I, 'Juliet', Notebook 1, p. 57.
16. *Letters of KM*, Vol. I, to Sylvia Payne, 24 January 1904.
17. *Memories of LM*, pp. 22–3.
18. *Letters of KM*, Vol. I, to Marion Tweed, 16 April 1903.
19. *Memories of LM*, p. 23.
20. *Notebooks*, Vol. 2, Notebook 45, p. 30.
21. *Notebooks*, Vol. 1, 'Juliet', Notebook 1, p. 61.
22. *Letters of KM*, Vol. I, to Sylvia Payne, 24 April 1906.
23. *Notebooks*, Vol. 1, 'Juliet', Notebook 1, p. 67.
24. Ibid., p. 55.
25. Ida Baker, Katherine Mansfield: Memoirs of LM, MS-Group-0035, ATL.
26. *Letters of KM*, Vol. I, to Sylvia Payne, 24 April 1906.
27. *Notebooks*, Vol. 1, Notebook 39, p. 110.

PART II – WANTED: A NEW WORLD

CHAPTER 4: 'THE WIZARD LONDON'

1. *Notebooks*, Vol. 1, Notebook 1, p. 88.
2. Edith K. Bendall (Mrs Robison), interviews 1983–86, audio tape, Oral History Centre, ATL.
3. *Notebooks*, Vol. 1, Notebook 1, pp. 79–80.
4. Chaddie Beauchamp to Sylvia Payne, quoted Antony Alpers, *The Life of Katherine Mansfield*, Jonathan Cape, London, 1980, p. 42.
5. *Letters of KM*, Vol. I, to Sylvia Payne, 8 January 1907.

6. *Notebooks*, Vol. 1, Notebook 1, 'At Sea', p. 79.
7. Ibid., Notebook 39, May 1908, p. 110.
8. *Free Lance*, 4 May 1907, quoted Alpers, p. 48.
9. *Notebooks*, Vol. 1, Notebook 39, 25 June 1907, p. 102.
10. Ibid., p. 103.
11. Ibid., pp. 100–1.
12. Ibid.
13. Edith K. Bendall interviews.
14. *Notebooks*, Vol. 1, Notebook 39, p. 101.
15. Ibid., 29 June 1907, p. 103.
16. Letter, Joseph Burney Trapp, 4 March 1947, MS-Papers-8618, ATL.
17. *Notebooks*, Vol. 1, Notebook 39, '29 June', pp. 103–4.
18. *Letters of KM*, Vol. I, undated to unknown recipient, *c.* 1909.
19. *Free Lance*, 13 April 1907, quoted Alpers, p. 47.
20. *Notebooks*, Vol. 1, Notebook 39, 25 June 1907, p. 102.
21. Ibid., p. 103.
22. Ibid., 27 August 1907, pp. 106–7.
23. *Notebooks*, Vol. 1, Notebook 2, 23 January 1907, p. 153.
24. *Notebooks*, Vol. 1, Notebook 39, June 1907, (Days Bay), p. 100.
25. Ibid., 22 October 1907, p. 109.
26. *Notebooks*, Vol. 1, Notebook 1, p. 58.
27. Ibid., p. 86.
28. Ibid., 'The Tale of Three', p. 73.
29. *Notebooks*, Vol. 1, Notebook 29, April 1907, p. 122.
30. *Notebooks*, Vol. 1, Notebook 39, 21 October 1907, p. 108.
31. Ibid., 2 September 1907, p. 107.
32. *Letters of KM*, Vol. I, to Edwin James Brady, 23 September 1907.
33. Letter, HB to Edwin James Brady, 1907 (undated), MS-Papers-4009, ATL.
34. *Letters of KM*, Vol. I, to Martha Putnam, December 1907 (undated).
35. *Notebooks*, Vol. 1, Notebook, New Year's Eve 1907–08, p. 151.
36. *Notebooks*, Vol. 1, Notebook 39, 21 October 1907, p. 108.
37. Ibid., 6 September 1907, p. 107.
38. Ibid., p. 108.
39. *Letters of KM*, Vol. I, to Charlotte Beauchamp, 18 November 1907.
40. *Notebooks*, Vol. 1, Notebook 2, 'The Urewera Notebook', p. 135.
41. *Notebooks*, Vol. 1, Notebook 2, pp. 136–7.
42. Ibid., p. 149.
43. Ibid., pp. 135–49.
44. *Letters of KM*, Vol. I, to Martha Putnam, December 1907 (undated).
45. Ibid., to Vera Beauchamp, late March 1908.
46. *Notebooks*, Vol. 1, Notebook 1, 'Juliet', p. 67.
47. *Notebooks*, Vol. 1, Notebook 39, p. 111.
48. *Notebooks*, Vol. 1, Notebook 2, pp. 159–60.
49. *The Journal of Marie Bashkirtseff*, Virago, London, 1985, preface, p. xxxv.
50. Ibid., p. 347.
51. *Letters of KM*, Vol. I, to Vera Beauchamp, May/June 1908 (undated).
52. Ibid., 19 June 1908.
53. *Evening Post* (Wellington), 4 July 1908, p. 15.

CHAPTER 5: FREEDOM AND EXPERIENCE

1. *Memories of LM*, p. 45.
2. Ibid., p. 30.

3. Ibid., p. 37.
4. Ibid., p. 39.
5. Katherine Mansfield, 'The Tiredness of Rosabel', *Something Childish and other stories*, JMM (ed.), Constable, London, 1924.
6. *Memories of LM*, p. 42.
7. Ibid., p. 43.
8. *Letters of KM*, Vol. I, to GT, 10 September 1908.
9. *Memories of LM*, p. 42.
10. *Letters of KM*, Vol. I, to GT, 16 September 1908.
11. Ibid.
12. Ibid., 17 September 1908.
13. Katherine Mansfield, 'Something Childish but Very Natural', *Something Childish and other stories*.
14. *Letters of KM*, Vol. 1, to GT, 2 November 1908.
15. *Notebooks*, Vol. 1, KM to Vera Beauchamp, 'October', pp. 202–3.
16. *Notebooks*, Vol. 1, Notebook 39, 12 October 1908, p. 111.
17. *Letters of KM*, Vol. 1, to GT, 3, 5 October 1908.
18. Ibid., 8 November 1908.
19. *Notebooks*, Vol. 1, Unbound Papers, 'Youth and Age', 1 October 1908, p. 203.
20. *Notebooks*, Vol. 1, Notebook 39, May 1908, p. 110; Notebook 2, p. 161.
21. *Letters of KM*, Vol. I, to GT, 23 September 1908.
22. Ibid., 4 November 1908.
23. *Memories of LM*, p. 39.
24. Margaret Woodhouse (née Wishart), interview with Antony Alpers, 1948–49, Oral History Centre, ATL.
25. Ibid.
26. *Letters of KM*, Vol. I, to GT, 15 October 1908.
27. *Notebooks*, Vol. 1, 19 October 1908, p. 211.
28. Diaries of DB, 1923, Charles Deering McCormick Library of Special Collections, Northwestern University Library.
29. *Letters of KM*, Vol. I, to Sylvia Payne, 24 April 1906.
30. Ibid., to GT, 16 September 1908.
31. Ibid., 12 October 1908.
32. *Notebooks*, Vol. 1, 29 October 1908, p. 213.
33. Ibid.
34. *Letters of KM*, Vol. I, to GT, 13 October 1908.
35. Ibid., 29 October 1908.
36. *Notebooks*, Vol. 1, mss 'Maata', p. 238.
37. Ibid., p. 245.
38. *Notebooks*, Vol. 1, Newberry Notebook 2, Chapter Plan for 'Maata', p. 252.
39. *Notebooks*, Vol. 1, Unbound Papers, Notebook I, dated 4.XII.08, p. 202.
40. *Letters of KM*, Vol. I, to GT, 3 October 1908.
41. *Notebooks*, Vol. 1, Newberry Notebook 2, Chapter Plan for 'Maata', pp. 252–3.

CHAPTER 6: THE LOST CHILD

1. *Memories of LM*, p. 45.
2. Margaret Woodhouse (née Wishart), interview with Antony Alpers, 1948–49, Oral History Centre, ATL.
3. An entry in her notebook for 1908 and the early part of 1909 is headed 'In the train. Liverpool'. This is obviously not the same visit as the probable trip made to Liverpool at the end of March. Other biographers have assumed that Katherine made only one trip to visit GT, but there are clearly two. On this occasion, which appears

to be the first visit, she travels to Liverpool via Hereford (i.e. from London). The only time she could have done this is at the end of January: she was definitely in London for the whole week when the Moody-Manners Opera Company visited Liverpool in the autumn of 1908. In March the company travelled to Liverpool from Glasgow. Katherine was with them in Glasgow – if she went to Liverpool with them on this occasion she would not have been travelling alone via Hereford. Also, in the journal entry on the train her mood is buoyant; on the second occasion her feelings were very different. The journal entry for Liverpool also precedes the one most likely to have been made in Glasgow.

4. *Memories of LM*, p. 48.
5. *Notebooks*, Vol. 1, Newberry Notebook 2, Chapter Plan for 'Maata', p. 253.
6. Letter, GB to A. Alpers, 16 November 1949, Letters relating to Katherine Mansfield, MS-Papers-3886, ATL. For a further description of GB's relationship with KM, see also letter, GB to Mrs Lucy O'Brien, MS-0262, ATL.
7. *Memories of LM*, pp. 45–6.
8. GB, 16 November 1949, MS-Papers-3886, ATL.
9. Ida Baker, Katherine Mansfield: Memoirs of LM, MS-Group-0035, ATL.
10. GB, 16 November 1949, MS-Papers-3886, ATL; Letters, GB to JMM, private collection.
11. *Memories of LM*, p. 47.
12. GB, 16 November 1949, MS-Papers-3886, ATL.
13. Just after her marriage on 2 March, Katherine tells Ida that she is expecting GT's child. The only way, then, of knowing for certain that you were pregnant was to count missed periods. After the second missed period you could go to a doctor who could make a physical examination or do a chemical test with urine injected into a rabbit to make sure. If Katherine knew by 2 March that she was pregnant, she had missed at least two periods and must certainly have known she was carrying GT's child by the time she married GB. This puts the latest time she could have conceived at the beginning of December (his visit to Carlton Hill from 22 to 30 November) or the first few days of January (the Christmas holiday). She was with GT during the last week in January, but if she had conceived the baby then, she would not have known she was pregnant before agreeing to marry GB. And Dolly Trowell said that the Trowell family threw Katherine out – at the beginning of January – because they discovered that she was pregnant with GT's child.
14. Robert Gathorne-Hardy (ed.), *Ottoline at Garsington: Memoirs of Lady Ottoline Morrell 1915–1918*, Faber & Faber, London, 1974, pp. 148–9.
15. *Notebooks*, Vol. 1, p. 162.
16. *Memories of LM*, p. 43; also Memoirs of LM, MS-Group-0035, ATL.
17. *Notebooks*, Vol. 1, Newberry Notebook 2, Chapter Plan for 'Maata', p. 254.
18. Ida Baker, Katherine Mansfield: Memoirs of LM, MS-Group-0035, ATL. See also *Memories of LM*, p. 48, for the edited version.
19. *Memories of LM*, p. 48; also *Notebooks*, Vol. 1, Notebook 2, p. 164 for KM's use of Veronal and its effect on her.
20. *Notebooks*, Vol. 1, Notebook 2, p. 162.
21. Ibid., p. 163.
22. Interview with Jeffrey Meyers, 1978, Oral History Centre, ATL. See Jeffrey Meyers, *Katherine Mansfield: A Darker View*, Cooper Square Press, New York, 2002, p. 49.
23. *Letters of KM*, Vol. IV, to JMM, 18 October 1920.
24. Katherine Mansfield, 'The Tiredness of Rosabel', *Something Childish and other stories*.
25. *Notebooks*, Vol. 1, Notebook 2, p. 164.
26. Ibid., pp. 164–5.
27. *Memories of LM*, p. 49.
28. Ibid.

29. Ida gave this as her reason in conversations with others later in her life. Some biographers have also argued that Annie Beauchamp cannot have known about the child. But this is ridiculous, and members of the Beauchamp family agree. Katherine must have been at least five months pregnant by the end of May – and possibly as much as six since she seems to have known or suspected she was pregnant at Christmas. Such an advanced pregnancy could not have been concealed from her mother's expert eye. Then there is also Katherine's honesty. When asked outright by her mother why she had married GB and what had happened with GT, Katherine would in the end have had to tell the truth. She was by then at her wits' end. And what point would there have been to lie? In a few months time the evidence would have been there for everyone to see. The fact that Katherine's siblings didn't know about it until later and her closest friends were never told, is characteristic of the way illegitimate babies were kept secret within families. For Katherine it was a story too painful to tell.
30. Margaret Woodhouse (née Wishart), interview with Antony Alpers, 1948–49, Oral History Centre, ATL.
31. *Notebooks*, Vol. 1, Unbound Papers, 1914, pp. 300–5.
32. Ibid., p. 234.
33. Two postcards Katherine sent in August 1909 show clearly the 'little white tower of the convent' behind the church and 'the Kinderasyl', both of which she mentioned to her mother in the note on the back. MS-Papers-0251-3, ATL.
34. *Notebooks*, Vol. 1, Unbound Papers, p. 227.
35. Ibid., pp. 235–6.
36. Ibid., 'The Grandmother', p. 235.
37. *Letters of KM*, Vol. I, to JMM, late July 1917.
38. Indian clubs were a fashionable way of keeping fit.
39. Katherine Mansfield, 'The Luft Bad', *In a German Pension*, Stephen Swift, London, 1911.
40. Katherine Mansfield, 'Germans at Meat', *In a German Pension*, Stephen Swift, London, 1911.
41. Katherine Mansfield, 'Frau Fischer', *In a German Pension*, Stephen Swift, London, 1911.
42. Katherine Mansfield, 'At Lehmann's', *In a German Pension*, Stephen Swift, London, 1911.
43. *Notebooks*, Vol. I, Unbound Papers, p. 227
44. Original letter from KM addressed to GT, private collection. Transcript as in Ibid., pp. 227–8.
45. *Notebooks*, Vol. II, p. 96.
46. *Notebooks*, Vol. II, p. 82, Printed in *Adelphi*, Vol. 1, No. 4, 1923.
47. *Adelphi*, Vol. 1, No. 9, February 1924, 'Ich muss straiten um vergessen zu konnen; ich muss bekampfen, um mich selbst wieder achten zu konnen.' Printed in JMM (ed.), *The Journal of Katherine Mansfield* (incorporating The Scrapbook), Constable, London, 1954.
48. Katherine Mansfield, 'The Advanced Lady', *In a German Pension*, Stephen Swift, London, 1911.

CHAPTER 7: COMING OF AGE IN BAVARIA

1. Her daughter Maria remembered them perfectly for Antony Alpers. See Alpers, *The Life of Katherine Mansfield*, p. 100.
2. Katherine Mansfield, 'Frau Brechenmacher Attends a Wedding', *In a German Pension*.
3. Katherine Mansfield Papers (Additions), Newberry Library, Chicago.
4. *Letters of KM*, Vol. I, to Jeanne Beauchamp, 10 November 1909.
5. Letter, Vere Bartrick-Baker to KM, 12 December 1909; GB, Letters relating to Katherine Mansfield, MS-Papers-3886, ATL.
6. Letter, Floryan Sobieniowski to Katherine Mansfield, MS-Papers-3886, ATL. Quoted Alpers, p. 102.

7. *Letters of KM*, Vol. I, unidentified recipient, [1909?].
8. Letter, Floryan Sobieniowski to Katherine Mansfield, 9 January 1909, quoted Alpers, p. 104.
9. In an unpublished letter to Antony Alpers held in the ATL GB states that 'For her own reasons K.M. urgently insisted on our living together normally as man and wife', MS-Papers-3886, MS-Papers-0263, ATL.
10. Ruth Mantz collaborated with JMM on a biography of Katherine and was given a great deal of information which she did not use in what became a bland, sanctified 'life'. She told Jeffrey Meyers that Katherine had been pregnant by Floryan, though at the time Meyers presumed she was talking about the 'phantom' pregnancy mentioned by Ida the following year, when Floryan could not have been the father. Meyers thought Mantz was deliberately misleading him to avoid the issue of paternity and did not realise what she might have been saying until it was too late.
11. George Bowden speculates that Katherine's family may have been putting pressure on her to return to him, but this is unlikely and Katherine is well able to resist their power to make her do anything she doesn't want to do. Nor is it simply a question of money: Katherine has an independent (though small) allowance, enough to provide a roof over her head, and she has good friends, like Ida and Vere, willing to provide practical and financial help. Some have put forward the theory that she left Floryan and came back to George because she realised that she had contracted gonorrhoea in Germany. But if you suspect that you have venereal disease, or any other unidentified gynaecological symptom, you go to a doctor, not to a husband you left ten months earlier because you couldn't bear to sleep with him. And you certainly don't ask him to consummate the marriage. It simply isn't credible. Besides, Katherine – like most ordinary people, and many doctors, at that time – is quite ignorant of the specific symptoms of venereal disease, believing it to be something suffered only by prostitutes. Freely available information about all aspects of sex, birth control and intimate health, pioneered by Marie Stopes, is still a decade in the future.
12. Ida Baker, Katherine Mansfield: Memoirs of LM, MS-Group-0035, ATL.
13. JMM (ed.), *Poems*, Constable, London, 1923; Knopf, New York, 1924.
14. MS-Papers-3886, ATL; Letters, GB to JMM, private collection.
15. *New Age*, 3 February 1910, p. 316.
16. Paul Selver, *Orage and the New Age Circle*, Allen & Unwin, London, 1959.
17. *Letters of KM*, Vol. I, to JMM, from Paris, 21 March 1915.
18. The *New Age* published several Chekhov stories during this period and had two east European specialists as contributors – Paul Selver and Carl E. Bechhofer. Both were aware of the German translations of Chekhov, which Bechhofer regarded as superior to the English and wrote to that effect in the *New Age*. Chekhov's version of the story appears in both the German and English collections available at this time. Yet no one picked up the similarities between Katherine's story and Chekhov's 'Spat Khochetsia' ('Sleepyhead' in the English version), or, if they did, did not feel it significant enough to comment on. See *Letters of KM*, Vol. V, 13 July 1922, to Arnold Gibbons, for KM's views on plagiarism.
19. A. R. Orage, 'On Sentimentality', *New Age*, 4 May 1911.
20. *New Age*, March 1910.
21. *Memories of LM*, p. 56.
22. *Letters of KM*, Vol. I, undated, undisclosed recipient, [1908–09?].
23. Some biographers have suggested that the note was found by GB in his flat immediately after their marriage in early 1909 before Katherine went to Bad Wörishofen, but all sources are perfectly clear that Katherine didn't move any of her belongings into GB's apartment until their reunion in January 1910. Her hasty

removal after the operation, supervised by Ida, meant that several things were left behind and it is much more likely that GB found the note on this occasion. He would have been unlikely to have agreed to give their marriage another chance if he'd read it nine months earlier. GB also had several other compromising letters in his possession – how he came by them is an interesting question.

24. Letter, IB to GT, University of Windsor, Ontario; copy in MS-Papers-3886, ATL.
25. *Notebooks*, Vol. 2, Unbound Papers, p. 204.

CHAPTER 8: IN SEARCH OF KATHERINE MANSFIELD

1. *New Age*, 11 and 25 August 1910.
2. Katherine Mansfield, 'Frau Fischer', *In a German Pension*.
3. Beatrice Campbell, Lady Glenavy, in conversation with Anthony Alpers, 1950, quoted Alpers, p. 114.
4. William Orton, *The Last Romantic*, Cassell & Co., London, 1937, pp. 269–70.
5. Walter Pater, *The Renaissance: Studies in Art and Poetry*, Oxford University Press, Oxford, 1998, p. 154.
6. Roger Fry, *Manet and the Post-Impressionists*, Introduction to the exhibition catalogue, November 1910, see Martha Kapos, *The Impressionists and their Legacy*, Barnes, New York, 1995, p. 645.
7. Arthur Symons, *The Symbolist Movement in Literature*, Dutton, London, 1958, p. 34.
8. *Letters of KM*, Vol. IV, to DB, 5 December 1921.
9. Pater, pp. 153–4.
10. Orton, pp. 276–7.
11. Katherine Mansfield Papers (MS), Newberry Library, Chicago.
12. *New Age*, Vol. 9, 4 May 1911, Literary Supplement.
13. *Notebooks*, Vol. 1, Notebook 8, 14 March 1911, p. 225.
14. R. H. Congreve (A. R. Orage), 'A Third Tale for Men Only', *New Age*, 8 February 1912.
15. Beatrice Hastings, *Straight-Thinker Bulletin*, June 1932, p. 7.
16. Congreve (A. R. Orage), 'A Third Tale for Men Only'.
17. *Notebooks*, Vol. 1, Notebook 8, p. 224.
18. *Memories of LM*, pp. 59–60.
19. Orton, pp. 269–70.
20. Ibid., p. 275.
21. *Memories of LM*, p. 63.
22. Congreve (A. R. Orage), 'A Fourth Tale for Men Only', *New Age*, May–June 1912.
23. Orton, p. 277.
24. Congreve (A. R. Orage), 'A Fourth Tale for Men Only'.
25. *Memories of LM*, p. 67.
26. *Notebooks*, Vol. 1, Newberry Notebook 2, pp. 225–7.
27. JMM (ed.), *The Journal of Katherine Mansfield*, Constable, London, 1927, p. 220.
28. *Memories of LM*, p. 67.
29. Ibid., p. 64.
30. Ibid., p. 65.
31. This can be read at www.katherinemansfield.net under 'The Writing', 'Writing in Periodicals', 'Pastiche by Katherine and Beatrice'.

CHAPTER 9: 'THE MODEL BOYS-WILL-BE-BOYS PSEUDO INTELLECTUAL MAGAZINE'

1. Orton, pp. 280–1.
2. JMM, 'Art and Philosophy', *Rhythm*, Summer 1911.
3. 'Present Day Criticism', *New Age*, 4 April 1912.

4. JMM, *Between Two Worlds*, Jonathan Cape, London, 1935, p. 173, quoting Thomas Hardy's 'Thoughts of Phena at News of Her Death'.
5. *Memories of LM*, p. 66.
6. Ida Baker, Katherine Mansfield: Memoirs of LM, MS-Group-0035, ATL.
7. *Memories of LM*, p. 67.
8. *Notebooks*, Vol. 1, Newberry Notebook 2, p. 249.
9. Orton, pp. 281–2.
10. Ibid., p. 283.
11. Ibid., pp. 282–4.
12. *Notebooks*, Vol. 1, 'Maata', p. 247.
13. *Between Two Worlds*, p. 184.
14. Reviews, *New Age*, 21 December 1911.
15. *Between Two Worlds*, p. 184.
16. Ibid.
17. Ibid., p. 186.
18. Ibid., p. 187.
19. *Memories of LM*, p. 68.
20. *Between Two Worlds*, p. 188.
21. Ibid., p. 189.
22. JMM, *The Things We Are*, Constable, London, 1922, p. 227.
23. *Between Two Worlds*, p. 11.
24. Ibid., p. 241.
25. Congreve (A. R. Orage), 'A Third Tale for Men Only'.
26. 'A Marriage of Passion' – a skit on contemporary marriage and smart dinner parties, featuring Mr and Mrs De Voted; and a 'Pastiche' set in a ladies club, ruthlessly sending up women's conversation.
27. *New Age*, 4 April 1912.
28. Lea, p. 38.
29. C. A. Hankin (ed.), *The Letters of John Middleton Murry to Katherine Mansfield*, Constable, London, 1983, 30 March 1912.
30. *Memories of LM*, p. 68; *Between Two Worlds*, p. 208.
31. Hankin (ed.), *Letters of JMM to KM*, 28 March 1912.
32. Ibid., 30 March 1912.
33. *Between Two Worlds*, p. 189.
34. *Memories of LM*, p. 68.
35. Jeanne Renshaw's daughter in conversation with Margaret Scott, 2007.
36. *Notebooks*, Vol.1, Notebook 8, 'The Youth of Rewa', p. 222.

PART III – THE TWO KATHERINES

CHAPTER 10: VIOLET

1. Lea, p. 122; JMM, Diaries and notebooks, 1947, MS-Group-0411, MSX-4162, ATL.
2. Unpublished papers, private collection.
3. Lea, p. 123; JMM, Diaries and notebooks, 1947, MS-Group-0411, MSX-4162, ATL.
4. JMM, Journal, 9 April 1924, private collection.
5. JMM, Diaries and notebooks, 1947, MS-Group-0411, MSX-4162, ATL.
6. JMM, Diaries and notebooks, March 1924, private collection.
7. JMM, *The Voyage*, Constable, London, 1924.
8. Quoted Lea, Part Two: 1923–31.
9. JMM, 'The Well at Cerne', *Adelphi*, Vol. II, No. 1, June 1924.
10. Hankin (ed.), *Letters of JMM to KM*, 30 March 1912.
11. Letter, JMM to Prudence Maufe, MS-Papers-3995, Folder 1, ATL.

12. Letter, JMM to Prudence Maufe; Prudence Maufe to Sydney Waterlow, MS-Papers-3995, ATL.
13. Huxley (ed.), *Letters of D. H. Lawrence*, to JMM, 16 May 1924.
14. JMM, Diaries and notebooks, 19 April 1924, private collection.
15. Ibid.
16. Henry King (one of JMM's pseudonyms), 'The Intruders', *Adelphi*, Vol. II, No. 6, November 1924.
17. *Beloved Quixote*.
18. Lea, p. 140; JMM, Diaries and notebooks, 1947, MS-Group-0411, MSX-4162, ATL.
19. *Between Two Worlds*, p. 493.
20. JMM, Diaries and notebooks, 1947, MS-Group-0411, MSX-4162, ATL.
21. Olivier Bell (ed.), *Diary of Virginia Woolf, Volume Two*, 17 October 1924.
22. Lea, p. 140.
23. *Beloved Quixote*, p. 48.
24. Violet le Maistre, writing as Mary Arden, 'The Dream', *Adelphi*, Vol. II, No. 8, January 1925.
25. JMM, Review of Amy Lowell, *Adelphi*, Vol. II, No. 11, April 1925.
26. *Notebooks*, Vol. II, Notebook 26, p. 181.
27. JMM, 'Katherine Mansfield', delivered as a lecture in America, 1935. Published in *Katherine Mansfield and Other Literary Studies*, Constable, London, 1959.
28. J. P. Hogan, quoted Lea, p. 139.
29. JMM, Diaries and notebooks, 1947, MS-Group-0411, MSX-4162, ATL.
30. *Adelphi*, Editorial, Vol. II, No. 11, April 1925.
31. Eighteen thousand, according to JMM, unpublished letter, papers of JMM, GB 0237 MSS 2506–2518, Special Collections and Archives, Edinburgh University Library.
32. Letter, S. Koteliansky to JMM, 7 October 1924, quoted Lea, p. 133.
33. Letter, Sydney Waterlow to JMM, 26 November 1924, MS-Papers-1157, ATL.
34. Huxley (ed.), *Letters of D. H. Lawrence*, to JMM, 17 November 1924.
35. Lea, p. 141; JMM, Diaries and notebooks, 1947, MS-Group-0411, MSX-4162, ATL.
36. Ibid.
37. *Beloved Quixote*, p. 36.

CHAPTER 11: THE FAILURE OF LOVE

1. Lea, p. 126; JMM, Diaries and notebooks, 1947, MS-Group-0411, MSX-4162, ATL.
2. *Adelphi*, Vol. IV, No. 9, March 1927.
3. Violet le Maistre, letters and diaries, private collection.
4. JMM, Diaries and notebooks, 1947, MS-Group-0411, MSX-4162, ATL; quoted Colin Middleton Murry, *One Hand Clapping*, Gollancz, London, 1975, p. 14.
5. Violet le Maistre, writing as Mary Arden, *Luck and Other Stories*, Jonathan Cape, London, 1928; also *Adelphi*, August 1926.
6. Huxley (ed.), *Letters of D. H. Lawrence*, to JMM, 9 January 1926.
7. Ibid., to DB, 25 January 1926.
8. Letter, D. H. Lawrence to S. Koteliansky, 28 June 1926, Ms, BL; *Beloved Quixote*, p. 49.
9. *One Hand Clapping*, p. 17.
10. Angela Carter, *Nothing Sacred*, Virago, London, 1982.
11. *Notebooks*, Vol. 2, Notebook 22, 12 January 1920.
12. JMM, Diaries and notebooks, 1953, MS-Group-0411, MSX-4158, ATL.
13. JMM (ed.), *Journal of Katherine Mansfield*, Introduction.
14. Ibid.
15. Waterlow's comment, quoted letter, S. Koteliansky to Sydney Waterlow, 12 December 1928, MS-Papers-1157, ATL.
16. JMM, Diaries and notebooks, 1947, MS-Group-0411, MSX-4162, MSX-4163, ATL; quoted Lea, p. 143.

17. Ibid., p. 144; quoted Lea, p. 144.
18. JMM, Diaries and notebooks, 1947, MS-Group-0411, MSX-4162, MSX-4163, ATL.
19. Violet le Maistre, 'Uncle Alfred', *Luck and Other Stories*.
20. Violet le Maistre, 'Eva', *Luck and Other Stories*.
21. M. Robinson, Review, *New Adelphi*, Vol. 1, No. 1, September 1927.
22. H. Tomlinson, Review of 'The Journal of Katherine Mansfield', *New Adelphi*, Vol. 1, No. 1, September 1927.
23. Unpublished letters of Violet Middleton Murry, private collection.
24. *Adelphi*, Vol. IV, No. 11, May 1927.
25. Lea, p. 148.
26. Letter, Florence Hardy to Edmund Gosse, private collection; Lea, p. 148.
27. Letter, Max Plowman to JMM, 1932, MS-Papers-5413, ATL.
28. *One Hand Clapping*, p. 22.
29. He was also notoriously unreliable as a judge of character. One of his co-editors on the *Adelphi* once remarked that he would have seriously doubted his own integrity had JMM appointed him to the post. Anecdote related Lea.
30. Violet le Maistre, Fragment of a story, MS-Papers-4025, ATL.
31. Ibid.
32. JMM, 30 October 1930, Diaries and notebooks, MS-Group-0411, MSX-4148, ATL.
33. Ibid., 26 April 1930.
34. Ibid., 20 December 1930.
35. Max Plowman, unpublished papers, private collection.
36. *One Hand Clapping*, p. 30.
37. JMM, autobiographical fragment, private collection; see also MS-Group-0411, MSX-4162, MSX-4163, ATL.
38. Huxley (ed.), *Letters of D. H. Lawrence*, to JMM, 20 May 1929, p. 801.
39. JMM, Diaries and notebooks, MS-Group-0411, ATL, quoted Lea, p. 165.
40. Byrne, *A Genius for Living*, p. 355.
41. JMM, 26 April 1930, Diary 1930–1933, MS-Group-0411, MSX-4148, ATL.
42. Letter, FL to JMM, copied into the Diary of JMM, JMM, Diaries and notebooks, 1955–1956, MS-Group-0411, MSX-4160, ATL.
43. JMM, Diaries and notebooks, 1955–1956, MS-Group-0411, MSX-4160, ATL; quoted Lea, p. 173.
44. JMM, autobiographical fragment, private collection; also MS-Group-0411, MSX-4162, MSX-4163, ATL.
45. JMM, Diaries and notebooks, 1931, MS-Group-0411, MSX-4148, ATL.
46. Letter from Violet Middleton Murry to JMM, February 1929, pasted into the Diary of JMM, Diaries and notebooks, 1931, MS-Group-0411, MSX-4148, ATL.
47. JMM, Diaries and notebooks, October 1930–1, 6–8 March 1931, MS-Group-0411, MSX-4148, ATL.
48. *One Hand Clapping*, p. 33.
49. *Beloved Quixote*, p. 61.
50. Ibid., p. 67.
51. JMM, Diaries and notebooks, 1930–1933, MS-Group-0411, MSX-4148, ATL.
52. Dorothy Plowman, unpublished papers, private collection.
53. Max Plowman, unpublished papers, private collection.
54. JMM, 31 March 1931, MSX-4148, ATL.
55. Dorothy Plowman, unpublished papers, private collection.
56. JMM, Diaries and notebooks, April 1931, MS-Group-0411, MSX-4148, ATL.
57. Ibid.
58. Ibid.
59. Ibid.; *Beloved Quixote*, p. 66.

PART IV – THE MEMBER OF A WANDERING TRIBE

CHAPTER 12: TIG AND WIG

1. JMM, *Between Two Worlds*, p. 202.
2. Letter, Rupert Brooke to Edward Marsh, Ms, BL.
3. Katherine Mansfield, Review, *Rhythm*, June 1912.
4. *New Age*, 13 June 1912.
5. *New Age*, May–June 1912.
6. *Rhythm*, June 1912.
7. *Between Two Worlds*, p. 181.
8. Katherine Mansfield, 'Psychology', *Bliss*, Constable, London, 1921.
9. *Between Two Worlds*, p. 214.
10. *Memories of LM*, p. 77.
11. *Between Two Worlds*, p. 214.
12. Ibid.
13. H. S. Ede, *A Savage Messiah: A Biography of the Sculptor Henri Gaudier-Brzeska*, Heinemann, London, 1931, p. 85.
14. Beatrice, Lady Glenavy, *Today we will only gossip*, Constable, London, 1964, pp. 57–8.
15. Ibid., p. 58.
16. *Adam International Review*, No. 300, 1966 (Katherine Mansfield edition).
17. Katherine Mansfield, 'Je ne Parle pas Francais', *Bliss*.
18. *Between Two Worlds*, p. 219; Diaries and miscellaneous papers, private collection.
19. *Letters of KM*, Vol. I, to GB, 23 May 1912.
20. GB, MS-Papers-3886, ATL.
21. Ede; *Between Two Worlds*, p. 225.
22. Ede, p. 84.
23. *Between Two Worlds*, p. 223.
24. Ibid., p. 225.
25. Enid Bagnold, *Enid Bagnold's Autobiography*, William Heinemann, London, 1969, p. 86.
26. *Between Two Worlds*, p. 226.
27. *Letters of KM*, Vol. I, to IB, 24 February 1914.
28. Ibid., 11 September 1912.
29. *Between Two Worlds*, p. 232.
30. JMM, 'I never made love to her – right to the end.', quoted Lea, p. 31.
31. Sophie Brzeska's diary, quoted Ede, p. 89.
32. Ibid., p. 90.
33. *Between Two Worlds*, p. 237.
34. Ibid., p. 242.
35. *Memories of LM*, p. 79.
36. *Notebooks*, Vol. 1, Notebook 8, p. 225.
37. James T. Boulton (ed.), *The Letters of D. H. Lawrence*, Vol. I, Cambridge University Press, 1979, 26 January 1913.
38. Katherine Mansfield, Mss notebook, private collection.
39. *Notebooks*, Vol. 1, Notebook 33, p. 266.
40. Bagnold. p. 86.
41. *Notebooks*, Vol. 2, Notebook 45, p. 32.
42. *Notebooks*, Vol. 1, Newberry Notebook 2, p. 264.
43. *Notebooks*, Vol. 1, Unbound Papers, p. 306.
44. *Letters of KM*, Vol. I, to JMM, May 1913 (undated).
45. Ibid., May/June 1913.
46. *Notebooks*, Vol. 1, Notebook 18, 1 April 1914.
47. *Between Two Worlds*, p. 249.

48. *Memoirs of LM*, MS-Group-0035, Folder 3, ATL.
49. *Between Two Worlds*, p. 210.
50. Ibid., p. 246.
51. *Letters of KM*, Vol. I, to JMM, 20 May 1913.
52. *Notebooks*, Vol. 1, Notebook 18.
53. *Memories of LM*, p. 86.
54. David Garnett, *The Golden Echo*, Chatto & Windus, London, 1954.
55. Frieda Lawrence, *Not I But the Wind*, Heinemann, London, 1935 (first published Viking Press, New York, 1934), p. 34.
56. Ibid., p. 58.
57. Beatrice, Lady Glenavy, p. 61.
58. *Between Two Worlds*, p. 269.
59. *Letters of KM*, Vol. I, to Jeanne Beauchamp, 11 October 1913.
60. Ibid., 22 December 1913.
61. Beatrice, Lady Glenavy, p. 58.
62. *Letters of KM*, Vol. I, to Charlotte Beauchamp Perkins, 22 December 1913.
63. *Notebooks*, Vol. 2, Notebook 4, 20 February 1915.
64. Francis Carco (trans. Stella Wynne-Edwards), *Montmartre à vingt ans*, Paris, 1938, pp. 195–6, quoted Alpers, p. 179.
65. *Notebooks*, Vol. 1, Notebook 19.
66. JMM, Diaries and notebooks, Journal 1913–1920, MS-Group-0411, MSX-4147, ATL.
67. *Letters of KM*, Vol. I, to JMM, 11 February 1914.
68. *Notebooks*, Vol. 1, Notebook 19.
69. Ibid., Notebook 33, p. 276.
70. Ibid., Notebook 23, p. 278.
71. Ibid., Notebook 23, p. 279.
72. Ibid., Notebook 18, p. 282.

CHAPTER 13: RANANIM

1. *Letters of KM*, Vol. I, to JMM, [7?] May 1915.
2. There are two accounts of this episode, which differ in detail. In *Between Two Worlds* (p. 280), JMM describes Katherine's collapse and the dash for the doctor, but not the 'death jacket'; the other account is in Beatrice Campbell's *Today we will only gossip* (p. 69). They may be two different episodes, but this would be unusual within such a short time frame and both accounts share critical details. JMM's memory was selective when he came to write his autobiography and he often left out things that he felt did not reflect well on Katherine. There are many inaccuracies of time and place.
3. *Notebooks*, Vol. 1, Notebook 18, March 1914.
4. Ibid.
5. Ibid., Notebook 23, p. 278.
6. Ibid., Notebook 18, 2 April 1914, p. 283.
7. Ibid., Notebook 18, pp. 282–4.
8. *Notebooks*, Vol. 2, Notebook 34, p. 57.
9. *Notebooks*, Vol. 1, Notebook 18, March 1914.
10. Ibid., pp. 282–3.
11. JMM, Diaries and notebooks, Journal 1913–1920, MS-Group-0411, MSX-4147, ATL.
12. *Notebooks*, Vol. 1, Notebook 18, 30 August 1914, p. 284.
13. Ibid., 6 April 1914, p. 284.
14. Huxley (ed.), *Letters of D. H. Lawrence*, to JMM, 8 May 1914.
15. Ibid.
16. *Notebooks*, Vol. 2, Notebook 12, 20 September 1914, p. 143.

17. Frieda Lawrence, *Not I but theWind*, p. 71.
18. JMM, Diaries and notebooks, Journal 1913–1920, MS-Group-0411, MSX-4147, ATL.
19. *Letters of KM*, Vol. I, to Beatrice Campbell, 4 May 1916.
20. *Letters of KM*, Vol. I, to Laura Bright, 21 September 1914.
21. *Notebooks*, Vol. 1, Unbound papers, p. 289.
22. *Memories of LM*, p. 82.
23. *Notebooks*, Vol. 1, Notebook 18, 3 November 1914.
24. Huxley (ed.), *Letters of D. H. Lawrence*, 18 January 1915.
25. *Notebooks*, Vol. 1, Notebook 4, 2 January 1915.
26. Huxley (ed.), *Letters of D. H. Lawrence*, 19 May 1913.
27. D. H. Lawrence, Ch IX, 'Low-Water Mark', *Aaron's Rod*, Martin Secker, London, 1933.
28. Koteliansky Papers, BL, quoted John Carswell, *Lives and Letters*, Faber & Faber, London, 1978, p. 100.
29. Ibid., pp. 88–9.
30. Letter, JMM to Beatrice Campbell, January 1955, quoted Beatrice, Lady Glenavy, p. 191.
31. S. Koteliansky to Sydney Waterlow, MS-Papers-1157, ATL, quoted Carswell, p. 101.
32. *Letters of KM*, Vol. I, to S. Koteliansky, 26 February 1915.
33. Letter, KM to S. Koteliansky, March 1915, Koteliansky Papers, BL, quoted Carswell, p. 102.
34. *Notebooks*, Vol. 1, Notebook 18, 16 November 1915, p. 285.
35. *Notebooks*, Vol. 1, Unbound Papers, p. 286.
36. Beatrice, Lady Glenavy, p. 81.
37. *Notebooks*, Vol. 1, Notebook 18, 30 August 1915, p. 284.
38. George J. Zytaruk and James T. Boulton (eds), *The Letters of D. H. Lawrence,Volume II, June 1913– October 1916*, Cambridge University Press, Cambridge, 1981, to BR, 12 February 1915.
39. *Notebooks*, Vol. 1, Unbound Papers, 18 December 1914, p. 286.
40. *Notebooks*, Vol. 1, Notebook 18, p. 283.
41. *Letters of KM*, Vol. I, to HB, December 1914.
42. Ibid., to Annie Burnell Beauchamp, 15 December 1914.
43. FL, *Not I but theWind*, p. 70.
44. *Notebooks*, Vol. 2, Notebook 4, p. 1.
45. *Notebooks*, Vol. 2, Unbound Papers. I am also indebted to an unpublished thesis for discussion of this enigmatic story: Jeannie Beauchamp, 'Bridging the Gulf, Taking the Risk: An Exploration of "Relationships" in Katherine Mansfield's "Juliet", "Brave Love", and "Prelude"', MA thesis, Victoria University of Wellington, 2007.
46. *Notebooks*, Vol. 2, Notebook 4, 2 January 1915.
47. Ibid., 6 to 8 January, 1915, p. 3.
48. Ibid.
49. *Notebooks*, Vol. 1, Unbound Papers, p. 305.
50. *Notebooks*, Vol. 2, Notebook 4, 21 January 1915, p. 6.
51. Ibid., p. 3.
52. Ibid., p. 9.
53. Leslie Beauchamp, Beauchamp Family Papers, MS-Papers-2063, ATL
54. Francis Carco, *Les Innocents*, Paris, 1916; also *Letters of KM*, Vol. I, to Francis Carco, [mid?] February 1915.
55. *Letters of KM*, Vol. I, to JMM, 21 March 1915.
56. *Notebooks*, Vol. 2, Notebook 4, p. 12.
57. Ibid.
58. Ibid.
59. JMM to Gordon Campbell, February 1915 (undated), private collection, quoted Beatrice, Lady Glenavy, pp. 65–6.

60. D. H. Lawrence, Ch IX, 'Low-Water Mark', *Aaron's Rod; Between Two Worlds*, p. 331.
61. *Between the Two Worlds*, p. 315.
62. *Notebooks*, Vol. 2, Unbound Papers 'The Dark Hollow'.
63. JMM, Diaries and notebooks, Journal 1913–1920, MS-Group-0411, MSX-4147, ATL.
64. *Between Two Worlds*, p. 340.
65. *Letters of KM*, Vol. I, [to S. Koteliansky, 8th March 1915?].
66. *Letters of KM*, Vol. I, to S. Koteliansky, 10 March 1915.
67. JMM, Diaries and notebooks, Journal 1913–1920, MS-Group-0411, MSX-4147, ATL.
68. *Letters of KM*, Vol. I, to JMM, 13 March 1915.
69. *Notebooks*, Vol. 2, Unbound Papers, 'Femme Seule', p. 23.
70. *Letters of KM*, Vol. I, to S. Koteliansky, 29 March 1915.
71. Ibid., to JMM, 21 March 1915.
72. Ibid.
73. *Letters of KM*, Vol. I, to JMM, 19 March 1915.
74. *Notebooks*, Vol. 2, Notebook 45, p. 24.
75. Walter Pater, 'The Poetry of Michelangelo', *The Renaissance: Studies in Art and Poetry*, 1893, reprinted by Dover Publications Inc, New York.
76. *Letters of KM*, Vol. I, to JMM, 25 March 1915.
77. Hankin (ed.), *Letters of JMM to KM*, 19 March 1915, p. 44.
78. Ibid., 29 March 1915, p. 56.
79. *Letters of KM*, Vol. I, to JMM, 28 March 1915.
80. Ibid., to S. Koteliansky, 4 May 1915.
81. *Letters of KM*, Vol. I, to JMM, 7 May 1915.
82. Ibid., 8–9 May, 1915
83. Ibid., 12 May 1915.
84. Ibid., 15 May 1915.
85. Ibid.
86. Ibid., 14 May 1915.
87. Ibid., to S. Koteliansky, 17 May 1915.
88. *Between Two Worlds*, p. 350.
89. Beatrice, Lady Glenavy, p. 68.
90. Anne Estelle Rice, 'Memories of Katherine Mansfield', *Adam International Review*, No. 300, 1966.
91. Zytaruk and Boulton (eds), *Letters of D. H. Lawrence*, Volume II, 5 September 1915.
92. FL, *Not I but the Wind*, p. 69.
93. Huxley (ed.), *Letters of D. H. Lawrence*, to Harriet Monroe, 18 September 1915.
94. Katherine Mansfield, 'Autumns', *Signature*, No. 1, 4 October 1915.
95. *Letters of KM*, Vol. I, to Leslie Beauchamp, 25 August 1915.
96. Letter, James Hibbert to the Beauchamps, Beauchamp Family Papers, MS-Papers-2063-07, ATL; discussed by C. K. Stead in *Book Self*, Auckland University Press, Auckland, 2008.
97. Beatrice, Lady Glenavy.
98. *Notebooks*, Vol. 2, Unbound Papers, October 1915, p. 14.
99. *Between Two Worlds*, p. 351.
100. Huxley (ed.), *Letters of D. H. Lawrence*, to OM, June 1915.
101. Beatrice, Lady Glenavy, p. 68.
102. Huxley (ed.), *Letters of D. H. Lawrence*, to Edward Marsh, 6 November 1915.
103. The Diaries of DB, Charles Deering McCormick Library of Special Collections, Northwestern University Library, quoted Hignett, *Brett*, pp. 75–7.
104. *Notebooks*, Vol. 2, Unbound Papers, 29 October 1915, p. 15.

CHAPTER14: PRELUDE

1. *Letters of KM*, Vol. I, to S. Koteliansky, 28 November 1915.
2. Ibid., to Anne Estelle Drey, 8 December 1915
3. Letter, Annie Beauchamp to Clara Palmer, 16 March 1916, MS-Papers-4005, ATL, quoted Alpers, p. 193.
4. Huxley (ed.), *Letters of D. H. Lawrence*, to JMM, 4 December 1915.
5. *Letters of KM*, Vol. I, to JMM, 10 December 1915.
6. Ibid., to S. Koteliansky, 28 November 1915.
7. Ibid., to Anne Estelle Drey, 8 December 1915.
8. *Between Two Worlds*, p. 374.
9. *Letters of KM*, Vol. I, to S. Koteliansky, 17 May 1915.
10. Ibid., to JMM, 12–13, 14–15 December 1915.
11. Letter, Frederick Goodyear to KM, 12 December 1915, JMM, MS-Papers-4005-07, ATL.
12. Hankin (ed.), *Letters of JMM to KM*, 20 December 1915, p. 75.
13. *Letters of KM*, Vol. I, to JMM, 14–15 December 1915.
14. Ibid., 11 December 1915.
15. Ibid., 16 December1915.
16. *Notebooks*, Vol. 2, Notebook 45, p. 29.
17. *Letters of KM*, Vol. I, to JMM, 12–13 December 1915.
18. *Notebooks*, Vol. 2, Notebook 34, 14 February 1916, p. 59.
19. Huxley (ed.), *Letters of D. H. Lawrence*, to KM, 12, 20 December 1915.
20. Ibid., 20 December 1915.
21. *Letters of KM*, Vol. I, to JMM, 19–20 December 1915.
22. Hankin (ed.), *Letters of JMM to KM*, 22 December 1915, pp. 82–3.
23. *Letters of KM*, Vol. I, to S. Koteliansky, December 1915 (undated).
24. Ibid., to JMM, 24 December 1915.
25. Ibid., 28 December 1915.
26. Letter, JMM to KM, 28 December 1915, MS-Papers-4003-07, ATL.
27. *Ottoline at Garsington*, pp. 84–5.
28. *Letters of KM*, Vol. I, to JMM, 29 December 1915.
29. Ibid., to JMM, 30 November–1 December 1915.
30. *Between Two Worlds*, pp. 398– 9.
31. *Notebooks*, Vol. 2, Notebook 34, letter to Frederick Goodyear, 4 March 1916, p. 60.
32. *Letters of KM*, Vol. I, letter to JMM, 22 March 1916; *Between Two Worlds*, p. 393.
33. *Notebooks*, Vol. 2, Notebook 34, p. 58.
34. *Notebooks*, Vol. 2, Unbound Papers, 'Camomile Tea', p. 68.
35. *Notebooks*, Vol. 2, Notebook 45, 22 January 1916, pp. 32–3.
36. Ibid., p. 29.
37. *Notebooks*, Vol. 2, Notebook 34, p. 58.
38. Ibid., Notebook 45, p. 33.
39. Ibid., p. 30.
40. *Letters of KM*, Vol. I, to Frederick Goodyear, 4 March 1916; Letters of Frederick Goodyear, letters to and from Katherine Mansfield and friends / collected and annotated by JMM, MS-Group-4003, ATL.
41. *Notebooks*, Vol. 2, Notebook 34, p. 60.
42. Ibid., Notebook 45, p. 25.
43. Ibid., Notebook 34, p. 60.
44. Katherine Mansfield, *The Aloe*, V. O'Sullivan (ed.), Port Nicholson Press, Wellington, 1982. Original ms in the Newberry Library, Chicago.
45. Ibid.
46. *Letters of KM*, Vol. I, to Vera Mackenzie Bell, 26 February 1916.
47. Ibid., to HB, 6 March 1916.

48. Huxley (ed.), *Letters of D. H. Lawrence*, to KM and JMM, 24 February 1916 (undated).
49. *Letters of KM*, Vol. I, to JMM, 26 December 1915.
50. Huxley (ed.), *Letters of D.H. Lawrence*, to KM, March 1916.
51. *Letters of KM*, Vol. I, to OM, 26 February 1916.
52. *Notebooks*, Vol. 2, Notebook 45, p. 28.
53. *Letters of KM*, Vol. I, to JMM, 22 March 1916.
54. Ibid., to HB, 6 March 1916.
55. Ibid., to OM, 26 February 1916.
56. Ibid., to OM, 7 April 1916.
57. FL, *Not I but the Wind*, p. 73.
58. *Between Two Worlds*, p. 409.
59. *Letters of KM*, Vol. I, to S. Koteliansky, 11 May 1916.
60. Ibid., to Beatrice Campbell, 4 May 1916.
61. Ibid., to S. Koteliansky, 11 May 1916.
62. FL to OM, 19 May 1915, ms, Stanford University, USA.
63. *Letters of KM*, Vol. I, to Beatrice Campbell, 4, 14 May 1916.
64. John Worthen and Lindeth Vasey (eds), *The First 'Women in Love'*, Cambridge Edition of the Works of D. H. Lawrence, Cambridge University Press, Cambridge, 1998.
65. Ibid.
66. *Between Two Worlds*, p. 411.
67. D. H. Lawrence, *Phoenix II, Uncollected, Unpublished and Other Prose Works*, Viking Press, New York, 1968.
68. Ibid.
69. *Between Two Worlds*, p. 412.
70. *Letters of KM*, Vol. I, to S. Koteliansky, 11 May 1916.
71. Ibid., to Frederick Goodyear, 4 March 1916; Letters of Frederick Goodyear, letters to and from Katherine Mansfield and friends /collected and annotated by JMM, MS-Group-4003, ATL.
72. Letter, OM to BR, quoted Paul Delaney, *Lawrence's Nightmare: The Writer and his Circle in the Years of the Great War*, Harvester Press, Brighton, 1979.
73. Huxley (ed.), *Letters of D. H. Lawrence*, to OM, 24 May 1916.
74. *Letters of KM*, Vol. I, to S. Koteliansky, 24 June 1916.
75. Huxley (ed.), *Letters of D. H. Lawrence*, to Catherine Carswell, 9 July 1916.
76. *Letters of KM*, Vol. I, to S. Koteliansky, 3 July 1916.

CHAPTER 15: THE 'BLOOMS BERRIES'

1. *Ottoline at Garsington*, p. 70.
2. *The Autobiography of Bertrand Russell*, Vol. I, Vol. II, George, Allen & Unwin Ltd, London, 1967, 1968.
3. Nicolson (ed.), *Letters of Virginia Woolf*, to Vanessa Bell, 27 November 1917.
4. *Ottoline at Garsington*, pp. 84, 148.
5. Letter, BR to OM, 1915, quoted *Ottoline at Garsington*, p. 57.
6. Diaries of DB, Charles Deering McCormick Library of Special Collections, Northwestern University Library, quoted Hignett, Brett, pp. 104–5.
7. Leonard Woolf and James Strachey (eds), *The Letters of Virginia Woolf & Lytton Strachey*, Hogarth Press, London, 1956.
8. *Autobiography of Bertrand Russell*, quoted *Ottoline at Garsington*, p. 43.
9. *Letters of KM*, Vol. I, to OM, 17 May 1916.
10. Diaries of DB, Charles Deering McCormick Library of Special Collections, Northwestern University Library, quoted Hignett, Brett, p. 105.
11. *Ottoline at Garsington*, p. 149.
12. *Notebooks*, Vol. 2, Notebook 45, p. 27.

13. Katherine Mansfield, *The Aloe*, V. O'Sullivan (ed.), Port Nicholson Press, Wellington, 1982. Original ms in the Newberry Library, Chicago.
14. Woolf and Strachey (eds), *Letters of Virginia Woolf & Lytton Strachey*.
15. *Letters of Virginia Woolf*, to Lytton Strachey, 25 July 1916.
16. *Ottoline at Garsington*, p. 150.
17. Ibid., p. 148.
18. Letter, DB to OM, 2 November 1916, quoted Alpers, p. 221.
19. Letter, D. H. Lawrence to JMM, quoted *Between Two Worlds*, p. 424.
20. *Letters of KM*, Vol. I, to Mary Hutchinson, 5 August 1916.
21. *Ottoline at Garsington*, p. 186.
22. *Letters of KM*, Vol. I, to OM, 20 August 1916. The reference is to nineteenth-century writer Thomas de Quincey's famous essay, 'Murder Considered as One of the Fine Arts'.
23. Ibid., to JMM, 18 August 1916.
24. Charlotte Mary Pickthall, Papers relating to KM, MS-Group-0036, ATL.
25. Vera MacKintosh Bell, MS-Group-0034, ATL.
26. *Letters of KM*, Vol. I, to OM, September 1916 (undated).
27. *Ottoline at Garsington*, p. 77.
28. *Letters of KM*, Vol. I, to OM, January 1916 (undated).
29. Letter, Mark Gertler to OM, 31 August 1916, quoted Alpers, p. 216.
30. *Ottoline at Garsington*, p. 150.
31. *Letters of KM*, Vol. I, to OM, 27 October 1916.
32. Letter, DB to OM, 2 November 1916, quoted Alpers, p. 221.
33. *Memories of LM*, p. 99.
34. Diaries of DB, Charles Deering McCormick Library of Special Collections, Northwestern University Library, quoted Hignett, *Brett*, pp. 86–7.
35. *Letters of KM*, Vol. I, to BR, 7 December 1916.
36. Ibid., 1 December 1916.
37. *Autobiography of Bertrand Russell*, p. 27.
38. *Letters of KM*, Vol. I, to BR, 17 December 1916.
39. *Ottoline at Garsington*, p. 149.
40. Nicolson (ed.), *Letters of Virginia Woolf*, to Vanessa Bell, 11 February 1917.
41. Anne Olivier Bell (ed.), *Diary of Virginia Woolf, Volume One, 1915–1919*, Hogarth Press, London, 1977, October 1917.
42. *Ottoline at Garsington*, p. 180.
43. Ibid., p. 150.
44. FL, *Not I but the Wind*, p. 77.
45. Noel Carrington (ed.), *Mark Gertler: Selected Letters*, Rupert Hart-Davis Ltd, London, 1965, D. H. Lawrence to Mark Gertler, 13 November 1916.
46. *Ottoline at Garsington*, p. 150.
47. *Notebooks*, Vol. 2, Unbound Papers, p. 76.
48. Letter, Aldous Huxley to Julian Huxley, Grover Smith (ed.), *The Letters of Aldous Huxley*, Chatto & Windus, London, 1969, quoted Alpers, p. 227.
49. *Letters of KM*, Vol. I, to OM, 14 January 1917.
50. Ibid., to BR, 21 January 1917.
51. Ibid., to JMM, January 1917 (undated).
52. Ibid., to OM, 14 January 1917.
53. Ibid., to JMM, January 1917 (undated).
54. *Ottoline at Garsington*, p. 128.
55. *Letters of KM*, Vol. I, to OM, 14 January 1917.
56. Ibid., to BR, 24 February 1917.
57. Ibid., to OM, 3 April 1917.
58. *New Age*, Vol. 20, No. 23, 19 April 1917.
59. *Memories of LM*, p. 102.

60. *Letters of KM*, Vol. I, to JMM, 19 May 1917.
61. *Between Two Worlds*, p. 433.
62. *Notebooks*, Vol. 2, Notebook 24, 30 May 1917, p. 94.
63. Marion C. Ruddick, Prologue, Incidents in the childhood of Katherine Mansfield, MS-Papers-1339, ATL.
64. *Letters of KM*, Vol. I, to OM, 24 June 1917.
65. Ibid., to VW, 24 June 1917.
66. Nicolson (ed.), *Letters of Virginia Woolf*, to Vanessa Bell, 27 June 1917.
67. Olivier Bell (ed.), *Diary of Virginia Woolf, Volume One*, 2 March 1918.
68. *Letters of KM*, Vol. I, to VW, June 1917 (undated).
69. Ibid., to DB, 11 October 1917.
70. Katherine Mansfield, *Poems*, JMM (ed.), Constable, London, 1923; Knopf, New York, 1924.
71. *Letters of KM*, Vol. I, to OM, 15 August 1917.
72. Ibid., to VW, 23 August 1917.
73. Ibid., to DB, 1 August 1917.
74. Katherine Mansfield, 'In Confidence', *New Age*, Vol. 21, No. 4, 24 May 1917.
75. *Ottoline at Garsington*, p. 188.
76. JMM, Diaries and notebooks, Journal 1913–1920, MS-Group-0411, MSX-4147, ATL. For KM's opinion of the poem see letter to JMM, *Letters of KM*, Vol. I, 10 August 1917.
77. *Letters of KM*, Vol. I, to OM, 11 August 1917.
78. *Ottoline at Garsington*, pp. 236–7.
79. *Letters of KM*, Vol. I, to VW, 23 August 1917.
80. Ibid., to OM, 15 August 1917.
81. Ibid., to OM, 22 or 29? October 1917; see Olivier Bell (ed.), *Diary of Virginia Woolf, Volume One*, 27 October 1917.
82. *Letters of KM*, Vol. I, to OM, 22 or 29? October 1917.
83. Olivier Bell (ed.), *Diary of Virginia Woolf, Volume One*, 12 November 1917.
84. *Letters of KM*, Vol. I, to JMM, late July 1917.
85. Ibid., to OM, 20 November 1917.
86. Letter, OM to KM, MS-Papers-4003, ATL.
87. *Memories of LM*, p. 105.
88. *Letters of KM*, Vol. I, to VW, December 1917 (undated).
89. Ibid., to JMM, 13 December 1917.
90. Ibid., 17 December 1917.
91. Ibid., 14, 23–4 December 1917.
92. Ibid., to Anne Estelle Drey, 22 December 1917.
93. *Between Two Worlds*, p. 449.
94. *Letters of KM*, Vol. I, to JMM, 14 December 1917.
95. *Between Two Worlds*, p. 450.
96. The tubercular bacillus was identified by Koch only six years before Katherine was born. The ability of tuberculosis to be latent for long periods of time and to hide itself behind symptoms of other conditions, such as pleurisy, pneumonia, rheumatism and digestive problems, made it very difficult to diagnose. Many cases, like Katherine's, went undetected until they were quite well advanced. As the only treatment that could be offered was the reinforcement of the immune system, clean air, rest and nourishing food, the prognosis was not good.
97. *Letters of KM*, Vol I, to JMM, 23 December 1917.
98. *Memories of LM*, p. 106.

PART V – BETTY

CHAPTER 16: IN LIMBO

1. MS 2515, Papers of JMM, GB 0237 MSS 2506–2518, Special Collections and Archives, Edinburgh University Library.
2. *Beloved Quixote*, p. 91.
3. JMM, Diaries and notebooks, 1936, MS-Group-0411, MSX?, ALT; quoted Lea, p. 210.
4. *Beloved Quixote*, p. 173.
5. JMM, Diaries and notebooks, 28 May 1945, MS-Group-0411, MSX-4156, MSX-4157, ATL.
6. JMM, Diaries and notebooks, 1947, MS-Group-0411, MSX-4162, MSX-4163, ATL, quoted Lea, p. 187.
7. JMM, Diaries and notebooks, 14 October 1931, MS-Group-0411, MSX?, ATL; quoted *Beloved Quixote*, p. 77.
8. Ruth Elvish Mantz, 'Tormentor and Tormented', in Jan Pilditch (ed.), *The Critical Response to Katherine Mansfield*, Greenwood Press, Westport, Connecticut, 1996.
9. Ruth Elvish Mantz, 'Katherine Mansfield – 50 years later', *Adam International Review*, Nos 370–75, 1972.
10. Elvish Mantz, 'Tormentor and Tormented'.
11. Elvish Mantz, 'Katherine Mansfield – 50 years later'.
12. Ruth Elvish Mantz and John Middleton Murry, *The Life of Katherine Mansfield*, Constable, London, 1933.
13. JMM, Diaries and notebooks, 9 December 1933, MS-Group-0411, MSX-4150, ATL.
14. *One Hand Clapping*, p. 58.
15. Ibid., p. 24.
16. Ibid., p. 87.
17. Ibid., p. 130.
18. *Beloved Quixote*, p. 91.
19. Ibid., p. 99.
20. JMM, Diaries and notebooks, 16 September 1931, MS-Group-0411, MSX-4148, ATL.
21. Spoken by Whickham, JMM's *The Voyage*; quoted *Beloved Quixote*, p. 53.
22. JMM, Diaries and notebooks, 30 March & 16 June 1932, MS-Group-0411, MSX-4149, ATL.
23. *Beloved Quixote*, p. 91.
24. JMM, Diaries and notebooks, 16 November 1934, MS-Group-0411, MSX-4151, ATL.
25. JMM, 'Notes on Modern Marriage', MS 2510, Papers of JMM, GB 0237 MSS 2506–2518, Special Collections and Archives, Edinburgh University Library.
26. JMM, Diaries and notebooks, 23 August 1932, MS-Group-0411, MSX-4150, ATL.
27. Letter, JMM to A.W.Votier, 7 January, 1932, quoted Lea, pp. 196–7.
28. D. H. Lawrence, *Fantasia of the Unconscious*.
29. Quoted Lea, p. 198.
30. William Gerhardi, Review, *Times Literary Supplement*, pasted into the Diary of JMM, Diaries and notebooks, June 1931, MS-Group-0411, MSX-4148, ATL.
31. Quoted Lea, p. 224.
32. Articles of Association, Adelphi School Company, quoted Lea, pp. 223–4. John MacMurray was a well-known and respected Scottish Quaker communitarian philosopher.
33. JMM, 'Katherine Mansfield', *Katherine Mansfield and Other Literary Studies*, London, Constable, 1959.
34. Letter, Professor Clarence Thorpe to F. A. Lea, quoted Lea, pp. 226–7.
35. Letter, JMM to Victor Cooley, 1 March 1936, quoted Lea, p. 227.
36. JMM, Diaries and notebooks, 1 April 1936, MS-Group-0411, MSX-4152, ATL.

37. *One Hand Clapping*, pp. 99–100.
38. Ibid., p. 14.

CHAPTER 17: 'THE LAST HELL'

1. JMM, Diaries and notebooks, May–June 1936, MS-Group-0411, MSX-4153, ATL.
2. *One Hand Clapping*, pp. 115–16.
3. Lea, p. 230.
4. Katherine Middleton Murry, private collection.
5. JMM, Diaries and notebooks, 6 September 1936, MS-Group-0411, MSX-4153, ATL.
6. Ibid., October 1936 (undated).
7. Ibid., 14 October 1936.
8. Ibid., 28 October 1936.
9. Quoted Lea, p. 239.
10. JMM, autobiography, part 2, 1947, Diaries and notebooks, MS-Group-0411, MSX-4162, MSX-4163, ATL.
11. Ibid.
12. Ibid.
13. Canon Charles Raven, quoted Lea, p. 250.
14. Colin Middleton Murry, *Shadows on the Grass*, Gollancz, London, 1977.
15. Letter, JMM to James Young, 9 May 1938, MS-Papers-5413, ATL.
16. 'Introduction', *Notebooks*, Vol. 1, p. xvii.
17. JMM (ed.), *The Scrapbook of Katherine Mansfield*.
18. JMM, letter to Grace Rogers, private collection.
19. *One Hand Clapping*, p. 183.
20. Mary Middleton Murry, *To Keep Faith*, Constable, London, 1959, p. 13.
21. Ibid., p. 20.
22. JMM, MS 2515, Papers of JMM, GB 0237 MSS 2506–2518, Special Collections and Archives, Edinburgh University Library.
23. JMM, 23 June 1937, MS-Group-0411, MSX-4154, ATL. See also Dunning Notebook, MSX-6920, ATL, for original poem and Katherine's comments on it.
24. JMM, autobiographical fragment, 1947, Diaries and notebooks, MS-Group-0411, MSX-4162, MSX-4163, ATL.
25. The Letters of Mary Gamble and JMM, private collection, quoted in *To Keep Faith*, p. 16.
26. *To Keep Faith*, p. 19.
27. *Beloved Quixote*, p. 192; and mss, private collection.

PART VI – THE DARK KATHERINE

CHAPTER 18: FACING OBLIVION

1. Hankin (ed.), *Letters of JMM to KM*, 9 January 1918, p. 95.
2. *Letters of KM*, to JMM, 9 January 1918.
3. *Notebooks*, Vol. 2, Unbound Papers, 19 February 1918, p. 125.
4. *Letters of KM*, Vol. II, to JMM, 11 January 1918.
5. Ibid.
6. *Letters of KM*, Vol. II, to Annie Burnell Beauchamp, 18 January 1918.
7. Ibid., to JMM, 19 January 1918.
8. Ibid., 20 January 1918.
9. Hankin (ed.), *Letters of JMM to KM*, 19 January 1918, pp. 105–6.
10. *Letters of KM*, Vol. II, to JMM, 6 February 1918.
11. Ibid., to JDF, 24 January 1918.

12. Ibid., to JMM, 3 February 1918.
13. Ibid., 3, 4 February 1918.
14. Ibid.
15. *Letters of KM*, Vol. II, to JMM, 8 February 1918.
16. *Between Two Worlds*, p. 463.
17. *Letters of KM*, Vol. II, to JMM, several dates, January and February 1918.
18. Hankin (ed.), *Letters of JMM to KM*, 8 February 1918, p. 115.
19. *Letters of KM*, Vol. II, to JMM, 10, 11 February 1918.
20. Ibid., to JMM, 10, 11, 12 February 1918.
21. Ibid., to JMM, 12,13 February 1918.
22. *Memories of LM*, p. 107.
23. *Letters of KM*, Vol. II, to JMM, 12, 13 February 1918.
24. Ibid., to JMM, 14, 16 February 1918.
25. *Notebooks*, Vol. 2, Unbound Papers, 19 February 1918, p. 125.
26. *Letters of KM*, Vol. II, to JMM, 19 February 1918.
27. Ibid., to JMM, 17, 18 February 1918.
28. Ibid., to KMM, 21, 23 March 1918.
29. Ibid., to JMM, 28 February 1918.
30. Hankin (ed.), *Letters of JMM to KM*, 10 March 1918, p. 135.
31. *Letters of KM*, Vol. II, to JMM, 18 March 1918.
32. Ibid., to JMM, 19 March 1918.
33. Ibid., 21, 22 March 1918.
34. *Notebooks*, Vol. 2, Unbound Papers, p. 127.
35. *Letters of KM*, Vol. II, to JMM, 25, 26 March 1918.
36. Ibid., to JMM, 28 March 1918.
37. Ibid., to IB, 12 April 1918.
38. Ibid., to IB, 18 April 1918.
39. Olivier Bell (ed.), *Diary of Virginia Woolf, Volume One*, 28 May 1918.
40. *Letters of KM*, Vol. II, to JDF, September 1918 (undated).
41. *Notebooks*, Vol. 2, Notebook 12, 25 April 1918, p. 133.
42. *Letters of KM*, Vol. II, to DB, 30 April 1918.
43. Ibid., to JMM, 27 May 1918.
44. Hankin (ed.), *Letters of JMM to KM*, 28 May 1918, p. 159.
45. *Notebooks*, Vol. 2, two versions – one in third person (Notebook 42, pp. 159–60) and one in the first person (Notebook 35, p. 240).

CHAPTER 19: AT THE BOTTOM OF THE SEA

1. *Letters of KM*, Vol. II, to JMM, 17 May 1918.
2. *Notebooks*, Vol. 2, Notebook 12, 21 May, 1918, p. 134.
3. *Notebooks*, Vol. 2, Unbound Papers, p. 129 & Notebook 12, June, p. 140.
4. *Notebooks*, Vol. 2, Unbound Papers, p. 127; MS-Papers-4006-06, 4006-15, ATL.
5. *Letters of KM*, Vol. II, to IB, 16 June 1918.
6. Letters of KM, Vol. II. to JMM, 8 June 1918, quoted *Between Two Worlds*, Ch. 32.
7. Hankin (ed.), *Letters of JMM to KM*, 24, 25 May 1918, pp. 152–6.
8. *Between Two Worlds*, p. 486.
9. *Letters of KM*, Vol. II, to IB, 14 June 1918.
10. *Memories of LM*, p. 122.
11. *Letters of KM*, Vol. II, to JMM, 9 June 1918.
12. *Notebooks*, Vol. 2, Notebook 12, p. 141.
13. Letter, Clive Bell to VW, quoted by VW, Olivier Bell (ed.), *Diary of Virginia Woolf, Volume One*, 16 July 1918.
14. *Letters of KM*, Vol. II, to VW, 27 May 1919.

15. Ibid., to VW, 1 November 1918.
16. Ibid., to IB, 3 August 1918.
17. Olivier Bell (ed.), *Diary of Virginia Woolf, Volume One*, 15 July, 7 August 1918.
18. *Notebooks*, Vol. 2, Notebook 12, p. 137.
19. *Letters of KM*, Vol. II, to DB, 22 July 1918.
20. Letter, Annie Beauchamp to Clara Palmer, 6 May 1918, MS-Papers-4005-4, ATL.
21. *Notebooks*, Vol. 2, Notebook 12, p. 139.
22. *Letters of KM*, Vol. II, to Anne Estelle Drey, 13 January 1919.
23. *Letters of KM*, Vol. II, to OM, 2 December 1918.
24. *Memories of LM*, p. 127.
25. *Notebooks*, Vol. 2, Notebook 12, 24 October 1918, p. 144.
26. *Letters of KM*, Vol. II, to Anne Estelle Drey, 15 October 1918.
27. *Memories of LM*, p. 127.
28. *Between Two Worlds*, p. 493.
29. *Notebooks*, Vol. 2, Notebook 12, 20 September 1918.
30. Ibid., Notebook 42, p. 160.
31. *Letters of KM*, Vol. II, to DB, 19 July 1918. WAAC was the Women's Auxiliary Army Corps; Wrens were members of the Women's Royal Naval Service.
32. *Letters of KM*, Vol. II, to DB, 27 October 1918.
33. *Notebooks*, Vol. 2, Notebook 12, p. 139.
34. Walter de la Mare, 'Horse in a Field', *Westminster Gazette*, 28 January 1922.
35. *Notebooks*, Vol. 2, Notebook 16, p. 166.
36. *Memories of LM*, p. 135.
37. Dunning Notebook, MSX-6920, ATL.
38. Ibid.
39. 'Realizing the marked tendency of tuberculosis toward latency and its tendency to masquerade under a great variety of trivial ailments or other misleading conditions, we must not overlook any symptom or complaint of the past. The correlation of preceding events, often widely separated in time, and the localisation of their focal symptoms will aid us in piecing together the story of the evolution of the tuberculous process in the individual in question.' J. A. Miller, *Pulmonary Tuberculosis in Adults and Children*, Thomas Nelson, New York, 1939.
40. *Letters of KM*, Vol. II, to VW, 10 November 1918.
41. Ibid., KM to Anne Drey, 13 January 1919.
42. *Notebooks*, Vol. 2, Notebook 42, p. 159, Notebook 16, p. 173.
43. Medical report, Dr Bouchage, private collection.
44. *Notebooks*, Vol. 2, Unbound Papers, p. 238.
45. Ibid., Notebook 16, p. 171.
46. Ibid., Notebook 26, p. 182.
47. Ibid., Notebook 12, 20 [September?], 1918, p. 143.
48. *Letters of KM*, Vol. II, to OM, 17 November 1918.
49. Ibid., to VW, 10 April 1919.
50. Ibid., to S. Koteliansky, 7 April 1919.
51. Ibid., to DB, 17 December 1918.
52. Unpublished Letter, IB to JMM, private collection.
53. *Notebooks*, Vol. 2, Notebook 16, pp. 165–7.
54. *Letters of KM*, Vol. II, to DB, 1 January 1919.
55. *Notebooks*, Vol. 2, Unbound Papers, 31 December 1918, p. 153–4.

CHAPTER 20: THE PERFECT FRIEND

1. *Notebooks*, Vol. 2, Unbound Papers, 19 May 1919, p. 154.
2. *Letters of KM*, Vol. II, to Anne Estelle Drey, 13 August 1919.

3. Letter, Lytton Strachey to VW, quoted Jeffrey Meyers, 'Murry's Cult of Mansfield'.
4. *Letters of KM*, Vol. II, to OM, 17 August 1919.
5. Ibid.
6. Ibid., to OM, 24 May 1918.
7. *Letters of KM*, Vol. III, to Richard Murry, 21 October 1919.
8. Ibid., to JMM, 11 October 1919.
9. Ibid., 7 November 1919.
10. *Letters of KM*, Vol. V, to JMM, 8 October 1922.
11. *Letters of KM*, Vol. III, to JMM, 10 November 1919.
12. JMM (ed.), *Novels and Novelists*, Constable, London, 1930. (This is a collection of KM's reviews in the *Athenaeum*.)
13. *Letters of KM*, Vol. III, to JMM, 13 October 1919.
14. Ibid., 13 January 1920; see also *Memories of LM*, p. 143.
15. *Letters of KM*, Vol. III, to JMM, 21 November 1919.
16. *Memories of LM*, p. 142.
17. *Notebooks*, Vol. 2, Notebook 16, 10 November 1919, p. 171.
18. *Letters of KM*, Vol. III, to JMM, 31 October 1919 and 6 November 1920.
19. Ibid., 11 November 1919.
20. Ibid., 12 November 1919, see also IB, Diary, MS-Group-0035, ATL.
21. Letter, HB to KM, from Menton, 13 November 1919, private collection.
22. *Letters of KM*, Vol. IV, to JMM, 4 October 1920.
23. Hankin (ed.), *Letters of JMM to KM*, 16 November 1919. For KM's reply, see *Letters of KM*, Vol. III, 21 November 1919.
24. Hankin (ed.), *Letters of JMM to KM*, 1 November 1919, p. 200.
25. *Letters of KM*, Vol. III, to JMM, 7 November 1919.
26. Ibid., 4 December 1919.
27. Hankin (ed.), *Letters of JMM to KM*, 5 November 1919, p. 203; 2 February 1920, pp. 261–2.
28. *Notebooks*, Vol. 2, Notebook 26, 17 December 1919, pp. 179–81.
29. Ibid., Notebook 22, January 1920, pp. 187–8.
30. *Letters of KM*, Vol. III, to JMM, 13 January 1920.
31. Letter, IB to JMM, 11 January 1920, private collection.
32. *Notebooks*, Vol. 2, Notebook 22, 11 January 1920, p. 188.
33. Hankin (ed.), *Letters of JMM to KM*, 9 February 1920, pp. 271–2.
34. *Letters of KM*, Vol. III, to JMM, 21 January 1920; *Notebooks*, Notebook 20, 23 January 1920.
35. *Letters of KM*, Vol. III, to JMM, 7 February 1920.
36. *Notebooks*, Vol. 2, Notebook 22, 6 February 1920, p. 192
37. *Letters of KM*, Vol. III, to IB, 4 March 1920.
38. Ibid., to JMM, 24–25 April 1920.
39. *Letters of KM*, Vol. IV, to OM, May 1920 (undated).
40. Hankin (ed.), *Letters of JMM to KM*, April 1920 (undated), p. 304.
41. JMM, Diaries and notebooks, 17 January 1918, MS-Group-0411, MSX-4147, ATL.
42. *Letters of KM*, Vol. IV, to S. & V. Schiff, 4 May 1920.
43. Valerie Eliot (ed.), *The Letters of T. S. Eliot*, Vol. 1, 1898–1922, Faber & Faber, London, 1988, to Ezra Pound.
44. Olivier Bell (ed.), *Diary of Virginia Woolf, Volume Two*, 20 February 1919.
45. *Letters of KM*, Vol. III, to JMM, 10 November 1919.
46. Bell (ed.), *Diary of Virginia Woolf, Volume Two*, 16 January 1923.
47. Ibid., 31 May, 5 June 1920.
48. Ibid., 5 June 1920.
49. Karen Usborne, *'Elizabeth': The Author of Elizabeth and Her German Garden*, Bodley Head Ltd, London, 1986.

50. 'I'd rather like to dine with her. Even to sleep with her afterwards. Would she be pale like that all over? But no. She'd have large moles. They go with that kind of skin. And I can't bear them. They remind me somehow, disgustingly, of mushrooms.' Je ne parle pas Francais, MS-Papers-3998, ATL.
51. Hankin (ed.), *Letters of JMM to KM*, 22 March 1920, pp. 296–7.
52. *Notebooks*, Vol. 2, Notebook 25, p. 219.
53. Diaries of DB, Charles Deering McCormick Library of Special Collections, Northwestern University Library, quoted Hignett, *Brett*, p. 111.
54. *Letters of KM*, Vol. IV, to DB, 19 August 1920.
55. JMM, autobiographical fragment, Diaries and notebooks, 1947, MS-Group-0411, MSX4162, MSX-4162, ATL.
56. *Notebooks*, Vol. 2, Notebook 25, p. 218.
57. Ibid., pp. 218–19.
58. Olivier Bell (ed.), *Diary of Virginia Woolf, Volume Two*, 25 August 1920.
59. *Memories of LM*, p. 149.

CHAPTER 21: 'A WRITER FIRST AND A WOMAN AFTER'

1. *Letters of KM*, Vol. IV, to JMM, 16 September 1920.
2. Ibid., to JMM, 7 October 1920.
3. Ibid., to JMM, 18 October 1920.
4. *Letters of KM*, Vol. III, to JMM, 15 October 1919.
5. *Notebooks*, Vol. 2, Unbound Papers, p. 204.
6. Ibid., Notebook 38, p. 209.
7. D. H. Lawrence, *Signature*, No. 2, 18 October 1915.
8. *Notebooks*, Vol. 2, Notebook 36, p. 255.
9. *Letters of KM*, Vol. IV, to JMM, 21 October 1920.
10. *Notebooks*, Vol. 2, Newberry Notebook 7, 14 July 1921, p. 280.
11. Ibid., Notebook 7, p. 260.
12. JMM to KM, private collection, early December 1920, see Hankin (ed.), *Letters of JMM to KM*, pp. 317–19. Only the first pages of John's letter remain and it ends as he puts EB's annoying dog out of the bedroom. John always maintained that he did not sleep with EB.
13. *Notebooks*, Vol. 2, Notebook 35, 27 December 1920, p. 240.
14. *Letters of KM*, Vol. IV, to JMM, 12 December 1920.
15. Ibid.
16. *Notebooks*, Vol. 2, Unbound Papers, p. 202.
17. Ibid., Notebook 35, 27 December 1920, p. 239.
18. Ibid., Notebook 35, p. 240.
19. Letter, JMM to KM, 11 January 1921, MS-Papers-4003-36, ATL.
20. *Letters of KM*, Vol. IV, to A. A. Knopf, 10 January 1921.
21. Nicolson (ed.), *Letters of Virginia Woolf*, VW to Vanessa Bell, March 1922 (undated).
22. *The Dial*, Vol. 71, September 1921, p. 365.
23. Ibid.
24. *Letters of KM*, Vol. IV, to Michael Sadleir, 7 February 1921.
25. Letter, John Galsworthy to KM, 2 August 1921, MS-Papers-4321-01, ATL.
26. *Letters of KM*, Vol. IV, to A. R. Orage, 9 February 1921.
27. Ibid., to S. Koteliansky, 19 February 1921.
28. Ibid., to Mr A. Kay, 6 February 1921.
29. *Notebooks*, Vol. 2, Notebook 9, p. 231.
30. *Letters of KM*, Vol. IV, to William Gerhardi, 23 June 1921.
31. *Memories of LM*, p. 153.
32. *Letters of KM*, Vol. IV, to Sydney Waterlow, 16 March 1921.

33. Ibid., to IB, 13 March 1921.
34. Ibid., 20 March 1921.
35. *Memories of LM*, p. 154.
36. *Notebooks*, Vol. 2, Notebook 25, p. 229.
37. The phrase is from W. B. Yeats, 'Prayer for my Daughter'.
38. *Letters of KM*, Vol. IV, to Anne Estelle Drey, 12 May 1921.
39. Ibid., to JMM, 7 May 1921.
40. Hankin (ed.), *Letters of JMM to KM*, 19 May 1921, pp. 332–3.
41. Ibid., 16 May 1921, p. 330.
42. *Letters of KM*, Vol. IV, to Anne Estelle Drey, 19 May 1921.
43. Ibid., to DB, 4 August 1921.
44. Olivier Bell (ed.), *Diary of Virginia Woolf, Volume Two*, 9 May 1921.
45. *Letters of KM*, Vol. IV, to DB, 29 July 1921. It somehow echoes A. A. Milne's nursery
    rhyme – 'half way up the stairs, is the stair where I sit . . . it isn't in the nursery,
    it isn't in the town . . . it isn't really anywhere, it's somewhere else instead' – but
    Milne's poem is not to be published for several years. For a further discussion of KM
    and the transitional, see Angela Smith, *A Public of Two: Katherine Mansfield and Virginia Woolf*,
    Clarendon Press, Oxford, 1999.
46. Ibid., to DB, 4 June 1921.
47. Ibid., to Richard Murry, 20 June 1921.
48. *Notebooks*, Vol. 2, Newberry Notebook 7, July 1921, p. 279.
49. *Letters of KM*, Vol. IV, to DB, 4 August 1921.
50. Ibid., 12 September 1921.
51. Ibid., to IB, 20 August 1921.
52. Ibid.
53. Ibid., to IB, 7 September 1921.
54. *Notebooks*, Vol. 2, Notebook 31, 16 October 1921, p. 290.
55. *Letters of KM*, Vol. V, to DB, 4 January 1922.
56. *Letters of KM*, Vol. IV, to Elizabeth Russell, 15 December 1921.
57. Ibid., to DB, 12 September 1921.
58. Letter, now lost, to Thomas Moult, 1920–1, quoted in *T.P.'s Weekly*, 1 December 1928.
59. *Letters of KM*, Vol. IV, to DB, 1 October 1921.
60. *Notebooks*, Vol. 2, Newberry Notebook 6, 13 November 1921, p. 277.
61. *Letters of KM*, Vol. IV, to Sylvia Lynd, 24 September 1921.
62. Ibid., to S. Koteliansky, 18 October 1921.
63. Ibid., to Ivan Manoukhine, 4 December 1921.
64. Ibid., to DB, 13 December 1921.
65. *Notebooks*, Vol. 2, Notebook 31, 24 November 1921, p. 291.
66. Ibid., Notebook 20, 30 January 1922, p. 322.
67. *Letters of KM*, Vol. V, to JMM, 3 February 1922.

PART VII – A RELIGION OF LOVE

CHAPTER 22: KEEPING FAITH

1. *Letters of KM*, Vol. III, to JMM, 5 December 1919.
2. JMM, *Between Two Worlds*, p. 480.
3. JMM, 3 September 1939, Diaries and notebooks, private collection.
4. *To Keep Faith*, p. 28.
5. JMM, Diaries and notebooks, MS-Group-0411, MSX-4155, ATL, quoted *To Keep Faith*,
   p. 61.
6. *To Keep Faith*, p. 29.
7. Letters of JMM, 1940, quoted *To Keep Faith*, pp. 67–8.

8. Ibid.
9. *To Keep Faith*, p. 33.
10. JMM, *Europe in Travail*, Sheldon Press, London, 1940, quoted Lea, p. 275.
11. The diaries of Mary Middleton Murry, private collection.
12. Parliamentary question asked by H.G. Strauss, MP for Norwich, Lea, p. 279.
13. Letter to F. A. Lea, quoted Lea, p. 296.
14. The diaries of Katherine Middleton Murry, private collection.
15. *One Hand Clapping*, p. 192.
16. Letter, JMM to Max Plowman, 2 April 1940, quoted Lea, p. 295.
17. The diaries of Katherine Middleton Murry, private collection.
18. *One Hand Clapping*, p. 193.
19. The diaries of Katherine Middleton Murry, 16 November 1980, private collection.
20. *One Hand Clapping*, p. 184.
21. The diaries of Katherine Middleton Murry, private collection.
22. *Beloved Quixote*, p. 203.
23. JMM, Diaries and notebooks, Diary 1940–50, MS-Group-0411, MSX-4155, ATL.
24. Ibid., 13 April 1936
25. Ibid., 13 November 1940.
26. *To Keep Faith*, p. 82.
27. JMM, Diaries and notebooks, 12 December 1941, Diary 1940–50, MS-Group-0411, MSX-4155, ATL.
28. Geoffrey Sinclair, the diaries of Katherine Middleton Murry, 26 April 1985, private collection.
29. The diaries of Katherine Middleton Murry, 26 April 1985, private collection.
30. The diaries of Mary Middleton Murry, private collection.
31. The diaries of Katherine Middleton Murry, private collection.
32. Ibid.
33. Ibid., 2 January 1987.
34. The diaries of Katherine Middleton Murry, 13 February 1931, private collection.
35. Ibid., 3 January 1983.
36. Ibid., 24 May 1957.
37. *One Hand Clapping*, p. 206.
38. *Letters of KM*, Vol. V, to JMM, 15 October 1922.
39. JMM, 23 October 1942, Diaries and notebooks, Diary 1940–50, MS-Group-0411, MSX-4155, ATL.
40. John Middleton Murry, *Community Farm*.
41. The letters of Katherine Middleton Murry, 2 October 1968, private collection.
42. Letter, JMM to unknown recipient, 12 October 1943, quoted Lea, p. 302.
43. The diaries of Katherine Middleton Murry, 27 November 1980, private collection.
44. *Democracy and War*, PPU pamphlet, 1940; *Christocracy*, Dakers, London, 1942; *The Economics of Peace*, PPU pamphlet, 1943.
45. JMM, *Christocracy*, p. 118.
46. JMM, 1946, Diaries and notebooks, MS-Group-0411, MSX-4155, ATL.
47. The diaries of Katherine Middleton Murry, private collection.
48. Ibid., 14 April 1981.
49. JMM, 1946, Diaries and notebooks, MS-Group-0411, MSX-4155, ATL.
50. Letters from GB to Antony Alpers concerning his relationship with Katherine Mansfield, MS-0263, ATL.
51. Joan Corbett, 2 October 1949, Patric Anthony Lawlor Papers, 77-067-8/23, ATL.
52. Antony Alpers, Preface, p. vii.
53. Letter, A. Alpers to J. D. Fergusson, Fergusson Archive, Box 7, 601–700, 604, Fergusson Gallery, Perth, Scotland.
54. Antony Alpers, Papers relating to Katherine Mansfield, MS-Papers-5079-421, ATL.

55. IB, Memoirs of LM, MS-Group-0035, Folder 3, ATL.
56. JMM, 15 June, 5 July 1948, Diaries and notebooks, Diary 1940–1950, MS-Group-0411, MSX-4155, ATL.
57. Ibid., 14 October 1948.
58. Ibid., 12 July 1948.
59. Ibid., 19 July 1948.
60. Ibid., 12 July 1948.
61. Ibid.
62. Ibid., 29 August 1947.
63. Ibid., 7 October 1947.
64. Sylvia Berkman, *Katherine Mansfield: A Critical Study*, Yale University Press, Connecticut, 1951.
65. Elisabeth Schneider, 'Katherine Mansfield and Chekhov', in Pilditch (ed.), *The Critical Response to Katherine Mansfield*.
66. *Letters of KM*, Vol. V, to Arnold Gibbons, 13 July 1922.
67. JMM, Diaries and notebooks, Diary 1940–1950, MS-Group-0411, MSX-4155, ATL.
68. Beatrice, Lady Glenavy, p. 188.
69. Ian A. Gordon, 'The Editing of Katherine Mansfield's Journal and Scrapbook', in Pilditch (ed.), *The Critical Response to Katherine Mansfield*.
70. *Beloved Quixote*, p. 202.
71. *Shadows on the Grass*, p. 81.
72. The diaries of Katherine Middleton Murry, 24 May 1957, private collection.
73. Ibid.
74. Beatrice, Lady Glenavy, p. 189.
75. JMM, 12 August 1956, Diaries and notebooks, Diary July 1955–December 1956, MS-Group-0411, MSX-4160, ATL.
76. The diaries of Katherine Middleton Murry, 14 March 1989, private collection.
77. JMM, 14 February 1953, Diaries and notebooks, MS-Group-0411, MSX-4160, ATL.
78. *To Keep Faith*, p. 190.
79. Letters of Anne Estelle Rice to JDF, Fergusson Archive, Fergusson Gallery, Perth, Scotland.
80. *To Keep Faith*, p. 11.
81. Ibid., p. 37.
82. The diaries of Katherine Middleton Murry, 16 March 1981, private collection.

PART VIII – 'THE LEVANTINE PSYCHIC SHARK'

CHAPTER 23: THE SOUL'S DESPERATE CHOICE

1. *Notebooks*, Vol. 2, Notebook 20, p. 311 (flyleaf).
2. Ibid., Notebook 20, 6 February 1922, p. 324.
3. Ibid., Notebook 20, 20 January 1922, pp. 318–19; 6 February 1922, p. 324.
4. *Letters of KM*, Vol. V, to JMM, 1 February 1922.
5. *Notebooks*, Vol. 2, Notebook 20, 31 January 1922, p. 322.
6. *Letters of KM*, Vol. V, to JMM, 2 February 1922.
7. Ibid., to JMM, 3, 4 February 1922.
8. *Notebooks*, Vol. 2, Notebook 20, 1 February 1922, p. 322.
9. Ibid., 4 February 1922, p. 323.
10. Ibid., 8 February 1922, p. 324.
11. Ibid., 3, 4 February 1922, p. 323.
12. Letter, 1922, quoted in Roland Merlin, 'The Drama of Katherine Mansfield', *L'Illustration*, No. 16, 19 January 1946.
13. *Notebooks*, Vol. 2, 'Room 135', Unbound Papers, p. 338.

14. *Memories of LM*, p. 181.
15. Ibid., p. 176.
16. *Letters of KM*, Vol. V, to IB, 14, 24 February 1922; Ida Baker, letter, 22 February 1922, private collection.
17. Ibid., to IB, 28 February 1922.
18. Olivier Bell (ed.), *Diary of Virginia Woolf, Volume Two*, 12 March 1922.
19. Leonard Woolf, *Beginning Again: An Autobiography of the Years 1911 to 1918*, Hogarth Press, London, 1964.
20. *Notebooks*, Vol. 2, Notebook 45, 2 January 1916, p. 33.
21. Orton, p. 274.
22. *The Freeman*, Vol. 5, 21 June 1922, p. 357.
23. *Letters of KM*, Vol. V, to Violet Schiff, 8 January 1922.
24. *Novels and Novelists*, review dated 25 June 1920.
25. JMM, 'Tuesday' [24 January?] 1922, Diaries and notebooks, MS-Group-0411, MSX-4146, ATL.
26. *Letters of KM*, Vol. V, to Elizabeth, Countess Russell, 31 December 1922.
27. Ibid., to Elizabeth Russell, January 1922 (undated).
28. *Notebooks*, Vol. 2, Notebook 20, 13 February 1922, p. 326.
29. Ibid., 17 February 1922, p. 326.
30. *Letters of KM*, Vol. V, to HB, 18 March 1922.
31. Ibid., to HB, 20 June 1922.
32. Ibid., to DB, 29 April 1922.
33. Ibid., to IB, 10 May 1922.
34. Ibid., to DB, 29 April 1922.
35. Ibid., to Sydney Schiff, 12 January 1922.
36. Ibid., to Violet Schiff, 1 April 1922, quoted Alpers, pp. 357–8.
37. Ibid., to Sydney Schiff, 12 January 1922.
38. Ibid., to DB, 26 February, 1922; Richard Murry, 3 March 1922.
39. Ibid., to Elizabeth Russell, 5 June 1922.
40. Autograph letter, dated 12 March 1922, Papers of JMM, GB 0237 MSS 2506–2518, Special Collections and Archives, Edinburgh University Library.
41. JMM, 20 April 1922, Diaries and Notebooks, MS-Group-0411, MSX-4146, ATL.
42. *Letters of KM*, Vol V, to IB, February 1922 (undated).
43. Ibid., undated.
44. Ibid., to IB, 27 May 1922.
45. Ibid., 7 June 1922.
46. *Memories of LM*, p. 206.
47. Katherine Mansfield, review, *Rhythm*, July 1912.
48. *Letters of KM*, Vol. V, to JMM, 5 July 1922.
49. *Notebooks*, Vol. 2, Unbound papers, p. 339.
50. *Memories of LM*, p. 207.
51. *Letters of KM*, Vol. V, to Elizabeth, Countess Russell, March 1922 (undated).
52. Ibid., to OM, 4 March 1922.
53. *Memories of LM*, p. 210.
54. *Notebooks*, Vol. 2, Notebook 30, pp. 287–8.
55. Quoted Moore, *Gurdjieff and Mansfield*, p. 128.
56. Ruth Mantz interview with Samuel Koteliansky, *Adam International Review*, Nos 370–5, 1972.
57. Annotations on the ms are in Katherine's hand, but *Dostoevsky: Letters and Reminiscences* was published in 1923, 'trans. by S. S. Koteliansky and J. Middleton Murry' with no acknowledgment of the work that Katherine had done.
58. Ruth Mantz interview with Samuel Koteliansky.
59. IB in conversation with Ruth Mantz, *Adam International Review*, Nos 370–5, 1972.

60. P. D. Ouspensky, *The Fourth Way, A collection of lectures, questions and answers*, Knopf, New York, 1957, p. 3.
61. *Letters of KM*, Vol. V, to JMM, September 1922 (undated).
62. Ibid., to Sydney Schiff, 18 January 1922.
63. Ibid., to Sarah G. Millin, March 1922 (undated).
64. Olivier Bell (ed.), *Diary of Virginia Woolf, Volume Two*, 16 January 1923.
65. Anne Estelle Rice, 'Memories of Katherine Mansfield', *Adam International Review*, No. 300, 1966.
66. Anne Estelle Rice, catalogue, exhibition at New Zealand House, London: 'Katherine Mansfield: Her letters and works', May 1958.
67. Anne Estelle Rice, 'Memories of Katherine Mansfield'.
68. Ouspensky, *In Search of the Miraculous*, quoted JMM's diary, 7 April 1946, Diaries and notebooks, MS-Group-0411, MSX-4157, ATL.
69. *Letters of KM*, Vol. V, to JMM, 27 September 1922.

CHAPTER 24: 'A CHILD OF THE SUN'

1. *Letters of KM*, Vol. V, to DB, 3 October 1922.
2. Ibid., to DB, 9 October 1922.
3. Ouspensky, *In Search of the Miraculous*, quoted JMM's diary, 7 April 1946, MS-Group-0411, MSX-4157, ATL.
4. *Letters of KM*, Vol. V, to JMM, 11 October 1922.
5. James Young, 'An Experiment at Fontainebleau', *New Adelphi*, Vol. 1, No. 1, September 1927, pp. 26–40.
6. *Notebooks*, Vol. 2, Notebook 30, October 1922, pp. 285–7.
7. James Moore, *Gurdjieff and Mansfield*.
8. Orton, p. 274.
9. *Notebooks*, Vol. 2, Notebook 30, October 1922, pp. 285–7.
10. Roland Merlin, 'The Drama of Katherine Mansfield'; *Notebooks*, Vol. 2, Notebook 30, 14 October 1922; Ibid., Notebook 20, Sunday 15 October 1922.
11. Hankin (ed.), *Letters of JMM to KM*, 14 October 1922, p. 365.
12. *Letters of KM*, Vol. V, to JMM, 18 October 1922.
13. Ibid., to JMM, 16 October 1922. The reference is to the Mad Hatter's tea party in Lewis Carroll's *Alice's Adventures in Wonderland*.
14. *Letters of KM*, Vol. V, to JMM, 24 October 1922.
15. Ibid., to IB, 10 November 1922.
16. Ibid., to JMM, 28 October 1922.
17. *Notebooks*, Vol. 2, Notebook 30, October 1922, pp. 285–7.
18. *Letters of KM*, Vol. V, to JMM, 18 October 1922.
19. *Notebooks*, Vol. 2, Notebook 20, 17 October 1922, p. 329. This is a reference to the famous 1888 two-volume book, *Travels in Arabia Deserta*, by English poet, traveller and writer Charles Montagu Doughty.
20. Letter, Wyndham Lewis to Violet Schiff, 20 September 1922, BL.
21. The recollections of Gurdjieff's interpreter, quoted James Moore, *Gurdjieff and Mansfield*.
22. IB, Diary 1922, MS-Group-2365, ATL.
23. *Letters of KM*, Vol. V, to JMM, 18 October 1922.
24. Ibid.
25. Ibid., to JMM, 7 November 1922.
26. Ibid., to JMM, 19 November 1922.
27. Olgivanna, 'The Last Days of Katherine Mansfield', *The Bookman*, March 1931.
28. Letter, Wyndham Lewis to Violet Schiff, 20 September 1922, BL.
29. *Letters of KM*, Vol. V, to JMM, 12 November 1922.
30. Ibid., to HB, 31 December 1922.
31. Ibid., to JMM, 19 November 1922.

32. Ibid., 1 December 1922.
33. A. R. Orage, 'A Last Talk with Katherine Mansfield', *The Century*, November 1924.
34. Ibid.
35. Raymond Mortimer, 'The Dove's Nest and Other Stories', in Pilditch (ed.), *The Critical Response to Katherine Mansfield*.
36. *Letters of KM*, Vol. V, to JMM, 2 November 1922.
37. Letter, Elizabeth, Countess Russell to Katherine Mansfield, 1 January 1923, MS-Papers-4003, Folder 39, ATL.
38. Last words in the printed edition of Katherine's notebooks. Also published as Katherine's 'last words' by JMM in the *Adelphi*, 1924. But not the last words in the notebook and probably written towards the end of 1922.
39. Newberry Notebook 3, Katherine Mansfield Papers (MS), Newberry Library, Chicago – microfilm; Selected manuscripts from the Newberry Library, Micro-MS-0251-1, ATL.

Bibliography

WORKS BY KATHERINE MANSFIELD

Complete Transcriptions

O'Sullivan, Vincent and Scott, Margaret (eds), *The Collected Letters of Katherine Mansfield*, Oxford University Press, Oxford, Volume I, 1903–17, 1984; Volume II, 1918–19, 1987; Volume III, 1919–20, 1993; Volume IV, 1920–21, 1996; Volume V, 1921–23, 2008

Scott, Margaret (ed.), *The Notebooks of Katherine Mansfield*, Vols 1 and 2, Lincoln University Press & Daphne Brasell Associates Ltd, Lincoln, 1997

Selections Edited by John Middleton Murry

The Journal of Katherine Mansfield, Constable, London, 1927; Knopf, New York, 1927

The Letters of Katherine Mansfield, Vols I & II, Constable, 1928; Knopf, New York, 1929

Novels and Novelists, Constable, London, 1930

The Scrapbook of Katherine Mansfield, Constable, London, 1937; Knopf, New York, 1939

Katherine Mansfield's Letters to John Middleton Murry, 1913–1922, Constable, London, 1951

The Journal of Katherine Mansfield (incorporating the Scrapbook), Constable, London, 1954

Fiction

In a German Pension, Stephen Swift, London, 1911

Prelude, Hogarth Press, London, 1918

Bliss and other stories, Constable, London, 1920; Knopf, New York, 1921

The Garden Party and other stories, Constable, London, Knopf, New York, 1922

The Dove's Nest and other stories, J. M. Murry (ed.), Constable, London, 1923; Knopf, New York, 1923

Something Childish and other stories, J. M. Murry (ed.), Constable, London, 1924; published as *The Little Girl*, Knopf, New York, 1924

The Aloe, J. M. Murry (ed.), Constable, London, 1930; Knopf, New York, 1930

The Collected Stories of Katherine Mansfield, (Omnibus edition), Constable, London, 1945; Penguin edition, 1981

Poetry

Poems, J. M. Murry (ed.), London, Constable, 1923; Knopf, New York, 1924

TEXTS ABOUT KATHERINE MANSFIELD

Biographies

Alpers, Antony, *Katherine Mansfield: A Biography*, Knopf, New York 1953

————, *The Life of Katherine Mansfield*, Jonathan Cape, London, 1980; Oxford University Press, Oxford, 1982

Baker, Ida, *Katherine Mansfield: The Memories of LM*, first published Michael Joseph, 1971; this edition, Virago, London, 1985

Berkman, Sylvia, *Katherine Mansfield: A Critical Study*, Yale University Press, Connecticut, 1951

Boddy, Gillian, *Katherine Mansfield*, Penguin, Auckland, 1988

Mantz, Ruth Elvish & John Middleton Murry, *The Life of Katherine Mansfield*, Constable, London, 1933

Meyers, Jeffrey, *Katherine Mansfield: A Biography*, Hamish Hamilton, London, 1978; reprinted as *Katherine Mansfield: A Darker View*, Cooper Square Press, New York, 2002

Tomalin, Claire, *Katherine Mansfield: A Secret Life*, Penguin, London, 1988

Plays and Films

Downes, Cathy, *The Case of Katherine Mansfield*, Women's Play Press, New Zealand, 1995

Leave All Fair, Pacific Films, 1985, New Zealand, screenplay, Stanley Harper, starring John Gielgud and Jane Birkin

Rosenthal, Amy, *On the Rocks*, Hampstead Theatre, London, July 2008

Tomalin, Claire, *The Winter Wife*, London, 1991

Novels

Keefer, Janice Kulyk, *Thieves: A Novel of Desire and Deception Shadowing the Life of Katherine Mansfield*, Harper Flamingo, Canada, 2004

Lappin, Linda, *Katherine's Wish*, Wordcraft of Oregon, 2008

Stead, C. K., *Mansfield*, Harvill Press, London, 2004; Vintage, London, 2005

Critical Texts

Beauchamp, Jeannie, 'Bridging the Gulf, Taking the Risk: An Exploration of "Relationships" in Katherine Mansfield's "Juliet", "Brave Love", and "Prelude"', MA thesis, Victoria University of Wellington, 2007.

Burgan, Mary, *Illness, Gender and Writing: The Case of Katherine Mansfield*, Johns Hopkins University Press, Baltimore, Maryland, 1995

Carter, Angela, *Nothing Sacred: Selected Writings*, Virago, London, 1982

Chatterjee, Atul Chandra, *The Art of Katherine Mansfield: An Enquiry into the Meaning and Technique of the Short Stories of Katherine Mansfield*, S. Chand & Co., New Delhi, 1980, 1991

Clarke, Brice, MD, 'Katherine Mansfield's Illness', *Proceedings of the Royal Society of Medicine*, Vol. 48, December 1955, pp. 1029–32

Dunbar, Pamela, *Radical Mansfield: Double Discourse in Katherine Mansfield's Short Stories*, St Martin's Press, New York, 1997

Fullbrook, Kate, *Katherine Mansfield: A Critical Study*, Harvester Press, Brighton, 1986

Gounelas, Ruth Parkin, *Fictions of the Female Self: Charlotte Brontë, Olive Schreiner, Katherine Mansfield*, Macmillan Press, London; St Martin's Press, New York, 1991

Gunsteren, Julia Van, *Katherine Mansfield and Literary Impressionism*, Rodopi BV Editions, Amsterdam, 1990

Hankin, C. A. (ed.), *Katherine Mansfield & Her Confessional Stories: Critical Essays on the New Zealand Novel*, St Martin's Press, New York, 1983

———, *Life in a Young Colony: Selections From Early New Zealand Writing*, Whitcoulls, Christchurch, 1981

Kaplan, Sydney Janet, *Katherine Mansfield and the Origins of Modernist Fiction*, Cornell University Press, New York, 1991

Kimber, Gerri, *Katherine Mansfield: The View from France*, Peter Lang, London, 2008

Michel, Paulette and Dupuis, Michel (eds), *Fine Instrument: Essays on Katherine Mansfield*, Dangaroo Press, Sydney, 1989

Modern Fiction Studies, Autumn 1978, Vol. 24, No. 3, special Katherine Mansfield issue

Morrow, Patrick D., *Katherine Mansfield's Fiction*, Popular Press, Bowling Green State University, Ohio, 1993

Murry, J. M., *Katherine Mansfield and other Literary Studies*, Constable, London, 1959

Norburn, Roger, *A Katherine Mansfield Chronology*, Palgrave Macmillan, London, 2008

O'Sullivan, Vincent (ed.), *Katherine Mansfield's New Zealand Stories*, Penguin, Auckland, 1988

———, *The Poems of Katherine Mansfield*, Oxford University Press, Auckland, 1991

Pilditch, Jan (ed.), *The Critical Response to Katherine Mansfield*, Greenwood Press, Westport, Connecticut, 1996

Raitt, Suzanne & Trudi Tate, *Women's Fiction and the Great War*, Oxford University Press, Oxford, 1997

Robinson, Roger (ed.), *Katherine Mansfield: In from the Margin*, Louisiana State University Press, Baton Rouge, Louisiana, 1994

Sellei, Nora, *Katherine Mansfield and Virginia Woolf: A Personal and Professional Bond*, Peter Lang, London, 1996

Smith, Angela, *Katherine Mansfield: A Literary Life*, Palgrave Macmillan, London, 2000

————, *Katherine Mansfield & Virginia Woolf: A Public of Two*, Oxford University Press, Oxford, 1999

Woods, Joanna, *Katerina: The Russian World of Katherine Mansfield*, Penguin, Auckland, 2001

TEXTS RELATING TO JOHN MIDDLETON MURRY

Arden, Mary (Violet le Maistre), *Luck and Other Stories*, Jonathan Cape, London, 1928

Hankin, C. A. (ed.), *The Letters of John Middleton Murry to Katherine Mansfield*, Constable, London, 1983

Lea, F. A., *John Middleton Murry: A Biography*, Methuen, London, 1959

Murry, Colin Middleton, *One Hand Clapping*, Gollancz, London, 1975

Murry, Colin Middleton, *Shadows on the Grass*, Gollancz, London, 1977

Murry, Katherine Middleton, *Beloved Quixote*, Souvenir Press, London, 1986

Murry, Mary Middleton, *To Keep Faith*, Constable, London, 1959

OTHER SOURCES

Adam International Review, No. 300, 1966 (Katherine Mansfield edition)

Bagnold, Enid, *Enid Bagnold's Autobiography*, William Heinemann, London, 1969

Bashkirtseff, Marie, *The Journal of Marie Bashkirtseff*, Virago, London, 1985

Beatrice, Lady Glenavy (Beatrice Campbell), *Today we will only gossip*, Constable, London, 1964

Boulton, James T., *The Letters of D. H. Lawrence*, Vol. I, Cambridge University Press, Cambridge, 1979

Boulton, J. T. & Vasey, L., *The Letters of D. H. Lawrence*, Vol. V, Cambridge University Press, Cambridge, 1989

Byrne, Janet, *A Genius for Living: The Life of Frieda Lawrence*, Bloomsbury, London, 1995

Carco, Francis, *Les Innocents*, Paris, 1916

————, *Montmartre a vingt ans*, (trans. Stella Wynne-Edwards), Paris, 1938

Carrington, Noel (ed.), *Mark Gertler: Selected Letters*, Rupert Hart-Davis Ltd, London, 1965

Carswell, John, *Lives and Letters: A. R. Orage, Katherine Mansfield, Beatrice Hastings, John Middleton Murry, S. S. Koteliansky, 1906–1957*, Faber & Faber, London, 1978

Delaney, Paul, *Lawrence's Nightmare: The Writer and his Circle in the Years of the Great War*, Harvester Press, Brighton, 1979

Ede, H. S., *A Savage Messiah: A Biography of the Sculptor Henri Gaudier-Brzeska*, Heinemann, London, 1931

Gathorne-Hardy, Robert (ed.), *Ottoline at Garsington: Memoirs of Lady Ottoline Morrell 1915–1918*, Faber & Faber, London, 1974

Gordon, Lyndall, *Virginia Woolf: A Writer's Life*, Virago, London, 2006

Hastings, Beatrice, *The Old New Age – Orage and Others*, Blue Moon Press, London, 1935

Hignett, Sean, *Brett: From London to New Mexico*, Hodder & Stoughton, London, 1984

Huxley, Aldous (ed.), *The Letters of D. H. Lawrence*, Heinemann, London, 1932

Lawrence, D. H., *Phoenix II, Uncollected, Unpublished and Other Prose Works*, Viking Press, New York, 1968.

Lawrence, Frieda, *Not I but the Wind*, Heinemann, London, 1935

Lee, Hermione, *Virginia Woolf*, Chatto & Windus, London, 1996

Moore, James, *Gurdjieff and Mansfield*, Routledge & Kegan Paul, London, 1980

Nicolson, Nigel (ed.), *The Letters of Virginia Woolf, Volume Two, 1912–1922*, Chatto & Windus, London, 1976

Olivier Bell, Anne (ed.), *The Diary of Virginia Woolf, Volume One, 1915–1919*, Hogarth Press, London, 1977

————, assisted by Andrew McNeillie, *The Diary of Virginia Woolf, Volume Two, 1920–1924*, Hogarth Press, London, 1978

Orton, William, *The Last Romantic*, Cassell & Co., London, 1937

Ouspensky, P. D., *In Search of the Miraculous*, Harcourt, Brace, New York, 1949; Routledge, London, 1949.

————, *The Fourth Way*, Knopf, New York, 1957

Pater, Walter, *The Renaissance: Studies in Art and Poetry*, Oxford University Press, Oxford, 1998

Roberts, Warren, James T. Boulton and Elizabeth Mansfield (eds), *The Letters of D. H. Lawrence, Volume IV, June 1921–March 1924*, Cambridge University Press, Cambridge, 1987

Russell, Bertrand, *The Autobiography of Bertrand Russell*, Allen & Unwin, London, Vol. I, 1967; Vol. II, 1968

Sankaran, Dr B., 'Tuberculosis of Bones and Joints', *Indian Journal of Tuberculosis*, No. 40, 1993, pp. 109–18

Scott, Margaret, *Recollecting Mansfield*, Random House, Auckland, 2001

Selver, Paul, *Orage and the New Age Circle*, Allen & Unwin, London, 1959

Sichel, Pierre, *Modigliani*, Dutton, London, 1967

Symons, Arthur, *The Symbolist Movement in Literature*, Dutton, London, 1958

Tuli, S. M., *Tuberculosis of the Skeletal System: Epidemiology and Prevalence, Clinical Features*, New Delhi, 1997, Jaypee Brothers Medical Publication

Usborne, Karen, *'Elizabeth': The author of Elizabeth and her German Garden*, Bodley Head Ltd, London, 1986

Woolf, Leonard, *Beginning Again: An Autobiography of the Years 1911–1918*, Hogarth Press, London, 1964

Woolf, Leonard and Strachey, James (eds), *The Letters of Virginia Woolf and Lytton Strachey*, Hogarth Press, London, 1956

SELECT LIST OF WORKS BY JOHN MIDDLETON MURRY

Still Life (novel), Constable, London, 1916

Doestoevsky: A Critical Study, Secker & Warburg, London, 1916

Poems: 1917–18, Heron Press, London, 1918

The Critic in Judgement (poetry), Hogarth Press, London, 1919

The Evolution of an Intellectual, Cobden Sanderson, London, 1920

Cinnamon and Angelica (verse play), Cobden Sanderson, London, 1920

Aspects of Literature, Collins, London, 1920

Poems: 1916–1920, Cobden Sanderson, London, 1921

The Problem of Style, Oxford University Press, Oxford, 1922

The Things We Are (novel), Constable, London, 1922

Countries of the Mind, Oxford University Press, Oxford, 1922

Pencillings, Collins, London, 1922

The Voyage (novel), Constable, London, 1924

Discoveries, Collins, London, 1924

To the Unknown God, Jonathan Cape, London, 1925

Keats and Shakespeare, Oxford University Press, London, 1925

The Life of Jesus, Jonathan Cape, London, 1926

Things to Come, Jonathan Cape, London, 1928

God, Jonathan Cape, London, 1929

D. H. Lawrence: Two essays, Gordon-Fraser, London, 1930

Studies in Keats, Oxford University Press, Oxford, 1931

Son of Woman (D.H. Lawrence), Jonathan Cape, London, 1931

The Necessity of Communism, Jonathan Cape, London, 1932

Reminiscences of D.H. Lawrence, Jonathan Cape, London, 1933

William Blake, Jonathan Cape, London, 1933

The Biography of Katherine Mansfield, J. M. Murry & Ruth E. Mantz, Constable, London, 1933

Between Two Worlds (autobiography), Jonathan Cape, London, 1935

Shakespeare, Jonathan Cape, London, 1936

The Necessity of Pacifism, Jonathan Cape, London, 1937

Heaven – and Earth, Jonathan Cape, London, 1938

The Pledge of Peace, H. Joseph, London, 1938

The Defence of Democracy, Jonathan Cape, London, 1939

Europe in Travail, Sheldon Press, London, 1940

The Betrayal of Christ by the Churches, Dakers, London, 1940

Christocracy, Dakers, London, 1942

Adam and Eve, Dakers, London, 1944

The Free Society, Dakers, London, 1948

Looking Before and After, Sheppard Press, London, 1948

The Challenge of Schweitzer, Jason Press, London, 1948

Katherine Mansfield and other Literary Portraits, Nevill, London, 1949

John Clare and other Studies, Nevill, London, 1950

The Conquest of Death, Nevill, London, 1951
Community Farm, Nevill, London, 1952
Jonathan Swift, Jonathan Cape, London, 1954
Unprofessional Essays, Jonathan Cape, London,1956
Love, Freedom and Society, Jonathan Cape, London, 1957
Not as the Scribes, SCM Press, London, 1959

Index